Lecture Notes in Computer Science 16070

Founding Editors

Gerhard Goos
Juris Hartmanis

Editorial Board Members

Elisa Bertino, *Purdue University, West Lafayette, IN, USA*
Wen Gao, *Peking University, Beijing, China*
Bernhard Steffen, *TU Dortmund University, Dortmund, Germany*
Moti Yung, *Columbia University, New York, NY, USA*

The series Lecture Notes in Computer Science (LNCS), including its subseries Lecture Notes in Artificial Intelligence (LNAI) and Lecture Notes in Bioinformatics (LNBI), has established itself as a medium for the publication of new developments in computer science and information technology research, teaching, and education.

LNCS enjoys close cooperation with the computer science R & D community, the series counts many renowned academics among its volume editors and paper authors, and collaborates with prestigious societies. Its mission is to serve this international community by providing an invaluable service, mainly focused on the publication of conference and workshop proceedings and postproceedings. LNCS commenced publication in 1973.

Walter Senn · Marcello Sanguineti ·
Ausra Saudargiene · Igor V. Tetko ·
Alessandro E. P. Villa · Viktor Jirsa ·
Yoshua Bengio
Editors

Artificial Neural Networks and Machine Learning – ICANN 2025

34th International Conference on Artificial Neural Networks
Kaunas, Lithuania, September 9–12, 2025
Proceedings, Part III

 Springer

Editors
Walter Senn
University of Bern
Bern, Switzerland

Ausra Saudargiene
Vytautas Magnus University
Kaunas, Lithuania

Alessandro E. P. Villa
University of Lausanne
Lausanne, Switzerland

Yoshua Bengio
Université de Montréal
Montréal, QC, Canada

Marcello Sanguineti
University of Genoa
Genoa, Italy

Igor V. Tetko
Helmholtz Zentrum München
Neuherberg, Germany

Viktor Jirsa
Aix-Marseille Université
Marseille, France

ISSN 0302-9743　　　　　　ISSN 1611-3349　(electronic)
Lecture Notes in Computer Science
ISBN 978-3-032-04548-5　　　ISBN 978-3-032-04549-2　(eBook)
https://doi.org/10.1007/978-3-032-04549-2

© The Editor(s) (if applicable) and The Author(s), under exclusive license
to Springer Nature Switzerland AG 2026

This work is subject to copyright. All rights are solely and exclusively licensed by the Publisher, whether the whole or part of the material is concerned, specifically the rights of translation, reprinting, reuse of illustrations, recitation, broadcasting, reproduction on microfilms or in any other physical way, and transmission or information storage and retrieval, electronic adaptation, computer software, or by similar or dissimilar methodology now known or hereafter developed.
The use of general descriptive names, registered names, trademarks, service marks, etc. in this publication does not imply, even in the absence of a specific statement, that such names are exempt from the relevant protective laws and regulations and therefore free for general use.
The publisher, the authors and the editors are safe to assume that the advice and information in this book are believed to be true and accurate at the date of publication. Neither the publisher nor the authors or the editors give a warranty, expressed or implied, with respect to the material contained herein or for any errors or omissions that may have been made. The publisher remains neutral with regard to jurisdictional claims in published maps and institutional affiliations.

This Springer imprint is published by the registered company Springer Nature Switzerland AG
The registered company address is: Gewerbestrasse 11, 6330 Cham, Switzerland

If disposing of this product, please recycle the paper.

Preface

The 34th International Conference on Artificial Neural Networks (ICANN 2025) was held in Kaunas, Lithuania, from September 9 to 12, 2025.

The International Conference on Artificial Neural Networks (ICANN) serves as a global platform for presenting the latest breakthroughs in artificial intelligence, neural networks, deep learning, and brain-inspired computing. Organized annually by the European Neural Network Society (ENNS), ICANN has, since its inception in 1992, evolved into one of Europe's most prestigious conferences at the intersection of Artificial Intelligence and Neuroscience. It offers researchers, practitioners, and industry professionals a unique opportunity to share innovations, discuss theoretical advances, and explore practical applications of neural computation. The conference strongly values the synergy between theoretical progress and impactful real-world applications, and actively encourages contributions that demonstrate how artificial neural networks are being used to address pressing societal and technological challenges.

We received 375 submissions for the main research track. The research track accepted 170 papers (45%). In addition, there were 42 papers submitted to workshops and special sessions, which were mainly invited contributions (of which 29 were accepted). Each paper was assigned three reviewers, although due to availability and completion rates, an average of 2.2 reviews per paper was obtained, totaling 807 reviews. The review process followed a double-blind peer-review model, and area chairs oversaw quality and fairness. The papers submitted to the main research track were presented over two days. Additionally, one day was devoted to tutorials and one day to workshops.

The General Co-chairs of ICANN 2025 were distinguished experts in the fields of Artificial Intelligence and Neuroscience:

- Yoshua Bengio (Université de Montréal, Canada) is one of the world's leaders in Artificial Intelligence and Deep Learning, the most cited computer scientist worldwide, the recipient of the 2018 A.M. Turing Award, considered to be the "Nobel prize of computing". He is Co-president and Scientific Director of LawZero, a nonprofit organization committed to advancing research and developing technical solutions for safe-by-design AI systems, the Founder and Scientific Advisor of Mila and a Canada CIFAR AI Chair.
- Viktor Jirsa (Aix-Marseille Université, France; EBRAINS Chief Science Officer) is renowned for his fundamental work in theoretical neuroscience, and for open-source simulation platform The Virtual Brain, used to build personalised brain models for epilepsy surgery and other brain disorders. He served as a lead investigator in the EU Flagship Human Brain Project and its successor infrastructure EBRAINS (European Brain REsearch INfrastructureS). Jirsa's contributions have been recognised with numerous honours, including the Human Brain Project Innovation Prize (2021).

The conference featured five keynote talks spanning a wide spectrum of topics, reflecting both emerging scientific challenges and the growing convergence of theoretical insights, real-world applications, and ethical considerations in AI and neuroscience. These talks addressed the frontiers of generative models, causality, brain simulation, ethics, and efficient deep learning, showcasing the diverse landscape ICANN 2025 aimed to represent:

- Bernhard Schölkopf (Max Planck Institute for Intelligent Systems, Tübingen, Germany): *AI Extracting Causality*
- Viktor Jirsa (Aix-Marseille University, France): *Virtual Brain Twins for Health and Disease*
- Gintarė Karolina Džiugaitė (DeepMind, USA): *On Memorization and Unlearning*
- Emmanuel Bengio (McGill University; Recursion/Valence Labs, Canada): *AI and Generative Models*
- Christiane Woopen (University of Bonn, Germany): *Ethics in AI, Neuroscience, Digital Twins, and Consciousness Research Neuroscience and AI for a Flourishing Life*
- Alessio Micheli (University of Pisa, Italy): *A Journey through Efficient Deep Learning on Graphs*

The invited speakers covered topics at the intersection of neuroscience and artificial intelligence such as neuromorphic computing, biophysical modeling, engineering network-based brain therapies, AI oversight, and reasoning-capable robotics in the physical world:

- Mihai Petrovici (NeuroTMA Lab, University of Bern, Switzerland): *Teacher Propagation Through Space, Time and the Brain*
- Mehmet Fatih Yanik (ETH Zürich, Switzerland): *Engineering Brain Activity Patterns for Therapeutics*
- Michael Deistler (Machine Learning in Science, University of Tübingen, Germany): *Building Mechanistic Models of Neural Computations with Simulation-based Machine Learning*
- Ameya Pandurang Prabh (Tübingen AI Center, University of Tübingen, Germany): *Scalable Strategies for AI Oversight of AI - Progress, Pitfalls and Path Forward*
- Ignas Budvytis (Resilient Robotics, UK): *Embodied Reasoning in the Physical World*

Participants had the exclusive opportunity to attend the public Panel Discussion 'Where Does AI Lead To? Opportunities and Risks', where the leading experts Yoshua Bengio, Viktor Jirsa, Christiane Woopen, Gintarė Karolina Džiugaitė, and Bernhard Schölkopf addressed the interaction between AI and Neuroscience, ethical challenges, AI's impact on human identity, and questions about the safe and responsible development of AI.

The ICANN 2025 Organizing Committee committed itself to supporting Diversity and Inclusion within the Artificial Intelligence and Neuroscience communities. As part of this commitment, ICANN 2025 awarded two scholarships of €1000 and €500 to early-career researchers from developing countries and/or underrepresented communities in science and technology. These scholarships were intended to support travel and accommodation costs, helping recipients attend the conference, present their research, and become active members of the ICANN community.

By enabling broader participation, ICANN 2025 continued efforts towards fostering a more inclusive and representative research environment, encouraging the exchange of ideas across cultures, disciplines, and career stages.

We extend our sincere thanks to all the authors, workshop and tutorial organizers, and participants whose scientific contributions and engagement made ICANN 2025 such a dynamic and inspiring event. Crafting a rich and interdisciplinary program would not have been possible without the dedication and significant commitment of the area chairs, the program committee led by Walter Senn (University of Bern, Switzerland) and the organizing committee, especially Ausra Saudargiene (Lithuanian University of Health Sciences/Vytautas Magnus University, Lithuania) and Linas Petkevičius (Vilnius University, Artificial Intelligence Association of Lithuania). We are also deeply grateful to the many volunteers and session chairs, whose behind-the-scenes work ensured the smooth running of the conference, as well as to all reviewers.

We thank Springer for their continued collaboration in publishing the conference proceedings, and Microsoft for providing access to the CMT conference management system and offering technical assistance throughout the organization process.

We deeply appreciate the ongoing support and guidance of the European Neural Network Society (ENNS), whose leadership and vision continue to shape the ICANN community.

September 2025

Ausra Saudargiene
Walter Senn
Igor V. Tetko
Alessandro E. P. Villa
Marcello Sanguineti
Viktor Jirsa
Yoshua Bengio

Organization

General Chairs

Yoshua Bengio — Université de Montréal, Canada
Viktor Jirsa — Aix-Marseille Université, France

Program Committee

Walter Senn (Chair) — University of Bern, Switzerland
Marcello Sanguineti — University of Genova, Italy
Igor V. Tetko — Helmholtz Munich, Germany and BIGCHEM GmbH, Germany
Alessandro E. P. Villa — University of Lausanne, Switzerland
Ausra Saudargiene — Lithuanian University of Health Sciences/Vytautas Magnus University, Lithuania

Honorary Chairs

Vera Kurkova — Czech Academy of Sciences, Czech Republic
Alessandro E. P. Villa — University of Lausanne, Switzerland
Stefan Wermter — University of Hamburg, Germany

Communication Committee

Sebastian Otte — University of Lübeck, Germany
Kristína Malinovská — Comenius University in Bratislava, Slovakia

Local Organizing Committee

Ausra Saudargiene — Lithuanian University of Health Sciences/Vytautas Magnus University, Lithuania
Linas Petkevičius — Vilnius University, Lithuania

Workshop, Tutorials and Special Session Chairs

Povilas Daniusis Vytautas Magnus University, Lithuania
Dalius Matuzevičius VilniusTech, Lithuania

Diversity and Inclusion Chair

Kamilė Dementavičiūtė Vinted, Lithuania

ICANN Steering Committee

Stefan Wermter University of Hamburg, Germany
Angelo Cangelosi University of Manchester, UK
Igor Farkaš Comenius University in Bratislava, Slovakia
Christina Jayne Teesside University, UK
Matthias Kerzel University of Hamburg, Germany
Alessandra Lintas University of Lausanne, Switzerland
Kristína Malinovská Comenius University in Bratislava, Slovakia
Jaakko Peltonen Tampere University, Finland
Brigitte Quenet ESPCI Paris, France
Roseli Wedemann Rio de Janeiro State University, Brazil
Sebastian Otte University of Lübeck, Germany
Ausra Saudargiene Lithuanian University of Health Sciences/Vytautas Magnus University, Lithuania

Keynote Talks Abstracts

Virtual Brain Twins for Health and Disease

Viktor Jirsa

Institut de Neurosciences des Systèmes (INS), Aix-Marseille Université (AMU), France

Abstract. In the past twenty years, we have made significant progress in creating digital models of an individual's brain, so called virtual brain twins. By combining brain imaging data with mathematical models, we can predict outcomes more accurately than using each method separately. Our approach has helped us understand normal brain states, their operation and conditions like healthy aging, dementia and schizophrenia. We illustrate the virtual brain workflow along the example of drug resistant epilepsy, the so-called Virtual Epileptic Patient (VEP): we reconstruct the connectome of an epileptic patient using DTI and co-register other potential imaging data from the same individual (anatomical MRI, computer tomography (CT)). Each brain region is represented by neural population models, which are derived using mean field techniques from statistical physics expressing ensemble activity via collective variables. Subsets of brain regions generating seizures in patients with refractory partial epilepsy are referred to as the epileptogenic zone (EZ). During a seizure, paroxysmal activity is not restricted to the EZ, but may recruit other healthy brain regions and propagate activity through large brain networks. The identification of the EZ is crucial for the success of neurosurgery and presents one of the historically difficult questions in clinical neuroscience. The application of Bayesian inference and model inversion, in particular Hamiltonian Monte Carlo, allows the estimation of the patient's EZ, including estimates of confidence and diagnostics of performance of the inference. In summary, the Virtual Brain Twin augments the value of empirical data by completing missing data, allowing clinical hypothesis testing and optimizing treatment strategies for the individual patient. Virtual Brain Twins are part of the European infrastructure called EBRAINS, which supports researchers worldwide in digital neuroscience.

Biography. Viktor Jirsa, PhD, is Director of the Inserm Institut de Neurosciences des Systèmes (INS U1106) at Aix-Marseille Université and Director of Research (DRCE) at CNRS in Marseille, France. Trained in theoretical physics and applied mathematics (PhD 1996), he pioneered large-scale brain-network models that combine biologically grounded neural dynamics with individual connectomes, establishing a mathematical framework now central to network science in medicine. He is the scientific architect of the open-source simulation platform The Virtual Brain and served as a lead investigator in the EU Flagship Human Brain Project and its successor infrastructure EBRAINS, driving clinical translation of personalised brain models for epilepsy surgery and other disorders. Jirsa's contributions have been recognised with numerous honours, including the Human Brain Project Innovation Prize (2021).

Causal Representations, World Models and Digital Twins

Bernhard Schölkopf[1,2]

[1] Max Planck Institute for Intelligent Systems & ELLIS Institute Tübingen, Germany
[2] Professor at ETH, Zürich, Switzerland

Abstract. Research on understanding and building artificially intelligent systems has moved from symbolic approaches to statistical learning, and is now beginning to study interventional models relying on concepts of causality. Some of the hard open problems of machine learning and AI are intrinsically related to causality, and progress may require advances in our understanding of how to model and infer causality from data, as well as conceptual progress on what constitutes a causal representation and a causal world model. I will present basic concepts and thoughts, as well some applications to astronomy.

Biography. Bernhard Schölkopf's studies machine learning and causal inference, with applications to fields ranging from astronomy to biomedicine, computational photography, music and robotics. Originally trained in physics and mathematics, he earned a Ph.D. in computer science in 1997 and became a Max Planck director in 2001. His awards include the ACM AAAI Allen Newell Award, the BBVA Foundation Frontiers of Knowledge Award, the Leibniz Award, and the Royal Society Milner Award. He is a Professor at ETH Zurich, a Fellow of the ACM and of the CIFAR Program "Learning in Machines and Brains", and a member of the German Academy of Sciences. He helped start the MLSS series of Machine Learning Summer Schools, the ELLIS society, and the Journal of Machine Learning Research, an early development in open access and today the field's flagship journal. In 2023, he founded the ELLIS Institute Tübingen, and acts as its scientific director.

On Memorization and Unlearning

Gintarė Karolina Džiugaitė

Google DeepMind, USA

Abstract. Deep learning models exhibit a complex interplay between memorization and generalization. This talk will begin by exploring the ubiquitous nature of memorization, drawing on prior work on "data diets", example difficulty, pruning, and other empirical evidence. But is memorization essential for generalization? Our recent theoretical work suggests that eliminating it entirely may not be feasible. Instead, I will discuss strategies to mitigate unwanted memorization by focusing on better data curation and efficient unlearning mechanisms. Additionally, I will examine the potential of pruning techniques to selectively remove memorized examples and explore their impact on factual recall versus in-context learning.

Biography. Gintarė is a senior research scientist at Google DeepMind, based in Toronto, an adjunct professor in the McGill University School of Computer Science, and an associate industry member of Mila, the Quebec AI Institute. Prior to joining Google, Gintarė led the Trustworthy AI program at Element AI/ServiceNow, and obtained her Ph.D. in machine learning from the University of Cambridge, under the supervision of Zoubin Ghahramani. Gintarė was recognized as a Rising Star in Machine Learning by the University of Maryland program in 2019. Her research combines theoretical and empirical approaches to understanding deep learning, with a focus on generalization, memorization, unlearning, and network compression.

AI and Generative Models

Emmanuel Bengio

McGill University; Recursion/Valence Labs, Montreal, Canada

Abstract. In this talk I will share some recent progress on training energy-based generative models using the GFlowNet framework and applying them to scientific problems, as well as speculate on the bigger picture; using GFNs to be good Bayesians, and create models that reason about their environment, concluding with an open discussion of next steps and open problems.

Biography. Emmanuel Bengio is a senior ML Scientist at Valence Labs @ Recursion, working on GFlowNet and drug discovery from Mila, Montreal, Canada. He is mainly interested in Machine Learning, especially Deep Learning and Reinforcement Learning and mixing both. Lately, he has been working at the intersection of ML and drug design using the new GFlowNet framework.

Neuroscience and AI for a Flourishing Life

Christiane Woopen

Heinrich Hertz Professor at the University of Bonn, Germany

Abstract. Neuroscience and artificial intelligence are rapidly advancing fields that combine remarkable scientific progress with ambitious visions for the future. At the same time, they face deep conceptual disagreements, ethical concerns, and dystopian anxieties. Their findings—and the methodological innovations they employ, such as digital twins—raise complex ethical questions concerning autonomy, justice, privacy, and sustainability. Moreover, they are grounded in contested assumptions about the brain and its significance for personal identity and agency. These debates inevitably lead to broader philosophical questions about the nature of human beings and their potential distinctiveness within the continuum of life and consciousness. This lecture examines the ethical implications of these interrelated developments and levels of thought, and it argues for the relevance of human flourishing as a guiding ethical principle in addressing them.

Biography. Christiane Woopen is Heinrich Hertz Chair for Life Ethics at the University of Bonn and founding director of the Center for Life Ethics since October 2021. In addition to leading national and international research projects on ethics in digital technologies, sciences and health she is involved in policy advice, including as Chair of the German Ethics Council (2012–2016), as President of the Global Summit of National Ethics Councils (2014–2016), as a member of the UNESCO International Bioethics Committee until 2017, as Co-speaker of the German Data Ethics Commission (2018–2019), and as Chair of the European Group on Ethics in Science and New Technologies (EGE, 2017–2021). Woopen is a member of several academies of sciences (NRW, BBAW, Academia Europaea, National Academy of Medicine in Mexico) and was awarded the Order of Merit of the State of North Rhine-Westphalia as well as the Federal Cross of Merit 1st Class.

A Journey Through Efficient Deep Learning on Graphs

Alessio Micheli

Head of the Computational Intelligence and Machine Learning Group, Department of Computer Science, University of Pisa, Italy

Abstract. Although the investigation on learning in structured domains started in the late 1990s, recently deep learning for graphs has attracted tremendous research interest and increasing attention for applications. Indeed, graphs are powerful and flexible tools for representing relationships among data at different levels of abstraction. Unsurprisingly, the range of applications includes many fields, including biology, chemistry, network science, computer vision, natural languages and many others. On the other hand, extending the data domain to graphs opens new challenges for the field of deep learning, particularly regarding efficiency, which is related to the important aspect of environmental sustainability. The talk will very briefly introduce the area of deep learning for graphs, with a focus on its origins. We will then move on to discuss advanced topics and current open issues by providing an overview of recent progress in my research group. We will pay particular attention to efficiency, the interplay between model depth and learning complex data representations, and explainability on graphs.

Biography. Alessio Micheli is Full Professor at the Department of Computer Science of the University of Pisa, where he is the head and scientific coordinator of the Computational Intelligence & Machine Learning Group (CIML), part of the CAIRNE.eu Research Network. His research interests include machine learning, neural networks, deep learning, learning in structured domains (sequence, tree, and graph data), recurrent and recursive neural networks, reservoir computing, and probabilistic and kernel-based learning for non-vectorial data, with a particular focus and pioneering works on efficient neural networks for learning from graphs. Micheli is the national coordinator of the "Italian Working group on Machine Learning and Data Mining" of the Italian Association for Artificial Intelligence and he has been co-founder/chair of the IEEE CIS Task Force on Reservoir Computing. He is an elected member of the Executive Committee of the European Neural Network Society – ENNS. He serves as an Associate Editor for Neural Networks and IEEE Transactions on Neural Networks and Learning Systems.

Teacher Propagation Through Space, Time and the Brain

Mihai Petrovici

NeuroTMA Lab, University of Bern, Switzerland

Abstract. Whether biological or artificial, intelligence ultimately boils down to the ability of physical substrates to perform (complex) computations efficiently. Which algorithms can "run" on the dynamics of a given substrate? And conversely, which substrates should we build to implement our algorithms of choice? In my talk, I will discuss variants of these questions that are inspired by recent insights from neurobiology and recent developments in neuromorphic engineering. In particular, I will address several challenges of credit assignment in physical neuronal networks and show how they can be met with rigorous math and creative physics.

Biography. Already since my earliest days as an aspiring physicist, I have worked in several fields that are marked by emergent phenomena arising from complex interactions, from high-multiplicity particle collisions to ultracold glasses and, ultimately, neuromorphic systems. It is this "science of complexity" that continues to intrigue and inspire me. Following my PhD with Karlheinz Meier at Heidelberg University, I moved to the University of Bern, where I am now leading the Neuro-inspired Theory, Modeling and Applications (NeuroTMA) Lab.

I believe there is much to learn from brains about cognition, but taking steps beyond biology may well be warranted when building physical substrates for artificial intelligence – there are good reasons for airplanes not to flap their wings. Therefore, in our group, we combine knowledge and methods from a variety of fields - neuroscience, mathematics, physics, machine learning and microelectronics - to understand biological intelligence and extract its key features for subsequent implementation in silico.

Engineering Brain Activity Patterns for Therapeutics

Mehmet Fatih Yanik

ETH Zurich, Chair of Neurotechnology Laboratories, NSC Study Director, Co-director of Institute of Neuroinformatics, ETH Artificial Intelligence Center

Abstract. Brain networks are disrupted in numerous disorders. I will first show how aberrant brain-wide activity patterns can be corrected by targeting distinct network motifs with multiple neuromodulators using a vertebrate model of human epilepsy and autism. This systematic approach rescues behavior unlike any other. Next, I will present two technologies to realize such network corrections in humans: (1) Biocompatible ultraflexible tentacle electrodes that allow single-neuron-resolution network recordings simultaneously from many brain areas, where we can track inter-areal neuronal ensembles year long, and we are currently starting the first human acute recordings. (2) AU-FUS technology that allows us to non-invasively deliver drugs/RNA to specific brain circuits with 1,300x enhanced focal concentration with millimeter precision across the BBB; we are performing the first pre-clinical large animal studies. I will show how targeting dorsal ACC reduces chronic anxiety without motor side effects.

Biography. Yanik received his BS and MS in Engineering and Physics at MIT in 2000, and PhD in Computational and Applied Physics at Stanford in 2006. He completed brief postdoctoral work in Stanford Bioengineering and Neurosurgery. He subsequently served as Assistant (2006) and later as Associate Professor (2009) till his tenure at MIT. He is currently a professor at ETH Zurich in the Institute for Neuroinformatics. His studies are recognized by a NIH Director's Pioneer Award, NIH Director's New Innovator Award, NIH Transformative Research Award, ERC Consolidator Award, SNSF (~ERC) Advanced, Bridge Discovery Award, Packard Award in Engineering and Science, Alfred Sloan Award in Neuroscience, NIH Eureka Award, NSF Career Award, Silicon Valley's Innovator's Challenge Award, Technology Review Magazine's "World's top 35 innovators under age 35", and Junior Chamber International's "Outstanding Young Person", among others. His work has been highlighted by The Economist, BBC, Popular Mechanics, Nature, Guardian, ABC, Boston Globe, Scientific American, MIT Technology Review, The Scientist, National Geographic, Blick, and others.

Building Mechanistic Models of Neural Computations with Simulation-Based Machine Learning

Michael Deistler

Machine Learning in Science, University of Tübingen, Germany

Abstract. A central challenge in neuroscience is that many properties of neural systems cannot be measured exactly. This limits our understanding of these systems and our ability to build simulations that match experimental recordings or predict neural responses to unseen stimuli. Inference allows scientists to identify parameters—the properties that cannot be measured exactly—such that biophysical simulations are consistent with experimental measurements of neural activity.

I will present machine learning-based inference methods for biophysical simulations in neuroscience. While the focus is on neuroscience, the methods are broadly applicable. First, I will discuss simulation-based Bayesian inference using neural networks. Second, I will introduce differentiable simulation as a powerful approach for parameter inference in large-scale biophysical models. This allows us to directly optimize parameters using gradient-based methods, even in morphologically detailed models of single cells or networks—overcoming the scalability barriers of previous approaches.

Together, these results demonstrate how machine learning opens new possibilities for constructing and fitting biophysical simulations in neuroscience, helping to bridge the gap between experimental data and mechanistic understanding.

Biography. My research lies at the intersection of machine learning and science. I build inference methods that enable the tuning of mechanistic simulators to match empirical measurements. I have a particular focus on biophysical simulations in neuroscience, where I develop machine learning methods to build large-scale and data-driven models of biological intelligence.

Scalable Strategies for AI Oversight of AI - Progress, Pitfalls and Path Forward

Ameya Pandurang Prabh

Tübingen AI Center, University of Tübingen, Germany

Abstract. As foundation models scale, the aspiration of "AI providing oversight for AI" is becoming practical reality. Recent advances, including large-language-model (LLM) judges that auto-grade outputs and weak-to-strong pipelines where smaller models critique larger ones, demonstrate that automated oversight can effectively augment limited human supervision. However, new evidence exposes a critical flaw: great models increasingly think alike. We show that model errors become more correlated as capabilities improve. The similarity that drives high accuracy also biases LLM judges towards models resembling themselves, and weak-to-strong training becomes less effective as supervisors and students share similar blind spots. This talk outlines a research agenda and practical engineering solutions to maintain trustworthy automated supervision despite model convergence.

Biography. Ameya Prabhu is a postdoctoral researcher at the Tübingen AI Center, hosted by Matthias Bethge. His work focuses on data-centric methodologies, scalable lifelong benchmarks, and oversight mechanisms for foundation models. He earned his PhD at the University of Oxford under the guidance of Adel Bibi and Philip Torr, studying foundations of continual learning, machine unlearning, and lifelong model benchmarking. His current research interests are centered around developing Scientist AI (also known as STEM AI), inspired by the vision of Yoshua Bengio and Evan Hubinger. Specifically, he is working towards creating large language models (LLMs) as non-agentic cognitive systems that explain observed data through generating theories, rather than imitating or pleasing humans. His goal is to build powerful, trustworthy AI systems designed explicitly for safe, sandboxed exploration of STEM problems, without external human modeling or intervention.

Embodied Reasoning in the Physical World

Ignas Budvytis

Resilient Robotics, Cambridge, UK

Abstract. Robotics has recently experienced several significant breakthroughs in various capabilities, including improvements in 3D shape estimation and re-rendering algorithms, open-world perception, video generation-based world models, and solving complex manipulation tasks via imitation learning. However, widespread adoption of generalist robotic systems in the physical world still requires further research breakthroughs. In particular, safely interacting with humans, adapting to changes in tasks or environments, and efficiently learning from human feedback remain critical challenges. All these capabilities rely on embodied reasoning—the ability to understand one's own form factor, action space, and impact on the operating environment.

This talk aims to examine AI reasoning from its origins to recent advancements, providing inspiration for novel embodied reasoning systems while highlighting past pitfalls. The presentation reviews early contributions by Turing, McCarthy, and Hayes, and discusses challenges such as the framing problem. Additionally, it covers key milestones in neurosymbolic AI, early visual reasoning, and current efforts in embodied reasoning, including multi-modal foundational models and agentic AI reasoning frameworks. The talk concludes with a brief overview of remaining challenges and future directions for systems that reason effectively in the physical world.

Biography. Ignas Budvytis is an independent researcher and former academic specialising in computer vision, machine learning, and robotics. He is dedicated to developing advanced technologies that enhance how machines perceive and interpret the world. Ignas holds a Bachelor's degree in Computer Science and a PhD in Computer Vision from the University of Cambridge. He recently served as an Assistant Professor of Computer Vision and Robotics in the Department of Engineering at the University of Cambridge.

Contents – Part III

ACGCN: A Sequence-Attention-Based Graph Convolutional Model for Enhanced Recommendation Systems 1
Mingke Liao, Feng Yao, and Yang Yang

Hyperparameter-Free Bi-level Knowledge Graph Optimization for Link Prediction 16
Hao Li, Tong Mei, and Jiaxin Fang

SWIFT: State-Space Wavelet Integrated Forecasting Technology for Enhanced Time Series Prediction 29
Wei Li

Federated Privacy-Preserving for Cross-Domain Sequential Recommendation 41
Su Chen, Yan Dong, Yanmin Shang, Xiaolin Xu, and Xixun Lin

An Enhanced Audio Feature Tailored for Anomalous Sound Detection Based on Pre-trained Models 53
Guirui Zhong, Qing Wang, Jun Du, Lei Wang, Mingqi Cai, and Xin Fang

Multimodal Sentiment Analysis with Parallel Attention and Correlation Fusion 65
Xiaoqiang Liu, Jie Lei, Jiaqi Wu, Zunlei Feng, and Ronghua Liang

A Hybrid Learning Approach for Continual Knowledge Graph Embedding: Contrastive Masking and Joint Anti-Forgetting 77
Nanhui Lai, Ke Jin, Yingchao Long, Weihao Yu, and Jin Huang

Leveraging Machine-Translated Data for Sentiment Analysis in Low-Resource Languages: A Case Study on Bengali 89
Nur-A-Alam Abir, Xiaowang Zhang, Rafiul Haq, and Sofonias Yitagesu

RRetFC: Leveraging Recursive Retrieval For LLM-Enhanced Complex Fact-Checking 101
Yuxuan Xie, Xiaoliang Liu, Peng Wu, and Li Pan

Feature-Aware Sequence Models for Tabular Data Processing with Missing Values 114
Yan Qian and Yiqing Shen

Topic-Driven Hyper-relational Knowledge Graphs with Adaptive
Reconstruction for Multi-hop Question Answering Using LLMs 127
   Yingying Zhang, Bo Cheng, and Yuli Chen

Toward Better Document-Level Relation Extraction: De-sampling
and Mixture of Experts in Action 139
   *Xiaojun Sheng, Shilong Wei, Yafei Wang, Minmin Li, Weixi Wang,
   Renzhong Guo, and Qi Yang*

ConSens: Assessing Context Grounding in Open-Book Question
Answering 151
   Ivan Vankov, Matyo Ivanov, Adriana Correia, and Victor Botev

ChiMDQA: Towards Comprehensive Chinese Document QA
with Fine-Grained Evaluation 164
   Jing Gao, Shutiao Luo, Yumeng Liu, Yuanming Li, and Hongji Zeng

Emotional Text-to-Speech via Style Decoder with Emotion Shared
Styleformer Block and RoPE Prior Encoder 180
   Wenhan Yao, Fen Xiao, Ye Xiao, Zexin Li, Xiarun Chen, and Weiping Wen

Can LLM-Generated Textual Explanations Enhance Model Classification
Performance? An Empirical Study 192
   *Mahdi Dhaini, Juraj Vladika, Ege Erdogan, Zineb Attaoui,
   and Gjergji Kasneci*

Early Acoustic and Vision Cross-Modal Interaction Learning for Multimal
Sentiment Analysis 205
   Xiongjian Lv, Yimin Wen, Yi Qian, and Xiaoyu Li

Uncovering Causal Relation Shifts in Event Sequences Under
Out-of-Domain Interventions 217
   *Kazi Tasnim Zinat, Yun Zhou, Xiang Lyu, Yawei Wang, Zhicheng Liu,
   and Panpan Xu*

Sustainable Techniques to Improve Data Quality for Training Image-Based
Explanatory Models for Recommender Systems 229
   *Jorge Paz-Ruza, David Esteban-Martínez, Amparo Alonso-Betanzos,
   and Bertha Guijarro-Berdiñas*

TimeFlowDiffuser: A Hierarchical Diffusion Framework with Adaptive
Context Sampling for Multi-horizon Time Series Forecasting 241
   Wei Li

ConDTab: Conditional Diffusion Transformer for Mixed-Type Tabular
Synthesis with Dual Attention Latent Encoding 253
   Ruoxuan Wang, Shiying Li, Liuyi Fan, Wei Ma, Zexi Li, and Xinbo Ai

SentiAug: Adaptive Keywords Replacement and Confidence-Guided
Self-training Selection for Robust Sentiment Classification 266
   *Luyuan Yang, Yan Chu, Qingchao Zhao, Hanlin Wang, Ximeng Zhao,
and Zhong Chu*

Real-Time and Personalized Product Recommendations for Large
E-Commerce Platforms 279
   Matteo Tolloso, Davide Bacciu, Shahab Mokarizadeh, and Marco Varesi

A Two-Stage Framework Integrating Prompt Learning and Fine-Tuning
for Code Summarization 294
   Xiaoshu Sun, Siqi Lv, Wei Wan, Yiming Qin, and Gang Hu

DialGACL: Nonlinear Graph Attention Reasoning with Contrastive
Learning for Complex Dialogue Fact Verification 307
   *Wei Xia, Yu Zhong, Linfeng Gong, Yulong Yang, Sifan Zhao,
and Shaoguo Cui*

TimbreAdv: Timbre Adversarial Attacks on Speaker Verification Systems 319
   *Ye Xiao, Wenhan Yao, Zexin Li, Jinsu Yang, Yuhao Chen, Xiandang Luo,
Fen Xiao, and Weiping Wen*

Time Series Generation for Augmenting Multi-channel Automotive Audio
Data 331
   *Philipp Engler, Ludger van Elst, Peter Schichtel, Andreas Dengel,
and Sheraz Ahmed*

PGD: Probe Guided Decoding for Alignment 343
   Changxin Chen

Long Abstracts from the ICANN

Dimensionality Reduction of Protein Language Model Embeddings
for Viral Clustering 359
   Brendonas Stakauskas and Virginijus Marcinkevičius

Author Index 361

ACGCN: A Sequence-Attention-Based Graph Convolutional Model for Enhanced Recommendation Systems

Mingke Liao, Feng Yao(✉), and Yang Yang

School of Computer Science and Engineering, Wuhan Institute of Technology,
Wuhan 430205, China
linuxyf@gmail.com

Abstract. In the field of recommendation systems, to address the problem of poor embedding representation quality and limited model generalization ability due to data sparsity, this paper proposes a sequence-attention-based graph convolutional model. In existing methods, there is still considerable room for improvement in recommendation effectiveness due to the neglect of high-order relationships between users and items and the capture of dynamic behaviors. The ACGCN model, through its designed MLP interest learning module, is able to better capture the sequential features in user behavior and dynamically adjust the weights of positive and negative samples through an attention mechanism, thereby enhancing the ability to capture user interests. In addition, the model enhances the understanding of user behavior through supervised contrastive learning, improving the generalization ability of the recommendation system. Validation on three public datasets shows that the ACGCN model outperforms current mainstream models in both Recall@20 and NDCG@20 metrics, demonstrating the effectiveness and performance advantages of this method.

Keywords: recommendation system · sequence attention · contrastive learning · collaborative filtering · graph convolutional network

1 Introduction

With the rapid development of Internet technology, information is growing explosively, often interspersed with a large amount of redundant and ineffective information, making it difficult for users to quickly and accurately find content of interest. A recommendation system is one of the effective methods to solve the problem of information overload. Its function is to recommend information of interest to users based on their interests and historical behaviors [1]. Collaborative filtering (CF) [2], as a fundamental recommendation task, has been widely studied in academia and industry. Collaborative filtering-based recommendation methods only need to use users' historical interaction data to recommend other items that users may be interested in, which is simple and effective, making it the most widely used personalized recommendation algorithm today.

In real-world recommendation scenarios, users' behaviors are dynamic and change over time. Therefore, capturing the sequential features of user behavior in sessions [3] is crucial for making appropriate recommendations, which is also the core goal of recommendation algorithms. With the rise of deep learning, many deep neural network-based recommendation models have emerged to capture the evolution of users' historical behaviors. Kang et al. [4] proposed SASRec, which captures the dependencies in user behavior sequences through self-attention mechanisms. However, since it primarily focuses on local relationships within the behavior sequence, it struggles to quickly adapt to dynamic changes in user interests. Hidasi et al. [5] proposed GRU4Rec, which leverages RNNs to capture the temporal sequences of user behaviors, but it tends to forget critical information from earlier parts of the sequence when dealing with long sequences. Recently, MLP-based architectures have made significant progress and show potential to surpass RNNs, GNNs, and Transformers in sequence modeling. FMLP-Rec [6] uses a filtering algorithm to reduce the impact of noise in the data, thereby enhancing the expressive power of the MLP architecture and improving recommendation performance. MLPs, with their multi-layer structure, automatically extract complex high-order features, strengthening the model's ability to capture nonlinear relationships, thus improving the accuracy and generalization capability of the recommendation system. Sequence attention mechanisms, by dynamically adjusting the weights of positive and negative samples and capturing the temporal dependencies of user behavior, can better adapt to changes in user interests and effectively handle information in long sequences. By combining both, these challenges can be addressed effectively, enhancing recommendation performance and system robustness.

Therefore, this paper proposes a sequence-attention-based [7] graph convolutional model (ACGCN). On the one hand, the interest learning module designed by MLP [8] can better capture the sequential features in user behavior, and dynamically adjust the weights of positive and negative samples by calculating the sequence attention scores. Especially in complex behavior sequences, this dynamic adjustment mechanism can more flexibly capture the dynamic behavior of users in sessions, not only limited to local sequential relationships but also reflecting changes in user interests more comprehensively [28], thereby enhancing the model's personalized recommendation effect. On the other hand, by selecting positive and negative samples from item pairs with good co-occurrence capability and using supervised contrastive learning [9], the model can better distinguish subtle differences between positive and negative samples, improving the understanding of user behavior and helping to enhance the model's generalization ability across different time spans. In addition, supervised contrastive learning can help the model make more efficient use of training data, reducing training time and computational resource consumption.

The main contributions of this paper are as follows:

– An interest learning module is designed based on MLP to capture the sequential features of user behavior in sessions. The sequence attention scores are calculated using the obtained sequential features, and weights are dynamically assigned to positive and negative samples, improving the model's ability to capture user interests and enhancing the personalized recommendation effect of the system.

– Positive and negative samples are selected from item pairs with good co-occurrence capability, and supervised contrastive learning is used to distinguish the characteristics of positive and negative samples, enhancing generalization ability.

– The model is validated on three public datasets, and the results show that the recommendation performance of the ACGCN model is superior to that of the current mainstream models.

2 Related Work

In this section, we will review two tasks related to this work: sequence-based recommendation and contrastive learning.

2.1 Sequence-Based Recommendation Models

Sequence-based recommendation models are a type of recommendation system that focuses on processing the sequential relationships in user behavior data (i.e., the temporal sequence of behaviors). These models assume that users' interests and preferences are dynamic and depend on their previous behavior sequences. Therefore, the model predicts the user's next action or point of interest by capturing the temporal sequence of user behaviors, thereby recommending more relevant content [4]. He et al. [10] proposed a general framework called NCF, which uses a multilayer perceptron (MLP) to learn interactions. This method replaces the inner product operation in the MF model with a multilayer neural network. However, due to the neglect of the high-order connectivity between users and items, it fails to fully exploit the performance of the recommendation system. Wu et al. [11] proposed the SR-GNN model, which represents user sessions as a directed graph and applies graph convolutional networks to capture the sequential relationships between items in sessions. Based on the above research ideas, this paper proposes a sequence attention mechanism that combines the sequential features captured by MLP with the attention mechanism to enhance the recommendation system's ability to capture user interests.

2.2 Contrastive Learning in Recommendation Models

The core of contrastive learning (CL) is to utilize unlabeled data in a self-supervised manner, requiring the model to identify and distinguish different data instances, thereby gaining a deep understanding of the internal structure of the data, aiming to alleviate data sparsity [12]. For example, Yu et al. [13] proposed a similar idea by generating contrastive views by adding uniform noise in the embedding space, which is a simple and effective contrastive method. Lin et al. [14] proposed the NCL model, using semantically similar prototypes and structural neighbors in the embedding space as positive instances. Xia et al. [15] proposed the S2-DHCN, which enhances the model's representation ability by contrasting two hypergraph channels. Cai et al. [16] proposed the LightGCL model, using matrix factorization (MF) to reconstruct the user-item interaction graph to generate contrastive instances, effectively utilizing the original graph information. While these models introduce innovative approaches in the design of recommendation systems, there are still unresolved issues, such as insufficient robustness to noise, problems in selecting positive and negative samples, poor generalization ability, and high computational complexity. To address these issues, this paper selects item pairs with good co-occurrence capability from the item co-occurrence matrix as positive and negative samples and distinguishes the characteristics of positive and negative samples through supervised contrastive learning.

3 Methodology

This section mainly introduces the proposed ACGCN model, as shown in Fig. 1, which can be divided into two parts:

- A multilayer perceptron (MLP) is used to extract the sequential relationship features between users and items and compute attention scores to dynamically assign weights to positive and negative samples;

- Combined with contrastive learning, it mainly distinguishes high-similarity and low-similarity item pairs through the similarity between positive and negative sample pairs, thus better understanding the relationship between users and items.

3.1 Sequence Attention Mechanism

Existing work often fixes the weights of positive and negative samples when calculating the similarity between users and samples, which may prevent the model from dynamically adjusting weights based on specific samples. This limitation hinders the model from fully utilizing the data features, thereby affecting classification accuracy and overall performance. In cases of data imbalance,

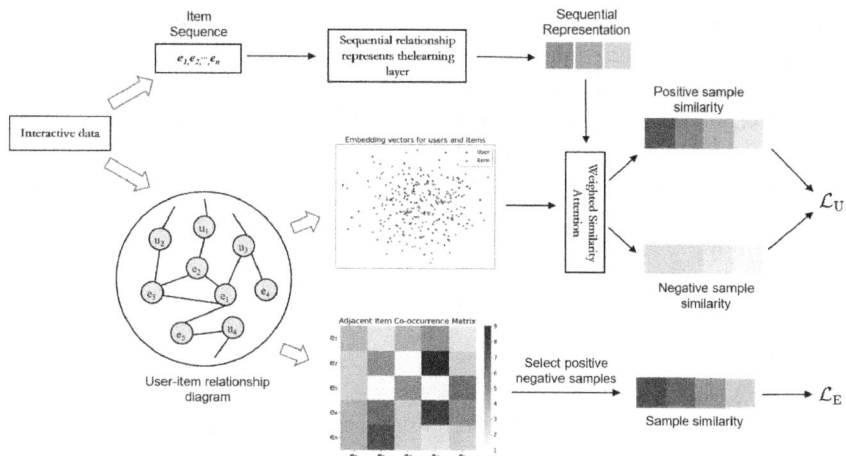

Fig. 1. Overall Framework of ACGCN

fixed weights can also cause the model to favor the majority class. To address these issues, this paper proposes an attention-based graph convolutional network, where the MLP is used to extract the sequential relationship features between users and items to reveal user interests and preferences. Then, attention scores are computed based on these features to dynamically assign weights to positive and negative samples.

UltraGCN [17] believes that the limitations potentially present in message passing in CF hinder the efficient training of models based on GCN in recommendation tasks. Therefore, it approximates an infinite layer graph convolutional state, directly receiving the embedding vector of user $e_u = \sum_{i \in \mathcal{N}(u)} \beta_{u,i} e_i$, where $\beta_{u,i} = \frac{1}{d_u}\sqrt{\frac{d_u+1}{d_i+1}}$, without formal message passing. Here, $\mathcal{N}(u)$ represents the set of neighboring items of user u, indicating all items that have interacted with user u, and $\beta_{u,i}$ denotes the initial weight between user u and item i. e_i represents the embedding vector of item i that is related to user u, and d_u and d_i represent the degrees of user u and item i, respectively. The goal is to maximize the weighted similarity sum between user u and its neighboring items: $\max \sum_{i \in \mathcal{N}(u)} \beta_{u,i} e_u^T e_i$, where $e_u^T e_i$ represents the dot product between the embedding vectors of user u and item i, indicating the similarity between the two. By minimizing the distance between users and items with higher similarity in embedding space, users and items with higher similarity can be placed closer together in the embedding space.

Sequence Relationship Learning. The sequence of item embeddings is denoted as $E = [e_1, e_2, \ldots, e_n]$, where $E \in \mathbb{R}^{D \times N}$, D is the embedding dimension, and N represents the maximum sequence length in the current session. To achieve this goal, This paper utilizes a sequential relationship representation learning layer, which consists of two MLP blocks. Specifically, the first MLP block is used to model the sequence relationship of the session sequence, revealing the dynamic changes in user interests over time, as shown in Fig. 2. The second MLP block is used to further extract the higher-level features [29] from the sequence, enabling the MLP to better understand the sequential features of the interaction sequence and learn more deeply about the sequence relationships. The chosen sequential embedding is then used as input, and the output is an embedding representation with the same dimension as the input. The process is defined as follows:

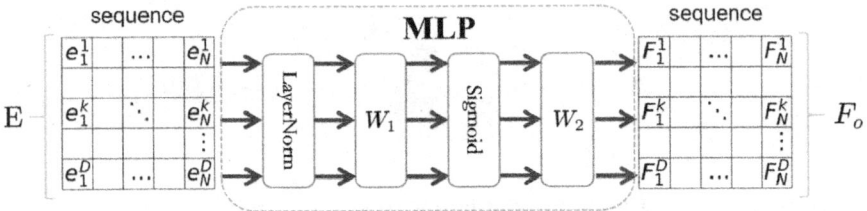

Fig. 2. Sequential MLP Structure

$$F_o = E + W_2\sigma(W_1 LayerNorm(E)) \tag{1}$$
$$S_o = (F_o)^T + W_4\sigma(W_3 LayerNorm((F_o)^T)) \tag{2}$$

Here, T represents the transpose, allowing the second MLP to integrate feature information in the sequence, σ is the Sigmoid activation function, and LayerNorm represents layer normalization. W_1, W_2, W_3, W_4 are all trainable weight matrices. For ease of representation, the above process is simplified as follows:

$$S_o = ORL(E) \tag{3}$$

Sequential representations are generated. To learn complex sequential relationships, a multi-layer encoding approach is used. The first layer of sequence encoding is defined as $S_o^{(l)} = S_o$, and the encoding layer for l ($l > 1$) is defined as:

$$S_o^{(l)} = ORL\left(S_o^{(l-1)}\right) \tag{4}$$

This paper uses a Weighted Similarity Attention Mechanism [21] to compute the sum of weighted similarities between the sequence relationship features and all neighboring items for each user, By calculating the similarity between the user and neighboring items, attention weights are assigned to each neighboring item, obtaining the user's preferences for neighboring items. For simplicity. we directly use S to represent the sequence relationship feature matrix $S_o^{(l)}$, and the attention score α_i is computed as follows:

$$\alpha_i = \frac{\exp(\beta_{u,i} e_u^\top e_i + S(u,i))}{\sum_{k \in \mathcal{N}(u)} \exp(\beta_{u,i} e_u^\top e_k + S(u,k))} \tag{5}$$

Finally, a regularization loss function $\mathcal{L}_U$ is introduced, which is used to minimize the difference between the user embedding e_u and the neighboring item embedding e_i. To simplify the optimization process, the maximum residual similarity between e_u and e_i is selected, and the Sigmoid activation function and negative log-likelihood [21] loss are introduced to represent the similarity loss:

$$\mathcal{L}_U = - \sum_{(u,i) \in N^+} \alpha_i \beta_{u,i} \log(\sigma(e_u^T e_i)) \qquad (6)$$

Dynamic weight adjustment. The weights of positive samples are adjusted dynamically. For each positive sample, the attention score α_i is used to dynamically adjust its weight. The weight of the positive sample is set as $w_i^+ = \alpha_i$. The weights of negative samples are adjusted similarly. For each negative sample, the attention score α_i of the negative sample is used to adjust its weight. The weight of the negative sample is set as $w_j^- = 1 - \alpha_i$.

In the learning of user-item interactions, in order to alleviate the over-smoothing problem, we choose to perform negative sampling [30] during the training process. For each positive sample pair $(u,i) \in N^+$ (i.e., item i that user u has actually interacted with), the model will randomly sample some items j that user u has not interacted with, forming negative sample pairs $(u,j) \in N^-$. This is inspired by the negative sampling strategy used in Word2Vec [18], which provides a simpler and more effective way to offset the over-smoothing problem. After negative sampling, we finally get the following constrained loss:

$$\mathcal{L}_U = - \sum_{(u,i) \in N^+} w_i^+ \beta_{u,i} \log(\sigma(e_u^T e_i)) - \sum_{(u,j) \in N^-} w_j^- \beta_{u,j} \log(\sigma(-e_u^T e_j)) \qquad (7)$$

where N^+ and N^- represent the sets of positive pairs and randomly sampled negative pairs.

Generally, CF models optimize item recommendations using pairwise BPR (Bayesian Personalized Ranking) loss [19] or pointwise BCE (Binary Cross Entropy) loss [10]. We formulate CF as a link prediction problem in graph learning. We choose the following BCE loss as the main optimization objective. To efficiently train our recommendation model, this is consistent with the following format:

$$\mathcal{L}_O = - \sum_{(u,i) \in N^+} w_i^+ \log(\sigma(e_u^T e_i)) - \sum_{(u,j) \in N^-} w_j^- \log(\sigma(-e_u^T e_j)) \qquad (8)$$

Finally, we obtain a constraint function that relies only on the user-item relationship:

$$\mathcal{L} = \mathcal{L}_O + \lambda \mathcal{L}_U \qquad (9)$$

where λ is the hyper-parameter to control the importance weights of two losse terms.

3.2 Contrastive Learning

Since the item-item co-occurrence matrix often requires a dense adjacency matrix for user-item graphs, directly comparing all items against each other may result in a large number of irrelevant item pairs. Therefore, this paper utilizes contrastive learning to optimize the similarity between positive and negative samples, enhancing the model's ability to distinguish between positive and negative samples. This helps the recommendation system gain a deeper understanding of the high-order relationships between users and items, thus improving the model's generalization and recommendation performance.

First, we construct the item-item co-occurrence matrix through the linkage of common items. It generates the weighted adjacency matrix of items based on $G = A^T A$, where G represents the number of items that appear in the same row under the same user in the interaction matrix. Each row of the matrix represents a user, and each column represents an item. The matrix element indicates the interaction between user i and item j. We then approximate the similarity matrix G using the infinite-layer graph convolution to derive the similarity between each pair of items: $\omega_{i,j} = \frac{G_{ij}}{g_i - G_{i,i}} \sqrt{\frac{g_i}{g_j}}$, where $\omega_{i,j}$ represents the similarity between item i and item j, and $G_{i,j}$ and G_j represent the frequency of occurrence of item i and item j, respectively.

Selection of Positive and Negative Samples. Wen [31] and others proposed a dynamic negative sample selection strategy, where negative samples become 'harder' during the model's learning process, thereby improving the model's generalization ability. To better select negative samples, we propose a sampling strategy. Positive sample pairs are selected from co-occurring item pairs. For example, for each item i, an item j with a high co-occurrence frequency is selected as the positive sample. Negative sample pairs are selected from non-co-occurring or low-co-occurrence item pairs. For example, for each item n, an item m with a low co-occurrence frequency is selected as the negative sample. Thus, for the positive sample pair (i, j) and the negative sample pair (n, m), their similarities are as follows:

$$\text{sim}(e_i, e_j) = \frac{G_{i,j}}{g_i - G_{i,i}} \sqrt{\frac{g_i}{g_j}}, \quad g_i = \sum_k G_{i,k} \tag{10}$$

where g_i and g_j denote the degrees (sum by column) of item i and item j in G, respectively.

Finally, a supervised contrastive learning loss function is used to simultaneously maximize the similarity of positive sample pairs and minimize the similarity of negative sample pairs:

$$\mathcal{L}_E = -\sum_{(i,j) \in P} \log\left(\sigma(\omega_{i,j})\right) - \sum_{(n,m) \in N} \log\left(1 - \sigma(\omega_{n,m})\right) \tag{11}$$

Among them, P represents the set of positive samples, N represents the set of negative samples, and σ is the sigmoid function. Finally, the recommendation model based on graph neural networks and the contrastive learning are integrated into a unified learning framework for joint optimization. The final learning objective is shown in formula (12). Among them, λ and δ are the hyperparameters that respectively adjust the relative importance of the user-item and item-item relationships.

$$\mathcal{L} = \mathcal{L}_O + \lambda \mathcal{L}_U + \delta \mathcal{L}_E \tag{12}$$

4 Experiments

4.1 Experimental Setup

Datasets and Evaluation Metrics. In order to validate the performance of the model, we use three publicly available datasets: Amazon-Book, Yelp2018, and Gowalla. Each dataset has its specific number of users, items, and interactions, as shown in Table 1.

Table 1. Statistics of the Datasets

Dataset	Users	Items	Interactions	Density
Amazon - Book	52,643	91,599	2,984,108	0.062%
Yelp2018	31,668	31,668	1,561,406	0.130%
Gowalla	29,858	40,981	1,027,370	0.084%

For the Evaluation Metrics. This paper adopts the widely used top-K recommendation method and employs Recall and Normalized Discounted Cumulative Gain (NDCG) as performance metrics, which are commonly used in recommendation system tasks. Recall represents the proportion of successfully predicted samples among the positive samples, while NDCG evaluates the accuracy of the recommendation results. Following common practice in the field of recommendation systems, K is set to 20.

Parameter Settings. The experimental environment used in this paper is based on the Anaconda environment, utilizing Python 3.10 and PyTorch 1.12.1 for the experiments. In terms of hardware, it includes an Intel(R) Xeon(R) CPU E5-2678 v3 @ 2.50 GHz processor, 64 GB of memory, and an NVIDIA RTX 8000 GPU with 48 GB of memory. All experiments and model training are conducted under this environment.

Generally, we adopt Gaussian distribution with 0 mean and 10^{-4} standard deviation to initialize embeddings. In many cases, we initialize using a Gaussian distribution with a mean of 0 and a standard deviation of 0.1. The Adam algorithm is employed to optimize model parameters, with an L2 regularization coefficient set to 10^{-4}, a learning rate of 10^{-4}, a batch size of 1024, a negative sampling ratio of 300, and an item neighbor size of 10. In particular, we fix the embedding size is fixed at 64, consistent with recent GCN-based [20] work, to maintain the same level of parameters for a fair comparison.

4.2 Comparison Experiment

The experimental results of the proposed ACGCN and other classical collaborative filtering recommendation algorithms on three real-world datasets are shown in Table 2. In this table, *Improv.* represents the improvement percentage of the proposed algorithm compared to the existing optimal baseline algorithm in each metric.

From the experimental results presented in Table 2, the following conclusions can be drawn:

- LR-GCCF [22] introduces a residual structure inspired by ResNet [23] to solve the performance degradation problem caused by increasing the depth of GCN layers, while simplifying some parameters. Its performance is slightly better than NGCF, but it has limitations, as some datasets are not suitable for very deep GCNs.
- IMP-GCN [24] introduces an interest-aware message-passing mechanism. This approach differentiates the importance of neighboring nodes based on user-specific interests during information aggregation, allowing for a more targeted feature representation that better captures fine-grained and diverse user preferences compared to models treating all neighbor information equally.
- DGCF [25], with its dynamic graph modeling, multi-hop information aggregation, and adaptive weight allocation mechanisms, performs excellently when handling time-varying user preferences and sparse data. In contrast, LightGCN's [27] is simpler and, although it performs well in certain scenarios, DGCF has a clear advantage when dealing with complex and dynamic recommendation tasks, making it the best performer among baseline models.
- IA-GCN [26] employs an interactive graph convolution mechanism to more precisely model the nuances within user-item interactions. By dynamically considering different interaction types or strengths during message passing, it aims to capture complex user preferences for more personalized and accurate recommendations, particularly in scenarios with diverse interaction patterns.
- UltraGCNbase [17] employs simplified graph convolution operations, filtering out noisy or ambiguous relations, and assigns more reasonable edge weights to capture user-item and item-item relations. This suggests its superiority in capturing user-item relations and generating recommendation results compared to DGCF.
- Despite the advantages of UltraGCNbase, which still fixes the weight distribution between positive and negative samples and performs better on user-item relations than item-item relations, the model proposed in this paper builds on UltraGCNbase by introducing a two-layer MLP to incorporate user preferences for item sequences. Attention scores are calculated to dynamically allocate weights between positive and negative samples. Supervised item-item co-occurrence modeling selects high-frequency positive samples and low-frequency negative samples, and contrastive learning is used to maximize the similarity of positive sample pairs while minimizing the similarity of negative sample pairs. On the three datasets, ACGCN outperforms the best-performing baseline model (IA-GCN) in terms of Recall@20 by 5.08%, 4.40%,

and 3.53%, and in terms of NDCG@20 by 5.36%, 3.91%, and 3.20%. ACGCN achieves the best results across all baseline algorithms on both Recall@20 and NDCG@20. We attribute such good performance of ACGCN to the following reasons: 1) By using a sequential relationship table Using a learning layer to capture the sequential evolution of historical interaction items in a conversation. 2) Compared with other baselines, ACGCN can leverage powerful graph convolution to exploit useful and deeper collaborative information in graphs. These advantages together lead to the superiority of ACGCN than compared state-of-the-art models.

Table 2. Experimental Results of ACGCN and Baseline Models

Model	Amazon-Book		Yelp2018		Gowalla	
	Recall@20	NDCG@20	Recall@20	NDCG@20	Recall@20	NDCG@20
NGCF	0.0344	0.0263	0.0579	0.0477	0.157	0.1327
LR-GCCF	0.0335	0.0265	0.0561	0.0443	0.1519	0.1285
LightGCN	0.0411	0.0315	0.0649	0.053	0.183	0.1554
IMP-GCN	0.0460	0.0357	0.0653	0.0531	0.1845	0.1567
DGCF	0.0422	0.0324	0.0654	0.053	0.1842	0.1561
IA-GCN	0.0472	0.0373	0.0659	0.0537	0.1839	0.1562
UltraGCNbase	0.0504	0.0393	0.0667	0.0552	0.1845	0.1566
ACGCN	0.0496	0.0393	0.0688	0.0558	0.1904	0.1612
Improv.	5.08%	5.36%	4.40%	3.91%	3.53%	3.20%

4.3 Ablation Study

To better understand the actual value of each component of the recommendation task in the model, the following ACGCN model variants were designed for comparative study:

- ACGCN/A: This variant removes the attention scores calculated from sequence features.
- ACGCN/C: This variant removes the supervised contrastive learning task.
- ACGCN/S: This variant removes the attention scores calculated from sequence features and adopts random positive and negative sample sampling in the item-item learning process, instead of supervised selection of item pairs with strong co-occurrence capabilities.

For a better understanding of the functionality of each part of the recommendation task, we conducted the ablation experiments on the Amazon-Book dataset. The experimental results of each model variant are shown in Fig. 3.

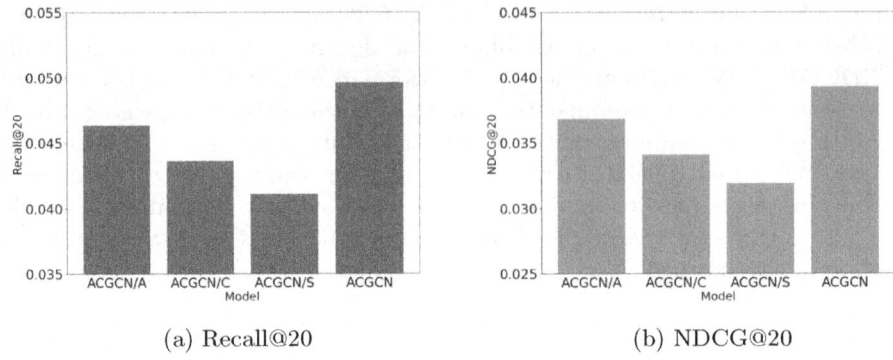

Fig. 3. Performance comparison of variants of ACGCN

The comparison between ACGCN/A and ACGCN/S shows that using random positive and negative sample sampling instead of supervised selection of item pairs with strong co-occurrence in the item-item learning process has a significant impact on the model's learning process, leading to a notable decrease in recommendation quality.

The comparison between ACGCN/C and ACGCN reveals that removing the attention scores calculated from sequence features weakens the model's ability to capture user behavior sequence information. This results in the model assigning similar weights to the samples, reducing its discriminative ability. Consequently, the model fails to effectively learn and adapt to complex user behavior patterns, leading to decreased recommendation accuracy.

When comparing ACGCN/A and ACGCN, we observe that the removal of the supervised contrastive learning task lowers the model's ability to differentiate between positive samples. This indicates that the contrastive learning task plays an important role in improving the model's discriminative ability.

In conclusion, ACGCN performs the best in all scenarios, which indicates that the model is effective and that each component of the model structure is indispensable.

4.4 Parameter Analysis

We first set δ to 0.20 and then tested $\lambda = [0.1, 0.5, 1.0, 1.5, 2.0, 2.5, 3.0]$; in this paper, we use δ to adjust the weight of the contrastive loss, and we set λ to 2.0. Then, we compared the results for $\delta = [0.01, 0.10, 0.20, 0.30, 0.40, 0.50]$. To study the impact of these two hyperparameters, we conducted experiments on the Yelp2018 dataset, and the results are shown in Fig. 4.

For λ, we found that smaller values limited the effect of the user-item constraint loss, and values around 2 were appropriate. As for δ, the trend was similar to λ, but more pronounced, with 0.2 being a suitable choice. Furthermore, as δ increased, the model's performance on the dataset declined. The likely reason for this is that the increase in δ caused gradient conflicts between the contrastive

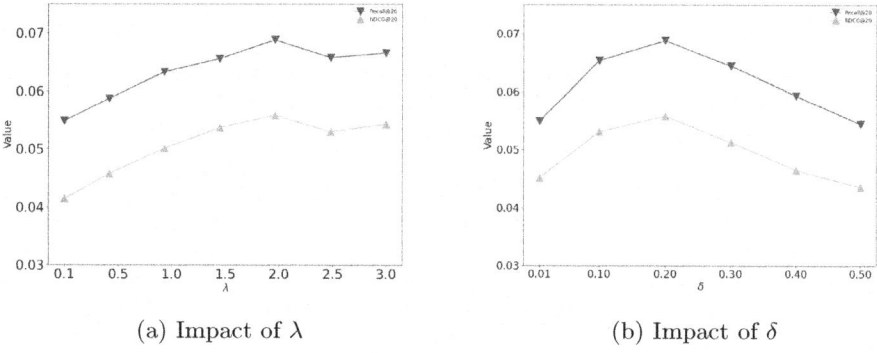

Fig. 4. Performance comparison with different λ and δ

task and the recommendation task, harming the optimization of the recommendation task. Overall, our study of these two parameters shows that they are crucial to ACGCN, allowing for flexible adjustment of the learning weights for different relationships, and should be carefully tuned.

Overall, our study of these two parameters shows that they are crucial to ACGCN, allowing for flexible adjustment of the learning weights for different relations, and should be carefully tuned.

5 Conclusion

This paper proposes a sequence-attention-based graph convolutional model aimed at improving the performance of recommendation systems. Specifically, it captures the sequential features in user behavior through an MLP-based interest learning module and utilizes an attention mechanism to dynamically adjust the weights of positive and negative samples, thereby more accurately reflecting changes in user interests. Moreover, by selecting positive and negative samples with strong co-occurrence from the item co-occurrence matrix and employing a supervised contrastive learning method, ACGCN is able to more precisely distinguish between positive and negative samples, thus enhancing the recommendation system's performance and generalization ability.

Experimental results demonstrate that the proposed ACGCN model outperforms existing mainstream models on several public datasets, especially achieving significant improvements in key performance metrics such as Recall@20 and NDCG@20. However, the model relies on user-item interaction data for learning, and in cold-start scenarios [32], where there is insufficient interaction information, the performance of such models may degrade. In future work, we will consider addressing this limitation by incorporating additional features such as content, context, and social information to complement the lack of user-item interaction data.

References

1. Zhou, K., et al.: S3-rec: self-supervised learning for sequential recommendation with mutual information maximization. In: Proceedings of the 29th ACM International Conference on Information Knowledge Management, pp. 1893–1902. ACM, New York (2020)
2. Koren, Y., Rendle, S., Bell, R.: Advances in collaborative filtering. In: Ricci, F., Rokach, L., Shapira, B. (eds.) Recommender Systems Handbook, vol. 42, pp. 91–142. Springer, New York (2021)
3. Quadrana, M., Cremonesi, P., Jannach, D.: Sequence-aware recommender systems. In: Proceedings of ACM Computing Surveys (CSUR), vol. 51, no. 4, pp. 1–36. ACM, New York (2018)
4. Kang, W.-C., McAuley, J.: Self-attentive sequential recommendation. In: Proceedings of the IEEE International Conference on Data Mining (ICDM), pp. 197–206. IEEE, New York (2018)
5. Hidasi, B.: Session-based recommendations with recurrent neural networks. arXiv preprint arXiv:1511.06939 (2015)
6. Zhou, K., Yu, H., Zhao, W.X., Wen, J.R.: Filter-enhanced MLP is all you need for sequential recommendation. In: Proceedings of the ACM Web Conference 2022, pp. 2388–2399. ACM (2022)
7. Cho, S.M., Park, E., Yoo, S.: MEANTIME: mixture of attention mechanisms with multi-temporal embeddings for sequential recommendation. In: Proceedings of the 14th ACM Conference on Recommender Systems, pp. 515–520. ACM, New York (2020)
8. Taud, H., Mas, J.-F.: Multilayer perceptron (MLP). In: Mas, J.-F. (ed.) Geomatic Approaches for Modeling Land Change Scenarios, pp. 451–455. Springer, Heidelberg (2018)
9. Khosla, P., et al.: Supervised contrastive learning. In: Advances in Neural Information Processing Systems, vol. 33, pp. 18661–18673 (2020)
10. He, X., Liao, L., Zhang, H., Nie, L., Hu, X., Chua, T.-S.: Neural collaborative filtering. In: Proceedings of the 26th International Conference on World Wide Web, pp. 173–182. ACM, New York (2017)
11. Wu, S., Tang, Y., Zhu, Y., Wang, L., Xie, X., Tan, T.: Session-based recommendation with graph neural networks. In: Proceedings of the AAAI Conference on Artificial Intelligence, vol. 33, no. 01, pp. 346–353. AAAI Press (2019)
12. Zhang, W., et al.: Mixed supervised graph contrastive learning for recommendation. arXiv preprint arXiv:2404.15954 (2024)
13. Yu, J., Yin, H., Xia, X., Chen, T., Cui, L., Nguyen, Q.V.H.: Are graph augmentations necessary? Simple graph contrastive learning for recommendation. In: Proceedings of the 45th International ACM SIGIR Conference on Research and Development in Information Retrieval, pp. 1294–1303. ACM, New York (2022)
14. Li, H., Luo, X., Yu, Q., Wang, H.: Session-based recommendation via contrastive learning on heterogeneous graph. In: Proceedings of the IEEE International Conference on Big Data (Big Data), pp. 1077–1082. IEEE, New York (2021)
15. Xia, X., Yin, H., Yu, J., Wang, Q., Cui, L., Zhang, X.: Self-supervised hypergraph convolutional networks for session-based recommendation. In: Proceedings of the AAAI Conference on Artificial Intelligence, vol. 35, no. 5, pp. 4503–4511. AAAI Press (2021)
16. Cai, X., Huang, C., Xia, L., Ren, X.: LightGCL: simple yet effective graph contrastive learning for recommendation. arXiv preprint arXiv:2302.08191 (2023)

17. Mao, K., Zhu, J., Xiao, X., Lu, B., Wang, Z., He, X.: UltraGCN: ultra simplification of graph convolutional networks for recommendation. In: Proceedings of the 30th ACM International Conference on Information and Knowledge Management, pp. 1253–1262. ACM, New York (2021)
18. Church, K.W.: Word2Vec. Nat. Lang. Eng. **23**(1), 155–162. Cambridge University Press (2017)
19. Rendle, S., Freudenthaler, C., Gantner, Z., Schmidt-Thieme, L.: BPR: Bayesian personalized ranking from implicit feedback. arXiv preprint arXiv:1205.2618 (2012)
20. Zhang, S., Tong, H., Xu, J., Maciejewski, R.: Graph convolutional networks: a comprehensive review. Comput. Soc. Netw. **6**(1), 1–23. Springer (2019)
21. Veličković, P., Cucurull, G., Casanova, A., Romero, A., Lio, P., Bengio, Y.: Graph attention networks. arXiv preprint arXiv:1710.10903 (2017)
22. Chen, L., Le, W., Hong, R., Zhang, K., Wang, M.: Revisiting graph based collaborative filtering: a linear residual graph convolutional network approach. In: AAAI (2020)
23. He, K., Zhang, X., Ren, S., Sun, J.: Deep residual learning for image recognition. In: Proceedings of the IEEE Conference on Computer Vision and Pattern Recognition, pp. 770–778. IEEE, New York (2016)
24. Liu, F., Cheng, Z., Zhu, L., Gao, Z., Nie, L.: Interest-aware message-passing GCN for recommendation. In: Proceedings of the Web Conference 2021, pp. 1296–1305. ACM (2021)
25. Wang, X., Jin, H., Zhang, A., He, X., Xu, T., Chua, T.-S.: Disentangled graph collaborative filtering. In: Proceedings of the 43rd International ACM SIGIR Conference on Research and Development in Information Retrieval, pp. 1001–1010. ACM, New York (2020)
26. Zhang, Y., et al.: IA-GCN: interactive graph convolutional network for recommendation. arXiv preprint arXiv:2204.03827 (2022)
27. He, X., Deng, K., Wang, X., Li, Y., Zhang, Y., Wang, M.: LightGCN: simplifying and powering graph convolution network for recommendation. In: Proceedings of the 43rd International ACM SIGIR Conference on Research and Development in Information Retrieval, pp. 639–648. ACM, New York (2020)
28. Schwab, I., Kobsa, A., Koychev, I.: Learning user interests through positive examples using content analysis and collaborative filtering. Internal Memo, GMD, St. Augustin, Germany (2001)
29. Salau, A.O., Jain, S.: Feature extraction: a survey of the types, techniques, applications. In: Proceedings of the 2019 International Conference on Signal Processing and Communication (ICSC), pp. 158–164. IEEE (2019)
30. Chen, T., Sun, Y., Shi, Y., Hong, L.: On sampling strategies for neural network-based collaborative filtering. In: Proceedings of the 23rd ACM SIGKDD International Conference on Knowledge Discovery and Data Mining, pp. 767–776. ACM (2017)
31. Wen, X., Wang, J., Yang, X.: Dynamic negative sampling for recommendation with feature matching. Multimedia Tools Appl. **83**(16), 49749–49766. Springer (2024)
32. Zhou, Z., Zhang, L., Yang, N.: Contrastive collaborative filtering for cold-start item recommendation. In: Proceedings of the ACM Web Conference 2023, pp. 928–937. ACM (2023)

Hyperparameter-Free Bi-level Knowledge Graph Optimization for Link Prediction

Hao Li[1], Tong Mei[2], and Jiaxin Fang[3(✉)]

[1] National University of Defense Technology, Changsha, China
[2] Qingdao University of Science and Technology, Qingdao, China
[3] Dalian University of Technology, Dalian, China
17527785317@163.com

Abstract. In this paper, we explore the challenges and advancements in Bi-level Knowledge Graphs, which extend traditional triplet-based representations to capture relationships between facts. While Bi-level KGs offer greater expressiveness, they encounter issues related to sparsity and the introduction of hyperparameters in data augmentation modules, designed to enrich the graph structure. Specifically, the hyperparameters τ and λ, which control the scale of augmented data and its loss weight, have been set empirically without sufficient exploration of their optimal values across different dataset sizes. To address this, we propose a method that eliminates these redundant hyperparameters by introducing functions $\mathcal{F}(\cdot)$ and $\mathcal{G}(\cdot)$ to determine the optimal scale of augmented data and loss weight. Our approach uses KL divergence to ensure alignment between the augmented and original datasets, and identifies a quadratic relationship between model performance and the loss weight. The effectiveness of our method is validated on three datasets, demonstrating significant improvements in triplet prediction and conditional link prediction tasks compared to existing models. This strategy not only improves model performance but also reduces reliance on empirical tuning, leading to more efficient and scalable knowledge graph reasoning models.

Keywords: Knowledge graph · Parameter elimination · Link prediction

1 Introduction

Knowledge Graph(KG) is a graphical structure that abstracts real-world entities and their relationships as nodes and edges [31]. It is typically represented in the form of (h, r, t), where h and t are entities and r is the relationship between them [28]. However, this simple triplet representation only captures the relationships between entities, overlooking the relationships between facts. Recently, researchers proposed a novel knowledge graph structure called the Bi-level Knowledge Graph (Bi-level KG). In this structure, triplets (facts) are represented as new nodes, and a set of relationships between these new nodes is defined. By extending the nodes and relationships, Bi-level KG can effectively represent the relationships between facts. Figure 1 illustrates the structure of Bi-level KG, where the left parts represents the relationships between entities,

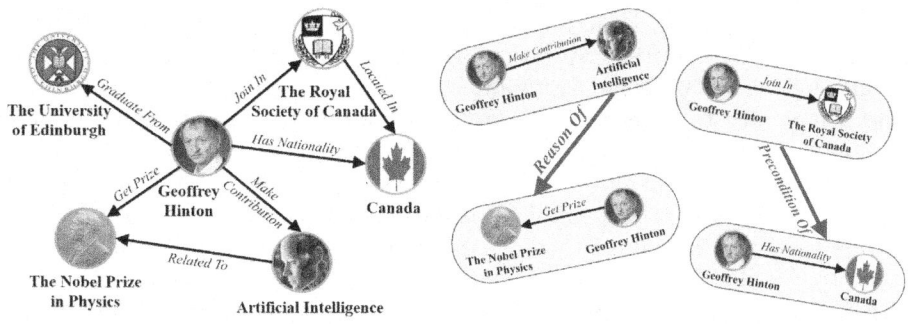

Fig. 1. Bi-level KG redefines each triplet as a node and then defines a new set of relationships between these nodes. The left part of figure corresponds to the traditional knowledge graph, while the right part corresponds to the fact-level knowledge graph.

and right parts represents the relationships between facts. Bi-level KG enables more complex link prediction tasks. The model can predict unknown facts based on known facts and relationships, or identify an unknown entity in a target fact.

However, the fact-level structure of Bi-level KG is highly sparse, as most facts in the real world do not have relationships between them. Therefore, to model the fact representations in Bi-level KG, existing approaches typically use dimensionality-reduced triplet representations (h, r, t) to express facts. To improve the representation of facts, uncovering hidden triplets in entity knowledge graphs has become a key research focus. To extract high-quality triplet data, BiVE [7] proposed a data augmentation module based on a random walk strategy, which achieved promising results. During model training, the data are not directly integrated into the training set but are instead incorporated into the model as an independent module.

Currently, existing data augmentation methods introduce additional hyperparameters. For example, in the data augmentation module from [7], two hyperparameters are introduced: τ, which controls the number of new data points generated, and λ, which represents the weight of the loss associated with the new data. A lower value of τ results in richer data, but may also introduce erroneous data that could interfere with the model; a higher value of τ generates less data, limiting its ability to enrich the graph structure. For the hyperparameter λ, its weight influences the model's ability to learn from new data. Both excessively high or low values of λ can have significant impacts on the model's performance (for more details, refer to the experimental section).

In existing works, the authors set the two hyperparameters as fixed values, without fully exploring the impact of the data augmentation module on model performance. We observe that the three data sets for Bi-level KG-FBH, FBHE, and DBHE - vary in scale, and therefore the hyperparameter values should differ depending on the data set. To date, no research has explored the relationship between the data augmentation components and the hyperparameters of the original datasets. As a result, determining how to adjust the number of augmented data points and the loss weight based on the dataset size has become a crucial issue. Through preliminary experiments, we found that the optimal number of augmented data can be explored by analyzing the graph structure information in the dataset. Additionally, the weight of the data augmentation module follows a nonlinear distribution, and we can use algorithms with low time complexity to determine the optimal parameters. Additionally, we have developed a model evaluation method based on the model's performance across various metrics, which allows for a comprehensive assessment of the model's performance in both triplet prediction and conditional link prediction tasks.

In this paper, to eliminate the redundant hyperparameters τ and λ introduced by the data augmentation module, we designed two functions, $\mathcal{F}(\cdot)$ and $\mathcal{G}(\cdot)$, which determine the scale of the generated augmented data and the loss weight of the module. This significantly improves the utilization of the data augmentation module in Bi-level KG. To comprehensively evaluate the model's performance in both triplet prediction and conditional link prediction, we developed a model evaluation method. We conducted extensive comparative experiments, ablation studies, hyperparameter experiments, and transferability tests, successfully demonstrating that our approach to eliminating hyperparameters is both feasible and effective. Our contributions can be summarized as follows:

- We are the first to investigate the external module parameters in knowledge graph reasoning models. Through parameter analysis, we discover a functional relation between the parameters and conduct reasoning validation.
- By introducing the concept of KI divergence, we ensure the credibility of the data generated by the data augmentation module. By solving function $\mathcal{F}(\tau)$, we eliminate the hyperparameter τ that controls the scale of the data.
- Through a series of experimental verifications and function fittings, we identify the performance variation patterns for each dataset across different tasks. By using the $\mathcal{G}(\lambda)$ function, we eliminate the weight hyperparameter λ.
- Extensive comparative experiments, ablation studies and hyperparameter experiments have validated that our proposed hyperparameter elimination method and model evaluation method are both feasible and effective.

2 Related Work

2.1 Hyper Knowledge Graph

To enhance the expressiveness of KGs, researchers have developed various types of hyper-knowledge graphs with different structures [30]. Temporal Knowledge Graphs [28,29] add timestamps to each triplet, enriching the semantic information [8,24,27]. ECEformer [1] uses a transformer encoder to effectively capture the temporal information in triplets, while TPmod [3] assigns different weights to triplets from different time points. Additionally, some hypergraph-based studies [4,5] expand triplets with key-value pairs. BiVE [7] integrated the relations between facts into traditional KGs and designed the BiVE [7] model, which enables more advanced prediction tasks. NextE [9] represents atomic facts and nested relations in a generalized four-dimensional hypercomplex space using matrices.

2.2 Knowledge Graph Representation Learning

Knowledge graph representation learning [21] is a technique aimed at mapping entities and relationships in a knowledge graph to a low-dimensional vector space [11,22]. Currently, knowledge graph representation learning methods can be broadly categorized into three types: Translational Models: These methods, exemplified by TransE [16], aim to minimize $||\mathbf{h} + \mathbf{r} - \mathbf{t}||$. Such methods include TransR [17] and TransW [18]. Tensor Decompositional Models: SimplE [20] enhances the canonical polyadic decomposition by incorporating two independent entity embeddings. Neural Network Models: RGCN [25] optimizes the aggregation methods through relation-specific aggregation, while CompGCN [12] uses three different types of message aggregation to facilitate the flow of information.

2.3 Parameter Optimization

As knowledge graph reasoning models become increasingly sophisticated, parameter selection has become an important issue, primarily in two aspects: 1) Internal model parameter. With the advancement of graph neural network technologies, models such as NBF-Net [10], CompGCN [12], and GraIL [13] have achieved significant success in link prediction. However, these methods have complex parameters, high sensitivity. 2) External model parameter. To address issues within the model, researchers often design independent modules to tackle specific problems [19,26]. Generally, the choice of hyperparameters for modules depends on human expertise and experience [2]. Existing research has proposed various innovative methods to reduce the reliance on hyperparameters. FreeGEM [15] reduces the need for manual hyperparameter tuning significantly by using an online-monitoring-offline architecture to update user and item embeddings in real-time. CoPER [14] leverages relationships as contextual generators for model parameters, replacing the traditional additive interaction method.

3 Methods

3.1 Preliminary

Definition 1 (Bi-Level Knowledge Graph). Traditional knowledge graphs are typically written as $\mathcal{G} = \{\mathcal{V}_e, \mathcal{E}_e, \mathcal{R}_e\}$, where $\mathcal{V}_e$ represents the set of entities, $\mathcal{E}_e$ represents the set of edges, and $\mathcal{R}_e$ represents the set of relationships. The construction process of Bi-level KG is as follows: first, a new set of nodes $\mathcal{V}_t$ is defined, where each element is drawn from $\mathcal{E}_e$, meaning each fact is redefined as a node. Then, a set of relationships between facts, $\mathcal{R}_t$, and a set of edges, $\mathcal{E}_t = \{(h_t, r_t, t_t) : h_t, t_t \in \mathcal{V}_t, r_t \in \mathcal{R}_t\}$, are defined. Ultimately, the Bi-level knowledge graph is written as $\mathcal{G}_t = \{\mathcal{V}_e, \mathcal{E}_e, \mathcal{R}_e, \mathcal{V}_t, \mathcal{E}_t, \mathcal{R}_t\}$.

Definition 2 (Triplet Prediction). In Bi-level knowledge graph $\mathcal{G}_t = \{\mathcal{V}_e, \mathcal{E}_e, \mathcal{R}_e, \mathcal{V}_t, \mathcal{E}_t, \mathcal{R}_t\}$, for a known fact $h_t \in \mathcal{V}_t$ and a relationship $r_t \in \mathcal{R}_t$, the task is to predict another unknown fact $? \in \mathcal{V}_t$. The triplet prediction problem is defined as $(h_t, r_t, ?)$ or $(?, r_t, t_t)$.

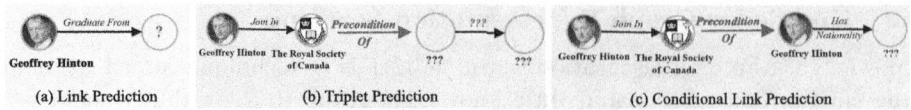

Fig. 2. Examples of the three type link prediction tasks

Definition 3 (Conditional Link Prediction). In Bi-level knowledge graph $\mathcal{G}_t = \{\mathcal{V}_e, \mathcal{E}_e, \mathcal{R}_e, \mathcal{V}_t, \mathcal{E}_t, \mathcal{R}_t\}$, for a known fact $h_t \in \mathcal{V}_t$, a relationship $r_t \in \mathcal{R}_t$, and incomplete fact $t_t \in \mathcal{V}_t$ the task is to predict an unknown entity $? \in t_t$. The conditional link prediction problem is defined as $(h_t, r_t, (?, r, t))$, $(h_t, r_t, (h, r, ?))$, $((?, r, t), r_t, t_t)$ or $((h, r, ?), r_t, t_t)$.

Figure 2 illustrates three types of link prediction tasks. While traditional knowledge graphs can only perform link prediction, Bi-level KG is capable of link prediction, triplet prediction, and conditional link prediction.

3.2 Bi-level KG Reasoning Backbone

Inspired by QuatE, we model Bi-level KG using quaternions. Entities are represented as vectors in the quaternion space, and relationships are represented as rotational vectors. Compared to traditional translation-based models, quaternions can capture complex relationships by leveraging higher-dimensional spaces. We represent each entity in the vector space with four vectors as:

$$Q_{entity} = \{s + x\mathbf{i} + y\mathbf{j} + z\mathbf{k} : s, x, y, z \in \mathbb{R}^d\}. \tag{1}$$

The role of a relationship in a quaternion-based representation is to rotate other quaternions in the vector space. Therefore, relationships are also encoded in the same way as entities with quaternions. However, to eliminate the scaling effect, the representation of relationships is typically normalized to unit length:

$$W_r = \{s_r + x_r\mathbf{i} + y_r\mathbf{j} + z_r\mathbf{k} : s_r, x_r, y_r, z_r \in \mathbb{R}^d\}. \tag{2}$$

Since the connections between facts are relatively sparse, facts cannot be represented in the vector space through random initialization. To provide higher-quality embeddings, we combine the entity and relationship representations within each fact and use dimensionality reduction techniques to ensure that the dimensionality of the fact's representation matches that of the entity representations. We define a function $f(\cdot)$ to implement this mapping. To ensure that the representation of each entity is as distinct as possible, we introduce an offset vector. Therefore, the representation of each fact is defined as:

$$Q_{triplet} = f(Q_h, W_r, Q_t) + b. \tag{3}$$

During training, the head entity h is rotated by the relationship r, causing the inner product between the rotated quaternion Q'_h and the tail entity Q_t

to increase. This indicates that the entities are moving closer together in the four-dimensional space. The rotation is computed as follows:

$$Q'_h(s'_h, x'_h, y'_h, z'_h) = Q_h \otimes W_r^\triangleleft = (s_h \circ p - x_h \circ q - y_h \circ u - z_h \circ v) + \\ (s_h \circ q + x_h \circ p + y_h \circ v - z_h \circ u)\mathbf{i} + (s_h \circ u - x_h \circ v + y_h \circ p + z_h \circ q)\mathbf{j} + \\ (s_h \circ v + x_h \circ u - y_h \circ q + z_h \circ p)\mathbf{k},$$
(4)

Here, $\circ$ represents the element-wise multiplication between two vectors. We employ the quaternion inner product as the scoring function:

$$\phi(h, r, t) = Q'_h \cdot Q_t = \langle s'_h, s_t \rangle + \langle x'_h, x_t \rangle + \langle y'_h, y_t \rangle + \langle z'_h, z_t \rangle.$$
(5)

It is important to note that Eq. (5) can be used to compute all data in our model, as we have unified the dimensionality of fact and entity representations through Eq. (3).

To improve the quality of factual embeddings, BiVE [7] proposes a data augmentation strategy based on random walks. This strategy is independent of the training process and functions as a plug-and-play module. It further uncovers latent factual data in the knowledge graph and is trained separately from the training set during the training process.

Specifically, the process begins by establishing reverse edges, allowing entities between two related facts to be connected via paths. Next, multiple random walks are performed, recording the i-th walk's starting and ending points as (s_i, t_i), and the sequence of relations in the path as p_i. All paths form a set of paths $\mathcal{W} = \{(s_i, p_i, t_i)\}$. Finally, the paths are sorted by the frequency of p, and for all paths with the same p_i, we count whether the starting point s_i and ending point t_i share the same relation r in the training set, recording their frequency. The ratio is then defined as the number of identical p_i paths as the denominator, and the number of related relations in the training set as the numerator:

$$c(p_i, r) := \frac{|\{(s_i, r, t_i) : (s_i, p_k, t_i) \in \mathcal{W}, (s_i, r, t_i) \in \mathcal{E}_{train}\}|}{|\{(s_i, p_i, t_i) : (s_i, p_i, t_i) \in \mathcal{W}\}|}.$$
(6)

The higher the value of $c(p_i, r)$, the closer the relationship sequence p_i is to the relation r in the training set. For all paths with a given relation sequence p_i, we can establish an edge with relation r between every pair of starting point s_i and ending point t_i. In this way, we construct a data augmentation file that records all the augmented data, denoted as $\mathcal{E}_{aug}$.

The existing approach sets a hyperparameter $\tau = 0.7$ and saves the triples that satisfy $c(p_i, k) > \tau$ as augmented data. After the data augmentation module enhances the data, the entire knowledge graph can be divided into three parts based on the source: entity triples, factual triples, and augmented triples. The total loss is defined as:

$$\mathcal{L} = \mathcal{L}_{entity} + \alpha \mathcal{L}_{fact} + \lambda \mathcal{L}_{aug}.$$
(7)

The hyperparameters λ and τ control the size of $\mathcal{E}_{aug}$ and the loss weight, respectively. Due to factors such as dataset size and graph density, the values of these two hyperparameters are ambiguous and can only be determined through empirical experience. BiVE [7] sets these two hyperparameters to fixed values without further exploration. NextE [9] changes their values, but applies the same hyperparameters across all datasets without in-depth investigation.

3.3 Hyperparameter Solving Function

Solving τ Based on KL Divergence. In the data augmentation module, the hyperparameter τ controls the size of the augmented dataset. Specifically, the smaller the value of τ, the larger the generated dataset. To ensure that the augmented data effectively supplements the original training data without causing a significant shift in the data distribution, we propose an optimization method based on Kullback-Leibler divergence.

To minimize the distributional difference between the augmented dataset and the original dataset, we use KL divergence to measure the relative information between them. KL divergence quantifies the distributional difference between the original dataset $\mathcal{E}train$ and the augmented dataset $\mathcal{E}aug$, and minimizing it helps ensure that the augmented data does not introduce excessive noise or deviate from the distribution of the original data. For each triple (h,r,t), we can calculate its probability distribution in both the original dataset and the augmented dataset using the model's scoring function $h(h,r,t)$. The probability distributions of the training set and the augmented dataset are denoted as $P_D(h,r,t)$ and $P_{D_{aug}}(h,r,t)$, respectively, and are represented by the following:

$$P_D(h,r,t) = \frac{\exp(h(h,r,t))}{\sum_{(h,r,t') \in \mathcal{C}} \exp(h(h,r,t'))}, \tag{8}$$

$$P_{D_{\text{aug}}}(h,r,t) = \frac{\exp(h_{\text{aug}}(h,r,t))}{\sum_{(h,r,t') \in \mathcal{C}} \exp(h_{\text{aug}}(h,r,t'))}. \tag{9}$$

Here, $h(h,r,t)$ represents the score in the training dataset, $h_{aug}(h,r,t)$ represents the score in the augmented dataset, and $\mathcal{C}$ denotes the candidate set, which includes negative triples such as (h,r,t). Next, we use KL divergence to measure the distributional difference between the original and the augmented dataset:

$$\mathcal{F}_{\text{KL}}(P_D \parallel P_{D_{\text{aug}}}) = \sum_{(h,r,t) \in \mathcal{C}} P_D(h,r,t) \log \frac{P_D(h,r,t)}{P_{D_{\text{aug}}}(h,r,t)}. \tag{10}$$

By minimizing the KL divergence, we can optimize the hyperparameter τ to make the augmented dataset as close as possible to the original dataset in terms of probability distribution. Specifically, our goal is to minimize the KL divergence between the augmented dataset and the original dataset:

$$\tau^* = \arg\min_{\tau} \mathcal{F}_{\text{KL}}(P_D \parallel P_{D_{\text{aug}}}), \tag{11}$$

Here, the optimal τ^* is the value that makes the distribution of the augmented dataset as close as possible to the distribution of the original dataset.

Table 1. More details for three Bi-level KG datasets

	$\mathcal{V}_e$	$\mathcal{R}_e$	$\mathcal{E}_e$	$\mathcal{R}_t$	$\mathcal{V}_t$	$\mathcal{E}_t$
FBH	14541	237	310117	6	27062	33157
FBHE	14541	237	310117	10	34941	33718
DBHE	12440	87	68296	8	6717	8206

Theoretical Justification. KL divergence is a principled way to measure the difference between two probability distributions. By minimizing the KL divergence between the augmented data distribution PD_{aug} and the original data distribution PD, we constrain the augmented data to remain close to the original data in statistical structure. This prevents distributional drift and ensures that the augmented data does not introduce significant noise. Such use of KL divergence has also been adopted in data augmentation and domain adaptation literature as a way to preserve semantic consistency between domains.

Solving λ Based on Fitting Function. To solve for the hyperparameter τ, we set its value range to $[0.5, 1.0]$ and discretized it with a step size of 0.05. Specifically, the values of τ are as follows: $0.50, 0.55, ..., 1.00$. For each value of τ, we conducted experiments and recorded the corresponding model performance.

Preliminary experimental results show a clear quadratic relationship between the hyperparameter τ and model performance. Specifically, when τ is small (e.g., close to 0.5), the model performance is relatively low. As τ increases, the weight of the augmented data gradually increases, leading to an improvement in model performance. However, when τ continues to increase, the model performance starts to stabilize and even shows a downward trend. This quadratic relationship can be expressed mathematically as follows:

$$\mathcal{H}(\lambda) = a\lambda^2 + b\lambda + c, \tag{12}$$

Here, a, b, and c are constants obtained through experimental fitting. The basic idea of the least squares method is to find the optimal parameters by minimizing the sum of the squared residuals. Specifically, given a set of data (λ_i, y_i), where $i = 1, 2, ..., n$ represents the index of the data, the goal of the least squares method is to minimize the following objective function:

$$S(a, b, c) = \sum_{i=1}^{n} \left(y_i - (a\lambda_i^2 + b\lambda_i + c)\right)^2. \tag{13}$$

We selected the DBHE dataset and conducted experiments using the hyperparameter $\tau = 0.9$ obtained in the previous step, following the procedure outlined above. Through fitting, we obtained the following coefficients for the quadratic function: $a = 12.45$, $b = -27.28$, and $c = 83.14$.

Remark on Dynamic Adjustment. While our method statically determines the optimal values of τ and λ before training, the optimization process is inherently based on dataset-specific statistics (e.g., graph density, score distribution).

Table 2. Table shows the experimental results of triplet prediction. Improvements that surpass the baseline models are highlighted in bold.

	FBH			FBHE			DBHE		
	MR	MRR	Hit@10	MR	MRR	Hit@10	MR	MRR	Hit@10
PTransE	111024.3	0.069	0.071	86793.2	0.249	0.274	18888.7	0.158	0.195
RPJE	113082.0	0.070	0.072	89173.1	0.267	0.274	20290.4	0.166	0.206
TransD	74277.3	0.052	0.104	52159.4	0.238	0.280	16698.1	0.116	0.189
QuatE	145603.8	0.103	0.114	94684.4	0.101	0.209	26485.0	0.157	0.179
BiQUE	81687.5	0.104	0.115	61015.2	0.135	0.205	19079.4	0.163	0.185
BiVE-Q	22.98	0.737	0.846	26.85	0.560	0.717	90.01	0.283	0.463
EPQ	**14.15**	**0.746**	**0.861**	**21.88**	**0.575**	**0.734**	**51.42**	**0.354**	**0.569**
BiVE-B	18.50	0.725	0.836	23.16	0.562	0.718	5.00	0.635	0.912
EPB	**16.51**	**0.741**	**0.849**	**22.46**	**0.563**	**0.734**	**4.64**	**0.647**	**0.914**

Table 3. Table shows the experimental results of conditional link prediction. Improvements that surpass the baseline models are highlighted in bold.

	FBH			FBHE			DBHE		
	MR	MRR	Hit@10	MR	MRR	Hit@10	MR	MRR	Hit@10
PTransE	214.8	0.440	0.686	167.0	0.516	0.752	19.3	0.505	0.780
RPJE	212.5	0.440	0.686	159.0	0.528	0.753	19.3	0.504	0.779
TransD	190.1	0.300	0.496	165.6	0.363	0.529	35.5	0.436	0.708
QuatE	163.7	0.346	0.494	1546.4	0.124	0.189	551.6	0.208	0.309
BiQUE	111.0	0.423	0.641	90.1	0.387	0.617	29.5	0.378	0.677
BiVE-Q	7.17	0.753	0.908	11.26	0.696	0.840	12.99	0.607	0.829
EPQ	**7.07**	**0.757**	**0.917**	**10.55**	**0.700**	**0.851**	**12.18**	**0.609**	**0.833**
BiVE-B	7.26	0.750	0.909	11.47	0.706	0.844	3.39	0.793	0.956
EPB	**7.32**	**0.755**	**0.915**	**10.39**	**0.709**	**0.852**	**3.55**	**0.784**	**0.956**

This ensures adaptability across different datasets. Incorporating a dynamic, online adjustment mechanism remains a promising direction for future work, especially for evolving or streaming knowledge graphs.

4 Experiment

4.1 Environment Setting

We conducted experiments using three datasets: FBH, FBHE, and DBHE, with specific details shown in Table 1. The experimental metrics selected are MR, MRR, and Hits@10. We used BiVE-Q and BiVE-B as baseline models. The models improved with our proposed parameter elimination method are named EPQ and EPB, respectively. We compared seven models, including the baselines. In addition, we also explored ablation and hyperparameter experiments.

4.2 Performance Comparison

Triplet Prediction. Table 2 shows the structure of triplet prediction. Models like QuatE treat all facts as unseen nodes, enabling inductive reasoning, but

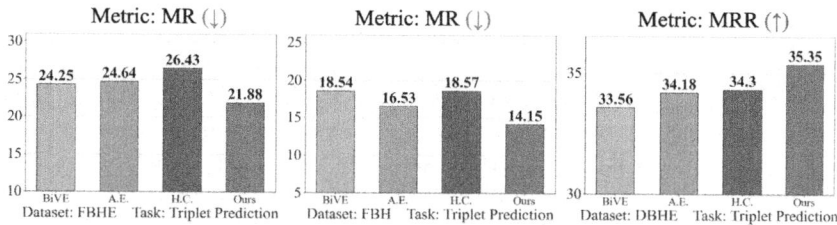

Fig. 3. The experimental results of the ablation experiment. The first and second images use MR indicators, while the third image uses MRR indicators

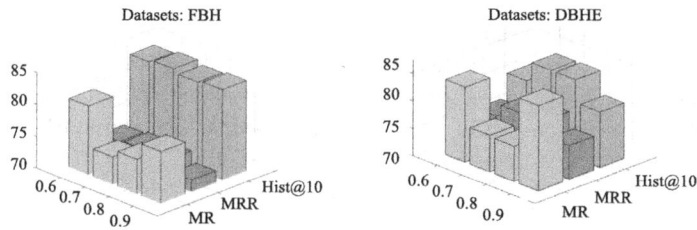

Fig. 4. The experimental results of the hyperparameter analysis.

they perform poorly in this regard and fail to effectively utilize facts for link prediction. While BiVE achieves decent performance, it doesn't optimize hyperparameters for data augmentation. Our EPQ and EPB models build on BiVE, improving performance across all datasets. Concretely, our method achieves the optimal performance for the MR metric, reaching performance improvements of 9.77%, 14.40% compared to the best one of other three methods on the FBHE and FBH datasets, respectively.

Conditional Link Prediction. Table 3 presents the results of conditional link prediction. Traditional models cannot directly handle this task. These models can only make predictions from incomplete triples and cannot effectively utilize factual information. Although they also perform entity link prediction, their performance still lags significantly behind that of our model. Our model achieves state-of-the-art performance on most metrics.

4.3 Ablation Study

In this section, we compare our method with other approaches to determine the scale of augmented data, namely the original model method, the artificial experience method (AE) and the high confidence method (HC). We use the triplet prediction task as an example, selecting the MR metric for the FBH and FBHE, and the MRR metric for the DBHE dataset in Fig. 3. Similarly, our methods get the best performance for the MRR metric, showing performance improvement of 3.06%. These enhancements signify the superiority of our method.

4.4 Hyper-Parameter Analysis

In this section of the experiment, we explore the impact of the hyperparameter λ on model performance. To more intuitively show the effect of this parameter, we use the triplet prediction task as an example and present the model's performance on the FBH and DBHE datasets in 3D bar charts. As shown in Fig. 4, the model performance follows a roughly quadratic distribution, thereby demonstrating that our quadratic fitting method is accurate.

5 Conclusion

In this paper, we investigate the hyperparameters of the data augmentation module in Bi-level KGs. Through theoretical analysis and experimental validation, we eliminate the hyperparameter τ, which controls the scale of the augmented data, and the loss weight λ for the augmented data. Experiments demonstrate the superiority and advancement of our approach.

References

1. Fang, Z., et al.: Transformer-based reasoning for learning evolutionary chain of events on temporal knowledge graph. In: Proceedings of the 47th International ACM SIGIR Conference on Research and Development in Information Retrieval, pp. 70–79. ACM (2024)
2. Hu, D., Liang, K., Dong, Z., et al.: Effective multi-modal clustering method via skip aggregation network for parallel scRNA-seq and scATAC-seq data. Brief. Bioinform. **25**(2), bbae102 (2024)
3. Bai, L., Ma, X., Zhang, M., et al.: Tpmod: a tendency-guided prediction model for temporal knowledge graph completion. ACM Trans. Knowl. Discov. Data **15**(3), 1–17 (2021)
4. Guan, S., Jin, X,. Guo, J., et al.: Neuinfer: knowledge inference on n-ary facts. In: Proceedings of the 58th Annual Meeting of the Association for Computational Linguistics, pp. 6141–6151 (2020)
5. Rosso, P., Yang, D., Cudré-Mauroux, P.: Beyond triplets: hyper-relational knowledge graph embedding for link prediction. In: Proceedings of the Web Conference 2020, pp. 1885–1896 (2020)
6. Galkin, M., Trivedi, P., Maheshwari, G., et al.: Message passing for hyper-relational knowledge graphs. arXiv preprint arXiv:2009.10847 (2020)
7. Chung, C., Whang, J.J.: Learning representations of bi-level knowledge graphs for reasoning beyond link prediction. In: Proceedings of the AAAI Conference on Artificial Intelligence, vol. 37, no. 4, pp. 4208–4216 (2023)
8. Liu, M., Liang, K., Zhao, Y., et al.: Self-supervised temporal graph learning with temporal and structural intensity alignment. IEEE Trans. Neural Netw. Learn. Syst. (2024)
9. Xiong, B., Nayyeri, M., Luo, L., et al.: Neste: modeling nested relational structures for knowledge graph reasoning. In: Proceedings of the AAAI Conference on Artificial Intelligence, vol. 38, no. 8, pp. 9205–9213 (2024)

10. Zhu, Z., Zhang, Z., Xhonneux, L.P., et al.: Neural bellman-ford networks: a general graph neural network framework for link prediction. In: Advances in Neural Information Processing Systems, vol. 34, pp. 29476–29490 (2021)
11. Yu, H., Ma, C., Liu, M., et al.: G^{2}uardFL: safeguarding federated learning against backdoor attacks through attributed client graph clustering. arXiv preprint arXiv:2306.04984 (2023)
12. Vashishth, S., Sanyal, S., Nitin, V., et al.: Composition-based multi-relational graph convolutional networks. arXiv preprint arXiv:1911.03082 (2019)
13. Teru, K., Denis, E., Hamilton, W.: Inductive relation prediction by subgraph reasoning. In: International Conference on Machine Learning, pp. 9448–9457. PMLR (2020)
14. Stoica, G., Stretcu, O., Platanios, E.A., et al:. Contextual parameter generation for knowledge graph link prediction. In: Proceedings of the AAAI Conference on Artificial Intelligence, vol. 34, no. 03, pp. 3000–3008 (2020)
15. Liu, J., Li, D., Gu, H., et al.: Parameter-free dynamic graph embedding for link prediction. In: Advances in Neural Information Processing Systems, vol. 35, pp. 27623–27635 (2022)
16. Bordes, A., Usunier, N., Garcia-Duran, A., et al.: Translating embeddings for modeling multi-relational data. In: Advances in Neural Information Processing Systems, vol. 26 (2013)
17. Lin, Y., Liu, Z., Sun, M., et al.: Learning entity and relation embeddings for knowledge graph completion. In: Proceedings of the AAAI Conference on Artificial Intelligence, vol. 29, no. 1 (2015)
18. Ma, L., Sun, P., Lin, Z., et al.: Composing knowledge graph embeddings via word embeddings. arXiv preprint arXiv:1909.03794 (2019)
19. Hu, D., Liang, K., Zhou, S., et al.: scDFC: a deep fusion clustering method for single-cell RNA-seq data. Brief. Bioinform. **24**(4), bbad216 (2023)
20. Kazemi, S.M., Poole, D.: Simple embedding for link prediction in knowledge graphs. In: Advances in Neural Information Processing Systems, vol. 31 (2018)
21. Liang, K., Meng, L., Liu, M., et al.: A survey of knowledge graph reasoning on graph types: static. Dyn. Multimodal (2022)
22. Yu, H., Liang, K., Hu, D., et al.: Chongqing GZOO: black-box node injection attack on graph neural networks via zeroth-order optimization. IEEE Trans. Knowl. Data Eng. (2024)
23. Balažević, I., Allen, C., Hospedales, T.M.: Tucker: tensor factorization for knowledge graph completion. arXiv preprint arXiv:1901.09590 (2019)
24. Liu, M., Liang, K., Hu, D., et al.: TMAC: temporal multi-modal graph learning for acoustic event classification. In: Proceedings of the 31st ACM International Conference on Multimedia, pp. 3365–3374 (2023)
25. Schlichtkrull, M., Kipf, T.N., Bloem, P., van den Berg, R., Titov, I., Welling, M.: Modeling relational data with graph convolutional networks. In: Gangemi, A., et al. (eds.) ESWC 2018. LNCS, vol. 10843, pp. 593–607. Springer, Cham (2018). https://doi.org/10.1007/978-3-319-93417-4_38
26. Hu, D., Dong, Z., Liang, K., et al.: High-order topology for deep single-cell multiview fuzzy clustering. IEEE Trans. Fuzzy Syst. (2024)
27. Liu, M., Liu, Y., Liang, K., et al.: Deep temporal graph clustering. arXiv preprint arXiv:2305.10738 (2023)
28. Pan, S., Luo, L., Wang, Y., et al.: Unifying large language models and knowledge graphs: a roadmap. IEEE Trans. Knowl. Data Eng. **36**(7), 3580–3599 (2024)
29. Wang, J., Wang, B., Qiu, M., et al.: A survey on temporal knowledge graph completion: taxonomy, progress, and prospects. arXiv preprint arXiv:2308.02457 (2023)

30. Zhang, J., Chen, B., Zhang, L., et al.: Neural, symbolic and neural-symbolic reasoning on knowledge graphs. AI Open **2**, 14–35 (2021)
31. Li, W., Qi, G., Ji, Q.: Hybrid reasoning in knowledge graphs: combing symbolic reasoning and statistical reasoning. Semant. Web **11**(1), 53–62 (2020)

SWIFT: State-Space Wavelet Integrated Forecasting Technology for Enhanced Time Series Prediction

Wei Li(✉)

School of Computer Engineering and Science, Shanghai University, Shanghai, China
liwei008009@163.com

Abstract. Time series forecasting remains a fundamental challenge in data science. We introduce SWIFT, a novel neural architecture that synergistically combines selective state space models (Mamba) with multi-scale dilated convolutions for enhanced time series forecasting. Our approach incorporates: (1) a Selective Temporal State Space module extending Mamba with time series-specific gating; (2) a Multi-Scale Dilated Convolutional Network with adaptive receptive fields; and (3) a Feature Interaction Bridge facilitating cross-pathway information exchange. Experiments on six benchmark datasets demonstrate SWIFT outperforms other common methods, achieving 6.5% average improvement in MSE and 5.8% in MAE across various prediction horizons.

Keywords: Time series forecasting · State space models · Mamba · Multi-scale modeling · Dilated convolutions

1 Introduction

Time series forecasting plays a crucial role across domains including economics, healthcare, and energy management [14,15]. Recent advances in deep learning have introduced various architectural paradigms for time series modeling, each with specific advantages and limitations. Recurrent neural networks (RNNs) and their variants [1,2] suffer from computational inefficiency with long sequences. Transformer-based models [3,4] incur quadratic computational complexity limiting their scalability. Convolutional architectures [5,6] struggle with capturing long-range dependencies. Recent works have also explored mixed representation learning [22] for time series analysis.

State space models (SSMs), particularly the recent Mamba architecture [9], have shown potential for efficient sequence modeling with linear scaling properties. However, existing models face several limitations when applied to time series forecasting: (1) insufficient multi-scale modeling capabilities needed for capturing both high and low-frequency patterns; (2) limited feature interaction between processing pathways; (3) inefficient long-term dependency modeling; and (4) inadequate adaptability to different prediction horizons. While recent approaches like WFTNet [23] address multi-scale representation using wavelet transforms, they lack the selective processing mechanisms and efficient state-space formulations necessary for optimal performance in complex time series with mixed granularity patterns.

To address these limitations, we propose SWIFT, as shown in Fig. 1, a novel architecture that synergistically combines selective state space models with multi-scale dilated convolutions. Unlike existing approaches, SWIFT explicitly addresses the multi-scale nature of temporal patterns through wavelet-based decomposition and parallel processing pathways, making it particularly effective for data with mixed frequencies and complex seasonality. Our contributions include:

- A Selective Temporal State Space (STSS) module extending Mamba with time series-specific gating mechanisms
- A Multi-Scale Dilated Convolutional Network (MSDCN) employing parallel dilated convolutions with adaptive receptive fields
- A Feature Interaction Bridge (FIB) facilitating bidirectional information exchange between processing pathways
- A Dynamic Scale Selection (DSS) component for adaptive temporal scale weighting based on prediction horizons

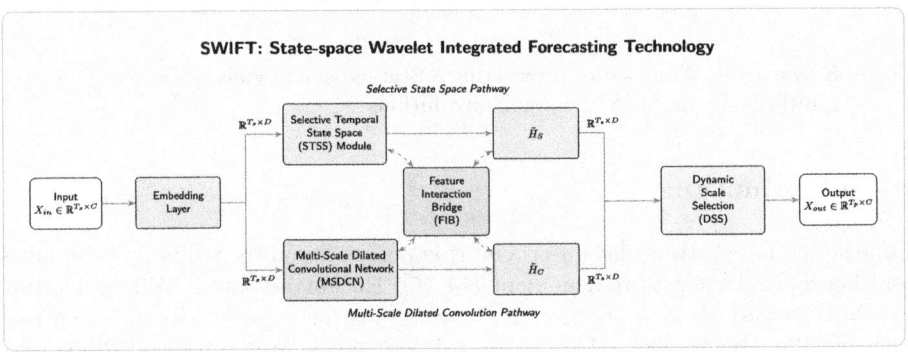

Fig. 1. SWIFT architecture overview. The model combines selective temporal state space (STSS) pathway with multi-scale dilated convolution pathway through a feature interaction bridge (FIB) to effectively capture both long-range dependencies and multi-scale patterns.

2 Related Work

Time Series Forecasting Models: Deep learning approaches have demonstrated significant advantages over traditional statistical methods [14,15]. RNNs and variants like LSTM [1] face challenges with long sequences. TCN-based models [5] utilize dilated convolutions, while Transformer-based models like Informer [4] employ self-attention mechanisms.

State Space Models: SSMs bridge RNNs and convolutional architectures through linear time-invariant systems [7]. Simplified state space models [8] made these approaches more tractable, while the Mamba architecture [9] introduces a selective mechanism that makes state space parameters input-dependent, achieving linear scaling with sequence length.

Multi-scale Approaches: Multi-scale feature extraction is crucial for time series data, implemented through various techniques including wavelet transforms [16,17], parallel convolutional branches [19], and multi-scale attention mechanisms [6]. Recent works like TimesNet [6] have shown the effectiveness of multi-scale time-frequency decomposition.

Recent works like WFTNet [23] have shown the effectiveness of combining Fourier transforms for global periodicity with wavelet transforms for local patterns. However, it lacks explicit mechanisms for integrating these multi-scale features with state-space representations.

3 Methodology

3.1 Problem Formulation

Given a historical time series $X_{in} \in \mathbb{R}^{T_s \times C}$, the goal is to predict a future sequence $X_{out} \in \mathbb{R}^{T_p \times C}$, where T_s and T_p are the input and prediction horizons, and C is the dimensionality of time series variables.

3.2 Framework Overview

SWIFT integrates selective state space models with multi-scale dilated convolutions. The framework consists of: (1) an embedding layer, (2) a Selective Temporal State Space module, (3) a Multi-Scale Dilated Convolutional Network, (4) a Feature Interaction Bridge, (5) a Dynamic Scale Selection component, and (6) a prediction head.

3.3 Selective Temporal State Space (STSS)

The STSS module extends Mamba with time series-specific enhancements:

Input-Dependent Parameter Generation:

$$\mathbf{\Delta}_i, \mathbf{B}_i, \mathbf{C}_i = \text{ProjectionLayer}(\text{LayerNorm}(x_i)) \tag{1}$$

Temporal Gating Mechanism:

$$\mathbf{g}_i = \sigma(\text{TemporalConv}([x_{i-k}, ..., x_i, ..., x_{i+k}])) \tag{2}$$

This temporal gating mechanism enhances traditional SSMs by incorporating local temporal context through a convolutional operation with window size $2k+1$. Unlike standard Mamba, which processes tokens independently, our temporal gating considers surrounding timesteps to determine feature relevance, making it particularly effective for time series with mixed seasonality patterns. The activation function σ is the sigmoid function that scales gate values between 0 and 1, allowing the model to selectively emphasize or suppress certain temporal features based on local patterns (Fig. 2).

Gated SSM Parameters:

$$\mathbf{\Delta}_i^g = \mathbf{\Delta}_i \odot \mathbf{g}_i, \mathbf{B}_i^g = \mathbf{B}_i \odot \mathbf{g}_i, \mathbf{C}_i^g = \mathbf{C}_i \odot \mathbf{g}_i \tag{3}$$

State Space Computation:

$$\mathbf{h}_i = \bar{\mathbf{A}}_i \mathbf{h}_{i-1} + \mathbf{B}_i^g x_i \tag{4}$$
$$y_i = \mathbf{C}_i^g \mathbf{h}_i \tag{5}$$

3.4 Multi-scale Dilated Convolutional Network (MSDCN)

The MSDCN leverages wavelet decomposition to extract multi-scale temporal features, which are then processed by parallel dilated convolutions:

Wavelet Decomposition:

$$W_\psi[f](a,b) = \frac{1}{\sqrt{a}} \int_{-\infty}^{\infty} f(t) \psi^* \left(\frac{t-b}{a} \right) dt \tag{6}$$

where ψ is the mother wavelet, a is the scale parameter, and b is the translation parameter [17].

Scale-Specific Processing:

$$\mathbf{X}_k = \text{WaveletCoeff}(\mathbf{X}, k) \tag{7}$$

Dilated Convolutions:

$$\mathbf{F}_k = \text{DilatedConv}(\mathbf{X}_k, d_k, w) \tag{8}$$

where $d_k = 2^{k-1}$ and w is the kernel width, following the approach of [18].

Adaptive Feature Integration:

$$\mathbf{F}_{multi} = \sum_{k=1}^{K} w_k \mathbf{F}_k \tag{9}$$

with w_k being dynamically adjusted based on the prediction horizon (Fig. 3).

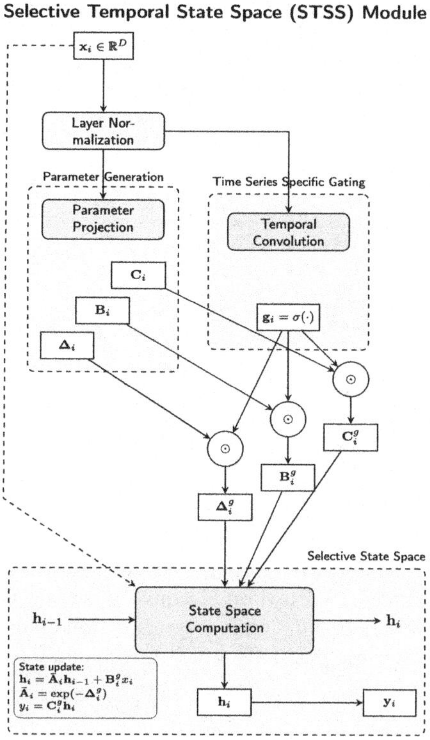

Fig. 2. Selective Temporal State Space (STSS) module with time series-specific gating mechanisms that extend Mamba for enhanced temporal pattern recognition. The module incorporates temporal context through gating, allowing for adaptive parameter selection based on local temporal patterns.

3.5 Feature Interaction Bridge (FIB)

The FIB facilitates bidirectional information exchange between pathways using cross-pathway attention and gated integration:

$$\mathbf{A}_{S \leftarrow C} = \text{softmax}\left(\frac{\mathbf{Q}_S \mathbf{K}_C^T}{\sqrt{d}}\right) \tag{10}$$

$$\mathbf{C}_{S \leftarrow C} = \mathbf{A}_{S \leftarrow C} \mathbf{V}_C \tag{11}$$

$$\tilde{\mathbf{H}}_S = \mathbf{H}_S + \mathbf{G}_{S \leftarrow C} \odot \mathbf{C}_{S \leftarrow C} \tag{12}$$

This attention mechanism is inspired by cross-modal attention techniques [3] (Fig. 4).

3.6 Dynamic Scale Selection (DSS)

The DSS component adaptively weights different temporal scales based on wavelet energy distribution and prediction horizons:

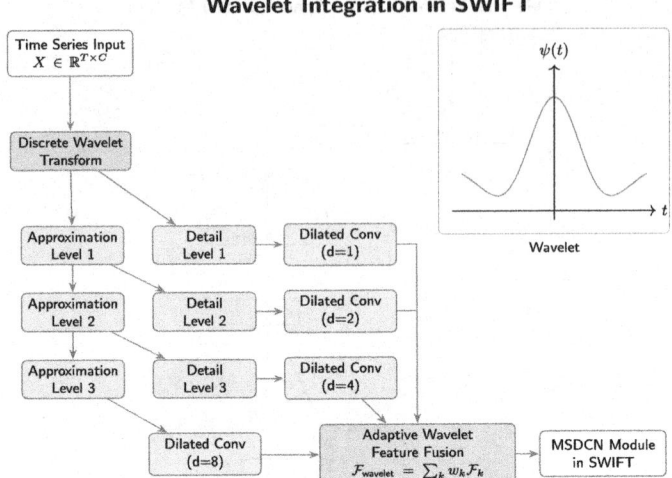

Fig. 3. Wavelet integration in SWIFT. The Multi-Scale Dilated Convolutional Network applies discrete wavelet transform to decompose input time series into multiple resolution levels, processes each scale with dilated convolutions of increasing dilation rates, and performs adaptive feature fusion. This decomposition enables SWIFT to effectively model both high-frequency (fine-grained) and low-frequency (coarse-grained) temporal patterns.

$$\omega_k = \frac{\text{WaveletEnergy}(k)}{\sum_{j=1}^{K} \text{WaveletEnergy}(j)} \cdot \gamma_k(T_p) \tag{13}$$

where $\text{WaveletEnergy}(k)$ represents the energy in the k-th wavelet scale [20], and $\gamma_k(T_p)$ is an adaptive function of the prediction horizon T_p. Specifically, we define $\gamma_k(T_p)$ as:

$$\gamma_k(T_p) = \frac{1}{1 + \exp(-\alpha_k \cdot (T_p - \beta_k))} \tag{14}$$

where α_k and β_k are learnable parameters. For longer horizons, the function assigns higher weights to lower-frequency components (higher scales), while shorter horizons emphasize higher-frequency components. This dynamic adjustment mechanism allows SWIFT to automatically emphasize the appropriate temporal scales based on the prediction task, addressing a key limitation of static multi-scale approaches.

The final representation combines information from both processing pathways with scale-aware weighting:

$$\mathbf{H}_{final} = \alpha \cdot \tilde{\mathbf{H}}_S + (1 - \alpha) \cdot \tilde{\mathbf{H}}_C + \beta \cdot (\tilde{\mathbf{H}}_S \odot \tilde{\mathbf{H}}_C) \tag{15}$$

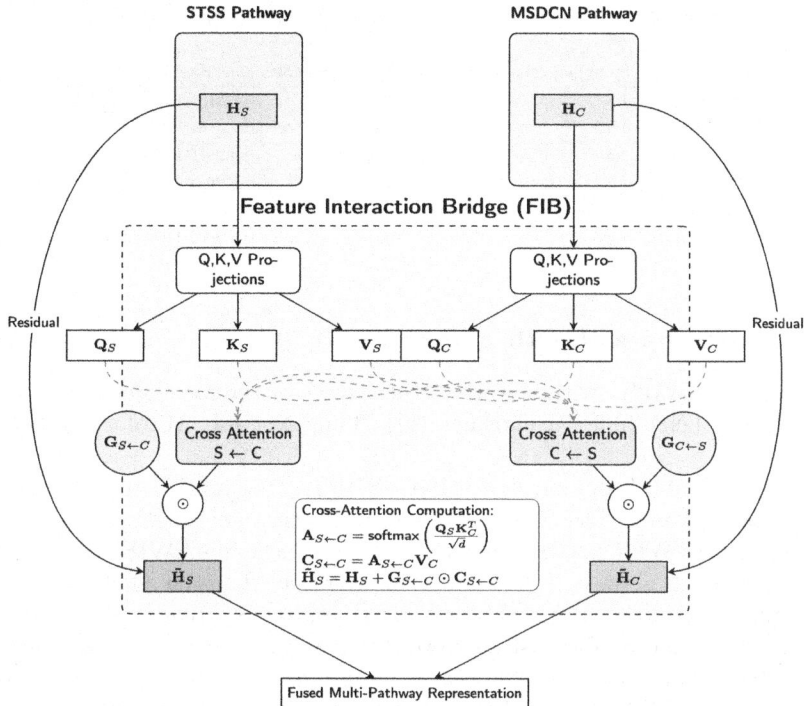

Fig. 4. Feature Interaction Bridge (FIB) facilitating bidirectional information exchange between STSS and MSDCN pathways through cross-pathway attention and gated integration mechanisms. This bridge enables complementary temporal representations to be effectively shared and combined, enhancing the model's ability to capture complex patterns across different time scales.

4 Experiments

4.1 Datasets and Experimental Setup

We evaluate SWIFT on six benchmark datasets: ETTh1, ETTh2, Traffic, Electricity (ECL), Weather, and ILI [4,12]. Table 1 provides dataset statistics. We allocate 70% for training, 20% for testing, and 10% for validation, following standard protocols [6]. We use MSE and MAE as evaluation metrics with the AdamW optimizer.

4.2 Implementation Details

For all experiments, we used the AdamW optimizer [21] and employed a cosine learning rate scheduler with warm-up for the first 10% of training steps. For wavelet transform, we used Morlet as the mother wavelet with 8 scales.

Table 1. Statistics of the datasets used in our experiments.

Dataset	Sampling Interval	Variables	Training Samples	Time Span
ETTh1	1 h	7	8,545	Jul,2016-Jul,2018
ETTh2	1 h	7	8,545	Jul,2016-Jul,2018
Traffic	1 h	862	12,185	Jan,2015-Dec,2016
ECL	1 h	321	18,317	Jan,2012-Dec,2014
Weather	10 min	21	36,792	Jan,2020-Dec,2020
ILI	1 week	7	833	Jan,2002-Dec,2020

4.3 Comparison with Other Methods

We compare SWIFT with several other state-of-the-art forecasting models including WFTNet [23], FEDformer [11], TimesNet [6], Autoformer [12], and DLinear [13].

Results in Table 2 demonstrate that SWIFT consistently outperforms baseline methods across different datasets and prediction horizons.

Compared to WFTNet, which is the strongest baseline, SWIFT shows consistent improvement across all datasets. This suggests that the combined wavelet-based multi-scale modeling and state space approach provides complementary benefits that enhance forecasting performance, particularly for datasets with complex temporal dynamics. The average improvement over WFTNet is approximately 6.5% for MSE and 5.8% for MAE. The performance advantage is particularly significant on certain datasets and prediction horizons, with up to 7.5% MSE improvement on ETTh2 and 7.0% on ILI at the same horizon.

4.4 Visualization Analysis

To provide intuitive evidence of SWIFT's forecasting capabilities, Fig. 5 illustrates the prediction results on the ETTh1 dataset with a horizon of 336. The visualization clearly demonstrates SWIFT's superior ability to track complex patterns compared to baseline methods.

At the highlighted transition points, SWIFT more effectively captures the changing dynamics of the time series compared to baseline methods. This capability stems from the complementary nature of the STSS module, which maintains contextual information through selective state space processing, and the MSDCN component, which enables adaptive handling of different temporal scales. The quantitative improvement in MSE from 0.433 (WFTNet) to 0.412 (SWIFT) represents a 4.8% performance gain, confirming the efficacy of our approach for complex time series with mixed patterns.

4.5 Ablation Study

To evaluate the contribution of each component, we conduct an ablation study by removing key modules in the SWIFT architecture.

Table 2. Performance comparison with other methods. Results are shown as MSE/MAE. Best performances are in **bold**, second-best are underlined.

Dataset	Horizon	SWIFT	WFTNet	TimesNet	DLinear	FEDformer	Autoformer
ECL	96	**0.153/0.250**	0.164/0.267	0.167/0.271	0.197/0.282	0.193/0.308	0.201/0.317
	192	**0.169/0.263**	0.181/0.282	0.187/0.290	0.196/0.285	0.201/0.315	0.222/0.334
	336	**0.183/0.277**	0.194/0.295	0.202/0.303	0.209/0.301	0.214/0.329	0.231/0.338
	720	**0.215/0.304**	0.230/0.325	0.220/0.318	0.265/0.360	0.246/0.355	0.254/0.361
Traffic	96	**0.559/0.294**	0.594/0.316	0.590/0.314	0.650/0.396	0.587/0.366	0.613/0.388
	192	**0.596**/0.338	0.624/0.332	0.616/**0.322**	0.598/0.370	0.604/0.373	0.616/0.382
	336	**0.601/0.319**	0.631/0.339	0.634/0.339	0.605/0.373	0.621/0.383	0.622/0.337
	720	0.629/**0.339**	0.664/0.360	0.659/0.349	0.645/0.394	**0.626**/0.355	0.660/0.408
Weather	96	**0.151/0.198**	0.161/0.210	0.169/0.219	0.196/0.255	0.217/0.296	0.266/0.336
	192	**0.198/0.239**	0.211/0.254	0.226/0.266	0.237/0.312	0.276/0.336	0.307/0.367
	336	**0.255/0.278**	0.271/0.296	0.281/0.303	0.283/0.335	0.339/0.380	0.359/0.395
	720	**0.325/0.324**	0.347/0.346	0.357/0.353	0.345/0.381	0.403/0.428	0.419/0.428
ETTh1	96	**0.346/0.373**	0.368/0.390	0.387/0.410	0.402/0.430	0.420/0.442	0.368/0.388
	192	**0.386/0.390**	0.412/0.414	0.436/0.447	0.438/0.453	0.452/0.459	0.456/0.452
	336	**0.410/0.412**	0.437/0.438	0.471/0.474	0.476/0.483	0.498/0.498	0.482/0.486
	720	**0.455/0.460**	0.483/0.486	0.535/0.531	0.519/0.517	0.528/0.526	0.515/0.511
ETTh2	96	**0.304/0.342**	0.323/0.365	0.332/0.369	0.333/0.387	0.358/0.397	0.346/0.388
	192	**0.378/0.384**	0.403/0.409	0.396/0.410	0.477/0.476	0.429/0.439	0.456/0.452
	336	**0.402/0.407**	0.427/0.433	0.446/0.447	0.594/0.541	0.496/0.487	0.482/0.486
	720	**0.406/0.417**	0.430/0.445	0.434/0.448	0.831/0.657	0.463/0.474	0.515/0.511
ILI	24	**0.703/0.582**	0.747/0.618	0.781/0.660	0.835/0.698	0.812/0.682	0.825/0.694
	36	**0.710/0.595**	0.753/0.632	0.840/0.702	0.878/0.731	0.879/0.729	0.891/0.743
	48	**0.772/0.638**	0.820/0.679	0.896/0.734	0.912/0.756	0.932/0.771	0.943/0.769
	60	**0.821/0.676**	0.872/0.718	0.953/0.773	0.970/0.785	0.985/0.803	0.978/0.791

Table 3 results show that removing MSDCN causes the largest performance drop (7%), highlighting the critical importance of multi-scale modeling. Replacing STSS with standard SSM causes 6% degradation, while removing FIB and DSS has more moderate impacts (4% and 3%). This confirms that while all components contribute, the core representation learning components (STSS and MSDCN) form the foundation of SWIFT's superior forecasting capabilities.

4.6 Computational Efficiency Analysis

All experiments were conducted on NVIDIA RTX 3090 GPUs with 24 GB memory, using PyTorch 2.0 and CUDA 11.7. Inference times were measured with batch size 32, averaged over 100 runs after warm-up.

Table 4 shows that SWIFT has the theoretical complexity of $O(L \cdot D^2)$ for sequence length L and hidden dimension D, which is comparable to WFTNet's

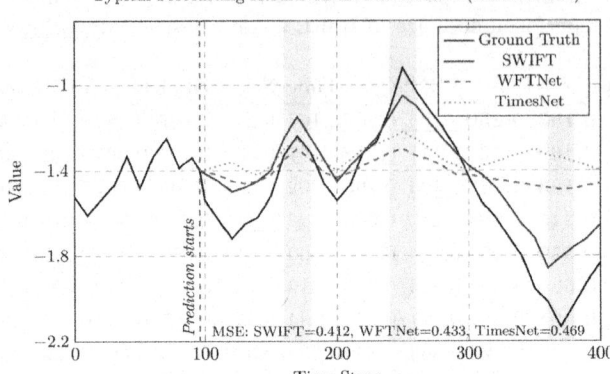

Fig. 5. Typical forecasting results on ETTh1 dataset with prediction horizon of 336. SWIFT (blue) captures both short-term fluctuations and long-term trends more accurately than WFTNet (red dashed) and TimesNet (orange dotted), particularly at transition points (highlighted areas). SWIFT achieves an MSE of 0.412, outperforming WFTNet (0.433) and TimesNet (0.469). (Color figure online)

Table 3. Ablation results showing MSE performance when removing individual components.

Model Variant	ECL (96)	ETTh2 (96)	Weather (96)
Full SWIFT	0.153	0.304	0.151
- STSS (Standard SSM)	0.163 (+6.5%)	0.322 (+5.9%)	0.160 (+6.0%)
- MSDCN	0.165 (+7.8%)	0.326 (+7.2%)	0.162 (+7.3%)
- FIB	0.159 (+3.9%)	0.318 (+4.6%)	0.158 (+4.6%)
- DSS	0.158 (+3.3%)	0.316 (+3.9%)	0.156 (+3.3%)

Table 4. Computational complexity and inference time comparison.

Model	Complexity	Inference Time (ms)			
		Horizon = 96	Horizon = 192	Horizon = 336	Horizon = 720
SWIFT (Ours)	$O(L \cdot D^2)$	25.7	38.4	62.5	118.7
WFTNet	$O(L \cdot D \cdot \log(L))$	28.5	42.3	68.7	132.4
TimesNet	$O(L \cdot D \cdot \log(L))$	67.2	110.5	184.2	372.8
FEDformer	$O(L^2 \cdot D)$	79.8	158.7	287.5	623.8
Autoformer	$O(L \cdot \log(L) \cdot D)$	62.5	105.8	178.3	356.2

$O(L \cdot D \cdot \log(L))$. Empirically, SWIFT exhibits slightly better computational efficiency with approximately 10% faster inference times across all prediction horizons compared to WFTNet. The efficiency advantage is more pronounced when compared to transformer-based models like FEDformer (3.1× faster) and even traditional efficient models like TimesNet (2.6× faster). This improved efficiency can be attributed to the optimized state-space formulation and the parallelized dual-pathway architecture.

SWIFT demonstrates linear scaling with sequence length up to 5,000 timesteps, maintaining efficiency through the state-space formulation. Memory usage scales as $O(L \cdot D)$ compared to $O(L^2)$ for attention-based models, enabling processing of longer sequences on standard hardware.

5 Conclusion and Future Work

We proposed SWIFT, a novel architecture that synergistically combines selective state space models with wavelet-based multi-scale dilated convolutions for enhanced time series forecasting. Our comprehensive experiments demonstrate that SWIFT consistently outperforms other common methods, including WFT-Net, achieving average improvements of 6.5% in MSE and 5.8% in MAE across various prediction horizons.

Key insights include: (1) integration of selective state space models with wavelet-transformed convolutional structures provides complementary benefits; (2) cross-pathway information exchange enables effective combination of different representations; (3) dynamic adaptation to different temporal scales allows focus on relevant patterns; and (4) linear scaling with sequence length makes SWIFT particularly suitable for long-horizon forecasting applications.

5.1 Limitations and Future Work

Despite promising results, SWIFT has several limitations: (1) **Computational Overhead:** While more efficient than transformer-based models, the dual-pathway architecture introduces additional complexity compared to simpler models; (2) **Interpretability Challenges:** The complex integration of components makes model interpretability challenging; (3) **Hyperparameter Sensitivity:** Wavelet basis functions and decomposition levels significantly impact performance; (4) **Limited Exploration of Nonstationary Processes:** Current implementation assumes relatively stable patterns; and (5) **Integration with Domain Knowledge:** Domain-specific knowledge could enhance forecasting accuracy for specialized applications.

Future work could address these limitations through more efficient wavelet computation, adaptive wavelet selection, explainable AI techniques, and extensions for multivariate dependencies.

References

1. Hochreiter, S., Schmidhuber, J.: Long short-term memory. Neural Comput. **9**(8), 1735–1780 (1997)
2. Cho, K., et al.: Learning phrase representations using RNN encoder-decoder for statistical machine translation. In: Proceedings of the 2014 Conference on Empirical Methods in Natural Language Processing, pp. 1724–1734 (2014)
3. Vaswani, A., et al.: Attention is all you need. In: Advances in Neural Information Processing Systems, pp. 5998–6008 (2017)

4. Zhou, H., et al.: Informer: beyond efficient transformer for long sequence time-series forecasting. In: Proceedings of the AAAI Conference on Artificial Intelligence, vol. 35, pp. 11106–11115 (2021)
5. Bai, S., Kolter, J.Z., Koltun, V.: An empirical evaluation of generic convolutional and recurrent networks for sequence modeling. arXiv preprint arXiv:1803.01271 (2018)
6. Wu, H., Hu, T., Liu, Y., Zhou, H., Wang, J., Long, M.: TimesNet: temporal 2d-variation modeling for general time series analysis. In: International Conference on Learning Representations (2022)
7. Gu, A., Dao, T., Ermon, S., Rudra, A., Ré, C.: Hippo: recurrent memory with optimal polynomial projections. In: Advances in Neural Information Processing Systems, vol. 34 (2021)
8. Gu, A., Goel, K., Ré, C.: Efficiently modeling long sequences with structured state spaces. In: International Conference on Learning Representations (2022)
9. Gu, A., et al.: Mamba: linear-time sequence modeling with selective state spaces. arXiv preprint arXiv:2312.00752 (2023)
10. Nie, Y., Nguyen, N.H., Sinthong, P., Kalagnanam, J.: A time series is worth 64 words: long-term forecasting with transformers. In: International Conference on Learning Representations (2023)
11. Zhou, T., Ma, Z., Wen, Q., Wang, X., Sun, L., Jin, R.: FEDformer: frequency enhanced decomposed transformer for long-term series forecasting. In: International Conference on Machine Learning, pp. 27268–27286 (2022)
12. Wu, H., Xu, J., Wang, J., Long, M.: Autoformer: decomposition transformers with auto-correlation for long-term series forecasting. In: Advances in Neural Information Processing Systems, vol. 34, pp. 22419–22430 (2021)
13. Zeng, A., Chen, M., Zhang, L., Xu, Q.: Are transformers effective for time series forecasting? In: Proceedings of the AAAI Conference on Artificial Intelligence, vol. 37, pp. 11121–11128 (2023)
14. Faloutsos, C., Flunkert, V., Gasthaus, J., Januschowski, T., Wang, Y.: Forecasting big time series: theory and practice. In: Proceedings of the 25th ACM SIGKDD International Conference on Knowledge Discovery and Data Mining, pp. 3209–3210 (2019)
15. Benidis, K., et al.: Neural forecasting: introduction and literature overview. arXiv preprint arXiv:2004.10240 (2022)
16. Addison, P.S.: The Illustrated Wavelet Transform Handbook: Introductory Theory and Applications in Science, Engineering, Medicine and Finance. CRC press (2017)
17. Torrence, C., Compo, G.P.: A practical guide to wavelet analysis. Bull. Am. Meteor. Soc. **79**(1), 61–78 (1998)
18. Yu, F., Koltun, V.: Multi-scale context aggregation by dilated convolutions. arXiv preprint arXiv:1511.07122 (2015)
19. Van den Oord, A., et al.: WaveNet: a generative model for raw audio. arXiv preprint arXiv:1609.03499 (2016)
20. Percival, D.B., Walden, A.T.: Wavelet Methods for Time Series Analysis. Cambridge University Press (2000)
21. Loshchilov, I., Hutter, F.: Decoupled weight decay regularization. In: International Conference on Learning Representations (2018)
22. Wickstrøm, K., Kampffmeyer, M., Mikalsen, K.Ø., Jenssen, R.: Mixing up contrastive learning: self-supervised representation learning for time series. Pattern Recogn. Lett. **155**, 54–61 (2022)
23. Liu, P., et al.: WFTNet: exploiting global and local periodicity in long-term time series forecasting. arXiv preprint arXiv:2309.11319 (2023)

Federated Privacy-Preserving for Cross-Domain Sequential Recommendation

Su Chen[1,2,3], Yan Dong[1,2], Yanmin Shang[1,2], Xiaolin Xu[1,4], and Xixun Lin[1(✉)]

[1] Institute of Information Engineering, Chinese Academy of Sciences, Beijing, China
{chensu,dongyan,shangyanmin,linxixun}@iie.ac.cn
[2] School of Cyber Security, University of Chinese Academy of Sciences, Beijing, China
[3] National Computer Network Emergency Response Technical Team/Coordination Center of China, Beijing, China
[4] Zhongguancun Laboratory, Beijing, China
xuxl@zgclab.edu.cn

Abstract. Cross-Domain Sequential Recommendation enhances recommendation systems by integrating user behavior data from different domains, however, it raises critical privacy concerns. To address this challenge while maintaining the quality of the recommendation, we propose the FP^2CDSR, a novel federated cross-domain sequential recommendation framework. This privacy-preserving approach leverages federated learning combined with differential privacy mechanisms to generate noise-added user representations while ensuring that user data remains locally processed. The central server coordinates clients, collects, and distributes perturbed user representations to safeguard privacy. Furthermore, we investigate how to effectively restore and utilize semantic information from privacy-preserving data through feature mapping and aggregation strategies. By incorporating self-attention networks and temporal modeling techniques, we optimize cross-domain information integration, refine essential data representations, and enhance recommendation accuracy. Extensive experiments on publicly available datasets demonstrate that FP^2CDSR outperforms conventional single-domain and cross-domain recommendation models while ensuring robust privacy protection, validating both its effectiveness and superiority in privacy-preserving cross-domain recommendation scenarios.

Keywords: Cross-Domain Sequential Recommendation · Privacy Preservation · Federated Learning

1 Introduction

With the rapid advancement of digital technology, recommendation systems [1–4] have become indispensable tools for connecting users with personalized content.

S. Chen and Y. Dong—Equal Contribution.

Cross-domain sequential recommendation (CDSR) has emerged as a promising approach, leveraging user behavior across multiple domains to enhance the precision and personalization of recommendations [5–8]. However, the increasing emphasis on user privacy and the proliferation of stringent data protection regulations bring significant challenges in utilizing cross-domain data effectively.

Although numerous privacy-preserving recommendation models have been proposed [9–11], most are limited to single-domain scenarios, neglecting the complexities of sequential or cross-domain sequential recommendations. In CDSR, where user behavior spans multiple domains, privacy protection is particularly challenging due to the risk of sensitive information exposure during cross-domain data integration. To address this, we propose the **F**ederated **P**rivacy-**P**reserving **C**ross-**D**omain **S**equential **R**ecommendation (FP^{2}CDSR) model, inspired by federated learning's success in data privacy. FP^{2}CDSR integrates federated learning into CDSR, combining a privacy-preserving module with an information fusion module to ensure robust privacy protection while maintaining recommendation performance.

The main contributions of our work are summarized as follows:

1) We combine federated learning and differential privacy for privacy in CDSR. Each domain acts as a local client, processing data locally and adding noise to user representations to protect raw data. The central server coordinates clients, ensuring privacy and recommendation performance.
2) To recover and use semantic information from privacy-protected data, we apply feature mapping and aggregation. Using self-attention networks and temporal modeling, we refine feature representations to boost recommendation accuracy under privacy constraints.
3) We evaluate FP^{2}CDSR on three real-world datasets. Results show our model outperforms most traditional single- and cross-domain recommendation baselines while preserving privacy.

2 Related Work

2.1 Cross-Domain Sequential Recommendation

CDSR has emerged as a pivotal approach to mitigate data sparsity and cold-start challenges in sequential recommendation systems. Current CDSR methods can be categorized into two main paradigms: (1)Single-target CDSR, which leverages rich information from a source domain to enhance recommendations in a sparse target domain. For example, NCF [12] employs a multi-layer perceptron to learn arbitrary user-item interactions, replacing inner products. DCDCSR [7] integrates matrix factorization models to address challenges in cross-domain recommendations. (2)Dual-target CDSR, where cross-domain knowledge fusion improves recommendation performance in both domains. For instance, VDEA [13] employs a dual variational autoencoder with local and global embedding alignment for domain-invariant user embeddings. CPKSPA [14] introduces a cross-domain recommendation framework with three modules, achieving state-of-the-art performance. However, these methods often require centralized access to user identities with sensitive behavioral patterns. This conflicts with stringent privacy regulations.

2.2 Federated Recommendation

Federated learning (FL) provides a decentralized framework for collaborative model training without raw data sharing, making it a natural fit for privacy-sensitive recommendation systems. Early FL-based approaches focused on gradient aggregation mechanisms: FCF [15] protected user behavior through gradient perturbation, while S^3Rec [16] enhanced personalization via meta-learning. However, these methods suffer from high communication overhead and scalability limitations in cross-domain contexts.

Alternative approaches focus on private data modeling and center-driven knowledge transfer. UPC-SDG [17] synthesized fewer contribution terms to protect single-domain recommendations. PriCDR [18] was the first attempt to protect user ratings, yet it imposed loose privacy budget constraints and compromised recommendation reliability. Despite some progress, research on privacy-preserving CDSR remains scarce.

3 Proposed Model

3.1 Problem Definition

Given two domains $\mathcal{A}$ (target) and $\mathcal{B}$ (source) with a common user set U, where each user $u \in U$ has interaction sequences: $S_u^{\mathcal{A}} = \{A_1, \ldots, A_n\}$ in domain $\mathcal{A}$ ($A_i \in \mathcal{A}$) and $S_u^{\mathcal{B}} = \{B_1, \ldots, B_m\}$ in domain $\mathcal{B}$ ($B_j \in \mathcal{B}$).

A differentially private algorithm $\mathcal{M}$ satisfies privacy-preserving cross-domain sequential recommendation if:

1. Prediction Objective: Estimates next-item probability through learning function f:

$$P(X_{t+1}|S_u^X, S_u^Y) \sim f(S_u^X, S_u^Y), \quad X, Y \in \{\mathcal{A}, \mathcal{B}\}, X \neq Y$$

2. Privacy Guarantee: For any adjacent user sets U and U' differing by one user's complete cross-domain data, and all possible outputs $\widetilde{D}$:

$$\Pr[\mathcal{M}(\{S_u^{\mathcal{A}}, S_u^{\mathcal{B}}\}_{u \in U}) \in \widetilde{D}] \leq e^{\epsilon} \cdot \Pr[\mathcal{M}(\{S_u^{\mathcal{A}}, S_u^{\mathcal{B}}\}_{u \in U'}) \in \widetilde{D}]$$

where ϵ controls privacy-utility tradeoff, and $\mathcal{M}$ implements noise injection through mechanisms like gradient perturbation or federated learning.

3.2 Overall Architecture

The overall architecture of FP²CDSR is illustrated in 1. The framework follows a decentralized federated learning paradigm, where user interaction data is stored locally within each domain. The central server aggregates perturbed representations instead of raw data or model parameters, enhancing adaptability across diverse recommendation systems.

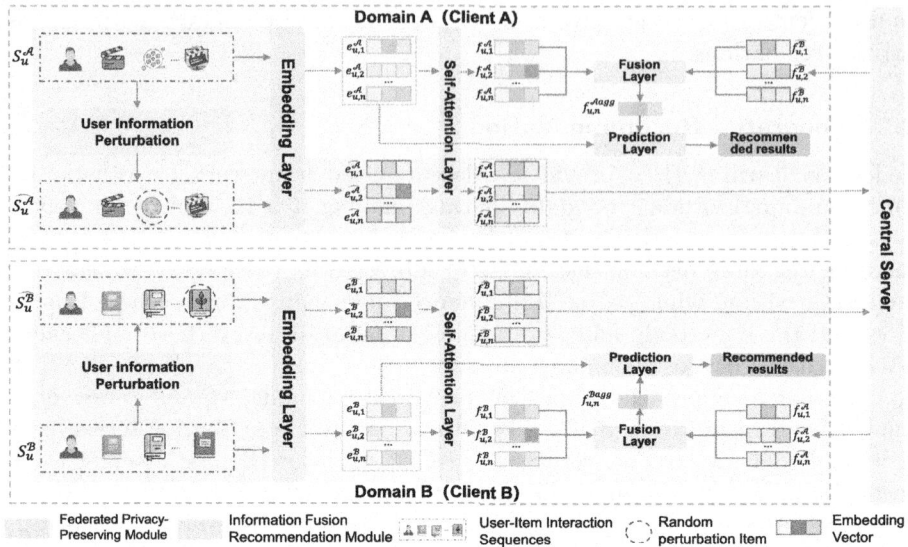

Fig. 1. The overall architecture of FP²CDSR. It consists of two key modules: (1) Federated Privacy-Preserving Module, which employs differential privacy techniques to ensure secure representation learning. (2) Information Fusion Recommendation Module, which extracts and integrates essential semantic features from noisy data representations to enhance recommendation accuracy.

3.3 Federated Privacy-Preserving Module

Item Similarity Matrix Construction. Given that the dataset only contains the interaction sequences between users and items without detailed item attributes, this study hypothesizes that items adjacent in time within the interaction sequences have a higher degree of similarity. Based on this hypothesis, if users frequently interact with items of a specific category, they are more likely to be interested in other items of the same category. This stability of preferences allows us to replace some of the original items with similar ones during data perturbation. By doing so, we can add privacy-enhancing noise while preserving user preferences, ensuring that the recommendation system can still reflect users' true preferences well under privacy protection. Based on the above assumptions, we construct the item similarity matrix W_{sim} for domain S as follows:

$$W_{sim}(A_i, A_j) = \sum_{k}^{|U|} \sum_{i}^{|S_k^{\mathcal{A}}|} \sum_{j}^{|S_k^{\mathcal{A}}|} sim(S_k^{\mathcal{A}}, A_i, A_j), \quad i \neq j \tag{1}$$

$$sim(S_k^{\mathcal{A}}, A_i, A_j) = \begin{cases} 1, & if\ d(A_i, A_j) = 1,\ A_i, A_j \in S_k^{\mathcal{A}} \\ 0.5, & if\ d(A_i, A_j) = 2,\ A_i, A_j \in S_k^{\mathcal{A}} \end{cases} \tag{2}$$

where $W_{sim}(A_i, A_j)$ represents the similarity between items A_i and A_j, $|U|$ denotes the total number of users, and $sim(S_k^{\mathcal{A}}, A_i, A_j)$ represents the similarity between A_i and A_j in sequence $S_k^{\mathcal{A}}$. The distance $d(A_i, A_j)$ between items in the sequence is considered, and for computational efficiency, the model only calculates similarities for items with a distance of 1 or 2. Based on the assumption, the similarity of an item with itself should be the highest, so it is defined as:

$$W_{sim}(A_i, A_i) = \max_{i \neq j, 1 \leq j \leq |\mathcal{A}|} W_{sim}(A_i, A_j) + 1 \tag{3}$$

The matrix W_{sim} is row-normalized via min-max to obtain:

$$W_{n-s}(A_i, A_j) = \frac{W_{sim}(A_i, A_j) - \min_{1 \leq k \leq |\mathcal{A}|}(W_{sim}(A_i, A_k))}{\max_{1 \leq k \leq |\mathcal{A}|}(W_{sim}(A_i, A_k)) - \min_{1 \leq k \leq |\mathcal{A}|}(W_{sim}(A_i, A_k))} \tag{4}$$

where $|\mathcal{A}|$ is the total number of items in domain $\mathcal{A}$. The item similarity matrix for domain $\mathcal{B}$ can be obtained in the same way.

Perturbation of User-Item Interaction Sequences

Based on the item similarity matrix W_{n-s} and the exponential mechanism, the perturbation of user-item interaction sequences is performed as follows. Taking domain $\mathcal{A}$ as an example, assume that the interaction sequence of user u with items in domain $\mathcal{A}$ is $S_u^{\mathcal{A}} = \{A_1, A_2, \ldots, A_{n-1}, A_n\}$. The utility function q and sensitivity Δq are defined as:

$$q(S_u^{\mathcal{A}}, A_k) = \max_{1 \leq i \leq n}(W_{n-s}(A_i, A_k)), \quad A_k \in \mathcal{A} \tag{5}$$

$$\Delta q = \max_{S_u^{\mathcal{A}} \sim \widehat{S_u^{\mathcal{A}}}} |q(S_u^{\mathcal{A}}, A_k) - q(\widehat{S_u^{\mathcal{A}}}, A_k)| = 1 \tag{6}$$

The utility function $q(S_u^{\mathcal{A}}, A_k)$ represents the utility of outputting A_k given the interaction sequence $S_u^{\mathcal{A}}$, where A_k is any item in the candidate set (the set of all items in domain $\mathcal{A}$). Intuitively, the more similar A_k is to the items in $S_u^{\mathcal{A}}$, the higher the probability of it being selected, which aligns with the assumption in the previous section. The sequences $S_u^{\mathcal{A}}$ and $\widehat{S_u^{\mathcal{A}}}$ are adjacent datasets, meaning they differ by only one item. According to the exponential mechanism, the probability of selecting A_k is:

$$\Pr(A_k) = \frac{\exp\left(\frac{\epsilon q(S_u^{\mathcal{A}}, A_k)}{2\Delta q}\right)}{\sum_{A_i \in \mathcal{A}} \exp\left(\frac{\epsilon q(S_u^{\mathcal{A}}, A_i)}{2\Delta q}\right)} \tag{7}$$

where ϵ is the privacy budget, a non-negative real number that determines the level of noise added. Notably, since the candidate set $\mathcal{A}$ often contains a large number of items, only the top 20 items most similar to A_k are considered in the candidate set for computational efficiency. By repeating this selection process, a certain proportion (set to 10% in experiments) of items in $S_u^{\mathcal{A}}$ are randomly replaced, resulting in the final perturbed sequence $\widehat{S_u^{\mathcal{A}}}$. This sequence is then converted into a user representation (details will be provided in the next section) and sent to the central server.

3.4 Information Fusion Recommendation Module

Acquisition and Fusion of User Latent Features. Taking domain $\mathcal{A}$ as an example, given the input sequences $S_u^{\mathcal{A}}$ and the perturbed sequences $\widehat{S_u^{\mathcal{A}}}$ for $|U|$ users, assume the longest sequence length is n, i.e., $S_u^{\mathcal{A}} = \{A_1, A_2, \ldots, A_{n-1}, A_n\}$. For sequences shorter than n, they are padded with zeros at the beginning. Let the item embedding matrix for domain $\mathcal{A}$ be $E^{\mathcal{A}}$. Thus, the sequence $S_u^{\mathcal{A}}$ can be encoded as $\{e_{u,1}^{\mathcal{A}}, \ldots, e_{u,n}^{\mathcal{A}}\} \in \mathbb{R}^{n \times d}$. Adding the positional information $P \in \mathbb{R}^{n \times d}$, the sequence feature $E_u^{\mathcal{A}}$ for user u can be represented as:

$$E_u^{\mathcal{A}} = \{e_{u,1}^{\mathcal{A}}, e_{u,2}^{\mathcal{A}}, \ldots, e_{u,n}^{\mathcal{A}}\} + P \tag{8}$$

Further, inspired by SASRec [9], since self-attention mechanisms can capture long-range dependencies in sequences by focusing on different parts of the sequence, the model introduces a self-attention layer to process the user's interaction sequence in the target domain, generating latent features that reflect the user's behavior patterns:

$$F_u^{\mathcal{A}} = FFN(SA(E_u^{\mathcal{A}})) \tag{9}$$

where $FFN(\cdot)$ represents a point-wise feedforward network, and $SA(\cdot)$ represents the self-attention layer. The output of the self-attention module is considered as the user's latent feature $F_u^{\mathcal{A}} = (f_{u,1}^{\mathcal{A}}, f_{u,2}^{\mathcal{A}}, \ldots, f_{u,n}^{\mathcal{A}})$. The same method is applied to obtain the latent features $\widehat{F_u^{\mathcal{A}}}$ from the perturbed sequence, which are then sent to the central server for use by other clients. Assuming that the latent features $\widehat{F_u^{\mathcal{B}}}$ from domain $\mathcal{B}$ are obtained from the central server, the model aggregates the locally generated $F_u^{\mathcal{A}}$ and the received $\widehat{F_u^{\mathcal{B}}}$ to produce the global user latent feature:

$$F_u^{\mathcal{A}agg} = w \cdot F_u^{\mathcal{A}} + (1-w) \cdot \widehat{F_u^{\mathcal{B}}} \tag{10}$$

where w is a hyperparameter that controls the proportion of features transferred from the source domain.

User-Item Interaction Recommendation. Given the global user latent feature $F_u^{\mathcal{A}agg} = (f_{u,1}^{\mathcal{A}agg}, f_{u,2}^{\mathcal{A}agg}, \ldots, f_{u,n}^{\mathcal{A}agg})$, where $f_{u,n}^{\mathcal{A}agg}$ represents the user's preference feature at time n, the probability of user u interacting with a candidate item $A_{n+1} \in \mathcal{A}$ (with embedding $e_{u,n+1}^{\mathcal{A}} \in E^{\mathcal{A}}$) at the next time step $n+1$ is:

$$\widehat{p}_{u,n} = \sigma(f_{u,n}^{\mathcal{A}agg} \odot e_{u,n+1}^{\mathcal{A}}) \tag{11}$$

where $\odot$ is the dot product operator, and σ is the sigmoid function, mapping the value to the range $[0, 1]$.

3.5 Model Training

Our method uses binary cross-entropy loss to train the model, capturing users' latent preferences and behavior patterns. At time t, items with actual interactions are positive samples, while items randomly sampled from the non-positive set are negative samples. The loss function is:

$$\mathcal{L} = -\sum_{u \in U} \sum_{A_i \in A^T \cup A^F} (p_{u,t} \cdot \log \widehat{p}_{u,t} + (1 - p_{u,t}) \cdot \log(1 - \widehat{p}_{u,t})) \tag{12}$$

4 Experiments

4.1 Experimental Setup

Datasets. For evaluation, we utilize three publicly available datasets from Douban and Amazon, reflecting real-world application scenarios. In the Douban dataset, we select the movie category as the source domain and the book category as the target domain. This choice is consistent with existing mainstream work([6,12,19,20]). It should be noted that these datasets only contain item IDs, without related semantic information (such as item descriptions or attributes). In the Amazon dataset, we consider two domain pairs: Movies-Books and Sports-Cloth. To ensure data quality, interactions in the source domain exceed 10 per user/item, while those in the target domain exceed 5. The statistics of these datasets are summarized in Table 1.

Table 1. Dataset Statistics

Dataset	User	Items	Interactions	Avg. Seq. Length
Douban Movies[S]	1599	13712	826844	517.10
Douban Books[T]		6778	90846	56.81
Amazon Movies[S]	4250	20542	103816	24.43
Amazon Books[T]		74107	119493	28.12
Amazon Sports[S]	3322	10200	36151	10.88
Amazon Cloth[T]		7685	23589	7.10

Baseline Models. To evaluate the performance of FP²CDSR, we compare it with two groups of baseline models: (1)Sequential recommendation methods: GMF [12], NCF [12], GRU4Rec [21] and SASRec [9]. (2)Cross-domain sequential recommendation methods: EMCDR [10], DCDCSR [6], DAAN [19], C2DSR [12] and TPUF [20].

4.2 Evaluation Metrics

Following previous research [12], we adopt the leave-one-out strategy to evaluate recommendation performance. The primary metrics are: (1) Hit Ratio @N (HR@N): Measures whether the test item appears in the top-N recommendations. (2) Normalized Discounted Cumulative Gain @N (NDCG@N): Evaluates the ranking quality of test items in the recommendation list.

4.3 Recommendation Performance

This chapter compares the performance of the FP²CDSR model with single-domain and cross-domain sequential baseline models. The experimental results are presented in Table 2, where the best-performing model is highlighted in bold. On three real-world datasets, although the FP²CDSR model perturbs user information for privacy protection, its recommendation performance in the target domain still outperforms most baseline methods. Compared with the advanced cross-domain sequential recommendation method TPUF [20], the FP²CDSR model shows an average performance improvement of approximately 0.5% in most cases, verifying that the model can effectively enhance the recommendation quality while ensuring user privacy.

However, on the Amazon (Sports→Apparel) dataset, the FP²CDSR model did not perform best in all metrics. Through analysis, it was found that the relatively short average sequence lengths of the source and target domains in this dataset may make the recommendation performance more vulnerable to perturbations. Nevertheless, considering the importance of privacy protection, such minor performance losses are acceptable.

To explore the impact of privacy protection on recommendation performance, this experiment constructed the SASRec + P² model by applying the privacy-preserving strategy (P²) proposed in this paper to the single-domain model SASRec [9]. The experimental data shows that after the introduction of P², the recommendation performance decreased slightly compared with the original SASRec model, which confirms the effectiveness of the privacy-preserving strategy and ensures the protection of user preference information.

4.4 Ablation Experiments

This subsection focuses on the role of the item similarity matrix in the federated privacy-protection module. During differential privacy perturbation, a random selection and replacement strategy (rd) is adopted to replace the privacy protection strategy (P²) based on the similarity matrix.

Table 2. Overall Performance Comparison

Dataset	Metrics	Single-domain Methods					Cross-domain Methods					
		GMF	NFC	GRU4Rec	SASRec	SASRec+P²	EMCDR	DCDCSR	DAAN	C2DSR	TPUF	**FP²CDSR**
Douban Movie → Book	HR@5	0.1859	0.2390	0.2610	0.3267	0.3178	0.2321	0.2278	0.2215	0.2634	0.3648	**0.3711**
	NDCG@5	0.1260	0.1659	0.1821	0.2346	0.2289	0.1586	0.1545	0.1479	0.1835	0.2583	**0.2593**
	HR@10	0.2985	0.3611	0.3655	0.4568	0.4411	0.3392	0.3454	0.3367	0.3748	0.5137	**0.5150**
	NDCG@10	0.1621	0.2049	0.2157	0.2767	0.2485	0.1929	0.1923	0.1849	0.2193	**0.3061**	0.3054
Amazon Movie → Book	HR@5	0.1067	0.1396	0.1349	0.1198	0.1127	0.1149	0.1297	0.1236	0.1339	0.1523	**0.1596**
	NDCG@5	0.0681	0.1020	0.0966	0.0836	0.0794	0.0799	0.0877	0.0869	0.0990	0.1090	**0.1157**
	HR@10	0.1685	0.1874	0.1840	0.1812	0.1692	0.1676	0.1919	0.1796	0.1895	0.2078	**0.2132**
	NDCG@10	0.0877	0.1173	0.1124	0.1034	0.0976	0.0970	0.1076	0.1048	0.1168	0.1271	**0.1329**
Amazon Sport → Cloth	HR@5	0.1205	0.1223	0.1425	0.1865	0.1797	0.1579	0.1591	0.1162	0.1425	0.1992	**0.2034**
	NDCG@5	0.0885	0.0872	0.1113	0.1580	0.1521	0.1097	0.1065	0.0737	0.0933	0.1669	**0.1669**
	HR@10	0.1803	0.2039	0.1932	0.2265	0.2242	0.2310	0.2334	0.1957	0.2165	**0.2596**	0.2534
	NDCG@10	0.1073	0.1128	0.1274	0.1709	0.1663	0.1331	0.1306	0.0991	0.1170	**0.1861**	0.1839

In the single-domain scenario, the experimental results of three datasets (Table 3) show that the random selection and replacement strategy causes significant perturbations to the sequences, is likely to introduce strong-noise interactions, disrupts user preference information, and leads to a substantial decline in the performance of sequential recommendation. In contrast, the item similarity matrix designed in this paper can better preserve the original user preference information.

Table 3. Single-domain Results

Methods	Metrics	Dataset		
		Douban Movie	Amazon Movie	Amazon Sport
SASRec+rd	HR@10	0.6038	0.4245	0.2095
	NDCG@10	0.3895	0.2694	0.1423
SASRec+P²	HR@10	**0.6420**	**0.4651**	**0.2309**
	NDCG@10	**0.4062**	**0.2996**	**0.1581**

In the cross-domain scenario, the experimental results of three cross-domain datasets (Table 4) indicate that the random selection and replacement strategy also damages user preference information. By comparison, the item similarity matrix is more conducive to preserving the original preference information. However, due to the native distribution biases and user preference biases between dif-

Table 4. Cross-domain Results

Methods	Metrics	Dataset		
		Douban Movie→Book	Amazon Movie→Book	Amazon Sport→Cloth
FP²CDSR+rd	HR@10	0.4974	0.1976	0.2531
	NDCG@10	0.3044	0.1155	0.1792
FP²CDSR	HR@10	**0.5150**	**0.2132**	**0.2534**
	NDCG@10	**0.3054**	**0.1329**	**0.1839**

ferent domains, the improvement in cross-domain recommendation performance by the item similarity matrix is less than that in the single-domain scenario.

4.5 Privacy Budget Analysis

The dataset, limited to item IDs without semantic info, makes privacy attack experiments (e.g., attribute inference) tough: embedding-to-ID mapping is non-linear with no semantic aid, and traditional attacks fail to generalize to new IDs, yielding near-random accuracy. Therefore, privacy attack experiments on the current cross-domain dataset struggle to provide reliable privacy metrics.

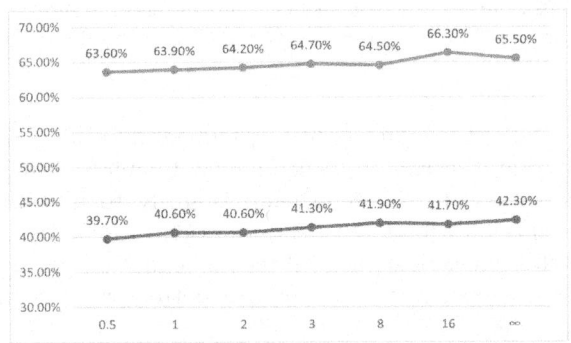

Fig. 2. Impact of Privacy Budget on Recommendation Accuracy. The x-axis is the privacy budget ε, the green line represents HR@10, and the blue line represents NDGC@10. (Color figure online)

Similar to most federated recommendation methods [15,22], we did not directly conduct privacy attack experiments. However, in Sect. 3.3, we ensure the algorithm satisfies ϵ-differential privacy, providing theoretical privacy guarantees for user data. Additionally, we analyze the impact of the privacy budget ϵ on recommendation performance in this section, indirectly reflecting the data protection effectiveness of our method.

To isolate confounding factors arising from user preference heterogeneity across domains, experiments were conducted in a single-domain recommendation scenario. Using the Douban Movie dataset with the SASRec+P^2 model, experimental results (Figure 2) demonstrate that recommendation accuracy improves with increasing privacy budgets (i.e. reduced noise addition). Maximum accuracy occurs when the privacy budget approaches infinity (noise-free conditions). Balancing privacy protection and recommendation quality, we empirically set the default privacy budget to 2 for cross-domain recommendation experiments.

5 Conclusion

In this paper, we propose a cross-domain sequence recommendation algorithm (FP^{2}CDSR) that combines federated learning and differential privacy techniques, aiming to enhance the accuracy and personalization capability of recommendation systems while protecting user privacy. The effectiveness of the algorithm is verified through experiments on three real datasets, proving its wide applicability in the field of recommendation systems and sequence modeling. Despite the results, the model still has its limitations. In the future, we can collect and create semantically rich cross-domain sequential recommendation datasets, based on which comprehensive privacy inference experiments can be conducted to further quantify the privacy protection effectiveness of this method. In addition, the research can be extended to a wider range of cross-domain recommendation scenarios, especially recommendation techniques for cross-user groups to meet the diverse and personalized needs in the real world.

Acknowledgments. This work is supported by the National Natural Science Foundation of China (No.62192785,No.62402491) and the National Key Research and Development Program of China (NO.2022YFB3102200).

References

1. Lin, X., Wu, J., Zhou, C., Pan, S., Cao, Y., Wang, B.: Task-adaptive neural process for user cold-start recommendation. In: Proceedings of the Web Conference 2021, pp. 1306–1316 (2021)
2. Lin, X., et al.: Towards flexible and adaptive neural process for cold-start recommendation. IEEE Trans. Knowl. Data Eng. **36**(4), 1815–1828 (2023)
3. Lin, X., et al.: Contrastive modality-disentangled learning for multimodal recommendation. ACM Trans. Inf. Syst. (2025)
4. Zhu, S., Li, M., Pan, G., Lin, X.: TTGL: large-scale multi-scenario universal graph learning at TikTok. In: Proceedings of the 31st ACM SIGKDD Conference on Knowledge Discovery and Data Mining (2025). https://doi.org/10.1145/3711896.3737269
5. Cao, J., Lin, X., Cong, X., Ya, J., Liu, T., Wang, B.: DisenCDR: learning disentangled representations for cross-domain recommendation. In: Proceedings of the 45th International ACM SIGIR Conference on Research and Development in Information Retrieval, pp. 267–277 (2022)
6. Zhu, F., Wang, Y., Chen, C., Liu, G., Orgun, M., Wu, J.: A deep framework for cross-domain and cross-system recommendations. arXiv preprint arXiv:2009.06215 (2020)
7. Zhu, F., Wang, Y., Chen, C., Liu, G., Orgun, M., Wu, J.: A deep framework for cross-domain and cross-system recommendations. arXiv preprint arXiv:2009.06215 (2020)
8. Wu, Y., et al.: FairCDR: transferring fairness and user preferences for cross-domain recommendation. In: Proceedings of the 31st ACM SIGKDD Conference on Knowledge Discovery and Data Mining (2025). https://doi.org/10.1145/3711896.3736951
9. Kang, W.C., McAuley, J.: Self-attentive sequential recommendation. In: 2018 IEEE International Conference on Data Mining (ICDM), pp. 197–206. IEEE (2018)
10. Man, T., Shen, H., Jin, X., Cheng, X.: Cross-domain recommendation: an embedding and mapping approach. In: IJCAI, vol. 17, pp. 2464–2470 (2017)

11. McMahan, B., Moore, E., Ramage, D., Hampson, S., y Arcas, B.A.: Communication-efficient learning of deep networks from decentralized data. Artif. Intell. Stat., 1273–1282. PMLR (2017)
12. He, X., Liao, L., Zhang, H., Nie, L., Hu, X., Chua, T.S.: Neural collaborative filtering. In: Proceedings of the 26th International Conference on World Wide Web, pp. 173–182 (2017)
13. Liu, W., Zheng, X., Su, J., Hu, M., Tan, Y., Chen, C.: Exploiting variational domain-invariant user embedding for partially overlapped cross domain recommendation. In: Proceedings of the 45th International ACM SIGIR Conference on Research and Development in Information Retrieval, pp. 312–321 (2022)
14. Liu, W., Zheng, X., Su, J., Zheng, L., Chen, C., Hu, M.: Contrastive proxy kernel stein path alignment for cross-domain cold-start recommendation. IEEE Trans. Knowl. Data Eng. **35**(11), 11216–11230 (2023)
15. Ammad-Ud-Din, M., Ivannikova, E., Khan, S.A., Oyomno, W., Fu, Q., Tan, K.E., Flanagan, A.: Federated collaborative filtering for privacy-preserving personalized recommendation system. arXiv preprint arXiv:1901.09888 (2019)
16. Lin, Y., et al.: Meta matrix factorization for federated rating predictions. In: Proceedings of the 43rd International ACM SIGIR Conference on Research and Development in Information Retrieval, pp. 981–990 (2020)
17. Liu, F., Cheng, Z., Chen, H., Wei, Y., Nie, L., Kankanhalli, M.: Privacy-preserving synthetic data generation for recommendation systems. In: Proceedings of the 45th International ACM SIGIR Conference on Research and Development in Information Retrieval, pp. 1379–1389 (2022)
18. Chen, C., Wu, H., Su, J., Lyu, L., Zheng, X., Wang, L.: Differential private knowledge transfer for privacy-preserving cross-domain recommendation. In: Proceedings of the ACM Web Conference 2022, pp. 1455–1465 (2022)
19. Liu, H., Guo, L., Li, P., Zhao, P., Wu, X.: Collaborative filtering with a deep adversarial and attention network for cross-domain recommendation. Inf. Sci. **565**, 370–389 (2021)
20. Ding, Y., Li, H., Chen, K., Shou, L.: TPUF: enhancing cross-domain sequential recommendation via transferring pre-trained user features. In: Proceedings of the 32nd ACM International Conference on Information and Knowledge Management, pp. 410–419 (2023)
21. Hidasi, B., Karatzoglou, A., Baltrunas, L., Tikk, D.: Session-based recommendations with recurrent neural networks. arXiv preprint arXiv:1511.06939 (2015)
22. Wu, J., et al.: Hierarchical personalized federated learning for user modeling. In: Proceedings of the Web Conference 2021, pp. 957–968 (2021)

An Enhanced Audio Feature Tailored for Anomalous Sound Detection Based on Pre-trained Models

Guirui Zhong[1], Qing Wang[1(✉)], Jun Du[1], Lei Wang[2], Mingqi Cai[3], and Xin Fang[3]

[1] University of Science and Technology of China, Hefei, China
qingwang2@ustc.edu.cn
[2] National Intelligent Voice Innovation Center, Hefei, China
[3] iFLYTEK Research, Hefei, China

Abstract. Anomalous Sound Detection (ASD) aims at identifying anomalous sounds from machines and has gained extensive research interests from both academia and industry. However, the uncertainty of anomaly location and much redundant information such as noise in machine sounds hinder the improvement of ASD system performance. This paper proposes a novel audio feature of filter banks with evenly distributed intervals, ensuring equal attention to all frequency ranges in the audio, which enhances the detection of anomalies in machine sounds. Moreover, based on pre-trained models, this paper presents a parameter-free feature enhancement approach to remove redundant information in machine audio. It is believed that this parameter-free strategy facilitates the effective transfer of universal knowledge from pre-trained tasks to the ASD task during model fine-tuning. Evaluation results on the Detection and Classification of Acoustic Scenes and Events (DCASE) 2024 Challenge dataset demonstrate significant improvements in ASD performance with our proposed methods.

Keywords: DCASE · Anomalous Sound Detection · Feature Extraction · Feature Enhancement

1 Introduction

The goal of Anomalous Sound Detection (ASD) is to detect whether the sound produced by a target machine is normal or anomalous. With the widespread use of machines, timely identification of mechanical faults is not only beneficial for machine maintenance, but also helps reduce property losses and protect personal safety. In factories, experienced workers can assess whether a machine is functioning normally or not based on the sound it emits. However, this method is highly subjective and may not consistently detect the machine's condition. Hence, developing an intelligent ASD system is essential to replace manual detection and improve reliability.

In recent years, the Detection and Classification of Acoustic Scenes and Events (DCASE) Challenge has attracted extensive attention from scholars in the fields of signal processing and machine learning, effectively driving advancements in acoustic scene classification, acoustic event detection, and related fields. The ASD task was first introduced into the competition in 2020 and has been held five times so far. The purpose of this task is to use machine learning models to detect whether a machine's sound is abnormal, thereby enabling intelligent monitoring of machine state [6,13].

Due to the scarcity of abnormal sounds in realistic scenarios, only normal sounds emitted from machines can be used for model training, making ASD a self-supervised learning (SSL) task rather than a simple binary classification problem (i.e., normal or abnormal). To address this challenge, scholars have explored various auxiliary tasks to accomplish ASD. These auxiliary methods can be broadly divided into two main categories: discriminative learning and generative learning. Discriminative learning approach assumes that if models classify a specific machine type's sound as other types, this sound will be considered anomalous. Alternatively, generative learning approach evaluates anomalous likelihood based on reconstruction error: the higher the error, the more likely the sound is anomalous. Both methods operate on the premise that models trained solely on normal sounds struggle with anomalous audio due to distribution differences between normal and abnormal data.

Recently, methods based on pre-trained models have achieved significant progress compared to previous non-pre-trained approaches. These methods leverage a Vision Transformer (ViT) backbone pre-trained on AudioSet and fine-tune it on machine audio, aiming to transfer the model's general audio processing capabilities to the specific domain of machine audio [8,12]. However, there are still some obstacles that impede further performance improvements in ASD. Firstly, due to diverse causes of machine anomalies, it is difficult to determine the exact position of abnormal sounds on the spectrogram, which means that anomalous sounds can appear across different frequency ranges of the spectrogram. Furthermore, machine sounds often contain a great deal of trivial information, making it challenging for models to effectively learn machine-related features.

To address the first challenge, we use Mel filter banks with evenly distributed intervals to ensure equal attention across all frequency ranges in machine sounds. Since machine anomalies can arise from various causes, they may appear in different frequency ranges. For the second challenge, a straightforward solution is to incorporate attention modules into pre-trained models. Nevertheless, training new module parameters from scratch in a pre-trained model often yields minimal benefits or can even be detrimental due to knowledge inconsistency between the newly added parameters and the existing pre-trained ones. To mitigate this issue and enhance ASD performance, we instead employ a parameter-free attention module. We highlight three key contributions of this paper as follows:

– We design a novel audio feature to ensure equal attention across all frequency ranges and better capture the anomaly in machine sounds.

- We propose a parameter-free feature enhancement framework to remove redundant information and strengthen the relevant feature in machine audio.
- Evaluation results on the DCASE 2024 ASD dataset demonstrate significant improvements in ASD performance with our proposed methods. As a result, our system reaches a new state-of-the-art (SOTA) performance on the DCASE 2024 ASD evaluation dataset.

2 Related Works

2.1 Discriminative Learning

Although anomalous sound detection is trained exclusively on normal machine sounds, these sounds contain categorical information such as machine type, domain, and attribute. The discriminative learning method leverages this information to accurately classify normal sounds, enabling the model to effectively characterize normal audio features and learn meaningful representations through classification tasks (e.g., machine type or machine attributes). During training, the model continuously optimizes its classification accuracy for normal data. As a result, during testing, sounds that cannot be correctly classified into the expected machine type or attribute are more likely to be identified as anomalous.

Wilkinghoff [17] explores a simple yet effective SSL approach for ASD, based on a convolutional neural network (CNN) that integrates both time-domain and frequency-domain information from audio. Wang et al. [16] introduce a two-stage multi-attribute classification framework tailored for ASD in real scenarios, facilitating the extraction of discriminative representations of machine sounds. Recently, Jiang et al. [8] propose to utilize a ViT backbone pre-trained on AudioSet and fine-tune it on machine audio, which has made great progress in ASD. Notably, the first-place entries in the DCASE ASD challenge have predominantly relied on discriminative learning method, highlighting its effectiveness in ASD.

2.2 Generative Learning

The generative learning method is one of the earliest approaches used to detect anomalous sounds, with auto-encoder (AE) being a typical example. AE reconstructs the original signal by encoding and decoding the input sound signal through a neural network. Anomalous sounds are then detected based on the reconstruction error. Specifically, for normal sounds, because we have seen the normal sound samples when training the AE, the signal recovered by encoding and decoding closely resembles the input signal. In contrast, for anomalous sounds, which the AE has not encountered during training and which differ from normal sounds, the reconstructed signal deviates significantly from the original input. This discrepancy enables the detection of anomalous sounds.

Zhou et al. [21] design an auxiliary classifier into AE in a multi-task learning manner and a group-based decoder structure to enhance ASD. Guan et al. [5] introduce an ID-constrained Transformer-based AE architecture, which

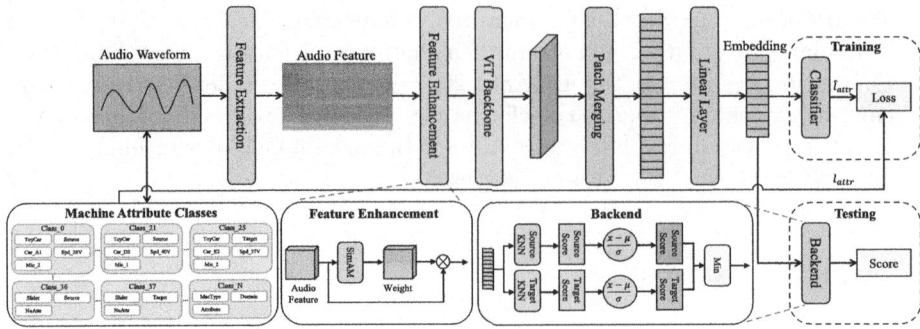

Fig. 1. The proposed ASD model consists of a modified feature extraction module, a feature enhancement module, a network backbone to classify machine attributes, and a backend with domain normalization technique.

mitigates the generalization of AE for anomalous sounds and enhances the distinguishing ability for different machines of the same type. Moreover, Jiang et al. [9] utilize a generative adversarial network (GAN) to detect anomalous sounds.

3 Proposed Method

The overall flowchart of the proposed ASD framework is illustrated in Fig. 1, mainly consisting of a modified feature extraction module, a feature enhancement module, a ViT backbone, and a backend with domain normalization technique. The feature extraction module uses a set of evenly distributed filter banks to extract the audio feature based on the conventional process of extracting FBank. Meanwhile, as shown in the lower middle box of Fig. 1, the feature enhancement module comprises an attention module to obtain weights using the Simple, Parameter-Free Attention Module (SimAM) [18]. Then, in the bottom-right box, we introduce K-Nearest Neighbors (KNN) detectors with a simple domain normalization strategy to generate the anomaly score, which is less affected by domain shift. By means of these techniques and the network backbone, we carry out machine attribute classification task to realize ASD. These proposed methods are elaborated in the following subsections.

3.1 Feature Extraction

In this section, we review the extraction process of the original filter banks (FBank) feature. The process can be mainly divided into the following steps: pre-emphasis, framing, applying window functions, Fast Fourier Transform (FFT), Mel filtering, and logarithmic operation. As frequency increases, the spacing between adjacent Mel filters gradually widens when Mel filtering. This design prioritizes low-frequency information, aligning with the human ear's greater sensitivity to low frequencies and reduced sensitivity to high frequencies.

However, this Mel filter intervals arrangement does not apply to the ASD task. On the one hand, some machine sounds are primarily distributed in higher frequency ranges. On the other hand, due to the unpredictability of real-world scenarios, there are many different reasons that can make the machine anomalous, causing that the anomaly will occur at random, unfixed frequency ranges. To address this, we propose a modified FBank feature tailored for ASD task by adjusting the intervals between adjacent Mel filters to be evenly spaced. In other words, all adjacent Mel filters are distributed uniformly to enhance anomaly detection in machine sounds. Notably, except for the change of intervals, the process of extracting modified FBank features is consistent with the original process.

3.2 Feature Enhancement

Parameter-Free Attention Module Due to the presence of redundant information in sounds, such as background noises, it is necessary to enhance the features of machine sounds to enable the model to focus on crucial information. One straightforward and widely used approach is to incorporate attention modules within the network. These attention modules can be categorized into two classes: the first class involves designing specific trainable layers distinct from the backbone network, known as parameter-requiring modules; the second class involves obtaining the corresponding weights through elaborate formulas, which usually do not require training, referred to as parameter-free modules.

Because we use pre-trained models, which have been proven to be more effective in contrast with previous non-pre-trained ways, as our baseline, parameter-free attention modules are applied in the network as the feature enhancement layer. This choice serves two key purposes. On the one hand, it is usually unreasonable to add new trainable parameters to pre-trained models, as there is knowledge inconsistency between the newly added parameters and the existing pre-trained parameters, making it difficult for the attention modules to perform their expected functions. Notably, this differs from the common practice of replacing the pre-trained decoder with specific modules for downstream tasks during fine-tuning. For instance, linear layers are used to replace the original decoder to perform downstream classification tasks. However, attention modules are generally placed within or before encoder, with only slight adjustments made during fine-tuning. On the other hand, even though it is feasible to freeze the pre-trained parameters and then fine-tune the newly added attention parameters to achieve knowledge consistency, this method is still more complex than directly adding parameter-free attention modules and fine-tuning the model only once, and it cannot guarantee effectiveness.

Feature Enhancement Module For the feature enhancement layer, we deploy SimAM as the attention module. SimAM assigns a corresponding weight to each neuron, calculated using a formula based on the spatial suppression phenomenon. The SimAM calculates the respective weights of all neurons on a single channel. Thus, giving an audio spectrogram $\mathbf{X} \in \mathbb{R}^{1 \times F \times T}$, where F denotes the frequency dimension and T denotes the time dimension, we refer to the weights obtained from the SimAM as $\mathbf{W} \in \mathbb{R}^{1 \times F \times T}$. Given the target neuron z and other neurons x_i in $\mathbf{X}$, the process of SimAM can be defined below:

$$e_z^* = \frac{4(\hat{\sigma}^2 + \lambda)}{(z - \hat{\mu})^2 + 2\hat{\sigma}^2 + 2\lambda} \quad (1)$$

$$w_z^* = \text{sigmoid}(1/e_z^*) \quad (2)$$

where $\hat{\mu} = \frac{1}{M}\sum_{i=1}^{M} x_i$, $\hat{\sigma}^2 = \frac{1}{M}\sum_{i=1}^{M}(x_i - \hat{\mu})^2$, λ is a hyperparameter, and $M = F \times T$ is the number of neurons on the single channel of $\mathbf{X}$. It is noted that we set $\lambda = 10^{-4}$ (the default value of the original paper) in all experiments and do not tune it. e_z^* and w_z^* represent the minimal energy and the weight of target neuron z; the lower energy e_z^*, the greater the weight w_z^*. sigmoid($\cdot$) is the sigmoid activation function to restrict too large value. Finally, we obtain $\mathbf{W}$ by grouping all target neurons weights w_z^* across the channel. In fact, the weight represents the linear separability between the target neuron and other neurons; the higher the linear separability, the greater the weight. Specific derivation process can be found in [18].

3.3 KNN Backend with Domain Normalization

In real-world scenarios, machine operational states and the environmental noises are not constant, which causes the domain shift problem and greatly restricts the performance of the ASD system. To address this, we introduce a simple domain normalization strategy in the backend KNN detector to alleviate the problem during inference, building upon a similar method from [20]. The concrete operation is presented in the bottom-right box of Fig. 1.

To start with, we train two KNN detectors for each machine type, one using the embeddings from all samples in the source domain and the other using the embeddings from all samples in the target domain. Subsequently, two anomaly scores for a given testing machine audio are obtained by computing the cosine distance between the embedding of the testing audio and its closest neighbor (k = 1). Then, score normalization is performed between the two domains. In the end, the minimum anomaly score for each testing machine audio is adopted as the audio's final score. The aforementioned process is shown below:

$$\text{Score}_i = d(\mathbf{E}_{test}, \mathbf{E}_i) \quad (3)$$

$$\text{Score}_i^N = (\text{Score}_i - \mu_i)/\sigma_i \quad (4)$$

$$\text{Score} = \text{Min}(\text{Score}_s^N, \text{Score}_t^N) \quad (5)$$

where d($\cdot$) denotes the cosine distance, the subscript 'i' is the domain indicator, Score_i represents the anomaly score of the testing audio in the source ($i = s$) or target ($i = t$) domain, and $\mathbf{E}_{test}$ denotes the test embedding of machine audio acquired by the fine-tuned model. Score_i^N represents normalized anomaly score. Variables μ_i and σ_i indicate the mean and standard deviation of anomaly scores in the source or target domain. Min($\cdot$) is the minimum operation.

3.4 Machine Attribute Classification

In this section, we explain the whole process of ASD system used in this paper. The machine attribute classification schematic diagram can be found in Fig. 1. To begin with, the machine audio waveform **x** is transformed into the modified FBank feature **X** by the feature extraction module. What this feature extraction process distinguishes from the original FBank extraction process is the use of evenly distributed filter banks. Subsequently, this audio feature is input to the feature enhancement layer to remove redundant information in the feature. So far, we have obtained the enhanced audio feature $\mathbf{X}_e$ tailored for ASD system, the process can be defined below:

$$\mathbf{X} = \text{Extract}(\mathbf{x}) \tag{6}$$

$$\mathbf{X}_e = \text{SimAM}(\mathbf{X}) \times \mathbf{X} \tag{7}$$

where **X** can be original or modified FBank feature as described above, Extract(·) represents the feature extraction process, and SimAM(·) denotes the used attention module in the feature enhancement layer.

Then, the enhanced audio feature is split into multiple patches and input into the ViT backbone pretrained on the AudioSet [4]. The backbone models each patch and outputs embeddings for all patches. Thereafter, the attentive statistics pooling layer [14] is used to merge all patches information into an utterance embedding. Lastly, the utterance embedding is mapped into low-dimensional embedding. This embedding is utilized for machine attribute classification by ArcFace [2] classifier during fine-tuning. We combine each machine type, domain, and its corresponding attributes as a separate class and perform classification tasks. For those machine types without attributes, we combine their machine types and domains as separate classes. The details can be found in the dataset introduction section later. After fine-tuning, this embedding is used for anomaly detection in the KNN backend with the domain normalization technique during testing. The training stage can be defined below:

$$\mathbf{E} = \mathcal{F}(\mathbf{X}_e) \tag{8}$$

$$\hat{l}_{attr} = \mathcal{C}_{attr}(\mathbf{E}) \tag{9}$$

$$\mathcal{L}_{\text{ASD}} = \text{CE}(\hat{l}_{attr}, l_{attr}) \tag{10}$$

where **E** and $\mathcal{F}(\cdot)$ denote the embedding of machine audio and the map function including ViT, patch merging, and linear mapping operation, separately. $\mathcal{C}_{attr}(\cdot)$ indicates the ArcFace attribute classifier, CE(·) is the cross-entropy loss, and $\mathcal{L}_{\text{ASD}}$ is the ASD loss to be optimized. l_{attr} and $\hat{l}_{attr}$ represent the ground truth and predicted attribute labels. After training, the embedding will pass through backend to obtain anomaly score.

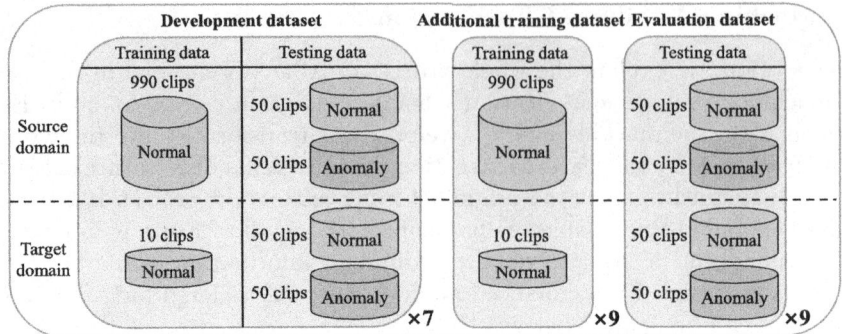

Fig. 2. The structure of the DCASE 2024 ASD dataset.

4 Experiments

4.1 Dataset and Metrics

We evaluate the ASD task on the DCASE 2024 ASD dataset [3,7], a widely accepted public benchmark for many papers in the ASD area. The structure of the dataset can be found in Fig. 2. It is noted that there are seven and nine machine types in the development and additional (including additional training and evaluation) datasets, respectively. Each machine type has 1000 clips for training and 200 clips for testing. Some machine types have corresponding attribute information as metadata. For instance, as shown in the bottom-left box of Fig. 1, the ToyCar has car model (Car), speed (Spd), and microphone number (Mic) attributes. Unique value of attributes, combining with machine type and domain, is considered as a separate class. Additionally, for those machine types without attributes, we combine their machine types and domains as separate classes. We evaluate all methods with the area under the receiver operating characteristic (ROC) curve (AUC) and the partial AUC (pAUC) using the anomaly score that indicates the anomaly degree. Meanwhile, we compare the harmonic mean performance on the development set, evaluation set and all machine types, which we all refer to as score. The harmonic mean calculated on the evaluation set serves as the official score according to the challenge rules [6,13].

4.2 Implementation Details

The overall framework used in this work is based on the public open-source Efficient Audio Transformer (EAT) project [1]. All audio waveforms are padded or truncated to 10s, and then converted to log-mel spectrograms with a frame length of 25ms, a frame shift of 10ms, and 128 mel bins. We use the Adam optimizer, and the pre-trained EAT is fine-tuned for appropriate epochs to converge with a batch size of 32. A cosine learning rate scheduler is adopted with an upper limit of 5e-5 and a warm-up step of 120. Mixup [19] and SpecAugment [15] data augmentation techniques are utilized to generate more diverse data during the

Table 1. Performance comparison for different audio features and domain normalization (DN) method. Mean and standard deviation over five runs are reported.

Feature	DN	Development set				Evaluation set				All
		AUC_s	AUC_t	pAUC	score	AUC_s	AUC_t	pAUC	score	score
o-FB	-	78.21±1.04	56.85±0.35	56.47±0.83	62.39±0.37	71.43±2.06	62.11±0.33	57.91±0.48	63.33±0.82	62.91±0.29
	✓	69.64±1.19	67.69±0.44	55.65±1.07	63.68±0.56	66.13±1.05	72.16±0.81	57.02±0.34	64.49±0.59	64.13±0.12
g-FB	-	70.10±0.37	49.85±0.89	55.36±0.55	57.26±0.45	70.79±1.13	48.05±1.40	53.43±0.46	55.90±0.74	56.48±0.22
	✓	64.57±0.33	63.78±1.04	**56.70±0.53**	61.47±0.44	62.27±1.02	63.18±0.37	52.71±0.09	58.98±0.33	60.04±0.09
m-FB	-	78.38±0.74	59.01±0.40	55.08±0.58	62.68±0.14	**74.44±1.73**	64.24±0.55	**59.03±0.41**	65.29±0.55	64.12±0.25
	✓	70.76±0.43	**68.93±0.48**	54.73±0.55	**63.95±0.28**	70.01±0.11	**73.78±0.42**	58.05±0.52	**66.57±0.32**	**65.40±0.11**

training step with mixup α of 0.8 and mask ratio of 0.2 on the time and frequency axes, respectively. We execute all experiments 5 times independently and report the mean and standard deviation.

4.3 Experimental Results and Analysis

Feature Extraction Module. We use the EAT pre-trained on the AudioSet with original FBank feature and fine-tune it using different FBank features. In the fine-tuning stage, we validate the effect of different audio features by modifying the distribution of filter banks. We refer to original FBank and modified FBank as o-FB and m-FB, separately. Meanwhile, we also compare another filter bank, Gammatone filter, referred to as g-FB. AUC_s, AUC_t, and pAUC represent the AUC in the source domain, the AUC in the target domain, and the pAUC across both domains. From Table 1, we can find that using m-FB to fine-tune the model achieves the best performance compared with others, which aligns with our motivation for designing the evenly distributed filter banks, i.e., better capturing the anomalies in machine sounds. Besides, the reason for g-FB's performance is that it is too different from o-FB used in pre-training, which makes the model unable to adapt in fine-tuning, while m-FB has good adaptability.

Domain Normalization Method. As shown in Table 1, it can be found that greater performance is achieved by using domain normalization. Upon closer inspection of the AUC values between the two domains, it is evident that the domain normalization technique primarily enhances the performance by bridging and narrowing the gap between them. This aligns with our motivation for designing the domain normalization method, which aims to alleviate the domain shift problem. Due to the higher score, we use the m-FB feature and domain normalization method for later experiment validation.

Feature Enhancement Module. We validate the effect of feature enhancement module in the way of the last row of Table 1. We first apply the original SimAM, which is a form of global feature enhancement from the view of the whole spectrogram, to the audio spectrogram, which only leads to improvements of 0.28% on all machine types. After further analysis of this phenomenon, as shown in the Fig. 3, we know that from the global view, the characteristic

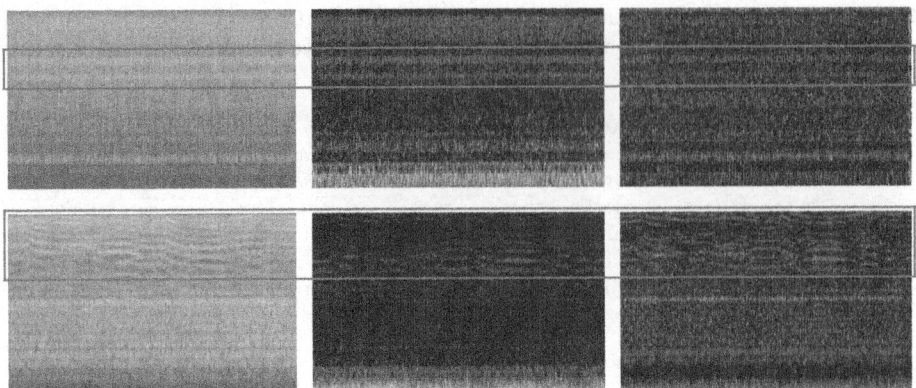

Fig. 3. Visualization of the audio spectrogram, the global weight from the original SimAM, and the local weight obtained by the improved SimAM, are shown in the left, middle, and right sides, respectively. The first and second rows represent Brushless-Motor and HoveringDrone machines, respectively. The key distinguishing features of different machine types are framed in the red rectangular boxes. (Color figure online)

lines of some machine types cannot be well captured because their characteristic lines are small or complex and easily disturbed by noise. Therefore, we split the whole spectrogram into multiple small spectrograms with a size of 32 × 32 to utilize feature enhancement from the local view. As shown in the third row of Table 2, the local feature enhancement has further improvements on the overall performance (all score). From spectrograms of different machine types and experimental results, we can find that some machine types and others are suitable from the local and global views, respectively. Moreover, machine condition detection is performed under a specific machine type, which is known to us during both training and testing. This distinguishes ASD approaches from other classification tasks. Thus, we further utilize the prior knowledge of machine types to apply a certain feature enhancement method (global or local) for each machine type, which we call customized feature enhancement. Specifically, as shown in the Fig. 3, global feature enhancement is applied to machine types such as BrushlessMotor, which have simple and easily identifiable feature lines, while local feature enhancement is performed on types like HoveingDrone, which exhibit fine and difficult-to-detect feature lines. As shown in the last row of Table 2, the customized feature enhancement approach gains further improvements and achieves the best performance among all feature enhancement modes.

Comparison with Other SOTA Models. As shown in Table 3, we compare our methods and other ASD SOTA models by the performance on the DCASE 2024 ASD dataset according to the challenge rules. Here the baseline represents the official system of the DCASE 2024 ASD Challenge. Meanwhile, some of the previous SOTA systems use multiple subsystems to ensemble, so here we also list their size of overall parameters. It can be found that with our proposed methods in this paper, we achieve a new SOTA performance on the DCASE 2024 ASD

Table 2. Performance comparison for different feature enhancement modes. Mean and standard deviation over five runs are reported.

Mode	Development set				Evaluation set				All
	AUC_s	AUC_t	pAUC	score	AUC_s	AUC_t	pAUC	score	score
Vanilla	70.76±0.43	68.93±0.48	54.73±0.55	63.95±0.28	70.01±0.11	73.78±0.42	58.05±0.52	66.57±0.32	65.40±0.11
Global	72.02±1.25	69.11±1.07	55.75±0.17	64.80±0.51	**70.57±0.80**	72.65±1.00	57.95±0.39	66.38±0.24	65.68±0.15
Local	**72.87±1.51**	70.32±0.52	56.86±0.99	65.88±0.78	69.77±1.31	73.00±0.55	57.77±0.26	66.16±0.57	66.03±0.39
Customized	72.25±0.89	**70.55±0.42**	**57.15±0.86**	**65.91±0.50**	70.26±1.02	**74.00±0.15**	**58.26±0.74**	**66.80±0.59**	**66.40±0.10**

Table 3. Comparison between our proposed methods and other SOTA models on the DCASE 2024 ASD dataset.

System	Size	Development set				Evaluation set				All
		AUC_s	AUC_t	pAUC	score	AUC_s	AUC_t	pAUC	score	score
Official baseline [6]	267K	65.00	50.28	52.84	55.35	**71.51**	50.58	51.72	56.50	55.99
Lv (No. 1) [12]	700M	**73.97**	**72.41**	59.16	**67.82**	71.03	73.66	56.70	66.24	**67.02**
Jiang (No. 2) [11]	360M	-	-	59.60	67.67	69.56	72.34	56.51	65.36	66.50
Zhao (No. 3) [20]	-	60.25	61.50	53.26	58.10	68.65	63.91	54.94	61.96	59.97
AnoPatch [8]	90M	-	-	-	62.47±0.77	-	-	-	65.58±1.12	63.98±0.38
Jiang [10]	90M	-	-	-	64.05±0.55	-	-	-	66.01±0.66	65.01±0.18
Ours	90M	72.25±0.89	70.55±0.42	57.15±0.86	65.91±0.50	70.26±1.02	**74.00±0.15**	**58.26±0.74**	**66.80±0.59**	66.40±0.10

evaluation dataset with fewer number parameters and a score comparable to the No. 1 and No. 2 teams on all machine types. It is noted that our methods only use one system, while No. 1 and No. 2 teams use 7 and 4 subsystems, respectively.

5 Conclusion

In this paper, we propose two simple yet effective methods to enhance the performance of pre-trained models in ASD. By using modified FBank audio feature, the ASD system can better capture the anomaly in machine audio, resulting in improved performance. Meanwhile, by incorporating with parameter-free and customized feature enhancement, the ASD system can better learn the crucial features of machine audio. Finally, we achieve great increases and a new SOTA performance on the DCASE 2024 ASD evaluation dataset.

References

1. Chen, W., Liang, Y., Ma, Z., Zheng, Z., Chen, X.: Eat: self-supervised pre-training with efficient audio transformer. arXiv preprint arXiv:2401.03497 (2024)
2. Deng, J., Guo, J., Xue, N., Zafeiriou, S.: Arcface: additive angular margin loss for deep face recognition. In: Proceedings of the IEEE/CVF Conference on Computer Vision and Pattern Recognition, pp. 4690–4699 (2019)
3. Dohi, K., et al.: Mimii dg: sound dataset for malfunctioning industrial machine investigation and inspection for domain generalization task. arXiv preprint arXiv:2205.13879 (2022)

4. Gemmeke, J.F., et al.: Audio set: an ontology and human-labeled dataset for audio events. In: 2017 IEEE International Conference on Acoustics, Speech and Signal Processing (ICASSP), pp. 776–780. IEEE (2017)
5. Guan, J., et al.: Transformer-based autoencoder with id constraint for unsupervised anomalous sound detection. EURASIP J. Audio Speech Music Process. **2023**(1), 42 (2023)
6. Harada, N., Niizumi, D., Ohishi, Y., Takeuchi, D., Yasuda, M.: First-shot anomaly sound detection for machine condition monitoring: a domain generalization baseline. In: 2023 31st European Signal Processing Conference (EUSIPCO), pp. 191–195. IEEE (2023)
7. Harada, N., Niizumi, D., Takeuchi, D., Ohishi, Y., Yasuda, M., Saito, S.: Toyadmos2: another dataset of miniature-machine operating sounds for anomalous sound detection under domain shift conditions. arXiv preprint arXiv:2106.02369 (2021)
8. Jiang, A., et al.: Anopatch: towards better consistency in machine anomalous sound detection. arXiv preprint arXiv:2406.11364 (2024)
9. Jiang, A., Zhang, W.Q., Deng, Y., Fan, P., Liu, J.: Unsupervised anomaly detection and localization of machine audio: a GAN-based approach. In: ICASSP 2023-2023 IEEE International Conference on Acoustics, Speech and Signal Processing (ICASSP), pp. 1–5. IEEE (2023)
10. Jiang, A., et al.: Adaptive prototype learning for anomalous sound detection with partially known attributes. In: ICASSP 2025 - 2025 IEEE International Conference on Acoustics, Speech and Signal Processing (ICASSP), pp. 1–5 (2025). https://doi.org/10.1109/ICASSP49660.2025.10889514
11. Jiang, A., et al.: Thuee system for first-shot unsupervised anomalous sound detection. Technical report, DCASE2024 Challenge (2024)
12. Lv, Z., eta l.: Aithu system for first-shot unsupervised anomalous sound detection. Technical report, DCASE2024 Challenge (2024)
13. Nishida, T., et al.: Description and discussion on dcase 2024 challenge task 2: first-shot unsupervised anomalous sound detection for machine condition monitoring. arXiv preprint arXiv:2406.07250 (2024)
14. Okabe, K., Koshinaka, T., Shinoda, K.: Attentive statistics pooling for deep speaker embedding. arXiv preprint arXiv:1803.10963 (2018)
15. Park, D.S., et al.: Specaugment: a simple data augmentation method for automatic speech recognition. arXiv preprint arXiv:1904.08779 (2019)
16. Wang, S., et al.: Representation learning using machine attribute information for anomalous sound detection in real scenarios. In: 2024 International Joint Conference on Neural Networks (IJCNN), pp. 1–7. IEEE (2024)
17. Wilkinghoff, K.: Self-supervised learning for anomalous sound detection. In: ICASSP 2024-2024 IEEE International Conference on Acoustics, Speech and Signal Processing (ICASSP), pp. 276–280. IEEE (2024)
18. Yang, L., Zhang, R.Y., Li, L., Xie, X.: Simam: a simple, parameter-free attention module for convolutional neural networks. In: International Conference on Machine Learning, pp. 11863–11874. PMLR (2021)
19. Zhang, H., Cissé, M., Dauphin, Y., Lopez-Paz, D.: mixup: Beyond empirical risk minimization. arXiv preprint arXiv:1710.09412 (2017)
20. Zhao, R., Ren, K., Zou, L.: Enhanced unsupervised anomalous sound detection using conditional autoencoder for machine condition monitoring. Technical report, DCASE2024 Challenge (2024)
21. Zhou, Y., Xu, D., Wei, H., Long, Y.: Autoencoder with group-based decoder and multi-task optimization for anomalous sound detection. arXiv preprint arXiv:2311.08829 (2023)

Multimodal Sentiment Analysis with Parallel Attention and Correlation Fusion

Xiaoqiang Liu[1], Jie Lei[1(✉)], Jiaqi Wu[1], Zunlei Feng[2], and Ronghua Liang[1]

[1] College of Computer Science, Zhejiang University of Technology, Hangzhou 310000, China
jasonlei@zjut.edu.cn
[2] College of Computer Science, Zhejiang University, Hangzhou 310000, China

Abstract. Multimodal Sentiment Analysis (MSA) has received increasing attention in recent years but faces some challenges: Information conflicts between unimodal tokens and multimodal sentiment labels lead to errors in sentiment analysis, while inter-modal correlation learning is equally difficult when multimodal fusion is performed. In this paper, we propose a new framework, PamSA, which incorporates parallel attention and correlation fusion. Specifically, we first propose parallel attention, which utilises parallel cross-fusion modules to implicitly guide cross-modal learning, correcting the sentiment information for each modality. After that, proceed to correlation fusion. We use distance-aware contrastive learning to further exploit the obtained intermodal features to learn the mixed-modal correlations. Finally, we perform a weighted fusion of mixed modalities to obtain multimodal fusion features to identify sentiment information. Experimental results show that our proposed PamSA achieves state-of-the-art performance on three datasets, including CMU-MOSI, CMU-MOSEI, and CH-SIMS. The code link is https://github.com/lxq666666/PamSA

Keywords: Sentiment analysis · Multimodal · Parallel · Attention · Correlation

1 Introduction

With the widespread popularity of social media, videos containing multiple modalities have become the main information carriers. Significant progress has been made in sentiment analysis in recent years, which focuses on the three modalities of text [1], visual [2] and audio [3] in video, so that human emotional characteristics can be effectively exploited.

Traditional approaches to sentiment analysis [4,5] tend to focus on a single modality, which may result in incomplete and limited information acquisition. Unlike unimodal sentiment analysis [6], multimodal sentiment analysis explores their interrelationships. Multimodal sentiment analysis is a challenging

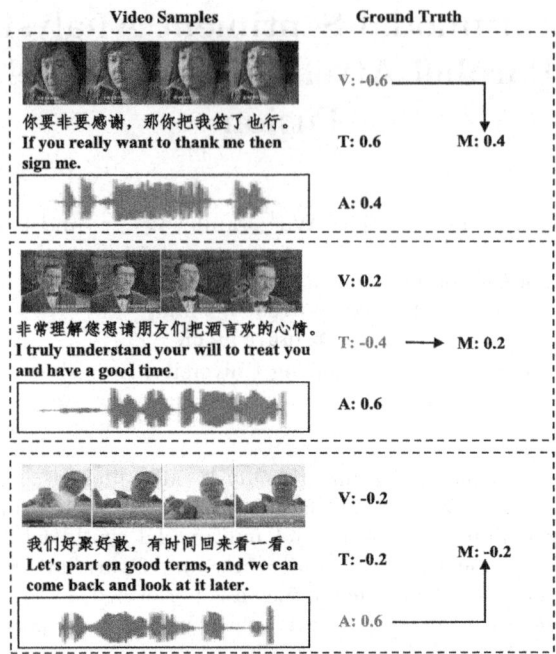

Fig. 1. Three video samples with information conflicts between visual, text, or audio modal tokens and multimodal sentiment labels from CH-SIMS dataset. In the Ground Truth, V, T and A denote the visual, text and audio, respectively. M is the overall sentiment label of the video sample. The values of all labels are from −1 (negative) to 1 (positive).

task that requires the combined processing of multiple information sources such as text, visual and audio to identify sentiment [7]. Due to the heterogeneity and complementarity between different information sources, joint representations are involved in reasoning about multimodal messages and can improve the performance of a given task [8].

Researchers have proposed a variety of MSA fusion methods. In traditional MSA schemes, early fusion [9], intermediate fusion [10,11] and late fusion [12,13] were investigated to integrate multimodal features. Later, deep neural networks were used for feature extraction and fusion in MSA [14–16]. Multimodal correlations were also explored by learning modal features [17].

Compared to the other two modalities (visual and audio), text is a high-level semantics that is easy to analyse during computation, but the result is a heavy dependency on text, which may be affected by the information conflict between text and sentiment. Sun [18] proposed a counterfactual framework to eliminate the direct influence of textual modalities. Unlike Sun [18], Ma [19] consider this problem from a fusion perspective and address the issue of conflicting information between text and sentiment. But it still uses text modality as the primary modality to implicitly guide cross-modal learning, ignoring the problem of

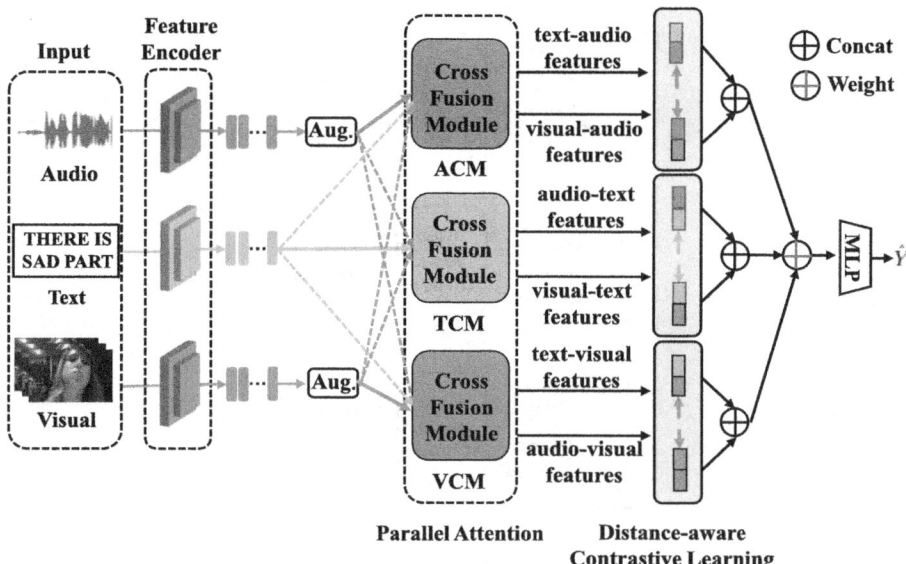

Fig. 2. Overview of our proposed PamSA. We extract deep features from each modality. We then correct the modal sentiment information by parallel attention and learn the correlation of the hybrid modalities through correlation fusion. The resulting fused features are used for sentiment analysis.

information conflict between both audio and visual modalities and sentiment labels. And according to our investigation, as shown in Fig. 1, there is an information conflict problem between unimodal tokens and multimodal sentiment labels on Chinese Multimodal Sentiment Analysis Datase (CH-SIMS) [15]. Meanwhile, we also analysed the data on the CH-SIMS dataset and counted the proportion of data with conflicting information on multimodal sentiment labels as 8.15%, 7.01% and 6.05% for the three modalities of text, visual and audio, respectively.

The contribution of this work is we propose a new framework, PamSA, to address these issues. In our framework, a three-branch parallel structure is designed that no longer prefers a single modality. This means that our method treats text, audio, and visual modalities equally and effectively exploits the complementary relationship between the three modalities to solve the problem of conflicting unimodal tokens with information from multimodal sentiment labels. Our proposed PamSA outperforms the state-of-the-art methods on three datasets.

2 Method

An overview of our PamSA framework is shown in Fig. 2. We first extract deep features of each modality with the corresponding pretrained feature extractors. Then, since visual and audio modalities are not high-level semantics like text modality, we augment the features of visual and audio modalities to facilitate

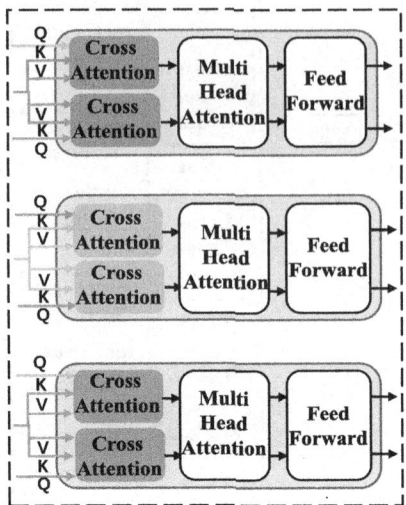

Fig. 3. The parallel attention module solves the problem of conflicting information by correcting each modality through a three-branch parallel structure.

subsequent contrastive learning. In Fig. 2, 'Aug' indicates the augmentation of features to improve the generalisation ability and robustness of the model by increasing the diversity of features. 'Aug' supports a variety of feature enhancement methods, including crop, cutout, reverse, multiscale and disorder. Next, we feed the extracted deep features into a parallel attention module where inter-modal correlations are exploited in parallel to correct the conflicting sentiment information for three modalities. The resulting inter-modal features are further passed to the distance-aware contrastive learning to learn the correlation of the hybrid modalities. Finally, we perform weighted fusion of mixed-modal features to obtain multimodal fusion features and output sentiment analysis information after multilayer perceptron processing.

2.1 Parallel Attention

Our parallel attention module (PAM), shown in Fig. 3, The PAM consists of three cross-fusion modules, ACM, TCM and VCM, in parallel, for correcting audio, text and visual modalities, respectively. The cross-fusion module is based on the attention module of transformer [20] and consists of three sub-layers: cross-attention, multi-head attention and feed-forward.

We explore inter-modal correlations by involving both primary and secondary modalities in the attention manipulation. We fused the three matrices in the module to the primary and secondary modalities. In this way, the attention function in our cross-fusion module is:

$$Cro\left(Q^s, K^p, V^p\right) = \sigma \left(\frac{Q^s W^{(Q^s)} \left(K^p W^{(K^p)}\right)^T}{\sqrt{d}} \right) V^p W^{(V^p)} \quad (1)$$

where Q as a query, K as a key, and V as a value. $W^{(Q)}$, $W^{(K)}$ and $W^{(V)}$, σ are the linear projection weight matrices of Q, K and V, and the softmax activation function, respectively, and d is the common dimension for three modalities, the superscripts s and p indicate that the matrices are from the secondary modality and the primary modality. Here we take the example of TCM, a cross-fusion module with text as the primary modality, where we use the secondary modalities (audio and visual) as the query and the primary modality (text) as the key and value in the cross-attention layer, in order to enforce modal invariance on the common space of the query and key-value pairs, as well as to reduce distributional gaps between the modalities. Finally, we obtain two fusion features, h^{at} and h^{vt}. The former is used for fusion of audio and text, and the latter is used for fusion of vision and text. The cross-fusion modules ACM and VCM are similar in principle to TCM. The cross-fusion module ACM with audio as the primary modality obtains two fusion features, h^{ta} and h^{va}. The cross-fusion module VCM with vision as the primary modality obtains two fusion features, h^{tv} and h^{av}.

h^{at} and h^{vt}, h^{ta} and h^{va}, h^{tv} and h^{av}, these six fusion features are then processed through a multi-head attention layer, which can significantly improve the representation of the fusion features so that they contain richer contextual information. And finally through the feed-forward layer, which further processes the output of the multi-head attention layer, and usually consists of two fully connected layers and a nonlinear activation function.

The proposed PAM employs a three-branch architecture to address inter-modal heterogeneity and conflicts between unimodal tokens and multimodal sentiment labels. Each branch functions as a cross-fusion module, utilizing a cross-attention mechanism to align the query-key-value spaces across modalities. This alignment minimizes the distribution gap between modalities. Crucially, within each branch, two modalities serve as the query to correct the information of the third (primary) modality, which acts as key and value. This cross-modal correction process enables implicit learning from the other modalities, refining the primary modality's representations to extract task-relevant information while mitigating the influence of conflicting information. By leveraging this parallel architecture, PAM simultaneously corrects erroneous information across all three modalities without relying solely on any single one, thereby effectively resolving the conflict between unimodal tokens and the multimodal sentiment labels.

2.2 Correlation Fusion

After Correcting the sentiment information of each modality, we then perform multimodal fusion in the correlation fusion module. Our correlation fusion module requires two sub-layers: Distance-aware contrastive learning (DACL) and weighted fusion.

Inspired by Ma [19], we use DACL to learn the correlation of mixed modality. As shown in Fig. 4, we select positive and negative samples within a batch based on the distance between the labels of the mixed modality. Specifically, we compute the label distances between the anchor sample (instance 1) and other samples in the batch. Samples with label distances less than a threshold d (Instance 2) are considered positive samples, while samples with distances greater than d (Instance 3, Instance 4) are considered negative samples. An example of fusion features h^{at} and h^{vt} for DACL, formally, the distance-aware contrast loss $\mathcal{L}_{DACL}$ (based on InfoNCE [21]) can be derived as:

$$\mathcal{L}_{DACL}\left(h_i^{at}, h_i^{vt}\right) = -\log \frac{\sum_{j \in p} exp\left(\Phi \frac{(h_i^{vt}, h_j^{at})}{\tau}\right)}{\sum_{k \notin p} exp\left(\Phi \frac{(h_i^{vt}, h_k^{at})}{\tau}\right)} \quad (2)$$

where Φ is the cosine similarity scoring function, τ is the temperature, p is the set of positive sample metrics selected based on the label distance, and i, j, k are metrics for different samples. We consider using different fusion pairs as anchors, so the final contrast loss $\mathcal{L}_{CL}$ is:

$$\begin{aligned}\mathcal{L}_{CL} = &\mathcal{L}_{DACL}\left(h_i^{at}, h_i^{vt}\right) + \mathcal{L}_{DACL}\left(h_i^{vt}, h_i^{at}\right) \\ &+ \mathcal{L}_{DACL}\left(h_i^{av}, h_i^{tv}\right) + \mathcal{L}_{DACL}\left(h_i^{tv}, h_i^{av}\right) \\ &+ \mathcal{L}_{DACL}\left(h_i^{ta}, h_i^{va}\right) + \mathcal{L}_{DACL}\left(h_i^{va}, h_i^{ta}\right)\end{aligned} \quad (3)$$

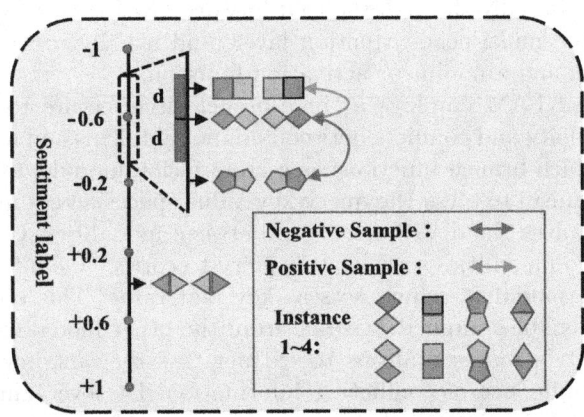

Fig. 4. The distance-aware contrastive learning avoids false positives and sampling of negative samples by introducing distance information of sentiment labels into traditional contrastive learning.

DACL selects positive/negative samples based on label distance thresholds d. This strategy bounds the generalization error. By avoiding false positives and sampling of negative samples, DACL ensures tighter clustering of same-sentiment features, improving robustness. Then, we splice the features h^{vt} and h^{at} into a mixture of features f_t, the features h^{tv} and h^{av} into a mixture of features f_v, and the features h^{ta} and h^{va} into a mixture of features f_a. This results in the multimodal feature F_{multi} as:

$$F_{multi} = w_t \cdot f_t + w_v \cdot f_v + w_a \cdot f_a \quad (4)$$

where w_t, w_v, and w_a are learnable parameters.

2.3 Loss Function

Our task losses include the regression task loss and the classification task loss, the loss is calculated as:

$$\mathcal{L}_{task} = \begin{cases} \frac{1}{N}\sum_{i=1}^{N}|\hat{y}_i - y_i| & \text{for regression} \\ -\frac{1}{N}\sum_{i=1}^{N} y_i \log \hat{y}_i & \text{for classification} \end{cases} \tag{5}$$

where N is the size of the smallest batch, y_i and $\hat{y}_i$ denote the true and predicted labels of the i-th sample, respectively. Overall loss include task loss and contrastive loss:

$$\mathcal{L} = \mathcal{L}_{task} + \alpha \mathcal{L}_{CL} \tag{6}$$

where α is a parameter that balances the contribution of different losses.

3 Experiments And Results

3.1 Datasets and Implementatoin Details

The CMU-Multimodal Opinion Sentiment and Emotion Intensity (CMU-MOSI) dataset consists of 2,199 multimodal samples, each of which is assigned a mood score ranging from −3 (indicating strongly negative) to 3 (indicating strongly positive).

The CMU-Multimodal Sentiment Analysis (CMU-MOSEI) is an extended version of CMU-MOSEI. It includes 22,856 video clips collected from YouTube. Their mood scores for each sample ranged from −3 to 3 indicating the most negative to the most positive.

The Chinese Multimodal Sentiment Analysis Dataset (CH-SIMS) includes the same modalities in Mandarin: audio, text, and video, collected from 2281 annotated video segments. It includes data from TV shows and movies, making it culturally distinct and diverse, and provides multiple labels for the same utterance based on different modalities, which adds an extra layer of complexity and richness to the data.

We divided the experimental objectives into two categories: classification and regression. For classification, we used weighted F1 scores (Has0_F1/Non0_F1), and binary classification accuracy (Has0_Acc-2/Non0_Acc-2). For regression, we used Mean Absolute Error (MAE) and Pearson Correlation (Corr), where higher values (except MAE) indicate better performance. During training, we used the Adam optimiser in conjunction with the StepLR scheduler. All experiments were performed on NVIDIA RTX 3090 GPUs.

Table 1. Performance on the MOSI dataset. ∗: The results are reproduced from code provided by their authors. ⋄: Model using unaligned data. The best results are in bold.

Model	MOSI			
	MAE (↓)	Corr (↑)	Acc-2 (↑)	F1 (↑)
LF_DNN [22]	0.978	0.658	-/79.3	-/79.3
MulT [17]	0.871	0.698	-/83.0	-/82.8
TFN⋄ [25]	0.901	0.698	-/80.8	-/80.7
LMF⋄ [26]	0.917	0.695	-/82.5	-/82.4
MCTN [23]	0.909	0.676	79.3/-	79.1/-
TCSP [24]	0.908	0.710	-/80.9	-/81.0
MFN [27]	0.951	0.665	77.9/80.0	77.8/80.0
TFR-Net [28]	0.721	0.789	82.7/84.0	82.7/84.0
MISA [14]	0.777	0.778	81.8/83.5	81.8/83.6
Self-MM⋄∗ [16]	0.737	0.794	82.7/84.2	82.6/84.3
PriSA⋄∗ [19]	0.739	0.789	82.2/83.8	82.2/83.8
PamSA⋄ (Ours)	**0.719±0.002**	**0.796±0.001**	**83.1/85.1±0.3**	**83.0/85.1±0.2**

Table 2. Performance on the MOSEI dataset. ∗: The results are reproduced from code provided by their authors. ⋄: Model using unaligned data. The best results are in bold.

Model	MOSEI			
	MAE (↓)	Corr (↑)	Acc-2 (↑)	F1 (↑)
LF_DNN [22]	0.561	0.723	-/82.3	-/82.2
MulT [17]	0.580	0.703	-/82.5	-/82.3
TFN⋄ [25]	0.593	0.700	-/82.5	-/82.1
LMF⋄ [26]	0.623	0.677	-/82.0	-/82.1
MCTN [23]	0.609	0.670	79.8/-	80.6/-
TCSP [24]	0.576	0.715	-/82.8	-/82.7
MFN [27]	0.575	0.720	81.8/84.0	81.9/83.9
TFR-Net [28]	0.551	0.756	81.8/83.5	81.6/83.8
MISA [14]	0.558	0.752	80.7/84.7	81.1/84.7
Self-MM⋄∗ [16]	0.535	0.763	81.4/84.4	81.8/84.3
PriSA⋄∗ [19]	**0.527**	0.770	82.5/85.8	82.9/85.7
PamSA⋄ (Ours)	0.529±0.002	**0.775±0.003**	**83.5/86.3±0.5**	**83.7/86.1±0.2**

Table 3. Performance on the SIMS dataset. ∗: The results are reproduced from code provided by their authors. ⋄: Model using unaligned data. The best results are in bold.

Model	MAE (↓)	Corr (↑)	Acc-2 (↑)	F1 (↑)
LF_DNN [22]	0.446	0.555	77.0	77.3
MulT [17]	0.440	0.582	77.5	77.4
TFN⋄ [25]	0.434	0.584	78.1	77.9
LMF⋄ [26]	0.441	0.576	77.8	77.9
MFN [27]	0.435	0.582	77.9	77.9
TFR-Net [28]	0.437	0.583	78.0	78.1
MISA [14]	0.447	0.563	76.5	76.6
Self-MM⋄∗ [16]	0.421	0.588	78.2	78.3
PriSA⋄∗ [19]	0.437	0.584	77.5	77.9
PamSA⋄ (Ours)	**0.419±0.001**	**0.601±0.002**	**78.8±0.4**	**78.8±0.3**

3.2 Results

The experimental results are shown in Tables 1, 2 and 3. Because three modalities in these datasets are sequences, there is an alignment problem. In general, models using aligned corpora usually produce better results. Although the unaligned data setting is more challenging for task performance, our method follow the unaligned data setting in order to validate the performance of our model under difficult conditions and to ensure a fair and detailed comparison.

PamSA achieves state-of-the-art or comparable results on most of the metrics for the MOSI, MOSEI and SIMS datasets, boosting 0.5%-2% on almost all metrics. Notably, our model shows significant improvement on the MOSI dataset. This may be due to the fact that the dataset is small, and the impact on the task of the presence of the anomalies of conflicting information between unimodal tokens and multimodal sentiment labels is magnified. Our PamSA achieves state-of-the-art results on datasets of different sizes and languages, indicating that our method can be applied to different data scenarios.

3.3 Ablation Studies

The results of the ablation studies are shown in Table 4. The row 1 is the performance of our method. We analyse each component of the PamSA framework in detail. These components include the PAM (rows 2–8), DACL in correlation fusion (row 9) and weighted fusion (row 10). All these ablation experiments were performed on the three datasets.

In row 2 of Table 4, instead of using the corrected modality to implicitly guide cross-modal learning (IGCL) in the three cross-fusion modules of parallel attention, we use an explicitly guided cross-modal learning approach where the one modality as query and the remaining two modalities as the keys and values.

Table 4. Ablation studies of the MOSI, MOSEI and SIMS datasets. The best results are in bold.

Model	MOSI				MOSEI				SIMS			
	MAE	Corr	Acc-2	F1	MAE	Corr	Acc-2	F1	MAE	Corr	Acc-2	F1
1 PamSA (Ours)	**0.719**	**0.796**	**85.1**	**85.1**	**0.529**	**0.775**	**86.3**	**86.1**	**0.419**	**0.601**	**78.8**	**78.8**
2 w/o IGCL	0.728	0.789	84.6	84.6	0.535	0.773	85.5	85.5	0.433	0.591	77.2	77.4
3 TCM &VCM	0.730	0.788	84.0	84.0	0.533	0.768	85.9	85.8	0.420	0.598	78.5	78.6
4 TCM &ACM	0.763	0.786	82.9	83.0	0.537	0.766	85.4	85.4	0.445	0.571	76.8	77.3
5 VCM &ACM	0.733	0.792	84.3	84.3	0.530	0.772	85.2	85.2	0.436	0.584	76.1	76.6
6 only TCM	0.753	0.772	83.4	83.4	0.531	0.766	85.7	85.5	0.582	0.454	68.9	56.6
7 only VCM	0.755	0.788	83.8	83.9	0.546	0.763	85.5	85.4	0.441	0.582	76.6	77.0
8 only ACM	0.737	0.792	84.0	84.0	0.535	0.768	85.5	85.3	0.440	0.580	78.6	78.4
9 w/o DACL	0.739	0.786	84.0	84.0	0.539	0.769	85.8	85.6	0.422	0.599	78.6	78.5
10 w/o Weight	0.755	0.782	84.0	84.0	0.541	0.766	85.4	85.1	0.439	0.594	78.1	78.4

This means that one modality is used to correct the other two modalities. This leads to a reduction in the amount of correct sentiment information that provides correction. We can observe a decrease in row 2. The reason is that the model learns some false correlations and ambiguous information in it. It also proves the validity of our method.

Our parallel attention is using a three-branch parallel structure, and in rows 3–5 of Table 4, we show the model performance of the PAM taking a two-branch structure. In rows 6–8 of Table 4, we show the model performance of the PAM taking a single-branch structure. The results demonstrate that parallel attention missing cross-fusion modules of any branch causes an overall performance degradation of the model. This demonstrates the presence of modal tokens in each modality with conflicting multimodal sentiment labels information. It also demonstrates the effectiveness of the PAM of our three-branch structure.

After using DACL, our framework is able to further learn the relevance of mixed modalities. In row 9 of Table 4, we show the effect of removing DACL on model performance. Our results show that removing this contrastive learning will decrease the performance of the model. Despite the drop, the performance of the model is still comparable to other state-of-the-art methods. This indicates that our parallel attention strategy is effective, and contrastive learning can further build mixed-modality correlations to improve performance on this basis.

Weighted fusion can give more weight to important mixed modal features and facilitate accurate analysis of sentiment. In row 10 of Table 4, it is demonstrated that removing the weighted fusion will also degrade the performance of the model. In particular, the performance degradation on the MOSI and MOSEI datasets is obvious, proving the effectiveness of weighted fusion.

4 Conclusion

In this paper, we address the problem of conflicting information between unimodal tokens and multimodal sentiment labels resulting in wrong sentiment analysis. To address this problem, we propose a PamSA framework in which parallel attention uses a three-branch parallel structure avoiding preference for a single modality and correct the sentiment information for each modality. We also invoke a distance-aware contrastive learning method to learn mixed-modal correlations, and weighted fusion of mixed modalities to obtain multimodal features that can effectively analyse sentiment. Finally, we evaluate our PamSA on three datasets of MSA, and our PamSA outperforms other state-of-the-art methods on three datasets.

Acknowledgments.. This work was supported in part by Zhejiang Provincial Natural Science Foundation of China (No.LDT23F0202, No. LDT23F02021F02, No. LQ22F020013), and the National Natural Science Foundation of China (No. 62432014, No. 62036009, No. 62106226, No. 62432014).

References

1. Ali, Y., Ameneh, G.S., Osmar, R.Z.: Current state of text sentiment analysis from opinion to emotion mining. ACM Comput. Surv. **50**(2), Article 25, 33 p. (2018)
2. Kahou, S.E., Bouthillier, X., Lamblin, P., et al.: EmoNets: multimodal deep learning approaches for emotion recognition in video. J Multimodal User Interfaces **10**, 99–111 (2016)
3. Luo, Z., Xu, H., Chen, F.: Audio sentiment analysis by heterogeneous signal features learned from utterance-based parallel neural network. In: AffCon@AAAI (2018)
4. Lu, Z.Y., Cao, L.l., Zhang, Y., Chiu, C.C., Fan, J.: Speech sentiment analysis via pre-trained features from end-to-end ASR models, 7149–7153 (2020)
5. Zhang, L., Hong, X., Arandjelovic, O., Zhao, G.: Short and long range relation based spatio-temporal transformer for micro-expression recognition. IEEE Trans. Affect. Comput. **13**, 1973–1985 (2021)
6. Zhang, L., Wang, S., Liu, B.: Deep learning for sentiment analysis: a survey. Wiley Interdisc. Rev. Data Min. Knowl. Discov. **8** (2018)
7. Han, W., Chen, H., Poria, S.: Improving Multimodal Fusion with Hierarchical Mutual Information Maximization for Multimodal Sentiment Analysis (2021)
8. Hanai, T.A., Ghassemi, M.M., Glass, J.R.: Detecting depression with audio/text sequence modeling of interviews. In: Interspeech (2018)
9. Poria, S., Chaturvedi, I., Cambria, E., Hussain, A.: Convolutional MKL based multimodal emotion recognition and sentiment analysis. In: 2016 IEEE 16th International Conference on Data Mining (ICDM), pp. 439–448 (2016)
10. Han, J., Zhang, Z., Ringeval, F., Schuller, B.: Strength modelling for real-world automatic continuous affect recognition from audiovisual signals. Image Vision Comput. **65** (2016)
11. Delbrouck, J., Tits, N., Dupont, S.: Modulated Fusion using Transformer for Linguistic-Acoustic Emotion Recognition (2020)

12. Ho, N., Yang, H., Kim, S., Lee, G.: Multimodal approach of speech emotion recognition using multi-level multi-head fusion attention-based recurrent neural network. IEEE Access **8**, 61672–61686 (2020)
13. Tzirakis, P., Chen, J., Zafeiriou, S., Schuller, B.: End-to-end multimodal affect recognition in real-world environments. Inf. Fusion **68**, 46–53 (2021)
14. Hazarika, D., Zimmermann, R., Poria, S.: MISA: modality-invariant and -specific representations for multimodal sentiment analysis. In: Proceedings of the 28th ACM International Conference on Multimedia (2020)
15. Yu, W., et al.: CH-SIMS: a Chinese multimodal sentiment analysis dataset with fine-grained annotation of modality. In: Annual Meeting of the Association for Computational Linguistics (2020)
16. Yu, W., Xu, H., Yuan, Z., Wu, J.: Learning modality-specific representations with self-supervised multi-task learning for multimodal sentiment analysis. In: AAAI Conference on Artificial Intelligence (2021)
17. Tsai, Y.H., Bai, S., Liang, P.P., Kolter, J.Z., Morency, L., Salakhutdinov, R.: Multimodal transformer for unaligned multimodal language sequences. In: Proceedings of the Conference. Association for Computational Linguistics. Meeting, 2019, pp. 6558–6569 (2019)
18. Sun, T., Wang, W., Jing, L., Cui, Y., Song, X., Nie, L.: Counterfactual reasoning for out-of-distribution multimodal sentiment analysis. In: Proceedings of the 30th ACM International Conference on Multimedia (2022)
19. Ma, F., Zhang, Y., Sun, X.: Multimodal sentiment analysis with preferential fusion and distance-aware contrastive learning. In: 2023 IEEE International Conference on Multimedia and Expo (ICME), pp. 1367–1372 (2023)
20. Vaswani, A., et al.: Attention is all you need. In: Neural Information Processing Systems (2017)
21. v. d. Oord, A., Li, Y., Vinyals, O.: Representation learning with contrastive predictive coding. arXiv preprint arXiv:1807.03748 (2018)
22. Williams, J., Comanescu, R., Radu, O., Tian, L.: DNN Multimodal Fusion Techniques for Predicting Video Sentiment (2018)
23. Pham, H., Liang, P.P., Manzini, T., Morency, L., Póczos, B.: Found in translation: learning robust joint representations by cyclic translations between modalities. IN: AAAI Conference on Artificial Intelligence (2018)
24. Wu, Y., Lin, Z., Zhao, Y., Qin, B., Zhu, L.: A Text-centered shared-private framework via cross-modal prediction for multimodal sentiment analysis. In: Findings (2021)
25. Zadeh, A., Chen, M., Poria, S., Cambria, E., Morency, L.: Tensor fusion network for multimodal sentiment analysis. In: Conference on Empirical Methods in Natural Language Processing (2017)
26. Liu, Z., Shen, Y., Lakshminarasimhan, V.B., Liang, P.P., Zadeh, A., Morency, L.: Efficient Low-rank Multimodal Fusion With Modality-Specific Factors (2018)
27. Zadeh, A., Liang, P.P., Mazumder, N., Poria, S., Cambria, E., Morency, L.: Memory Fusion Network for Multi-view Sequential Learning (2018)
28. Yuan, Z., Li, W., Xu, H., Yu, W.: Transformer-based feature reconstruction network for robust multimodal sentiment analysis. In: Proceedings of the 29th ACM International Conference on Multimedia (2021)

A Hybrid Learning Approach for Continual Knowledge Graph Embedding: Contrastive Masking and Joint Anti-Forgetting

Nanhui Lai[1], Ke Jin[2], Yingchao Long[1], Weihao Yu[3], and Jin Huang[2](✉)

[1] School of Artificial Intelligence, South China Normal University, Foshan, Guangdong, China
{2023025196,2022024919}@m.scnu.edu.cn
[2] School of Computer Science, South China Normal University, Guangzhou, Guangdong, China
{2023023198,huangjin}@m.scnu.edu.cn
[3] Research Institute of China Telecom Corporate Ltd., Guangzhou, Guangdong, China
yuwh3@chinatelecom.cn

Abstract. Knowledge graphs (KGs) in real-world applications are inherently dynamic and continuously evolving. Continual Knowledge Graph Embedding (CKGE) aims to integrate new knowledge while preserving previously acquired knowledge, which ensures an optimal balance between learning and retention. However, existing CKGE methods predominantly focus on mitigating catastrophic forgetting but neglect the continuous performance improvement from the efficient integration of new knowledge. In this work, we propose a novel model based on **C**ontrastive **M**asked KG Autoencoder with **J**oint **A**nti-Forgetting module, termed CMJA. It facilitates the integration of new knowledge and strengthens the retention of previous knowledge. To effectively acquire new knowledge, CMJA incorporates a contrastive masked KG autoencoder, which improves the ability of the embeddings to capture distinguishing features. Additionally, to consolidate the retention of previously learned knowledge, we introduce a joint anti-forgetting module, which imposes stricter control over minor discrepancies and enhances the model's robustness to noise. It mitigates catastrophic forgetting more comprehensively. Experimental results show that CMJA achieves superior performance in the link prediction task. Subsequent experiments show that CMJA achieves a more desirable balance between plasticity and stability.

Keywords: Knowledge graph embedding · Continual learning · Contrastive learning

1 Introduction

As the structured semantic knowledge bases, knowledge graphs (KGs) [6] are designed to represent concepts from the physical world and their relationships efficiently. In the real world, KGs are not static but constantly evolve as new entities, relations, and triples emerge. Between 2021 and 2022, Wikidata [20] was enriched with more than 5 million entities, approximately 500 new relationships, and 50 million triples. To accommodate the intrinsic evolution of KGs, traditional knowledge graph embedding (KGE) [16,24] methods must retrain the entire graph to incorporate new knowledge, which results in significant computational and training costs. If simple fine-tuning of new facts is applied, it would quickly disrupt previously acquired knowledge leading to catastrophic forgetting.

To address this issue, the continual knowledge graph embedding (CKGE) task [4,19] has emerged to address these challenges. It enables the incremental integration of new knowledge without the necessity of retraining the entire knowledge graph. CKGE reduces training costs by effectively integrating new knowledge (plasticity) while maintaining prior information (stability), striving to achieve an optimal balance between these two aspects.

Current CKGE methods primarily focus on mitigating catastrophic forgetting. However, they often overlook the enhancement of plasticity, which is crucial for promoting efficient adaptation to new knowledge and supporting continuous performance improvement. For instance, snapshot 1 contains the triple *(Tom, father of, John)*, while snapshot 3 introduces a new triple *(Tom, grandpa of, Sophia)*. Existing approaches may successfully preserve previous knowledge but fail to effectively integrate new facts, such as the fact that Tom is Sophia's grandfather. They neglect the critical need to facilitate the learning of new knowledge. Additionally, some regularization-based CKGE methods mitigate catastrophic forgetting by adding penalty terms to prevent substantial changes in the entities and relations embeddings. However, when only a single embedding regularization [2,18] or distillation method [7,22] is employed, these approaches often fail to impose sufficient constraints on the subtle distinctions between old and new knowledge. This limitation hinders the ability of these methods to manage the distinctions between old and new knowledge effectively and increases their vulnerability to noise interference. As new knowledge continuously accumulates, these methods encounter increasing difficulties in maintaining previously acquired knowledge, resulting in a gradual degradation in performance over time.

To overcome these shortcomings, we propose CMJA, a novel approach designed to optimize the acquisition of new knowledge while substantially mitigating catastrophic forgetting for continuous performance improvement. First, to preserve the inherent semantics conveyed by KGs, we employ the hierarchical ordering method [11] to identify the optimal sequence for integrating new triples into the learning process. Second, we propose a contrastive masked KG autoencoder that masks and reconstructs entities or relations within newly added facts. It enhances representation learning and adaptability. Unlike the traditional masked KG autoencoder, it incorporates a contrastive loss function [8] to improve embedding discrimination by pulling positive samples closer and pushing negative samples apart. This strengthens the model's ability to distinguish semantic differences. Third, a joint anti-forgetting module is proposed, which integrates embedding regularization and distillation methods. This module balances knowledge retention and adaptability to mitigate catastrophic forgetting.

We evaluate CMJA on several datasets, showing that it outperforms existing methods. Ablation studies confirm that both the contrastive masked KG autoencoder and the joint anti-forgetting module are essential for performance gains. The main contributions of this paper are:

- We propose a contrastive masked KG autoencoder designed to enhance the model's ability to efficiently incorporate new knowledge.
- To further mitigate catastrophic forgetting, we introduce a joint anti-forgetting module that enhances the model's stability.
- Extensive experiments on existing datasets demonstrate the superiority of CMJA over various state-of-the-art models.

2 Related Work

Continual learning [5,23] is a machine learning paradigm that enables a model to retain previously acquired knowledge while continuously integrating new information. Existing CKGE methods can generally be categorized into three types.

Dynamic architecture-based methods [12,17]. These methods dynamically adjust the network structure to accommodate new knowledge, either by extending the network or adding additional neurons and layers. CWR [12] preserves prior knowledge by incrementally allocating new neurons and weights without modifying existing structures. While the growth of knowledge requires continuous model expansion, it also limits scalability for large knowledge graphs and constrains practical deployment.

Memory replay-based methods [10,13,21]. This approach stores examples from previous knowledge to replay during the learning of new knowledge, which mitigates catastrophic forgetting. GEM [13] stores samples from previous snapshots and selectively replays them during learning, using gradient constraints to prevent interference with prior knowledge. The main drawback of these methods is the significant increase in computational cost with more knowledge updates, along with data security and privacy risks from storing past data.

Regularization-based methods [3,9,11,25]. These methods enhance knowledge retention by adding regularization terms to the loss function and constraining model parameters. SI [25] assesses the importance of each parameter based on its contribution to previous tasks and constrains substantial updates to these parameters when learning new tasks. EWC [9] uses the Fisher information matrix to identify important parameters and applies stronger regularization to preserve prior knowledge. They avoid storing previous knowledge and enable incremental updates without the need for past data. But this may excessively constrain parameter adjustments, which limits adaptability to new tasks.

However, existing methods overlook the enhancement of new knowledge acquisition. To overcome this limitation, this paper proposes a contrastive masked KG autoencoder to facilitate more effective knowledge learning, along with a joint anti-forgetting module to mitigate catastrophic forgetting better.

3 Methodology

3.1 Preliminary and Problem Statement

Growing Knowledge Graph. A growing knowledge graph is represented as a series of sequential snapshots, i.e., $\mathcal{G} = \{\mathcal{S}_0, \mathcal{S}_1, ..., \mathcal{S}_n\}$. Each snapshot $\mathcal{S}_i$ is characterized as a triplet $(\mathcal{E}_i, \mathcal{R}_i, \mathcal{T}_i)$, where $\mathcal{E}_i$, $\mathcal{R}_i$ and $\mathcal{T}_i$ represent the sets of entities, relations, and triples, respectively. The entities $\mathcal{E}_i$, relations $\mathcal{R}_i$, and triples $\mathcal{T}_i$ in snapshot $\mathcal{S}_i$ are subsets of those in snapshot $\mathcal{S}_{i+1}$. Additionally, we define $\Delta\mathcal{E}_i = \mathcal{E}_i - \mathcal{E}_{i-1}$, $\Delta\mathcal{R}_i = \mathcal{R}_i - \mathcal{R}_{i-1}$, $\Delta\mathcal{T}_i = \mathcal{T}_i - \mathcal{T}_{i-1}$ as the new entities, relations and triples. Each triple $(h, r, t) \in \mathcal{T}_i$ consists of a head entity h and a tail entity t, both belonging to $\mathcal{E}_i$, with $r \in \mathcal{R}_i$ representing their relation.

Continual Knowledge Graph Embedding. Knowledge graph embedding maps entities and relations into a low-dimensional vector space $\mathbb{R}$, capturing semantic and structural information. A typical KGE model includes embedding layers for vector representation and a scoring function to evaluate triples during training. Continual knowledge graph embedding seeks to update the embeddings of existing entities $\mathcal{E}_{i-1}$ and relations $\mathcal{R}_{i-1}$, acquire the embeddings of new entities $\Delta\mathcal{E}_i$ and new relations $\Delta\mathcal{R}_i$, and ultimately attain the embeddings for all entities $\mathcal{E}_i$ and relations $\mathcal{R}_i$, by learning from the training datasets $\mathcal{D}_1, \mathcal{D}_2, \ldots, \mathcal{D}_t$. As CKGE does not retrain on old data, $\mathcal{D}_i$ is considered old knowledge after training and does not participate in future snapshots.

3.2 Overview of CMJA

In this section, we describe the proposed model for continual knowledge graph embedding, termed CMJA.

Figure 1 illustrates the CMJA architecture. When new knowledge emerges at snapshot $\mathcal{S}_i$, CMJA performs hierarchical ordering inspired by IncDE [11] on new triples to get optimal learning sequences. Then, CMJA facilitates new knowledge acquisition and mitigates catastrophic forgetting through two novel components: (1) a contrastive masked KG autoencoder, which improves representation quality by reconstructing masked graph components under a contrastive learning framework; and (2) a joint anti-forgetting module, which preserves old knowledge by combining embedding regularization with distillation methods.

3.3 Contrastive Masked KG Autoencoder

To balance new knowledge acquisition and prior knowledge retention in CKGE tasks, we propose the Contrastive Masked KG Autoencoder (CMKGA). CMKGA employs masking and reconstruction to learn robust embeddings while integrating contrastive learning to enhance their discriminative power. This improves the model's ability to distinguish similar and dissimilar entities and relations, which leads to higher-quality embeddings and more accurate knowledge learning.

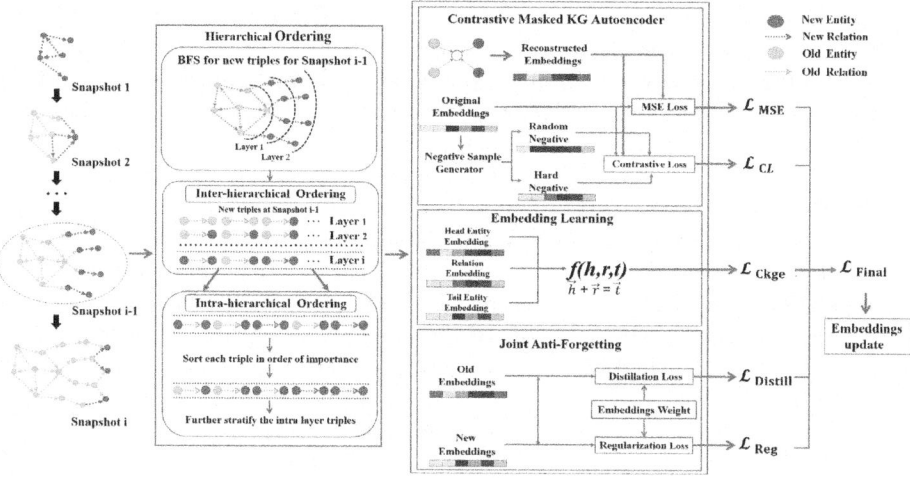

Fig. 1. Overview of the CMJA. It mainly consists of three parts: contrastive masked KG autoencoder, embedding learning module and joint anti-forgetting module.

In our setup, CMKGA learns embeddings by reconstructing masked embeddings from their corresponding masked subgraph. We use the first-order subgraph of an entity or a relation to reconstruct its embedding x_k^{rec}. We define the reconstruction process as follows:

$$x_k^{rec} = \text{MAE}\left(\bigcup_{j=1}^{i} \mathcal{N}_j(x_k)\right), \tag{1}$$

where x_k represents either an entity e_k or a relation r_k, and $N_j(x_k)$ denotes the set of facts associated with x_k within the j-th snapshot. MAE() as an encoder to capture the representation of the input subgraph. In this paper, CMKGA draws on the concept of TransE [1], utilizing an encoder similar to that of the traditional masked KG autoencoder [3]. It can avoid the introduction of additional parameters that make it an ideal choice for CKGE. CMKGA needs to align the entity or relation embedding with the reconstructed representation as follows:

$$\mathcal{L}_{\text{Mse}} = \frac{1}{|\mathcal{E}_i|} \sum_{j=1}^{|\mathcal{E}_i|} \left\| \mathbf{e}_j^{rec} - \mathbf{e}_j \right\|_2^2 + \frac{1}{|\mathcal{R}_i|} \sum_{k=1}^{|\mathcal{R}_i|} \left\| \mathbf{r}_k^{rec} - \mathbf{r}_k \right\|_2^2, \tag{2}$$

$\mathbf{e}_j$ and $\mathbf{r}_k$ denote the entity and relation embeddings in the current snapshot. $\mathbf{e}_j^{rec}$ and $\mathbf{r}_k^{rec}$ denote the reconstructed entity and relation embeddings, respectively. This loss function encourages the reconstructed embedding $\mathbf{e}_j^{rec}$ and $\mathbf{r}_k^{rec}$ to closely approximate the original embedding $\mathbf{e}_j$ and $\mathbf{r}_k$, effectively learning both new and existing knowledge representations. Compared to the traditional masked knowledge graph autoencoder, CMKGA incorporates contrastive learning to enhance its ability to distinguish entities and relations across different contexts. By drawing positive samples closer and pushing negative samples apart, it improves the model's sensitivity to subtle differences.

Within this framework, negative samples include both random negatives and hard negatives, where hard negatives [15] are defined as samples that exhibit high semantic similarity to the reconstructed embeddings. This method of constructing negative samples not only reduces computational complexity but also enhances the model's discriminative capability. To identify such hard negatives, cosine similarity is utilized to identify the negative samples that are the most semantically aligned with the reconstructed embeddings. Hard negatives will be selected each epoch. The hard negative sampling formula is as follows:

$$e_j^{hard} = \text{top-K}_{n=1}^{|\mathcal{E}_i|} \text{sim}\left(\mathbf{e}_j^{rec}, \mathbf{e}_n\right), \tag{3}$$

$\text{sim}(\cdot, \cdot)$ denotes cosine similarity. In this process, the positive samples are excluded from the calculation. The K most semantically similar negative samples, with K set to 5, are then selected as hard negatives. e_j^{hard} is the hard negatives set of e_j. e_j^{neg} is the negative sample set of e_j that includes e_j^{hard} and random negatives that are randomly chosen in the current entity set. The contrastive loss [8] is then defined as follows:

$$\mathcal{L}_{CL}^j = -\log \frac{\exp\left(\frac{\text{sim}(\mathbf{e}_j^{rec}, \mathbf{e}_j)}{\tau}\right)}{\exp\left(\frac{\text{sim}(\mathbf{e}_j^{rec}, \mathbf{e}_j)}{\tau}\right) + \sum_{e'_j \in e_j^{neg}} \exp\left(\frac{\text{sim}(\mathbf{e}_j^{rec}, \mathbf{e}'_j)}{\tau}\right)}, \tag{4}$$

where τ is the temperature parameter and e_j is the original embedding, which is the positive sample. $\mathcal{L}_{CL}^j$ denotes the loss of contrastive learning for $\mathbf{e}_j$. The final contrastive loss [8] for snapshot S_i is:

$$\mathcal{L}_{CL} = \frac{1}{|\mathcal{E}_i|} \sum_{j=1}^{|\mathcal{E}_i|} \mathcal{L}_{CL}^j. \tag{5}$$

For each snapshot, TransE [1] is applied to incorporate new data and iteratively update the learned embeddings. The loss for TransE [1] is:

$$\mathcal{L}_{Ckge} = \sum_{(h,r,t) \in \mathcal{D}_i} \max\left(0, f(h,r,t) - f(h',r,t') + \gamma\right), \tag{6}$$

where γ is the margin, (h', r, t') is the negative sample of (h, r, t) and $f(h, r, t) = |h + r - t|_{L1/L2}$ is the score function of TransE [1]. Moreover, we retain the embeddings of existing entities $\mathcal{E}_{i-1}$ and relations $\mathcal{R}_{i-1}$ derived from the model at snapshot $\mathcal{S}_{i-1}$, while the embeddings of newly introduced entities $\Delta\mathcal{E}_i$ and relations $\Delta\mathcal{R}_i$ are initialized randomly.

3.4 Joint Anti-Forgetting Module

To further mitigate catastrophic forgetting, we propose the joint anti-forgetting module that combines regularization and distillation methods. When the embedding update is substantial, the module effectively maintains penalty strength while enhancing resistance to noise interference. This prevents drastic shifts in parameters that could lead to catastrophic forgetting and ensures more robust continual learning. In contrast, when updates are minimal, the joint anti-forgetting module can precisely adjust subtle differences between new and old knowledge, further reducing the risk of catastrophic forgetting. In addition, different entities and relations have different levels of importance, and we need to prioritize entities and relations that have greater importance and retention.

Inspired by LKGE [3], we calculate the weight of each entity or relation by the number of new and past facts containing it:

$$\omega(x_k) = 1 - \frac{|\mathcal{N}_i(x_k)|}{\sum_{j=1}^{i} |\mathcal{N}_j(x_k)|}, \tag{7}$$

it retains only the aggregated count of trained facts associated with each entity or relation. The regularization weights are updated exactly once per snapshot. The loss function of regularization methods is as follows:

$$\mathcal{L}_{\text{Reg}} = \sum_{j=1}^{|\mathcal{E}_i|} \omega(e_j) \|\mathbf{e}_j - \overline{\mathbf{e}}_j\|_2^2 + \sum_{k=1}^{|\mathcal{R}_i|} \omega(r_k) \|\mathbf{r}_k - \overline{\mathbf{r}}_k\|_2^2, \tag{8}$$

where e_j and r_k denote the representation in the current snapshot. $\overline{e}_j$ and $\overline{r}_k$ denote the representation from the previous snapshot. $\omega(e_j)$ is the regularization weight for entity e_j and $\omega(r_k)$ is the regularization weight for relation r_k. Then, we distill the entity representation in the current snapshot using entities from the previous snapshot. The loss of the distillation method is:

$$\mathcal{L}_{\text{Distill}}^{j} = \begin{cases} \frac{1}{2} \cdot \omega(e_j)(\mathbf{e}_j - \overline{\mathbf{e}}_j)^2, & |\mathbf{e}_j - \overline{\mathbf{e}}_j| \leq 1 \\ \omega(e_j)|\mathbf{e}_j - \overline{\mathbf{e}}_j| - \frac{1}{2}, & |\mathbf{e}_j - \overline{\mathbf{e}}_j| > 1 \end{cases} \tag{9}$$

$$\mathcal{L}_{\text{Distill}} = \sum_{j=1}^{|\mathcal{E}_i|} \mathcal{L}_{\text{Distill}}^{j}, \tag{10}$$

where $\mathcal{L}_{\text{Distill}}^{j}$ denotes the loss of distillation for $\mathbf{e}_j$ and $\mathcal{L}_{\text{Distill}}$ denotes the final distillation loss for snapshot $\mathcal{S}_i$. The combination of $\mathcal{L}_{\text{Distill}}$ and $\mathcal{L}_{\text{Reg}}$ forms a joint loss function that significantly reduces the risk of catastrophic forgetting.

3.5 Final Learning Objective

To ensure the incorporation of new knowledge while preserving old knowledge, the comprehensive continual learning objective $\mathcal{L}_{Final}$ is defined as follows:

$$\mathcal{L}_{Final} = \mathcal{L}_{Ckge} + \alpha \mathcal{L}_{Mse} + \beta \mathcal{L}_{CL} + \gamma(\mathcal{L}_{Reg} + \mathcal{L}_{Distill}), \tag{11}$$

where α, β and γ are hyperparameters used to balance the various objectives.

Table 1. The statistics of datasets. N_E, N_R and N_T denote the number of cumulative entities, cumulative relations, and current triples at each time i

Dataset	Snapshot 1			Snapshot 2			Snapshot 3			Snapshot 4			Snapshot 5		
	N_E	N_R	N_T	N_E	N_R	N_T	N_E	N_R	N_T	N_E	N_R	N_T	N_E	N_R	N_T
ENTITY	2,909	233	46,388	5,817	236	72,111	8,275	236	73,785	11,633	237	70,506	14,541	237	47,326
RELATION	11,560	48	98,819	13,343	96	93,535	13,754	143	66,136	14,387	190	30,032	14,541	237	21,594
FACT	10,513	237	62,024	12,779	237	62,023	13,586	237	62,023	13,894	237	62,023	14,541	237	62,023
HYBRID	8,628	86	57,561	10,040	102	20,873	12,779	151	88,017	14,393	209	103,339	14,541	237	40,326
GraphEqual	2,908	226	57,636	5,816	235	62,023	8,724	237	62,023	11,632	237	62,023	14,541	237	66,411
GraphHigher	900	197	10,000	1,838	221	20,000	3,714	234	40,000	7,467	237	80,000	14,541	237	160,116
GraphLower	7,505	237	160,000	11,258	237	80,000	13,134	237	40,000	14,072	237	20,000	14,541	237	10,116

4 Experiment

This section outlines the baselines and experimental setup, presents the results highlighting the advantages of our approach, and concludes with an in-depth analysis. It provides key insights from the experimental data.

4.1 Datasets

We use seven datasets [3,11] for CKGE: ENTITY, RELATION, FACT, HYBRID, GraphEqual, GraphHigher and GraphLower. In ENTITY, RELATION, and FACT, the number of entities, relations, and triples increases uniformly per snapshot. In HYBRID, their total growth remains consistent over time. These datasets require new triples to include at least one existing entity, which limits knowledge expansion. In contrast, GraphEqual, GraphHigher, and GraphLower allow new triples to exclude existing entities. GraphEqual maintains a constant increase in triples per snapshot, while GraphHigher accelerates, and GraphLower decelerates in growth. The number of snapshots is set to 5 for all datasets. For each dataset, the data are further divided into training, validation, and test sets with a ratio of 3:1:1. A detailed overview of the dataset is presented in Table 1.

4.2 Baselines

We select three types of continual learning-based methods: dynamic architecture-based, memory replay-based, and regularization-based methods, as comparative baselines for evaluation. In detail, memory replay-based approaches are represented by GEM [13], EMR [21], and DiCGRL [10], while dynamic architecture-based methods include PNN [17] and CWR [12]. On the other hand, regularization-based methods comprise SI [25], EWC [9], LKGE [3] and IncDE [11].

4.3 Metrics

We evaluate the performance of our model using the link prediction task. In this process, either the head or the tail entity of a triple is replaced with all candidate

Table 2. Main experimental results on ENTITY, RELATION, FACT, HYBRID, GraphEqual, GraphHigher, and GraphLower. The best result is highlighted in bold.

Method	ENTITY			RELATION			FACT			HYBRID			GraphEqual			GraphHigher			GraphLower		
	MRR	H@1	H@10	MRR	H@1	H@10	MRR	H@1	H@10	MRR	H@1	H@10	MRR	H@1	H@10	MRR	H@1	H@10	MRR	H@1	H@10
PNN	0.229	0.130	0.425	0.167	0.096	0.305	0.157	0.084	0.290	0.185	0.101	0.349	0.212	0.118	0.405	0.186	0.097	0.364	0.213	0.119	0.407
CWR	0.088	0.028	0.202	0.021	0.010	0.043	0.083	0.030	0.192	0.037	0.015	0.077	0.122	0.041	0.277	0.189	0.096	0.374	0.032	0.005	0.080
GEM	0.165	0.085	0.321	0.093	0.040	0.196	0.175	0.092	0.345	0.136	0.070	0.263	0.189	0.099	0.372	0.197	0.109	0.372	0.170	0.084	0.346
EMR	0.171	0.090	0.330	0.111	0.052	0.225	0.171	0.090	0.337	0.141	0.073	0.267	0.185	0.099	0.359	0.202	0.113	0.379	0.188	0.101	0.362
DiCGRL	0.107	0.057	0.211	0.133	0.079	0.241	0.162	0.084	0.320	0.149	0.083	0.277	0.104	0.040	0.226	0.116	0.041	0.242	0.102	0.039	0.222
SI	0.154	0.072	0.311	0.113	0.055	0.224	0.172	0.088	0.343	0.111	0.049	0.229	0.179	0.092	0.353	0.190	0.099	0.371	0.186	0.099	0.366
EWC	0.229	0.130	0.423	0.165	0.093	0.306	0.201	0.113	0.382	0.186	0.102	0.350	0.207	0.113	0.400	0.198	0.106	0.385	0.210	0.116	0.405
LKGE	0.234	0.136	0.425	0.192	0.106	0.366	0.210	0.122	0.387	0.207	0.121	0.379	0.214	0.118	0.407	0.207	0.120	0.382	0.210	0.116	0.403
IncDE	0.253	0.151	0.448	0.199	0.111	0.370	0.216	0.128	0.391	0.224	0.131	0.401	0.234	0.134	0.432	0.227	0.132	0.412	0.228	0.129	0.426
CMJA	**0.272**	**0.171**	**0.471**	**0.213**	**0.124**	**0.386**	**0.217**	**0.131**	**0.395**	**0.230**	**0.138**	**0.404**	**0.247**	**0.148**	**0.451**	**0.239**	**0.146**	**0.430**	**0.238**	**0.139**	**0.435**

entities. We will compute a score for each triple and subsequently rank them accordingly. Then, we compute the Mean Reciprocal Rank (MRR), Hits@1, and Hits@10 as our evaluation metrics. Higher values of these metrics indicate better performance. For each snapshot i, we compute the average of the aforementioned metrics across all test sets from both the current and previous snapshots. The final results are based on the model generated in the last snapshot.

4.4 Setting

All experiments are conducted on the NVIDIA RTX 3090Ti GPU, using the PyTorch [14] framework. We set TransE [1] as the base model and the number of snapshots to 5. We tune the batch size in [256, 512, 1024] and set the embedding size for entities and relations to 200. We choose the Adam as the optimizer and set the learning rate from [1e-5, 1e-4, 1e-3]. The hyperparameters for the final learning objective are set to $\alpha = 0.1$, $\beta = 0.1$, and $\gamma = 0.01$ in all experiments. To maintain consistency and objectivity, all results are averaged over five running times, and early stopping with patience of 5 is applied across all methods.

4.5 Main Results

We compare CMJA with all baselines for the link prediction task. The results of the experiments across seven datasets are summarized in Table 2. CMJA consistently outperforms existing CKGE approaches, which demonstrates strong adaptability across different datasets. It surpasses existing methods and achieves significant improvements in key evaluation metrics.

Its effectiveness is particularly evident in the ENTITY dataset, where it aligns well with the dataset's homogeneous entity growth. In contrast, its performance gain on the FACT dataset is minimal due to the increasing complexity of entity and relation embeddings, which weakens the impact of the contrastive masked KG autoencoder. In GraphEqual, GraphHigher, and GraphLower, CMJA maintains robust performance, effectively managing large-scale knowledge expansion and continual updates. These results demonstrate CMJA's effectiveness in balancing new knowledge acquisition and prior knowledge retention.

Table 3. Ablation experimental results on ENTITY, RELATION, FACT, HYBRID, GraphEqual, GraphHigher and GraphLower.

Method	ENTITY			RELATION			FACT			HYBRID			GraphEqual			GraphHigher			GraphLower		
	MRR	H@1	H@10	MRR	H@1	H@10	MRR	H@1	H@10	MRR	H@1	H@10	MRR	H@1	H@10	MRR	H@1	H@10	MRR	H@1	H@10
w/o CMKGA	0.261	0.158	0.456	0.205	0.115	0.376	0.215	0.127	0.389	0.217	0.124	0.393	0.239	0.139	0.438	0.228	0.134	0.413	0.228	0.130	0.426
w/o J-Anti	0.167	0.083	0.321	0.037	0.017	0.071	0.139	0.068	0.275	0.132	0.069	0.252	0.199	0.112	0.373	0.236	0.140	0.422	0.197	0.108	0.373
CMJA	**0.272**	**0.169**	**0.468**	**0.213**	**0.124**	**0.389**	**0.217**	**0.131**	**0.395**	**0.230**	**0.138**	**0.404**	**0.247**	**0.146**	**0.446**	**0.239**	**0.145**	**0.426**	**0.242**	**0.146**	**0.430**

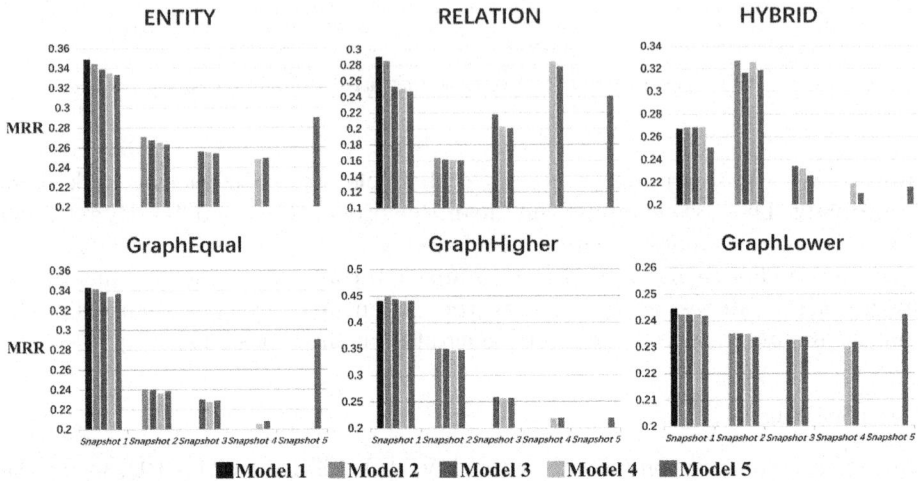

Fig. 2. Results of CMJA's dynamic learning capability at each time. Model i is trained on the i-th snapshot and evaluated using test data from snapshots 1 through i.

4.6 Ablation Study

To evaluate the effectiveness of the contrastive masked KG autoencoder (CMKGA) and the joint anti-forgetting module (J-Anti), we conduct an ablation study by introducing two CMJA variants: w/o CMKGA and w/o J-Anti. The results are presented in Table 3, which indicate a notable performance decline when either component is removed. Excluding the joint anti-forgetting module leads to significant performance degradation. This effect is especially evident in RELATION with evolving relationships, where retaining prior knowledge becomes increasingly challenging. However, this impact is less substantial in GraphHigher. This is likely because its early snapshots contain limited prior knowledge, which reduces catastrophic forgetting. Similarly, removing CMKGA causes a significant performance decline across all datasets. This underscores its crucial role in enhancing representation learning and improving model adaptability. These findings highlight the critical contributions of these two key components.

4.7 Performance of CMJA in Each Snapshot

To assess knowledge retention, the model trained on the i-th snapshot is evaluated using test data from previous snapshots. Figure 2 presents the experimental results. First, we observe that the performance of CMJA experiences only minimal degradation over time in the ENTITY, RELATION and GraphEqual test datasets, suggesting that the model effectively preserves prior knowledge across these datasets. Furthermore, in the HYBRID, GraphHigher and GraphLower, the performance of CMJA remains consistently stable throughout the majority of the evaluation period. Notably, the continuous updating of knowledge seems to facilitate the retention of prior knowledge, which leads to improved performance on earlier test data and sustained overall performance improvements.

5 Conclusion

This paper presents CMJA, a novel approach to continual knowledge graph embedding. Inspired by IncDE, we first apply hierarchical ordering to updated triples for optimal learning sequences. Then, we enhance knowledge acquisition with the contrastive masked KG autoencoder. Finally, we mitigate catastrophic forgetting through the joint anti-forgetting module. In the future, we will explore CKGE learning in multi-modal scenarios and its application in few-shot learning.

Acknowledgements. This work is supported by the National Nature Science Foundation of China (Project No.62177015).

References

1. Bordes, A., Usunier, N., Garcia-Duran, A., Weston, J., Yakhnenko, O.: Translating embeddings for modeling multi-relational data. In: Advances in Neural Information Processing Systems, vol. 26 (2013)
2. Cortes, C., Mohri, M., Rostamizadeh, A.: L2 regularization for learning kernels. arXiv preprint arXiv:1205.2653 (2012)
3. Cui, Y., et al.: Lifelong embedding learning and transfer for growing knowledge graphs. In: Proceedings of the AAAI Conference on Artificial Intelligence, vol. 37, pp. 4217–4224 (2023)
4. Daruna, A., Gupta, M., Sridharan, M., Chernova, S.: Continual learning of knowledge graph embeddings. IEEE Robot. Autom. Lett. **6**(2), 1128–1135 (2021)
5. De Lange, M., et al.: A continual learning survey: defying forgetting in classification tasks. IEEE Trans. Pattern Anal. Mach. Intell. **44**(7), 3366–3385 (2021)
6. Dong, X., et al.: Knowledge vault: a web-scale approach to probabilistic knowledge fusion. In: Proceedings of the 20th ACM SIGKDD International Conference on Knowledge Discovery and Data Mining, pp. 601–610 (2014)
7. Gou, J., Yu, B., Maybank, S.J., Tao, D.: Knowledge distillation: a survey. Int. J. Comput. Vis. **129**(6), 1789–1819 (2021)
8. Khosla, P., et al.: Supervised contrastive learning. Adv. Neural. Inf. Process. Syst. **33**, 18661–18673 (2020)
9. Kirkpatrick, J., et al.: Overcoming catastrophic forgetting in neural networks. Proc. Natl. Acad. Sci. **114**(13), 3521–3526 (2017)
10. Kou, X., Lin, Y., Liu, S., Li, P., Zhou, J., Zhang, Y.: Disentangle-based continual graph representation learning. arXiv preprint arXiv:2010.02565 (2020)

11. Liu, J., et al.: Towards continual knowledge graph embedding via incremental distillation. In: Proceedings of the AAAI Conference on Artificial Intelligence, vol. 38, pp. 8759–8768 (2024)
12. Lomonaco, V., Maltoni, D.: CORe50: a new dataset and benchmark for continuous object recognition. In: Conference on Robot Learning, pp. 17–26. PMLR (2017)
13. Lopez-Paz, D., Ranzato, M.: Gradient episodic memory for continual learning. In: Advances in Neural Information Processing Systems, vol. 30 (2017)
14. Paszke, A., et al.: PyTorch: an imperative style, high-performance deep learning library. In: Advances in Neural Information Processing Systems, vol. 32 (2019)
15. Robinson, J., Chuang, C.Y., Sra, S., Jegelka, S.: Contrastive learning with hard negative samples. arXiv preprint arXiv:2010.04592 (2020)
16. Rossi, A., Barbosa, D., Firmani, D., Matinata, A., Merialdo, P.: Knowledge graph embedding for link prediction: a comparative analysis. ACM Trans. Knowl. Discov. Data (TKDD) **15**(2), 1–49 (2021)
17. Rusu, A.A., et al.: Progressive neural networks. arXiv preprint arXiv:1606.04671 (2016)
18. Schmidt, M., Fung, G., Rosales, R.: Fast optimization methods for L1 regularization: a comparative study and two new approaches. In: Kok, J.N., Koronacki, J., Mantaras, R.L., Matwin, S., Mladenič, D., Skowron, A. (eds.) ECML 2007. LNCS (LNAI), vol. 4701, pp. 286–297. Springer, Heidelberg (2007). https://doi.org/10.1007/978-3-540-74958-5_28
19. Song, H.J., Park, S.B.: Enriching translation-based knowledge graph embeddings through continual learning. IEEE Access **6**, 60489–60497 (2018)
20. Vrandečić, D., Krötzsch, M.: Wikidata: a free collaborative knowledgebase. Commun. ACM **57**(10), 78–85 (2014)
21. Wang, H., Xiong, W., Yu, M., Guo, X., Chang, S., Wang, W.Y.: Sentence embedding alignment for lifelong relation extraction. arXiv preprint arXiv:1903.02588 (2019)
22. Wang, K., Liu, Y., Ma, Q., Sheng, Q.Z.: MulDE: multi-teacher knowledge distillation for low-dimensional knowledge graph embeddings. In: Proceedings of the Web Conference 2021, pp. 1716–1726 (2021)
23. Wang, L., Zhang, X., Su, H., Zhu, J.: A comprehensive survey of continual learning: theory, method and application. IEEE Trans. Pattern Anal. Mach. Intell. (2024)
24. Wang, Q., Mao, Z., Wang, B., Guo, L.: Knowledge graph embedding: a survey of approaches and applications. IEEE Trans. Knowl. Data Eng. **29**(12), 2724–2743 (2017)
25. Zenke, F., Poole, B., Ganguli, S.: Continual learning through synaptic intelligence. In: International Conference on Machine Learning, pp. 3987–3995. PMLR (2017)

Leveraging Machine-Translated Data for Sentiment Analysis in Low-Resource Languages: A Case Study on Bengali

Nur-A-Alam Abir, Xiaowang Zhang(✉), Rafiul Haq, and Sofonias Yitagesu

College of Intelligence and Computing, Tianjin University, Tianjin 300350, China
{abirmoy,xiaowangzhang}@tju.edu.cn

Abstract. Sentiment analysis involves identifying the polarity of text, determining whether the sentiment is positive or negative. Bengali, the seventh most spoken language globally, remains a low-resource language, which poses challenges for sentiment analysis tasks. This research thus explores the application of machine translation (MT) to generate large datasets for low-resource languages. Specifically, we translate the IMDB review dataset (IMDB-EN) from English to Bengali and Hindi using Google Translator, word-by-word translation, and the "bridge-translation" method. The translated datasets are then used to train models, which are compared to those trained on native datasets for performance evaluation. We extensively evaluate the performance of various traditional machine learning, deep learning, including transformer-based algorithms, alongside large language models (LLM) such as GPT-4o, and Gemini-1.5 Flash. Additionally, 173 Bengali samples from the Google-translated dataset are manually translated to analyze the model's performance when trained on both translated and native data. A similar experiment is conducted for Hindi, where the IMDB-EN dataset is translated to Hindi (IMDB-HN) and used to train a model, followed by testing against the Hindi Amazon reviews corpus. Our findings indicate that the "bridge-translation" method indeed positively effects classifier's performance. The model trained on the bridge-translated dataset achieves an accuracy of 90.23% when tested on the native Bengali dataset, demonstrating the potential of using machine translation to boost performance in sentiment analysis for low-resource languages. Our data and code are available (https://github.com/abirmoy/Bengali-Sentiment-Analysis-on-MT-Dataset).

Keywords: Sentiment analysis · Bengali · Machine translation

1 Introduction

Over the past decade, the growing popularity of social media platforms like Facebook and Twitter has enabled people to share their opinions on various topics [1]. Analyzing the sentiments expressed in people's comments about a particular movie or TV show can provide insights into whether it is being perceived positively or negatively. Movie reviews are a significant source of subjective judgments and are of great interest to researchers in sentiment analysis. It contains domain-specific terminology and references, and their length, structure, and use of language can vary widely making it an intricate task [2]. Bengali is the seventh most spoken language in the world, it is still considered a low-resource language due to the lack of high-quality large-scale publicly available datasets, pre-trained models, and other resources compared to high-resource languages such as English [3,4]. The use of Bengali on online platforms has grown significantly, yet there remains a noticeable absence of large-scale, high-quality movie review datasets tailored for sentiment analysis in Bengali.

The development of a dataset requires data collection and annotation labelling the data into respective categories which is carried out by human annotators [5]. As an alternative to the lack of language-specific text or data labelling material, a multilingual approach to dataset development is suggested in [6,7]. This approach utilizes machine translation methods for dataset transfer from high-resource languages to low-resource languages. For instance, although there are many high-quality datasets available in the English language, however, the presence of such datasets in Bengali is relatively few. Transformer-based models have played a vital role in the advancement of translation quality, leading machine translation to be considered as a mature field [7]. This research explores the machine translation approach to create a large dataset for low-resource languages by translating the English dataset into Bengali, and Hindi. We then applied various classification algorithms, including Bangla-Bert [8], Hindi-Bert [9], a hybrid model of long short-term memory and convolutional neural network (LSTM-CNN) [10], support vector machine (SVM) [11], and random forest (RF) [12]. The overall contribution of this research is as follows:

- The IMDB-EN dataset translated into Bengali (IMDB-BN) using Google translator, and offline word-by-word translation (IMDB-Word-BN). Additionally, a different multi-step translation process "bridge-translation" has also been explored where, instead of directly translating from source language to target language, we first translate from English to an intermediate language, Chinese (IMDB-CN-BN) and Hindi (IMDB-HN-BN) separately and then from the intermediate language to target language Bengali.
- To evaluate the performance of the model trained on the translated dataset, we conducted a cross-dataset evaluation using a dataset developed in the native language, Bangla (BN-Drama) [13].
- We manually translated 173 misclassified samples from the translated datasets to analyze the effectiveness of the models trained on both translated and native language datasets.
- Finally, to assess whether translating a dataset from one language to another is viable, we also translated the IMDB dataset [14] from English to Hindi. Using this translation, we then trained a model applying Hindi-Bert [9] and tested its performance against the HSAC: a Hindi sentiment analysis corpus derived from Amazon reviews[1].

---

[1] https://github.com/Udrasht/Hindi-Sentiment-Analysis-Corpus-from-Amazon-Reviews.

2 Related Work

Sentiment analysis in the context of Bengali language presents a unique challenge due to the limited availability of resources. Addressing this low-resource challenge, several studies have introduced datasets. These datasets are typically small in size and rely on human annotations. An annotated sentiment corpus proposed in [15], consisting of 158K Book reviews collected from online bookstores. The annotations are based on the rating of the reviews. However, the dataset in the highly imbalanced majority (89.6%) being in the positive class. Islam et al. [16] introduced a dataset of 15K instances for analyzing sentiment in Bangla text. This dataset was created by annotating comments on news and videos from different domains. In [17], Hafizur et al. developed a dataset consisting of 800 comments collected from Bangla movie review sites and social media by using web crawling methods. Mahtab et al. [18] presented a research work on Sentiment Analysis on Bangladesh Cricket with Support Vector Machine. The dataset named ABSA that was used here contains 2979 data samples. The data samples were labelled as three classes, namely Positive, Negative and Neutral. The authors also collected a dataset of their own and it contains 1601 data samples with three classes.

The authors of [6] compare language-specific sentiment analysis methods and uses machine translation systems to translate non-English text to English and then apply English sentiment analysis methods to evaluate the performance. The study suggests, machine translation is an easy and efficient baseline to conduct language-specific sentiment analysis. In addition, they propose that this method may provide competitiveness in the context of multilingual sentiment analysis. In [19], Shalunts et al. translated an original corpus from German, Russian, and Spanish to English in order to investigate the potential of machine translation on sentiment analysis and combine two sentiment analysis techniques.

3 Methodology

3.1 Dataset

We collected three publicly available datasets for sentiment analysis and the statistics of the datasets are presented in Table 1. The IMDB-EN [3] is a collection of 50,000 reviews from IMDB contains a balanced number of positive and negative reviews 2500 each making it an excellent choice for training model. Moving on to BN-Drama [13] a publicly available dataset that contains 11807 annotated reviews of Bengali drama collected from various YouTube channel's comments section. It is comprised of 3307 negative and 8500 positive reviews. Finally, HSAC is an Amazon product review dataset for Hindi sentiment analysis, a collection of 4411 reviews in total, among them 1596 positive and 1965 negative samples.

Table 1. Overview of Datasets

Dataset	Language	Size
IMDB movie reviews	English	50K
Bengali drama reviews	Bengali	11.8K
Hindi Amazon reviews	Hindi	4.4K

3.2 Translation Process

The IMDB-EN review dataset is originally in English, for our analysis purpose we have translated it into Bengali and Hindi. The translation has been carried out by machine translation including bridge-translation, and word by word translation. We first translated IMDB-EN dataset directly from English to Bengali (IMDB-BN), and Hindi (IMDB-HN) using Google translation. The architecture of translation has been presented in Fig. 1.

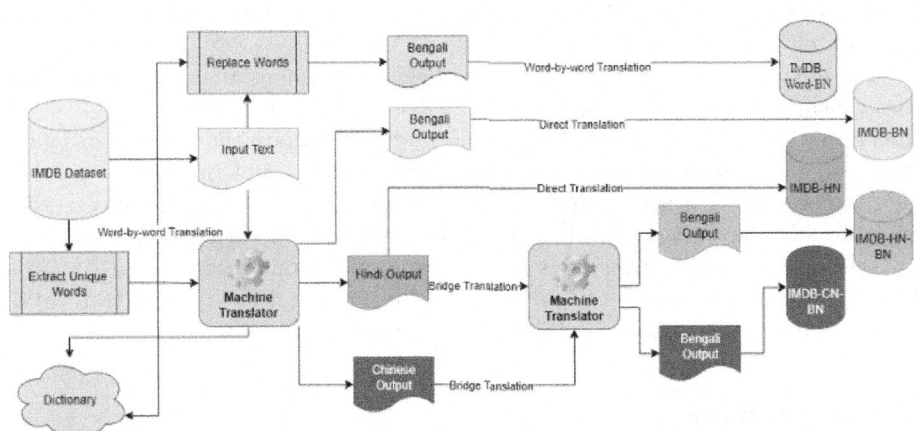

Fig. 1. Translation architecture.

Moving ahead, an offline word-by-word translation was done to translate from English to Bengali (IMDB-Word-BN). Here first we create a list of unique words, then translate them into Bengali using Google translator to create dictionary and finally replace each English word with their corresponding Bengali meaning.

Lastly, we applied "bridge-translation" method, where instead of directly translating from source language to target language, we first translate from English to an intermediate language and then intermediate language to target language (Bengali). So why do we add an extra step to translate through an intermediate language? The hypothesis is the better the translation quality the higher the model's performance. Therefore, we have carefully selected two languages among them one is considered as high resource language (Chinese), and the other one is a mid-resource language (Hindi). Among Hindi and Chinese, Hindi shares a similar sentence structure as Bengali: subject–object–verb (SOV) pattern [20,21]. The goal is to investigate that if the translation quality improves when the data from source language (English) goes through an intermediate language that is resource rich and or has similar structure (in this case Hindi, and Chinese) to the target language (Bengali).

To sum up, after applying the above described method for translation now we have direct translated datasets, bridge translated datasets, word-by-word translated dataset and native dataset for training models.

3.3 Models

We have conducted classification experiments using diverse range of algorithms including classical models as well as both small and large language models. For the classical algorithms, we used SVM [11], and RF [12] the two most widely used algorithms. As for deep learning algorithms, we used a hybrid model LSTM-CNN [10], and transformers-based models such as Bangla-Bert [8] for Bengali and Hindi-Bert [9] for Hindi language. To conduct the experiments, we split data into training, and test sets with a proportion of 80%, and 20%, respectively. Finally, we investigated LLMs performance with in-context zero-shot and few-shot learning. We used the following models: GPT-4o, and Gemini-1.5 Flash. We randomly selected 200 data points from each of the translated Bengali dataset to assess the effectiveness of zero-shot and the few-shot prompts. To evaluate the performance we computed accuracy, precision, recall, and F1-score to measure the performance of each classifier using python sklearn.

4 Results and Discussion

4.1 Results

This section explains the results after evaluating the sentiment analysis using machine translation and native data to classify sentiments in multiple languages.

Native Dataset. Table 2 presents the performance of Bangla and Hindi native datasets. For Bengali language among the models trained using BN-Drama dataset the Bangla-Bert model achieved highest performance with 96.11 accuracy, and 97.15 recall. Followed by SVM with 94.75 accuracy and the highest recall of 97.6. LSTM-CNN achieved an accuracy of 92.76, while RF had the lowest performance 86.72 but maintained high recall of 94.9. Overall, the models were able to achieve fairly higher performance when trained on native datasets.

Moving on, it is evident from the experiment results presented in Table 2 and Table 3 on Hindi language that the models trained on machine-translated data generally performed better than those trained on native data. Within the same dataset, IMDB-HN (English to Hindi machine-translated IMDB) achieves higher accuracy than HSAC across all classifiers. Notably, SVM performs best on IMDB-HN (89.89 accuracy), while it achieves 85.69 on HSAC. Similarly, Hindi-Bert struggles with HSAC (74.61) but improves on IMDB-HN (81.46).

Table 2. Performance of Native Dataset

Dataset	Classifier	Accuracy	F1	Recall
BN-Drama	Bangla-Bert	96.11	97.27	97.15
BN-Drama	LSTM-CNN	92.76	92.6	92.76
BN-Drama	RF	86.72	91.26	94.9
BN-Drama	SVM	94.75	96.42	97.6
HSAC	Hindi-Bert	74.61	67.03	57.5
HSAC	LSTM-CNN	82.75	82.8	82.75
HSAC	RF	80.59	80.26	80.59
HSAC	SVM	85.69	83.33	87.32

Translated Dataset. Performance of the models trained on direct machine and word-by-word translated dataset are presented in Table 3. In the direct English to Bangla machine translated dataset IMDB-BN, SVM achieved highest accuracy of 88.93, F1-score of 89.08, and a recall of 89.66. Bangla-Bert follows closely behind with an accuracy of 86.32, F1-score of 86.35, and a recall of 86.06. On the other hand, LSTM-CNN and RF shows lower results, with LSTM-CNN and RF achieving an accuracy of 82.58, and 76.7 respectively.

Table 3. Performance of Direct Machine Translation and Word-by-Word Translation

Dataset	Classifier	Accuracy	F1	Recall
IMDB-BN	Bangla-Bert	86.32	86.35	86.06
IMDB-BN	LSTM-CNN	82.58	82.58	82.58
IMDB-BN	RF	76.7	76.65	76.19
IMDB-BN	SVM	88.93	89.08	89.66
IMDB-Word-BN	Bangla-Bert	86.11	86.53	89.42
IMDB-Word-BN	LSTM-CNN	82.45	82.43	82.45
IMDB-Word-BN	RF	78.21	78.65	79.92
IMDB-Word-BN	SVM	89.12	89.31	90.25
IMDB-HN	Hindi-Bert	81.46	80.84	78.17
IMDB-HN	LSTM-CNN	81.05	81.05	81.05
IMDB-HN	RF	80.77	80.7	80.49
IMDB-HN	SVM	89.89	89.98	89.42

Moving on to word-by-word translation, SVM achieves highest accuracy of 89.12, an F1-score of 89.31, and a recall of 90.25 when trained on IMDB-Word-BN dataset. Bangla-Bert shows a slight decrease in accuracy, dropping to 86.11, but improves in terms of recall 89.42 and F1-score of 86.53. In contrast, LSTM-CNN and RF performed less effectively, with LSTM-CNN achieving 82.45 and RF reaching 78.21 in accuracy, although RF shows an improvement in recall 79.92. It is evident that traditional word-by-word translation can by no means be undervalued in the sentiment analysis. In fact, word-by-word translation could be a good option for low-resource languages if the translation dictionary is large enough.

Finally, to understand how translating through an intermediate language impacts translation quality thus affect the classifier's performance we adapted "bridge-translation" method, we first translate the IMDB dataset from English to Hindi and then from Hindi and to Bangla (IMDB-HN-BN), similarly from English to Chinese then from Chinese to Bangla (IMDB-CN-BN). As presented in Table 4, among bridge translated datasets SVM remains the top classifier, demonstrating higher accuracy values of 89.28 when trained on IMDB-HN-BN and 89.26 on IMDB-CN-BN dataset. Its F1-scores and recalls are also among the highest, with 89.47 F1 and 90.43 recall for the IMDB-HN-BN and 89.47 F1 and 90.55 recall for the IMDB-CN-BN. Bangla-Bert performs well in this task as well, with accuracy value of 87.16 for IMDB-HN-BN and 87.19 for IMDB-CN-BN. On contrary, LSTM-CNN and RF showed lower performance, with LSTM-CNN achieving accuracy between 82.9 and 83.15 and RF underperforming with accuracy below 78.0 across both datasets. The bridge translated datasets IMDB-HN-BN and IMDB-CN-BN outperformed both direct machine translation and word-by-word in terms of accuracy, F1-score, and recall. Specifically, SVM showed slight improvements in accuracy and recall, surpassing both other methods, yielding an accuracy of 89.28 on IMDB-HN-BN and 89.26 on IMDB-CN-BN. Bangla-Bert also benefited from this approach, showing a small gain in performance. While the improvements were marginal, bridge-translation was particularly advantageous for SVM and Bangla-Bert, suggesting that leveraging an intermediate language can contribute enhancing model's performance in polarity detection.

Table 4. Performance of Bridge Translation

Dataset	Classifier	Accuracy	F1	Recall
IMDB-HN-BN	Bangla-Bert	87.16	87.39	88.48
IMDB-CN-BN	Bangla-Bert	87.19	87.31	87.61
IMDB-HN-BN	LSTM-CNN	82.9	82.89	82.9
IMDB-CN-BN	LSTM-CNN	83.15	83.12	83.15
IMDB-HN-BN	RF	77.06	76.94	76.19
IMDB-CN-BN	RF	77.5	77.47	77.02
IMDB-HN-BN	SVM	89.28	89.47	90.43
IMDB-CN-BN	SVM	89.26	89.47	90.55

Cross-Dataset Evaluation. Table 5 compares the top performance of cross dataset evaluation. The results highlight the impact of various translation methods on the performance of sentiment analysis. For Bengali cross-dataset evaluation the models trained on direct machine-translated dataset IMDB-BN, and word-by-word translated dataset IMDB-Word-BN, tested on native BN-Drama dataset, the Bangla-Bert achieved an accuracy of 89.32 with IMDB-BN and 89.99 with IMDB-Word-BN. However, training on bridge-translated datasets (IMDB-HN-BN and IMDB-CN-BN) improved the generalization, yielding slightly higher accuracy of 90.23 and 90.06, respectively, about 6.0% behind the accuracy of

Bangla-Bert on BN-Drama (Table 5). Among traditional machine learning models, SVM performed well particularly when trained on bridge-translated datasets, achieving 82.64 accuracy with IMDB-CN-BN. Fig. 2 presents cross-dataset testing accuracy with their respective classifier's name.

On contrary, when models were trained on the native dataset and tested on translated datasets, the Bangla-Bert's accuracy reached to 77.51 when trained using IMDB-BN and tested on BN-Drama. Interestingly the performance on bridge translated dataset IMDB-HN-BN was higher (78.63) than on direct translated IMDB-BN dataset. This clearly suggests that the "bridge-translation" method indeed positively affected the classifier's performance. While models trained on native data BN-Dama underperform during cross-dataset evaluation, however, it is noteworthy to highlight that the goal of cross-dataset evaluation

Table 5. Top Performance of Cross-Dataset Testing

Training Dataset	Testing Dataset	Classifier	Accuracy
BN-Drama	IMDB-BN	Bangla-Bert	77.51
BN-Drama	IMDB-HN-BN	Bangla-Bert	78.63
IMDB-HN-BN	BN-Drama	Bangla-Bert	90.23
IMDB-CN-BN	BN-Drama	Bangla-Bert	90.06
IMDB-BN	BN-Drama	Bangla-Bert	89.32
IMDB-Word-BN	BN-Drama	Bangla-Bert	89.99
IMDB-CN-BN	BN-Drama	SVM	82.64
IMDB-HN	HSAC	SVM	75.9
IMDB-HN	HSAC	Hindi-Bert	69.78
HSAC	IMDB-HN	SVM	71.64

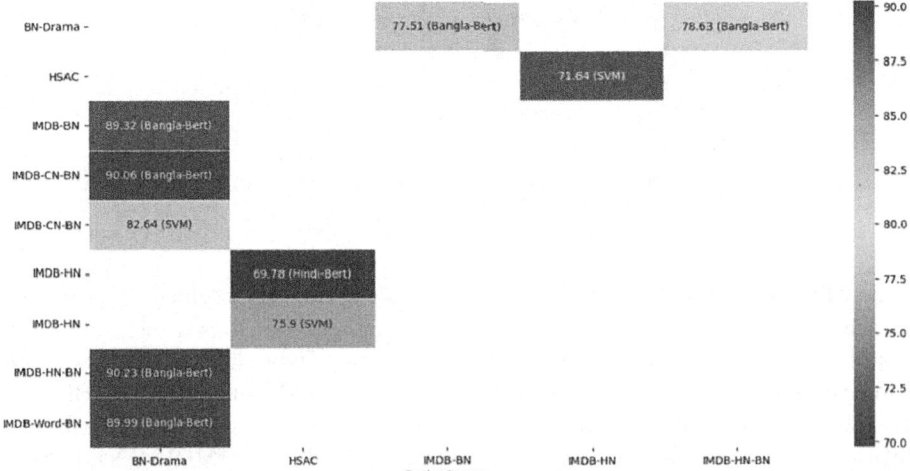

Fig. 2. Cross-dataset testing accuracy with classifier names.

is to investigate whether the models trained on machine translated dataset can outperform the accuracy achieved by native dataset, not the other way around.

Overall, it can be inferred that bridge-translation can enhance model performance, improving linguistic generalization across different datasets. Among the classifiers, Bangla-Bert and SVM consistently achieved higher accuracy.

Finally, in cross-dataset testing scenario for Hindi language, a similar trend has been observed, among the models trained on machine translated IMDB-HN and tested on native HSAC, the SVM achieved the highest accuracy of 75.9 accuracy (Table 5) failing to surpass SVM's performance on HSAC 85.69 (Table 2).

LLM. In our experiment we investigated LLMs performance with zero-shot and few-shot learning on GPT-4o, and Gemini-1.5 Flash. From Table 6 it can be observed that IMDB-CN-BN dataset achieves perfect accuracy of 100 with Gemini-1.5 Flash in both settings. A dramatic improvement is observed on Hindi IMDB-HN where accuracy increases from 80.5 in zero-shot to 94.5 in 10-shot when tested with Gemini-1.5 Flash. On the other hand, GPT-4o remains the most stable across both zero-shot and 10-shot settings with minimal fluctuations in accuracy. Additionally, similar trends have been observed on machine translated Hindi benefiting from 10-shot learning.

Overall, all the models achieve more than 90% accuracy of zero-shot prompt across all the dataset except from IMDB English to Hindi translated data. However, its accuracy also surpasses 90% on 10-shot learning. The higher accuracy on IMDB-CN-BN and IMDB-HN-BN in zero-shot setting also suggests that bridge-translation method has some level of contribution in producing data that are generally understandable by the LLMs.

Table 6. Accuracy of Zero-Shot, and 10-Shot Learning with GPT, and Gemini

Dataset	GPT-4o Zero-shot	GPT-4o 10-shot	Gemini-1.5 Zero-shot	Gemini-1.5 10-shot
BN-Drama	93.0	93.5	95.0	95.0
IMDB-BN	93.00	93.50	95.00	95.00
IMDB-Word-BN	97.50	98.50	94.50	97.00
IMDB-CN-BN	99.00	99.00	100.00	100.00
IMDB-HN-BN	96.00	96.00	95.50	95.50
HSAC	90.0	91.5	96.0	94.5
IMDB-HN	89.00	91.50	80.50	94.50

Manual Translation. We collected 400 machine translated Bengali samples that were commonly mis-classified during the evaluation and manually translated 173 samples out of 400 for better understanding. The performance of the models improved after manual translation; the experiment result presented in Table 7 shows the top performance of Bangla-Bert model trained on machine translated dataset (IMDB-BN) reaching merely 63.0 accuracy. Our investigation on further misclassified 65 samples found that despite being trained on five times larger data (machine translated), the model still struggles to correctly predict sentiment when there exists negation, sarcasm, and or ambiguous words in the given input text.

Table 7. Performance on Manual Translated Data

Training Dataset	Classifier	Accuracy
IMDB-BN	Bangla-Bert	63.0
IMDB-CN-BN	Bangla-Bert	63.0
IMDB-HN-BN	Bangla-Bert	59.53
IMDB-Word-BN	Bangla-Bert	56.64

4.2 Discussion

This study has conducted a thorough investigation into the effectiveness of machine translated data for training models and presented detailed analysis of experimental results. Performance fluctuation has been observed both during inter-dataset and intra-dataset evaluation for both Bangla and Hindi languages. Tables 4, 5 and 6 reports the changes in the performance of classifiers when trained and or tested by adapting "bridge-translation" method. Finally, our experimental findings on cross-dataset evaluation suggest that machine translation can be particularly useful when there is little or no data available in native language. While, such approach can significantly reduce the cost of manual data collection and annotation, however, machine translation is still not mature enough to be an alternative method to develop large-scale dataset for low-resource languages like Bangla.

5 Conclusion

In this study, we conducted experiments on machine-translated datasets by translating the IMDB movie review dataset from English to Bengali using various translation methods, including direct machine translation, bridge translation, and word-by-word translation for sentiment analysis. Our findings reveal that large language models (LLMs) performed significantly better than other models. Among the other models tested, Bangla-BERT and SVM consistently yielded higher accuracy in both Bengali and Hindi, indicating their superiority in capturing complex sentiment nuances. Furthermore, an investigation of 65 manually translated misclassified samples showed that despite being trained on a dataset five times larger, the model trained on machine-translated data still struggled to correctly identify sentiment polarity, particularly in the presence of negation, sarcasm, or ambiguous terms. This suggests that while machine translation can be a helpful tool, it still faces limitations in accurately capturing complex linguistic features. Our study indicates that the machine translation approach is not yet a suitable substitute for building high-quality datasets. However, machine translation can still be effective, particularly when little or no data is available. Translation methods like bridge translation and word-by-word translation can save time and effort compared to manual data collection and annotation.

In the future, we aim to explore the potential of using large language models (LLMs) such as Llama and DeepSeek for translation tasks, and investigate the performance of transformer-based models on these translated texts.

References

1. Latif, D., Samad, M.A., Rinawulandari, R., Kadir, S.: Social media in shaping public opinion roles and impact: a systematic review. Jurnal Komunikasi: Malays. J. Commun. **40**, 205–223 (2024)
2. Sharma, H., Pangaonkar, S., Gunjan, R., Rokade, P.: Sentimental analysis of movie reviews using machine learning. In: ITM Web of Conferences, p. 02006. EDP Sciences, (2023)
3. Sengupta, S., Ghosh, S., Mitra, P., Tamiti, T.I.: Milestones in Bengali Sentiment Analysis leveraging Transformer-models: Fundamentals, Challenges and Future Directions. CoRR abs/2401.07847 (2024)
4. Hasan, M., Islam, L., Jahan, I., Meem, S.M., Rahman, R.M.: Natural language processing and sentiment analysis on Bangla social media comments on Russia-Ukraine war using transformers. Vietnam J. Comput. Sci. **10**, 329–356 (2023)
5. Ghafoor, A., Imran, A.S., Daudpota, S.M., Kastrati, Z., Batra, R., Wani, M.A.: The impact of translating resource-rich datasets to low-resource languages through multi-lingual text processing. IEEE Access **9**, 124478–124490 (2021)
6. Araújo, M., Pereira, A., Benevenuto, F.: A comparative study of machine translation for multilingual sentence-level sentiment analysis. Inf. Sci. **512**, 1078–1102 (2020)
7. Cattoni, R., Gangi, M.A.D., Bentivogli, L., Negri, M., Turchi, M.: MuST-C: a multilingual corpus for end-to-end speech translation. Comput. Speech Lang. **66**, 101155 (2021)
8. Kowsher, M., Sami, A.A., Prottasha, N.J., Arefin, M.S., Dhar, P.K., Koshiba, T.: Bangla-BERT: transformer-based efficient model for transfer learning and language understanding. IEEE Access **10**, 91855–91870 (2022)
9. Joshi, R.: L3Cube-HindBERT and DevBERT: pre-trained BERT transformer models for Devanagari based Hindi and Marathi languages. CoRR abs/2211.11418 (2022)
10. Zhang, J., Li, Y., Tian, J., Li, T.: LSTM-CNN hybrid model for text classification. In: 2018 IEEE 3rd Advanced Information Technology, Electronic and Automation Control Conference (IAEAC), pp. 1675–1680. IEEE (2018)
11. Mullen, T., Collier, N.: Sentiment analysis using support vector machines with diverse information sources. In: Proceedings of the 2004 Conference on Empirical Methods in Natural Language Processing , EMNLP 2004, A meeting of SIGDAT, a Special Interest Group of the ACL, held in conjunction with ACL 2004, 25-26 July 2004, Barcelona, Spain, pp. 412–418 (2004)

12. Breiman, L.: Random forests. Mach. Learn. **45**, 5–32 (2001)
13. Sazzed, S.: Cross-lingual sentiment classification in low-resource Bengali language. In: Proceedings of the Sixth Workshop on Noisy User-generated Text (W-NUT 2020), pp. 50–60 (2020)
14. Maas, A.L., Daly, R.E., Pham, P.T., Huang, D., Ng, A.Y., Potts, C.: Learning Word Vectors for Sentiment Analysis. In: The 49th Annual Meeting of the Association for Computational Linguistics: Human Language Technologies, Proceedings of the Conference, 19-24 June, 2011, Portland, Oregon, USA, pp. 142–150 (2011)
15. Kabir, M., Mahfuz, O.B., Raiyan, S.R., Mahmud, H., Hasan, M.K.: BanglaBook: A Large-scale Bangla Dataset for Sentiment Analysis from Book Reviews, pp. 1237–1247 (2023)
16. Islam, K.I., Kar, S., Islam, M.S., Amin, M.R.: SentNoB: A Dataset for Analysing Sentiment on Noisy Bangla Texts, pp. 3265–3271 (2021)
17. Banik, N., Rahman, M.H.H.: Evaluation of naïve bayes and support vector machines on Bangla textual movie reviews. In: 2018 International Conference on Bangla Speech and Language Processing (ICBSLP), pp. 1–6. IEEE (2018)
18. Mahtab, S.A., Islam, N., Rahaman, M.M.: Sentiment analysis on Bangladesh cricket with support vector machine. In: 2018 International Conference on Bangla Speech and Language Processing (ICBSLP), pp. 1–4. IEEE (2018)
19. Shalunts, G., Backfried, G., Commeignes, N.: The impact of machine translation on sentiment analysis. Data Analytics **63**, 51–56 (2016)
20. Ali, M.N.Y., Rahman, M.L., Sorwar, G.: Bangla DeConverter for extraction of BanglaText from universal networking language. Information **10**, 324 (2019)
21. Rajput, A.S.: Scientific writing: the predicament of weather and climate scientists in India. Bull. Am. Meteor. Soc. **100**, 399–402 (2019)

RRetFC: Leveraging Recursive Retrieval For LLM-Enhanced Complex Fact-Checking

Yuxuan Xie[1,2], Xiaoliang Liu[3], Peng Wu[1,2(✉)], and Li Pan[1,2]

[1] School of Computer Sciences, Shanghai Jiao Tong University, Shanghai, China
catking@sjtu.edu.cn
[2] Shanghai Key Laboratory of Integrated Administration Technologies for Information Security, Shanghai Jiao Tong University, Shanghai, China
[3] School of Politics, National Defense University, Shanghai, China

Abstract. Fake claims spreading in social media are often carefully crafted and complex, so that multi-source evidence and reasoning are required for checking their authenticity. To this end, we propose RRetFC, a Recursively Retrieval enhanced method for complex Fact Checking with LLMs, which has a multi-step recursive retriever and an LLM-enhanced reader. Specifically, for the evidence retriever, as the long-range semantic dependencies between explicit entities of a complex claim may involve some other hidden entities, it is hard for traditional retrieval methods to get all necessary evidence for fact-checking in once retrieval. Thus RRetFC designs a recursive retriever which gets all necessary evidence recursively with the help of LLM. For the reader, as the evidence retrieved from some external knowledge sources may inevitably contain noise which may undermining the judgment, RRetFC firstly employs an LLM to filter out noise from the retrieved evidence and carefully reason to generate an analysis report. Subsequently, RRetFC fine-tunes a SLMs based on the analysis text to produce the final prediction label. Our experiments on two public fact-checking datasets show that RRetFC outperforms state-of-the-art baseline methods and exhibits superior evidence retrieval capabilities.

Keywords: automatic fact-checking · LLM · evidence retrieval

1 Introduction

The wide and rapid spread of misinformation on social media has raised grade concerns, highlighting the growing importance of fact-checking [7]. Existing automatic fact-checking pipelines typically follow a retriever-reader structure, where the former retrieves relevant evidence, and the latter makes a judgment of "support" or "refute" based on the evidence. Although many works on fact-checking have achieved certain successes, most of them are often limited to simple claims that can be directly verified with a single piece of evidence. In contract, real-world claims are usually logically complex and involve information from multiple aspects, so that they typically require multiple pieces of evidence from diverse documents and involve complex logical reasoning to reach a final authenticity judgment. This poses challenges for both the retriever and the reader.

For evidence retriever, traditional retrieval approaches often try to retrieve several pieces of evidence about the explicit entities involved in a complex claim. However, they may neglect the long-range semantic dependencies between entities, making it difficult to retrieve all necessary evidence required to verify intricate relationships between entities. With the widespread application of LLMs, some have tried to adopt LLMs to decompose any complex claim into multiple simpler sub-claims with one-hop relationship, each of which is used to precisely retrieve partial evidence [3,17]. In this way, evidence verifying one-hop relationships between entities can be retrieved. Although these decomposition based methods have made significant progress, they still face some challenges. Firstly, decomposition without explicit rules or guiding knowledge may inevitably introduce errors. In addition, the long-range semantic dependencies between entities still cannot be effectively resolved through decomposition, so that some key evidence may still be missing. In fact, the essence of long-range semantic dependencies between entities in a complex claim is that their multi-hop relationships are built on multiple hidden intermediate entities. As a result, some pieces of evidence about the hidden intermediate entities, though crucial for fact-checking, cannot be retrieved solely based on the explicit information within the claim itself. Instead, they require recursive retrieval after the missing information about the hidden intermediate entities in the claim is further supplemented. An example can be seen in Fig. 1, where the claim is hard to further decompose without the information about the hidden intermediate entities, i.e., the player's club SD Eibar. This information should be retrieved through the player's name and then used to retrieve the evidence about its league.

For the reader, the result is obtained by comparing the consistency between the claim and the evidences. For claims with complex logic, multiple steps of decomposition and reasoning may be required, such as graph-based models [2] and some LLM-based methods [10,12]. However, since the evidences retrieved from some external knowledge sources may inevitably contain noise and information that may cause ambiguity, so trained-based model may inadvertently learn from such noise, thereby undermining the credibility of the judgments. While the LLM-based models have been demonstrated that although they excel at reasoning the rationales for the authenticity of claims, they struggle to directly provide their authenticity judgment labels because of lacking task-specific knowledge, resulting in suboptimal performance. Therefore, both trained-based models and LLM-based models have certain limitations.

To this end, we proposed RRetFC, an automatic fact-checking pipeline with a multi-step recursive retriever and an LLM enhanced reader, which improves the handling of complex claims. Specifically, due to the hidden intermediate entities in complex claims, traditional retrieval methods based on entity queries

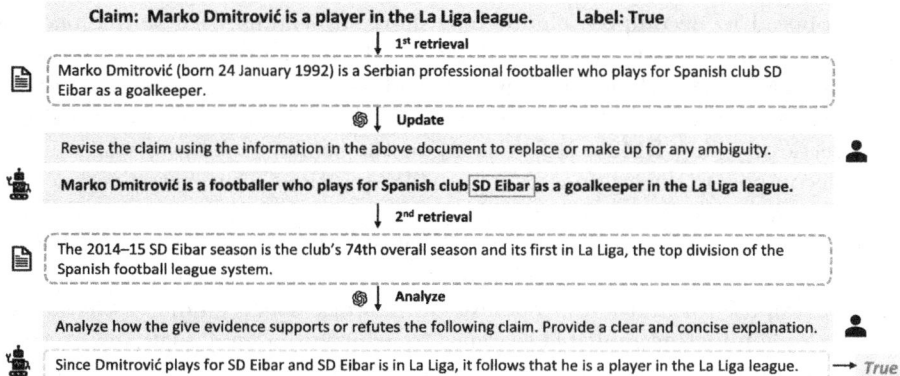

Fig. 1. A complex fact-checking example of RRetFC on HOVER dataset. We first retrieved the evidence about the player, in which we found information about his club SD Eibar for the second retrieval.

or semantic similarity often struggle to retrieve all related evidence to verify intricate relationships in complex claims when lacking information of hidden entities. To effectively retrieve more comprehensive relevant evidence, we propose a multi-step recursive retrieval method based on LLM. Evidence related to explicit entities can be successfully retrieved by traditional retrieval methods. Since hidden entities often have certain relationships to some explicit entities, information about hidden entities can be extracted from retrieved evidence of explicit entities. Thus, we adopt LLMs to extract the key information and update the claim with it to retrieve evidence related to hidden entities using traditional retrieval methods. The above evidence retrieval and claim updating steps are iterated until all necessary evidence is extracted. The evidence retrieved through multi-step recursive retriever more comprehensively covers the necessary information for verifying the claim. However, it may also inevitably introduce noise and ambiguous information that could affect the accuracy of the verification process. To filter out noise and ambiguous information in the retrieved evidence and enhance semantics, we then use LLM to further analyze the claim and evidence and reason rationales while focusing on different entities in the claim and their relationships. As the LLM is not good at directly giving judgment labels, ultimately we fine-tune small language models(SLMs) like BERT based on those analysis for final judgment. We conducted comprehensive experiments on two complex datasets and results demonstrate that RRetFC outperforms existing baseline methods, showcasing its effectiveness in complex fact-checking.

2 Related Works

2.1 Evidence Retriever

Complex claims often describe multiple entities with intricate relationships and hidden intermediate entities, making retrieval difficult. To handle this, some have proposed to decompose claims into short sub-claims with simple one-hop relationships and conduct multiple retrieval. [17] decomposes claims into first-order predicate logic (FOL) and uses Google search for sub-claims' evidence retrieval. [3], on the other hand, decomposes a claim into 10 questions and performs retrieval using BM25. [13] focuses on the semantic roles of words in the claim, decomposing the original claim into 5W questions. However, direct decomposing can not solve the problem of long-range semantic dependencies between entities, which may make the claim hard to clearly decompose or make it difficult to retrieve key evidence for sub-claims. Apart from the methods of decomposing, [11] proposed a multi-step retrieval framework which emulates the human behavior of conducting multiple searches to achieve the final goal when retrieving information. However, its claim updating process is limited to direct contact of the claim and retrieved results, which may overlook complex semantic logic. In addition, like many other methods [9,14] that use dense retrievers to enhance semantic understanding during retrieval, [11] also trains a dense retriever to perform retrieval at the vector level. However, training a dense retriever requires a large amount of gold evidence annotated data for training and incurs high computational overhead. Compared to the above methods, our multi-step recursive retriever performs retrieval using only BM25 and an LLM, without the need for training. Additionally, due to the powerful capabilities of LLM, it can accurately leverage the information from the previous retrieval to enrich the query.

2.2 LLM in Fact Verification

Recently, LLMs have been shown to have excellent capabilities in various tasks. Due to their outstanding semantic understanding and reasoning abilities, LLMs have demonstrated huge potential in fact-checking.

[12] utilize the in-context learning and code generation abilities of LLM to transform complex claims into pre-defined programs with three functions. The programs are then executed to retrieve evidence and obtain the final judgment. [10] proposed a framework totally based on LLM, including claim detection, query generation, evidence retrieval and final judgment. [4,17] also employ LLM to generate human-readable explanations for model prediction.

However, LLMs itself have unsolved problems like hallucination and prompt sensitivity. Moreover, some studies have pointed out that LLMs struggle to effectively integrate multiple evidence and process complex reasoning. As a result, there remains a performance gap between LLMs and fine-tuning SLMs. [8] found that LLMs are suboptimal at giving a final prediction but good at generating useful rationales. So they proposed a model using these rationales to enhance model training. In addition, [16] employ LLMs to generate explanations for both support and refute side, and then fine-tune BERT to evaluate the relative defense strength to select the stronger side. Our propose reader in RRetFC followed these researches and has a LLM-SLM structure.

The problem of fact-checking is first formulated. Given a claim c and a relevant knowledge source $\mathcal{K}$. E^* represents the smallest evidence set needed to verify the claim(with $E^* \in \mathcal{K}$) and the target of a retriever is retrieving a set of

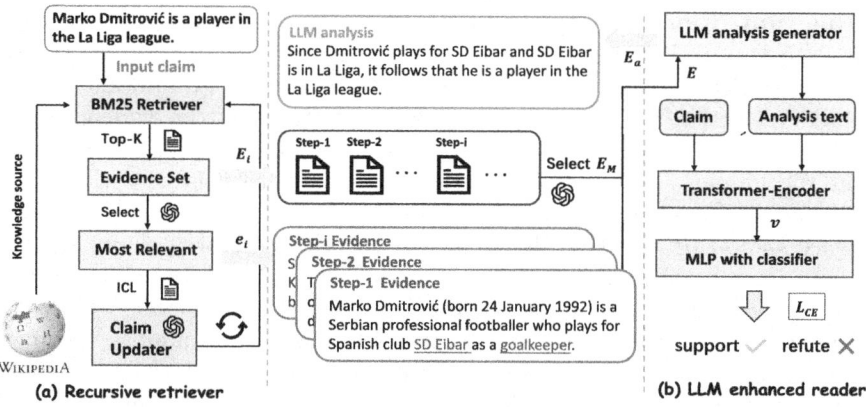

Fig. 2. The overview of RRetFC, which is consist of two modules:(a) recursive retriever iteratively retrieves evidence to overcome long-range semantic dependencies; (b) LLM enhanced reader employs an LLM to analyze and fine-tunes a SLM to classify.

evidence E from $\mathcal{K}$ where $E \in \mathcal{K}$ and $E^* \subseteq E$. Then the reader predicts a label y to determine whether evidence E refutes or supports the claim c. In this paper, we set $\mathcal{K}$ as a large textual corpus such as Wikipedia or Science documents. The overview of two components of RRetFC is shown in Fig. 2.

2.3 Recursive Retriever

BM25 Retriever. For complex claims, we usually have $|E^*| \geq 2$. In addition, the long-range semantic dependencies between entities often exist, making part of the evidence can not be retrieved until the missing information about the hidden intermediate entities is supplemented. As a result, traditional and widely used methods like BM25 [3,12] are unable to retrieve all of the needed evidence. Nonetheless, they are good at retrieving evidences in E^* related to explicit entities in the claim. Since hidden entities and explicit entities in a claim often have certain relationships, information of hidden entities close to certain explicit entities can be found in their retrieved evidence, and can be further used to retrieve evidence related to hidden entities. Therefore, we propose to conduct recursive multiple retrieval using BM25, where the useful evidence retrieved from previous step will assist in the next retrieval of missing evidence.

In step i, we directly use the claim c_i as query and calculate the query-document relevance score for all paragraphs in $\mathcal{K}$. Then we only reserve the top-k result set E_i as the evidence retrieved in this step for further process. Notably, since the c_i used in the i-th retrieval still has some semantic connection with the previous claims, the retrieval results of c_i inevitably contain some repeated evidence in $\bigcup_{j=1}^{i-1} E_j$. As a result, such repeated evidence should be neglected when collecting E_i with top-k reservation strategy.

Relevant Evidence Selection. Since hidden intermediate entities are related to the explicit entities in the claim, the evidence set E_i retrieved by querying explicit entities in claim c_i is likely to contain useful information about the hidden entities. Relevant evidence selection is to select the evidence e_i in E_i that is most relevant to the claim for querying and contains useful information about the hidden entities. Traditional methods regard this as a classification task, training models with annotated gold evidence to determine which piece of evidence should be selected. However, training the selector requires additional computational overhead. Moreover, gold evidence may not always be available. Given the few-shot capability and strong semantic understanding of long texts exhibited by LLM, we employ an LLM to select without training. Specifically, for the evidence E_i retrieved in step i, we make LLM select the most relevant and informative evidence $e_i = \mathcal{LLM}(P_{select}(c_i, E_i))$ for c_i, where P_{select} is our designed prompt for evidence selection:

"Here is a claim to be verified: [claim] Here are some paragraphs: [evidence set] Please select the most relevant one from the above paragraphs as evidence to help verify. Response with the selected paragraph directly."

Claim Updater. Claim updating is to utilize the relevant information about hidden intermediate entities in e_i to revise c_i. Then the revised claim c_{i+1} may introduce new cues that benefit further retrieval. Claim updating can be considered a challenging text generation task, as models need to extract useful information in e_i and make appropriate revisions without altering the core semantics of the sentence. Moreover, such revisions do not follow a fixed pattern, they could involve adding information, rephrasing, or simplifying redundant details. This requires the model to have strong semantic understanding and creativity capability. Fortunately, LLMs have shown strong few-shot generalization capability, often referred to as in-context learning (ICL). This allows them to understand and adapt to new tasks based on a few human annotated examples. Inspired by many work that utilizing LLMs for customized tasks, we also employ an LLM to conduct claim updating. Moreover, since we restrict the LLM's focus to useful information only, retrieval bias introduced at specific previous steps has little chance to propagate to subsequent queries. Specifically, for the evidence e_i selected in step i, we use a prompt P_{revise} to generate the new claim for next retrieval step $c_{i+1} = \mathcal{LLM}(P_{revise}(ICL, c_i, e_i))$. ICL here is a set of human-annotated successful examples $\{(c'_j, e'_j, c'_{j+1})\}$ that contain various revisions. The templete of P_{revise} is as follows:

"Here is a claim: [claim]. And this is a relevant document: [selected evidence]. Please revise the claim using the information in the above document to replace or make up for any ambiguity. Below are some examples: [ICL examples]. Response with the revised claim directly."

We perform N rounds of retrieval for each claim, where N is a hyperparameter adjusted based on the complexity of the claim. After recursive retrieval is terminated, to reduce omissions, the retriever performs a secondary filtering on all retrieved evidence and select a subset $E_M \subset \bigcup_{i=1}^{N} E_i$, where $|E_M| = M$. Finally, the retriever returns $E = \{e_1, e_2, \ldots, e_N\} \cup E_M$ as final result.

2.4 LLM Enhanced Reader

Analysis Generation. Evidence retrieved from open-domain sources inevitably introduces irrelevant evidence as noise. On one hand, [6] points out that such irrelevant evidence may reduce the model's classification performance. On the other hand, a trained model may make decisions based on the noise, reducing credibility of predicted results.

To filter out the irrelevant noise, we use LLM to perform an initial prediction of the claim based on the retrieved evidence, providing an analysis of how the evidence supports or refutes the claim as an explanation $E_a = \mathcal{LLM}(P_{analyze}(c, E))$. $P_{analyze}$ is our designed prompt for analysis generation, where we prevent LLM from focusing on irrelevant information and restrict its explanation on evidence only to avoid hallucination. To enhance the performance of LLMs in analyzing complex claims, we also guide LLM to clearly identify the entities while eliminating the impact of ambiguous references and carefully reason out their relationships. The templete of $P_{analysis}$ is as follows:

"Analyze how the give evidence supports or refutes the following claim. Provide a clear and concise explanation. You can focus on different entities and their relationships to make your decision more accurate. Remember to clearly identify vague references to people or places. Input: [claim][evidence]. Instruction: Directly provide your explanation without any preamble or conclusion. Only use information present in the evidence to support your analysis."

SLM-Based Inference. However, LLMs have been proved suboptimal in giving a final prediction label [8]. With the claim c and analysis E_a derived from LLM, we develop a SLM-based claim classifier. This model aims to fully leverage the claim text and the LLM's preliminary prediction and analysis, ultimately determining the truthfulness of the claim. Concretely, we concatenate the claim text and analysis text, and then feed them into a Transformer encoder for a contextual representation v:

$$v = Transformer - Enc([[CLS]; c; [SEP]; E_a]; \theta^{enc}) \quad (1)$$

where θ^{enc} represents the encoder parameters. Then v will be fed to a MLP model for classification:

$$p^{ver} = softmax(MLP(v; \theta^{ver})) \quad (2)$$
$$\hat{y} = argmax(p^{ver}) \quad (3)$$

where p denotes the probability distribution of predicted label, and $\hat{y}$ denotes the finally predicted label for claim c. The training loss is as follows:

$$\mathcal{L} = -\sum log p_{[\hat{y}=y]}, \quad y \in \{0, 1\} \quad (4)$$

3 Experiment

3.1 Experimental Setup

Datasets. Since we focused on complex fact-checking, we choose to evaluate our model on two eligible datasets. HOVER is a multi-hop fact-checking dataset contains three subsets: 2-hop, 3-hop and 4-hop with increasing levels of complexity. SciFact [15] is a scientific fact-checking dataset. We followed the work in [17] and collected claims that require evidence support and have a global label for testing. A total of 692 claims were chosen, with more than half requiring support from multiple pieces of evidence. In terms of corpus selection, we use the official corpus provided by the author of these two datasets.

Baselines We compare RRetFC with seven baselines and categorize them into three groups following [8]:

SLM-only methods. 1) **BERT** [5] is a widely used pre-trained SLM, and here we fine-tune it on the training set. 2) **MUSER** [11] first encodes the corpus and claims for multi-step dense retrieval, and then trains an NLI model for judgment.

LLM-only methods. 1) **COT** [18] (Chain of Thought) is a popular prompt engineering method which guides LLM to explicitly show its reasoning process. 2) **ProgramFC** [12] uses LLMs to convert claims into predefined programs and execute them by selected plug-in model. 3) **FOLK** [17] uses LLMs to decompose claims into first-order predicate logic to verify.

SLM+LLM methods. 1) **ARG** [8] uses LLMs to generate textual descriptions and commonsense rationales for given claims and trains a model for prediction. 2) **SuperICL** [19] first trains a model to make an initial prediction, obtaining labels and confidence scores, which are then used to construct in-context learning examples for LLMs to verify.

Implementation Details. We employ `Qwen-long` [1] as our LLM used for evidence retrieval and analysis generation and `bert-base` as our base model. We also use them for other baselines to maintain fairness. For baseline methods that do not specify an evidence retrieval process, we uniformly use BM25 to retrieve evidence from the corpus. During the retrieval phase, we set retrieval round N same as the hop for the HOVER dataset and $N = 3$ for the SciFact dataset. All results are obtained by averaging over three tests to reduce errors.

3.2 Main Results

Table 1 presents the accuracy and macro-F1 score of RRetFC and seven baselines on the HOVER dataset with different hops and the SciFact dataset. Based on the experiment results, we have the following major observations:

First, RRetFC achieves the best classification performance across all datasets, demonstrating its effectiveness in complex fact-checking tasks. A Wilcoxon

Table 1. The macro-F1 score and accuracy of RRetFC and other 7 baseline methods on three subsets of HOVER dataset and SciFact dataset.

Models	HOVER (2-hop)		HOVER (3-hop)		HOVER (4-hop)		SciFact	
	Acc	Macro-F1	Acc	Macro-F1	Acc	Macro-F1	Acc	Macro-F1
BERT	60.51	60.82	55.64	55.92	51.71	51.41	56.92	47.38
MUSER	58.30	59.46	59.78	60.18	53.13	53.12	56.45	49.02
CoT	67.96	68.68	58.99	60.39	55.61	57.11	84.14	84.70
ProgramFC	70.18	70.30	59.02	60.96	61.00	59.16	67.02	70.70
FOLK	66.27	66.26	55.10	54.80	60.61	60.35	69.79	67.59
ARG	66.28	65.45	63.94	63.79	60.83	59.47	71.85	66.33
SuperICL	69.78	69.79	58.86	60.19	56.48	57.53	85.73	85.92
RRetFC	**73.00**	**74.22**	**67.68**	**67.82**	**61.31**	**62.03**	**87.15**	**88.02**

signed-rank test was conducted to compare our model against second-best baseline. The result (p = 0.008) indicates a significant improvement at the 0.05 level. Notably, our method achieves relatively larger improvements on the HOVER dataset, indicating its advantage in handling complex claims that require reasoning.

Secondly, results on SciFact show that all methods involving LLMs perform significantly better than the two SLM-only methods. We believe this is due to the characteristics of the SciFact dataset. SciFact focuses on a specific domain and has relatively fewer training data, which makes it difficult for SLMs to acquire relevant knowledge and effectively learn through training. However, LLMs overcome these challenges through their comprehensive knowledge, thereby enhancing models' performance in such scenarios.

Finally, we found that although MUSER has a multi-step retriever similar to ours, its performance on the HOVER 2-hop is even worse than the method of one-step BM25 and fine-tuning BERT, indicating its designing flaws. Upon analysis, we found that the evidence retrieved by MUSER contains a significant amount of noise. In contrast, our multi-step retrieval module utilizes LLM for precise claim updating and LLM analysis. Experiment results demonstrate that it is more robust and efficient.

According to our statistics following the experiment, the API consumed approximately 7,000 tokens for evidence retrieval and 1,000 tokens for analysis generation per claim on average across all datasets, which is affordable.

3.3 Impact of Multi-step Retrieval

Recursive multi-step retriever is a crucial module in our model design. To further investigate its role, we conducted ablation study by replacing it with one-step BM25 for comparison. As shown in Fig. 3, the overall performance of the model significantly declines compared to the full version of RRetFC.

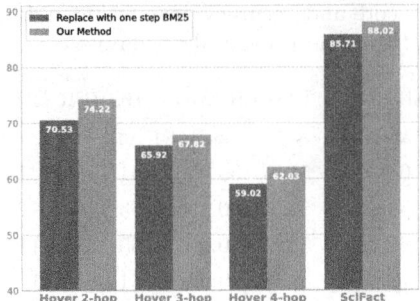

Fig. 3. Ablation study of replacing our proposed recursive retriever with one step BM25

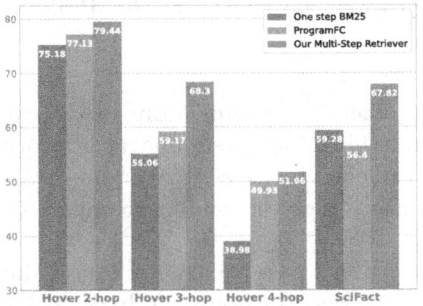

Fig. 4. Recall of gold evidence in retrieved evidence

To further verify the effectiveness of the retriever, we followed the experiment in [12], calculating the recall of gold evidence for the retrieved evidence with fixed number. Since FOLK utilizes a search engine and MUSER retrieves snippet level evidence, it is hard for them to compare with the gold evidence. Therefore, we compare only with one-step BM25 and ProgramFC.

As shown in Fig. 4, our method achieves the highest recall, demonstrating its strong retrieval capability. Compared to the second-best baseline method, our retriever achieves improvements of 4.26, 13.24, 12.68 and 8.54 on HOVER and SciFact datasets, with larger improvements on the 3-hop and 4-hop HOVER subsets. This indicates that recursive multi-step retrieval is more advantageous for handling long-range semantic dependencies in complex claims.

3.4 Impact of LLM Analysis

Utilizing LLM for the preliminary analysis of retrieved evidence is another key module in our model design. Figure 5 presents the experiment results after removing the LLM analysis. As shown, there is a significant performance drop compared to the full version. Notably, the performance drop on SciFact is par-

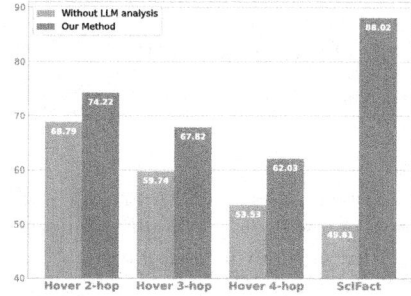

Fig. 5. Ablation of removing LLM analysis in the reader

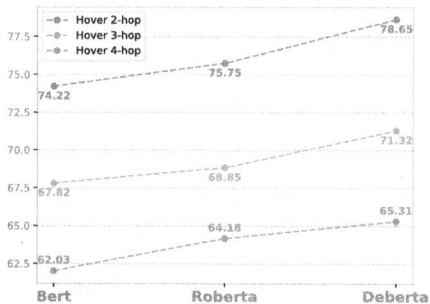

Fig. 6. Macro F1 score of changing different small LM on HOVER dataset

ticularly significant, reaching 43.41%, which aligns with our conclusion in 4.2 that LLM can effectively enhance performance on SciFact.

In the main experiment, we trained BERT to learn from the LLM analysis and perform the final classification. To further demonstrate the generalizability of LLM analysis across different base models, we conducted experiments using two other widely used SLMs: Roberta and Deberta. The macro-F1 scores of the three models on the HOVER dataset are shown in Fig. 6. From the results, we can observe that LLM analysis is effective for other models as well, enabling them to learn effectively. Additionally, improvements in the performance of the base models also improve the final classification performance.

4 Conclusion

We proposed RRetFC, which retrieves all necessary evidence by a recursive retriever and refines the retrieved evidence for final claim verification and explanation by an LLM enhanced reader. The method is equipped with good expressiveness because: (i) using recursive, RRetFC successfully eliminates the impact of long-range semantic dependencies in complex claims and retrieves necessary evidence about hidden intermediate entities; (ii) benefiting from the reasoning capability of LLM, RRetFC can filter noise out from the evidence and handle the intricate relationships in complex claims better. The results on HOVER and SciFact dataset indicate the effectiveness of RRetFC in verifying complex claims.

References

1. Bai, J., et al.: Qwen technical report (2023). https://arxiv.org/abs/2309.16609
2. Barnabò, G., Siciliano, F., Castillo, C.: Fbmultilingmisinfo: challenging large-scale multilingual benchmark for misinformation detection. In: 2022 International Joint Conference on Neural Networks (IJCNN), pp. 1–8 (2022)
3. Chen, J., Kim, G., Sriram, A., Durrett, G., Choi, E.: Complex claim verification with evidence retrieved in the wild. In: Proceedings of the 2024 Conference of the North American Chapter of the Association for Computational Linguistics. pp. 3569–3587 (2024)
4. Dai, S.C., Hsu, Y.L., Xiong, A.: Ask to know more: Generating counterfactual explanations for fake claims. In: Proceedings of the 28th ACM SIGKDD Conference on Knowledge Discovery and Data Mining, pp. 2800–2810. KDD '22, ACM (2022)
5. Devlin, J., Chang, M.W., Lee, K., Toutanova, K.: BERT: pre-training of deep bidirectional transformers for language understanding. In: Proceedings of the 2019 Conference of the North American Chapter of the Association for Computational Linguistics: Human Language Technologies, pp. 4171–4186 (2019)
6. Guan, J., Dodge, J., Wadden, D., Huang, M., Peng, H.: Language models hallucinate, but may excel at fact verification (2024). https://arxiv.org/abs/2310.14564
7. Guo, Z., Schlichtkrull, M., Vlachos, A.: A survey on automated fact-checking. Transactions of the Association for Computational Linguistics, pp. 178–206 (2022)
8. Hu, B., Sheng, Q., Cao, J., Shi, Y., Li, Y., Wang, D., Qi, P.: Bad actor, good advisor: Exploring the role of large language models in fake news detection. In: Proceedings of the AAAI Conference on Artificial Intelligence, pp. 22105–22113 (2024)
9. Karisani, P., Ji, H.: Fact checking beyond training set. In: Proceedings of the 2024 Conference of the North American Chapter of the Association for Computational Linguistics: Human Language Technologies, pp. 2247–2261 (2024)
10. Li, M., Peng, B., Galley, M., Gao, J., Zhang, Z.: Self-checker: plug-and-play modules for fact-checking with large language models. In: Findings of the Association for Computational Linguistics: NAACL 2024, pp. 163–181 (2024)
11. Liao, H., Peng, J., Huang, Z., Zhang, W., Li, G., Shu, K., Xie, X.: Muser: a multi-step evidence retrieval enhancement framework for fake news detection. In: Proceedings of the 29th ACM SIGKDD Conference on Knowledge Discovery and Data Mining, pp. 4461–4472. KDD '23 (2023)
12. Pan, L., Wu, X., Lu, X., Luu, A.T., Wang, W.Y., Kan, M.Y., Nakov, P.: Fact-checking complex claims with program-guided reasoning. In: Proceedings of the 61st Annual Meeting of the Association for Computational Linguistics, pp. 6981–7004, July 2023
13. Rani, A., et al.: FACTIFY-5WQA: 5W aspect-based fact verification through question answering. In: Proceedings of the 61st Annual Meeting of the Association for Computational Linguistics, pp. 10421–10440 (2023)
14. Soleimani, A., Monz, C., Worring, M.: Bert for evidence retrieval and claim verification, pp. 359–366. Berlin, Heidelberg (2020)

15. Wadden, D., Lin, S., Lo, K., Wang, L.L., van Zuylen, M., Cohan, A., Hajishirzi, H.: Fact or fiction: verifying scientific claims. In: Proceedings of the 2020 Conference on Empirical Methods in Natural Language Processing (EMNLP), pp. 7534–7550 (2020)
16. Wang, B., Ma, J., Lin, H., Yang, Z., Yang, R., Tian, Y., Chang, Y.: Explainable fake news detection with large language model via defense among competing wisdom. In: Proceedings of the ACM Web Conference 2024, pp. 2452–2463 (2024)
17. Wang, H., Shu, K.: Explainable claim verification via knowledge-grounded reasoning with large language models. In: Findings of the Association for Computational Linguistics: EMNLP 2023, pp. 6288–6304 (2023)
18. Wei, J., Wang, X., Schuurmans, D., Bosma, M., Ichter, B., Xia, F., Chi, E., Le, Q., Zhou, D.: Chain-of-thought prompting elicits reasoning in large language models (2023). https://arxiv.org/abs/2201.11903
19. Xu, C., Xu, Y., Wang, S., Liu, Y., Zhu, C., McAuley, J.: Small models are valuable plug-ins for large language models. In: Findings of the Association for Computational Linguistics: ACL 2024, pp. 283–294 (2024)

Feature-Aware Sequence Models for Tabular Data Processing with Missing Values

Yan Qian[1] and Yiqing Shen[2(✉)]

[1] Shenzhen Campus of Harbin Institute of Technology, Shenzhen, China
23s151150@stu.hit.edu.cn
[2] Department of Computer Science, Johns Hopkins University, Baltimore, MD, USA
yiqingshen1@gmail.com

Abstract. Tabular data remains fundamental in diverse domains including finance, healthcare, multimedia, and industrial applications. While deep learning approaches have shown promise for analyzing tabular data, current architectures face high complexity and suboptimal performance when processing high-dimensional tabular datasets and handling missing values. Recent sequence modeling architectures like Mamba and Hyena have demonstrated computational efficiency advantages, but their direct application to tabular data is limited by the inherent heterogeneity of features and complex interdependencies. We propose two novel architectures, FT-Mamba and FT-Hyena, which enhance these sequence models with feature-aware components specifically designed for tabular data processing. These architectures incorporate specialized tokenization and encoding mechanisms that explicitly account for numerical and categorical feature types while maintaining computational efficiency. To address missing values, we introduce an innovative adaptive masking strategy that combines type-aware masking with dynamic probability adjustment based on feature-specific statistical properties. This is complemented by learnable missing value representations and a teacher-guided distillation approach that enables robust handling of incomplete data during inference without requiring separate imputation steps. Experimental evaluation across five real-world datasets demonstrates that our architectures, particularly FT-Hyena, achieve nearly twice the processing efficiency of existing approaches while maintaining competitive performance with state-of-the-art Transformer-based models. The adaptive masking strategy consistently outperforms conventional imputation methods while reducing computational overhead during inference. The code is available at https://github.com/Gudesoy/Models-for-Tabular-Data.

Keywords: Tabular Data · Deep Learning · Model Architectures · Missing Value Processing

1 Introduction

Tabular data, characterized by its structured format of rows and columns, remains fundamental in diverse domains, including finance, healthcare, multimedia and industrial applications. While traditional machine learning approaches such as decision trees [13], random forests [5], and gradient-boosting machines [15] have long been the standard methods for tabular data analysis, they often struggle to handle the increasing complexity of modern datasets [11], particularly when confronted with high dimensionality and missing values [25]. Deep learning (DL) has emerged as a promising alternative, offering automatic feature extraction and end-to-end learning capabilities that reduce the need for manual feature engineering [4,18]. Previous work [7] has achieved substantial progress in adapting various DL architectures for tabular data [7], from basic multilayer perceptrons (MLPs) [19] to more sophisticated models such as Residual Networks (ResNets) [10] and Transformers [23]. Among these, the Feature Tokenizer Transformer (FT-Transformer) [7], which specifically adapts the Transformer architecture for tabular data, has established itself as a benchmark model due to its exceptional generalization capabilities in various tasks. However, FT-Transformer's computational efficiency deteriorates when processing high-dimensional tabular data, prompting the exploration of alternative architectures. Recent sequence modeling architectures based on state space models (SSMs), particularly Mamba [8] and Hyena [20], have shown promising efficiency when processing high-dimensional data [1,22]. While these models show potential, their direct application to tabular data presents challenges. Specifically, the inherent heterogeneity of tabular features and their complex inter-dependencies require specialized processing beyond simple token-based approaches. Furthermore, these architectures lack mechanisms to handle the diverse characteristics of numerical and categorical features that are fundamental to tabular data. To address these limitations, we propose two novel architectures, FT-Mamba and FT-Hyena, which enhance Mamba [8] and Hyena [20] with feature-aware components specifically designed for tabular data processing. Our architectures incorporate specialized tokenization and encoding mechanisms that explicitly account for different feature types while maintaining the computational efficiency of their base models.

Another major challenge in tabular data analysis is the frequent occurrence of missing values, which can impairs model performance by disrupting the learning of feature relationships [3]. Traditional DL models typically cannot process incomplete tabular data directly, requiring preliminary imputation steps that often introduce additional complexity and computational overhead. While conventional imputation approaches like zero or mean imputation are computationally efficient, they frequently fail to preserve the underlying feature dependencies, resulting in suboptimal model performance [24]. Recent advances have introduced more sophisticated solutions, such as treating missing values as prediction targets [16] or employing two-stage approaches like DiffImpute [24]. These methods first learn the data distribution before generating imputed values. However, such two-stage approaches [14,21,25] introduce substantial computational overhead during inference, limiting their practical applicability, especially for large-scale datasets. This increased complexity also poses challenges for seamless integration into existing data processing pipelines. While random masking techniques during model training offer a simpler alternative to two-stage methods, they present their own set of limitations. Current approaches typically implement uniform masking across all feature types, failing to account for the fundamental distinctions between numerical and categorical features. Additionally, their use of fixed masking rates overlooks the varying importance of different features, disregarding crucial statistical properties such as information content and predictive power relative to the target variable. To overcome these challenges, we propose an efficient single-stage approach that integrates adaptive masking with learnable missing value representations and teacher-guided distillation. Our method employs feature-aware masking that distinguishes between numerical and categorical features, with masking probabilities dynamically adjusted based on feature-specific statistical properties. The learnable parameters for missing value representations adapt to the underlying data distribution through gradient-based optimization, enabling the model to discover context-aware representations that optimize downstream task performance. We further enhance this approach through distillation, where a teacher model pre-trained on complete data guides the training process on adaptively masked data.

In brief, the major contributions are three-fold. First, we introduce FT-Mamba and FT-Hyena which enhance sequence modeling capabilities for tabular data by incorporating feature-aware components. Second, we propose an adaptive masking method that enables model to handle missing value during the inference stage. It innovatively moves beyond conventional random masking by incorporating both feature-type awareness and statistical properties of the data. Third, we propose a learnable missing value representation with a corresponding distillation guidance. Rather than relying on static imputation, our approach employs trainable parameters that adapt to the underlying data distribution, guided by a teacher model pre-trained on complete data.

2 Methods

2.1 Network Architectures

While Mamba and Hyena have demonstrated their performance in sequence modeling tasks, their direct application to tabular data presents challenges for the inherent heterogeneity and complex inter-dependencies in tabular features. To address these limitations, we propose FT-Mamba and FT-Hyena, novel architectures that incorporate a feature-aware tokenizer specifically designed for tabular data processing, as illustrated in Fig. 1. Our architectures differs from traditional Mamba and Hyena models by moving beyond simple token-based processing to explicitly account for the diverse characteristics of tabular features.

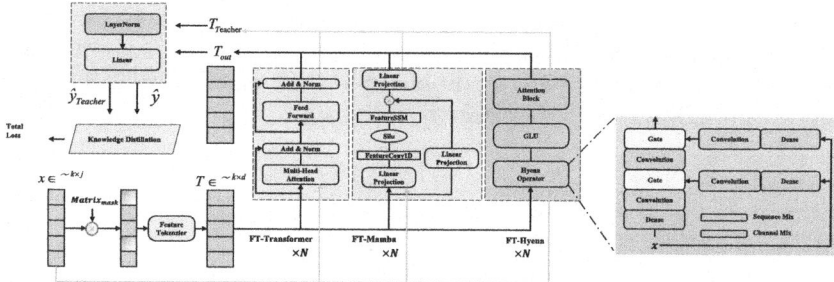

Fig. 1. Overview of the proposed architectures for tabular data processing. The diagram illustrates the common structure shared by the FT-Transformer, FT-Mamba, and FT-Hyena models, including the random masking process for handling missing values, the feature tokenizer for embedding generation, and the architecture-specific feature processing units (FPUs). The Transformer, Mamba, and Hyena blocks are shown in detail, highlighting their unique components such as multi-head attention, state space models, and Hyena operators. The final output layers for prediction are also depicted.

Feature-Aware Tokenizer. The feature-aware tokenizer transforms heterogeneous tabular features $x = [x_1, \cdots, x_k]$ into a unified embedding space $T \in \mathbb{R}^{k \times d}$, where k represents the number of features and d denotes the embedding dimension [6]. For each feature $x_j \in \mathbb{X}_j$, the embedding is computed as:

$$T_j = b_j + f_j(x_j) \in \mathbb{R}^d, \tag{1}$$

where b_j represents the learnable feature-specific bias and $f_j : \mathbb{X}_j \to \mathbb{R}^d$ implements type-specific embedding functions. For numerical features, f_j employs an adaptive linear projection $f_j(x_j) = W_j x_j$, where $W_j \in \mathbb{R}^{d \times 1}$ represents a learnable weight matrix. Categorical features are handled through a context-aware embedding lookup mechanism, expressed as $f_j(x_j) = E_j[x_j]$, with $E_j \in \mathbb{R}^{|C_j| \times d}$ representing the learnable embedding matrix for a feature with cardinality $|C_j|$.

Feature-Aware Encoder. Following afterwards the feature-aware tokenizer is the feature-aware encoders. Our encoder architecture enhances the standard Mamba and Hyena blocks with specialized modifications designed specifically for tabular data processing. In FT-Mamba, we extend the original Mamba block by integrating feature-aware SSMs [8] with custom convolutional layers that preserve and leverage feature relationships. The computational flow within each FT-Mamba encoder block follows:

$$y = \texttt{LayerNorm}(x + \texttt{FeatureSSM}(\texttt{FeatureConv1D}(x))),$$

where x and y represent the block's input and output respectively. The FeatureConv1D operation implements feature-type-specific processing through grouped convolutions:

$$\texttt{FeatureConv1D}(x) = \begin{cases} W_n * x & \text{for numerical features} \\ W_c * x & \text{for categorical features} \end{cases}, \tag{2}$$

where $*$ denotes the convolution operation, and W_n, W_c represent distinct learnable kernels optimized for numerical and categorical features respectively. The FeatureSSM component extends traditional SSMs by incorporating feature-type awareness through the following state equations:

$$\begin{aligned} h_{t+1} &= A(x_t)h_t + B(x_t)u_t \\ y_t &= C(x_t)h_t + D(x_t)u_t \end{aligned} \tag{3}$$

where the state matrices $A(x_t)$, $B(x_t)$, $C(x_t)$, and $D(x_t)$ are dynamically generated based on feature types according to

$$A(x_t) = \texttt{MLP}(\texttt{TypeEmb}(x_t)), \tag{4}$$

where $\texttt{TypeEmb}(x_t)$ produces feature-type-specific embeddings, which are then transformed by an MLP into appropriate state transition parameters.

For FT-Hyena, each block extends the original Hyena architecture with feature-specific gating mechanisms [20]:

$$y = x + \texttt{FeatureGatedAttn}(\texttt{FeatureGatedConv}(x)). \tag{5}$$

The FeatureGatedConv is formulated as

$$\texttt{FeatureGatedConv}(x) = \sigma(G(x)) \odot (W_h * x), \tag{6}$$

where σ represents the sigmoid activation function, W_h denotes the learnable convolution kernels, and $\odot$ indicates element-wise multiplication (*i.e.* Hadamard product). The feature-type-dependent gating function $G(x)$ is defined as:

$$G(x) = W_g[\texttt{TypeEmb}(x); x], \tag{7}$$

with W_g representing a learnable weight matrix that integrates feature-type embeddings with input features. The FeatureGatedAttn mechanism computes attention weights conditioned on feature types:

$$\texttt{FeatureGatedAttn}(x) = \texttt{softmax}(\frac{QK^T}{\sqrt{d}} + M(x))V, \tag{8}$$

where Q, K, and V are the query, key, and value matrices derived from linear transformations of input x, d is the dimensionality of the key vectors used to scale the attention scores, and $M(x) = W_m \texttt{TypeEmb}(x)$ is a mask of learned characteristic types with W_m being a learnable weight matrix.

2.2 Adaptive Masking for Missing Values

We introduce an adaptive masking strategy during model training to handle missing values during inference. This approach advances beyond traditional random masking techniques through two innovations that account for both feature types and their statistical properties. The first innovation is a type-aware masking scheme that distinguishes between numerical and categorical features, recognizing their inherent differences in representation and behavior. This contrasts with conventional approaches that apply uniform masking across all feature types. The masking operation can be formally expressed as:

$$x_{\text{masked}} = \text{stack}\left[x^{\text{num}} \odot M_{\text{mask}}^{\text{num}}, x^{\text{cat}} \odot M_{\text{mask}}^{\text{cat}}\right], \tag{9}$$

where x_{masked} are the resulting masked training data, x^{num} and x^{cat} represent the numerical and categorical characteristics in x, $M_{\text{mask}}^{\text{num}}$ and $M_{\text{mask}}^{\text{cat}}$ are binary random mask matrices for the numerical and categorical characteristics. The second innovation is a dynamic masking probability adjustment based on feature-specific statistical properties. Rather than employing fixed masking rates, we compute feature-specific probabilities using:

$$p_j = \alpha \cdot \texttt{entropy}(x_j) + \beta \cdot \texttt{correlation}(x_j, y), \tag{10}$$

where p_j denotes the masking probability for feature j. This probability is determined by two components: $\texttt{entropy}(x_j)$, which quantifies the information content of the feature, and $\texttt{correlation}(x_j, y)$, which measures its predictive power with respect to the target variable y. Correlation of these statistics help us to better filter the mask features for learning, and effectively avoid instability due to random masks during the training process. The learnable parameters α and β automatically balance these components during training to optimize the masking strategy. This adaptive approach ensures that the model learns robust representations by experiencing realistic missing-data scenarios during training, with masking patterns that reflect both the structural and statistical properties of the underlying data distribution.

2.3 Learnable Missing Value Representations with Teacher-Guided Training

We combine learnable missing value representations with distillation to improve the performance on missing values. Instead of using static replacement strategies (such as using all zeros), our method dynamically learns optimal representations for missing values through trainable parameters that adapt to the underlying data distribution. This approach can be formalized as:

$$x_{\text{masked}} = x \odot (1 - M) + \theta \odot M, \tag{11}$$

where $M = M_{\text{mask}}^{\text{cat}} + M_{\text{mask}}^{\text{num}}$ denotes the masking matrix and θ represents a learnable parameter matrix that adapts to different missing data patterns. Through gradient-based optimization, this formulation enables the model to discover context-aware representations for missing values that optimize downstream task performance. To further enhance the learning process, we incorporate distillation where a teacher model, pre-trained on complete data, guides the training of our primary model on data with adaptive masking. The combined loss function integrates both distillation and task-specific objectives:

$$\text{Loss} = \alpha \cdot F\left(\frac{y_{\text{teacher}}}{T}, \frac{y}{T}\right) + (1 - \alpha) \cdot F(y, \tilde{y}_{True}) \tag{12}$$

where α controls the contribution of knowledge distillation, T represents the temperature parameter that smooths the teacher's predictions, and F denotes the task-specific loss function.

3 Experiments

Datasets and Implementations. The experiments are conducted on five public tabular datasets, namely California Housing (CA) [17], Adult (AD) [12], Helena (HE) [9], Higgs Small (HI) [2], and Jannis (JA) [9]. Additionally, a synthetic dataset was used to assess the efficiency of each architecture in handling high-dimensional tabular data. All experiments were implemented with PyTorch 2.3.0, CUDA 11.8, and Python 3.9.19, on one NVIDIA A100 GPU.

Table 1. Performance comparison of three architectures. '↓' denotes RMSE for regression tasks, where the lower the better; '↑' denotes accuracy for classification task, where the higher the better. GPU memory on CA dataset for comparison.

Model	CA ↓	AD ↑	HE ↑	JA ↑	HI ↑	GPU Mem/Mibs
FT-Transformer	0.464	0.854	**0.389**	**0.729**	**0.730**	**627**
FT-Mamba	0.476	**0.860**	0.379	0.723	0.722	755
FT-Hyena	**0.452**	0.853	0.381	0.720	0.716	1431

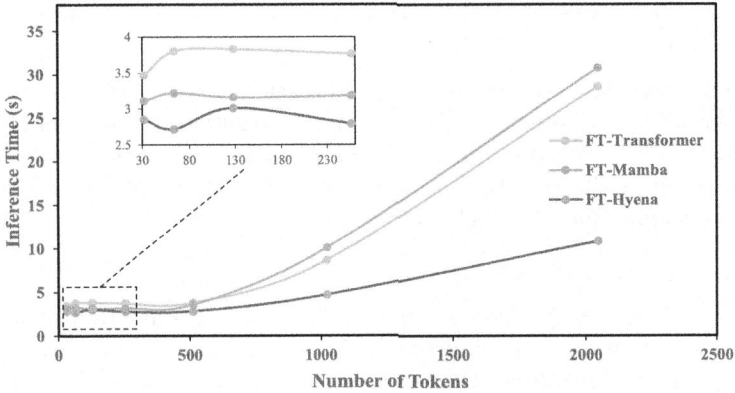

Fig. 2. Comparison of inference time for FT-Transformer, FT-Mamba, and FT-Hyena with the different numbers of token count (30-2000).

Performance Analysis of Model Architectures. Table 1 presents the performance comparison of FT-Mamba and FT-Hyena versus the FT-Transformer in five different data sets. Our results demonstrate that the proposed architectures achieve performance comparable to FT-Transformer. Specifically, FT-Hyena exhibits the best performance on the CA dataset, with an RMSE score of 0.452 outperforming both FT-Transformer and FT-Mamba. Conversely, FT-Mamba shows superior performance on the AD dataset, achieving the highest classification accuracy of 0.860. Notably, FT-Transformer maintains strong performance, excelling in three out of five datasets while consuming fewer GPU resources. These findings suggest that although our proposed architectures offer competitive alternatives, FT-Transformer remains a robust choice for specific tabular data tasks. However, with technological advancements, the dimensionality of data has grown exponentially, and efficiency is now often prioritized over marginal accuracy losses.

Computational Efficiency Analysis. Figure 2 illustrates the inference time performance of FT-Transformer, FT-Mamba, and FT-Hyena as the number of input dimensionality (*i.e.* number of features/token counts) increases from 30 to 2000. As shown in the inset graph, all three models perform similarly for lower token counts (30–230), though FT-Transformer is slower. Differences emerge when tokens exceed 500: FT-Hyena maintains the lowest inference time across all counts, scaling efficiently with only a modest increase at 2000 tokens (11s). FT-Transformer and FT-Mamba perform similarly up to 1000 tokens, but FT-Mamba slows slightly afterward. Both show steep inference time rises at 2000 tokens (31s for FT-Mamba, 29s for FT-Transformer), while FT-Hyena's time is less than half. This highlights its efficiency in high-dimensional tabular data.

Table 2. Comparison of adaptive masking with conventional imputation methods for handling missing values. Performance metrics (RMSE for CA, accuracy for others) are shown for FT-Transformer (Trans.), FT-Mamba (Mam.), and FT-Hyena with varying percentages of missing data during inference. 'Z' denotes zero value imputation, 'M' denotes mean value imputation, and 'K' denotes our proposed random masking method during training. The best results for each metric and missing data percentage are in **bold**.

		10%			20%			30%			40%			50%			60%			70%		
		Trans.	Mam.	Hyena	Trans.	Mam.	Hyena	Trans.	Mam.	Hyena	Trans.	Mam.	Hyena	Trans.	Mam.	Hyena	Trans.	Mam.	Hyena	Trans.	Mam.	Hyena
CA ↓	Z	1.025	1.080	0.840	1.246	1.334	1.030	1.348	1.440	1.157	1.406	1.490	1.240	1.411	1.506	1.267	1.423	1.515	1.340	1.427	1.520	1.406
	M	0.721	**0.726**	0.702	0.899	0.898	0.882	1.045	1.029	1.053	1.142	1.125	1.173	1.266	1.215	1.299	1.354	1.292	1.411	1.426	1.349	1.506
	K	**0.684**	0.765	**0.688**	**0.724**	**0.806**	**0.734**	**0.773**	**0.845**	**0.786**	**0.825**	**0.883**	**0.835**	**0.901**	**0.940**	**0.895**	**0.965**	**0.985**	**0.948**	**1.029**	**1.025**	**0.999**
AD ↑	Z	0.841	0.781	0.841	0.820	0.795	0.822	0.803	0.634	0.804	0.789	0.567	0.791	0.781	0.512	0.783	0.773	0.455	0.774	0.769	0.399	0.769
	M	0.847	**0.842**	0.844	**0.834**	0.826	0.831	0.823	0.813	0.819	0.809	0.803	0.808	0.802	0.798	0.815	0.792	0.788	0.803	0.782	0.779	0.790
	K	**0.850**	0.838	**0.849**	0.843	**0.832**	**0.843**	0.834	**0.827**	**0.836**	0.827	**0.817**	**0.824**	0.820	**0.813**	**0.815**	0.807	**0.802**	**0.803**	0.795	**0.790**	**0.790**
HE ↑	Z	0.245	0.264	0.267	0.163	0.191	0.198	0.114	0.141	0.152	0.079	0.103	0.113	0.055	0.079	0.086	0.040	0.058	0.069	0.026	0.039	0.054
	M	**0.331**	**0.308**	**0.312**	0.276	0.248	0.251	0.229	0.203	0.201	0.183	0.161	0.162	0.140	0.123	0.123	0.109	0.098	0.097	0.082	0.074	0.076
	K	0.261	0.268	0.284	**0.257**	**0.259**	**0.275**	**0.258**	**0.247**	**0.266**	**0.240**	**0.233**	**0.253**	**0.221**	**0.214**	**0.230**	**0.206**	**0.193**	**0.202**	**0.185**	**0.167**	**0.167**
JA ↑	Z	0.626	0.657	0.647	0.564	0.606	0.596	0.524	0.561	0.552	0.495	0.529	0.521	0.476	0.501	0.498	0.462	0.478	0.483	0.448	0.461	0.464
	M	**0.706**	**0.693**	**0.684**	**0.671**	0.662	0.639	0.634	0.624	0.590	0.598	0.576	0.535	0.551	0.530	0.478	0.510	0.480	0.422	0.451	0.424	0.363
	K	0.666	0.688	0.675	0.659	**0.679**	**0.667**	**0.648**	**0.663**	**0.656**	**0.639**	**0.650**	**0.642**	**0.616**	**0.616**	**0.617**	**0.593**	**0.597**	**0.590**	**0.573**	**0.545**	**0.558**
HI ↑	Z	0.665	0.677	0.681	0.624	0.643	0.644	0.587	0.610	0.613	0.562	0.582	0.584	0.558	0.562	0.561	0.542	0.543	0.543	0.530	0.523	0.527
	M	**0.706**	**0.702**	**0.696**	**0.680**	**0.679**	0.668	0.653	0.653	0.646	0.632	0.629	0.624	0.616	0.620	0.608	0.600	0.600	0.592	0.578	0.582	0.576
	K	0.682	0.688	0.683	0.673	0.676	**0.669**	**0.664**	**0.660**	**0.657**	**0.645**	**0.643**	**0.643**	**0.631**	**0.632**	**0.630**	**0.612**	**0.614**	**0.612**	**0.591**	**0.593**	**0.596**

Analysis of Missing Value Handling Strategies. Table 2 presents a comparison of our proposed adaptive masking method without learnable parameters and

Table 3. Impact of random masking on FT-Hyena's performance with Missing Data. RMSE results on the CA dataset for different masking probabilities during training and missing values percentages during inference. Lower values (↓) indicate better performance. The best results for each column are in **bold**.

Masking Probability	Percentage of Missing Values in Inference						
	10%	20%	30%	40%	50%	60%	70%
5%	**0.660**	**0.707**	**0.761**	**0.819**	0.896	0.959	1.033
10%	0.688	0.734	0.786	0.835	0.895	0.948	0.999
15%	0.707	0.748	0.790	0.830	**0.895**	**0.941**	**0.993**
20%	0.712	0.750	0.792	0.832	0.896	0.945	0.995
30%	0.738	0.782	0.829	0.867	0.926	0.969	1.015
40%	0.797	0.831	0.865	0.898	0.949	0.986	1.024

knowledge distillation against the conventional imputation methods *i.e.* zero imputation (Z) and mean imputation (M). We evaluated these methods on three model architectures: FT-Transformer, FT-Mamba, and FT-Hyena, with varying percentages of missing values during inference, ranging from 10% to 70%. Our findings demonstrate the superior performance of the adaptive masking method across most scenarios. For the CA dataset, adaptive masking consistently outperforms both zero and mean imputation across all percentages of missing data for all three models. The improvement is notable at higher missing data rates, with RMSE reductions of up to 30% compared to zero imputation and 15% compared to mean imputation at 70% missing data. In the AD dataset, adaptive masking shows a slight but consistent advantage over mean imputation, particularly as the percentage of missing data increases. It also outperforms zero imputation, especially for the FT-Mamba. Across all datasets, the adaptive masking method exhibits consistency, often achieving the best results as the percentage of missing data increases. Finally, we compare the proposed methods in terms of full setting (with adaptive masking, learnable missing value representation and distillation) with more established imputation methods in Table 4. It demonstrates the exceptional effectiveness of our approach across all missing data scenarios. On the CA dataset, our method consistently achieves the lowest RMSE values, ranging from 0.677 at 10% missing data to 0.997 at 70% missing data. This performance represents a substantial improvement over traditional statistical methods like mean imputation and more sophisticated approaches like MICE. Notably, our method outperforms recent deep learning-based solutions, including GAIN and various DiffImpute [24] implementations, with improvements of up to 30% in RMSE across different missing data proportions. The performance advantage becomes particularly pronounced as the percentage of missing values increases, with our method maintaining robust performance even under extreme conditions where 70% of data is missing.

Table 4. Comparison of missing value handling capability on CA dataset in terms of RMSE. For each missing setting, the best results are in **bold**.

Imputation Methods	10%	20%	30%	40%	50%	60%	70%
Mean Imputation	0.870	1.011	1.097	1.168	1.218	1.253	1.268
Median Imputation	0.898	1.044	1.131	1.203	1.248	1.275	1.279
Mode Imputation	0.998	1.332	1.355	1.642	1.558	1.627	1.399
0 Imputation	1.166	1.451	1.669	1.836	1.963	2.073	2.148
1 Imputation	1.350	1.652	1.808	1.888	1.926	1.952	1.981
LOCF Imputation	1.534	1.801	1.946	1.144	1.723	1.752	1.782
NOCB Imputation	1.531	1.651	1.692	1.419	1.744	1.778	1.802
MICE (linear)	0.764	1.025	1.954	1.035	1.146	1.183	1.203
GAIN	0.846	0.947	0.999	1.154	1.240	1.311	1.344
DiffImpute w/ MLP	0.998	1.232	1.415	1.567	1.701	1.823	1.926
DiffImpute w/ ResNet	0.791	0.891	0.963	1.038	1.123	1.256	1.502
DiffImpute w/ Transformer	0.761	0.836	0.895	0.963	1.028	1.087	1.146
DiffImpute w/ U-Net	1.273	1.612	1.847	2.014	2.131	2.226	2.292
Ours	**0.677**	**0.707**	**0.769**	**0.819**	**0.880**	**0.933**	**0.997**

Ablation Study. We conducted comprehensive ablation studies to evaluate two aspects of our approach, namely the impact of masking probability during training and the contribution of individual components (missing value representation and distillation) to model performance. Our first analysis investigated how varying masking probabilities during training affect FT-Hyena's ability to handle different proportions of missing data during inference on the CA dataset, as shown in Table 3. The results reveal distinct optimal masking strategies depending on the expected proportion of missing values during deployment. For lower percentages of missing values (10-40%), a 5% masking probability during training yields the best performance, with RMSE values ranging from 0.660 to 0.819. This suggests that for datasets with a moderate amount of missing data, a conservative masking strategy during training is more effective. As the percentage of missing values increases beyond 40%, we observe a shift in the optimal masking probability. For 50-70% missing data, a 15% masking probability during training produces the best results, with RMSE values between 0.895 and 0.993. This indicates that for datasets with a high proportion of missing values, a more aggressive masking strategy during training better prepares the model to handle incomplete data during inference. Interestingly, very high masking probabilities (30-40%) during training consistently lead to poorer performance across all levels of missing value. This suggests that there is a balance to be struck, while some masking is beneficial for robustness, excessive masking can hinder the model's ability to learn useful patterns from the data. Our second analysis, presented in Table 5, examined the individual and combined effects of learnable parameters and knowledge distillation on FT-Hyena's performance. The learnable missing value representation alone improves performance by 2-4.5% across different missing data scenarios, with particularly strong gains under high missing data ratios. Distillation in isolation provides improvements of 1.3–3.9%, showing particular strength in moderate missing data scenarios. The combination of both components yields the strongest results, delivering performance improvements of up to 5.4% and showing particular effectiveness in scenarios with high proportions of missing data. These findings yield practical insights. First, masking probability during training should be calibrated based on the expected proportion of missing values in the target application. Second, while both learnable missing value representation and distillation provide individual benefits, their combination offers the most robust solution for handling missing values in real-world applications.

Table 5. Impact of learnable missing value representation and distillation on FT-Hyena's performance with missing data. We report the results on the CA dataset in terms of RMSE for different masking probabilities during training and inference. Lower values (↓) indicate better performance. The best results for each column are in **bold**.

Learnable Parameters	Knowledge Distillation	Percentage of Missing Values in Inference						
		10%	20%	30%	40%	50%	60%	70%
✗	✗	0.688	0.734	0.786	0.835	0.895	0.948	0.999
✓	✗	0.657	0.704	0.754	0.805	0.881	0.929	0.973
✗	✓	0.661	0.712	0.754	0.811	0.874	0.935	0.981
✓	✓	**0.651**	**0.697**	**0.747**	**0.799**	**0.860**	**0.911**	**0.966**

4 Conclusion

The widespread adoption of DL approaches across tabular data has been hindered by challenges in efficiently processing high-dimensional tabular datasets and handling missing values effectively. Hence, we introduce FT-Mamba and FT-Hyena architectures that enhance sequence modeling with feature-aware components, with FT-Hyena achieving twice the processing efficiency of existing approaches while maintaining competitive performance. We propose adaptive masking with learnable representations and teacher-guided distillation to handle missing values, enabling robust performance without separate imputation steps. Future work could extend these approaches to other deep learning architectures and explore their theoretical foundations to develop even more effective solutions for tabular data analysis.

References

1. Ahamed, M.A., Cheng, Q.: Mambatab: a plug-and-play model for learning tabular data. In: 2024 IEEE 7th International Conference on Multimedia Information Processing and Retrieval (MIPR), pp. 369–375. IEEE (2024)

2. Baldi, P., Sadowski, P., Whiteson, D.: Searching for exotic particles in high-energy physics with deep learning. Nat. Commun. **5**(1), 4308 (2014)
3. Baraldi, A.N., Enders, C.K.: An introduction to modern missing data analyses. J. Sch. Psychol. **48**(1), 5–37 (2010)
4. Borisov, V., Leemann, T., et al.: Deep neural networks and tabular data: a survey. IEEE Trans. Neural Netw. Learn. Syst. (2022)
5. Breiman, L.: Random forests. Mach. Learn. **45**, 5–32 (2001)
6. Chen, H., Perozzi, B., Al-Rfou, R., Skiena, S.: A tutorial on network embeddings. arXiv preprint arXiv:1808.02590 (2018)
7. Gorishniy, Y., Rubachev, I., Khrulkov, V., Babenko, A.: Revisiting deep learning models for tabular data. Adv. Neural. Inf. Process. Syst. **34**, 18932–18943 (2021)
8. Gu, A., Dao, T.: Mamba: Linear-time sequence modeling with selective state spaces. arXiv preprint arXiv:2312.00752 (2023)
9. Guyon, I., et al.: Analysis of the automl challenge series. Autom. Mach. Learn. **177**, 177–219 (2019)
10. He, K., Zhang, X., et al.: Deep residual learning for image recognition. In: Proceedings of the IEEE Conference on Computer Vision and Pattern Recognition, pp. 770–778 (2016)
11. Johnstone, I.M., Titterington, D.M.: Statistical challenges of high-dimensional data (2009)
12. Kohavi, R., et al.: A decision-tree hybrid: Scaling up the accuracy of naive-bayes classifiers In: Kdd, vol. 96, pp. 202–207 (1996)
13. Kotsiantis, S.B.: Decision trees: a recent overview. Artif. Intell. Rev. **39**, 261–283 (2013)
14. Lloret Carbonell, E., Shen, Y., Yang, X., Ke, J.: Covid-19 pneumonia classification with transformer from incomplete modalities. In: International Conference on Medical Image Computing and Computer-Assisted Intervention, pp. 379–388. Springer (2023). https://doi.org/10.1007/978-3-031-43904-9_37
15. Natekin, A., Knoll, A.: Gradient boosting machines, a tutorial. Front. Neurorobot. **7**, 21 (2013)
16. Neves, D.T., Alves, J., Naik, M.G., Proença, A.J., Prasser, F.: From missing data imputation to data generation. J. Comput. Sci. **61**, 101640 (2022)
17. Pace, R.K., Barry, R.: Sparse spatial autoregressions. Statist. Probability Lett. **33**(3), 291–297 (1997)
18. Paliwal, S.S., Vishwanath, D., et al.: Tablenet: deep learning model for end-to-end table detection and tabular data extraction from scanned document images. In: 2019 International Conference on Document Analysis and Recognition (ICDAR), pp. 128–133. IEEE (2019)
19. Pinkus, A.: Approximation theory of the mlp model in neural networks. Acta Numer **8**, 143–195 (1999)
20. Poli, M., et al.: Hyena hierarchy: towards larger convolutional language models. In: International Conference on Machine Learning, pp. 28043–28078. PMLR (2023)
21. Shen, Y., He, G., Unberath, M.: Promptable counterfactual diffusion model for unified brain tumor segmentation and generation with mris. arXiv preprint arXiv:2407.12678 (2024)
22. Thielmann, A.F., Kumar, M., Weisser, C., Reuter, A., Säfken, B., Samiee, S.: Mambular: A sequential model for tabular deep learning. arXiv preprint arXiv:2408.06291 (2024)
23. Vaswani, A., Shazeer, N., et al.: Attention is all you need. Adv. Neural Inform. Process. Syst. **30** (2017)

24. Wen, Y., Yi, K., Ke, J., Shen, Y.: Diffimpute: Tabular data imputation with denoising diffusion probabilistic model. arXiv preprint arXiv:2403.13863 (2024)
25. Zhang, D., Wang, C., Chen, T., Chen, W., Shen, Y.: Scalable swin transformer network for brain tumor segmentation from incomplete mri modalities. Artif. Intell. Med. **149**, 102788 (2024)

Topic-Driven Hyper-relational Knowledge Graphs with Adaptive Reconstruction for Multi-hop Question Answering Using LLMs

Yingying Zhang, Bo Cheng(✉), and Yuli Chen

State Key Laboratory of Networking and Switching Technology, Beijing University of Posts and Telecommunications, Beijing 100876, China
{YingyingZhang,chengbo,chenyuli}@bupt.edu.cn

Abstract. Large language models (LLMs) perform well on single-hop question answering (QA) tasks but face significant challenges in multi-hop QA tasks that require multi-step reasoning across multiple paragraphs. Although prompt-based LLMs leveraging the chain-of-thought (CoT) mechanism have improved multi-hop reasoning, they still suffer from performance degradation and hallucinations when critical knowledge is missing or outdated. To address these challenges, we propose a novel Topic-driven Hyper-relational Knowledge Graph with an Adaptive Reconstruction method that dynamically retrieves and prunes contextually relevant facts. Our approach employs a topic-driven pruning strategy to refine relevant facts and reduce noise, thus improving the reasoning ability of LLMs. Additionally, we introduce an adaptive reconstruction mechanism that dynamically supplements missing knowledge and optimizes the input during the reasoning process, preventing interruptions in reasoning chains. Experiments on the HotpotQA and MuSiQue datasets demonstrate that our approach significantly outperforms state-of-the-art baselines across multiple metrics, achieving superior results and validating its effectiveness in tackling complex multi-hop reasoning challenges.

Keywords: Multi-hop Question Answering · Hyper-Relational Knowledge Graphs · Topic-Driven Pruning · Adaptive Reconstruction

1 Introduction

Multi-hop question answering (QA) is a critical and challenging task in the field of natural language processing (NLP), which has gained significant attention in recent years. The task aims to enable models to integrate information across multiple paragraphs and perform deep comprehension and multi-step reasoning to answer complex questions and identify relevant chains of evidence [11,24]. This task not only tests the model's language understanding capabilities but also demands advanced abilities in information integration and reasoning. Traditionally, researchers have applied graph neural networks (GNNs) to multi-hop QA tasks [4,7,17]. In recent years, with the growing capabilities of large language models (LLMs), researchers have begun exploring the integration of LLMs with knowledge graphs to enhance performance on this task [9,15].

LLMs have made significant progress in natural language understanding and reasoning tasks [1,21], demonstrating strong performance on single-hop QA tasks [5,28]. However, when dealing with multi-hop QA tasks that require integrating information and reasoning across multiple steps, especially in scenarios that require a deep understanding of multiple entities and their relationships, LLMs still face limitations [9,26]. Multi-hop reasoning tasks not only depend on complex information integration but also demand strong contextual understanding and reasoning abilities.

Although LLMs enhanced by the chain-of-thought (CoT) mechanism [23] and its variants (CoT-Sc [22] and ToT [25]) can generate better answers and reasoning chains, their performance significantly decreases when the required knowledge is beyond the model's scope or outdated. Moreover, end-to-end methods that rely solely on CoT are prone to hallucinations, leading to incorrect reasoning results. To address this issue, StructQA [9] utilizes information extraction (IE) techniques to extract structured knowledge from unstructured text and construct semantic graphs, which are then combined with CoT reasoning to generate higher-quality and more faithful reasoning chains. However, the semantic graph structure in StructQA is not tailored to the question, failing to capture the essential contextual information, thereby reducing LLMs' performance. Additionally, StructQA feeds the constructed semantic graphs and the original text into the LLMs, causing prompt lengthening and information redundancy, limiting further performance improvements.

To overcome these challenges, we propose a novel method for multi-hop QA that constructs a context-aware hyper-relational knowledge graph centered around a topic-driven mechanism, aiming to explore the potential of LLMs in complex reasoning tasks. Specifically, we first select a relevant subset of paragraphs from the candidate set and extract context-aware structured information to build the hyper-relational knowledge graph. We then apply a topic-driven pruning strategy to refine and optimize the knowledge graph, preserving key information related to the question and eliminating redundant or irrelevant nodes and facts. Subsequently, the question and the pruned knowledge graph are then input to LLMs for reasoning. To further enhance reasoning robustness, we design an adaptive reconstruction mechanism that dynamically supplements missing knowledge and optimizes inputs, addressing disruptions in the reasoning chain due to insufficient information, thus further improving LLMs' performance on complex reasoning tasks. The main contributions of our work are as follows:

- We propose an effective and novel approach for multi-hop QA by constructing a context-aware hyper-relational knowledge graph that dynamically retrieves and integrates contextually relevant information, enabling efficient multi-step reasoning across multiple paragraphs.
- We introduce a topic-driven pruning strategy to refine the hyper-relational knowledge graph, retaining only the most relevant information to the question and eliminating redundant or irrelevant nodes.

– We present an adaptive reconstruction mechanism that dynamically supplements missing knowledge and optimizes inputs, effectively addressing reasoning interruptions due to insufficient information and improving the robustness and accuracy of LLMs in reasoning tasks.
 – We conduct extensive experiments on the HotpotQA [24] and MuSiQue [20] datasets, and experimental results demonstrate that our proposed method significantly outperforms state-of-the-art baselines [9] across multiple metrics, validating its effectiveness in multi-hop reasoning tasks.

2 Related Work

2.1 Multi-hop Question Answering

Multi-hop QA is a challenging task that requires integrating information across multiple paragraphs and performing multi-step reasoning to answer complex questions [9,11,26]. In recent years, high-quality multi-hop QA datasets such as HotpotQA [24], 2WikiMultiHopQA [6], and MuSiQue [20] have driven significant advancements in multi-hop QA models. The previous methods can be divided into three categories. Question Decomposition Methods, which break complex questions into simpler sub-questions (e.g., DecompRC [12], QFE [13], ONUS [16]). Graph-based Methods, which construct graphs from questions and context, apply GNNs for reasoning (e.g., DFGN [17], HGN [4], BFR-Graph [7], AMGN [8]). Graph-free Methods, which do not rely on graph structures and perform reasoning directly through the model (e.g., C2F Reader [18], FE2H [10], R^3 [27], Beam Retrieval [26]). Unlike these methods, our work proposes a topic-driven strategy to construct hyper-relational knowledge graphs, providing a new perspective for addressing the multi-hop QA task.

2.2 Knowledge Graphs for Multi-hop QA

In multi-hop QA, researchers often construct graphs by extracting structured knowledge from raw text to support reasoning and information integration. Traditional knowledge graphs represent documents, paragraphs, sentences, and entities as nodes, with edges defined by co-occurrences or logical relationships [4,8,17]. However, these edges often lack semantic depth and fail to capture complex reasoning relationships. To address this limitation, KIFGraph [3] introduces semantic edges derived from structured knowledge to enhance reasoning between nodes. Similarly, StructQA [9] employs semantic graphs to enhance the model's multi-hop reasoning capabilities. However, existing semantic graphs rely on simple triples (e_s, r, e_o). In contrast, our hyper-relational knowledge graphs incorporate contextual qualifiers (e.g., time, topic) to capture deeper semantic information, thereby improving the quality of inputs to LLMs.

3 Methodology

In this section, we propose a topic-driven and adaptive hyper-relational knowledge graph approach based on LLMs for complex reasoning in multi-hop QA

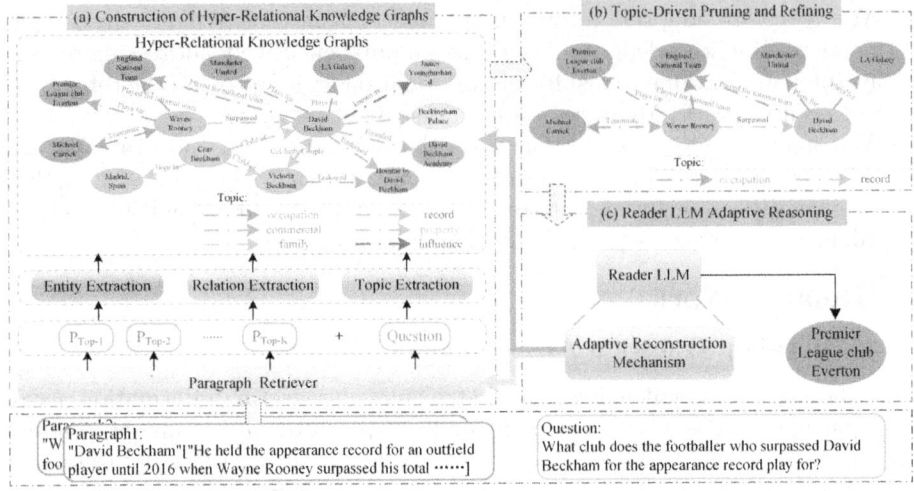

Fig. 1. An overview of our method. (a) Construction of hyper-relational knowledge graphs (Sect. 3.1). (b) Topic-driven pruning and refining (Sect. 3.2). (c) Reader LLM adaptive reasoning (Sect. 3.3).

tasks. Figure 1 illustrates the overall architecture of the proposed method. Specifically, we first filter a subset of paragraphs relevant to the question from the candidate paragraph set and extract context-aware structured information to construct the hyper-relational knowledge graph (Sect. 3.1). Next, we employ a topic-driven mechanism to prune and refine the hyper-relational knowledge graph, retaining only the most relevant information to the question and eliminating redundant or irrelevant nodes (Sect. 3.2). Then, the question and the pruned hyper-relational knowledge graph are fed into the LLM-based reader for reasoning. During the reasoning process, we introduce an adaptive reconstruction mechanism that dynamically fills in missing information and optimizes the input, addressing issues of reasoning chain breakage or insufficient information, thereby enhancing the robustness of LLMs in complex reasoning tasks (Sect. 3.3).

3.1 Construction of Hyper-relational Knowledge Graphs

Paragraph Retrieval. In multi-hop reasoning tasks, constructing a high-quality knowledge graph is a crucial step for enabling multi-step semantic reasoning. Although multi-hop QA datasets typically provide multiple candidate paragraphs for each question, only a small subset is actually relevant during the reasoning process. Therefore, to improve the efficiency and quality of subsequent knowledge extraction and graph construction, we first employ BM25 as a retriever to select the Top-K most relevant paragraphs to the question Q from the candidate paragraph set P.

$$P_{Top-K} = BM25 - Retriever(Q, P) \qquad (1)$$

Entity and Relation Extraction. Next, we utilize LLMs to extract entity-relation triples (e_s, r, e_o) from the retrieved paragraph set P_{Top-K}. To ensure both the quality and consistency of the extracted triples, we design a structured prompt template that guides the model to output triples in the desired format. The specific prompt template is as follows:

Task:
> *Comprehensively extract ALL the triples (subject, relation, object) from below given paragraph.*

Paragraphs:
> *< paragraph title >: < paragraph text >*

Triples :
> $(< subject\ e_s^1 >, < relation\ r^1 >, < object\ e_o^1 >)$
> $(< subject\ e_s^2 >, < relation\ r^2 >, < object\ e_o^2 >)$
> ......

Topic Extraction and Graphs Construction. To more effectively capture the complex multiple relationships between entities, we further introduce topic information T. Specifically, we first utilize LLMs to extract topics from the sentence containing each triple (e_s, r, e_o) to identify its core semantics. Then, we associate each triple with the most relevant contextual topic t to enrich the context of the triple and enhance the semantic expression capability of the knowledge graph. Finally, the hyper-relational knowledge graph $\mathcal{H}$ is defined as:

$$\mathcal{H} = \{(e_s, r, e_o, t) \mid e_s, e_o \in E, r \in R, t \in T\} \tag{2}$$

where E, R, and T denote the sets of entities, relations, and topics, respectively. This formulation not only links the subject e_s and object e_o via the relation r but also integrates the topic attributes t of the corresponding sentences, thereby embedding richer contextual semantic information into the knowledge graph.

3.2 Topic-Driven Pruning and Refining

After the construction of the hyper-relational knowledge graph, the next step is to prune and refine it to make it more effective for multi-hop reasoning. Although the entities and relations in the knowledge graph are relevant to the question, there may still be some information that is unrelated to the question's answer. For example, if the question asks about a person's occupation, the information about that person's hobbies captured in the knowledge graph does not help answer the question. To remove such redundant and irrelevant information, we design a topic-driven pruning mechanism that filters the nodes and edges in the hyper-relational knowledge graph based on the question's topic, retaining only the parts that are highly relevant to the question topic and thus reducing interference from redundant information.

Assuming the core topic extracted from the question Q is t_Q. We aim to retain the triples highly relevant to the topic t_Q in the knowledge graph. To measure the relevance of each hyper-triple (e_s, r, e_o, t) to the question topic t_Q, we define a relevance metric function S:

$$S\left((e_s, r, e_o, t), t_Q\right) = Sim\left(t, t_Q\right) \tag{3}$$

$$Sim\left(t, t_Q\right) = \frac{v_t \cdot v_{t_Q}}{\|v_t\| \|v_{t_Q}\|} \tag{4}$$

where $\cdot$ denotes the dot product, $\|\cdot\|$ denotes the Euclidean norm, and v_t and v_{t_Q} denote the embedding of the topic t and the question topic t_Q, respectively.

Based on the relevance metric S, we prune the hyper-relational knowledge graph by retaining only those hyper-triples with a relevance score greater than or equal to a predefined threshold τ_{sim} for further reasoning:

$$\mathcal{H}_{refined} = \{(e_s, r, e_o, t) \in \mathcal{H} | S\left((e_s, r, e_o, t), t_Q\right) \geq \tau_{sim}\} \tag{5}$$

Through this pruning and refinement process, we obtain a hyper-relational knowledge graph that is highly relevant to the question, providing effective knowledge support for the subsequent reasoning stage and enhancing the efficiency and accuracy of LLMs in generating answers.

3.3 Reader LLM Adaptive Reasoning

Reader LLM Prompt Construction. We then feed the question Q and the pruned hyper-relational knowledge graph $\mathcal{H}_{refined}$ into the reader LLM to perform multi-step reasoning and generate the answer. Given that LLMs are optimized for processing natural language, we linearize the hyper-relational graph $\mathcal{H}_{refined}$ into a structured textual format. Specifically, each hyper-triple (e_s, r, e_o, t) is transformed into a natural sentence such as: *Topic t, the relationship between subject e_s and object e_o is r*. These generated sentences are then ranked by their semantic relevance to the question Q, with more relevant facts positioned earlier in the input. This relevance-based ordering enhances the LLM's focus on salient information and reduces answer bias during generation.

Adaptive Reconstruction Mechanism. While information extraction and topic-driven pruning significantly reduce noise, information gaps in multi-hop reasoning may still hinder LLM performance. To mitigate this, we introduce a dynamic adaptive reconstruction mechanism that iteratively enriches the input prompt by identifying and compensating for missing facts during the reasoning process, thereby improving robustness and answer accuracy.

As the LLM processes the input graph, it may recognize missing facts involving certain named entities or topics. When such gaps are detected, the adaptive mechanism is triggered. We retrieve a set of relevant hyper-triples $\mathcal{H}_{missing}$ from the original hyper-relational graph $\mathcal{H}$, corresponding to the missing elements. These are then integrated with the pruned graph $\mathcal{H}_{refined}$ to construct an enhanced input for subsequent reasoning.

$$\mathcal{H}'_{refined} = \mathcal{H}_{refined} \cup \mathcal{H}_{missing} \tag{6}$$

If the missing facts cannot be supplemented from the existing hyper-relational knowledge graph $\mathcal{H}$, we fall back to the candidate paragraph set and perform global retrieval. We re-extract hyper-triples $\mathcal{H}_{missing}$ from paragraphs containing the relevant named entities or topics, and integrate them into the original knowledge graph as follows:

$$\mathcal{H}' = \mathcal{H} \cup \mathcal{H}_{missing} \tag{7}$$

The updated graph $\mathcal{H}'$ is subsequently pruned to generate a new refined version $\mathcal{H}'_{refined} = Prune(\mathcal{H}')$, which is used as the final input. This mechanism ensures both the completeness of the knowledge graph and the provision of more focused and relevant reasoning inputs.

4 Experiments

4.1 Experimental Settings

Datasets and Metrics. We evaluate the effectiveness of our proposed method on the HotpotQA [24] and MuSiQue [20] datasets, both of which are widely used multi-hop QA datasets in state-of-the-art multi-hop QA baselines. Table 1 shows the statistics for these two datasets. For each question, HotpotQA provides 10 candidate paragraphs, while MuSiQue provides 20 candidate paragraphs. In the experiments, we follow the strategy outlined in [9,19], randomly selecting 500 questions from the original dev set of each dataset for hyperparameter tuning. Additionally, we randomly sampled 2000 questions from the dev set to construct the test sets. To comprehensively evaluate the model's performance, we use four widely adopted metrics: Exact Match (EM), F1, Precision, and Recall [9,11], which measure the accuracy and completeness of the model's predicted answers.

Table 1. Statistics of benchmark datasets.

Datasets	#Train	#Dev	#Test
HotpotQA	90564	7405	7405
MuSiQue	19938	2417	2459

Baselines. To evaluate the effectiveness of our proposed method, we compared it with the following baseline approaches: (*i*) **Base (only ques)**: LLM receives only the question, assessing its reasoning ability solely based on internal knowledge without any external information. (*ii*) **Base (ques + paras)**: LLM receives the question and supporting paragraphs, evaluating its performance using unstructured external information. (*iii*) **StructQA** [9]: utilizes semantic graphs to improve multi-hop reasoning by guiding models to generate higher-quality and more faithful reasoning chains. (*iv*) **Holmes** [15]: Utilizes a context-aware hyper-relational knowledge graph to improve the multi-hop reasoning performance of large language models.

Implementation Details. In this experiment, we selected two mainstream LLMs as reader LLMs for comparative evaluation: GPT-3.5 [2] and GPT-4 [14]. To ensure fairness in the information processing stage across different models, we consistently used OpenAI's GPT-3.5-turbo[1] for structured knowledge extraction in all models. All experiments were conducted on 2 × Tesla A40 GPUs (80 GB total memory). For the HotpotQA [24] and MuSiQue [20] datasets, we set the Top-K values to 4 and 5, respectively, to control the number of paragraphs involved in graph construction based on dataset complexity. During the pruning phase, we set the similarity threshold τ_{sim} to 0.4 to retain only the hyper-triples most relevant to the question topic, effectively balancing noise reduction with reasoning coverage. We further limited the maximum number of reconstruction iterations to 2, ensuring bounded computational cost while the model refines the reasoning path when necessary.

4.2 Experimental Results

Table 2 reports the performance of our method on HotpotQA and MuSiQue using GPT-3.5-turbo as the reader. The results demonstrate that our approach achieves state-of-the-art or competitive performance across all metrics, confirming its strong overall effectiveness in multi-hop QA. Compared to StructQA [9] and Holmes [15], which also leverage structured knowledge, our method shows clear advantages, particularly in F1 and Recall on both datasets. These results confirm the efficacy of the topic-driven pruning strategy and adaptive reconstruction mechanism in jointly minimizing semantic redundancy and improving reasoning performance. By dynamically selecting and refining the most relevant information, our method furnishes the LLM with a concise and semantically complete context, enabling more faithful and precise answer generation.

Table 2. Performance comparison on HotpotQA and MuSiQue datasets.

Datasets	HotpotQA				MuSiQue			
Methods	EM	F1	Precision	Recall	EM	F1	Precision	Recall
Base (only ques)	0.22	0.38	0.36	0.41	0.08	0.17	0.19	0.16
Base (ques + paras)	0.52	0.68	0.66	0.71	0.31	0.47	0.44	0.51
StructQA [9]	0.57	0.68	0.65	0.72	0.33	0.49	0.45	**0.53**
Holmes [15]	0.58	0.70	**0.68**	0.73	**0.35**	0.49	0.46	0.52
Our Method	**0.59**	**0.72**	0.67	**0.78**	**0.35**	**0.50**	0.47	**0.53**

To evaluate the impact of different LLMs as readers on the performance of multi-hop QA tasks, we compared GPT-3.5-turbo and GPT-4-turbo readers on the HotpotQA dataset, as shown in Table 3. The experimental results indicate that our method significantly outperforms the current state-of-the-art baseline method, StructQA [9], regardless of whether GPT-3.5-turbo or GPT-4-turbo is used. Moreover, GPT-4-turbo demonstrates overall superior performance compared to GPT-3.5-turbo, further validating the potential of more powerful LLMs

---
[1] https://platform.openai.com/docs/models/gpt-3.5-turbo.

Table 3. Performance comparison of different LLMs as readers.

Methods	EM	F1	Precision	Recall
Reader LLM: gpt-3.5-turbo				
StructQA	0.57	0.68	0.65	0.72
Our Method	**0.59**	**0.72**	**0.67**	**0.78**
Reader LLM: gpt-4-turbo				
StructQA	0.63	**0.80**	**0.78**	0.82
Our Method	**0.64**	**0.80**	0.76	**0.85**

in enhancing multi-hop reasoning capabilities. Additionally, these results highlight the adaptability and robustness of our method across different model settings, demonstrating its ability to effectively leverage the capabilities of different LLMs for improved reasoning performance.

4.3 Ablation Studies

The Effect of Different Components. To assess the contribution of each module, we conducted ablation experiments on the HotpotQA dataset by comparing the full model with its variants. As shown in Table 4, removing any individual component leads to a noticeable performance degradation. Notably, excluding the topic-driven pruning module results in a substantial drop in EM and Precision, underscoring its effectiveness in eliminating irrelevant information and enhancing answer accuracy. Additionally, the absence of the adaptive reconstruction mechanism most severely affects Recall, emphasizing its role in supplementing missing facts and increasing reasoning coverage. These results comprehensively validate the effectiveness of the proposed model's three key components.

Table 4. Ablation study of different components in our Method.

Methods	EM	F1	Precision	Recall
Our Method	**0.59**	**0.72**	**0.67**	**0.78**
w/o Hyper-relational Knowledge Graph	0.54	0.66	0.62	0.71
w/o Topic-driven Pruning	0.51	0.64	0.57	0.73
w/o Adaptive Reconstruction	0.53	0.65	0.64	0.67

The Effect of the Parameter Top-K. To analyze the impact of the Top-K parameter used during the topic-driven pruning phase, we perform a grid search on HotpotQA and MuSiQue validation sets, varying K in $\{1, 2, 3, 4, 5, 6, 7, 8\}$ and select the value that yields the highest EM score. Top-K controls the number of top-ranked paragraphs (or triples) passed into the graph construction module, thus influencing reasoning input quality. As shown in Fig. 2, the best performance is achieved when $K = 4$ on HotpotQA and $K = 5$ on MuSiQue. This variation likely reflects differences in dataset complexity and the degree of cross-paragraph reasoning required. Notably, due to the subsequent adaptive pruning steps, setting a relatively higher K at this stage ensures better recall of relevant content, enabling richer graph construction and improved final performance.

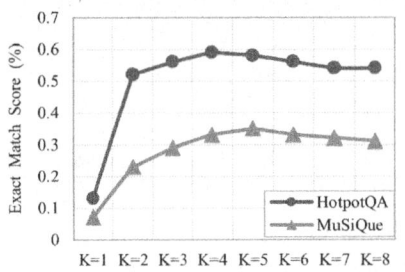
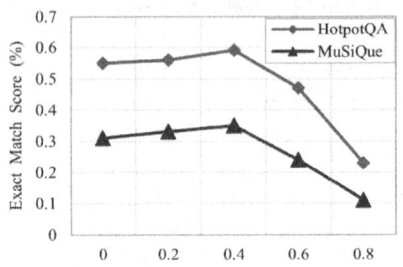

Fig. 2. Effect of the parameter Top-K. **Fig. 3.** Effect of pruning threshold τ_{sim}.

The Effect of Pruning Threshold τ_{sim}. We also tune the similarity threshold τ_{sim} via grid search on the validation sets, selecting from $\{0, 0.2, 0.4, 0.6, 0.8\}$. This threshold determines the pruning strength during the graph refinement phase. As shown in Fig. 3, performance improves as τ_{sim} increases up to 0.4, beyond which it starts to decline. This indicates that an optimal threshold effectively suppresses noisy triples while preserving context crucial to multi-hop reasoning. Conversely, excessive pruning may remove essential information, degrading overall accuracy.

4.4 Computational Cost Analysis

To evaluate the efficiency and practical feasibility of our approach, we compare its computational cost with StructQA [9], a representative structured reasoning baseline. All experiments are conducted on a server equipped with 2 × Tesla A40 GPUs (80 GB total memory). For consistency, GPT-3.5-turbo is used as the reader LLM in both methods. We report the average processing time per sample and peak GPU memory usage, evaluated on 100 examples from the HotpotQA development set. As shown in Table 5, our method achieves a 25.4% reduction in total runtime and a 13.0% decrease in peak GPU memory consumption compared to StructQA. These improvements stem primarily from the topic-driven pruning strategy, which effectively filters out irrelevant nodes and edges early in the pipeline, thereby reducing graph complexity and computational overhead.

Table 5. Time cost and GPU usage comparison.

Models	Graph Process Time (s)	LLM Reasoning Time (s)	Total Time (s)	Peak GPU Memory (GB)
StructQA	3.4	2.5	5.9	25.4
Our Method	**2.1**	**2.3**	**4.4**	**22.1**

5 Conclusion

In this paper, we propose a novel and efficient multi-hop QA method that leverages a topic-driven strategy to minimize noise and extract relevant facts, constructing a context-aware hyper-relational knowledge graph to enhance LLM input quality. Additionally, we design an adaptive reconstruction mechanism to dynamically supplement missing critical knowledge, further optimizing the reasoning chain and improving model performance. Experimental results demonstrate that our method achieves significant performance improvements on the HotpotQA and MuSiQue datasets, consistently outperforming state-of-the-art baseline methods across multiple evaluation metrics. These results validate the accuracy and robustness of our approach in complex reasoning tasks. In the future, we plan to integrate the graph with retrieval-augmented generation (RAG) to handle open-domain complex reasoning scenarios.

Acknowledgments. This research was supported by the National Key Research and Development Program of China under Grant 2022YFF0902701, the National Natural Science Foundation of China under Grants U21A20468, 62372058, U22A2026.

References

1. Biancini, G., Ferrato, A., Limongelli, C.: Multiple-choice question generation using large language models: methodology and educator insights. In: ACM Conference on User Modeling, Adaptation and Personalization, pp. 584–590 (2024)
2. Brown, T., et al.: Language models are few-shot learners. In: Neural Information Processing Systems, vol. 33, pp. 1877–1901 (2020)
3. Deng, Z., Zhu, Y., Qi, Q., Witbrock, M.J., Riddle, P.: Explicit graph reasoning fusing knowledge and contextual information for multi-hop question answering. In: Deep Learning on Graphs for Natural Language Processing, pp. 71–80 (2022)
4. Fang, Y., Sun, S., Gan, Z., Pillai, R., Wang, S., Liu, J.: Hierarchical graph network for multi-hop question answering. In: EMNLP, pp. 8823–8838 (2020)
5. Guan, X., et al.: Mitigating large language model hallucinations via autonomous knowledge graph-based retrofitting. In: AAAI Conference on Artificial Intelligence, vol. 38, pp. 18126–18134 (2024)
6. Ho, X., Nguyen, A.K.D., Sugawara, S., Aizawa, A.: Constructing a multi-hop QA dataset for comprehensive evaluation of reasoning steps. In: International Conference on Computational Linguistics, pp. 6609–6625 (2020)
7. Huang, Y., Yang, M.: Breadth first reasoning graph for multi-hop question answering. In: North American Chapter of the Association for Computational Linguistics, pp. 5810–5821 (2021)
8. Li, R., Wang, L., Wang, S.: Asynchronous multi-grained graph network for interpretable multi-hop reading comprehension. In: IJCAI, pp. 3857–3863 (2021)
9. Li, R., Du, X.: Leveraging structured information for explainable multi-hop question answering and reasoning. In: EMNLP, pp. 6779–6789 (2023)
10. Li, X.Y., Lei, W.J., Yang, Y.B.: From easy to hard: two-stage selector and reader for multi-hop question answering. In: ICASSP, pp. 1–5. IEEE (2023)

11. Mavi, V., Jangra, A., Jatowt, A., et al.: Multi-hop question answering. Found. Trends® Information Retr. **17**(5), 457–586 (2024)
12. Min, S., Zhong, V., Zettlemoyer, L.: Multi-hop reading comprehension through question decomposition and rescoring. In: ACL, pp. 6097–6109 (2019)
13. Nishida, K., Nishida, K., Nagata, M.: Answering while summarizing: multi-task learning for multi-hop QA with evidence extraction. In: ACL, pp. 2335–2345 (2019)
14. OpenAI, et al.: GPT-4 technical report. arXiv preprint arXiv:2303.08774 (2023)
15. Panda, P., Agarwal, A., Devaguptapu, C., Kaul, M.: Holmes: hyper-relational knowledge graphs for multi-hop question answering using LLMs. In: Annual Meeting of the Association for Computational Linguistics, pp. 13263–13282 (2024)
16. Perez, E., Lewis, P., Yih, W.t., Cho, K., Kiela, D.: Unsupervised question decomposition for question answering. In: EMNLP, pp. 8864–8880 (2020)
17. Qiu, L., et al.: Dynamically fused graph network for multi-hop reasoning. In: ACL, pp. 6140–6150 (2019)
18. Shao, N., Cui, Y., Liu, T., Wang, S., Hu, G.: Is graph structure necessary for multi-hop question answering? In: EMNLP, pp. 7187–7192 (2020)
19. Trivedi, H., Balasubramanian, N., Khot, T.: Interleaving retrieval with chain-of-thought reasoning for knowledge-intensive multi-step questions. In: Annual Meeting of the Association for Computational Linguistics, pp. 10014–10037 (2023)
20. Trivedi, H., Balasubramanian, N., Khot, T., Sabharwal, A.: MuSiQue: multihop questions via single-hop question composition. TACL **10**, 539–554 (2022)
21. Wadhwa, S., Amir, S., Wallace, B.C.: Revisiting relation extraction in the era of large language models. In: ACL, vol. 2023, p. 15566. NIH Public Access (2023)
22. Wang, X., Wei, J., Schuurmans, D., Le, Q., Chi, E.: Self-consistency improves chain of thought reasoning in language models. arXiv preprint arXiv:2203.11171 (2022)
23. Wei, J., et al.: Chain-of-thought prompting elicits reasoning in large language models. Neural Inf. Process. Syst. **35**, 24824–24837 (2022)
24. Yang, Z., et al.: HotpotQA: a dataset for diverse, explainable multi-hop question answering. In: Empirical Methods in Natural Language Processing, pp. 2369–2380 (2018)
25. Yao, S., et al.: Tree of thoughts: deliberate problem solving with large language models. Neural Inf. Process. Syst. **36** (2024)
26. Zhang, J., Zhang, H., Zhang, D., Yong, L., Huang, S.: End-to-end beam retrieval for multi-hop question answering. In: NAACL, pp. 1718–1731 (2024)
27. Zhangyue, Y., et al.: Rethinking label smoothing on multi-hop question answering. In: Computational Linguistics, pp. 611–623 (2023)
28. Zheng, X., et al.: KS-LLM: knowledge selection of large language models with evidence document for question answering. arXiv preprint arXiv:2404.15660 (2024)

Toward Better Document-Level Relation Extraction: De-sampling and Mixture of Experts in Action

Xiaojun Sheng[1,2], Shilong Wei[1,2], Yafei Wang[1,2], Minmin Li[1,3(✉)], Weixi Wang[2], Renzhong Guo[2], and Qi Yang[1]

[1] Guangdong Laboratory of Artificial Intelligence and Digital Economy (SZ), Shenzhen 518123, China
`liminmin@gml.ac.cn`
[2] Shenzhen University, Shenzhen 518060, China
[3] Key Laboratory of Urban Land Resources Monitoring and Simulation, Ministry of Natural Resources, Shenzhen 518034, China

Abstract. Document-level Relation Extraction aims to identify relationships between entity pairs in long texts, which is crucial for building knowledge graphs. However, it faces long-tail problem and evidence focus problem. To address these issues, this paper proposes the ATLOP-DME (De-Sampling and Mixture of Experts) model, building on the ATLOP method. The model introduces two core components: 1) **De-Sampling** to balance the relation category distribution and alleviate the long-tail problem, and 2) a **Mixture of Experts** system to focus on evidence. We conducted training on the DocRED, Re-DocRED, CDR, and GDA datasets. The experimental results demonstrate that, compared to the ATLOP model, the ATLOP-DME model achieved improvements of 24.02%, 10.19%, 7.5%, and 2.9% on the respective datasets. Notably, it sets new SOTA performance on the DocRED and Re-DocRED datasets. The code is now publicly available on GitHub (https://github.com/Shenjingbang/ATLOP-DME).

Keywords: DocRE · ATLOP · De-Sampling · MoE

1 Introduction

Document-level Relation Extraction (DocRE) aims to identify entity relationships across documents, essential for deep semantic understanding and cross-sentence reasoning, with applications in knowledge graph construction and information retrieval [1]. Unlike sentence-level tasks, DocRE requires capturing global semantics, increasing task complexity. With the emergence of large-scale pre-trained models such as BERT [2], and DeBERTa [5], significant improvements have been made in DocRE methods. Zhou et al. [30] proposed the ATLOP model based on BERT and RoBERTa, which employs adaptive thresholds and local context pooling techniques. Subsequently, Wang et al. [19] introduced co-reference distillation to ATLOP, resulting in the ATLOP+KIRE model. To enhance transparency, Ru et al. [14] proposed the ATLOP+LogiRE model, which improves model interpretability by learning logical rules. To address the semi-supervised challenges in DocRE, Tan et al. [17] proposed a semi-supervised framework that incorporates an axial attention module, adaptive focus loss, and knowledge distillation. Ma et al. [11] introduced the DREEAM method, which leverages evidence information and an ER self-training strategy to automatically generate evidence for learning from data without evidence annotations. Despite recent advances, DocRE faces two key challenges: 1) **Long-tail problem**: The uneven distribution of relation categories and insufficient low-frequency samples hinder learning of minority relations [3]. 2) **Evidence focus problem**: Models struggle to capture key evidence due to background noise in long texts [24].

To tackle these issues, we propose **ATLOP-DME**, an improved model based on ATLOP [23]. ATLOP-DME incorporates two key components: 1) **De-Sampling strategy**: Balances sample distribution by controlling unrelated entity pair frequency, mitigating the long-tail problem. 2) **Mixture of Experts (MoE)**: Dynamically selects expert networks to focus on key evidence and relevant entity pairs, enhancing reasoning ability.

Contributions: 1) Introduction of a **De-Sampling method** to improve low-frequency relation learning. 2) First application of **MoE** in DocRE, achieving improved target relation evidence modeling. 3) Significant performance gains on multiple datasets, with metrics such as F1, IgnF1, and EviF1 surpassing existing methods.

2 Methodology

2.1 Problem Formulation

Given a set of entities $E = \{e_i\}_{i=1}^{n}$ with subject e_s and object e_o, the goal of DocRE is to predict the relationship category between e_s and e_o in a document. The entity pairs are partitioned into two sets: 1) **Relation entity pairs** (R), where each pair has at least one non-empty relation; and 2) **Non-relation entity pairs** (NR), labeled as "no relation".

2.2 Model Architecture

As illustrated in Fig. 1, the proposed ATLOP-DME model consists of four modules: data preprocessing, feature extraction, relation classification, and evidence classification. - **Data preprocessing** applies De-Sampling to mitigate class imbalance. - **Feature extraction** uses a PLM to generate contextual embeddings and entity representations. - **Relation classification** leverages a MoE with Adaptive Threshold Loss to improve long-tail relation modeling. - **Evidence classification** employs Kullback–Leibler divergence to enhance reasoning by optimizing evidence distribution.

De-sampling. The imbalance between R and NR leads to over-reliance on non-relation pairs, weakening generalization. To address this, we propose a frequency-based random undersampling method [16], termed De-Sampling. By limiting

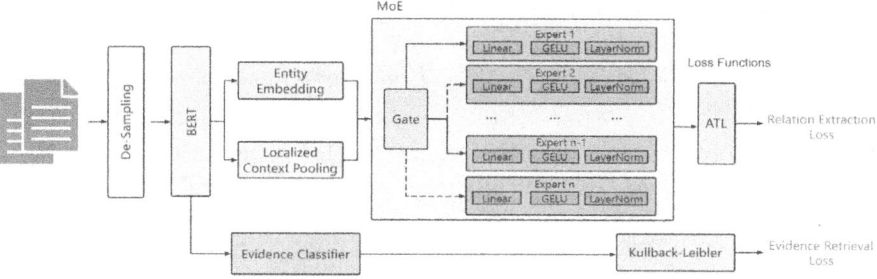

Fig. 1. Model Architecture

each entity's frequency in NR to a threshold k, the algorithm reduces redundancy while preserving R, improving long-tail relation learning.

Text Encoding. We employ a PLM as the encoder. For a document $D = [x_t]_{t=1}^{l}$, special tokens "*" mark entity boundaries [29]. The PLM generates contextual embeddings H and attention weights A:

$$H, A = \text{PLM}(D) \tag{1}$$

where $H \in \mathbb{R}^{l \times d}$ and $A \in \mathbb{R}^{h^* \times l \times l}$, with d as the embedding dimension and h^* the number of attention heads.

Entity Encoding. Following [8], we use logsumexp pooling for global entity representation:

$$h_{e_i} = \log \left(\sum_{j=1}^{N_{e_i}} \exp(h_{m_j^i}) \right), \tag{2}$$

where $h_{m_j^i}$ represents the j-th occurrence of entity e_i.

Localized Context Embedding. For each entity e_i, attention weights are aggregated via mean pooling:

$$A_{e_i} = \frac{1}{N_{e_i}} \sum_{j=1}^{N_{e_i}} A_{m_j^i}, \tag{3}$$

where $A_{m_j^i} \in \mathbb{R}^{h^* \times l}$ represents the self-attention weights. Entity pair attention is combined using the Hadamard product:

$$q^{(s,o)} = \frac{A_{e_s} \circ A_{e_o}}{A_{e_s}^T A_{e_o}}. \tag{4}$$

The local context embedding is obtained by weighted pooling:

$$r^{(s,o)} = H^T q^{(s,o)}. \tag{5}$$

MoE. We adopt a sparse gating MoE model [15], where a gating mechanism selects the top k experts dynamically:

$$H_{out} = \sum_{i=1}^{k} g_i(x) \cdot E_i(x), \tag{6}$$

where $g_i(x)$ is the gating weight and $E_i(x)$ is the i-th expert's output. To ensure load balancing, we use an auxiliary loss with Kullback–Leibler (KL) divergence:

$$L_{aux} = -\text{KL}(P(g)||U), \tag{7}$$

where $P(g)$ is the gating distribution and U is a uniform distribution.

Joint features for subject–relation and object–relation are computed as:

$$H_{sub-rel} = \text{MoE}(h_{e_s}, r^{(s,o)}), \tag{8}$$

$$H_{obj-rel} = \text{MoE}(h_{e_o}, r^{(s,o)}), \tag{9}$$

with the final relation score:

$$logit = W_1 \cdot H_{sub-rel} + W_2 \cdot H_{obj-rel}, \tag{10}$$

where W_1 and W_2 are learnable parameters.

Loss Function. We adopt Adaptive Threshold Loss [30] with a virtual threshold TH for multi-label classification. The loss encourages relation scores to exceed TH while suppressing non-relation scores:

$$L_{RE} = -\sum_{r \in R} \frac{\exp(logit_r)}{\sum_{r \in R \cup \{TH\}} \exp(logit_r)} - \frac{\exp(logit_{TH})}{\sum_{r \in N R \cup \{TH\}} \exp(logit_r)} + L_{aux} \tag{11}$$

Evidence Classification. We follow [22] to incorporate evidence retrieval. For each entity pair (e_s, e_o), local context embedding $q^{(s,o)}$ generates evidence scores:

$$p^{(s,o)} = \sum_{j=start(x_i)}^{end(x_i)} q^{(s,o)}. \tag{12}$$

The evidence distribution is computed as:

$$v^{(s,o)} = \frac{\sum_{r \in R \cup NR} v^{(s,r,o)}}{\sum_{r \in R \cup NR} 1^T v^{(s,r,o)}}, \qquad (13)$$

with a KL divergence loss for minimizing statistical distance:

$$L_{ER} = -\mathrm{KL}(v^{(s,o)} || p^{(s,o)}). \qquad (14)$$

The total loss is balanced by a hyperparameter λ:

$$L = L_{RE} + \lambda L_{ER}. \qquad (15)$$

3 Experiments

3.1 Research Questions

To evaluate the effectiveness and robustness of ATLOP-DME, we designed experiments to address the following research questions (RQs):

- **RQ1: Overall Performance**—How does ATLOP-DME compare to baseline models in DocRE?
- **RQ2: Component Effectiveness**—What is the impact of De-Sampling and Mixture of Experts on performance?
- **RQ3: Generalization**—How well does ATLOP-DME generalize across different DocRE datasets?
- **RQ4: Error Analysis**—What insights can be drawn from the model's error distribution?

3.2 Setting

Dataset. We evaluate model on the widely-used DocRED dataset [27], constructed by Tsinghua University using Wikipedia and Wikidata. DocRED consists of two subsets: human-annotated data (HAD) and distant supervision data (DSD).

Configuration. The experimental configuration is detailed as follows:

Model Architecture. The encoder is based on DeBERTa [5]. The MoE module comprises 4 experts, each with a 1-layer structure that includes a linear transformation, a GELU activation function, and layer normalization. The gating mechanism consists of a linear layer with a Tanh activation function, and the Top-K threshold is set to 2. The evidence classifier follows the DREEAM method [11], with the hyperparameter λ set to 0.15. In the De-Sampling method, the frequency threshold k is set to 1.

Table 1. Results on HAD and DSD subsets of DocRED dataset. "—" denotes unreported metrics.

Model	HAD			DSD		
	IgnF1 (%)	F1 (%)	EviF1 (%)	IgnF1 (%)	F1 (%)	EviF1 (%)
SSAN [23]	60.25	62.08	—	63.76	65.69	—
ATLOP [30]	**61.32**	**63.18**	—	—	—	—
MDP GPT-4 [31]	—	21.33	—	—	—	—
REPLM GPT-3.5 [13]	—	59.66	—	—	—	—
SAIS [21]	62.23	64.27	55.84	—	—	—
KD-DocRE [17]	—	—	—	65.27	67.12	—
DREEAM [11]	62.29	64.20	54.15	65.52	67.41	57.55
LMRC-LLaMA2-13B [10]	—	—	—	58.16	59.97	—
MSKI [6]	62.33	64.31	—	65.50	67.53	—
DocRE-CLip [7]	—	—	—	66.43	68.13	—
Ours (ATLOP-DME)	**86.45**$_{\pm0.07}$	**87.20**$_{\pm0.06}$	**75.67**$_{\pm0.07}$	**84.95**$_{\pm0.06}$	**84.12**$_{\pm0.08}$	**73.32**$_{\pm0.05}$

Training Parameters. The model was trained for 30 epochs using the Adam optimizer with a learning rate of 1×10^{-5} and a warm-up ratio of 0.06.

Evaluation. We use DocRED's official metrics [27] for evaluation: Relation Extraction (RE): Measured by F1 and IgnF1, where IgnF1 excludes relations appearing in the training set. Evidence Retrieval (ER): Measured by EviF1, following EIDER [22], where sentences with a probability >0.2 are considered evidence.

We report the mean and standard error from five independent runs with different random initializations.

3.3 Performance on DocRED

This section addresses RQ1.

As shown in Table 1, ATLOP-DME outperforms the baseline ATLOP model, with IgnF1 and F1 improving by 26% and 23% on HAD, respectively, confirming the effectiveness of our enhancements.

Compared to SOTA models like MSKI [6] and DREEAM [11], ATLOP-DME achieves a 16%-24% improvement, demonstrating a clear performance advantage.

The gains mainly stem from two factors: **De-Sampling** alleviates class imbalance by balancing relation distributions, while **MoE** enhances focus on key evidence, improving reasoning capability.

3.4 Ablation Studies

In this section, we focus on discussing RQ2. The experimental settings are largely consistent with those in Sect. 3.2, except for the parameter adjustments specific to the methods being ablated.

Table 2. The impact of different values of k in the De-Sampling method on the performance of the ATLOP-DME model. A value of $k =$ "—" indicates that the De-Sampling method is not applied.

k	NR ↑	F1 (%) ↓	IgnF1 (%) ↓	EviF1 (%) ↓
1	33100	$\mathbf{84.27_{\pm 0.07}}$	$\mathbf{82.49_{\pm 0.09}}$	$\mathbf{65.32_{\pm 0.06}}$
2	63110	$82.40_{\pm 0.06}$	$81.52_{\pm 0.08}$	$63.08_{\pm 0.09}$
4	121649	$79.38_{\pm 0.03}$	$78.34_{\pm 0.05}$	$61.43_{\pm 0.02}$
8	237053	$75.07_{\pm 0.09}$	$74.82_{\pm 0.04}$	$59.46_{\pm 0.07}$
16	464645	$69.25_{\pm 0.02}$	$68.73_{\pm 0.06}$	$57.52_{\pm 0.05}$
32	893218	$64.01_{\pm 0.08}$	$63.26_{\pm 0.03}$	$55.95_{\pm 0.09}$
—	$\mathbf{1163035}$	$63.49_{\pm 0.01}$	$61.71_{\pm 0.10}$	$54.01_{\pm 0.06}$

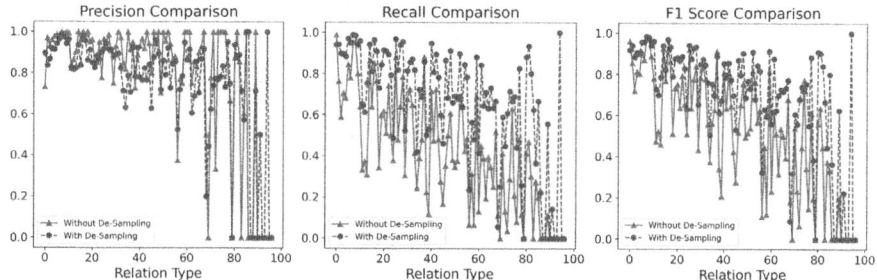

Fig. 2. Comparison of Performance with and without De-Sampling Method

De-sampling. We analyze the effect of varying k in De-Sampling on ATLOP-DME's performance. As k increases, non-relation entity pairs grow, causing performance degradation.

As shown in Table 2, small k has minimal impact (e.g., $k = 2$ reduces F1 by 2.55%), but with $k \geq 4$, performance declines sharply. At $k = 32$, F1 drops to 65.01%, and without De-Sampling (i.e., $k =$ "—"), F1 is 63.49%. Figure 2 shows: (1) **Category 0 (Non-relation)**: De-Sampling lowers Precision, reducing over-focus on non-relation pairs. (2) **Categories 1–96 (Low-frequency)**: It improves Recall, with some categories showing 100% gains, boosting F1.

De-Sampling mitigates the long-tail problem by balancing data distribution, enhancing generalization, and improving performance across relation types.

MoE. We examine the impact of MoE configuration on ATLOP-DME performance, focusing on the number of experts and the Top-K parameter.

As shown in Table 3: (1) **Limitations of Dense Configuration**: Without MoE, the Dense setup (195.75M parameters) achieves F1, IgnF1, and EviF1 scores of 84.30%, 83.47%, and 65.35%, indicating limited capacity to capture complex document-level relations. (2) **MoE Performance Gains**: Adding MoE (4 experts, Top-K $= 2$, 195.72M parameters) boosts F1 to 86.95%, showing

Table 3. Impact of different MoE configurations on ATLOP-DME. "—" indicates the absence of the MoE system. The "Dense" configuration replaces MoE with a fully connected layer as a control experiment.

Parameter	Experts	TopK	F1 (%)	IgnF1 (%)	EviF1 (%)
190.97M	—		$84.27_{\pm 0.07}$	$83.49_{\pm 0.09}$	$65.32_{\pm 0.06}$
195.75M	Dense		$84.30_{\pm 0.08}$	$83.47_{\pm 0.05}$	$65.31_{\pm 0.07}$
200.80M	Dense		$84.28_{\pm 0.06}$	$83.50_{\pm 0.07}$	$65.35_{\pm 0.08}$
195.72M	**4**	**2**	$\mathbf{86.95_{\pm 0.04}}$	$\mathbf{86.23_{\pm 0.03}}$	$\mathbf{75.28_{\pm 0.05}}$
198.09M	6	2	$86.68_{\pm 0.07}$	$85.92_{\pm 0.05}$	$74.95_{\pm 0.06}$
198.09M	6	4	$87.00_{\pm 0.02}$	$86.25_{\pm 0.03}$	$75.20_{\pm 0.04}$
200.46M	8	4	$86.94_{\pm 0.03}$	$86.18_{\pm 0.05}$	$75.14_{\pm 0.06}$
209.95M	16	8	$86.93_{\pm 0.04}$	$86.20_{\pm 0.03}$	$75.23_{\pm 0.05}$
228.92M	**32**	**8**	$\mathbf{87.20_{\pm 0.01}}$	$\mathbf{86.45_{\pm 0.02}}$	$\mathbf{75.67_{\pm 0.03}}$
266.86M	64	8	$87.00_{\pm 0.04}$	$86.26_{\pm 0.05}$	$75.21_{\pm 0.04}$
342.76M	128	8	$86.80_{\pm 0.06}$	$86.05_{\pm 0.07}$	$75.05_{\pm 0.05}$

Table 4. Comparative Performance Evaluation

(a) Re-DocRED Dataset			(b) CDR and GDA		
Model	IgnF1	F1	Model	CDR (F1)	GDA (F1)
MDP GPT-4 [31]	—	14.2	LSR [12]	64.8	82.2
AutoRE-Vicuna-7B [25]	—	53.84	**ATLOP** [30]	**69.4**	**83.9**
ATLOP [30]	78.52	79.46	Seq2rel [4]	67.2	84.9
KD-DocRE [17]	80.32	81.04	**SAIS** [21]	**79.0**	**87.1**
DREEAM [11]	78.67	79.35	RADM-DRE [28]	69.78	84.38
DocRE-CLiP [7]	**80.57**	**81.55**	CRFLOE [26]	69.98	84.12
Ours	$89.95_{\pm 0.08}$	$90.37_{\pm 0.05}$	Ours	$77.2_{\pm 0.06}$	$86.8_{\pm 0.08}$

improved handling of heterogeneous information. (3) **Effect of Expert Count and Top-K**: With 32 experts (Top-K = 8), F1 peaks at 87.20%, but performance slightly declines at 128 experts due to overfitting or redundancy. The 4-expert, Top-K = 2 setup offers the best efficiency-performance trade-off.

Attention Heatmap Analysis. Figure 3 shows the attention heatmap analysis. Without MoE, the model overemphasizes irrelevant entities, leading to incorrect evidence predictions. With MoE, experts collaboratively allocate attention, reducing focus on irrelevant entities and improving evidence identification. Sparse MoE's dynamic routing, specialized experts, and efficient computation enhance relation and evidence prediction performance. This aligns with the EviF1 score improvement in Table 3, confirming MoE's ability to mitigate evidence focus bias and improve generalization, crucial for tasks like knowledge graph construction.

```
subject:Prince Edmund; object:The Black Adder;          subject:Prince Edmund; object:The Black Adder;
gold-relation:present in work; pred-relation:present in work;   gold-relation:present in work; pred-relation:present in work;
gold-evidence:1,2; pred-evidence:1,2,6                  gold-evidence:1,2 ; pred-evidence:1,2
[1]" * The Archbishop * " is the third episode of the first series of the   [1]" * The Archbishop * " is the third episode of the first series of the
* BBC * sitcom * Black adder * [ * The Black Adder * ) . [2]It   * BBC * sitcom * Black adder * [ * The Black Adder * ) . [2]It
is set in * England * in * the late 15 th century * , and follows the   is set in * England * in * the late 15 th century * , and follows the
exploits of the fictitious * Prince Edmund as he is invested as *   exploits of the fictitious * Prince Edmund as he is invested as the
Archbishop of Canterbury * amid a * Machiavellian * plot by the King   Archbishop of Canterbury * amid a * Machiavellian * plot by the King
to acquire lands from the * Catholic Church * . [3]Most of the humour   to acquire lands from the * Catholic Church * . [3]Most of the humour
in the episode relies on religious satire . [4]The script pays tribute to the   in the episode relies on religious satire . [4]The script pays tribute to the
real - life * 12 th century * Archbishop of Canterbury , * Thomas Becket   real - life * 12 th century * Archbishop of Canterbury , * Thomas Becket
* . [5]* Edmund * , faced with the threat of assassination , attempts   * . [5]* Edmund * , faced with the threat of assassination , attempts
to escape to * France * into self - imposed exile ; and in a later scene ,   to escape to * France * into self - imposed exile ; and in a later scene ,
* two * drunk knights overhear King * Richard IV * exclaiming " Who   * two * drunk knights overhear King * Richard IV * exclaiming " Who
will rid me of this turbulent priest ? [6]" , the words attributed to King   will rid me of this turbulent priest ? [6]" , the words attributed to King
* Henry II * which led to * Becket * ' s death in * 11 70 * , and embark   * Henry II * which led to * Becket * ' s death in * 11 70 * , and embark
on a mission to murder * Edmund [7]" * The Archbishop * " won   on a mission to murder * Edmund * . [7]" * The Archbishop * " won
an * International Emmy Award * in * 1983 * in the * Popular Arts *   an * International Emmy Award * in * 1983 * in the * Popular Arts *
category . [8]The * Catholic Church * was to be satirize d again in the   category . [8]The * Catholic Church * was to be satirize d again in the
second series , * Black adder II * , in the * 1986 * episode " * Money   second series , * Black adder II * , in the * 1986 * episode " * Money
* " .
```

Fig. 3. The left image shows results without MoE, while the right image shows results with MoE. "gold-relation" and "pred-relation" denote the true and predicted relationship categories, respectively. "gold-evidence" and "pred-evidence" represent the true and predicted evidence sentence labels.

3.5 Evaluation on Multiple Datasets

To address RQ3, we evaluated ATLOP-DME on Re-DocRED, CDR, and GDA datasets using parameters consistent with Sect. 3.2.

On **Re-DocRED** [18], which addresses false negatives in DocRED, ATLOP-DME outperforms other models, achieving nearly 9% gains in IgnF1 and F1 over the SOTA model DocRE-CLiP [7], demonstrating enhanced generalization and robustness. For **CDR** [9] and **GDA** [20], biomedical datasets for chemical-disease and gene-disease interactions, ATLOP-DME achieves F1 scores of 77.2% and 86.8%, respectively, surpassing ATLOP (69.4% and 83.9%) and approaching the SOTA model SAIS (79.0% and 87.1%).

The smaller gains on CDR and GDA reflect their binary classification nature, with less room for improvement compared to the more complex multi-class setting in DocRED. Overall, ATLOP-DME demonstrates strong generalization across diverse datasets.

3.6 Error Analysis

To address RQ4, we categorized errors into four types: **Correct (C)**, **Wrong (W)**, **Missed (MS)**, and **More (MR)**.

As shown in Table 5a, 5.63% of cases were misclassified as MR, indicating "relationship generalization" errors where no-relationship pairs are incorrectly predicted as positive. This reflects difficulty in distinguishing between relationship and no-relationship pairs.

The binary classification results (relationship vs. non-relationship) in Table 5b demonstrate that ATLOP-DME achieved 91.62% F1, but in multi-class extraction, F1 dropped to 87.20%, highlighting the impact of class imbalance and long-tail issues. The primary performance bottleneck stems from misclassifying no-relationship pairs and handling low-frequency relations.

Table 5. Model Performance Analysis

(a) Error Type Distribution

	R	NR
R	C: 9815 (80.75%) W: 461 (3.79%)	MR: 685 (5.63%)
NR	MS: 1194 (9.82%)	10,823

(b) Evaluation Metrics

Model	P(%)	R(%)	F1(%)
Binary	93.75	89.59	91.62
Original	88.97	85.43	87.20

4 Conclusion

This study presents the ATLOP-DME model, an enhancement of the ATLOP framework, designed to address the long-tail and evidence focusing issues in DocRE. The model incorporates De-Sampling to alleviate the long-tail problem, improving prediction for low-frequency relations, and MoE to dynamically allocate experts for better handling of complex documents. Experimental results demonstrate that ATLOP-DME achieves SOTA performance on DocRED and Re-DocRED datasets, significantly outperforming existing models in F1 and IgnF1 metrics. Ablation studies confirm that both De-Sampling and MoE improve performance and adaptability. ATLOP-DME offers an effective solution for DocRE, providing valuable insights for future research.

Acknowledgments. This work was supported by National Key R&D Program of China (2022YFB3903705) and the Open Fund of Key Laboratory of Urban Land Resources Monitoring and Simulation, Ministry of Natural Resources (KF-2023-08-17).

References

1. Delaunay, J., et al.: A comprehensive survey of document-level relation extraction (2016-2023) (2023)
2. Devlin, J., Chang, M.W., Lee, K., Toutanova, K.: BERT: pre-training of deep bidirectional transformers for language understanding. In: Proceedings of the 2019 Conference of the North American Chapter of the Association for Computational Linguistics: Human Language Technologies, Minneapolis, Minnesota, pp. 4171–4186. Association for Computational Linguistics (2019)
3. Du, Y., et al.: Improving long tailed document-level relation extraction via easy relation augmentation and contrastive learning (2022)
4. Giorgi, J., Bader, G., Wang, B.: A sequence-to-sequence approach for document-level relation extraction. In: Proceedings of the 21st Workshop on Biomedical Language Processing, Dublin, Ireland, pp. 10–25. Association for Computational Linguistics (2022)
5. He, P., Gao, J., Chen, W.: DeBERTaV3: improving DeBERTa using electra-style pre-training with gradient-disentangled embedding sharing (2023)
6. Hou, W., Wu, W., Liu, X., Zhao, W.: Document-level relation extraction with multi-semantic knowledge interaction. Inf. Sci. **679**, 121083 (2024)

7. Jain, M., Mutharaju, R., Kavuluru, R., Singh, K.: Revisiting document-level relation extraction with context-guided link prediction. Proc. AAAI Conf. Artif. Intell. **38**(16), 18327–18335 (2024)
8. Jia, R., Wong, C., Poon, H.: Document-level n-ary relation extraction with multiscale representation learning. In: Proceedings of the 2019 Conference of the North American Chapter of the Association for Computational Linguistics: Human Language Technologies, Minneapolis, Minnesota, pp. 3693–3704. Association for Computational Linguistics (2019)
9. Li, J., et al.: BioCreative V CDR task corpus: a resource for chemical disease relation extraction. Database J. Biol. Databases Curation **2016**, baw068 (2016). https://europepmc.org/articles/PMC4860626
10. Li, X., Chen, K., Long, Y., Zhang, M.: LLM with relation classifier for document-level relation extraction (2024)
11. Ma, Y., Wang, A., Okazaki, N.: DREEAM: guiding attention with evidence for improving document-level relation extraction. In: Proceedings of the 17th Conference of the European Chapter of the Association for Computational Linguistics, Dubrovnik, Croatia, pp. 1971–1983. Association for Computational Linguistics (2023)
12. Nan, G., Guo, Z., Sekulic, I., Lu, W.: Reasoning with latent structure refinement for document-level relation extraction. In: Proceedings of the 58th Annual Meeting of the Association for Computational Linguistics, pp. 1546–1557. Association for Computational Linguistics, Online (2020)
13. Ozyurt, Y., Feuerriegel, S., Zhang, C.: Document-level in-context few-shot relation extraction via pre-trained language models (2024)
14. Ru, D., et al.: Learning logic rules for document-level relation extraction. In: Proceedings of the 2021 Conference on Empirical Methods in Natural Language Processing, Online and Punta Cana, Dominican Republic, pp. 1239–1250. Association for Computational Linguistics (2021)
15. Shazeer, N., et al.: Outrageously large neural networks: the sparsely-gated mixture-of-experts layer (2017)
16. Spelmen, V.S., Porkodi, R.: A review on handling imbalanced data. In: 2018 International Conference on Current Trends towards Converging Technologies (ICCTCT), pp. 1–11 (2018)
17. Tan, Q., He, R., Bing, L., Ng, H.T.: Document-level relation extraction with adaptive focal loss and knowledge distillation. In: Findings of the Association for Computational Linguistics: ACL 2022, Dublin, Ireland, pp. 1672–1681. Association for Computational Linguistics (2022)
18. Tan, Q., Xu, L., Bing, L., Ng, H.T., Aljunied, S.M.: Revisiting DocRED: addressing the false negative problem in relation extraction. In: Proceedings of the 2022 Conference on Empirical Methods in Natural Language Processing, Abu Dhabi, United Arab Emirates, pp. 8472–8487. Association for Computational Linguistics (2022)
19. Wang, X., Wang, Z., Sun, W., Hu, W.: Enhancing document-level relation extraction by entity knowledge injection. In: Sattler, U., et al. (eds.) ISWC 2022. LNCS, vol. 13489, pp. 39–56. Springer, Cham (2022). https://doi.org/10.1007/978-3-031-19433-7_3
20. Wu, Y., Luo, R., Leung, H.C.M., Ting, H.-F., Lam, T.-W.: RENET: a deep learning approach for extracting gene-disease associations from literature. In: Cowen, L.J. (ed.) RECOMB 2019. LNCS, vol. 11467, pp. 272–284. Springer, Cham (2019). https://doi.org/10.1007/978-3-030-17083-7_17

21. Xiao, Y., Zhang, Z., Mao, Y., Yang, C., Han, J.: SAIS: supervising and augmenting intermediate steps for document-level relation extraction. In: Proceedings of the 2022 Conference of the North American Chapter of the Association for Computational Linguistics: Human Language Technologies, Seattle, United States, pp. 2395–2409. Association for Computational Linguistics (2022)
22. Xie, Y., Shen, J., Li, S., Mao, Y., Han, J.: Eider: empowering document-level relation extraction with efficient evidence extraction and inference-stage fusion. In: Findings of the Association for Computational Linguistics: ACL 2022, Dublin, Ireland, pp. 257–268. Association for Computational Linguistics (2022)
23. Xu, B., Wang, Q., Lyu, Y., Zhu, Y., Mao, Z.: Entity structure within and throughout: modeling mention dependencies for document-level relation extraction. In: Proceedings of the AAAI Conference on Artificial Intelligence, vol. 35, pp. 14149–14157 (2021)
24. Xu, W., Chen, K., Mou, L., Zhao, T.: Document-level relation extraction with sentences importance estimation and focusing. In: Carpuat, M., de Marneffe, M.C., Meza Ruiz, I.V. (eds.) Proceedings of the 2022 Conference of the North American Chapter of the Association for Computational Linguistics: Human Language Technologies, Seattle, United States, pp. 2920–2929. Association for Computational Linguistics (2022)
25. Xue, L., Zhang, D., Dong, Y., Tang, J.: AutoRE: document-level relation extraction with large language models. In: Proceedings of the 62nd Annual Meeting of the Association for Computational Linguistics (Volume 3: System Demonstrations), Bangkok, Thailand, pp. 211–220. Association for Computational Linguistics (2024)
26. Yang, D., Li, X., Wu, H., Zhou, A., Liu, P.: CRFLOE: context region filter and relation word aware for document-level relation extraction. In: Huang, D.S., Si, Z., Zhang, Q. (eds.) ICIC 2024. LNCS, vol. 14877, pp. 102–114. Springer, Singapore (2024). https://doi.org/10.1007/978-981-97-5669-8_9
27. Yao, Y., et al.: DocRED: a large-scale document-level relation extraction dataset. In: Proceedings of the 57th Annual Meeting of the Association for Computational Linguistics, Florence, Italy, pp. 764–777. Association for Computational Linguistics (2019)
28. Zhang, Q., et al.: RADM-DRE: retrieval augmentation for document-level relation extraction with diffusion model. In: 2023 International Conference on Asian Language Processing (IALP), pp. 19–24 (2023)
29. Zhang, Y., Zhong, V., Chen, D., Angeli, G., Manning, C.D.: Position-aware attention and supervised data improve slot filling. In: Conference on Empirical Methods in Natural Language Processing (2017)
30. Zhou, W., Huang, K., Ma, T., Huang, J.: Document-level relation extraction with adaptive thresholding and localized context pooling. In: Proceedings of the AAAI Conference on Artificial Intelligence (2021)
31. Zhu, W., Wang, X., Chen, X., Luo, X.: Refining chatGPT for document-level relation extraction: a multi-dimensional prompting approach. In: Huang, D.S., Si, Z., Zhang, Q. (eds.) ICIC 2024. LNCS, vol. 14877, pp. 190–201. Springer, Singapore (2024). https://doi.org/10.1007/978-981-97-5669-8_16

ConSens: Assessing Context Grounding in Open-Book Question Answering

Ivan Vankov[1,3](✉), Matyo Ivanov[1], Adriana Correia[2], and Victor Botev[1]

[1] Iris.ai BG, Sofia, Bulgaria
{ivan,matyo,viktor}@iris.ai
[2] Iris.ai, Oslo, Norway
adriana@iris.ai
[3] Institute of Neurobiology, BAS, Sofia, Bulgaria

Abstract. Large Language Models (LLMs) have demonstrated considerable success in open-book question answering (QA), where the task requires generating answers grounded in a provided external context. A critical challenge in open-book QA is to ensure that model responses are based on the provided context rather than its parametric knowledge, which can be outdated, incomplete, or incorrect. Existing evaluation methods, primarily based on the LLM-as-a-judge approach, face significant limitations, including biases, scalability issues, and dependence on costly external systems. To address these challenges, we propose a novel metric that contrasts the perplexity of the model response under two conditions: when the context is provided and when it is not. The resulting score quantifies the extent to which the model's answer relies on the provided context. The validity of this metric is demonstrated through a series of experiments that show its effectiveness in identifying whether a given answer is grounded in the provided context. Unlike existing approaches, this metric is computationally efficient, interpretable, and adaptable to various use cases, offering a scalable and practical solution to assess context utilization in open-book QA systems.

Keywords: Deep learning · LLM evaluation · Open-book QA · Faithfulness

1 Introduction

With the development of Large Language Models (LLMs), the promise of automation and revolution in the way we handle human knowledge has become closer to reality. An area still left for improvement is knowledge-intensive (KI) tasks. There are several requirements that have not yet been fulfilled to guarantee full trustworthiness in real-world scenarios. We will define here four such key requirements that, when fulfilled, will boost the adoption of LLMs for KI tasks in business cases dramatically:

- **Utilizing the latest state of knowledge:** using up-to-date information that may not necessarily be present in the pre-trained data of the LLMs.
- **Handling of long-tail and rare knowledge:** many business cases require nuanced, domain specific or rare knowledge, which is crucial for accurate results (currently not present in pre-training data).
- **Handling diverse contexts:** many applications require domain-specific knowledge (e.g., medicine, finance, law) that is defined in common English but may have entirely different meanings in a specialized context. For instance, the phrase *"Blue Roof"* might refer to "tiles reflecting heat" in a business scenario, but would simply be understood as "blue-colored tiles" by an LLM without the relevant context.
- **Hallucination mitigation:** LLMs are prone to generate plausible but incorrect or unsupported by given information answers. Not only that but because of the high plausibility, they are also hard to flag as wrong and fix, making LLMs unreliable and hard to adopt for KI tasks.

Today, LLMs can address these requirements using two main approaches: weight modifying techniques [21,33] and input knowledge embedding techniques [13,30]. Weight modification techniques are powerful, but lack scalability due to the need to keep up with new or frequently updated information. Modifying weights every time new information is ingested can be expensive and can lead to an uncontrolled degradation of the original abilities [10,15]. For these reasons, these techniques become less practical for solving the business requirements defined above. Input knowledge embedding techniques like Retrieval Augmented Generation (RAG) embed external knowledge into the LLM input, which is significantly less expensive than weight modification, making it much more scalable and practical. Embedding knowledge in the input addresses all the requirements above, it gives the LLM the extra necessary information and context to answer the question and the desired focus to limit hallucinations. However, this method assumes that the LLMs are able to answer open-book questions - questions that are based on the presented knowledge and not on the pre-trained data. This makes open-book questions and answers (QA) evaluation an essential component for ensuring that LLMs can practically be useful for KI applications, and improve real-world implementations of LLMs for complex tasks.

The ability of an LLM to generate text that is grounded in the provided context is recognized as one of its defining characteristics [11,20] and is particularly important for building open-book QA systems [27]. However, the factors and underlying mechanisms that determine whether a model will base its output on the provided context rather than on its parametric knowledge are complicated and still not entirely understood [4,19,28,29]. Given that there is no reliable way to predict whether the provided context will be used to guide the model output, it is important to have a way to determine this after the output is generated.

1.1 Contribution

This work makes three main contributions. First, we introduce ConSens, a novel metric for assessing the effect of context on LLM-generated answers in open-book QA tasks. Second, we validate its effectiveness through extensive experiments across three different datasets. Third, we demonstrate that ConSens is not constrained by the choice of evaluator model—it achieves strong results even with lightweight generative LLMs, making it broadly applicable and efficient.

1.2 Related Work

The traditional way to evaluate the quality of LLMs output is to compare it to a reference text ('ground truth') using metrics which quantify the degree of lexical, e.g. ROUGE [14], or semantic [3,34] overlap. The same approach can be applied to identifying the role of the context on the generated answer in open-book QA by simply computing the similarity of the two texts (answer and context). Indeed, if the context was utilized by the LLM during generation then the resulting text should share lexical (e.g. named entities) and conceptual features with the context. The problem with metrics based on text similarity is that they tend to work at the surface level and struggle to account for the expressive abilities of modern LLMs [9]. More generally, similarity based metrics do not address the specifics of the open-book QA task such as how the relation between the answer and the context is conditioned on the question asked.

The state-of-the-art method for determining the faithfulness (i.e. the level of 'grounding') of a model answer with respect to a provided context is to delegate the task to an external LLM [6,11,22]. For example, [6] proposed a faithfulness metric that uses GPT-3.5 [18] to check whether all claims in the answer can be inferred from the context provided. A similar metric is also implemented in the Tonic Validate software development kit [25]. A more general approach is to define faithfulness as a custom evaluation criterion in general purpose LLM-as-a-judge evaluation frameworks such as GPTScore [8] and Prometheus [12]. The common characteristic of these metric implementations is that they rely on prompting an external, typically commercial, LLM accessed through an API. Consequently, they tend to be relatively slow and potentially costly, while also being influenced by LLM biases [31] and prompt sensitivity [23].

An alternative approach to quantifying faithfulness is to evaluate the conditional probability of generated tokens given the preceding context [5,32]. For example, [5] demonstrated that such a measure can be used to train a lightweight surrogate model for context attribution. We build on this idea by addressing some of the inherent problems of using token probabilities as a measure of model output quality and providing further evidence that manipulating the provided context can reveal its role in generating a given output.

2 ConSens

The goal of the ConSens metric is to provide a way to determine to what extent an LLM generated text is grounded in the context provided given a user query and a prompt. To do this, we contrast the perplexity of the model output in two conditions: when the context is provided (P_C) and when the context is empty (P_E). The ratio of these two perplexities, P_E/P_C, represents the effect of providing context on the probability of output tokens. The larger the ratio, the stronger the effect.

The final value of ConSens is scaled to the interval (-1, 1) applying a sigmoid transformation:
$$ConSens = \frac{2}{1+e^{-r}} - 1,$$
where
$$r = \ln\left(\frac{P_E}{P_C}\right).$$

A value of ConSens close to 1 indicates that providing the context increases the likelihood of generating the given output. Values around and below 0 suggest that the context is not contributing to the output.

The perplexity of a generated text is computed by averaging the perplexity of the individual tokens:
$$P_{\text{text}} = \frac{1}{N} \sum_{i=1}^{N} e^{-\ln(p(token_i|token_{j<i}))}$$

, where $p(token_i|token_{j<i})$ is the probability of generating $token_i$ at step i given $token_{j<i}$ - the sequence of $i-1$ tokens which preceeds $token_i$.

In order to highlight the contrast between two conditions, we discard closed set words such as pronouns, determiners, and conjunctions (e.g., 'it', 'the', 'and'), as well as words which also appear in the user query. The rationale of filtering the set of words is to exclude words that are a priori likely to have similar perplexities in the two conditions and can thus lead to underestimating the effect of the provided context. Importantly, ConSens is not dependent on the absolute perplexity of the answer text, but rather on the ratio of its conditional perplexity in the two conditions. Therefore, ConSens is not directly affected by the problems of using perplexity as a general proxy of the qualities of generated text [7, 26]. A sample calculation of the metric is shown in Table 1.

3 Validation

We hereby present a series of experiments that aim to evaluate the performance of the proposed metric. We assume that the metric is used in a conventional open-book QA setting. In this setting, an LLM is tasked with responding to a user query given a context text (e.g., a list of retrieved documents). Each evaluation example consists of a query, a context, and a model output (answer). ConSens values are calculated using Llama 3.2 1B[1] from the Meta LLama 3 family [16]. The choice of the evaluator model is justified by evidence that small models are more likely to adhere to the provided context than to respond using parametric knowledge [2]. The following template was used for prompting the model during evaluation:

---

[1] https://huggingface.co/meta-llama/Llama-3.2-1B-Instruct.

Table 1. Example of how the ConSens is calculated. The user question and the LLM generated answer are shown at the top. The words that are included in the calculation of the perplexity are underlined. "David Baker" and "is" are excluded because they also appear in the question and will result in relatively low perplexity regardless of the context condition. Closed set words such as 'a' (determiner), 'and' (conjunction) and punctuation marks are also excluded. The perplexities of the resulting three words are computed in four different contexts, starting with an empty one. The ConSens scores are given for the non-empty contexts only.

Question: What is David Baker known for?
Answer: David Baker is a biochemist and computational biologist.

Context	Word perplexities			ConSens
	"biochemist"	"computational"	"biologist"	
(empty)	4814.38	7117.1	1.61	
David Baker is an American scientist who has pioneered methods to design proteins and predict their three-dimensional structures.	263.73	293.92	1.72	0.91
Colorless green ideas sleep furiously.	3098.83	14517.0	2.01	−0.19
David Baker is an English professional footballer.	234191.27	61734.0	1.63	−0.92

```
Consider the following context:
Context:
{{context}}
Please answer the following question:
{{question}}
Answer:
```

3.1 Experiments

Experiment 1: Evaluation of Grounded Versus Ungrounded Answers. In the first experiment, we evaluated the ability of the metric to distinguish between answers that are based on the given context and those that are not by using the publically available WikiEval dataset [6]. Each example contains a question, a context (excerpt from Wikipedia), and two answers generated using an unspecified version of ChatGPT. The first answer (referred to as the 'grounded' answer) was generated by providing the corresponding context, while the second answer ('ungrounded') was based on parametric knowledge of the model; that is, the model did not have access to the context. For each example, we computed the value of the metric for each of the answers.

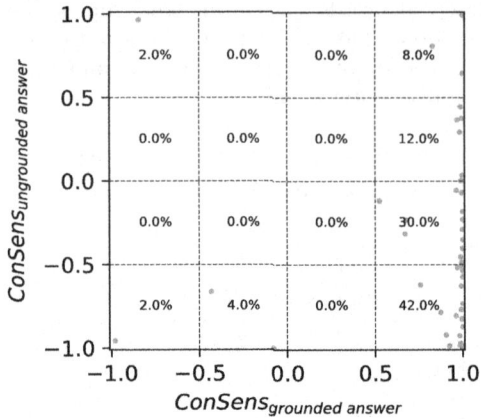

Fig. 1. Experiment 1 results. The x-axis represents the ConSens value for the grounded answer, while the y-axis corresponds to the ConSens value for the ungrounded answer. The percentage values indicate the proportion of scores that fall within the respective ranges of the two ConSens scores.

The results of Experiment 1 are presented in Fig. 1. The distribution of the metric scores clearly shows that ConSens results in higher values when grounded answers are evaluated (mean value m = 0.83, HDI[2]: [0.67, 1]) compared to ungrounded answers (m = −0.34, HDI: [−1.00, 0.45]). The average difference between conditions was 1.17 (HDI: [0.2, 2.00]). The value of the ROC AUC was 0.92 suggesting that the metric provides a reliable signal to differentiate answers that are based on the context provided from those that are not.

Experiment 2: Evaluation of Full Versus Partial Context. The second experiment aims to assess the sensitivity of the metric to removing a critical section of the provided context. A new dataset was constructed using a publicly available collection of biomedical abstracts [1]. For each abstract, we used OpenAI's GPT-4o to select two consecutive sentences and generate a question that could be answered using those sentences. The same model was then used to generate an answer to each of the questions using the entire abstract. The result of the procedure was a set of 657 questions paired with a full context (i.e. the whole abstract), partial context (the abstract with the two key sentences removed), and a model answer (generated by providing the full context).

The rationale for creating this dataset is to test the ability of the metric to distinguish the effect of two contexts on a generated answer when the contexts

---

[2] The highest density interval (HDI) stands for the shortest interval which contains a certain proportion of the data. The 90% HDI is used in all cases in this article.

are very similar as far as topic and terminology go. The difference between the full and partial context condition is only in those two consecutive sentences that are used to generate the question (note that the answer is always generated using the full context). This setting makes a stronger test of the ConSens metric than the WikiEval data set used in Experiment 1.

The results (Fig. 2) indicate that ConSens maxed out when the full context is provided. The value of ConSens was reliably higher in the full context condition (m = 0.95, HDI: [0.91, 1.0]) than in the partial context condition (m = 0.27, HDI: [−0.63, 1.0]). The mean difference between conditions was 0.69 (HDI: [0.0, 1.75]) and the ROC AUC was 0.93. Compared to the results of Experiment 1, there was an increased number of cases in which the metric resulted in similar scores, reflecting the increased difficulty to differentiate the effects of the full context and the partial context on the answer.

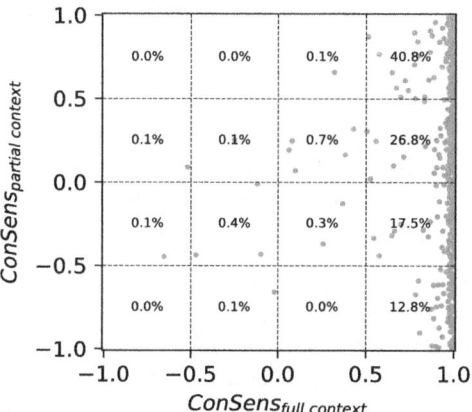

Fig. 2. Experiment 2 results. Values on the x axis represent the ConSens value when the full context was provided and the y axis represents the ConSens scores in the partial context condition. The high concentration of data points in the top-right region indicates that ConSens struggled to differentiate between the effects of partial and full contexts on the generated answers.

Experiment 3: Context Grounding in RAG Setting. The goal of the last experiment was to validate the use of ConSens in a typical RAG setting, in which the context consists of more than one document. The dataset consisted of the same questions and documents as in Experiment 2. The abstracts were vectorized using sentence embeddings[3] and fed into a vector database[4]. For each example, the question was used to retrieve the three most similar documents from the database. The context was constructed by concatenating the retrieved

---

[3] https://huggingface.co/sentence-transformers/all-MiniLM-L6-v2.
[4] https://github.com/chroma-core/chroma.

documents in randomized order. The answer was generated by providing the question and the context (consisting of the three documents) to gpt-4o.

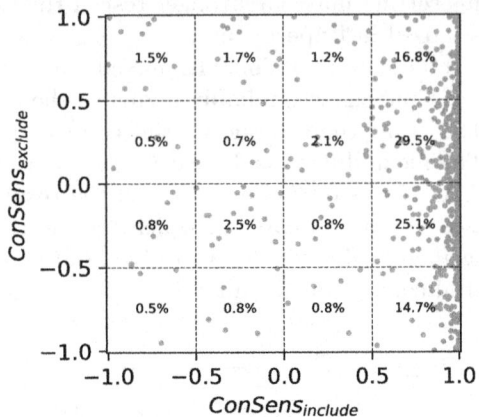

Fig. 3. Experiment 3 results. The x axis represents the minimum value of ConSens when the correct document (i.e. the abstract which was used to generate the question) was included in the context. Accordingly, the y axis stands for the value of ConSens when the correct document was not part of the context.

Only the retrieval hits were considered for evaluating ConSens, i.e. the cases in which the correct document (i.e., the abstract which was used to generate the question) was retrieved, which amounted to 88.21% of the examples. The validity of ConSens was tested by checking whether it can be used to identify which of the three retrieved documents was the most influential on the response. To do this, we manipulated the context by repeatedly excluding each of the documents from it and calculated the metric for each of the resulting three contexts. The idea of this manipulation is to examine the sensitivity of the metric to the exclusion of the most relevant context segment, compared to the other two.

The results of Experiment 3 are presented in Fig. 3. Removing the correct context resulted in the lowest ConSens score in 89.43% of the cases. Including the correct document in the context lead to a higher score (m = 0.77, HDI: [0.11, 1]) compared to when it was not included (m = 0.06, HDI: [−0.67, 1]). The mean difference between conditions was 0.72 (HDI: [−0.08, 1.98]). The ROC AUC was 0.88.

3.2 Comparison with Other Metrics

In order to gain further insight into the usefulness of the ConSens metric, the three experiments were repeated with the LLM-as-a-judge metric 'answer consistency' available in the Tonic Validate LLM/RAG evaluation framework [25]. The consistency score of the answers is calculated using OpenAI 'gpt-4-turbo-preview' to create a bulleted list of the main points in the response text and check the proportion of points that can be attributed to the provided context. The implementation of this metric therefore results in multiple calls to the evaluator model, the exact number depending on the number of main points extracted.

Furthermore, we also checked whether the performance of a ConSens across the three experiments can be explained in terms of the similarity between the context and the answer texts. To do this, we computed the cosine similarity of the vector embeddings of the two texts using the OpenAI 'text embedding-3-large' model.

The resulting ROC AUC scores for each of the metrics (Table 2) demonstrate that the performance of ConSens is comparable and, in some cases, superior to a much slower and more expensive LLM-as-a-judge metric and cannot be attributed to the mere similarity between the answer and the context texts.

Table 2. ROC AUC scores across the three experiments.

	ConSens	Tonic Answer Consistency	Answer-Context Similarity
Experiment 1	**0.92**	**0.92**	0.62
Experiment 2	**0.93**	0.75	0.68
Experiment 3	0.88	**0.91**	0.76

3.3 Evaluator Model

All the ConSens scores presented thus far have been based on token perplexity calculations using Llama 3.2 1B. We selected this model because it is one of the smallest industrial-grade models capable of following instructions and integrating information from relatively large texts. To demonstrate that ConSense's performance is not dependent on this specific model, we repeated the three experiments using three other models from the Llama family as well as two Gemma models ([24]) and phi-3-mini ([17]). The results, shown in Table 3, indicate that ConSense's performance remained largely independent from the choice of evaluator model. In other words, employing a larger (and slower and more expensive to deploy) model did not significantly impact ConSense's ability to distinguish between grounded and ungrounded generations of LLM.

4 Discussion

The pattern of results in all three experiments supports the validity of the ConSens metric. In Experiment 1, we show that ConSens can distinguish answers which are based on a given context from those which are not. In Experiment 2, the metric is used to determine which context is more likely to lead to generating a fixed answer. Finally, in Experiment 3, we demonstrate that ConSens can be used in RAG systems to identify which part of a given context contributes

Table 3. ConSens ROC AUC scores as a function of the evaluator model.

Evaluator Model	Experiment 1	Experiment 2	Experiment 3
Llama 3.2 1B	0.92	0.93	**0.88**
Llama 3.2 3B	0.97	**0.94**	0.87
Llama 3.1 8B	0.93	0.93	0.86
Llama 3.1 70B	0.92	0.92	0.82
Gemma 2 2B	0.95	0.90	0.85
Gemma 3 1B	0.90	0.91	0.76
phi-3-mini 4B	**0.98**	0.92	0.87

the most to a generated answer. It is worth noting that Experiments 2 and 3 are based on a dataset which has been constructed to be especially challenging for the metric. Importantly, the observed distribution of the ConSens scores between experiments and conditions indicates that the precision of the metric is high enough to be practically useful in real-world applications.

Although ConSens shows great promise for evaluating open-book QA systems, it does have certain limitations. Notably, it requires access to the model's raw outputs (i.e., logits), which are typically only available for open-source models and are difficult to obtain from LLMs accessed via API. However, in this paper, we demonstrate that the metric performs well even with one of the most lightweight LLMs available, making it suitable for efficient on-premise deployment across a variety of platforms, including edge and mobile devices.

Another limitation is that the metric scale is non-linear, which means that care must be taken when drawing conclusions from its data. For example, the metric cannot be used to show that the effect of document A on the answer is twice the effect of document B or that the difference between the effects of document A and B is the same as the difference between the effects of document C and D.

The idea of ConSens gives a lot of room for improvement and possible other use cases. For example, the same approach can be used to assess whether an auto-generated summary adequately covers all parts of the input. Another potential application is identifying critical segments of an LLM prompt that significantly influence the model's output. More broadly, the metric is applicable in any open-book QA scenario where the goal is to evaluate how the output of a generative LLM is conditioned on a specific segment of its input.

Unlike LLM-as-a-judge methods, ConSens doesn't require access to advanced LLM APIs, making it easy to deploy securely and privately. It's computationally efficient, works with lightweight models (not necessarily the one generating the answers), and avoids model-specific prompt tuning. Built on a simple, intuitive idea, ConSens is easy to interpret and implement. We believe it represents a valuable step toward effective evaluation of open-book QA systems in knowledge-intensive tasks.

Disclosure of Interests. The authors have no competing interests to declare that are relevant to the content of this article. Or: Author A has received research grants from Company W.

References

1. Attal, K., Ondov, B., Demner-Fushman, D.: A dataset for plain language adaptation of biomedical abstracts. Sci Data **10**(1), 8 (2023). https://www.nature.com/articles/s41597-022-01920-3
2. Bi, B., et al.: Context-dpo: Aligning language models for context-faithfulness. CoRR (2024). https://doi.org/10.48550/arXiv.2412.15280
3. Botev, V., Marinov, K., Schäfer, F.: Word importance-based similarity of documents metric (WISDM): fast and scalable document similarity metric for analysis of scientific documents. In: Proceedings of the 6th International Workshop on Mining Scientific Publications, pp. 17–23. ACM (2017), https://dl.acm.org/doi/10.1145/3127526.3127530
4. Chen, H.T., Zhang, M.J.Q., Choi, E.: Rich knowledge sources bring complex knowledge conflicts: Recalibrating models to reflect conflicting evidence. In: EMNLP 2022, Abu Dhabi, United Arab Emirates, 7-11 December 2022, pp. 2292–2307. ACL (2022), https://doi.org/10.18653/v1/2022.emnlp-main.146
5. Cohen-Wang, B., Shah, H. abd Georgiev, K., Madry, A.: Contextcite: Attributing model generation to context (2024). http://arxiv.org/abs/1904.09675
6. ES, S., James, J., Anke, L.E., Schockaert, S.: Ragas: Automated evaluation of retrieval augmented generation. In: EACL 2024 - System Demonstrations, St. Julians, Malta, 17-22 March 2024, pp. 150–158. ACL (2024), https://aclanthology.org/2024.eacl-demo.16
7. Fang, L., et al.: What is wrong with perplexity for long-context language modeling? CoRR (2024). https://doi.org/10.48550/arXiv.2410.23771
8. Fu, J., Ng, S., Jiang, Z., Liu, P.: Gptscore: Evaluate as you desire. In: NAACL 2024 (Volume 1: Long Papers), Mexico City, pp. 6556–6576. ACL (2024), https://doi.org/10.18653/v1/2024.naacl-long.365
9. Gao, M., Hu, X., Ruan, J., Pu, X., Wan, X.: LLM-based NLG evaluation: Current status and challenges (2024). http://arxiv.org/abs/2402.01383
10. Hawkins, W., Mittelstadt, B.D., Russell, C.: The effect of fine-tuning on language model toxicity. CoRR (2024). https://doi.org/10.48550/arXiv.2410.15821
11. Jacovi, A., et al.: The FACTS Grounding Leaderboard: Benchmarking LLMs' Ability to Ground Responses to Long-Form Input (2025). https://arxiv.org/abs/2501.03200
12. Kim, S., et al.: Prometheus 2: An open source language model specialized in evaluating other language models. In: Proceedings of the 2024 EMNLP (EMNLP), pp. 4334–4353. Miami, Florida, USA (2024). https://doi.org/10.18653/v1/2024.emnlp-main.248
13. Lewis, P.S.H., et al.: Retrieval-augmented generation for knowledge-intensive NLP tasks. In: NeurIPS 2020 (2020). https://proceedings.neurips.cc/paper/2020/hash/6b493230205f780e1bc26945df7481e5-Abstract.html
14. Lin, C.Y.: ROUGE: A package for automatic evaluation of summaries. In: Text Summarization Branches Out, pp. 74–81. ACL (2004). https://aclanthology.org/W04-1013/

15. Luo, Y., Yang, Z., Meng, F., Li, Y., Zhou, J., Zhang, Y.: An empirical study of catastrophic forgetting in large language models during continual fine-tuning. CoRR (2023). https://doi.org/10.48550/arXiv.2308.08747
16. Meta, L.T.A..: The llama 3 herd of models. CoRR (2024). https://doi.org/10.48550/arXiv.2407.21783
17. Microsoft: Phi-3 technical report: A highly capable language model locally on your phone (2024). https://arxiv.org/abs/2404.14219
18. OpenAI: Gpt-4 technical report (2024). https://arxiv.org/abs/2303.08774
19. Pham, Q., Ngo, H., Luu, A.T., Nguyen, D.Q.: Who's who: Large language models meet knowledge conflicts in practice. In: Findings of the Association for Computational Linguistics: EMNLP 2024, Miami, Florida, USA, 12-16 November 2024, pp. 10142–10151. ACL (2024), https://aclanthology.org/2024.findings-emnlp.593
20. Rashkin, H., et al.: Measuring attribution in natural language generation models. Comput. Linguistics **49**(4), 777–840 (2023). https://doi.org/10.1162/coli_a_00486
21. Roberts, A., Raffel, C., Shazeer, N.: How much knowledge can you pack into the parameters of a language model? In: EMNLP 2020, pp. 5418–5426. ACL (2020), https://doi.org/10.18653/v1/2020.emnlp-main.437
22. Saad-Falcon, J., Khattab, O., Potts, C., Zaharia, M.: ARES: an automated evaluation framework for retrieval-augmented generation systems. In: NAACL 2024 , (Volume 1: Long Papers), Mexico City, Mexico, pp. 338–354. ACL (2024), https://doi.org/10.18653/v1/2024.naacl-long.20
23. Sclar, M., Choi, Y., Tsvetkov, Y., Suhr, A.: Quantifying language models' sensitivity to spurious features in prompt design or: How I learned to start worrying about prompt formatting. In: ICLR 2024, Vienna, Austria, 2024. OpenReview.net (2024). https://openreview.net/forum?id=RIu5lyNXjT
24. Team, G.: Gemma: Open models based on gemini research and technology (2024), https://arxiv.org/pdf/2403.08295
25. Tonic.ai: Tonic Validate guide | Tonic Validate — docs.tonic.ai. https://docs.tonic.ai/validate (2023), Accessed 28 March 2025
26. Wang, Y., Deng, J., Sun, A., Meng, X.: Perplexity from PLM is unreliable for evaluating text quality. CoRR (2022). https://doi.org/10.48550/arXiv.2210.05892
27. Wu, K., Wu, E., Zou, J.: ClashEval: Quantifying the tug-of-war between an LLM's internal prior and external evidence (2024). https://arxiv.org/abs/2404.10198
28. Xie, J., Zhang, K., Chen, J., Lou, R., Su, Y.: Adaptive chameleon or stubborn sloth: Revealing the behavior of large language models in knowledge conflicts. In: ICLR 2024, Vienna, Austria, 7-11 May 2024. OpenReview.net (2024). https://openreview.net/forum?id=auKAUJZMO6
29. Xu, R., et al.: Knowledge conflicts for llms: A survey. In: Proceedings of the 2024 EMNLP, EMNLP 2024, Miami, FL, USA, 12-16 November 2024, pp. 8541–8565. ACL (2024), https://aclanthology.org/2024.emnlp-main.486
30. Yang, Z., Zhu, Z.: Curiousllm: Elevating multi-document QA with reasoning-infused knowledge graph prompting. CoRR (2024). https://doi.org/10.48550/arXiv.2404.09077
31. Ye, J., et al.: Justice or prejudice? quantifying biases in llm-as-a-judge. CoRR (2024). https://doi.org/10.48550/arXiv.2410.02736
32. Yuan, W., Neubig, G., Liu, P.: Bartscore: evaluating generated text as text generation. In: NeurIPS 2021, NeurIPS 2021, 6-14 December 2021, virtual, pp. 27263–27277 (2021). https://proceedings.neurips.cc/paper/2021/hash/e4d2b6e6fdeca3e60e0f1a62fee3d9dd-Abstract.html

33. Zhang, T., et al.: RAFT: adapting language model to domain specific RAG. CoRR (2024). https://doi.org/10.48550/arXiv.2403.10131
34. Zhang, T., Kishore, V., Wu, F., Weinberger, K.Q., Artzi, Y.: BERTScore: Evaluating text generation with BERT (2020). http://arxiv.org/abs/1904.09675

ChiMDQA: Towards Comprehensive Chinese Document QA with Fine-Grained Evaluation

Jing Gao[1,4], Shutiao Luo[2,4], Yumeng Liu[3,4], Yuanming Li[4(✉)], and Hongji Zeng[4]

[1] Beijing Jiaotong University, Beijing, China
jennygao@bjtu.edu.cn
[2] Beijing University of Posts and Telecommunications, Beijing, China
luoshutiao@bupt.edu.cn
[3] Beijing University of Technology, Beijing, China
liuyumeng-2021@emails.bjut.edu.cn
[4] Foxit Software Co. Ltd, Fuzhou, China
{yuanming_li,hongji_zeng}@foxitsoftware.com

Abstract. With the rapid advancement of natural language processing (NLP) technologies, the demand for high-quality Chinese document question-answering datasets is steadily growing. To address this issue, we present the Chinese Multi-Document Question Answering Dataset (ChiMDQA), specifically designed for downstream business scenarios across prevalent domains including academic, education, finance, law, medical treatment, and news. ChiMDQA encompasses long-form documents from six distinct fields, consisting of 6,068 rigorously curated, high-quality question-answer (QA) pairs further classified into ten fine-grained categories. Through meticulous document screening and a systematic question-design methodology, the dataset guarantees both diversity and high quality, rendering it applicable to various NLP tasks such as document comprehension, knowledge extraction, and intelligent QA systems. Additionally, this paper offers a comprehensive overview of the dataset's design objectives, construction methodologies, and fine-grained evaluation system, supplying a substantial foundation for future research and practical applications in Chinese QA. The code and data are available at: https://anonymous.4open.science/r/Foxit-CHiMDQA/

Keywords: Natural Language Processing · Document QA · Retrieval-Augmented Generation

1 Introduction

The rapid development of NLP technology has significantly accelerated the application of intelligent question-answering (QA) systems. Breakthroughs in pre-trained language models, such as BERT [29] and the GPT [25] series, have unlocked remarkable potential in domains including information retrieval, intelligent customer service, and knowledge management. However, current research predominantly focuses on English-language scenarios, and the development of Chinese question-answering systems is confronted with numerous challenges.

Although notable datasets such as CMRC [5] and DuReader [16] have contributed to the Chinese QA field, they reveal notable deficiencies in document diversity and question type comprehensiveness. These inherent limitations restrict their effectiveness in navigating the complex demands of real-world, multi-domain, and multi-task environments. Consequently, the development of a robust, multi-dimensional Chinese QA dataset represents a pivotal advancement for expanding the frontiers of Chinese NLP research.

Early QA datasets exhibited significant limitations in document coverage and question design depth. Mainstream datasets like SQuAD [24] predominantly rely on Wikipedia as a singular data source, resulting in a critical absence of specialized domain documents such as academic papers and legal texts. MS MARCO [13], while integrating web page data, presents substantial challenges with 90% of documents in HTML format, impeding effective handling of nested tables and cross-page formulas in PDF documents. DuReader [16] introduces a real Chinese search corpus, yet its documents average less than 400 words and fail to encompass structured long-form texts like financial and medical reports. In the domain of long document processing, MMLongBench-Doc [21] supports cross-page reasoning for 47.5 pages of English documents, but suffers from vague problem classification and limited cross-domain applicability. These fundamental constraints significantly hinder existing models' capabilities to parse multi-domain, rich-format long documents in real-world scenarios.

This paper presents the following contributions: (1) Chinese Multi-Topic Long Document Coverage: A comprehensive integration of six thematic document types comprising academic, financial, legal, medical, educational, and news, containing 6,068 QA pairs, providing a high-quality, diverse data resource for Chinese document question-answering. (2) Hierarchical Question Classification System: Grounded in the explicit and implicit fact theoretical framework [10], the question system encompasses two primary categories and ten subcategories, achieving two significant breakthroughs: Expanding the explicit fact category beyond SQuAD [24] and HotpotQA [32] by introducing three novel complex task types: filtering, statistical analysis, and computational reasoning; Developing implicit fact-based questions covering open-domain tasks such as generation and recommendation, extending assessment dimensions by 300% compared to DuReader [16]'s fact-based approach. (3) Fine-Grained Evaluation System: An innovative evaluation framework combining factual and open questions, comprising 21 comprehensive metrics for the Retrieval-Augmented Generation (RAG) system. This approach enables holistic performance assessment of QA systems across diverse question types, establishing a crucial foundation for Chinese QA research and application.

2 ChiMDQA Dataset

2.1 Motivation

As illustrated in Table 1, existing QA datasets primarily focus single-topic documents, thereby significantly constraining their applicability to the complex,

Table 1. Comparison of ChiMDQA with existing QA datasets.

Datasets	Data Source	Size	Language	PDF-Based	Stratification
SQuAD [24]	Wikipedia	100,000	English	No	No
MMLU-Pro [30]	STEM Website	12,032	English	No	No
Natural Questions [18]	Google search, Wikipedia	307,373	English	No	No
MS MARCO [13]	Bing's search	1,010,916	English	No	No
TriviaQA [17]	Wikipedia	95,956	English	No	No
HotpotQA [32]	Wikipedia	113,000	English	No	No
ScienceQA [20]	Elementary and high school science curricula	21,208	English	No	No
MULongBench-Doc [21]	lengthy PDF-formatted documents	1,091	English	Yes	No
DuReader [16]	Baidu Search, Baidu Zhidao documents	200,000	Chinese	No	6
DRCD [6]	Wikipedia	30,000	Chinese	No	7
ChiMDQA	lengthy PDF-formatted documents	6,068	Chinese	Yes	10

multi-domain document processing requirements of real-world scenarios. In addition, many of these datasets lack a fine-grained categorization of question types, failing to capture the full spectrum of question complexity—from straightforward fact retrieval to multi-step reasoning and semantic inference. To address these limitations, we propose ChiMDQA, a dataset designed to bridge this gap by incorporating multi-topic documents and a diverse set of well-defined, fine-grained question types. ChiMDQA is intended to serve as a more challenging and practically relevant benchmark, supporting the advancement of research and development in Chinese document-level QA.

2.2 Document Topics and Question Types

Document Topics. The ChiMDQA dataset covers six representative domains, namely academic, education, finance, law, medical treatment, and news to ensure broad topical coverage and real-world applicability. Academic documents consist of peer-reviewed research papers, which disseminate research findings and support academic endeavors. Educational documents focus on textbooks and instructional materials, covering various disciplines to facilitate teaching and educational research. Financial documents include financial reports that reflect corporate economic activities, aiding in financial analysis and decision-making. Legal documents comprise legal documents essential for legal practice, research, and case management. Medical documents involve clinical guidelines that inform medical practice. News documents feature journalistic articles that disseminate societal information. These domains were selected for their topical richness, representativeness, and relevance to real-world applications. Collectively, they offer comprehensive coverage of core knowledge required across a wide range of QA scenarios.

Question Types. ChiMDQA's question typology is grounded in Microsoft's two-level framework of explicit and implicit facts [10], refined for single-document QA. We use a two-tier system: Level 1 (L1) for explicit facts requiring direct extraction, and Level 2 (L2) for implicit facts needing inference or integration of information. For instance, "Where will the 2024 Olympics be held?" is an

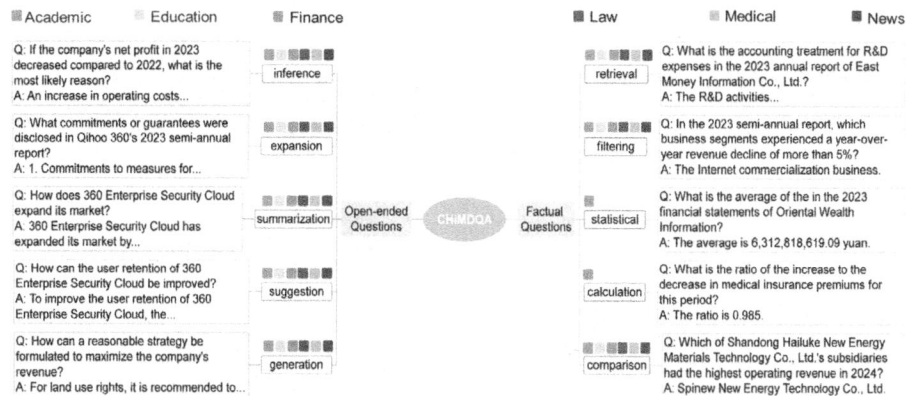

Fig. 1. Examples of Question Types and Their Topic Coverage in the ChiMDQA Dataset.

L1 question, while "What is the ruling party in the country where Canberra is located?" is an L2 question, as it requires synthesizing multiple pieces of information.

QA pairs in ChiMDQA are evenly divided between L1 and L2 and further categorized into factual and open-ended types, refined into ten subtypes to align with downstream tasks. Examples are shown in Fig. 1.

Factual Questions. Factual questions are those whose answers can be directly extracted from the document or obtained through simple calculations or filtering, without subjective reasoning or generative capabilities. This category includes the following subtypes:**(1) Retrieval Questions:** These are straightforward queries requiring the extraction of specific information explicitly stated in the document. No inference or summarization is involved. **(2) Filtering Questions:** These involve selecting target entities based on multiple conditions, such as Boolean logic, numeric ranges, classification constraints, or relational attributes. **(3) Statistical Questions:** These require basic statistical analysis of document content, including operations such as computing frequency, mean, maximum, minimum, median, mode, range, variance, standard deviation, and coefficient of variation. **(4) Computational Questions:** These involve arithmetic manipulation of numerical data within the document, including addition, subtraction, multiplication, division, percentage, and ratio calculations. **(5) Comparison Questions:** These questions require comparing entities of the same type along one or more dimensions, often necessitating a lightweight evaluation framework to assess differences in characteristics.

Open-Ended Question. Open-ended questions require reasoning, creative generation, or the integration of domain-specific knowledge. Answers are not constrained to a fixed template but instead emphasize semantic relevance, logical soundness, and contextual alignment. These questions typically demand a deeper understanding of document content and more comprehensive analytical capabilities. The open-ended category includes the following subtypes: **(1) Inference**

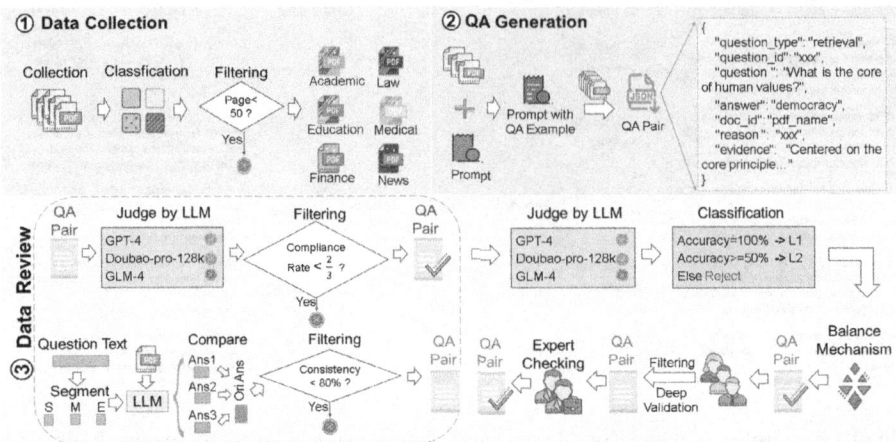

Fig. 2. The Framework of ChiMDQA Dataset Construction Process. (S: Start; M: Middle; E: End; Ori Ans: Original Answer)

Questions: These questions involve synthesizing dispersed information through logical reasoning and commonsense inference to uncover implicit facts. Examples include causal inference, multi-hop reasoning, or latent fact identification. **(2) Expansion Questions:** These require systematic elaboration of information to build hierarchical or structured representations, such as reconstructing organizational charts, taxonomies, or document section relationships. **(3) Summarization Questions:** These call for compressing and restructuring document content to distill key features or underlying patterns. Tasks may involve summarization, pattern identification, or concept clustering. **(4) Suggestion Questions:** These involve generating recommendations or decisions grounded in factual evidence from the document, often enhanced by domain-specific insights or contextual interpretation. **(5) Generation Questions:** These involve creative construction of new content based on the source document. Examples include imaginative extrapolation, cross-format transformation, or information synthesis.

In summary, ChiMDQA offers a comprehensive collection of documents across six domains, systematically categorizing questions into factual and open-ended types. By providing a structured approach to question answering, it provides a robust framework for evaluating and advancing question-answering methodologies across diverse computational linguistic research and applied scenarios.

2.3 Dataset Construction

ChiMDQA was constructed through a multi-stage pipeline, encompassing: data collection, QA pair generation, data review, and validation and statistics. An overview of the process is shown in Fig. 2.

Step 1: Data Collection. We collected approximately 15,000 multilingual PDF documents through web crawling and manual acquisition. Non-Chinese documents were filtered out using automated language detection tool. The remaining documents were further screened based on the following guidelines: **(1) File Format:** Only high-resolution, original (non-scanned) PDF files were retained to ensure extractable text and structural integrity. **(2) Timeliness and Relevance:** Documents were required to be published within the last five years and demonstrate clear relevance to one of the six target domains.**(3) Source Authority and Copyright Compliance:** All documents were obtained from credible sources with verified copyright compliance.

Following these criteria, we curated 60 representative documents—10 from each domain. Each selected PDF was processed through text extraction (using the PyMuPDF library), format normalization, and content cleaning. Text was segmented into logical blocks, and non-informative elements were removed via rule-based filtering to enhance data usability.

Step 2: QA Pair Generation. For each of the ten predefined question type, we designed specialized prompts that included task descriptions, generation requirements, JSON formatting specifications, and illustrative examples to guide large language models (LLMs) in producing high-quality QA pairs. After iterative refinement through pilot runs, we incorporated three validated JSON samples into the final prompt template used for large-scale generation.

We also conducted detailed document-level statistics, analyzing page count, word count, and token length across domains. Based on this analysis, we determined that models must support context windows of at least 64k tokens to effectively process long-form documents. As ChiMDQA is a Chinese-language dataset, we prioritized LLMs that have demonstrated strong performance in Chinese NLP and complex reasoning tasks. The selected models include: moonshot-v1-128k [27], doubao-pro-128k [4], qwen-plus [9], deepseek-chat [7] and glm-4-pro [11]. All models support context lengths of 64k tokens or more, making them well-suited for long-document comprehension.

Using the finalized prompts, we generated an initial batch of 250 QA pairs. We then randomly sampled 20% of the generated pairs for manual evaluation to assess their alignment with quality standards. Based on performance, consistency, and overall generation quality, GLM-4-Pro [11] was selected as the final model for generating the full set of QA pairs.

Step 3: Data Review. To ensure the quality and reliability of ChiMDQA, we implemented a hybrid verification pipeline combining automated evaluation with human-in-the-loop review. This multi-layered framework was designed to rigorously assess the factual accuracy, coherence, and structural diversity of the generated QA pairs.

Step 3.1: Automated Evaluation. To support large-scale quality assurance and efficient filtering, we design a multi-dimensional collaborative auditing framework that balances both efficiency and accuracy. The system leverages heterogeneous model verification, context robustness testing, and a dynamic difficulty-balancing mechanism. The pipeline includes: **(1) Multi-model Collaborative Pre-screening:** Three heterogeneous LLMs—GPT-4 [22], Doubao-

Table 2. Dataset statistics of ChiMDQA.

Statistics	Number	Statistics	Number
#Problems	6,068	**Length**	
Topics		**Question Length**	
- Academic	922	- maximum length	393
- Education	1,028	- minimum length	8
- Finance	980	- avg length	37.31
- Law	972	**Reference Answer Length**	
- Medical	1,107	- maximum length	4,726
treatment		- minimum length	2
- News	1,059	- avg length	162.44

Table 3. Statistical Analysis of Document Details within the Dataset.

Topic	Max Pages	Min Pages	Avg Pages	Max Length	Min Length	Avg Length
Academic	283	176	229.2	635,756	201,912	326,905
Education	129	60	102.1	154,363	65,796	97,356
Finance	275	118	167.7	247,067	107,265	156,131
Law	354	46	150.1	216,258	19,282	88,536
Medical treatment	181	64	102.5	335,273	4,061	96,088
News	160	60	100.7	728,287	317,266	593,027
Average	230.33	87.33	142.13	386,167.33	119,263.67	226,340.43

Pro-128k [4], and GLM-4 [11]—are employed for parallel inference and validation of QA pairs. Each model assigns a confidence score to the generated answer. Only QA pairs that receive confidence scores above 0.85 from at least two models are retained for further review. **(2) Context Sensitivity Screening:** To test robustness, we apply controlled context truncation (e.g., extracting the beginning, middle, or end of the document) and compare the model-generated responses across these segments to those generated from full context. QA pairs are flagged if answer consistency drops below an 80% threshold. **(3) Difficulty Calibration and Distribution Balancing:** We construct a gradient-based test set that classifies questions into two predefined difficulty levels, where L1 encompasses explicit fact retrieval and L2 involves single-step reasoning or knowledge integration. The distribution of these levels was continuously monitored. If a significant imbalance was detected (e.g., L1 exceeding 60%), sampling and generation strategies were adjusted accordingly to maintain diversity and prevent skewed learning dynamics.

Step 3.2: Manual Review. To further ensure the accuracy, clarity, and diversity of QA pairs, we conducted a comprehensive manual review following a strict five-stage cross-validation approach. The review procedure adhered to strict evaluation guidelines—namely, question clarity, answer correctness, and coverage across question types—and was implemented through a five-stage cross-validation framework: **(1) Initial Screening:** A team of three reviewers performed an initial evaluation using standardized templates to assess question clarity, grammatical correctness, and logical coherence. QA pairs that failed to meet baseline quality criteria were discarded. **(2) Deep Verification:** Two auditors independently examined the semantic accuracy of the answers, checked for logical coherence, and flagged ambiguous or unsupported claims. The focus was on ensuring alignment with the document and factual correctness. **(3) Dispute Arbitration:** In cases where reviewers disagreed, a third reviewer conducted a double-blind cross-validation, making the final decision on whether to retain, revise, or discard the QA pair. **(4) Diversity Review:** Reviewers assessed the semantic similarity of QA pairs to identify and flag redundant or duplicate questions. Based on their evaluations and optimization suggestions, the question generation strategy was refined to enhance diversity and reduce content overlap. **(5) Experts Validation:** A final round of domain-specific review was conducted by experts, who assessed the appropriateness and credibility of both questions and answers. They also resolved edge cases and resolved remaining disputes to ensure domain fidelity and factual accuracy.

Step 4: Data Validation and Statistics. To assess the quality and correctness of the dataset, we randomly sampled 100 QA pairs from each domain and conducted a manual validation process following the internal verification guideline and the Google Proof standard. The evaluation was carried out by members of the author team. Results indicated an overall error rate of approximately 3%, with most questions requiring contextual understanding rather than relying on memorized or easily retrievable internet knowledge. In addition, a comprehensive review was performed to ensure that the dataset contained no sensitive personal information or copyright-infringing content.

Overall, statistics related to question length and reference answer length are summarized in Table 2, while document-level statistics are presented in Table 3.

2.4 Future Expansion of the Dataset

While the current version of ChiMDQA provides a robust foundation for evaluation, we recognize the importance of continuous growth to keep pace with the evolving capabilities of LLMs. We have established a clear roadmap for future expansion, focusing on both increasing the dataset's scale and broadening its scope. Our expansion strategy will follow a semi-automated pipeline: (1) **Domain Expansion:** We plan to incorporate new high-value domains such as engineering, environmental science, and government reports. (2) **Automated Candidate Generation:** We will leverage state-of-the-art LLMs to generate a large pool of candidate QA pairs for new documents, using the same structured prompting techniques developed for the initial dataset. (3) **Rigorous Human-in-the-Loop Verification:** Crucially, all automatically generated candidates will undergo the same multi-stage human review and validation process detailed in Sect. 2.3. This ensures that any new additions meet the high standards of quality, accuracy, and diversity that define ChiMDQA. This hybrid approach will allow us to scale the dataset efficiently while maintaining its integrity as a reliable and challenging benchmark.

3 Experiments

3.1 Experimental Setup

We evaluate eight closed-source LLMs, each supporting a context window size of at least 128k tokens. The models include GPT-4 [22], GPT-4o [23], GLM-4-Plus [11], GLM-4-Air [11], GLM-4-Flash [11], YAYI-30B [14], Qwen-Plus [9] and Doubao-Pro-128k [4]. These models represent some of the most advanced LLMs currently available, primarily developed by the Chinese research and open-source communities. In addition to these models, we also conducted preliminary tests on other leading models from large technology companies, such as Google's Gemini series [15], Baichuan's models [31], and Meta's Llama series [1]. Our observations indicate that their performance trends are largely consistent with the results presented in this paper, with top-tier models like Gemini-1.5-Pro showing competitive performance comparable to GPT-4o. To maintain the clarity and focus of our result tables, we have centered our detailed analysis on the selected eight models, which provide a representative and diverse sample of the current state-of-the-art for Chinese long-document QA. They provide a strong foundation for evaluating both non-RAG and RAG-based question-answering systems.

3.2 Evaluation Metrics

To comprehensively assess the performance of non-RAG and RAG systems, we introduce a suite of evaluation metrics tailored to each setting. These fine-grained metrics enable more precise measurement of model capabilities and serve as guidance for downstream optimization.

For Non-RAG Evaluation for Factual Questions, We adopt the following evaluation metrics: Correct (CO) [8]: The predicted answer fully includes the reference answer and introduces no contradictory information. Not Attempted (NA) [8]: The predicted answer does not include the reference answer but also does not introduce contradictions. Incorrect (IN) [8]: The predicted answer contradicts the reference answer. Correct Given Attempted (CGA) [8]: The proportion of correctly answered questions among all attempted questions. F1-Score: The harmonic mean between Correct and CGA, calculated as:

$$F1 - \text{Score} = 2 \times \frac{\text{CO} \times \text{CGA}}{\text{CO} + \text{CGA}} \quad (1)$$

For open-ended questions, we apply the following automatic evaluation metrics: METEOR (M) [2]: Measures semantic similarity between generated and reference answers. ROUGE-L (R-L) [2]: Evaluates lexical overlap based on the longest common subsequence. CIDEr (C) [28]: Captures consensus and semantic consistency between generated and reference answers. Perplexity (PPL) [3]: Reflects the model's confidence when generating text; lower values indicate more fluent and confident output. BERTScore-F1 (B-F1) [12]: Assesses semantic similarity using contextual embeddings from BERT. We use the bert-base-chinese model in this study. The BERTScore-F1 is calculated using the following formulas:

$$\text{B-Precision} = \frac{\sum_i \text{sim}(g_i, r_i) \times \mathbb{I}(g_i \in r)}{\sum_i \mathbb{I}(g_i \in g)} \quad (2)$$

$$\text{B-Recall} = \frac{\sum_i \text{sim}(g_i, r_i) \times \mathbb{I}(r_i \in r)}{\sum_i \mathbb{I}(r_i \in r)} \quad (3)$$

$$\text{B-F1} = 2 \times \frac{\text{B-Precision} \times \text{B-Recall}}{\text{B-Precision} + \text{B-Recall}} \quad (4)$$

Here, g_i and r_i represent tokens in the generated and reference answers, respectively. $\text{sim}(g_i, r_i)$ denotes the cosine similarity between token embeddings, and $\mathbb{I}(\cdot)$ is the indicator function.

For RAG systems, in addition to adopting the same evaluation metrics as non-RAG systems for factual and open-ended questions, we also incorporate the RAGChecker [26] framework to conduct fine-grained evaluation of the retrieval and generation modules. The retrieval module metrics [26] include "Claim Recall" and "Context Precision", which measure the coverage and precision of the retrieved information required to generate a correct answer. The generation module metrics [26] include Faithfulness, which assesses the extent to which the generated answer relies on the retrieved content; Relevant Noise Sensitivity and Irrelevant Noise Sensitivity, which evaluate the model's sensitivity to semantically related and unrelated distractors, respectively; Hallucination, which detects statements in the generated response that are unrelated to both the reference answer and the retrieved context; Self-Knowledge, which measures the model's ability to answer based on its own pretrained knowledge; and Context Utilization, which evaluates how effectively the retrieved content is used during generation. Overall metrics [26] are computed by calculating the proportion of correct factual claims in the predicted answer (Precision) and the proportion of reference claims that are correctly predicted (Recall), and further integrating them into a comprehensive F1-Score to assess the quality of the generated response.

In summary, our evaluation framework offers a comprehensive, multi-perspective approach to measuring both the retrieval and generation performance of QA systems, supporting rigorous assessment and optimization.

4 Results and Analysis

4.1 Baselines

Table 4 and Table 5 present the evaluation results of various LLMs on the ChiMDQA dataset. These tables provide overall performance metrics for both factual and open-ended questions, including five evaluation indicators, as well as F1-Score and BERTScore-F1 across six distinct domains. From these results, we observe several insightful and noteworthy findings.

Table 4. Results of different models on factual questions in the ChiMDQA dataset. For metrics, **CO**, **NA**, **IN**, **CGA**, and **F1** denote "Correct", "Not attempted", "Incorrect", "Correct given attempted", and "F1-Score", respectively. **Bold** denotes the best model scores, and underline denotes the second-best model scores.

Models	Overall results on 5 metrics					F1-Score↑ on 6 topics					
	CO↑	NA↓	IN↓	CGA↑	F1↑	Acad	Edu	Fin	Law	Med	News
GPT-4 [22]	66.7	11.3	22.0	74.2	70.5	63.5	87.8	53.9	84.5	67.0	73.0
GPT-4o [23]	**73.2**	9.3	17.5	81.4	**76.5**	69.0	90.7	**57.6**	**87.4**	74.9	**77.8**
GLM-4-Plus [11]	69.5	10.0	20.5	77.0	73.2	65.8	89.2	56.0	86.0	70.0	74.5
GLM-4-Air [11]	67.1	10.2	22.8	74.7	70.6	64.0	87.2	54.0	85.3	67.5	73.5
GLM-4-Flash [11]	61.8	15.4	22.8	73.1	65.9	**71.2**	89.5	46.5	80.5	70.9	50.7
YAYI-30B [14]	61.4	24.8	**13.8**	81.6	70.1	44.8	**94.6**	56.3	81.2	77.8	64.5
Qwen-Plus [9]	68.5	17.9	**12.6**	**84.7**	76.3	61.5	**97.4**	52.1	84.9	**87.5**	60.6
Doubao-Pro-128k [4]	69.4	11.4	19.2	78.3	73.6	70.4	89.7	54.5	78.9	79.5	65.7

Table 5. Results of different models on open-ended questions in the ChiMDQA dataset. For metrics, **M**, **R-L**, **C**, **PPL**, and **B-F1** denote "METEOR", "ROUGE-L", "CIDEr", "Perplexity", and "BERTScore-F1", respectively. **Bold** denotes the best model scores, and underline denotes the second-best model scores.

Models	Overall results on 5 metrics					BERTScore-F1↑ on 6 topics					
	M↑	R-L↑	C↑	PPL↓	B-F1↑	Acad	Edu	Fin	Law	Med	News
GPT-4 [22]	24.9	29.8	34.7	30.3	74.9	74.8	77.9	76.8	77.6	76.5	75.3
GPT-4o [23]	**27.7**	**33.2**	**37.0**	25.8	**81.2**	**80.9**	81.9	79.7	**81.3**	79.8	**80.9**
GLM-4-Plus [11]	27.4	32.9	36.9	25.0	80.4	80.5	81.5	79.4	80.7	79.6	80.7
GLM-4-Air [11]	25.4	31.9	27.7	30.1	78.5	73.0	81.3	78.5	80.5	78.9	78.6
GLM-4-Flash [11]	26.0	32.5	28.0	27.8	79.3	74.0	**82.0**	79.0	81.0	79.5	79.5
YAYI-30B [14]	26.3	25.7	14.4	**20.8**	78.0	75.4	79.6	77.9	80.0	76.8	78.9
Qwen-Plus [9]	26.0	28.2	18.2	25.0	78.0	73.9	80.8	77.7	79.9	77.2	79.0
Doubao-Pro-128k [4]	22.7	26.4	12.3	53.1	76.1	74.5	78.4	75.3	73.7	76.0	78.5

- **GPT-4o Achieves Superior Overall Performance**: As shown in Table 4, GPT-4o achieves the highest scores in overall metrics for factual questions, with a CGA rate of 81.4 and an F1 of 76.5. These results indicate that GPT-4o not only attempts more questions correctly but also maintains high precision, outperforming other leading models in factual QA tasks. Table 5 further reveals that GPT-4o excels in open-ended questions, achieving top scores in M, R-L, C, and B-F1, with a B-F1 of 81.2. These results demonstrate GPT-4o's superior generative capabilities and semantic fluency.
- **High Perplexity Across Models**: Table 5 indicates that all models exhibit relatively high PPL scores on open-ended questions. For instance,

Table 6. Overall, Retrieval, and Generator Metrics for RAG Systems on ChiMDQA. For retrieval metrics, **Claim-R** and **Context-P** denote "Claim Recall" and "Context Precision", respectively. For generator metrics, **Fth**, **RNS**, **INS**, **Hlc**, **SK**, and **CU** denote "Faithfulness", "Relevant Noise Sensitivity", "Irrelevant Noise Sensitivity", "Hallucination", "Self-knowledge", and "Context Utilization", respectively. **Bold** denotes the best model scores, and underline denotes the second-best model scores.

Models	Overall Metrics			Retrieval Metrics		Generator Metrics					
	Precision$^\uparrow$	Recall$^\uparrow$	F1-Score$^\uparrow$	Claim-R$^\uparrow$	Context-P$^\uparrow$	Fth$^\uparrow$	RNS$^\downarrow$	INS$^\downarrow$	Hlc$^\downarrow$	SK$^\downarrow$	CU$^\uparrow$
GPT-4 [22]	37.8	39.7	31.9	59.1	50.2	50.3	24.8	6.9	26.2	4.9	68.4
GPT-4o [23]	**43.9**	44.4	**37.8**	**63.7**	**54.7**	57.6	25.9	7.8	22.3	5.3	**74.6**
GLM-4-Plus [11]	43.0	43.5	36.5	62.3	53.5	54.0	27.0	7.0	21.0	6.0	72.0
GLM-4-Air [11]	42.7	44.0	35.7	59.6	52.8	53.6	26.5	7.5	**20.6**	5.5	71.8
GLM-4-Flash [11]	43.1	38.9	31.3	59.4	50.6	46.5	**22.0**	6.6	27.0	5.6	66.3
YAYI-30B [14]	37.7	**49.6**	36.1	59.9	52.6	**59.6**	27.2	8.0	24.0	4.8	68.6
Qwen-Plus [9]	40.6	43.1	34.1	59.2	52.3	54.4	26.4	7.3	23.3	**4.4**	71.0
Doubao-Pro-128k [4]	43.7	38.0	28.3	61.3	52.5	45.1	23.9	**6.2**	23.3	4.2	70.0

GLM-4-Flash records a PPL of 27.8, while Doubao-Pro-128k reaches 53.1. High perplexity values suggest greater uncertainty in text generation, likely attributable to the inherent diversity of open-ended questions, which often lack a single correct answer. Consequently, models must generate responses within a broad semantic spectrum, leading to increased uncertainty.

- **Variability in Domain-Specific Performance**: Model performance varies significantly across domains. For example, in the financial domain, YAYI-30B achieves a B-F1 of 77.9 on open-ended questions but only an F1 of 56.3 on factual questions. Conversely, Qwen-Plus attains an F-Score of 84.7 on factual questions in the legal domain but records a BERTScore of just 79.9 on open-ended questions. This variability underscores the limitations of current models in handling domain-specific knowledge and highlights the need for further optimization to enhance adaptability and accuracy in specialized fields.

4.2 Retrieval-Augmented Baseline Model

In this study, we explore the effectiveness of the RAG strategy in improving the accuracy of LLMs on different types of questions. Specifically, we implemented a RAG system based on Langchain [19], with the following improvements:

- **Replacement of Embedding Model**: We replaced the original piccolo-base-zh model with the BCEmbedding model. This improvement aims to enhance the accuracy of vector representation and retrieval efficiency, thereby improving the model's ability to understand input queries.
- **Introduction of a Rerank Model**: We introduced the bce-reranker-base model to rerank the retrieved document snippets. This step helps to improve

the relevance of the retrieval results, ensuring that the model can obtain information from the most relevant document snippets.
- **Implementation of Intelligent Segmentation**: We implemented intelligent segmentation features, including automatic completion of affiliations for headings, paragraph titles, and hierarchical levels. This feature helps the model to better understand and organize the document structure, thereby improving the accuracy of retrieval and generation.

Using the RAGChecker framework, we evaluate system performance (see Table 6). Overall, GPT-4o achieved the best scores across all metrics, with Precision, Recall, and F1-Score reaching 43.9, 44.4, and 37.8, respectively, indicating superior alignment between generated answers and factual content. However, none of the models surpassed 40 in F1-Score, suggesting that RAG systems still have room for improvement when handling complex questions. In terms of retriever performance, GPT-4o scored 63.7 and 54.7 in Claim Recall and Context Precision, respectively, while GLM-4-Plus closely followed, demonstrating strong accuracy in identifying relevant document segments. For generator performance, YAYI-30B achieved the highest Faithfulness score (59.6), reflecting strong reliability of generated answers, whereas GPT-4o scored highest in Context Utilization (74.6), indicating its ability to more effectively leverage retrieved content for answer generation. Nevertheless, all models exhibited a Hallucination rate exceeding 20, revealing that RAG systems still face challenges in controlling factuality and hallucinations in generated content.

As shown in Fig. 3, all models showed notable improvements under the RAG setting. Specifically, for factual questions, all models saw improvements in F1-Score after applying the RAG strategy. For instance, GPT-4o improved from 76.5 to 81.2, GLM-4-Plus from 73.2 to 77.1, and YAYI-30B from 70.1 to 74.0, with an average gain of 4.6%. This demonstrates that RAG strategies effectively enhance model comprehension and factual answer generation. For open-ended

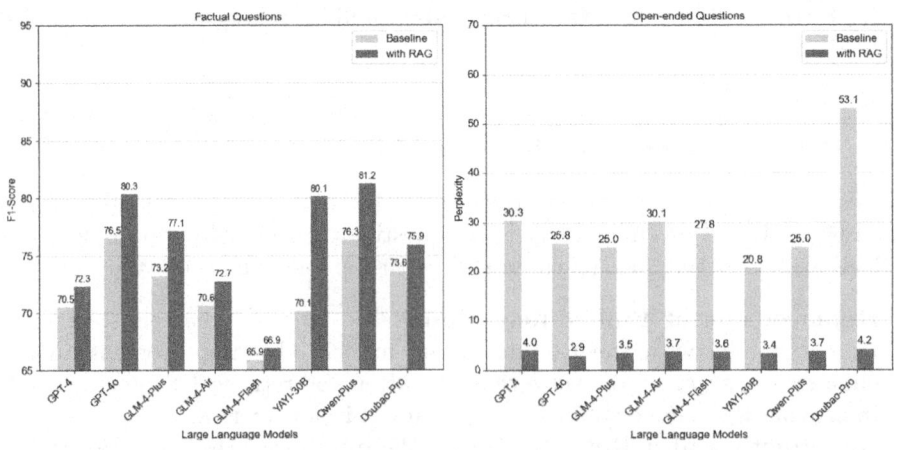

Fig. 3. Performance Comparison of Models with and without RAG.

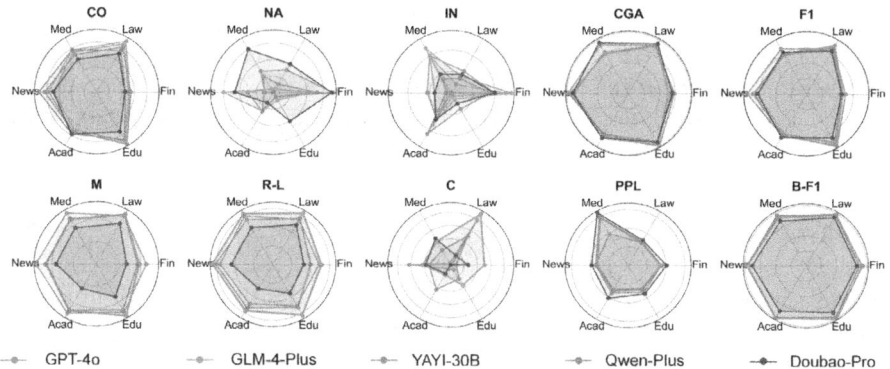

Fig. 4. Results of different models for six topics. (Top: Evaluation metrics for factual questions; Bottom: Evaluation metrics for open-ended questions)

questions, RAG significantly reduced model perplexity, indicating lower uncertainty and complexity in generated text. For example, Doubao-Pro-128k's perplexity dropped from 53.1 to 42.0, and GPT-4's from 30.3 to 24.0. Overall, the average perplexity decreased by 81.2%, suggesting that RAG not only improves the accuracy of generated answers, but also reduces model uncertainty, thereby yielding more fluent and coherent outputs for both factual and open-ended question types.

4.3 Domain-Wise Results Analysis

As discussed in Sect. 2.2, ChiMDQA spans six major domains, allowing for comprehensive assessment of model knowledge across diverse fields. Figure 4 presents a comparison of GPT-based models across all domains under the RAG setting.

GPT-4o consistently outperformed other models across all domains, achieving high scores in both CO and F1 metrics. For instance, in the legal domain, GPT-4o achieved a CO of 92.84 and an F1 of 90.32. GLM-4-Plus also demonstrated competitive performance, especially in CGA and B-F1, showing high alignment between generated answers and both factual and contextual content. YAYI-30B and Qwen-Plus performed well in some domains, but had limited knowledge coverage in areas such as finance. Doubao-Pro-128k exhibited lower performance across domains, with a relatively high Incorrect rate and a higher proportion of NA answers, indicating poor knowledge retrieval and question interpretation in certain areas.

For open-ended questions, models performance varied more significantly across domains. GPT-4o and GLM-4-Plus achieved better performance in metrics like M and R-L, indicating their responses were more consistent and better aligned with reference answers. YAYI-30B and Qwen-Plus also performed reasonably well in some domains, though they exhibited more volatility in performance across tasks. Doubao-Pro-128k showed the weakest overall results in open-ended tasks, with low scores in M and R-L, indicating significant challenges in generating coherent and relevant long-form responses. In conclusion, GPT-4o and GLM-4-Plus demonstrated more balanced and robust performance across both question types and domains, whereas other models showed more variation in quality depending on the specific task or field.

5 Conclusion

The construction of the ChiMDQA dataset aims to address the limitations in document types and question diversity within existing Chinese QA datasets, thereby satisfying the complex multi-domain and multi-type QA requirements in real-world scenarios. Through rigorous document screening and a systematic question design process, ChiMDQA contains six fields and 6,068 high-quality QA pairs. The design, construction, and fine-grained evaluation system of the dataset lay a solid foundation for related research and applications in Chinese QA. Experimental findings demonstrate that ChiMDQA effectively evaluate the processing capabilities of LLMs across different question types and business domains. Our exploration of the RAG strategy revealed that it substantially improves the models' F1-Score on factual questions and mitigates uncertainty for open-ended questions, thereby enhancing the accuracy and coherence of generated responses. However, there remains scope for improvement in handling complex questions and alleviating hallucinations.

Acknowledgments. This study was funded by Foxit Software Co. Ltd, Fuzhou, China. We are grateful to our colleagues at Foxit Software Co. Ltd, Fuzhou, China, for their valuable support and contributions. Special thanks also go to the reviewers for their insightful feedback.

References

1. AI@Meta. The llama 3 herd of models (2024). https://ai.meta.com/blog/meta-llama-3/
2. Banerjee, S., Lavie, A.: METEOR: an automatic metric for MT evaluation with improved correlation with human judgments (2005)
3. Brown, P.F., et al.: Class-based n-gram models of natural language. Comput. Linguist. **18**(4), 467–480 (1992)
4. ByteDance. Doubao-pro-128k. https://www.doubao.com
5. Cui, Y., et al.: A span-extraction dataset for Chinese machine reading comprehension
6. Shao, C.-C., et al.: DRCD: a Chinese machine reading comprehension dataset. *CoRR*, abs/1806.00920 (2018). http://arxiv.org/abs/1806.00920
7. DeepSeek-AI, et al.: DeepSeek-V3 technical report (2025). https://arxiv.org/abs/2412.19437
8. Wei, J., et al.: Measuring short-form factuality in large language models (2024). https://arxiv.org/abs/2411.04368

9. Bai, J., et al.: Qwen technical report. *arXiv preprint* arXiv:2309.16609 (2023)
10. Zhao, S., et al.: Retrieval augmented generation (RAG) and beyond: a comprehensive survey on how to make your LLMs use external data more wisely (2024). https://arxiv.org/abs/2409.14924
11. Team GLM, et al.: ChatGLM: a family of large language models from GLM-130B to GLM-4 all tools (2024). https://arxiv.org/abs/2406.12793
12. Zhang, T., et al.: BERTScore: evaluating text generation with BERT (2020). https://arxiv.org/abs/1904.09675
13. Nguyen, T., et al.: MS MARCO: A human generated machine reading comprehension dataset. *CoRR*, abs/1611.09268 (2016). http://arxiv.org/abs/1611.09268
14. Luo, Y., et al.: YAYI 2: Multilingual open-source large language models (2023). https://arxiv.org/abs/2312.14862
15. Google Gemini Team: Gemini 1.5: Unlocking multimodal understanding across millions of tokens of context (2024). https://storage.googleapis.com/deepmind-media/gemini/gemini_v1_5_report.pdf
16. He, W., et al.: DuReader: a Chinese machine reading comprehension dataset from real-world applications
17. Joshi, M., et al.: TriviaQA: A large scale distantly supervised challenge dataset for reading comprehension
18. Kwiatkowski, T., et al.: Natural questions: a benchmark for question answering research. Trans. Assoc. Comput. Linguist. **7** (2019)
19. LangChain. Langchain (2023). https://www.langchain.com/
20. Lu, P., et al.: Learn to explain: multimodal reasoning via thought chains for science question answering. In: The 36th Conference on Neural Information Processing Systems (NeurIPS) (2022)
21. Ma, Y., et al.: MMLongBench-Doc: benchmarking long-context document understanding with visualizations. In: Advances in Neural Information Processing Systems, vol. 37, pp. 95963–96010. Curran Associates, Inc. (2024)
22. OpenAI: GPT-4 (2023). https://openai.com/index/gpt-4
23. OpenAI. GPT-4O (2024). https://openai.com/index/hello-gpt-4o
24. Rajpurkar, P., et al.: SQuAD: 100,000+ questions for machine comprehension of text
25. Rathje, S., et al.: GPT is an effective tool for multilingual psychological text analysis. Proc. Natl. Acad. Sci. **121**(34), e2308950121 (2024)
26. Ru, D., et al.: RAGChecker: a fine-grained framework for diagnosing retrieval-augmented generation. In: Globerson, A., et al. (eds.) Advances in Neural Information Processing Systems, vol. 37, pp. 21999–22027. Curran Associates, Inc. (2024)
27. Kimi Team. Moonshot-v1-128k. https://kimi.moonshot.cn
28. Vedantam, R., et al.: CIDEr: consensus-based image description evaluation. In: 2015 IEEE Conference on Computer Vision and Pattern Recognition (CVPR), pp. 4566–4575 (2015)
29. Wang, J., et al.: Utilizing BERT for information retrieval: survey, applications, resources, and challenges. ACM Comput. Surv. **56**(7), 1–33 (2024)
30. Wang, Y., et al.: MMLU-Pro: a more robust and challenging multi-task language understanding benchmark. In: Globerson, A., et al. (eds.) Advances in Neural Information Processing Systems, vol. 37, pp. 95266–95290. Curran Associates, Inc. (2024)
31. Yang, A., et al.: Baichuan 2: open large-scale language models. *arXiv preprint* arXiv:2309.10305 (2023)
32. Yang, Z., et al.: HotpotQA: a dataset for diverse, explainable multi-hop question answering

Emotional Text-to-Speech via Style Decoder with Emotion Shared Styleformer Block and RoPE Prior Encoder

Wenhan Yao[1], Fen Xiao[1], Ye Xiao[1], Zexin Li[1], Xiarun Chen[2], and Weiping Wen[2(✉)]

[1] XiangTan University, Xiangtan, Hunan, China
wenhanyao@smail.xtu.edu.cn
[2] Peking University, Beijing, China
weipingwen@pku.edu.cn

Abstract. Emotional Text-to-Speech (E-TTS) aims to generate speech that not only sounds natural but also conveys rich emotional expressions. Unlike traditional TTS, E-TTS must capture complex elements such as pitch, prosody, rhythm, and timbre variations to accurately convey emotions. Recently, some classical deep learning-based methods, such as Tacotron2, Transformer-TTS, FastSpeech2, and VITS, have significantly improved speech synthesis quality. However, these models still face challenges like alignment instability, strict duration constraints, and difficulties in generalizing across emotions and styles. The VITS model, while capable of high-quality speech synthesis, struggles with integrating emotional information due to its complex architecture. To address this, we propose RoStyleVITS, an end-to-end emotional TTS model built on VITS. RoStyleVITS incorporates emotion-infused styleformer blocks and replaces the standard attention layer with a self-attention layer using Rotary Position Embedding (RoPE) to enhance text sequence modeling. Our method outperforms existing state-of-the-art emotional speech synthesis models in both subjective and objective evaluations, demonstrating improved emotional expression and synthesis quality.

Keywords: Emotion Speech · VITS · Style Transfer · RoPE

1 Introduction

Emotional Text-to-Speech (E-TTS) is a crucial branch of text-to-speech [1–6] that aims to generate speech that not only exhibits high naturalness but also conveys rich emotional expressions. Unlike traditional Text-to-Speech (TTS) systems, E-TTS needs to model more complex speech elements, including pitch, prosody, rhythm, and timbre variations [7,8], to accurately express target emotions. This technology has broad applications in intelligent voice assistants, virtual character dubbing, gaming, and education.

In recent years, research on emotional speech synthesis has mainly focused on two categories: parametric modeling methods and deep learning-based methods. Parametric modeling approaches, such as Hidden Markov Models (HMMs) [9] and rule-based methods like PSOLA [10], are difficult to achieve high naturalness and expressive speech. In contrast, most deep learning methods are based on several classical speech synthesis architectures [11–19], such as Tacotron2 [1], Transformer-TTS [4], FastSpeech2 [3], and VITS [5]. E-TTS methods that are built on these models have significantly improved synthesis quality and efficiency. However, these methods still suffer from certain limitations. For example, Tacotron2 and Transformer-TTS rely on an attention mechanism for alignment, which can lead to instability in synthesized speech, such as frame skipping and misalignment. FastSpeech2, while addressing alignment issues, enforces strict duration constraints, making it difficult to control speech timing flexibly. Moreover, existing approaches often struggle with cross-emotion generalization and multi-style speech modeling. The VITS model is trained based on variational autoencoder (VAE) theory, achieving exceptionally high-quality synthesized speech and allowing for stochastic prediction of speech duration. However, due to its complex architecture, it is not easy to integrate emotional information.

We aspire to create high-quality synthesized speech, so this paper chooses VITS as the foundation for our proposed model. To address the challenge of integrating emotional styles, we propose RoStyleVITS, an end-to-end novel emotional text-to-speech model that combines the advantages of both autoregressive and non-autoregressive models. Previous studies have demonstrated the effectiveness of self-attention models in speech generation [20]. Accordingly, we proposed to utilize emotion-shared double styleformer blocks on both sides of the decoder's MRF layer for emotion infusing. Additionally, we replace the standard attention layer in the original text prior encoder with a self-attention layer based on Rotary Position Embedding (RoPE). This substitution improves the effectiveness of text sequence modeling. Experiments demonstrate that our proposed method outperforms existing state-of-the-art emotional speech synthesis methods in both subjective and objective metrics.

2 Background

2.1 Text-to-Speech

Modern deep learning-based speech synthesis models can be broadly categorized into autoregressive methods (which learn $P_\theta([y_{t+1}]|[y_t, w_1, w_2, ..., w_N])$) and non-autoregressive methods (which learn $P_\theta([y_1, y_2, ..., y_T]|[w_1, w_2, ..., w_N])$) based on their implementation principles. The y_t denotes a speech signal point, and the w_n denotes a text unit. Tacotron2 [1], Large Language Model based TTS (LLM-TTS) [6], and Transformer-TTS [4] fall into the autoregressive category, while VITS [5] and FastSpeech2 [3] belong to the non-autoregressive category. Emotional speech synthesis needs to generate speech with highly variable emotional prosody, so models that allow flexible control over speech duration are better suited for this task.

2.2 VITS

VITS (Variational Inference Text-to-Speech) is a deep learning-based model for text-to-speech (TTS) synthesis. It combines the strengths of variational autoencoders (VAEs), normalizing flows, and recurrent neural networks to generate high-quality, natural-sounding speech. VITS is designed to handle both prosody and content simultaneously, making it more efficient and capable of generating expressive and diverse speech. By using a probabilistic framework, VITS can model the uncertainty in speech synthesis, allowing for more flexible and robust TTS systems. Its end-to-end architecture eliminates the need for complex, hand-engineered features, enabling seamless and fast training. Since the duration of the generated speech can vary randomly (depending on the speaker or emotional control conditions), the VITS model is well-suited as an emotional TTS architecture.

3 Method

3.1 Framework Based on VITS

Our proposed framework is built on VITS, as shown in 1, We added a style encoder (G_{senc}) and the well-designed decoder in VITS as the style decoder (G_{sdec}). The other modules include the Normalizing Flow ($G_{f\theta}$) [21], Monotonic Alignment Search (MAS) [5], the text encoder (G_{text}, including a projection layer), the Stochastic Duration Preditor (SDP), and the posterior encoder(G_q). Then, we introduce the framework's overview and individual modules. The whole model G_θ can accept an input text x_{text} and the emotional reference utterance y_{ref}, the model synthesizes speech y_{syn} with emotional style taken from the reference speech. The text's true waveform is y.

Overview. Our proposed framework can be formulated as a conditional VAE, aiming to maximize the variational lower bound (also known as the evidence lower bound, or ELBO) of the intractable marginal log-likelihood of the $log[G_\theta(y_{syn}|x_{text}, y_{syn})]$:

$$log[G_\theta(y|x_{text}, y_{ref})] \geq E_{G_q}\left[log[G_{sdec}(y|zq, y_{syn})] - log\frac{G_q(zq|y)}{G_{text}(zp|x_{text})}\right] \quad (1)$$

where $G_{text}(zp|x_{text})$ denotes a prior distribution of the text's latent variables zp. The $G_{sdec}(y|zq, y_{syn})$ is the likelihood function of a true waveform with the emotion condition y_{syn}, making it generate target emotion speech. In the VAE, first, we incorporated a posterior encoder $G_q(zq|y)$, which estimates the posterior distribution zq of real speech, helping it achieve point-to-point probability distribution space alignment between true speech and the text.

Posterior Encoder. The posterior encoder G_q consists of multiple residual blocks used in Glow-TTS [22]. A Glow-TTS residual block consists of layers of dilated convolutions with a gated activation unit and skip connection. We add speaker embedding into the residual blocks as global conditioning van2016wavenet. In the output step, the linear projection layer above the blocks produces the mean and variance of the normal posterior distribution μ_q, σ_q, which means $zq = \mu_q + \epsilon \cdot \sigma_q$.

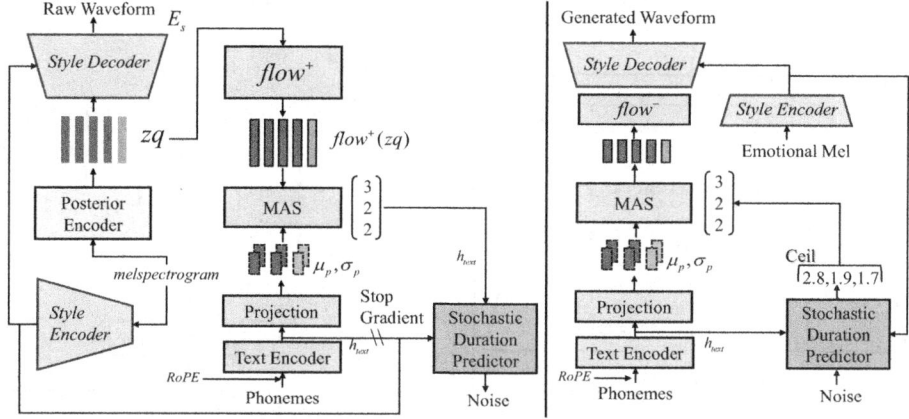

Fig. 1. Proposed framework.

Prior Modules. The prior encoder consists of a text encoder G_{text} and a normalizing flow $G_{f\theta}$. The text encoder accepts the phoneme index sequences and outputs the linguistic hidden representation's prior distribution μ_p, σ_p with a linear projection. We constructed the G_{text} and $G_{f\theta}$ by Rofomer's encoder [23] that utilizes Rotary Position Embedding (RoPE) to enhance the linguistic relationships. Under the guidance of RoPE, the Transformer-based speech emotion synthesis model achieves lower sequence loss, meaning that the reconstruction quality of the speech spectrogram is improved.

Other Modules. Monotonic Alignment Search (MAS) to align input phonemes with the target waveform by maximizing the ELBO rather than the exact log-likelihood. This redefined MAS ensures the alignment remains monotonic and non-skipping, reflecting natural speech patterns. Additionally, we introduce a Speaker and Emotion-Dependent Projection (SDP) module, where a linear layer integrates speaker and emotion embeddings—extracted from the style decoder—into the text representation, enabling the model to generate expressive speech conditioned on emotional prompts.

3.2 Style Encoder and Decoder

Our proposed core modules are the style encoder that encodes the input utterance's emotion information into the embedding and the style decoder that expands the lengths of zq and squeezes the dimension to a single-channel waveform.

Style Encoder. We apply the CAM++ model [24] as the emotion encoder. The style encoder accepts a speech spectrogram and outputs an emotion embedding. The entire model consists of two parts: a residual convolutional network as the

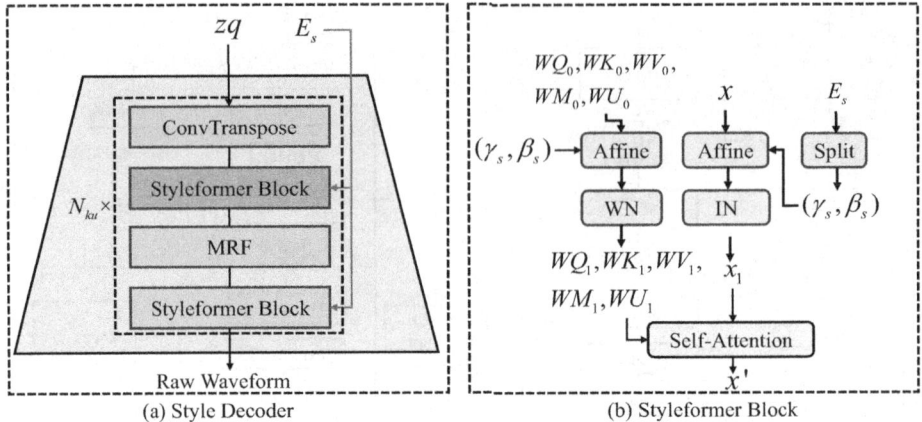

Fig. 2. The style decoder and the styleformer block. The decoder and the generator of HiFi-GAN have the same architecture. The styleformer block uses emotion embedding to compute an attention mechanism with emotional style.

front end and a time-delay neural network structure as the backbone. The front-end module is a 2D convolutional structure designed to extract more localized and detailed time-frequency features. The backbone module uses dense connections to reuse hierarchical features and improve computational efficiency. At the same time, each layer incorporates a lightweight context-aware mask module, which extracts contextual information at multiple scales through pooling operations. The mask helps remove irrelevant noise from the features while retaining key emotion information.

Style Decoder. As shown in Fig. 2, the style decoder consists of multiple expanding layers which include a transposed convolution, a front styleformer block, a multi-receptive field fusion (MRF) module, and a shared styleformer block. Based on the innovations in the StyleFormer [20], we share the emotional style embedding vector with the style transfer modules of the two twoStyle-Formerr blocks as shown in Fig. 2, indicated by the red arrow. Then, we will describe the styleformer block.

We assume the style block accepts input spectrograms $x \in R^{b,t,d}$ and emotion embedding $E_s \in R^{b,2d}$, the E_s is splitter split into two equal-length vectors, which serve as affine coefficients $(\gamma_s, \beta_s) \in R^{b,1,d}$. We create some trainable weights $\{WQ_0, WK_0, WV_0, WM_0, WU_0\} \in R^{b,d,d}$ during the model initialization phase. Then, these weight matrices are infused with the emotional style of the target speech through linear operations (Using WQ_0 matrix as an example) and used the weight normalization [25] (WN) for better training convergence:

$$WQ' = \gamma_s \cdot WQ_0 + \beta_s \quad (2)$$

$$WQ_1 = \frac{WQ'}{\sqrt{\sum_{k=0}^{d} WQ'^2_{i,j,k}}} \quad (3)$$

Then the input x is also infused with the emotional style:

$$x = \gamma_s \cdot \left(\frac{x - \mu_{b,t}}{\sigma^2_{b,t} + \epsilon} \right) + \beta_s \quad (4)$$

where $\mu_{b,t}$ denotes the mean of x along the d-dimension, $\sigma^2_{b,t}$ denotes the variance of x along the d-dimension, and ϵ represents a small constant (e.g., 1^{-5}) to prevent division by zero. Finally, we adopt the self-attention process with the style weights and style input sequence:

$$x' = \left[\frac{x \cdot (WQ_1) \cdot (x \cdot WK_1)^t}{\sqrt{d}} \cdot (x \cdot WV_1) \right] \cdot WM_1 + (x \cdot WU_1) \quad (5)$$

The style block outputs the stylized hidden spectrogram x'. We set two styleformer blocks before and after the MRF in each layer for learning the acoustic emotion information from the emotional target speech, which shares the same emotion embedding. Considering the transposed convolutions and MRFs, we set the same weight parameters as the HiFi-GAN generator. Thus, the style decoder can generate the emotional raw waveform with the reference speech.

4 Experiments Setup and Metrics

4.1 Dataset

A successfully trained speech synthesis model generally requires a dataset with a total duration of more than 3 h, and each speaker should have at least 50 utterances. Based on this, we chose to use the **ESD** [8]. The ESD database consists of 350 parallel utterances spoken by 10 native English and 10 native Chinese speakers and covers 5 emotion categories (neutral, happy, angry, sad and surprise). Each audio sample has a sampling rate of 16 kHz and a 32-bit floating-point depth. Beside, **EmoV-DB** [26] is also considered. The database covers 5 emotion classes for four speakers, containing two males and two females.

4.2 Training Configuration

Since the input to the posterior encoder is the Short-Time Fourier Transform (STFT) spectrograms, the parameters for extracting the STFT spectrograms are as follows. We use a window length of 1024 (equal to FFT banks) and a hop length of 160. The absolute amplitude of each audio sample is constrained between 0 and 1. During training, all the learning rates and other parameters are kept consistent with the settings of VITS.

4.3 Baseline Models

We chose the following baselines. (1) TP-GST [27] + FS2 [3]. The model is based on FastSpeech2 and a global style-token emotion encoder. (2) EmoQ-TTS [12]. (3) MsEmoTTS [18]. (4) METTS [15]. Most of these models are based on the FastSpeech2 model and have advanced capabilities for stylized emotional speech synthesis.

4.4 Metrics

Subject Metrics. The subjective evaluation metrics mainly reflect human perception of the naturalness and quality of generated speech. We use the **Mean Opinion Score (MOS)** and the **A/B preference test** to assess the naturalness of generated emotional speech and human emotional preference for different models. The MOS is measured by some annotators to evaluate sound quality on a 5-point scale. The higher the speech quality, the higher the MOS score. In the test, the subjects are asked to choose which of the two speeches in the same sentence by different models is perceptually more expressive.

Objective Metrics. Objective metrics evaluate the quality and emotional category of speech through speech feature comparison and model-based automatic classification. We computed **Mel Cepstral Distortion (MCD)** [28], **Root Mean Squared Error of Log $f0$** ($RMSE_{f0}$) [29] metrics for objective evaluation. The $f0$ denotes the pitch. The MCD measures the spectral difference between generated and real speech, while $RMSE_{f0}$ measures the fundamental frequency difference. The lower these two metrics are, the better the quality of the generated speech.

Additionally, we use a series of pre-trained models to evaluate the quality of generated utterances. We employ the NISQA model [30] to automatically predict the objective MOS score of utterances, referred to as **N-MOS**, which reflects the objective quality of the utterances. Furthermore, a speech emotion recognition model CAM++ [24], which is pre-trained on the ESD dataset, is used to predict the emotional category of generated utterances, and we compute the **Emotion Classification Macro F1 Score (Emo-F1)**, which reflects the accuracy of emotional expression in the generated utterances. Finally, we use the Whisper [31] model to calculate the **Word Error Rate (WER)** of the generated speech, which reflects the overall generation quality of the synthesis model. The higher the N-MOS and Emo-F1 metrics, the closer the speech's objective quality and emotional tendency are to real speech. Conversely, the lower the WER metric, the more successful the training of the speech synthesis model.

5 Ablation Study

As shown in the bottom two rows of the Tables 1 and 2, we constructed some model configurations for the proposed model: (1) **eVITS**. A VITS model that only additionally includes the speaker encoder layer. (2) **StyleVITS (w/o RoPE)**. The VITS with style modules but does not contain the RoPE text encoder. (3) **RoVITS (w/o style)**. The VITS with RoPE text encoder but does not contain the style modules. (4) **RoStyleVITS**. Proposed model, which contains style modules and RoPE text encoder.

Table 1. Results on ESD dataset

Model	MOS/N-MOS↑	MCD↓	$RMSE_{f0}$ ↓	Emo-F1↓ ↑	WER↓
Ground Truth	4.25/4.02	–	–	99.51%	2.10%
TP-GST + FS2 [3]	3.68/3.44	4.89	54.43	98.16%	3.64%
EmoQ-TTS [12]	3.72/3.53	4.81	53.15	99.39%	3.52%
MsEmoTTS [18]	4.02/3.83	4.76	53.04	99.51%	3.48%
METTS [15]	4.02/3.84	4.74	52.67	99.48%	3.41%
eVITS	3.52/3.48	4.96	54.56	97.89%	3.70%
StyleVITS (w/o RoPE)	3.79/3.67	4.87	49.56	98.54%	3.21%
RoVITS (w/o style)	3.84/3.72	4.67	54.37	97.51%	3.57%
RoStyleVITS	4.12/3.96	4.45	47.98	99.65%	2.78%

Table 2. Results on EmoV-DB dataset

Model	MOS/N-MOS↑	MCD↓	$RMSE_{f0}$ ↓	Emo-F1↓ ↑	WER↓
Ground Truth	4.27/4.01	–	–	99.47%	2.08%
TP-GST + FS2 [3]	3.65/3.42	4.82	53.98	98.12%	3.59%
EmoQ-TTS [12]	3.70/3.52	4.79	53.19	99.35%	3.48%
MsEmoTTS [18]	4.04/3.78	4.75	53.10	99.53%	3.38%
METTS [15]	4.07/3.90	4.70	52.43	99.59%	3.37%
eVITS	3.48/3.39	4.90	54.72	93.72%	3.82%
StyleVITS (w/o RoPE)	3.75/3.67	4.75	48.76	98.66%	3.16%
RoVITS (w/o style)	3.82/3.70	4.68	55.73	96.89%	3.37%
RoStyleVITS	4.10/4.02	4.39	47.56	99.42%	2.74%

6 Results

6.1 Objective Metrics Results

As shown in Tables 1 and 2, the experiments demonstrate that the MOS scores of our proposed method reached approximately 4.10, surpassing those of the more advanced baseline models. This indicates that the emotional speech generated by our proposed method is perceived as high-quality by human listeners. In the MOS evaluation, our analysis takes the ESD dataset as an example, as it contains a longer total duration of speech data, making it more representative for drawing accurate conclusions. The eVITS model lacks a proper emotional vector fusion module and suffers from convergence difficulties, resulting in lower synthesized speech quality. As a result, it only achieves a MOS score of 3.52. The StyleVITS (w/o RoPE) model does not include the RoPE module in its prior encoder, but it features a style transfer module that promotes model convergence and emotional fusion, achieving a better MOS score of 3.79 compared to eVITS. The RoVITS (w/o style) model lacks the emotional fusion module but includes the RoPE module, which enhances the effectiveness of text encoding, thereby reaching a MOS score of 3.84. This demonstrates that the RoPE module positively influences the quality of synthesized speech. The RoStyleVITS model incorporates both of our proposed key modules and thus achieves a higher MOS score of 4.12, outperforming the baseline models. Through these experiments, we demonstrate that both the RoPE and style blocks contribute positively to the quality of speech synthesis. A similar conclusion can be derived from the EmoV-DB dataset. Due to the shorter total duration of speech in EmoV-DB, the final experimental metrics are lower than those obtained on the ESD dataset.

In the Fig. 3, we present the A/B preference test between the baseline model and the proposed method. In the test, the subjects are asked to choose which of the two speeches for the same sentence, by different models, is perceptually more expressive. The experiment proves that RoStyleVITS is preferred over the baseline models.

6.2 Subjective Metrics Results

As shown in Tables 1 and 2, in the objective metric experiments, lower MCD, RMSE, and WER values indicate higher generated speech quality, while a higher Emo-F1 score demonstrates the model's ability to successfully generate utterances with reference emotion. We analyze the emotion-related metrics. The experimental results show that models lacking the effective emotional fusion blocks, such as eVITS and RoVITS (w/o style), perform poorly on $RMSE_{f0}$ and emo-F1 metrics. This indicates that the generated target emotional styles are either less distinguishable or exhibit noticeable deviation, highlighting the importance of our proposed style transfer block.

Next, we consider the semantics-related metrics. The results show that both the RoPE and the emotional style transfer block lead to improvements in these metrics. This indicates that they improve reconstruction quality in two ways: efficient textual sequence encoding and weight normalization.

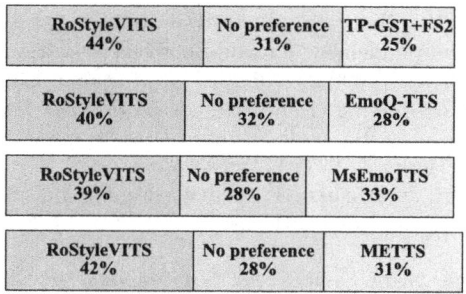

Fig. 3. A/B preference test

7 Conclusion

This paper proposes RoStyleVITS, a model built upon VITS that enhances text prior encoding using RoPE. Additionally, it employs a styleformer module with shared emotional embedding to construct an end-to-end multi-emotion and multi-speaker text-to-speech model. We propose replacing the standard attention layer with the RoPE attention layer to enhance the text encoder. Additionally, we design a dual-layer styleformer module with shared emotional embeddings in the decoder of the VITS model, which effectively injects the style of the reference speech during the decoding process. Experimental results show that our proposed method outperforms the baseline model in both subjective and objective metrics, indicating that our model can synthesize high-quality emotional speech. Furthermore, due to the use of the emotional encoder, it also has zero-shot generation capabilities.

References

1. Shen, J., et al.: Natural TTS synthesis by conditioning WaveNet on mel spectrogram predictions. In: IEEE International Conference on Acoustics, Speech and Signal Processing (ICASSP), pp. 4779–4783. IEEE (2018)
2. Ren, Y., et al.: Fastspeech: fast, robust and controllable text to speech. In: Advances in Neural Information Processing Systems, vol. 32 (2019)
3. Ren, Y., et al.: Fastspeech 2: fast and high-quality end-to-end text to speech. arXiv preprint arXiv:2006.04558 (2020)
4. Li, N., Liu, S., Liu, Y., Zhao, S., Liu, M.: Neural speech synthesis with transformer network. In: Proceedings of the AAAI Conference on Artificial Intelligence, vol. 33, no. 01, pp. 6706–6713 (2019)
5. Kim, J., Kong, J., Son, J.: Conditional variational autoencoder with adversarial learning for end-to-end text-to-speech. In: International Conference on Machine Learning, pp. 5530–5540. PMLR (2021)
6. Wang, C., et al.: Neural codec language models are zero-shot text to speech synthesizers. arXiv preprint arXiv:2301.02111 (2023)

7. Chan, C.H., Qian, K., Zhang, Y., Hasegawa-Johnson, M.: Speechsplit2. 0: unsupervised speech disentanglement for voice conversion without tuning autoencoder bottlenecks. In: ICASSP 2022-2022 IEEE International Conference on Acoustics, Speech and Signal Processing (ICASSP), pp. 6332–6336. IEEE (2022)
8. Zhou, K., Sisman, B., Liu, R., Li, H.: Emotional voice conversion: theory, databases and ESD. Speech Commun. **137**, 1–18 (2022)
9. Nose, T., Yamagishi, J., Masuko, T., Kobayashi, T.: A style control technique for hmm-based expressive speech synthesis. IEICE Trans. Inf. Syst. **90**(9), 1406–1413 (2007)
10. Toma, Ş.-A., Târşa, G.-I., Oancea, E., Munteanu, D.-P., Totir, F., Anton, L.: A td-psola based method for speech synthesis and compression. In: 2010 8th International Conference on Communications, pp. 123–126. IEEE (2010)
11. Bott, T., Lux, F., Vu, N.T.: Controlling emotion in text-to-speech with natural language prompts. arXiv preprint arXiv:2406.06406 (2024)
12. Im, C.-B., Lee, S.-H., Kim, S.-B., Lee, S.-W.: Emoq-TTS: emotion intensity quantization for fine-grained controllable emotional text-to-speech. In: ICASSP 2022-2022 IEEE International Conference on Acoustics, Speech and Signal Processing (ICASSP), pp. 6317–6321. IEEE, 2022
13. Diatlova, D., Shutov, V.: Emospeech: guiding fastspeech2 towards emotional text to speech. arXiv preprint arXiv:2307.00024 (2023)
14. Cui, C., et al.: Emovie: a mandarin emotion speech dataset with a simple emotional text-to-speech model. arXiv preprint arXiv:2106.09317 (2021)
15. Zhu, X., et al.: Metts: multilingual emotional text-to-speech by cross-speaker and cross-lingual emotion transfer. IEEE/ACM Trans. Audio Speech Lang. Process. **32**, 1506–1518 (2024)
16. Li, X., et al.: Umetts: a unified framework for emotional text-to-speech synthesis with multimodal prompts. In: ICASSP 2025-2025 IEEE International Conference on Acoustics, Speech and Signal Processing (ICASSP), pp. 1–5. IEEE (2025)
17. Liu, R., Sisman, B., Li, H.: Reinforcement learning for emotional text-to-speech synthesis with improved emotion discriminability. arXiv preprint arXiv:2104.01408 (2021)
18. Lei, Y., Yang, S., Wang, X., Xie, L.: Msemotts: multi-scale emotion transfer, prediction, and control for emotional speech synthesis. IEEE/ACM Trans. Audio Speech Lang. Process. **30**, 853–864 (2022)
19. Alemayehu, Y., Yadav, R.K., Mohammed, A.R., Thapa, S., Chauhan, S.: Infusing emotion in text to speech model. In 2024 4th International Conference on Technological Advancements in Computational Sciences (ICTACS), pp. 712–716. IEEE (2024)
20. Park, J., Kim, Y.: Styleformer: transformer based generative adversarial networks with style vector. In: Proceedings of the IEEE/CVF Conference on Computer Vision and Pattern Recognition, pp. 8983–8992 (2022)
21. Rezende, D., Mohamed, S.: Variational inference with normalizing flows. In: International Conference on Machine Learning, pp. 1530–1538. PMLR (2015)
22. Kim, J., Kim, S., Kong, J., Yoon, S.: Glow-TTS: a generative flow for text-to-speech via monotonic alignment search. In: Advances in Neural Information Processing Systems, vol. 33, pp. 8067–8077 (2020)
23. Su, J., Ahmed, M., Lu, Y., Pan, S., Bo, W., Liu, Y.: Roformer: enhanced transformer with rotary position embedding. Neurocomputing **568**, 127063 (2024)
24. Wang, H., Zheng, S., Chen, Y., Cheng, L., Chen, Q.: Cam++: a fast and efficient network for speaker verification using context-aware masking. arXiv preprint arXiv:2303.00332 (2023)

25. Salimans, T., Kingma, D.P.: Weight normalization: a simple reparameterization to accelerate training of deep neural networks. In: Advances in Neural Information Processing Systems, vol. 29 (2016)
26. Adigwe, A., Tits, N., Haddad, K.E., Ostadabbas, S., Dutoit, T.: The emotional voices database: Towards controlling the emotion dimension in voice generation systems. arXiv preprint arXiv:1806.09514 (2018)
27. Wang, Y., et al.: Style tokens: unsupervised style modeling, control and transfer in end-to-end speech synthesis. In: International Conference on Machine Learning, pp. 5180–5189. PMLR (2018)
28. Kubichek, R.: Mel-cepstral distance measure for objective speech quality assessment. In: Proceedings of IEEE Pacific Rim Conference on Communications Computers and Signal Processing, vol. 1, pp. 125–128. IEEE (1993)
29. Chai, T., Draxler, R.R.: Root mean square error (RMSE) or mean absolute error (MAE)?-arguments against avoiding RMSE in the literature. Geoscientific Model Dev. **7**(3), 1247–1250 (2014)
30. Mittag, G., Naderi, B., Chehadi, A., Möller, S.: Nisqa: a deep CNN-self-attention model for multidimensional speech quality prediction with crowdsourced datasets (2021)
31. Radford, A., Kim, J.W., Xu, T., Brockman, G., McLeavey, C., Sutskever, I.: Robust speech recognition via large-scale weak supervision. In: International Conference on Machine Learning, pp. 492–518. PMLR (2023)

Can LLM-Generated Textual Explanations Enhance Model Classification Performance? An Empirical Study

Mahdi Dhaini[✉], Juraj Vladika, Ege Erdogan, Zineb Attaoui, and Gjergji Kasneci

School of Computation, Information and Technology, Department of Computer Science, Technical University of Munich, Munich, Germany
mahdi.dhaini@tum.de

Abstract. In the rapidly evolving field of Explainable Natural Language Processing (NLP), textual explanations, i.e., human-like rationales, are pivotal for explaining model predictions and enriching datasets with interpretable labels. Traditional approaches rely on human annotation, which is costly, labor-intensive, and impedes scalability. In this work, we present an automated framework that leverages multiple state-of-the-art large language models (LLMs) to generate high-quality textual explanations. We rigorously assess the quality of these LLM-generated explanations using a comprehensive suite of Natural Language Generation (NLG) metrics. Furthermore, we investigate the downstream impact of these explanations on the performance of pre-trained language models (PLMs) and LLMs across natural language inference tasks on two diverse benchmark datasets. Our experiments demonstrate that automated explanations exhibit highly competitive effectiveness compared to human-annotated explanations in improving model performance. Our findings underscore a promising avenue for scalable, automated LLM-based textual explanation generation for extending NLP datasets and enhancing model performance.

Keywords: Explainable natural language processing · Natural language explanations · Natural language inference · Large language models

1 Introduction

Recent NLP advancements are driven by PLMs and LLMs, achieving state-of-the-art results across various tasks [1]. However, their black-box nature limits understanding of their predictions, prompting increased interest in Explainable NLP, where methods from Explainable AI explain model decision-making [2] to enhance trust and transparency, which is essential for advancing practical applications in sensitive domains.

A key challenge in Explainable NLP is the lack of definitive ground-truth explanations [3]. Researchers address this by collecting human-generated textual explanations, creating *explainable datasets* [4]. These datasets serve both as benchmarks for evaluating model-generated explanations and as training data to improve models' predictive performance [5]. However, human annotation is resource-intensive, impacting dataset scale and quality [6]. Recently, leveraging LLMs' text-generation capabilities for explanations has gained attention [7], though evaluating these explanations' quality and effectiveness in downstream tasks remains an open research question.

In this paper, we address these critical gaps by focusing on two primary objectives. First, we leverage multiple LLMs to automatically generate textual explanations and rigorously evaluate their quality using a comprehensive suite of metrics. Second, we investigate how the incorporation of these LLM-generated explanations impacts the performance of various PLMs and LLMs on downstream tasks, particularly within the NLI framework.

Our work is guided by the following research question: *How do LLM-generated textual explanations impact the performance of PLMs and LLMs on downstream predictive tasks?* Our contributions are as follows:

- We employ four LLMs of varying sizes and complexity to automatically generate explanations for two explainable NLI datasets in both zero-shot and few-shot settings.
- We evaluate the quality of the generated explanations using multiple metrics, including both reference-based measures and an innovative LLM-based evaluation approach.
- We examine the impact of incorporating LLM-generated explanations during both fine-tuning and inference, comparing their effects against human-annotated explanations and a no-explanation baseline across four distinct BERT-based models and three LLMs.[1]

2 Background and Related Work

Natural Language Inference (NLI) is one of the most fundamental NLP tasks [8]. The goal is, given two pieces of text, a premise and a hypothesis, to determine a logical relation between them as one of the three classes: entailment, contradiction, or neutral. The turning point in NLI was the construction of the Stanford NLI (SNLI) corpus in 2015 [9], a dataset of half a million examples, constructed with crowd-sourced effort where photos were captioned and then paired with entailed, contradicted, or neutral sentences written by annotators. Modern PLMs like BERT [10] and RoBERTa [11], as well as autoregressive LLMs like GPT, can often solve popular NLI datasets with an above-human performance, owing to the linguistic patterns and world knowledge acquired during their pre-training on huge corpora.

---

[1] We release our code on **GitHub**.

Explainable NLP and Datasets. The growing interest in Explainable NLP is evident from multiple surveys like [12,13], some addressing specific tasks or methods [14]. Interest in explainable NLP has led to the creation of explainable datasets for tasks such as hate-speech classification [15] and claim verification [16]. A comprehensive review of these datasets is provided in [13]. Textual explanations typically fall into highlights, structured, or free-text (natural language) categories and are annotated by authors, experts, and crowd-sourcing with most datasets relying on human annotators. However, human annotation presents several challenges. Collecting high-quality explanations is time-consuming and resource-intensive [17]. Human annotators' explanations may also suffer from subjectivity and inconsistency, potentially hindering model performance rather than aiding it [28]. Additionally, the diversity in explanation types introduces further complexities [18].

Generating LLM-Explanations. Due to the limitations of human-annotated explanations, recent research has explored using LLMs to generate Natural Language Explanations (NLE) and justifications for model decisions. Compared to traditional post-hoc feature attribution methods, NLEs provide human-readable justifications, which can enhance transparency and user understanding. [19] employed LLMs as rationalizers for knowledge-intensive tasks such as multiple-choice question answering. [20] investigated improving LLM-generated NLE quality through a tandem learning setup. [21] examined how various prompting techniques, such as CoT, can improve NLEs on commonsense reasoning tasks. These studies demonstrate the growing interest in leveraging LLMs to generate and refine NLEs, particularly for tasks requiring explanation-driven reasoning. However, none of the previously mentioned works investigate how extending datasets with LLM-generated explanations can impact the performance of PLMs and LLMs on downstream tasks.

Evaluating NLEs. NLEs are text snippets and can be evaluated with standard NLG metrics [22]. When human-written (gold) references exist, *reference-based* metrics are applicable. Traditional metrics, such as BLEU [23] and ROUGE [24], assess word overlaps between generated and reference texts. However, these metrics have become less suitable with the rise of LLMs, as they penalize expressive variations in wording. Consequently, semantic metrics like the embedding-based BERTScore [25] and distribution-based MAUVE [26] have gained popularity. Recently, evaluation methods using *LLM-as-judge* metrics have emerged, employing crafted prompts for LLMs to return numerical scores assessing generated texts, exemplified by G-Eval [27].

Closely Related Work. Among the previously mentioned works, the closest to ours is [28], which investigates how human explanations can impact the predictions of two PLMs. However, their study is limited to BART and T5 and focuses solely on human explanations. Additionally, [29] reviews studies employing different types of human explanations (highlights, structured, and free-text) to improve NLP models. However, they solely review studies incorporating human-annotated explanations. In contrast, while we also incorporate human explanations, our primary focus is on generating and investigating LLM-generated

NLEs. We evaluate the impact of these explanations on four PLMs, including the recent ModernBERT [30], as well as three LLMs of varying sizes.

3 Experimental Setup

We designed a comprehensive experimental framework that systematically integrates both human- and LLM-generated explanations into two benchmark datasets. For reproducibility, we provide all prompt templates for explanation generation, evaluation, and LLM performance evaluation in the repository.

3.1 Datasets

We use two datasets in our experiments. The first dataset, e-SNLI [31], is an extension of the SNLI dataset [32] with human-annotated natural language explanations. It contains premise-hypothesis pairs labeled as entailment, neutral, or contradiction, depending on how the premise relates to the hypothesis. The second dataset is the HealthFC dataset [33]. It consists of 750 health-related claims, labeled by medical experts and backed with evidence from systematic reviews and clinical trials. Each claim is paired with pieces of evidence and includes a verdict (supported, refuted, not enough information), as well as brief explanations for the verdict. For our experiments, we extracted a balanced subset of e-SNLI consisting of 840 examples, ensuring an equal representation of entailment, neutral, and contradiction instances. This subset size was deliberately chosen to closely match the 750-instance HealthFC dataset, enabling a fair and controlled comparison across our evaluation framework. Even though HealthFC is officially a dataset for automated fact-checking (claim verification), it is common to model this task as an NLI task.

3.2 Generating Natural Language Explanations with LLMs

In our pipeline, we focus on generating NLEs using multiple LLMs. We further extend both datasets we consider with explanations we generate using GPT-4o mini Mixtral-7B Gemma2-9B and LLama3-70B. For Mixtral-7B, Gemma2-9B, and LLama3-70B we use the APIs provided by Groq while for GPT-4o mini we use OpenAI APIs. We selected LLMs ranging in size from 7B to 70B parameters[2], to analyze how these factors influence both the quality of the generated text and the impact of generated explanations on downstream task performance. The rationale for selecting diverse LLMs, rather than models within the same family differing only in size, is to ensure a broader variety in the *sources of explanations*. We discuss later in the paper how this approach could be expanded in future work.

We generate explanations from the four LLMs under two settings: few-shot and zero-shot. After initial prompt validation, we explicitly instructed LLMs not

---

[2] along with GPT-4o mini, whose exact size is unknown.

to reveal or hint at labels in their explanations to avoid biasing the evaluation during inference. The few-shot setting examines if LLM explanations improve after exposure to human-written examples and evaluates the impact of these explanations on downstream tasks. Both zero-shot and few-shot prompts are provided in our repository; the few-shot prompts include four (*premise-hypothesis-explanation*) examples from the dataset. Due to our hardware constraints, we do not perform any memory-heavy approaches like fine-tuning of LLMs or reinforcement learning. We leave these for future work.

3.3 Evaluating LLM-Natural Language Explanations

We compare LLM-generated explanations with human-provided explanations from our selected datasets. Specifically, we employ the widely used BLEU, ROUGE, and BERTScore metrics. Beyond these conventional metrics, we incorporate the recent MAUVE. and the *LLM-as-judge* G-Eval framework that has been increasingly used in recent NLG research. We use G-Eval to measure human likeness in LLM-generated explanations, in particular, the clarity, coherence, and structure of the LLM-generated explanation. We provide the implementation details and metrics libraries in the repository.

3.4 Models for NLI Predictions

Fine-Tuning PLMs. For the downstream NLI task predictions, we use four PLMs (BERT, DeBERTa [34], RoBERTa, and ModernBERT [30]). For each run with a certain kind of or without explanations, we perform a 80/20 train/test split and fine-tune the PLMs on the train set for 10 epochs using the AdamW optimizer with a learning rate of 3e-6 for ModernBERT and 1e-5 for the other PLMs. We repeat this five times with a stratified 5-fold cross-validation and report results averaged over the five splits.

Experiments with LLMs. We also use three LLMs: GPT-4o mini Qwen 2.5 (7B) and Llama3.3-70B. For GPT, we use the OpenAI API, and for the two open-source LLMs, we use the API provided by Together AI. We give the LLM the premise-hypothesis (or claim-evidence) pairs as input, and optionally add the human- or LLM-generated explanations at the end of the hypothesis for e-SNLI and the claim for HealthFC. We adopt a zero-shot inference approach without fine-tuning. Instead, the generated explanations are directly appended to the hypothesis in the prompt. Zero-shot inference is well established in current literature as a resource-efficient method that leverages the inherent generalization capabilities of LLMs without additional overhead. Moreover, we do not adopt resource-intensive approaches such as fine-tuning for LLMs, even with the existence of lighter approaches like PEFT, as the primary focus of this study is to measure the impact of different explanations on the performance, rather than to compare zero-shot with fine-tuned LLMs performance. Our experimental setup covers the complete cross-product of explanation methods and classification models, covering all possible combinations, including cases where identical LLMs function in both explainer and classifier roles.

4 Analysis and Discussion

Our results stem from an extensive experimental design covering multiple dimensions. Specifically, we evaluated two NLI datasets (e-SNLI and HealthFC), employed four different LLMs to generate explanations, and tested each in both zero-shot and few-shot settings, yielding 16 distinct explanation generation scenarios. We present the evaluation results in Table 1. Furthermore, we assessed downstream classification performance across four PLMs and three LLM classifiers. By analyzing metrics such as accuracy and macro F1 across these diverse combinations spread across Fig. 1 and Tables 2, 3, our study offers a comprehensive insight into how various explanation generation strategies affect NLI performance. While possible that our insights are specific only to the two chosen datasets, we try to make our takeaways general and widely applicable.

4.1 Generation and Evaluation of LLM-Explanations

Table 1 presents average metric scores for LLM-generated explanations. GPT-4o mini generally scores highest on e-SNLI, while Llama3-70B leads on HealthFC. GPT-4o mini outperforms others on e-SNLI in BLEU, ROUGE-1, and BERTScore-F1, whereas Llama3-70B excels in these metrics for HealthFC. GPT-4o mini consistently achieves top G-Eval scores, suggesting its explanations align closely with human judgment. However, G-Eval score differences across models are small, indicating similar overall quality. Mistral-7B achieves the highest MAUVE scores in multiple settings, implying greater diversity and coherence. Scores slightly improve from zero-shot to few-shot settings, particularly BLEU and ROUGE-1 on e-SNLI, but these improvements are minor, indicating limited benefit from in-context examples. Additionally, model size alone doesn't ensure better performance; smaller models like Gemma2-9B and Mistral-7B sometimes perform competitively or better. Our analysis shows LLMs do not consistently prefer their own explanations. Human explanations generally provide more significant performance gains, especially on e-SNLI. GPT-4o mini excels on e-SNLI and Llama3-70B on HealthFC, with BLEU, ROUGE, and BERTScore strongly correlating with downstream improvements.

Overall, while scores improve slightly between zero-shot and few-shot settings (notably in BLEU and ROUGE-1 on e-SNLI), these improvements are marginal. This indicates that providing in-context examples from the dataset does not significantly enhance the generated explanations according to these metrics. Furthermore, model size alone does not guarantee better performance, as seen when comparing Gemma2-9B, Mistral-7B, and Llama3-70B, where smaller models sometimes achieve competitive or even higher scores.

4.2 Influence of Explanations on the Performance of PLMs

Both Human and LLM Explanations Improve PLMs' Performance. Results in Figs. 1a, 1b show that for both of our datasets, incorporating explanations generated both by humans and LLMs result in better predictive performance compared to the baseline of no explanations independent of the LLM

Table 1. Average scores of the evaluation metrics across different LLMs on e-SNLI and HealthFC datasets in zero-shot and few-shot settings. The highest value for each metric is highlighted in **bold**.

Dataset	Metric	Gemma2-9B	Mistral-7B	Llama3-70B	GPT4o-mini
e-SNLI (zero-shot)	BLEU	0.032	0.033	0.029	**0.039**
	ROUGE-1	0.295	0.314	0.277	**0.333**
	BERTScore F1	0.876	0.876	0.872	**0.881**
	MAUVE	0.004	**0.047**	0.013	0.029
	G-Eval	0.171	0.166	0.165	**0.176**
e-SNLI (few-shot)	BLEU	0.037	0.043	0.037	**0.051**
	ROUGE-1	0.299	0.352	0.316	**0.366**
	BERTScore F1	0.878	0.882	0.878	**0.885**
	MAUVE	0.004	**0.107**	0.040	0.084
	G-Eval	0.163	0.170	0.160	**0.174**
HealthFC (zero-shot)	BLEU	0.017	0.022	**0.030**	0.024
	ROUGE-1	0.269	0.285	**0.313**	0.292
	BERTScore F1	0.881	0.878	**0.883**	0.883
	MAUVE	0.004	**0.115**	0.083	0.023
	G-Eval	0.197	0.194	0.192	**0.214**
HealthFC (few-shot)	BLEU	0.018	0.023	**0.030**	0.023
	ROUGE-1	0.261	0.294	**0.309**	0.291
	BERTScore F1	0.884	0.881	**0.886**	0.884
	MAUVE	0.004	0.180	**0.197**	0.095
	G-Eval	0.199	0.187	0.192	**0.205**

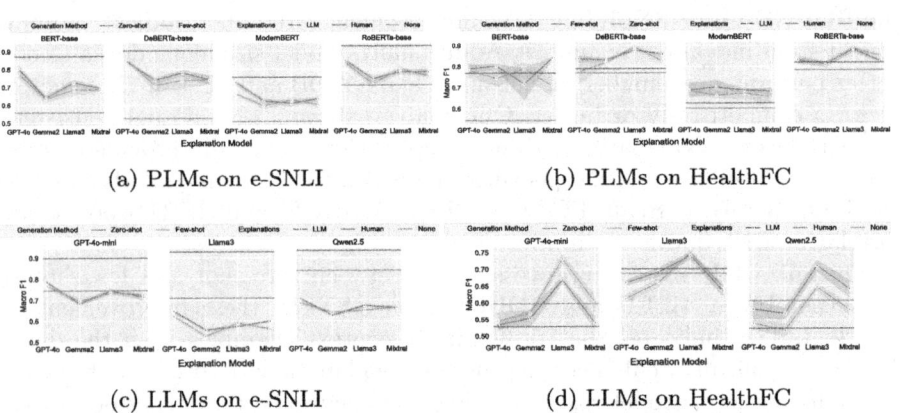

(a) PLMs on e-SNLI (b) PLMs on HealthFC

(c) LLMs on e-SNLI (d) LLMs on HealthFC

Fig. 1. (Zoom in for better reading) Plots of the models' performance on e-SNLI and HealthFC. **Top row (a–b)** shows average *Macro F1* for the four PLMs (BERT-base, DeBERTa-base, ModernBERT, RoBERTa-base); **bottom row (c–d)** shows average *Macro F1* for the three LLMs (GPT-4o mini, Llama3, Qwen2.5). In each panel, bars are grouped by explanation input condition: no explanations (gray), human explanations (green), and explanations generated by four LLMs in zero-shot (**blue**) vs. few-shot (orange) settings.

used to generate the explanations. This could be related to the explanations providing additional information beneficial for the task, and the models learning to use that information since they are trained with the explanations as well.

Relative benefit from human and LLM explanations varies between datasets. Table 2 displays the change in performance after incorporating LLM-generated explanations, compared to human explanations and the no-explanation baseline. Most significantly, LLM-generated explanations lead to better performance than human explanations with the HealthFC dataset, but worse performance on e-SNLI. This indicates that even though LLM-generated explanations are consistently more beneficial than having no explanations, humans can write more beneficial explanations than LLMs on certain datasets.

Table 2. Performance **impact** by LLM-generated explanations over the baseline of no explanations and human-written explanations, **averaged over the four PLMs** we have used as classifiers. Subscripts indicate standard deviations.

(a) e-SNLI

Explainer	Method	Improvement over No Explanations		Improvement over Human Explanations	
		Accuracy	Macro F1	Accuracy	Macro F1
GPT-4o	Few-shot	0.171	0.179	−0.119	−0.120
	Zero-shot	0.194	0.204	−0.096	−0.095
Gemma2	Few-shot	0.083	0.091	−0.207	−0.208
	Zero-shot	0.087	0.095	−0.204	−0.204
Llama3	Few-shot	0.142	0.151	−0.148	−0.148
	Zero-shot	0.113	0.122	−0.177	−0.177
Mixtral	Few-shot	0.110	0.117	−0.180	−0.182
	Zero-shot	0.119	0.128	−0.171	−0.171

(b) HFC

Explainer	Method	Improvement over No Explanations		Improvement over Human Explanations	
		Accuracy	Macro F1	Accuracy	Macro F1
GPT-4o	Few-shot	0.037	0.074	0.010	0.027
	Zero-shot	0.046	0.092	0.019	0.044
Gemma2	Few-shot	0.037	0.076	0.010	0.028
	Zero-shot	0.039	0.082	0.011	0.035
Llama3	Few-shot	0.070	0.119	0.042	0.071
	Zero-shot	0.060	0.095	0.033	0.047
Mixtral	Few-shot	0.037	0.066	0.009	0.019
	Zero-shot	0.056	0.107	0.028	0.059

4.3 Influence of Explanations on the Performance of LLMs

LLM Explanations Struggle to Outperform the No-Explanation Baseline. As both Table 3 and Figs. 1c, 1d show, in most cases, providing the classifier LLMs with LLM-generated explanations does not lead to better performance than having no explanations. This is in stark contrast to the results for the PLMs, where having explanations always led to benefits over the baseline. This difference might be because the LLMs used as classifiers are not explicitly trained on the explanations, and thus do not learn to use that information. The logic-based explanations of e-SNLI are akin to the CoT mechanism that LLMs deploy when answering reasoning questions. These explanations only improved the performance of PLMs, which seemingly do not have such a mechanism in their predictive process, but hurt the performance of LLMs, where the explanations clashed with their internal reasoning. Conversely, the summary-style explanations of HealthFC serve to provide additional context and background knowledge, and helped the PLMs and only Llama among LLMs. Our findings highlight the importance of tailoring explanation strategies to both the model type and task characteristics.

Table 3. Performance **impact** by LLM-generated explanations over the baseline of no explanations and human-written explanations, **averaged over the three LLMs** we have used as classifiers. Subscripts indicate standard deviations.

(a) e-SNLI

Explainer	Method	Improvement over No Explanations		Improvement over Human Explanations	
		Accuracy	Macro F1	Accuracy	Macro F1
GPT-4o	Few-shot	−0.072	−0.078	−0.226	−0.233
	Zero-shot	−0.071	−0.078	−0.226	−0.234
Gemma2	Few-shot	−0.137	−0.149	−0.292	−0.304
	Zero-shot	−0.155	−0.169	−0.310	−0.325
Llama3	Few-shot	−0.119	−0.130	−0.274	−0.285
	Zero-shot	−0.100	−0.113	−0.255	−0.269
Mixtral	Few-shot	−0.106	−0.116	−0.261	−0.271
	Zero-shot	−0.125	−0.135	−0.280	−0.291

(b) HFC

Explainer	Method	Improvement over No Explanations		Improvement over Human Explanations	
		Accuracy	Macro F1	Accuracy	Macro F1
GPT-4o	Few-shot	−0.067	−0.045	0.023	0.055
	Zero-shot	−0.076	−0.044	0.014	0.056
Gemma2	Few-shot	−0.039	−0.036	0.051	0.063
	Zero-shot	−0.043	−0.026	0.047	0.074
Llama3	Few-shot	0.014	0.055	0.104	0.155
	Zero-shot	0.052	0.098	0.142	0.198
Mixtral	Few-shot	−0.075	−0.038	0.015	0.061
	Zero-shot	−0.037	0.006	0.053	0.106

LLM Explanations Come Close to Human Explanations. Averaged over the classifier LLMs, the results in Table 3 show that on e-SNLI human explanations are considerably more beneficial than LLM explanations, with improvements in accuracy around 20–30%. On the HealthFC dataset, LLM explanations are more helpful, but with smaller differences in accuracy ranging from as low as 1% to 20%. These results, combined with the comparisons per model in

Figs. 1c, 1d indicate that human explanations are more helpful for LLMs than LLM-generated explanations in more cases and more strongly. Averaged over the classifier LLMs, the results in Table 3 show that on e-SNLI human explanations are considerably more beneficial than LLM explanations, with improvements in accuracy around 20–30%.

Effect of Human Explanations on LLMs Varies Strongly Between Datasets and Models. Finally, Figs. 1c, 1d show that while human explanations consistently lead to improvements over the baseline on e-SNLI, they only improve the performance of Llama 3 on HFC, and to a smaller extent. With both GPT-4o mini and Qwen 2.5, human explanations instead lead to performance decreases of around 10%. These results again support the claim that LLMs are less successful in using the provided explanations to their benefit compared to PLMs fine-tuned on the explanations, and that the extent to which the LLMs make use of the explanations varies between datasets and LLMs.

LLMs do not Necessarily Favor Their Own Explanations. We show in Figs. 1c, 1d that particularly comparing GPT-4o mini and Llama3, providing explanations generated by the models from the same model family as the classifier model do not necessarily lead to better performance than providing explanations generated by models from different families. On e-SNLI both models perform best with explanations generated by GPT-4o, and on HFC, with explanations generated by Llama3. This implies that the impact of the explanations rely more on the model generating the explanations rather than whether the explanation and the classifier models belong to the same family.

4.4 Different Types of Explanations

The explanations in the two datasets serve a different purpose. For e-SNLI, the explanations aim to clarify the *logical reasoning* process using which an entailment label was determined (e.g., *The person is standing, therefore they cannot be sitting*). On the other hand, explanations in the HealthFC dataset serve as a *summary* of the full-text evidence articles and aim to describe what was discovered (e.g., *Analyzed studies have found a positive effect of the drug on the illness*). This could explain the differences between performances of different models for different explanations. The logic-based explanations of e-SNLI are akin to the chain-of-thought (CoT) mechanism that LLMs deploy when answering reasoning questions. These explanations only improved the performance of PLMs, which seemingly do not have such a mechanism in their own predictive process, but hurt the performance of LLMs, where the explanations clashed with their internal reasoning process. Conversely, the summary-style explanations of HealthFC serve to provide additional context and background knowledge to the models, which could explain why they improved the performance of PLMs and, in some cases, even LLMs. Providing additional evidence in prompts to models in an explanatory way augments their knowledge state and leads to improved final reasoning predictions.

In addition, we also experimented with providing randomly chosen explanations from the datasets but observed worse performance than providing actual explanations. This implies that, unsurprisingly, the content of the explanations influences the models' predictions

5 Conclusion

In this work, we introduced a novel LLM-based framework for automatically generating textual explanations for NLI tasks. Our evaluation demonstrates that these automated rationales exhibit competitive quality to human annotations and can significantly enhance downstream model performance. This framework presents new opportunities for leveraging LLM explanations to augment non-explainable datasets and improve downstream model classification performance for both PLMs and LLMs. This work in particular highlights the potential of leveraging NLEs to improve LLMs' reasoning performance.

Future work will explore extending the framework to a broader set of datasets to encompass a wider range of tasks and complexities and further refine prompt engineering and explanation generation via refinement techniques [20], verification and refinement [35], and consistency fine-tuning [36]. Additionally, incorporating emerging evaluation metrics such as TIGERScore [37] and Prometheus [38] will enable more comprehensive quality assessments, while comparisons with advanced reasoning LLMs like OpenAI o3 and DeepSeek R1 could further validate our approach. In addition, we plan to extend our selection of LLMs used for generating explanations by experimenting with LLMs from the same family of different sizes (e.g., Gemma-9b vs Gemma-27b) to measure the impact of size on the quality of explanations per the metrics used in this study. Finally, another point of improvement is measuring and improving the faithfulness of self-explanations by LLMs [39], as we have observed that when asked to output the most important words for their predictions, LLMs frequently assign high importance to peripheral words in the prompt such as those describing the labels or denoting parts of the input such as the explanations provided.

Limitations. Our study is constrained by the sizes of the datasets considered and by the inherent challenges of evaluation metrics (e.g., MAUVE requires large output samples, and API costs for G-Eval can be prohibitive). In addition, the selection of LLMs we employed for generating explanations is limited by using one size per model family, as discussed in the future work, the study could benefit from extending this selection to models from the same family and of different sizes to systematically measure the effect of size on LLMs of same family. Despite these limitations, our findings underscore the strong potential of natural language explanations by LLM from different families and sizes in extending datasets with rationales and improving PLMs and LLMs performance in classification tasks.

Acknowledgments. We would like to thank the anonymous reviewers for their helpful suggestions. This research has been supported by the German Federal Ministry of Education and Research (BMBF) grant 01IS23069 Software Campus 3.0 (TU München).

References

1. Brown, T.B., et al.: Language Models are Few-Shot Learners (2020). arXiv preprint arXiv:2005.14165
2. Søgaard, A.: Explainable Natural Language Processing (Springer, 2022)
3. Lei, T., et al.: Rationalizing neural predictions. In: Proc. EMNLP, pp. 107–117 (2016)
4. DeYoung, Z., et al.: ERASER: a benchmark to evaluate rationalized NLP models. In: Proc. EMNLP, pp. 4443–4458 (2020)
5. Wiegreffe, S., et al.: A survey of annotated datasets for explainable natural language processing. arXiv preprint arXiv:2006.02366 (2020)
6. Rajani, N.F., et al.: Explain yourself! leveraging language models for commonsense reasoning. arXiv preprint arXiv:1906.02361 (2019)
7. Wei, J., et al.: Chain-of-thought prompting elicits reasoning in large language models. arXiv preprint arXiv:2201.11903 (2022)
8. Gubelmann, R., et al.: Capturing the varieties of natural language inference: a systematic survey of existing datasets and two novel benchmarks. J. Logic Lang. Inform. **33**, 21–48 (2024)
9. Bowman, S.R., et al.: A large annotated corpus for learning natural language inference. In: Proc. EMNLP, pp. 632–642 (2015)
10. Devlin, J., et al.: Bert: pre-training of deep bidirectional transformers for language understanding. In: Proc. NAACL-HLT, pp. 4171–4186 (2019)
11. Liu, Y., Ott, M., et al. Roberta: a robustly optimized bert pretraining approach. arXiv preprint arXiv:1907.11692 (2019)
12. Madsen, A., et al.: Post-hoc interpretability for neural NLP: A Survey. ACM Comput. Surv. **55** (2022)
13. Wiegreffe, S., Marasović, A.: Teach me to explain: a review of datasets for explainable NLP. In: Proc. NeurIPS Datasets and Benchmarks (2021)
14. Mardaoui, D., Garreau, D.: An analysis of LIME for text data. In: Proc. AISTATS, pp. 3493–3501 (2021)
15. Mathew, B., et al.: HateXplain: a benchmark dataset for explainable hate speech detection. In: Proc. AAAI, pp. 14867–14875 (2021)
16. Vladika, J., et al.: Step-by-step fact verification system for medical claims with explainable reasoning. In: Proc. 2025 NAACL-HLT (Association for Computational Linguistics, Albuquerque, New Mexico, 2025), pp. 805–816
17. Hartmann, J., et al.: Survey on how human explanations improve model learning. In: Proc. EMNLP, pp. 1000–1010 (2022)
18. Tan, C., et al.: The diversity of explanation types in natural language processing: implications and challenges. In: Proc. NAACL, pp. 3456–3465 (2021)
19. Mishra, A., et al.: Characterizing Large Language Models as Rationalizers of Knowledge-intensive Tasks in Findings of ACL (2024), 8117–8139
20. Wang, Q., et al.: Cross-Refine: improving natural language explanation generation by learning in tandem. In: Proc. COLING, pp. 1150–1167 (2025)
21. Wei Jie, Y., et al.: How interpretable are reasoning explanations from prompting large language models? In: Findings of NAACL, pp. 2148–2164 (2024)
22. Schmidtova, P., et al.: Automatic metrics in natural language generation: a survey of current evaluation practices. In: Proc. INLG, pp. 557–583 (2024)
23. Papineni, K., et al.: Bleu: a method for automatic evaluation of machine translation In: Proc. ACL, pp. 311–318 (2002)

24. Lin, C.-Y.: ROUGE: A Package for Automatic Evaluation of Summaries in Text Summarization Branches Out, pp. 74–81 (2004)
25. Zhang, T., et al.: BERTScore: evaluating text generation with BERT. In: Proc. ICLR (2020)
26. Pillutla, K., et al.: MAUVE: measuring the gap between neural text and human text using divergence frontiers. In: Proc. NeurIPS (2021)
27. Liu, Y., et al.: G-Eval: NLG Evaluation using Gpt-4 with Better Human Alignment. In: Proc. EMNLP, pp. 2511–2522 (2023)
28. Yao, B., et al.: Are human explanations always helpful? Towards objective evaluation of human natural language explanations. In: Proc. ACL, pp. 14698–14713 (2023)
29. Hartmann, M., Sonntag, D.: A survey on improving NLP models with human explanations. In: Proc. Workshop on Learning with Natural Language Supervision, pp. 40–47 (2022)
30. Warner, B., Chaffin, A., et al.: Smarter, better, faster, longer: a modern bidirectional encoder for fast, memory efficient, and long context finetuning and inference. arXiv preprint arXiv:2412.13663 (2024)
31. Camburu, O.-M., et al.: e-SNLI: Natural Language Inference with Natural Language Explanations. In: Proc. NeurIPS, pp. 9539–9549 (2018)
32. Bowman, S. R. et al.: A large annotated corpus for learning natural language inference. arXiv preprint arXiv:1508.05326 (2015)
33. Vladika, J. et al.: HealthFC: verifying health claims with evidence-based medical fact-checking. In: Proc. LREC-COLING, pp. 8095–8107 (2024)
34. He, P. et al.: Deberta: decoding-enhanced bert with disentangled attention. arXiv preprint arXiv:2006.03654 (2020)
35. Quan, X., et al.: Verification and refinement of natural language explanations through LLM-symbolic theorem proving. In: Proc. EMNLP, pp. 2933–2958 (2024)
36. Chen, Y., et al.: Towards Consistent Natural-Language Explanations via Explanation-Consistency Finetuning. In: Proc. COLING (2025), pp. 7558–7568
37. Jiang, D., et al.: TIGERScore: Towards Building Explainable Metric for All Text Generation Tasks. Trans, Machine Learning Research (2024)
38. Kim, S. et al.: Prometheus: inducing fine-grained evaluation capability in language models. In: Proc. ICLR (2024)
39. Parcalabescu, L., Frank, A.: On measuring faithfulness or self-consistency of natural language explanations. arXiv preprint arXiv:2311.07466 (2023)

Early Acoustic and Vision Cross-Modal Interaction Learning for Multimal Sentiment Analysis

Xiongjian Lv[1], Yimin Wen[1,2(✉)], Yi Qian[1], and Xiaoyu Li[1]

[1] Guangxi Key Laboratory of Image and Graphic Intelligent Processing, Guilin University of Electronic Technology, Guilin 541004, Guangxi, China
[2] School of Electronics and Information Engineering, Wuyi University, Jiangmen 529020, Guangdong, China
ymwen@guet.edu.cn

Abstract. Current methods for multimodal sentiment analysis task usually overlook the early interaction between acoustic and vision modalities before fusing with text modality. To overcome this problem, this paper proposed a model with a BAG-LSTM module, which consists of a bimodal adaption gate (BAG) and two modality-specific LSTM units, and other two attention modules focusing on improving the input and output sequences of BAG-LSTM. Through early interaction between acoustic and vision modalities, BAG calculates two shift vectors for these two modalities, respectively, to stimulate interactive sentimental information and facilitate implicit alignment of acoustic and vision modalities. The comprehensive experiments demonstrated that the proposed method has achieved the new state-of-the-art (SOTA) results. Our code is publicly available at https://github.com/mlmmwym/BAG-LSTM.

Keywords: Multimodal Sentiment Analysis · Multimodal Interaction · Multimodal Adaptation Gate

1 Introduction

Multimodal sentiment analysis (MSA) has been widely used in many applications, such as public opinion monitoring, social media analysis, and age rating of short video content, and so on [1,2]. Traditional unimodal sentiment analysis only considers extracting sentimental information from a single type of data, which often limits the accuracy of sentiment analysis due to the singularity of the data. MSA leverages the richness and complementary of cross-modal data, such as text, acoustic, and vision data, significantly enhancing the accuracy of sentiment analysis [3,4]. However, when conducting MSA, one often encounters

---

This work was partially supported by the National Natural Science Foundation of China (62366011) and the Natural Science Foundation of Guangxi District (2024GXNSFDA010066).

a series of troubles, such as the complexity and subtlety of sentiment, consistency and conflicts between modalities, and issues related to data missing and alignment. Solving these problems and integrating different modalities of data into a unified model and enabling these heterogeneous data to complement and interact with each other pose significant challenges.

Current methods for MSA task [5,6] mostly employ the Transformers trained on large text datasets as backbone, such as Bert [7], T5 [8], etc. Based on the position of modality fusion relative to the Transformer encoder, it can be divided into internal fusion methods (fusion within the encoder) [9,10] and external fusion methods (fusion at the input or output stages of the encoder) [5,6]. These methods usually identified text as main modality [11], and the way of its modality fusion is usually to inject multimodal information into text. For example, multimodal adaptation gate (MAG) [5] is a commonly used and effective multimodal fusion mechanism, which interprets the influence of acoustic and vision information on textual semantics as a shift within the latent semantic space of the text. However, these methods largely overlook a fact: before fusing acoustic and vision features with textual features, acoustic and vision signals require precise interaction. Sentiments evoked by the interaction of video and audio are called interactive sentiments, this specific sentimental information can only be fully captured when auditory and visual information interact. For example, consider a movie where the audience first closes their eyes to experience it relying solely on hearing, and then covers their ears to watch it using only vision. Although this separated modality of viewing still receives visual, auditory, or textual information, the experience it provides is far inferior to watching the movie normally. This is because the lack of interaction between auditory and visual information leads to the loss of interactive sentimental information. In the field of neuroscience, some studies have pointed out that the interaction between vision and hearing occurs before humans receive textual information [12]. However, in fact, acoustic and vision features without interaction are often difficult to be aligned implicitly during fusion, which may deteriorate model performance.

To handle the aforementioned problems, this paper proposed to improve MSA through early interaction between acoustic and vision modalities before fusing with text modality. The core of the proposed method is BAG-LSTM which consists of a bimodal adaption gate (BAG) and two modality-specific LSTM units. Two attention modules focused on improving the input and output sequences of BAG-LSTM, namely UA and BA are also proposed. The BAG-LSTM module processes acoustic and vision signals with two modality-specific LSTM units, respectively. In each LSTM unit, the output of the cell state is bypassed and input into the BAG. Through interaction between the acoustic and vision modalities, BAG calculates two shift vectors for these two modalities, respectively. Each shift vector is added with the output of its corresponding cell state to achieve semantic shift and then the addition is sent back as a new cell state to its corresponding LSTM unit to process subsequently. Thus, BAG-LSTM not only captures the temporal features of acoustic and vision modalities but also facilitates the interaction and implicit alignment of these two modalities. Although LSTM

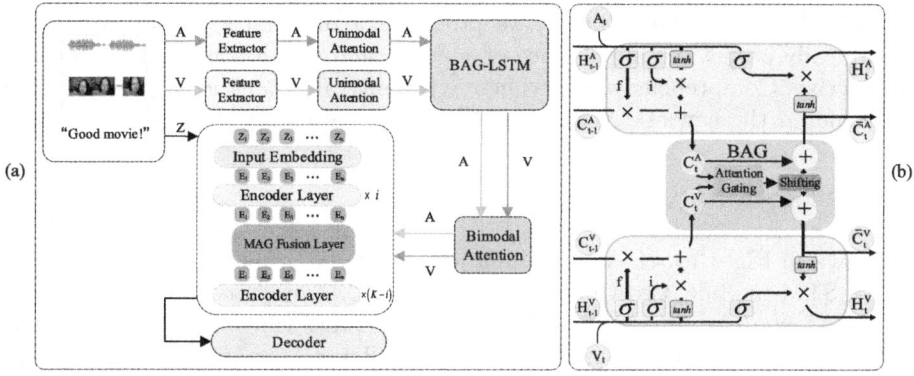

Fig. 1. (a) The overall architecture of the proposed model; (b) The network structure of the BAG-LSTM module.

offers certain advantages over traditional recurrent neural networks in processing sequence data, BAG-LSTM still faces the issue of information attenuation [13], which can significantly misconduct sentiment analysis tasks, as sentimental information may be distributed at any point in a sequence [14]. For example, in movies, it often requires a long time to gradually accumulate sentiments. To address this issue, this paper proposed a unimodal attention (UA) module to process the input sequence of each modality before inputting into the BAG-LSTM module. The proposed UA module first make the lengths of the two input sequences the same through average pooling and linear interpolation on adjacent features in each sequence. By calculating the attention weights of the input sequence from both temporal and representational dimensions and performing matrix multiplication, the UA module can enhance the sentimental information in the sequence, thus counteracting the effect of information attenuation.

Since MAG is primarily conducted at the word level, lacking a global perspective to adjust the importance of acoustic and vision features at different moments contradicts with how humans process sentimental information—often considering overall context [15]. Therefore, this paper proposed a bimodal attention (BA) module to apply attention mechanism to process the output of BAG-LSTM module before inputting into the MAG. BA calculates attention weights from three dimensions: temporal, representation, and modality. Through this approach, BA enhances the relevance of acoustic-vision features to sentiments and reduces irrelevant information, thereby improving the fusion effect with text modality in MAG.

The main contributions of this paper are as follows: first, we proposed the BAG-LSTM module, which effectively facilitates the interaction and implicit alignment of acoustic and vision modalities by integrating LSTM with an bimodal adaptation gate and two modality-specific LSTM units. Second, we proposed an unimodal attention module to make the lengths of the two input sequences the same and alleviate information attenuation before inputting into the BAG-LSTM module. Third, we proposed a bimodal attention module to dynamically adjust the importance of acoustic and vision features from a global perspective. Comprehensive experiments demonstrate that the proposed method has achieved the new state-of-the-art (SOTA) results.

2 Methodology

As shown in Fig. 1(a), the overall architecture of the proposed model includes a BAG-LSTM module, two Unimodal Attention (UA) modules, a Bimodal Attention (BA) module, and a T5 model with 12 Transformer layers and in which a MAG module is applied at the ith encoder layer ($i = 9$ in this paper). Initially, the acoustic and vision features are extracted separately by unified feature extractors. Subsequently, The UA module is used to enhance the sentimental information in the acoustic and vision sequences separately. Thereafter, the BAG-LSTM module facilitates the interaction between acoustic and vision modalities and implicit aligning them. Next, the BA module adjusts the importance of the acoustic and vision features. T5 is employed to extract contextual information in the text modality, and the MAG module is deployed to inject the acoustic and vision information extracted from the BA module into the text features.

2.1 BAG-LSTM

As shown in Fig. 1(b), A and V is respectively used to represent acoustic and vision modality. Both A and V are initially assumed to have the same sequence length L. For the input acoustic and vision features $\boldsymbol{A}_t$ and $\boldsymbol{V}_t$ at the time t, the following operations are performed:

$$\boldsymbol{f}_t^M = \sigma(\boldsymbol{W}_f \cdot [\boldsymbol{H}_{t-1}^M, \boldsymbol{M}_t] + \boldsymbol{b}_f) \tag{1}$$

$$\boldsymbol{i}_t^M = \sigma(\boldsymbol{W}_i \cdot [\boldsymbol{H}_{t-1}^M, \boldsymbol{M}_t] + \boldsymbol{b}_i) \tag{2}$$

$$\tilde{\boldsymbol{C}}_t^M = \tanh(\boldsymbol{W}_c \cdot [\boldsymbol{H}_{t-1}^M, \boldsymbol{M}_t] + \boldsymbol{b}_c) \tag{3}$$

$$\boldsymbol{C}_t^M = \boldsymbol{f}_t^M \odot \boldsymbol{C}_{t-1}^M + \boldsymbol{i}_t^M \odot \tilde{\boldsymbol{C}}_t^M \tag{4}$$

where $M \in \{A, V\}$ represents the acoustic or vision modalities, and $\boldsymbol{M}_t$ represents the input acoustic feature $\boldsymbol{A}_t$ when $M = A$, while $\boldsymbol{M}_t$ represents the input vision feature $\boldsymbol{V}_t$ when $M = V$. $\boldsymbol{f}$ and $\boldsymbol{i}$ respectively represent the activation vectors of the forget gate and input gate. $\boldsymbol{W}$ is the weight matrix, and $\boldsymbol{b}$ stands for the bias.

After obtaining the latest cell state features $\boldsymbol{C}_t^M$ ($\boldsymbol{C}_t^A$ and $\boldsymbol{C}_t^V$) for acoustic and vision modalities, respectively, they interact with each other through the BAG module as follows:

$$\boldsymbol{g}_t^M = \tanh(\boldsymbol{W}_g \cdot [\boldsymbol{C}_t^M, \boldsymbol{C}_t^{M'}] + \boldsymbol{b}_g) \tag{5}$$

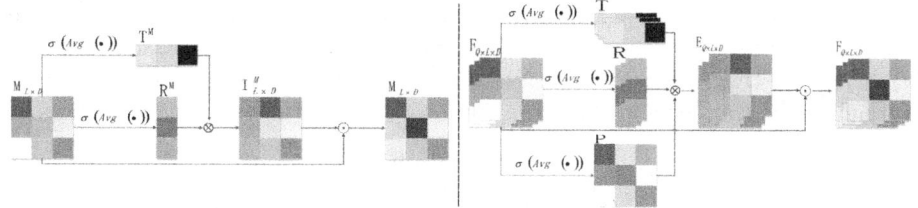

Fig. 2. Unimodal attention (left) and Bimodal Attention (right) model.

$$S_t^M = g_t^M \odot (W_h \cdot C_t^{M'} + b_h) \tag{6}$$

$$\overline{C}_t^M = C_t^M + a S_t^M \tag{7}$$

$$\alpha = \min\left(\frac{\|C_t^M\|_2}{\|S_t^M\|_2 + \epsilon}\beta, 1\right) \tag{8}$$

where, M' means the modality that interacts with M, which when $M = A$, $M' = V$, and vice versa. S represents the shift vector, and $\overline{C}_t^M$ represents the cell feature after the shift. The scaling factor α is used to control the impact of audio-visual interaction, ensuring it remains within an appropriate range, β is a hyperparameter selected through cross-validation and set to 0.9. $\|\cdot\|_2$ denotes the L_2 norm. ϵ is set to $1e-8$ to prevent the case where S_t^M becomes a zero vector. We use the scaling factor a so that the effect of non-verbal shift S_t^M remains within a desirable range. Finally, we apply a layer normalization and dropout layer to $\overline{C}_t^M$.

The subsequent hidden state features H_t^M will be calculated from the cell state features $\overline{C}_t^M$ that contain interaction information, with specific operations as follows:

$$H_t^M = \sigma(W_o \cdot [H_{t-1}^M, M_t] + b_o) \odot \tanh(\overline{C}_t^M) \tag{9}$$

Finally, we use the acoustic and vision hidden state sequences H^A and H^V as the input sequences of $A_{L \times D}$ and $V_{L \times D}$ for the subsequent BA module.

Here, it is noteworthy to mention why we choose to propose BAG for modality interaction instead of two AG modules. If two AG modules are used to handle acoustic-vision interaction separately, the first AG would adjust the semantic position of the video based on audio information, followed by the second AG adjusting the audio based on video information. This serial approach could cause the audio information originally integrated into the video to flow back into the audio features during the second step, not only failing to achieve effective interaction but possibly leading to feature confusion.

2.2 Unimodal Attention

To make the BAG-LSTM module performs more effectively, the UA module is proposed to make the lengths of the two input sequences the same to alleviate information attenuation.

Firstly, to make the lengths of the two input sequences the same, for the input acoustic sequence $\boldsymbol{A}_{L_A \times D}$ with the length of L_A and the input vision sequence $\boldsymbol{V}_{L_V \times D}$ with the length of L_V, we adjust them to the same length L through average pooling and linear interpolation on adjacent vectors in each sequence:

$$\boldsymbol{A}_{L \times D} = Adjust(\boldsymbol{A}_{L_A \times D}) \quad (10)$$

$$\boldsymbol{V}_{L \times D} = Adjust(\boldsymbol{V}_{L_V \times D}) \quad (11)$$

where D denotes representational dimension.

Secondly, as illustrated in the left side of Fig. 2, to alleviate information attenuation, both the acoustic and vision sequences are then adaptively re-calibrated by explicitly modelling their inter-dependencies information from both temporal and representational dimensions. Specifically, for the sake of simplicity, in the following, $\boldsymbol{M}_{L \times D}$ is used to present the sequence of $\boldsymbol{A}_{L \times D}$ when M = A, and $\boldsymbol{V}_{L \times D}$ when M = V, respectively. Subsequently, we squeeze the information from the sequence $\boldsymbol{M}_{L \times D}$ along both the temporal and representational dimensions separately, modeling their respective dependency relationship vectors as $\boldsymbol{T}^M$ and $\boldsymbol{R}^M$. The specific operations are as follows:

$$\boldsymbol{T}^M = \sigma(\boldsymbol{W}_L \cdot Avg_T(\boldsymbol{M}_{L \times D}) + \boldsymbol{b}_L) \quad (12)$$

$$\boldsymbol{R}^M = \sigma(\boldsymbol{W}_D \cdot Avg_R(\boldsymbol{M}_{L \times D}) + \boldsymbol{b}_D) \quad (13)$$

where $Avg_T(\cdot)$ and $Avg_R(\cdot)$ mean pooling operation is performed along temporal and representational dimensions, respectively. Subsequently, both $\boldsymbol{T}^M$ and $\boldsymbol{R}^M$ are used to solve the dependency relationships in each sequence, as follows:

$$\boldsymbol{I}^M_{L \times D} = \boldsymbol{T}^M \otimes \boldsymbol{R}^M \quad (14)$$

$$\boldsymbol{M}_{L \times D} = \boldsymbol{M}_{L \times D} \odot \boldsymbol{I}^M_{L \times D} \quad (15)$$

where $\otimes$ represents tensor product, $\odot$ means element-wise multiplication, and $\boldsymbol{I}^M_{L \times D}$ represents the dependency relationship modeled from each input sequence. $\boldsymbol{M}_{L \times D}$ is updated from the old $\boldsymbol{M}_{L \times D}$ element-wisely multiplied with $\boldsymbol{I}^M_{L \times D}$. Thus, the sentimental information in each sequence is enhanced to overcome information attenuation.

2.3 Bimodal Attention

Considering that in MAG not all acoustic and vision features have the same importance, we proposed a Bimodal Attention (BA) module, due to human's perception of text modality is influenced by acoustic or vision modalities with different intensity at different moments.

As shown at the right side in Fig. 2, $\boldsymbol{A}_{L \times D}$ and $\boldsymbol{V}_{L \times D}$ output from the BAG-LSTM module are concatenated along the modality dimension to obtain the bimodal matrix $\boldsymbol{F}_{Q \times L \times D}$ ($Q = 2$ represents the modalities of acoustic and vision). To model the dependency relationship in each sequence, $\boldsymbol{F}_{Q \times L \times D}$ is first pooled and then input into an output layer with a non-linear activation function. The operations are as follows:

$$P = \sigma(W_Q \cdot Avg_Q(F_{Q \times L \times D}) + b_Q) \quad (16)$$

$$T = \sigma(W_L \cdot Avg_L(F_{Q \times L \times D}) + b_L) \quad (17)$$

$$R = \sigma(W_D \cdot Avg_D(F_{Q \times L \times D}) + b_D) \quad (18)$$

where $Avg_Q(\cdot)$, $Avg_L(\cdot)$, and $Avg_D(\cdot)$ represents performing global average pooling across three dimensions, respectively. After obtaining the dependency relationship P, T, and R, we calculate the dependency relationship matrix E to the old bimodal matrix F and use them to obtain a new F which has adjusted the importance of acoustic and vision features:

$$E_{Q \times L \times D} = P \otimes T \otimes R \quad (19)$$

$$F_{Q \times L \times D} = F_{Q \times L \times D} \odot E_{Q \times L \times D} \quad (20)$$

At last, F is split along the modality dimension to obtain two input sequences of acoustic and vision for MAG.

It is worth mentioning that our proposed UA and BA modules are designed differently from self-attention pooling. UA models both temporal and semantic dimensions, constructing a richer attention matrix through tensor product operations, capturing more complex intra-modal relationships. Self-attention pooling primarily models the temporal dimension, with limited information interaction. Additionally, using pre-trained Transformer encoders may introduce bias towards the textual modality, reducing attention to visual and audio features. Therefore, we designed the UA and BA modules to ensure that the model fairly focuses on information from each modality.

3 experiments

3.1 Datasets and Metrics

CMU-MOSI is one of the most widely used benchmark dataset in the field of MSA. It contains 2199 utterance video segments, and each segment is manually annotated with a sentiment score ranging from -3 to +3 to indicate the sentiment polarity and relative sentiment strength of the segment. CMU-MOSEI is an upgraded version of CMU-MOSI. It comprises 23,453 video segments from 3,228 videos, similar to CMU-MOSI, each utterance-level sample in CMU-MOSEI is annotated a sentiment label on a scale of -3 to 3. Following the prior work, five metrics are used to evaluate models, which are binary classification accuracy (Acc-2), seven classification accuracy (Acc-7), F1 Score, Mean Absolute Error (MAE), and Pearson Correlation Coefficient (Corr). IEMOCAP comprises 7,532 samples, in which six emotions of happiness, sadness, anger, neutrality, excitement, and frustration are selected to evaluate models. For IEMOCAP, six classification accuracy (Acc.) and F1 Score (F1.) are used for evaluation.

Table 1. Performance Comparison on CMU-MOSI and CMU-MOSEI.

Models	CMU-MOSI					CMU-MOSEI				
	Acc7↑	Acc2↑	F1↑	Corr↑	MAE↓	Acc7↑	Acc2↑	F1↑	Corr↑	MAE↓
MAG-BERT$_{2020,ACL}$	45.1	84.6	84.6	0.789	0.730	52.8	85.1	85.1	0.761	0.558
Self-MM$_{2021,AAAI}$	45.8	84.9	84.8	0.785	0.731	53.0	85.2	85.2	0.763	0.540
MMIM$_{2021,EMNLP}$	45.0	85.1	85.0	0.781	0.738	53.1	85.1	85.0	0.752	0.547
FDMER$_{2022,MM}$	44.1	84.6	84.7	0.788	0.724	54.1	86.1	85.8	0.773	0.536
MVCL$_{2022,ICASSP}$	-	83.7	84.2	0.783	0.769	-	85.0	85.0	0.741	0.573
HyCon$_{2023,IEEE}$	46.6	85.2	85.1	0.790	0.713	52.8	85.4	85.6	0.776	0.601
EMT$_{2023,TAC}$	47.4	85.0	85.0	0.798	0.705	54.5	86.0	86.0	0.774	0.527
ALMT$_{2023,EMNLP}$	49.4	86.4	86.5	0.805	0.683	54.2	86.8	86.9	0.779	0.526
PEST$_{2024,KBS}$	-	86.1	86.1	0.796	0.723	-	85.3	85.1	0.761	0.542
MCL-MCF$_{2024,IEEE}$	-	87.3	**87.2**	0.799	0.692	-	86.4	86.3	0.767	0.536
KEBR$_{2024,MM}$	47.8	87.2	**87.2**	0.819	0.683	54.3	86.7	86.6	**0.799**	0.517
GLoMo$_{2024,MM}$	48.3	86.7	86.6	0.782	0.718	55.0	86.5	86.4	0.771	0.539
HyDiscGAN$_{2024,IJCAI}$	43.2	86.7	86.3	0.782	0.749	54.4	86.3	86.2	0.761	0.533
TCHFN$_{2025,KBS}$	44.7	86.1	86.3	0.780	0.748	53.1	86.2	86.4	0.770	0.538
Ours	**52.1**	**87.4**	87.1	0.782	**0.656**	**56.3**	**88.9**	**88.7**	0.760	**0.516**

3.2 Experimental Settings

To ensure fairness in experiments, we follow the recent SOTA methods to set our proposed method. For the text, audio, and visual information in the dataset, we use T5, librosa, and OpenFace to perform the feature extraction, respectively. Our proposed model runs on a single NVIDIA A100 GPU with the PyTorch framework for all datasets. We employed the Adam optimizer with an initial learning rate of 1e-5, a batch size of 64, and implemented a learning rate decay strategy that reduces the learning rate when the validation loss plateaus.

3.3 Results

Comparison to State-of-the-art To evaluate the effectiveness of our method, we compare the proposed method with the following recent and competitive baselines: MAG-BERT [5], Self-MM [16], MMIM [11], FDMER [17], EMT [18], MVCL [19], HyCon [20], ALMT [21], PEST [22], MCL-MCF [23], KEBR [24], GLoMo [25], HyDiscGA-N [26], and TCHFN [27]. The performance of our method and baselines on two datasets is shown in Table 1. It can be observed that our method matches or even outperforms these baselines on these two datasets. Our model excelled on four metrics: Acc7, Acc2, F1, and MAE, achieving 52.1%, 87.4%, 87.1%, and 0.656, respectively. Regarding the relatively low Corr metric, we attribute this to the MAG fusion method's inadequate learning capability for extreme samples with limited quantities. Nonetheless, our method demonstrates significant improvements in other key metrics.

Table 2. Ablation Results on CMU-MOSI and IEMOCAP.

Models	CMU-MOSI					IEMOCAP	
	Acc7↑	Acc2↑	F1↑	Corr↑	MAE↓	Acc.↑	F1.↑
w/o BAG	45.7	84.1	83.9	0.712	0.693	66.7	65.8
w/o UA	50.4	87.0	86.3	0.774	0.676	68.5	67.8
w/o BA	51.1	87.2	86.9	0.779	0.658	68.9	68.2
Ours	**52.1**	**87.4**	**87.1**	**0.782**	**0.656**	**70.1**	**69.3**

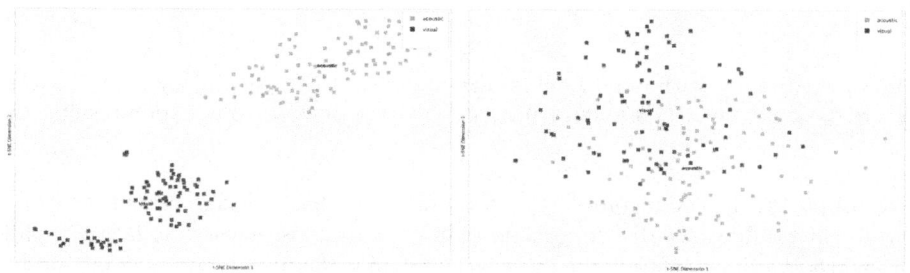

Fig. 3. t-SNE visualization. The left figure shows the raw data distributions of the visual and auditory modalities, and the right shows the aligned features produced through their interaction in the BAG-LSTM module.

Ablation Study To evaluate the rationality of our method, three cases are considered in Table 2. **w/o BAG** means the acoustic and vision modalities are not interacted only by employing two separate LSTM units. **w/o UA** means both the BAG-LSTM and BA modules are employed while the UA module is dropped. **w/o BA** means both the UA and BAG-LSTM modules are employed while the BA module is dropped. From Table 2, it can be observed that dropping BAG will led to significant decline on all performance metrics, underscoring the critical importance of the BAG-LSTM module, dropping the UA or BA module will deteriorate performance on all performance metrics too but with small degrees. The same ablation on IEMOCAP illustrated also illustrate the effectivity of the modules of BAG, UA, and BA.

3.4 Representation Visualization

Fig. 3 demonstrates the effectiveness of the BAG-LSTM component through private-shared semantic visualization. Specifically, we employ t-SNE to project diverse features into a 2D space, with color-coded semantic clusters. To ensure fairness, the perplexity parameter was fixed at 1.0. The left figure in Fig. 3 reveals clear separation boundary between visual and auditory features, consistent with the original data distribution. The right figure in Fig. 3 shows significant overlap between visual and auditory features—indicating that BAG-LSTM implicitly aligns features through cross-modal interaction to enhance fusion effective-

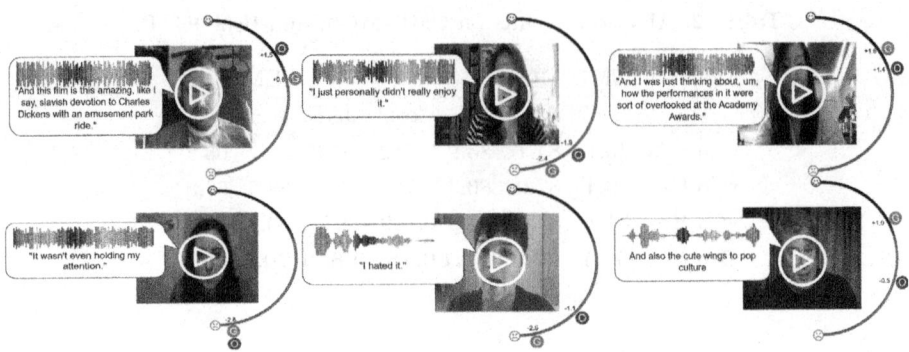

Fig. 4. Predictions with our model on samples from CMU-MOSEI and CMU-MOSI. Where 'G' represents the ground truth, and 'O' represents the prediction results.

ness. Importantly, the incomplete overlap aligns with our design objective: forced alignment would cause disproportionate information loss across modalities, while our method maintains essential alignment while maximally preserving modal-specific information.

3.5 Case Study

Figure 4 presents our model's results across different examples. The top-left and top-center figures show that when emotional information primarily resides in the textual modality, the model's predictions closely align with the ground-truth values. The top-right and bottom-left figures illustrate when emotional cues predominantly emerge from non-textual modalities, our proposed model generate accurate predictions—consistent with BAG-LSTM's designed effectiveness for cross-modal interaction. Further, when both textual and non-textual modalities exhibit strong emotional signals (bottom-center and bottom-right figures), BAG-LSTM, along with UA and BA components, continues to mine interactive emotional features.

4 Conclusions

This paper proposed a model with a BAG-LSTM module, which consists of a bimodal adaption gate (BAG) and two modality-specific LSTM units, and other two attention modules focusing on improving the input and output sequences of BAG-LSTM. Through early interaction between acoustic and vision modalities, BAG calculates two shift vectors for these two modalities, respectively, to stimulate interactive sentimental information and facilitate implicit alignment of acoustic and vision modalities. The ablation results illustrated the effectiveness of the proposed modules of BAD, UA, and BA, and the comprehensive experiments demonstrated that the proposed method has achieved the new state-of-the-art (SOTA) results.

References

1. Li, M., et al.: A unified self-distillation framework for multimodal sentiment analysis with uncertain missing modalities. In: Proceedings of the AAAI Conference on Artificial Intelligence, pp. 10074–10082 (2024)
2. Huang, J., Ji, Y., Yang, Y., Shen, H.T.: Cross-modality representation interactive learning for multimodal sentiment analysis. In: Proceedings of the 31st ACM International Conference on Multimedia, pp. 426–434 (2023)
3. Zong, D., Ding, C., Li, B., Li, J., Zheng, K., Zhou, Q.: Acformer: an aligned and compact transformer for multimodal sentiment analysis. In: Proceedings of the 31st ACM International Conference on Multimedia, pp. 833–842 (2023)
4. Guo, Z., Jin, T., Zhao, Z.: Multimodal prompt learning with missing modalities for sentiment analysis and emotion recognition. In: Ku, L.-W., Martins, A., Srikumar, V. (eds.) Proceedings of the 62nd Annual Meeting of the Association for Computational Linguistics (Volume 1: Long Papers), Bangkok, Thailand, pp. 1726–1736, Association for Computational Linguistics (Aug. 2024)
5. Rahman, W., et al.: Integrating multimodal information in large pretrained transformers. In: Jurafsky, D., Chai, J., Schluter, N., Tetreault, J. (eds.) Proceedings of the 58th Annual Meeting of the Association for Computational Linguistics (Online), pp. 2359–2369. Association for Computational Linguistics (July 2020)
6. Hwang, Y., Kim, J.-H.: Easum: enhancing affective state understanding through joint sentiment and emotion modeling for multimodal tasks. In: Proceedings of the IEEE/CVF Winter Conference on Applications of Computer Vision, pp. 5668–5678 (2024)
7. Devlin, J., Chang, M.-W., Lee, K., Toutanova, K.: BERT: Pre-training of deep bidirectional transformers for language understanding. In: Proceedings of the 2019 Conference of the North American Chapter of the Association for Computational Linguistics: Human Language Technologies, pp. 4171–4186 (2019)
8. Raffel, C., et al.: Exploring the limits of transfer learning with a unified text-to-text transformer. J. Mach. Learn. Res. **21**, 1–67 (2020)
9. Liu, Z., Zhou, B., Chu, D., Sun, Y., Meng, L.: Modality translation-based multimodal sentiment analysis under uncertain missing modalities. Inform. Fusion **101**, 101973 (2024)
10. Hu, G., Lin, T.-E., Zhao, Y., Lu, G., Wu, Y., Li, Y.: Unimse: Towards unified multimodal sentiment analysis and emotion recognition. In: Proceedings of the 2022 Conference on Empirical Methods in Natural Language Processing, pp. 7837–7851 (2022)
11. Han, W., Chen, H., Poria, S.: Improving multimodal fusion with hierarchical mutual information maximization for multimodal sentiment analysis. In: Proceedings of the 2021 Conference on Empirical Methods in Natural Language Processing, pp. 9180–9192 (2021)
12. Kaya, U., Kafaligonul, H.: Audiovisual interactions in speeded discrimination of a visual event. Psychophysiology, 13777 (2021)
13. Zhang, H., Zhang, Q., Shao, S., Niu, T., Yang, X.: Attention-based lstm network for rotatory machine remaining useful life prediction. IEEE Access **8**, 132188–132199 (2020)
14. Arbane, M., Benlamri, R., Brik, Y., Alahmar, A.D.: Social media-based covid-19 sentiment classification model using bi-lstm. Expert Syst. Appl. **212**, 118710 (2023)
15. Lu, G., Xie, K., Liu, Q.: What influences student situational engagement in smart classrooms: perception of the learning environment and students' motivation. Br. J. Edu. Technol. **53**, 1665–1687 (2022)

16. Yu, W., Xu, H., Yuan, Z., Wu, J.: Learning modality-specific representations with self-supervised multi-task learning for multimodal sentiment analysis. In: Proceedings of the AAAI Conference on Artificial Intelligence, pp. 10790–10797 (2021)
17. Yang, D., Huang, S., Kuang, H., Du, Y., Zhang, L.: Disentangled representation learning for multimodal emotion recognition. In: Proceedings of the 30th ACM International Conference on Multimedia, pp. 1642–1651 (2022)
18. Sun, L., Lian, Z., Liu, B., Tao, J.: Efficient multimodal transformer with dual-level feature restoration for robust multimodal sentiment analysis. IEEE Trans. Affect. Comput. **15**, 309–325 (2023)
19. Liu, P.: Improving the modality representation with multi-view contrastive learning for multimodal sentiment analysis. In: ICASSP 2023 - 2023 IEEE International Conference on Acoustics, Speech and Signal Processing (ICASSP), pp. 1–5 (2023)
20. Mai, S., Zeng, Y., Zheng, S., Hu, H.: Hybrid contrastive learning of tri-modal representation for multimodal sentiment analysis. IEEE Trans. Affect. Comput. **14**, 2276–2289 (2022)
21. Zhang, H., Wang, Y., Yin, G., Liu, K., Liu, Y., Yu, T.: Learning language-guided adaptive hyper-modality representation for multimodal sentiment analysis. In: Proceedings of the 2023 Conference on Empirical Methods in Natural Language Processing, pp. 756–767, 2023
22. Gan, C., Tang, Y., Fu, X., Zhu, Q., Jain, D.K., García, S.: Video multimodal sentiment analysis using cross-modal feature translation and dynamical propagation. Knowl.-Based Syst. **299**, 111982 (2024)
23. Fan, C., Zhu, K., Tao, J., Yi, G., Xue, J., Lv, Z.: Multi-level contrastive learning: hierarchical alleviation of heterogeneity in multimodal sentiment analysis. IEEE Trans. Affect. Comput. **16**, 207–222 (2025)
24. Zhu, A., Hu, M., Wang, X., Yang, J., Tang, Y., Ren, F.: Kebr: knowledge enhanced self-supervised balanced representation for multimodal sentiment analysis. In: Proceedings of the 32nd ACM International Conference on Multimedia, pp. 5732–5741 (2024)
25. Zhuang, Y., Zhang, Y., Hu, Z., Zhang, X., Deng, J., Ren, F.:Glomo: global-local modal fusion for multimodal sentiment analysis. In: Proceedings of the 32nd ACM International Conference on Multimedia, pp. 1800–1809 (2024)
26. Wu, Z., Zhang, Q., Miao, D., Yi, K., Fan, W., Hu, L.: Hydiscgan: a hybrid distributed cgan for audio-visual privacy preservation in multimodal sentiment analysis. In: Proceedings of the 33rd International Joint Conference on Artificial Intelligence (IJCAI), pp. 6550–6558 (2024)
27. Hou, J., Omar, N., Tiun, S., Saad, S., He, Q.: Tchfn: multimodal sentiment analysis based on text-centric hierarchical fusion network. Knowl.-Based Syst. **300**, 112220 (2024)

Uncovering Causal Relation Shifts in Event Sequences Under Out-of-Domain Interventions

Kazi Tasnim Zinat[1](✉), Yun Zhou[2], Xiang Lyu[2], Yawei Wang[2], Zhicheng Liu[1], and Panpan Xu[2]

[1] University of Maryland, College Park, MD 20740, USA
{kzintas,leozcliu}@umd.edu
[2] Amazon Web Services, Seattle, USA
{yunzzhou,xianglyu,yawenwan,xupanpan}@amazon.com

Abstract. Inferring causal relationships between event pairs in a temporal sequence is applicable in many domains such as healthcare, manufacturing, and transportation. Most existing work on causal inference primarily focuses on event types within the designated domain, without considering the impact of exogenous out-of-domain interventions. In real-world settings, these out-of-domain interventions can significantly alter causal dynamics. To address this gap, we propose a new causal framework to define average treatment effect (ATE), beyond independent and identically distributed (i.i.d.) data in classic Rubin's causal framework, to capture the causal relation shift between events of temporal process under out-of-domain intervention. We design an unbiased ATE estimator, and devise a Transformer-based neural network model to handle both long-range temporal dependencies and local patterns while integrating out-of-domain intervention information into process modeling. Extensive experiments on both simulated and real-world datasets demonstrate that our method outperforms baselines in ATE estimation and goodness-of-fit under out-of-domain-augmented point processes. The supplementary materials are available here.

Keywords: Sequential Data · Causal Estimation · Transformer

1 Introduction

Multivariate event sequences are prevalent across diverse domains, capturing time-stamped data from shared environments or subjects, such as Electronic Health Records [21] and industrial maintenance records [26]. Real-world data generation is often implicitly conditioned on unobserved out-of-domain variables, leading to generalization failures due to distribution shifts [11,25].

Causal relation analysis within event sequences aims to quantify how changes in one event influence another [7,16]. The Rubin Causal Model [9] characterizes causal relations through the average treatment effect (ATE), representing the average difference between treatment & control potential outcomes. However, existing work focuses on causal relations within designated domains, overlooking the influence of known exogenous out-of-domain interventions that can induce causal relationship shifts. For instance, while meal ingestion increases blood glucose, insulin injection (an out-of-domain intervention) can counteract this effect [3].

To address this gap, we propose a novel approach to detect causal relation shifts in temporal processes under out-of-domain interventions. Our framework extends ATE to account for unique intervention scenarios, enabling comparison across such contexts. To our knowledge, this is the first work to explicitly model out-of-domain intervention impact on causal relations in temporal event data.

Our main contributions are multi-fold. First, we develop a theoretical framework of ATE that moves beyond i.i.d. assumptions to explicitly condition on intervention states and temporal dependencies. Second, we develop a propensity score-based treatment effect estimator to mitigate confounder bias. We justify its estimation consistency under our new ATE framework. Third, we propose a new Transformer architecture that captures intervention-induced temporal pattern changes. The architecture consists of several new network components: 1) a novel out-of-domain intervention embedding mechanism that enables direct influence modeling on event sequences; b) a weighted combination module that adaptively balances intervention and event embeddings; 3) a hybrid Transformer-CNN structure to simultaneously capture global dependencies and local temporal patterns specific to intervention effects, 4) a multi-objective loss function that jointly optimizes for intensity estimation and event type prediction. Fourth, we provide comprehensive experimental validation on simulated and real-world datasets, demonstrating improved performance in both causal effect estimation and temporal process representation compared to existing methods.

2 Related Work

Point processes [4] model labeled event sequences, with Hawkes processes [8] capturing excitation/inhibition effects of past events on current occurrences. Neural approaches include RNNs [6,22] for handling time and labels simultaneously, and Transformers [23,27] for long-range dependencies [18].

Causal analysis compares potential treatment and control outcomes using the Rubin Causal Model [17], with ATE as the primary metric. Propensity scores mitigate confounding bias in observational studies [9], while deep learning advances causal estimation [15,19]. Temporal causal inference extends these concepts through Granger causality [24] and point process-based causal modeling [7,16]. A detailed discussion with other methods is provided in the supplementary materials

3 Out-of-Domain Intervention Augmented Causal Inference

3.1 Notation

Let us consider a set of n individual sequences $\{s_1, , \ldots, s_n\}$. In a generic event sequence scenario, for a single sequence s_k, the observation we collect for the i-th event can be expressed as a tuple $(e_{k,i}, t_{k,i})$. Here, $t_{k,i}$ represents the timestamp of the i-th event in sequence $\mathbf{s}_k$, and $e_{k,i}$ denotes the corresponding event type which belongs to a set of events $\mathbb{E}$. The count of observed events of sequence $\mathbf{s}_k$ is denoted by L_k. The time duration of each sequence is T. We categorize the events based on their types: cause events c, outcome events o, out-of-domain interventions v, and other measured events $\mathbf{x}$.

3.2 Temporal Point Process

We focus on temporal point processes, where both event type and timestamp are observed. Hawkes processes, known for their self-excitation property, are commonly used to model real-world event sequences [14,23]. Specifically, for an n-dimensional Hawkes process, the conditional intensity function (CIF) of outcome event o_i at time t is expressed as:

$$\lambda(t) = \mu(t) + \sum_{k=1}^{n} \sum_{t_{k,i} < t} \phi(t - t_{k,i}), \qquad (1)$$

where μ denotes the baseline intensity function, ϕ is the excitation function capturing the influence of past events on outcome event. Note that $\lambda(t)$ is not observable. In this work, we estimate it from sequence data.

3.3 Out-of-Domain Intervention Augmented Causal Framework

We extend the Rubin causal framework to incorporate out-of-domain interventions, leveraging two key concepts.

First, we adopt the notion of process independence from graphical models [5], to establish direct causal relationships in multivariate point processes. For event variables (x, y, z), x is process independent of y given z if CIF of x is not functionally dependent on the history of y given the history of z. Consequently, a set of events $\mathbb{X}$ is considered a direct cause of event y if y is process independent of all other events given $\mathbb{X}$. We exclude the trivial case where y is constant over $\mathbb{X}$. s, we introduce the concept of proximal history, a time-based simplification widely used in point process literature [2]. Proximal history posits that cause events only within a recent time window influences the outcome event, allowing earlier history to be disregarded.

Combining these notions, we establish a causal framework and define ATE under out-of-domain interventions, drawing inspiration from [7] while adapting the theoretical assumptions for unbiasedness to accommodate out-of-domain interventions. We further incorporate these interventions into the propensity score-adjusted estimator, modifying the score definition.

Definition 1. *For an event tuple (c, o, v), binary cause variable c_t^w at time t indicates whether cause event c has occurred at least once in the time window $[t-w, t)$. Similarly, binary out-of-domain intervention variable v_t^w indicates whether out-of-domain intervention v occurred within the same window. The potential outcome variable $\lambda^{(c_t^w, v_t^w)}(t)$ denotes the CIF of outcome event o at time t, given* the values of c_t^w and v_t^w. The binary vector $\mathbf{x}_t^w$ captures the occurrence of all other observed events in the time window $[t-w, t)$. The ATE of cause c_t^w on outcome $\lambda(t)$ under out-of-domain intervention v_t^w is defined as:

$$\tau(v_t^w) = \mathbb{E}\left[\frac{1}{T}\int_0^T \{\lambda^{(1,v_t^w)}(t) - \lambda^{(0,v_t^w)}(t)\}dt\right].$$

Unlike standard causal settings, $\lambda(t)$ is latent and estimated from event type and timestamp observations.

Cause and out-of-domain interventions may exhibit multiple occurrences prior to outcome within the time window. To focus on detecting causal relation shifts under interventions, we simplify the framework to study the treatment effect of occurrence, rather than count, as an initial step. Our real-world datasets validate this binary simplification. We defer continuous and ordinal cause and intervention modeling to future work. While not explicitly defined, process independence is crucial for linking the new ATE definition to causal relation shifts.

Theorem 1. *If event c is the direct cause of event o when out-of-domain intervention variable $v_t^w = 1$, and not if $v_t^w = 0$, then $\tau(1) \neq 0$ and $\tau(0) = 0$.*

Theorem 1 demonstrates that our new ATE effectively characterizes causal relations under out-of-domain interventions; the proof is provided in Appendix A of the supplementary materials.

3.4 Treatment Effect Estimation

In point process causal studies, cause event occurrences are typically not randomized, leading to potential imbalances between treatment groups. To address this, we propose a propensity score, adapted for our out-of-domain intervention augmented ATE framework, building on the established use of propensity scores for confounder adjustment in classical observational studies.

Definition 2. *The propensity score at time t for out-of-domain intervention variable v_t^w is*

$$e_t^w(v) = \mathbb{P}\{c_t^w = 1, v_t^w = v | \mathbf{x}_t^w\}, v \in \{0, 1\}.$$

Our novel propensity score, $e_t^w(v)$, incorporates both cause and out-of-domain intervention variables, conditioned on the proximal history of all other observed events. By treating binary out-of-domain interventions as alternative treatment assignments, rather than effect heterogeneity factors, we simplify the theoretical framework for estimation consistency.

We demonstrate that, with minor modifications to standard observational study assumptions to accommodate point process data and out-of-domain interventions, $e_t^w(v)$ effectively mitigates confounding bias, yielding an unbiased effect estimator.

Assumption 1 (SUTVA). *For each assignment pair (c_t^w, v_t^w) and any t, there is only a single version of population outcome $\lambda^{(c_t^w, v_t^w)}(t)$, and the time window receives the assignment will not affect the outcome of other time windows.*

The assumption is fundamental in causal inference. It ensures we can leverage observations under treatment assignment to infer potential outcomes.

Assumption 2 (unconfoundedness). For any t, we have

$$\{\lambda^{(0,0)}(t), \lambda^{(0,1)}(t), \lambda^{(1,0)}(t), \lambda^{(1,1)}(t)\} \perp\!\!\!\perp (c_t^w, v_t^w) | \mathbf{x}_t^w.$$

This assumption guarantees measured covariates sufficiently balance treatment groups and adjust for confounding bias across different out-of-domain interventions. While untestable, it is commonly postulated in observational studies.

Assumption 3 (overlap). There exists a constant ϵ such that $\epsilon < e_t^w(v) < 1 - \epsilon, \forall t, \forall v \in \{0,1\}$.

This assumption ensures sufficient observations across treatment groups under varying out-of-domain interventions for accurate estimation, and is verifiable in practice. Our real-world datasets satisfy this condition.

To simplify theoretical justification, we treat out-of-domain interventions as a second binary treatment variable, consistent with our framework's focus on the occurrence of cause and intervention events. This approach avoids the need for complex assumptions regarding potential outcomes and the impact of out-of-domain interventions on cause events, which would be overly intricate for our current framework and real-data applications.

We leverage propensity score $e_t^w(v)$ to construct weight

$$\alpha_t^w(v) = \frac{\mathbf{1}\{c_t^w=1, v_t^w=v\}}{e_t^w(v)} - \frac{\mathbf{1}\{c_t^w=0, v_t^w=v\}}{1-e_t^w(v)}.$$

We weight the outcome $\lambda(t)$ to derive the inverse probability weighting (IPW) estimator of ATE,

$$\hat{\tau}(v) = \mathbb{E}\left[\frac{1}{T}\int_0^T \alpha_t^w(v)\lambda(t)dt\right]. \tag{2}$$

We show that the IPW estimator is unbiased.

Theorem 2. *Under Assumptions 1, 2 and 3, we have $\mathbb{E}[\hat{\tau}(v)] = \tau(v), \forall v \in \{0,1\}$. The propensity score can be estimated by event duration ratio,*

$$\hat{e}_t^w(v) = \frac{\sum_{k=1}^n \sum_{i=1}^{L_k} \int_{t_{i-1}}^{t_i} \mathbf{1}\{c_t^w=1, v_t^w=v, \mathbf{x}_t^w\}dt}{\sum_{k=1}^n \sum_{i=1}^{L_k} \int_{t_{i-1}}^{t_i} \mathbf{1}\{\mathbf{x}_t^w\}dt}. \tag{3}$$

We obtain the effect estimate by plugging $\hat{e}_t^w(v)$ into the weight $\alpha_t^w(v)$ in Eq. (2). The outcome $\lambda(t)$ is estimated using a Transformer-based model on sequence data; see supplementary materials for the proof.

4 Transformer-Based Process Model

We propose a neural network model for learning temporal point processes and estimating the conditional intensity function (CIF) $\lambda(t)$ of outcome events under both cause and out-of-domain interventions. A key innovation is the integration of out-of-domain interventions into the input representation.

Our neural network model, illustrated in Fig. 1, adopts a hybrid Transformer-CNN architecture to capture long-range temporal dependencies and local patterns shaped by intervention dynamics. A self-attention block [20] models event interactions via attention weights, with multi-head attention enhancing expressiveness by capturing diverse relational patterns. To incorporate temporal context, we embed relative time differences $t_i - t_{i-1}$ using temporal positional encodings [27]. This architecture is used to model the logarithm of the outcome CIF, $\lambda(t)$, which is central to ATE estimation.

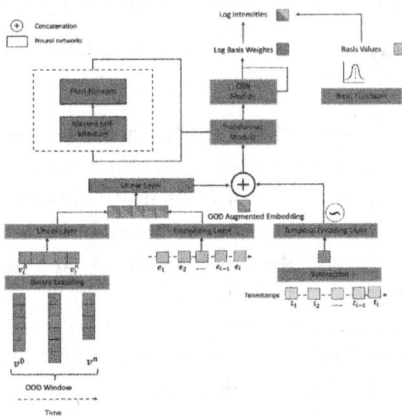

Fig. 1. Our neural network architecture for learning temporal point processes with out-of-domain interventions. It combines out-of-domain intervention-augmented (V_i) event embeddings (e_i) with positional encoding (Δt), uses Transformer and CNN modules for pattern extraction, and estimates the CIF $\lambda(t)$ for event prediction

Our model input comprises three encoded components: 1) binary indicators of out-of-domain interventions v occurring within the time window; 2) dense embeddings of event types (cause, outcome, and other observed events); and 3) relative event times, $t_i - t_{i-1}$, encoded using trigonometric positional encodings to capture temporal positions. We combine intervention and event type embeddings via a weighted sum to form a unified, intervention-aware event representation, which is then augmented with temporal positional encodings. The model outputs the conditional intensity function (CIF) for each event and timestamp, expressed as a sum over basis functions.

We optimize our model using three criteria combined into a single loss function. raining is performed on batches of sequences $B = \{s_1, s_2, ..., s_b\}$ where b is the batch size. For each batch, we compute the average loss across all sequences.

The first criterion is negative log likelihood (NLL) of event observations within the sequences.

$$L_{NLL} = \frac{1}{b}\sum_{k=1}^{b}\left[-\sum_{i=1}^{L_k}\log \lambda_{e_{k,i}}(t_{k,i}) + \sum_{e \in \text{outcome}}\int_0^T \lambda_e(t)dt\right], \quad (4)$$

where $\lambda_{e_{k,i}}(t_{k,i})$ is the conditional intensity function for event $e_{k,i}$ at timestamp $t_{k,i}$, and L_k is the length of sequence k. The first term represents the log-likelihood of observed events, while the second accounts for the probability of no events occurring in the remaining time intervals.

The second criterion is a prediction loss based on cross-entropy that measures how well the model predicts event types.

$$\mathcal{L}_{CE} = -\frac{1}{b} \sum_{k=1}^{b} \sum_{i=1}^{L_k} \sum_{e \in \mathbb{E}} y_{k,i,e} \log(p_{k,i,e}), \tag{5}$$

where $\mathbb{E}$ is the set of event classes, $y_{k,i,e}$ is the true binary indicator (0 or 1) of whether event e is the correct classification for i-th event in $\mathbf{s}_k$, $p_{k,i,e}$ is the predicted probability that i-th event belongs to class e.

The third criterion is L2 regularization term that penalizes large basis weights to prevent overfitting.

$$L_{reg} = \frac{1}{b} \sum_{k=1}^{b} \sum_{i=1}^{L_k} \sum_{l=1}^{\mathcal{B}} \exp(w_{l,k,i})^2, \tag{6}$$

where $w_{l,k,i}$ represents the log basis weights at time $t_{k,i}$ for basis function l, $\mathcal{B}$ denotes the total number of basis functions. The regularization prevents the basis weights from growing too large, which could lead to numerical instabilities.

Our final batch loss function combines the three criteria, (4), (5) and (6),

$$sL_{batch} = L_{NLL} + \alpha L_{CE} + \beta L_{reg}. \tag{7}$$

The hyperparameters α and β control the relative importance of the cross-entropy loss and regularization term, respectively. We minimize this batch loss using the Adam optimizer and evaluate convergence on a held-out validation set. Model selection is performed via 5-fold cross-validation. Additional hyperparameter and implementation details are provided in supplementary materials.

5 Numerical Study

We evaluated our method on both simulated and real-world data, comparing it against the CAUSE model [24] for ATE estimation and out-of-domain intervention-augmented process learning. CAUSE, which combines point processes and attribution methods for Granger causality inference, estimates the CIF without accounting for out-of-domain interventions. A comparative discussion with other models is provided in the supplementary materials.

5.1 Simulated Data

We generated synthetic event sequences with injected out-of-domain interventions, modeled as random events influencing specific cause–outcome pairs. Each intervention was assigned a random occurrence probability and time window, with dynamic injection based on these probabilities. Additional simulation details are provided in the supplementary materials.

We simulated three intervention impact types, increasing in complexity and coverage of out-of-domain intervention impact:

1. **No out-of-domain intervention (No OOD)**: we do not impose out-of-domain intervention on process, which also can serve as sanity check.

2. **Baseline out-of-domain intervention (Baseline)**: we modify the baseline intensity $\mu(t)$ of an outcome event CIF $\lambda(t)$ under out-of-domain intervention shown in Eq. 1. We implement 30 out-of-domain interventions per sequence.
3. **All out-of-domain intervention (All impact)**: we alter baseline intensity $\mu(t)$, the influence of cause and other observed events through $\phi(\cdot)$ on outcome event CIF $\lambda(t)$ under out-of-domain intervention. We implement 30 out-of-domain interventions per sequence.

We generate $1,000$ sequences for each intervention impact type, with sequence lengths drawn from a Poisson distribution (mean = 500). Each sequence includes 30 distinct event types: 20 used as causes and covariates, and the remaining 10 are designated as outcomes.

We compare our method with CAUSE in ATE estimation and process fitting in simulated data. The performance measures we adopt for ATE estimation are

1. **Bias**: the average of absolute difference between ATE estimate and true ATE across repetitions.
2. **Variance**: the variance of ATE estimate across repetitions.
3. **Mean squared error (MSE)**: the average of squared difference between ATE estimate and true ATE across repetitions.

Lower values indicate better ATE estimation. As shown in Table 1, our method significantly reduces bias across all scenarios, with slight increase in variance. This trade-off is beneficial, as it results in lower MSE in most cases.

Table 1. Simulated data ATE estimation performance comparison between our method and CAUSE for Baseline and All impact interventions. Lower values are better.

Out-of-Domain Intervention	Intervention Status	Bias		Variance		MSE	
		Ours	Cause	Ours	Cause	Ours	Cause
Baseline	0	**0.0155**	0.0522	0.0141	**0.00001**	**0.003**	0.0046
	1	**0.1561**	0.262	0.0002	**0.0002**	**0.027**	0.0708
All Impact	0	**0.0209**	0.0494	0.0027	**0.00001**	**0.0038**	0.0042
	1	**0.1615**	0.2192	0.0008	**0.0002**	**0.0283**	0.0498

We use the following performance measures for process fitting,

1. **Negative log likelihood (NLL)**: the NLL of fitted process model.
2. **Root mean squared error (RMSE)**: the square root of the average of squared outcome event occurrence time prediction error.
3. **Mean absolute error (MAE)**: the average of absolute outcome event prediction error.

Averaged across repetitions, Table 2 shows that our model consistently outperforms CAUSE across all scenarios by achieving lower NLL, RMSE, and MAE; demonstrating superior modeling of event distributions and predictive accuracy, even under varying intervention complexities.

Table 2. Simulated data process fitting performance comparison (NLL, RMSE, MAE) between our method and CAUSE with varying Out-of-Domain interventions. Lower values are better.

Out-of-Domain Intervention	NLL		RMSE		MAE	
	Ours	Cause	Ours	Cause	Ours	Cause
No OOD	**1009.06**	2456.53	**1.78**	3.89	**0.89**	2.60
Baseline	**852.48**	2438.36	**2.1**	3.84	**1.04**	2.56
All Impact	**1299.61**	2443.81	**2.18**	3.86	**1.17**	2.58

5.2 Real-World Data

We evaluated our method on two real-world datasets:

Predictive Maintenance [1]: This dataset contains hourly sensor readings (voltage, rotation, pressure, vibration) from 100 machines. Proactive maintenance events (scheduled component replacements) were modeled as out-of-domain interventions, while reactive maintenance events (failures requiring unscheduled replacements) served as outcomes. Continuous sensor readings were discretized into 625 bins based on mean deviation, with each bin treated as a potential cause event and others as time-varying covariates.

Diabetes [10]: This dataset includes lab events from 70 patients, such as insulin injections, glucose levels, meal consumption, physical activity, and hypoglycemia symptoms. We focused on glucose as the outcome and selected cause and OOD intervention events based on established medical knowledge. For example, in analyzing insulin-mediated effects of meals on glucose, we treated meal as the cause, insulin as the out-of-domain intervention, and activity and hypoglycemia symptoms as covariates. A baseline experiment without interventions was also conducted to assess model robustness.

Since ground truth ATEs and prior benchmarks are unavailable for the predictive maintenance dataset, we evaluated process fitting performance. As shown in Table 3, our model significantly outperformed CAUSE in future event prediction:achieving an 88% reduction in RMSE and a 90% reduction in MAE, while maintaining comparable distribution modeling (only 4% higher NLL). These improvements highlight the value of explicitly modeling out-of-domain interventions in capturing complex real-world dynamics.

Table 3. Predictive maintenance data process fitting performance (NLL, RMSE, MAE) comparison between our method and CAUSE, with proactive maintenance as out-of-domain intervention. Lower values are better.

NLL		RMSE		MAE	
Ours	Cause	Ours	Cause	Ours	Cause
300.66	**288.84**	**419.38**	3501.14	**59.88**	628.37

Table 4. ATE-estimated causal relations in diabetes dataset under Out-of-domain interventions, validated by medical literature.

Cause	Outcome	Out-of-Domain Intervention	Covariate	Our Conclusion & Literature Evidence
More than usual meal ingestion	Blood glucose decrease	Insulin	Activity, hypoglycemia symptopm	✓ Insulin injection, even when more than usual meal is ingested, may help to decrease blood glucose [3]
Hypoglycemia symptom	Blood glucose decrease	NPH insulin	Meal, activity	✓ Insulin injection, when hypoglycemic symptom is observed, may cause blood glucose to decrease further [13]
Insulin	Blood glucose decrease	Typical or more than usual activity	Meal, hypoglycemia symptom	✓ More activity increases the effect of insulin, boosting blood glucose decrease [12]

Table 5. Process fitting performance comparison between our method and CAUSE on the diabetes dataset, with activity and insulin as out-of-domain interventions. Sanity check: no intervention. Lower NLL, RMSE, and MAE indicate better performance.

Out-of-Domain Intervention	NLL		RMSE		MAE	
	Ours	Cause	Ours	Cause	Ours	Cause
Sanity Check	**613.21**	619.74	**15644.33**	15718.8	**2104.87**	2239.53
Activity	**563.47**	1345.61	**15729.25**	15770.73	**2108.1**	2111.2
Insulin	**181.57**	190.11	**342.74**	360.78	**55.81**	61.69

While ground truth ATEs for the diabetes dataset are unavailable, we validated the detected causal relation shifts against established medical literature. As shown in Table 4, the shifts identified by our method align with known findings. For example, our model captured the insulin-mediated effect where glucose levels decrease despite increased meal intake, consistent with results reported in [3]. Additionally, Table 5 demonstrates that our method outperforms CAUSE in process fitting across all intervention types, underscoring the benefits of incorporating out-of-domain interventions. The model also maintained strong performance in the baseline setting without interventions, confirming its robustness.

6 Discussion

While our method offers significant advantages in modeling causal relation shifts under out-of-domain interventions, two key limitations merit consideration.

First, our framework simplifies interventions to binary occurrence indicators, potentially limiting expressiveness for complex interventions with varying intensity or duration. Second, if interventions open backdoor causal paths between cause and outcome events, estimation accuracy may be compromised, requiring careful domain knowledge for intervention selection. Scalability concerns are discussed separately in the supplementary materials. Future work should extend the framework to continuous intervention variables for more fine-grained modeling and improved estimation precision.

7 Conclusion

We propose a novel causal framework leveraging out-of-domain interventions to analyze causal relation shifts in temporal process data. Our Transformer-based Hawkes process integrates intervention effects with an unbiased treatment effect estimator for accurate causal quantification. Extensive simulations and real-world validation, corroborated by literature, demonstrated superior performance in both process fitting and ATE estimation, enabling practical extraction of actionable causal knowledge for informed decision-making.

References

1. Azure: Ai predictive maintenance. https://github.com/Azure/AI-PredictiveMaintenance (2018)
2. Bhattacharjya, D., Subramanian, D., Gao, T.: Proximal graphical event models (2018)
3. Campbell, M.D., et al.: Metabolic implications when employing heavy pre-and post-exercise rapid-acting insulin reductions to prevent hypoglycaemia in type 1 diabetes patients: a randomised clinical trial. PLoS ONE **9**(5), e97143 (2014)
4. Daley, D.J., Vere-Jones, D., et al.: An introduction to the theory of point processes: volume I: elementary theory and methods. Springer (2003)
5. Didelez, V.: Graphical models for marked point processes based on local independence (2005)
6. Du, N., Dai, H., Trivedi, R., Upadhyay, U., Gomez-Rodriguez, M., Song, L.: Recurrent marked temporal point processes: embedding event history to vector. In: Proceedings of the 22nd ACM SIGKDD International Conference on Knowledge Discovery and Data Mining, pp. 1555–1564 (2016)
7. Gao, T., Subramanian, D., Bhattacharjya, D., Shou, X., Mattei, N., Bennett, K.P.: Causal inference for event pairs in multivariate point processes. Adv. Neural. Inf. Process. Syst. **34**, 17311–17324 (2021)
8. Hawkes, A.G.: Point spectra of some mutually exciting point processes. J. R. Stat. Soc. Ser. B Stat Methodol. **33**(3), 438–443 (1971)
9. Imbens, G.W., Rubin, D.B.: Causal Inference in Statistics, Social, and Biomedical Sciences. Cambridge University Press (2015)
10. Kahn, M.: Diabetes. UCI Machine Learning Repository (1994) .https://doi.org/10.24432/C5T59G
11. Koh, P.W., et al.: Wilds: a benchmark of in-the-wild distribution shifts. In: International Conference on Machine Learning, pp. 5637–5664. PMLR (2021)

12. Lawrence, R.: The effect of exercise on insulin action in diabetes. BMJ **1**(3406), 648 (1926)
13. Lee, S.J.: So much insulin, so much hypoglycemia. JAMA Intern. Med. **174**(5), 686–688 (2014)
14. Mei, H., Eisner, J.M.: The neural hawkes process: a neurally self-modulating multivariate point process. In: Advances in Neural Information Processing Systems, vol. 30 (2017)
15. Melnychuk, V., Frauen, D., Feuerriegel, S.: Causal transformer for estimating counterfactual outcomes. In: International Conference on Machine Learning, pp. 15293–15329. PMLR (2022)
16. Noorbakhsh, K., Rodriguez, M.: Counterfactual temporal point processes. Adv. Neural. Inf. Process. Syst. **35**, 24810–24823 (2022)
17. Schulam, P., Saria, S.: Reliable decision support using counterfactual models. In: Advances in Neural Information Processing Systems, vol. 30 (2017)
18. Shchur, O., Türkmen, A.C., Januschowski, T., Günnemann, S.: Neural temporal point processes: a review (2021)
19. Shi, C., Blei, D., Veitch, V.: Adapting neural networks for the estimation of treatment effects. In: Advances in Neural Information Processing Systems, vol. 32 (2019)
20. Vaswani, A., et al.: Attention is all you need. In: Advances in Neural Information Processing Systems, vol. 30 (2017)
21. Xiao, C., Choi, E., Sun, J.: Opportunities and challenges in developing deep learning models using electronic health records data: a systematic review. J. Am. Med. Inform. Assoc. **25**(10), 1419–1428 (2018)
22. Xiao, S., Yan, J., Yang, X., Zha, H., Chu, S.: Modeling the intensity function of point process via recurrent neural networks. In: Proceedings of the AAAI Conference on Artificial Intelligence, vol. 31 (2017)
23. Zhang, L.n., Liu, J.w., Song, Z.y., Zuo, X.: Temporal attention augmented transformer hawkes process. Neural Comput. Appl. 1–15 (2022)
24. Zhang, W., Panum, T., Jha, S., Chalasani, P., Page, D.: Cause: learning granger causality from event sequences using attribution methods. In: International Conference on Machine Learning, pp. 11235–11245. PMLR (2020)
25. Zheng, Y., Chen, G., Huang, M.: Out-of-domain detection for natural language understanding in dialog systems. IEEE/ACM Trans. Audio Speech Lang. Process. **28**, 1198–1209 (2020)
26. Zhou, Y., et al.: Deep sequence modeling for event log-based predictive maintenance. In: KDD 2023 International Workshop on Mining and Learning from Time Series (MileTS) (2023)
27. Zuo, S., Jiang, H., Li, Z., Zhao, T., Zha, H.: Transformer hawkes process. In: International Conference on Machine Learning, pp. 11692–11702. PMLR (2020)

Sustainable Techniques to Improve Data Quality for Training Image-Based Explanatory Models for Recommender Systems

Jorge Paz-Ruza[✉], David Esteban-Martínez, Amparo Alonso-Betanzos, and Bertha Guijarro-Berdiñas

Universidade da Coruña, CITIC, Campus de Elviña s/n 15071, A Coruña, Spain
{j.ruza,david.esteban.martinez,amparo.alonso.betanzos,
berta.guijarro}@udc.es

Abstract. Visual explanations based on user-uploaded images are an effective and self-contained approach to provide transparency to Recommender Systems (RS), but intrinsic limitations of data used in this explainability paradigm cause existing approaches to use bad quality training data that is highly sparse and suffers from labelling noise. Popular training enrichment approaches like model enlargement or massive data gathering are expensive and environmentally unsustainable, thus we seek to provide better visual explanations to RS aligning with the principles of Responsible AI. In this work, we research the intersection of effective and sustainable training enrichment strategies for visual-based RS explainability models by developing three novel strategies that focus on training Data Quality: 1) selection of reliable negative training examples using Positive-unlabelled Learning, 2) transform-based data augmentation, and 3) text-to-image generative-based data augmentation. The integration of these strategies in three state-of-the-art explainability models increases (∼5%) the performance in relevant ranking metrics of these visual-based RS explainability models without penalizing their practical long-term sustainability, as tested in multiple real-world restaurant recommendation explanation datasets.

Keywords: Machine Learning · eXplainable AI · Frugal AI · Recommender Systems · Positive-Unlabelled Learning · Data Quality

1 Introduction

Recommender Systems (RS) are a pillar of e-commerce, social networks and other fields by offering relevant suggestions to users that boost their engagement and trust [11]. However, their lack of explainability is also commonplace, making users sceptical to follow AI-powered recommendations [21]. Within explainability approaches for RS, visual-based ones see huge popularity [18], as human understanding has visual information as one of its cornerstones. Among the many existing visual explainability approaches, this work is contextualized in the use of user-provided images of items to offer visual explanations of recommendations to other users, which has been explored by different authors in search of more self-contained, relevant and realistic explanations [5].

Existing methodologies following this visual explainability approach, such as ELVis [5], MF-ELVis [8] or BRIE [7], model it as an authorship prediction task: predicting the image of an item that best explains the recommendation of the item to a user is equivalent to predicting the image of the item most likely to be uploaded or authored by that user; this way, the complete task can be modelled as top-N ranking task of user-image authorship.

The aforementioned existing approaches have improved the handling of existing training data through fixed similarity operators [8] and reformulation of the training as pairwise ranking [7], but have not tackled two fundamental data quality limitations of the dyadic user-image data used to achieve explainability: in most contexts, most users have uploaded few to none images to the RS, constituting a *cold start* situation, and data for training the explainability model lacks explicit negative examples, bringing noise into training examples if all unknown user-image pairs are considered cases of bad explanations [1].

While these explainability models could be improved with bigger, more expressive topologies or through massive training data gathering efforts, existing literature has proven this approach is not sustainable [16]: Energy efficiency and sustainability are key priorities for Machine Learning development, yet these -worryingly popular- approaches carry a unsustainable increase of greenhouse emissions and waste of computational resources. Aligning two different aspects of Responsible AI [4], it should be possible to further improve the explainability capabilities of these systems in a computationally sustainable manner.

In this work, we propose several sustainable techniques to increase the performance of visual RS explanation systems based on user-provided images while respecting their sustainability by focusing on improving the Data Quality (DQ) of the existing training data. The main contributions of this work include:

- We design and implement a novel model-agnostic, user-personalized two-step Positive-Unlabelled (PU) Learning model for visual-based RS explainability systems that selects reliable user-image non-authorship relations to act as negative examples within the authorship prediction task, increasing final model performance by refining the label quality of training data.
- We design and implement two data augmentation approaches for visual-based RS explainability systems based on image transforms and text-to-image Generative AI, increasing performance for low-activity users without massive data gathering efforts or model computational overhead.
- We evaluate these techniques integrating them in explainability models (ELVis, MF-ELVis, BRIE) and testing them on three real-world RS explainability datasets in restaurant recommendation contexts. The computational experiments prove that all three designed strategies not only significantly increase the performance of explanation models in relevant ranking metrics, but also maintain their long-term sustainability in terms of carbon emissions.

2 Background

This section introduces concepts and formalizations of the tasks and techniques that sustain this research work.

2.1 Ranking Images for Visual RS Explainability

Let $\mathcal{U}$ and $\mathcal{I}$ be the sets of users and items that interact in the RS forming (u, i) dyads where $u \in \mathcal{U}$ and $i \in \mathcal{I}$. In the approaches explored in this work, the set $\mathcal{P}$ of images of items taken by users are employed by equating the concepts of "explanation adequacy" to "authorship probability": for any user-image pair, the authorship probability $Pr(u, p)$ is defined as the likelihood that image p of item i could be likely authored by user u in the RS, such that:

$$Pr(u,p) \equiv Pr(u \in \mathcal{P}_u)$$

where $\mathcal{P}_u$ is the set of u's images. Therefore, a high predicted $Pr(u, p)$ is then thought as equivalent to predicting that p is a good explanation of a recommendation of item i to user u, and vice versa. Directly, to select from $\mathcal{P}_i$ -the set of images taken of item i- the best image p^* to represent a recommendation of i to u, we can maximize $Pr(u, p)$ as:

$$p^* = \arg max_{p \in \mathcal{P}_i} Pr(u,p)$$

Trivially, it is true that $Pr(u, p) = 1 \ \forall p \in \mathcal{P}_u$, but training data does not explicitly contain negative examples, i.e. bad image explanations s.t. $Pr(u, p) = 0$, forming then Positive and Unlabelled (PU) Data [1].

In the following, we describe existing state-of-the-art approaches ELVis, MF-ELVis and BRIE, that employ this visual-based RS explanation paradigm; their topological and optimization design is shown in Fig. 1.

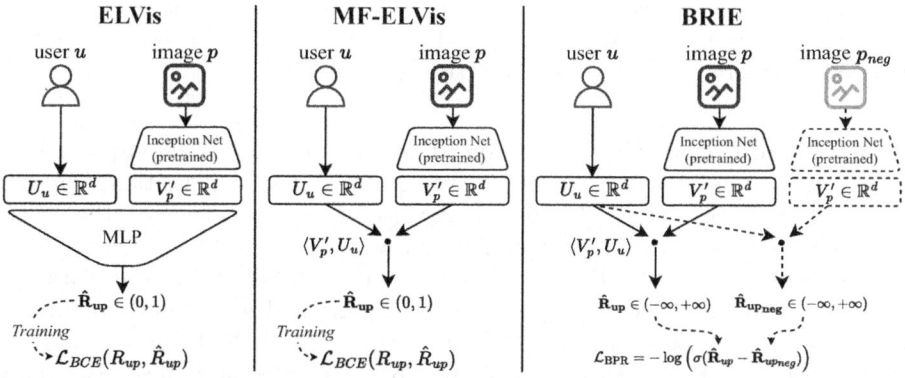

Fig. 1. Topologies and optimization of ELVis, MF-ELVis and BRIE [5,7,8].

ELVis. Diez et al. [5] proposed ELVis as a model that uses a neural network-based architecture to compute $Pr(u,p)$. To do this, u (the user id) is mapped into a d-dimensional latent embedding, while image p is projected to the same d-dimensional latent space with a *ResNet* image embedding network [17] coupled with a dense layer. The two d-dimensional vectors, representing u's and p's latent characteristics, are concatenated and projected through a Multi-Layer Perceptron and a final sigmoid activation to obtain as output the authorship probability $Pr(u,p) \in [0,1]$. While ELVis is able to achieve good explanatory performance by modelling users' latent explanatory preferences through implicit feedback, it surrogates training to a binary classification task distant from the real ranking problem, and uses a Deep Learning-oriented architecture that compromises sustainability due to high training and inference computational costs.

MF-ELVis. Paz-Ruza et al. [8] chose to replace ELVIs' MLP architecture by equipping MF-ELVis with fixed embedding similarity function computations (particularly, the inner product $\langle \mathbf{U_u}, \mathbf{V'_p} \rangle$ of u's and p's latent embeddings). MF-ELVis showed results competitive to the more expressive ELVis while reducing training time and emissions owing to a simpler yet effective architecture.

BRIE. BRIE [7] seeks to better handle existing training data by modelling learning as a pairwise ranking task [10] and resampling the paired random negative examples (unrelated image-user pairs) at the start of every epoch; BRIE is the current state-on-the-art in image ranking-based recommendation explainability and provides both significantly higher performance and lower training and inference execution time and greenhouse emissions than ELVis and MF-ELVis.

2.2 Data Quality on Dyadic Data

While BRIE and other models improve the handling of training data, they do not tackle some intrinsic quality issues of dyadic data: the *cold start* situation affecting most users, which do not upload many images into the system, and the unlabelled nature of the assumed negative examples.

Positive and Unlabelled Learning. Existing models assume any unrelated (u,p) pair can be considered a negative example (bad explanation) which is incompatible with images of a user being useful explanations for other users; ultimately, this produces noisy training and worse explanations.

In PU Data contexts, PU Learning is a semi-supervised learning paradigm that directly handles PU Data to improve training and model performance [1]. We focus on the most popular and flexible family of methods, named *two-step approaches*. Let $\mathcal{X}_P$ be the set of known positive examples (here, the set of past image uploads by users in the RS ($\mathcal{D} = \{(u,i,p),\dots\}$) and $\mathcal{X}_U$ the set of unlabelled examples (here, all other user-item-image combinations not in the original set ($\{(u,i,p),\dots\} \; p \in \mathcal{X}_P \setminus \mathcal{P}_u$), which considers both positive examples (good explanations) and negative examples (bad explanations). First, two-step PU Learning approaches obtain a refined set $RN \subset \mathcal{X}_U$ of "reliable" negative examples (in this work, images that are, with certainty, bad explanations for a given u). Then, as the second step, a final model is trained using $\mathcal{X}_P$ and RN to obtain a more accurate model trained with minimal noise; moreover, this also allows for shorter, more efficient model training with smaller and higher quality training sets (because $|RN| < |\mathcal{X}_U|$).

Data Augmentation. Data Augmentation is a popular approach to increase the availability of coherent training data without massive, costly data gathering [19], increasing the overall quality of existing data. We are interested in using data augmentation in some of its image variants to tackle the *cold start* problem in our task, where users have uploaded (typically few) images of items to the RS:

- **Transform-based augmentation**, which uses existing examples to introduce new coherent data in the domain, such as with geometric, contrast, deformations or cutout transforms [14]; these can replicate the variety and imperfections of user-uploaded images in RS.
- **Generative augmentation**, which can directly create new training examples; modal transform models, such as text-to-image [20], could potentially use existing textual data in the RS (e.g. users' reviews) to enrich training.

3 Proposed Sustainable Data Quality (DQ) Techniques

This section covers the three novel proposed methods (based on PU Learning, transform-based data augmentation, and generative data augmentation) to sustainably increase the performance of visual-based explainability of RS based on user-provided images through improvements in the quality of training data.

3.1 Reducing Label Noise with PU Learning

To overcome the labelling noise caused by the naive negativity assumptions on the task's PU Data made by existing approaches, we propose to apply PU Learning to properly handle unseen (user, image) pairs as unlabelled data.

One challenge compared to classic PU Learning is the complexity of dyadic user-image data that forms the unlabelled set $\mathcal{X}_U$. For instance, the same image uploaded by user u is unlabelled for users u' and u'' but can be respectively a good and bad explanation for those users. To overcome this limitation we model PU Learning user-wise, solving the PU task independently for each user; we choose to follow the two-step paradigm [1] for its flexibility. This choice is held by two basic assumptions: smoothness of the positive class (for each user, good explanations are images similar to those from the user), and separability with the negative class (for each user, bad explanations are images that differ from those from the user). We also assume SCAR (Selected Completely at Random) as the labelling mechanism [1], as it is reasonable to consider the user's own images are an i.i.d. sample of the distribution of good explanations for them.

To select reliable negative examples for each user we used discriminators based on a Rocchio classifier, which is light-weight and popular in classic PU Learning [12]. The selection of user-wise reliable negatives RN_u of each user is illustrated in Fig. 2 and proceeds as follows:

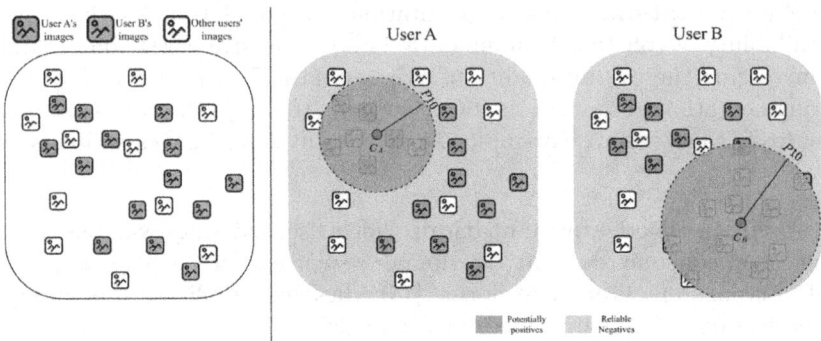

Fig. 2. User-personalized PU Learning technique proposed to select reliable negative examples (bad image explanations) for each user in recommendation personalization contexts. Here, the decision boundary for reliable negative selection is shown for two users A and B with different explanatory preferences.

1. Find the centroid of the embedding projections of u's images as obtained by an image embedding model ϕ to obtain a prototype of a good image explanation to u as $C_u = \frac{1}{|\mathcal{P}_u|} \sum_{p \in \mathcal{P}_u} \phi(p)$.
2. Discriminate reliable negatives through a similarity threshold; we employ the 10th percentile P_{10} of the cosine similarities SC between u's images and its centroid C_u to filter outliers in $\mathcal{P}_u$.
3. Admit unlabelled user-image pairs (u, p) with $p \notin \mathcal{P}_u$ to RN_u as reliable negative examples (i.e. p is a bad explanatory image for u because they would not author this image) if $SC(C_u, \phi(p)) \leq P_{10}$.

Finally, the explanation model can be seamlessly trained using the known positive examples $\mathcal{X}_P$ (i.e. $\mathcal{D}$, the user-image upload tuples originally in the data, representing good explanations) and the union of the reliable negative example sets RN_u (i.e. user-image pairs where the user would be very unlikely upload such an image, representing bad explanations). Since RN is a refined, smaller set of $\mathcal{X}_U$, the consequent lower labelling noise and increased quality of training data leads to more effective and efficient training of explanatory models.

3.2 Data Augmentation

To tackle the *cold start* problem (inability to learn from inactive users) due to the data sparsity in this task, we propose two Data Augmentation methods to enrich positive examples and increase training data quality for low-activity users by using either image transforms or text-to-image example generation.

Transform-Based Augmentation. We use three advanced transforms to user images: random cutouts, geometric transforms and Gaussian blur, mimicking imperfections in user-uploaded images, as seen in Fig. 3.

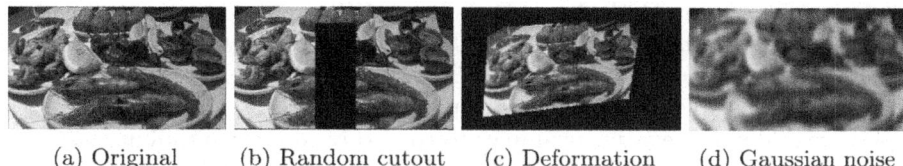

(a) Original (b) Random cutout (c) Deformation (d) Gaussian noise

Fig. 3. Example of transform-based data augmentation based on user's existing images, here to an image uploaded to a restaurant recommendation review.

Augmentation is most effective for low-activity users, so we set a user minimal activity threshold. For each user with $|P_u| < n$ images, we generate random transforms p' of images $p \in P_u$ and add them to P_u until reaching $|P_u| = n$, enriching in a personalized manner the existing data for each low-activity user.

Text-to-Image Generative Data Augmentation. We also propose the use of generative models to directly create new good explanation image data for less active users to enrich their training data. User reviews of items typically include a textual review representative of user preferences, so we employ a text-to-image Generative AI model to leverage the existing textual information in the RS.

For each user u with $|P_u| < n$ reviews, we consider the set of textual reviews R_u formed by reviews T written by user u. Using a generative text-to-image model G, and until an activity threshold $|P_u| = n$ is reached, we iteratively generate images $p_{gen} = G(T)$ for user u from randomly selected reviews $T \in R_u$ using the prompt exemplified in Fig. 4:

4 Experimental Setup

This section covers different aspects of the experimental configurations including datasets, evaluation protocols and other implementation details.

Photorealistic image, taken with a smartphone camera, uploaded with the following <type of item> review: <review text>

Fig. 4. Prompt structure (left) and examples of generated training images from reviews (right) through generative augmentation in a restaurant context.

4.1 Datasets

We evaluated our techniques using real-world datasets in restaurant recommendation explanation in TripAdvisor [9], following existing approaches, in three different cities (Gijon, Madrid, and Barcelona). We employed the user-wise leave-one-out dataset partitions provided by Díez et al. [5]: for each user with $N \geq 2$ images, one is used for training and the $N-1$ for testing; in the test set, for each (u, i, p) positive tuple (assumed good explanation), all (u, i, p') with $p' \in P_i \setminus \{p\}$ tuples are added as negative examples to conform each image ranking test case. This is, we assume an offline evaluation [13] where the system performs better the higher it ranks for a user u its real image p of item i, where p was not seen during training by the model. Table 1 shows basic dataset statistics.

Table 1. Summary of TripAdvisor datasets on image-based recommendation explanation in restaurant contexts.

Dataset	Users	Restaurants	Images	Images/User
Gijón	5,139	598	18,679	3.64
Barcelona	33,537	5,881	150,416	4.49
Madrid	43,628	6,810	203,905	4.67

4.2 Evaluation

With respect to explanation ranking quality, we followed recent works [7], and evaluated Recall@k and NDCG@k with $k = 10$, and AUC-ROC. Recall@10 and NDCG@10 only considered test cases with > 10 images, as trivially Recall@10=1 and NDCG@k>0 otherwise. Previous works also restrict evaluation to users with > 10 train images (active users), but we evaluate using all users as our techniques focus on improving training quality for low-activity users.

With respect to model sustainability, we analyze greenhouse emissions and execution times of the models and techniques, using CodeCarbon [3], by measuring the computational cost of applying our techniques to the datasets and training existing models on the original and refined datasets. Note that all techniques only affect the training dataset and consequent model training, so models' inference emissions and execution time are not affected by them.

Implementation Details. We now describe some finer implementation details regarding model configurations and experimental setup:

- We follow the respective best hyperparameter settings reported by the authors of each model and only re-optimize the number of training epochs used on the datasets refined with our techniques, using the same early-stopping policy with $p = 5$ and $\Delta = 0.001$ against the validation set of each dataset.
- We use aMuseD256 [6] for text-to-image in generative-based data augmentation, and ViT Large 14[1] to obtain image embeddings.
- Our improvement techniques for image-based RS explainability are made available in an open-source Python library[2] that is model-agnostic and modular to allow its research and commercial use.

5 Results

This section covers the results of performance and sustainability experiments with our techniques for improving image-based recommender explainability.

5.1 Explanation Ranking Performance

Table 2 shows the explanation ranking qualities of ELVis, MF-ELVis and BRIE with and without applying our techniques. For most datasets and metrics, the best results are obtained by applying our proposed techniques to the training data, with relative improvements up to 5% compared to not applying them.

Techniques do not clearly outperform others despite their diversity, but all increase performance in a majority of dataset and model combinations. Using our techniques, ELVis even surpasses the state-of-the-art model BRIE, thus we set a new highest performance in the task.

Despite the little effect on BRIE, this model employs a considerably strong dropout-based regularization –which can be considered an agressive training-time augmentation [2]– to allow generalization, which may negatively interact with our techniques. Re-optimizing BRIE's hyperparameters could allow our techniques to be more effective for this model, which we leave as future work.

5.2 Impact on Model Sustainability

Table 3 shows the training carbon emissions and execution time of the analyzed models with and without applying our techniques. Our PU-based technique produces 60% shorter, more effective training on refined and smaller training datasets with less label noise. Data augmentation approaches also increase model performance, but the larger training set and example generation carry higher computational overheads; we suggest these approaches could be prioritized when PU Learning is ineffective, or in data contexts with a high volume of unused textual data carrying valuable user preference knowledge.

---
[1] https://huggingface.co/openai/clip-vit-large-patch14.
[2] https://pypi.org/project/data-improvement-library/.

Table 2. Ranking quality results of ELVis, MF-ELVis and BRIE with and without applying our PU Learning (PU), transform-based data augmentation (T-DA) and generative data augmentation (Gen-DA) techniques, tested on TripAdvisor datasets. The best result for each dataset-metric combination is bolded and results with daggers † are significantly better than their no-technique counterparts.

	Gijon			Barcelona			Madrid		
	Recall@10	NDCG@10	AUCROC	Recall@10	NDCG@10	AUCROC	Recall@10	NDCG@10	AUCROC
ELVis	0.492	0.262	0.702	0.562	0.320	0.726	0.522	0.298	0.737
MF-ELVis	0.486	0.278	0.691	0.527	0.304	0.696	0.490	0.281	0.699
BRIE	**0.535**	**0.306**	0.736	0.584	0.342	0.745	0.538	**0.316**	0.752
Elvis + PU	0.517†	0.280†	0.715†	**0.587†**	0.334†	0.747†	0.524†	0.307†	0.752†
ELVis + T-DA	0.532†	0.290†	0.720†	**0.587†**	0.336†	0.745†	0.531†	0.315†	0.752†
ELVis + Gen-DA	0.527†	0.292†	0.722†	0.582†	**0.344†**	**0.750†**	0.534†	0.309†	**0.755†**
MF-Elvis + PU	0.490	0.276	0.692†	0.558†	0.315†	0.702†	0.499†	0.295†	0.716†
MF-ELvis + T-DA	0.495†	0.280†	0.699†	0.527	0.302	0.688	0.500†	0.287†	0.709†
MF-ELVis + Gen-DA	0.492	0.284†	0.705†	0.526	0.302	0.693	0.512†	0.298†	0.713†
BRIE + PU	0.531	0.299	0.731	0.586†	0.342	0.746†	0.538	0.314	0.753†
BRIE + T-DA	0.529	0.301	0.728	0.584	**0.344†**	0.745	0.535	0.312	0.748
BRIE + Gen-DA	**0.535**	**0.306**	0.737†	0.583	0.340	0.745	**0.540†**	0.315	0.752

Table 3. Training carbon emissions and execution time for explainability models ELVis, MF-ELVis and BRIE with and without the proposed techniques

	Time(hh m' s")	Emissions (gCO_2e)
ELVis	62' 11"	7.96
MF-ELVis	13' 24"	2.67
BRIE	12' 33"	1.49
ELVis + PU	22' 53"†	4.86†
ELVis + T-DA	36' 26"†	7.84†
ELVis + Gen-DA	5h 20' 10"	57.58
MF-Elvis + PU	**8' 32"†**	**1.17†**
MF-ELvis + T-DA	30' 12"	6.10
MF-ELVis + Gen-DA	3h 59' 28"	47.12
BRIE + PU	15' 31"	1.73
BRIE + T-DA	29' 25"	4.92
BRIE + Gen-DA	4h 03' 43"	47.71

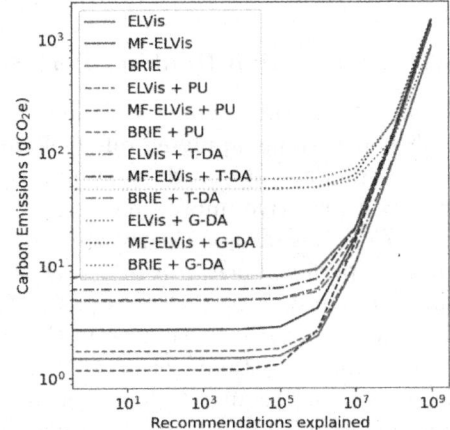

Fig. 5. Total carbon emissions (training and inference) depending on the number of inference cases for explainability methods ELVis, MF-ELVIs and BRIE with and without our techniques.

The long-term use of explainability models affects sustainability more than training (e.g. TripAdvisor sees 100M reviews p.a. [15]), and our techniques do not have effects on model inference. Figure 5 shows the long-term emissions (training+inference) of ELVis, MF-ELVis and BRIE with and without our techniques; clearly, the possible computational overheads of using data quality to improve model performance become negligible compared to inference-time emissions.

6 Conclusions

This work is framed at the intersection of three of the main modern challenges in Recommender Systems: explainability, sustainability and personalization. In the context of visual-based RS explainability through user-provided item images, we proposed to sustainably improve the performance of explainer models' performance by focusing on increasing Data Quality of the training data.

We proposed three novel techniques: one based in PU Learning, to tackle label noise from naive data assumptions, and two based in Data Augmentation (transform-based or text-to-image generation-based) to tackle *cold start* problems common to most users. Our computational experiments in real-world restaurant recommendation explanation datasets show that these techniques increase performance ($+ \sim 5\%$) of existing models (ELVis, MF-ELVis and BRIE) without compromising their long-term sustainability. Note that, while our experiments are framed on the restaurant domain, this approaches are applicable to any recommendation context where items have associated images uploaded by users.

With respect to further work, we identify different open ends: 1) a hyperparameter re-optimization of the used explainability models to increase effectiveness of our techniques; 2) the use of datasets with image-less textual reviews, to further prove the effects of generation-based augmentation 3) the design of PU Learning assumptions beyond single-prototype characterizations of users.

Acknowledgments. This work is funded by MICIU/AEI and ESF+ (FPU21/05783), ERDF A way of making Europe (PID2019-109238GB-C22, PID2023-147404OB-I00), ERDF/EU (PID2021-128045OA-I00), Ministry for Digital Transformation and Civil Service and 'Next-GenerationEU'/PRTR (TSI-100925-2023-1), and Xunta de Galicia (ED431C 2022/44). CITIC is funded by "Consellería de Cultura, Educación e Universidade" through ERDF and "Secretaría Xeral de Universidades" (ED431G 2023/01).

Disclosure of Interests. The authors have no competing interests to declare.

References

1. Bekker, J., Davis, J.: Learning from positive and unlabeled data: a survey. Mach. Learn. **109**(4), 719–760 (2020). https://doi.org/10.1007/s10994-020-05877-5
2. Bouthillier, X., Konda, K., Vincent, P., Memisevic, R.: Dropout as data augmentation. arXiv preprint arXiv:1506.08700 (2015)
3. Courty, B., et al.: MinervaBooks: mlco2/codecarbon: v2.4.1, May 2024. https://doi.org/10.5281/zenodo.11171501
4. Dignum, V.: Responsible artificial intelligence: how to develop and use AI in a responsible way, vol. 2156. Springer (2019)
5. Díez, J., Pérez-Núñez, P., Luaces, O., Remeseiro, B., Bahamonde, A.: Towards explainable personalized recommendations by learning from users' photos. Inf. Sci. **520**, 416–430 (2020). https://doi.org/10.1016/j.ins.2020.02.018

6. Patil, S., Berman, W., Rombach, R., Platen, P.V.: Amused: an open muse reproduction, January 2024. https://doi.org/10.48550/arXiv.2401.01808
7. Paz-Ruza, J., Alonso-Betanzos, A., Guijarro-Berdiñas, B., Cancela, B., Eiras-Franco, C.: Sustainable transparency on recommender systems: Bayesian ranking of images for explainability. Inf. Fusion **111**, 102497 (2024). https://doi.org/10.1016/j.inffus.2024.102497
8. Paz-Ruza, J., Eiras-Franco, C., Guijarro-Berdiñas, B., Alonso-Betanzos, A.: Sustainable personalisation and explainability in dyadic data systems. Procedia Comput. Sci. **207**, 1017–1026 (2022). https://doi.org/10.1016/j.procs.2022.09.157
9. Pérez-Núñez, P., Blanco, E., Bolon-Canedo, V., Remeseiro, B.: Tripadvisor restaurant reviews (2025). https://doi.org/10.5281/zenodo.14622324
10. Rendle, S., Freudenthaler, C., Gantner, Z., Schmidt-Thieme, L.: Bpr: Bayesian personalized ranking from implicit feedback, May 2012. https://doi.org/10.48550/arXiv.1205.2618
11. Ricci, F., Rokach, L., Shapira, B.: Introduction to recommender systems handbook. In: Ricci, F., Rokach, L., Shapira, B., Kantor, P.B. (eds.) Recommender Systems Handbook, pp. 1–35. Springer, Boston, MA (2011). https://doi.org/10.1007/978-0-387-85820-3_1
12. Rocchio, J.J.: Relevance feedback in information retrieval. In: Salton, G. (ed.) The Smart retrieval system - experiments in automatic document processing, pp. 313–323. Prentice-Hall, Englewood Cliffs, NJ (1971)
13. Shani, G., Gunawardana, A.: Evaluating recommendation systems. In: Ricci, F., Rokach, L., Shapira, B., Kantor, P.B. (eds.) Recommender Systems Handbook, pp. 257–297. Springer, Boston, MA (2011). https://doi.org/10.1007/978-0-387-85820-3_8
14. Shorten, C., Khoshgoftaar, T.M.: A survey on image data augmentation for deep learning. J. Big Data **6**(1), 1–48 (2019)
15. Statista research department: topic: Tripadvisor, https://www.statista.com/topics/3443/tripadvisor/
16. Strubell, E., Ganesh, A., McCallum, A.: Energy and policy considerations for deep learning in nlp, June 2019. https://doi.org/10.48550/arXiv.1906.02243
17. Szegedy, C., Ioffe, S., Vanhoucke, V., Alemi, A.: Inception-v4, inception-resnet and the impact of residual connections on learning, August 2016. https://doi.org/10.48550/arXiv.1602.07261
18. Tintarev, N., Masthoff, J.: Explaining recommendations: design and evaluation. In: Recommender Systems Handbook, pp. 353–382. Springer (2015)
19. Van Dyk, D.A., Meng, X.L.: The art of data augmentation. J. Comput. Graph. Stat. **10**(1), 1–50 (2001)
20. Yin, Y., et al.: Ttida: controllable generative data augmentation via text-to-text and text-to-image models. arXiv preprint arXiv:2304.08821 (2023)
21. Zhang, Y., Chen, X.: Explainable recommendation: a survey and new perspectives. Found. Trends^{TM} Inf. Retrieval **14**(1), 1–101 (2020). https://doi.org/10.1561/1500000066, arXiv:1804.11192 [cs]

TimeFlowDiffuser: A Hierarchical Diffusion Framework with Adaptive Context Sampling for Multi-horizon Time Series Forecasting

Wei Li(✉)

School of Computer Engineering and Science, Shanghai University, Shanghai, China
liwei008009@163.com

Abstract. Time series forecasting presents significant challenges in predicting complex temporal patterns across varying horizons. We introduce TimeFlowDiffuser, a novel framework that adapts diffusion models for time series forecasting through a hierarchical structure with adaptive context sampling. Our approach incorporates: (1) a Hierarchical Temporal Resolution module that processes time series at multiple scales; (2) an Adaptive Context Sampling mechanism that dynamically selects relevant historical context; (3) a Frequency-Aware Conditioning component that handles different frequency components; and (4) a Multi-Horizon Generation strategy for efficient prediction at various time horizons. Experiments on five benchmark datasets demonstrate that TimeFlowDiffuser consistently outperforms state-of-the-art methods, achieving average improvements of 7.2% in MSE and 6.3% in MAE, with particularly strong performance on long-horizon forecasting tasks. Our approach shows enhanced robustness to missing values and distributional shifts, with computational trade-offs discussed in Sect. 5.6.

Keywords: Time series forecasting · Diffusion models · Multi-scale modeling · Adaptive sampling · Multi-horizon prediction

1 Introduction

Time series forecasting is a critical task in numerous domains including energy management, healthcare, finance, and transportation [1]. While traditional statistical methods [2] have been widely used, recent deep learning advances have significantly improved forecasting through RNNs [3,4], Transformers [5–7], CNNs [8], and state space models [9,10]. However, these methods face limitations in long sequences, computational complexity, limited receptive fields, or linear scaling challenges.

However, existing methods face several critical limitations: (1) ineffective handling of multi-scale temporal patterns and mixed frequencies; (2) inability to adaptively focus on relevant historical context; (3) difficulty in modeling complex conditional distributions for uncertain futures; and (4) inefficient strategies for multi-horizon prediction, often requiring separate models for different forecast horizons.

Diffusion models [11,12,29] have emerged as a powerful paradigm for generative modeling, demonstrating exceptional capabilities in image [13], audio [14], and video generation [15]. Their ability to model complex data distributions through a gradual denoising process makes them promising candidates for time series forecasting. Initial explorations [16,17] have shown the potential of diffusion models for time series imputation and limited forecasting tasks, but a comprehensive framework leveraging the full potential of diffusion models for general time series forecasting remains unexplored.

In this paper, we introduce TimeFlowDiffuser, a novel diffusion-based framework specifically designed for time series forecasting challenges. As shown in Fig. 1, our approach significantly extends existing diffusion models with several key innovations to address the unique requirements of time series data:

- A **Hierarchical Temporal Resolution (HTR)** module that decomposes and processes time series at multiple temporal scales, enabling effective capture of both short-term fluctuations and long-term trends
- An **Adaptive Context Sampling (ACS)** mechanism that dynamically identifies and focuses on the most relevant historical context for each prediction, improving efficiency and performance
- A **Frequency-Aware Conditioning (FAC)** component that separately handles different frequency components of the time series, allowing specialized treatment of seasonal patterns, trends, and residuals
- A **Multi-Horizon Generation (MHG)** strategy that efficiently generates predictions at various time horizons without requiring separate models

Through extensive experiments on five benchmark datasets, we demonstrate that TimeFlowDiffuser consistently outperforms state-of-the-art methods across various forecast horizons. Our approach shows particularly strong performance in long-horizon forecasting scenarios, where uncertainty modeling becomes crucial. Additionally, TimeFlowDiffuser exhibits enhanced robustness to missing values and distributional shifts compared to existing methods.

2 Related Work

Deep Learning for Time Series: Deep learning has significantly advanced time series forecasting. Recurrent models like LSTM [3] and DeepAR [4] capture temporal dependencies. Transformer-based architectures including Informer [6], Autoformer [7], and FEDformer [19] have shown impressive results through attention mechanisms. Recent state space models like Mamba [9] and WFTNet [10] offer linear scaling properties.

Diffusion Models for Time Series: While diffusion models [11,12] have excelled in image, audio, and video generation, their application to time series is emerging. CSDI [17] adapts them for time series imputation, TimeGrad [16]

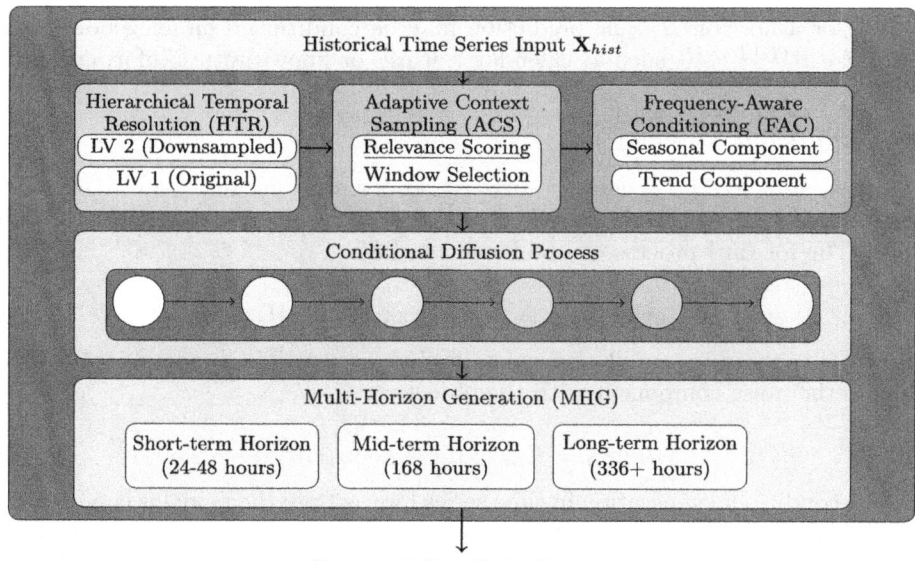

Fig. 1. TimeFlowDiffuser architecture overview. Our model combines a hierarchical diffusion process with adaptive context sampling and frequency-aware conditioning to generate multi-horizon forecasts. The framework consists of (a) a hierarchical temporal resolution module that processes time series at multiple scales, (b) an adaptive context sampling mechanism that identifies relevant historical segments, (c) a frequency-aware conditioning component that handles trend and seasonal patterns separately, and (d) a multi-horizon generation strategy that efficiently produces forecasts at different time ranges.

combines diffusion with autoregressive models, and SSSD [30] proposes a state space model with diffusion. However, these approaches have not fully addressed multi-scale, multi-horizon, and context-adaptive aspects that TimeFlowDiffuser targets.

Multi-scale Approaches: Multi-scale decomposition has been used in time series analysis through wavelet transforms [23] and hierarchical models like SOM-VAE [24]. While hierarchical structures in diffusion models have been explored for image generation [26], their application to time series forecasting with explicit temporal hierarchy remains underexplored.

3 Background

3.1 Problem Formulation

Given a historical multivariate time series $\mathbf{X}_{\text{hist}} = \{\mathbf{x}_1, \mathbf{x}_2, ..., \mathbf{x}_T\} \in \mathbb{R}^{T \times D}$, where T is the sequence length and D is the number of variables, the goal of time series forecasting is to predict future values $\mathbf{X}_{\text{future}} = \{\mathbf{x}_{T+1}, \mathbf{x}_{T+2}, ..., \mathbf{x}_{T+H}\} \in$

$\mathbb{R}^{H \times D}$ for a horizon H. The prediction may be conditioned on exogenous variables $\mathbf{Z} \in \mathbb{R}^{(T+H) \times D_z}$ such as calendar features or known future information.

3.2 Diffusion Models

Diffusion models [11,12] define a forward process that gradually adds Gaussian noise to data, and a reverse process that learns to recover the original data from noise. The forward process can be formulated as:

$$q(\mathbf{x}_t|\mathbf{x}_0) = \mathcal{N}(\mathbf{x}_t; \sqrt{\bar{\alpha}_t}\mathbf{x}_0, (1-\bar{\alpha}_t)\mathbf{I}) \quad (1)$$

where $\bar{\alpha}_t$ represents cumulative noise level at step t. The model is trained to predict the noise component with the objective:

$$L_{\text{simple}} = \mathbb{E}_{t,\mathbf{x}_0,\epsilon}\left[||\epsilon - \epsilon_\theta(\mathbf{x}_t, t)||^2\right] \quad (2)$$

For conditional generation in time series forecasting, the model is conditioned on historical context: $\epsilon_\theta(\mathbf{x}_t, t, \mathbf{c})$.

4 TimeFlowDiffuser Framework

We now describe our TimeFlowDiffuser framework, which extends standard diffusion models with hierarchical structure, adaptive context sampling, frequency-aware conditioning, and multi-horizon generation capabilities.

4.1 Hierarchical Temporal Resolution (HTR)

Time series often contain patterns at multiple time scales, from rapid fluctuations to long-term trends. Inspired by wavelet decomposition and hierarchical generative models, our HTR module explicitly processes time series at multiple temporal resolutions.

We define a set of L resolution levels, where each level l corresponds to a temporal downsampling factor $s_l = 2^{l-1}$. For each level, we create a downsampled version of the original time series:

$$\mathbf{X}^{(l)} = \text{Downsample}(\mathbf{X}, s_l) \quad (3)$$

The downsampling operation combines average pooling with skip connections to preserve both local details and global structure:

$$\mathbf{X}_i^{(l)} = \frac{1}{s_l} \sum_{j=(i-1)s_l+1}^{i \cdot s_l} \mathbf{X}_j + \lambda_l \cdot \mathbf{X}_{i \cdot s_l} \quad (4)$$

where λ_l is a learnable parameter controlling the importance of the skip connection.

Our diffusion process operates simultaneously across all resolution levels with shared parameters but level-specific noise schedules $\beta_t^{(l)}$:

$$\epsilon_\theta(\mathbf{X}_t^{(1)}, \mathbf{X}_t^{(2)}, ..., \mathbf{X}_t^{(L)}, t) \tag{5}$$

The hierarchical structure is maintained through resolution-specific attention blocks that communicate information across levels, allowing the model to capture dependencies between different time scales:

$$\mathbf{H}^{(l)} = \text{MSA}(\text{LN}(\mathbf{X}_t^{(l)})) + \mathbf{X}_t^{(l)} \tag{6}$$

$$\mathbf{X}_t^{(l)} = \text{MLP}(\text{LN}(\mathbf{H}^{(l)} + \sum_{k \neq l} \mathbf{A}^{(l,k)} \cdot \mathbf{H}^{(k)})) + \mathbf{H}^{(l)} \tag{7}$$

where MSA is multi-head self-attention, LN is layer normalization, MLP is a multi-layer perceptron, and $\mathbf{A}^{(l,k)}$ are learnable cross-level attention weights.

During generation, the predictions at each level are combined using learnable weights that depend on the prediction horizon:

$$\mathbf{X}_{\text{future}} = \sum_{l=1}^{L} w_l(H) \cdot \text{Upsample}(\mathbf{X}_{\text{future}}^{(l)}, s_l) \tag{8}$$

This hierarchical approach ensures that predictions incorporate patterns at all relevant time scales, from fine-grained details to long-term trends.

4.2 Adaptive Context Sampling (ACS)

Not all historical data points are equally relevant for forecasting. Our Adaptive Context Sampling mechanism dynamically identifies the most relevant historical segments for each prediction task. We define a set of K context windows with different spans, where each window k has length L_k and starting point S_k. The relevance of each window is determined by a trainable relevance function:

$$r_k = f_r(\mathbf{X}^{(k)}, \mathbf{Z}^{(k)}, H) \tag{9}$$

The final context representation is a weighted combination of all window representations:

$$\mathbf{C} = \sum_{k=1}^{K} r_k \cdot \text{Encoder}(\mathbf{X}^{(k)}, \mathbf{Z}^{(k)}) \tag{10}$$

4.3 Frequency-Aware Conditioning (FAC)

Time series often contain multiple frequency components, including trends, seasonality, and irregular patterns. Our Frequency-Aware Conditioning component explicitly decomposes the time series into trend (**T**), seasonal (**S**), and residual (**R**) components:

$$\mathbf{X}_{\text{hist}} = \mathbf{T} + \mathbf{S} + \mathbf{R} \tag{11}$$

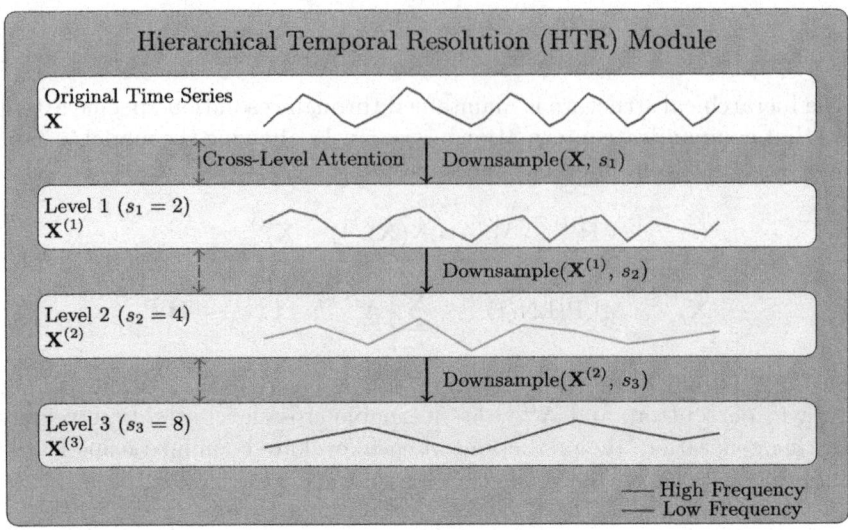

Fig. 2. Hierarchical Temporal Resolution (HTR) module. The time series is processed at multiple resolution levels simultaneously, with each level corresponding to a different temporal scale (increasing downsampling factors s_1, s_2, s_3). Cross-level attention mechanisms facilitate information exchange between different temporal scales, allowing the model to capture both fine-grained details and long-term trends. This hierarchical approach enables more effective modeling of complex temporal patterns.

Each component is encoded separately and used to condition the diffusion process through a component-aware cross-attention mechanism:

$$\epsilon_\theta(\mathbf{X}_t, t, \mathbf{C}_T, \mathbf{C}_S, \mathbf{C}_R, \mathbf{Z}) \tag{12}$$

This approach allows the model to handle different types of patterns in a specialized manner, improving prediction accuracy across diverse time series characteristics.

4.4 Multi-Horizon Generation (MHG)

Traditional forecasting models often require separate training for different prediction horizons or use autoregressive approaches that accumulate errors over long horizons. Our Multi-Horizon Generation strategy enables efficient prediction at various time horizons within a unified model.

We introduce a horizon-aware conditioning mechanism that adjusts the generation process based on the target horizon H:

$$\mathbf{E}_H = \text{Embedding}(H) \tag{13}$$

This horizon embedding is integrated throughout the model architecture, including:

1. A horizon-adaptive noise schedule that adjusts the diffusion process based on the prediction length:

$$\beta_t(H) = \beta_{\min} + (\beta_{\max} - \beta_{\min}) \cdot f_\beta(t, \mathbf{E}_H) \tag{14}$$

2. Horizon-specific attention masks that focus on relevant temporal context:

$$\mathbf{M}_{\text{attn}}(H) = \text{SoftMask}(\mathbf{E}_H) \tag{15}$$

3. Adaptive resolution weighting that emphasizes appropriate temporal scales:

$$w_l(H) = \text{Softmax}(g_w(\mathbf{E}_H))_l \tag{16}$$

During training, we use a curriculum strategy that gradually increases the prediction horizon, allowing the model to learn short-term patterns before tackling more challenging long-horizon predictions:

$$p(H) \propto H^{\gamma_t} \tag{17}$$

where γ_t increases over training iterations, shifting focus from short to long horizons.

For inference, we use a progressive generation strategy that allows reuse of computation for different horizons. Starting with a short horizon H_1, we generate predictions and then extend them to longer horizons $H_2, H_3, ..., H_n$ by conditioning each step on previously generated results:

$$\mathbf{X}_{T+1:T+H_1} = \text{Generate}(\mathbf{X}_{1:T}, H_1) \tag{18}$$

$$\mathbf{X}_{T+H_1+1:T+H_2} = \text{Generate}(\mathbf{X}_{1:T}, \mathbf{X}_{T+1:T+H_1}, H_2 - H_1) \tag{19}$$

This multi-horizon approach ensures efficient and accurate predictions across time scales without requiring separate models for each horizon.

5 Experiments

5.1 Datasets and Experimental Setup

We evaluate TimeFlowDiffuser on five widely-used benchmark datasets: ETTh1, ETTh2 (Electricity Transformer Temperature), Electricity, Traffic, and Weather [6]. Following standard protocols [8], we use a 7:1:2 split for training, validation, and testing with varying prediction horizons. We use MSE and MAE as evaluation metrics.

Implementation Details: All experiments were conducted on NVIDIA A100 GPUs with 40 GB memory. We use AdamW optimizer with learning rate 1e–4, batch size 32, and train for 100 epochs with early stopping. For fair comparison, we re-implemented all baseline methods using their official code repositories with consistent data preprocessing and evaluation protocols. The slight performance differences from original papers stem from unified experimental settings and consistent train/validation/test splits across all methods.

5.2 Baselines

We compare TimeFlowDiffuser with a comprehensive set of baselines:

- Statistical methods: ARIMA [2], Prophet [28]
- RNN-based methods: LSTM [3], DeepAR [4]
- CNN-based methods: TimesNet [8]
- Transformer-based methods: Autoformer [7], FEDformer [19], PatchTST [20]
- State space methods: Mamba [9], WFTNet [10]
- Diffusion-based methods: TimeGrad [16], CSDI [17], SSSD [30]

Due to space constraints and computational resources, we present results for the five most competitive baselines that have better implementations supporting all datasets and horizons.

5.3 Main Results

Table 1 presents the forecasting results on the ETTh1 and Electricity datasets. TimeFlowDiffuser consistently outperforms all baseline methods across different prediction horizons. On ETTh1, we observe an average improvement of 7.4% in MSE compared to the best baseline. For the Electricity dataset, the improvement is even more significant at 8.2% for MSE.

Table 1. Forecasting results on Mean Squared Error (MSE) across datasets and prediction horizons. Best results are in **bold**, and second-best results are underlined.

Method	ETTh1			ETTh2		Electricity		Traffic	Weather
	24	168	336	24	336	24	336	168	48
Autoformer	0.372	0.523	0.577	0.348	0.482	0.181	0.314	0.648	0.292
PatchTST	0.351	0.485	0.545	0.325	0.471	0.168	0.295	0.632	0.282
TimesNet	0.349	0.477	0.538	0.320	0.470	0.165	0.291	0.629	0.276
Mamba	0.347	0.471	0.528	0.317	0.467	0.160	0.283	0.627	0.273
WFTNet	0.339	0.456	0.514	0.311	0.465	0.158	0.275	0.625	0.269
TimeFlowDiffuser	**0.320**	**0.429**	**0.480**	**0.294**	**0.433**	**0.147**	**0.253**	**0.573**	**0.247**

5.4 Ablation Study

To understand the contribution of each component, we conducted an ablation study by removing key modules from TimeFlowDiffuser. Table 2 presents the results on the ETTh1 dataset with a 168-hour prediction horizon.

The results show that all components contribute significantly to the overall performance, with the Hierarchical Temporal Resolution (HTR) module providing the largest individual improvement (5.1% MSE reduction). The Adaptive Context Sampling (ACS) mechanism contributes a 4.2% MSE reduction,

Table 2. Ablation study on ETTh1 dataset with 168-hour prediction horizon.

Model Variant	MSE	MAE
Full TimeFlowDiffuser	0.429	0.421
- Hierarchical Temporal Resolution	0.451 (+5.1%)	0.438 (+4.0%)
- Adaptive Context Sampling	0.447 (+4.2%)	0.435 (+3.3%)
- Frequency-Aware Conditioning	0.445 (+3.7%)	0.434 (+3.1%)
- Multi-Horizon Generation	0.442 (+3.0%)	0.432 (+2.6%)
- All components (Base Diffusion)	0.485 (+13.1%)	0.464 (+10.2%)

while the Frequency-Aware Conditioning (FAC) and Multi-Horizon Generation (MHG) components provide 3.7% and 3.0% MSE reductions, respectively. When all components are removed, resulting in a basic diffusion model for time series, the performance drops by 13.1% in MSE and 10.2% in MAE, highlighting the substantial combined contribution of our innovations.

5.5 Robustness Analysis

We evaluate TimeFlowDiffuser's robustness to missing values and distributional shifts, which are common challenges in real-world time series data.
Missing Values: We randomly mask 10%, 30%, and 50% of the input data and measure the impact on forecasting performance. As shown in Fig. 3(a), TimeFlowDiffuser maintains higher accuracy than baseline methods as the missing rate increases, demonstrating superior robustness to incomplete data.
Distributional Shifts: We simulate distributional shifts by training on the first 70% of data and evaluating on the remaining 30%, which contains potential distribution changes. As shown in Fig. 3(b), TimeFlowDiffuser exhibits more stable performance compared to baselines, particularly on long-horizon predictions.

5.6 Computational Analysis

TimeFlowDiffuser requires approximately 2.3× more inference time than WFT-Net due to the iterative denoising process (50 steps). However, our parallel multi-horizon generation reduces the overhead for multiple forecast lengths. On ETTh1 with batch size 32: TimeFlowDiffuser takes 0.42 s per batch vs 0.18 s for WFT-Net, but generates all horizons simultaneously. Memory usage is 1.8× higher (6.2 GB vs 3.4 GB). For latency-critical applications, we provide a fast variant using DDIM sampling [27] with 10 steps, achieving 0.12 s inference with only 1.2% MSE increase.

5.7 Case Study: Energy Demand Forecasting

To demonstrate practical utility, we conducted a case study on energy demand forecasting using the Electricity dataset. Figure 4 shows TimeFlowDiffuser's predictions compared to actual values and baseline methods for a 168-hour forecast.

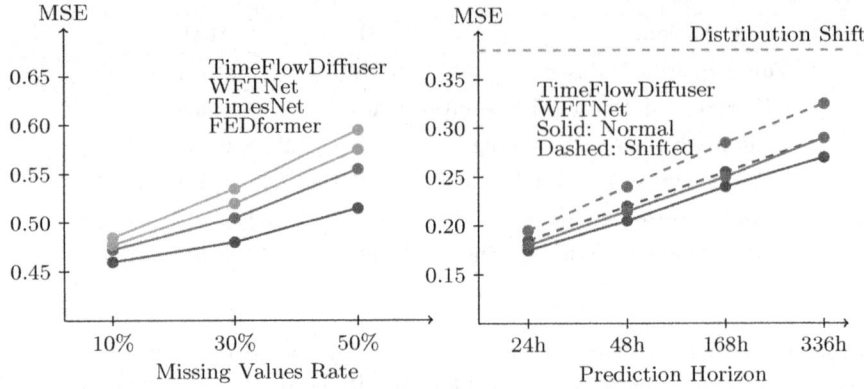

Fig. 3. Robustness analysis of TimeFlowDiffuser compared to baseline methods. (a) Performance with varying rates of missing values on ETTh1 dataset, showing that TimeFlowDiffuser maintains lower error rates even with 50% missing data compared to state-of-the-art methods. (b) Performance under distributional shift conditions on Electricity dataset, comparing normal test conditions (solid lines) with distribution shift scenarios (dashed lines). TimeFlowDiffuser exhibits more stable performance with a smaller gap between normal and shifted conditions compared to WFTNet, particularly for longer prediction horizons (168h and 336h).

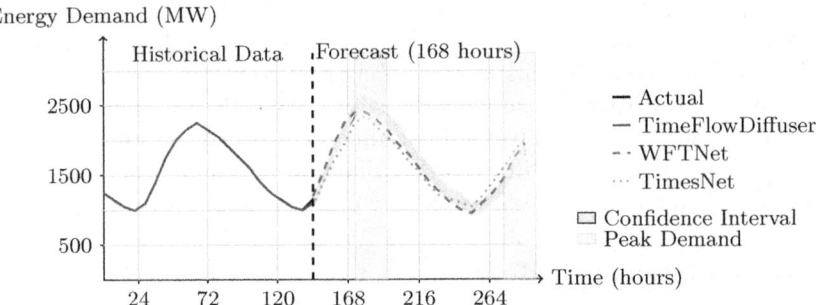

Fig. 4. Case study on energy demand forecasting using the Electricity dataset for 168-hour forecasts. TimeFlowDiffuser (blue) accurately captures daily patterns and peak demands (pink areas) with confidence intervals (shaded), outperforming WFTNet (red) and TimesNet (orange) compared to actual values (black). (Color figure online)

The results show that TimeFlowDiffuser effectively captures both regular patterns (daily cycles) and irregular events (demand spikes), with particularly strong performance during transitional periods and peak demand times.

5.8 Limitations and Future Work

Despite its strong performance, TimeFlowDiffuser has several limitations: (1) increased computational requirements compared to simpler models, and (2) challenges in incorporating structured domain knowledge in the diffusion process.

Future research directions include: (1) developing more efficient sampling strategies specifically optimized for time series data, and (2) integrating causal structure learning to improve interpretability.

References

1. Benidis, K., et al.: Neural forecasting: introduction and literature overview. arXiv preprint arXiv:2004.10240 (2020)
2. Box, G.E., Jenkins, G.M., Reinsel, G.C., Ljung, G.M.: Time Series Analysis: Forecasting and Control. Wiley (2015)
3. Hochreiter, S., Schmidhuber, J.: Long short-term memory. Neural Comput. **9**(8), 1735–1780 (1997)
4. Salinas, D., Flunkert, V., Gasthaus, J., Januschowski, T.: DeepAR: probabilistic forecasting with autoregressive recurrent networks. Int. J. Forecast. **36**(3), 1181–1191 (2020)
5. Vaswani, A., et al.: Attention is all you need. In: Advances in Neural Information Processing Systems, pp. 5998–6008 (2017)
6. Zhou, H., et al.: Informer: beyond efficient transformer for long sequence time-series forecasting. In: Proceedings of the AAAI Conference on Artificial Intelligence, vol. 35, pp. 11106–11115 (2021)
7. Wu, H., Xu, J., Wang, J., Long, M.: Autoformer: decomposition transformers with auto-correlation for long-term series forecasting. In: Advances in Neural Information Processing Systems, vol. 34, pp. 22419–22430 (2021)
8. Wu, H., Hu, T., Liu, Y., Zhou, H., Wang, J., Long, M.: TimesNet: temporal 2d-variation modeling for general time series analysis. In: International Conference on Learning Representations (2022)
9. Gu, A., et al.: Mamba: linear-time sequence modeling with selective state spaces. arXiv preprint arXiv:2312.00752 (2023)
10. Liu, P., et al.: WFTNet: exploiting global and local periodicity in long-term time series forecasting. arXiv preprint arXiv:2309.11319 (2023)
11. Ho, J., Jain, A., Abbeel, P.: Denoising diffusion probabilistic models. In: Advances in Neural Information Processing Systems, vol. 33, pp. 6840–6851 (2020)
12. Song, Y., Sohl-Dickstein, J., Kingma, D.P., Kumar, A., Ermon, S., Poole, B.: Score-based generative modeling through stochastic differential equations. In: International Conference on Learning Representations (2020)
13. Rombach, R., Blattmann, A., Lorenz, D., Esser, P., Ommer, B.: High-resolution image synthesis with latent diffusion models. In: Proceedings of the IEEE/CVF Conference on Computer Vision and Pattern Recognition, pp. 10684–10695 (2022)
14. Kong, Z., Ping, W., Huang, J., Zhao, K., Catanzaro, B.: DiffWave: a versatile diffusion model for audio synthesis. In: International Conference on Learning Representations (2021)
15. Ho, J., Salimans, T., Gritsenko, A., Chan, W., Norouzi, M., Fleet, D.J.: Video diffusion models. In: Advances in Neural Information Processing Systems, vol. 35 (2022)

16. Rasul, K., Seward, C., Schuster, I., Vollgraf, R.: Autoregressive denoising diffusion models for multivariate probabilistic time series forecasting. In: International Conference on Machine Learning, pp. 8857–8868 (2021)
17. Tashiro, Y., Song, J., Song, Y., Ermon, S.: CSDI: conditional score-based diffusion models for probabilistic time series imputation. In: Advances in Neural Information Processing Systems, vol. 34 (2021)
18. Cho, K., et al.: Learning phrase representations using RNN encoder-decoder for statistical machine translation. In: Proceedings of the 2014 Conference on Empirical Methods in Natural Language Processing, pp. 1724–1734 (2014)
19. Zhou, T., Ma, Z., Wen, Q., Wang, X., Sun, L., Jin, R.: FEDformer: frequency enhanced decomposed transformer for long-term series forecasting. In: International Conference on Machine Learning, pp. 27268–27286 (2022)
20. Nie, Y., Nguyen, N.H., Sinthong, P., Kalagnanam, J.: A time series is worth 64 words: long-term forecasting with transformers. In: International Conference on Learning Representations (2023)
21. van den Oord, A., et al.: WaveNet: a generative model for raw audio. arXiv preprint arXiv:1609.03499 (2016)
22. Wen, Z., Xu, G., Jiang, G., Zhang, H., Fu, Y., Liu, T.: DiffSTG: probabilistic spatio-temporal graph forecasting with denoising diffusion models. arXiv preprint arXiv:2301.13629 (2023)
23. Addison, P.S.: The Illustrated Wavelet Transform Handbook: Introductory Theory and Applications in Science, Engineering, Medicine and Finance. CRC Press (2017)
24. Fortuin, V., Hüser, M., Locatello, F., Strathmann, H., Rätsch, G.: SOM-VAE: Interpretable discrete representation learning on time series. In: International Conference on Learning Representations (2019)
25. Desai, A., Freeman, C., Wang, Z., Beaver, I.: TimeVAE: a variational auto-encoder for multivariate time series generation. In: Proceedings of the IEEE/CVF Conference on Computer Vision and Pattern Recognition, pp. 13807–13816 (2023)
26. Ho, J., Saharia, C., Chan, W., Fleet, D.J., Norouzi, M., Salimans, T.: Cascaded diffusion models for high fidelity image generation. J. Mach. Learn. Res. **23**(47), 1–33 (2022)
27. Song, J., Meng, C., Ermon, S.: Denoising diffusion implicit models. In: International Conference on Learning Representations (2021)
28. Taylor, S.J., Letham, B.: Forecasting at scale. Am. Stat. **72**(1), 37–45 (2018)
29. Lin, L., Li, Z., Li, R., Li, X., Gao, J.: Diffusion models for time-series applications: a survey. Front. Inf. Technol. Electron. Eng. **25**(1), 19–41 (2024)
30. Alcaraz, J.M.L., Strodthoff, N.: Diffusion-based time series imputation and forecasting with structured state space models. arXiv preprint arXiv:2208.09399 (2022)

ConDTab: Conditional Diffusion Transformer for Mixed-Type Tabular Synthesis with Dual Attention Latent Encoding

Ruoxuan Wang, Shiying Li, Liuyi Fan, Wei Ma, Zexi Li, and Xinbo Ai[✉]

School of Intelligent Engineering and Automation, Beijing University of Posts and Telecommunications, Beijing 100876, China
xinbo.ai@email.xx

Abstract. Diffusion models demonstrate superior capabilities in tabular data generation tasks, yet challenges remain in modeling heterogeneous features and maintaining global distribution consistency. Moreover, existing research has limited exploration of conditional diffusion for enhancing minority-class samples. This paper proposes ConDTab, a conditional diffusion-based framework built on unified latent encoding and dual attention mechanisms for mixed-type tabular data generation. A Variational Autoencoder enhanced with dual row-column attention facilitates heterogeneous feature fusion and global pattern modeling, yielding an informative latent space for diffusion-based generation. To achieve fine-grained conditional control, a dynamic condition fusion module aligns condition information (e.g., class constraints) with sample features and injects the resulting signals into both input and intermediate layers, guiding the generative process to enhance minority-class fidelity while maintaining global distributional coherence. We evaluate ConDTab on eight public datasets. ConDTab maintains superior stability across distribution alignment and downstream performance when transitioning to imbalanced data, it also achieves the highest efficiency in utility–privacy trade-offs.

Keywords: Tabular Synthesis · Latent Representation · Conditional Generation · Diffusion Transformers

1 Introduction

Tabular data plays a vital role in domains such as finance and healthcare. Tabular data synthesis techniques enhance its practicality by generating high-quality data to address challenges like class imbalance, missing values, and privacy concerns [2,14].

The rapid progress in generative modeling has empowered tabular data synthesis. While GANs [20,23] and VAEs [12,20] effectively capture complex feature dependencies in tabular data, they struggle with generation stability, class imbalance adaptation, and data fidelity [3].

To address these limitations, researchers have explored applying diffusion models to tabular data generation tasks. Diffusion models [4] were originally designed for continuous data, and adapting them to tabular data often involves encoding categorical features or using separate processes for different types [6, 8,9]. Recent methods map heterogeneous features into a unified latent space to model inter-column interactions [16,17,22], but they overlook global-local dependencies within rows, limiting alignment with real data distributions.

Another major challenge lies in the imbalanced class distribution of tabular data. Existing diffusion-based methods predominantly focus on unconditional generation, which causes minority classes to be overwhelmed by dominant ones during the noise injection and denoising processes. As a result, the class distribution of the generated data often deviates significantly from that of the real data.

Motivated by these challenges, our study proposes ConDTab, a novel conditional generative model with the following key contributions:

1)We construct a shared latent space based on a Transformer-VAE architecture, which integrates self-attention and cross-sample attention to jointly model feature dependencies and global sample relationships, effectively capturing the complex distribution of heterogeneous features.

2) We design a latent-space conditional fusion diffusion framework, which generates fine-grained condition information and injects it into both the input and intermediate layers of a Diffusion Transformer (DiT) to precisely guide the tabular data generation process.

3) We conducted extensive experiments on eight datasets, including imbalanced settings, and compared our model with eight classical or state-of-the-art methods. Our model outperforms existing approaches in distribution alignment, machine learning utility, and privacy balance, demonstrating its robustness in generating high-quality, condition-consistent synthetic tabular data.

2 Related Work

2.1 Tabular Representation Learning

Effective tabular representation methods enable generative models to better capture feature distributions and dependencies. To this end, researchers have proposed various representation learning approaches based on deep neural networks. Predictive models such as VIME [21] enhance feature representation by utilizing random masking and value replacement for feature reconstruction. While SCARF [1] and TransTab [19] leverage contrastive learning to enhance transferability and generalization. SAINT [15] integrates both strategies using cross-sample attention and combines reconstruction with InfoNCE contrastive loss for self-supervised pretraining.

However, most methods handle categorical and numerical features separately, lacking a unified latent space. VAE-based models like TVAE [20] and GOGGLE [12] address this issue by mapping heterogeneous features into a continuous space, but they often ignore global relationships among samples. This work combines hybrid learning with VAE to jointly model feature dependencies and sample-level structures in a shared latent space, providing more expressive representations for diffusion-based generation.

2.2 Conditional Tabular Generation

Early generative models such as VAEs and GANs have been applied to tabular data synthesis. However, their lack of class control mechanisms limits their performance when dealing with imbalanced data [7,10,12]. To address class imbalance, CTGAN [20] introduces a conditional vector mechanism, while CTAB-GAN+ [23] further incorporates hybrid modeling and frequency sampling. Diffusion models have gained traction in tabular data generation due to their stable training and high-quality synthesis capabilities [6,8,11]. TabDDPM [9] models tabular data distributions using two denoising diffusion probabilistic models [4,5]. AutoDiff [16] and TabSyn [22] integrate autoencoders with diffusion to address challenges in heterogeneous feature modeling.

Conditional mechanisms further improve the controllability and quality of diffusion-based tabular synthesis. Imb-FinDiff [14] improves minority class generation through class embeddings and conditional noise prediction, and MTab-Gen [18] applies conditional attention to reinforce class information. To our knowledge, this work is the first to explore the DIT-based conditional diffusion model [13] for tabular data generation. Our approach unifies the improvement of minority class synthesis with the mitigation of class imbalance, addressing key challenges in structured data generation.

3 Method

3.1 Task Definition

Given a tabular dataset with numerical features X_{num}, categorical features X_{cat}, and a set of constraints C specifying desired sample properties, our goal is to design a model that captures both local and global dependencies among heterogeneous features and generates high-quality synthetic data. To this end, we propose a conditional Transformer-VAE framework integrated with a diffusion model, as shown in Fig. 1. The framework first employs a VAE to encode the tabular data(Sect. 3.2), then performs conditional data generation using a diffusion process (Sect. 3.3). The task is formally defined as

$$\hat{X}_g = (\hat{X}_{\text{num}}, \hat{X}_{\text{cat}}) = \text{ConDTab}(X_{\text{num}}, X_{\text{cat}}, C). \tag{1}$$

3.2 Latent Space Learning

Feature Tokenization. To accommodate the Transformer architecture, we construct a unified representation of tabular data. Specifically, the numerical feature matrix $X_{\text{num}} \in \mathbb{R}^{B \times M_{\text{num}}}$ is first projected through a learnable linear

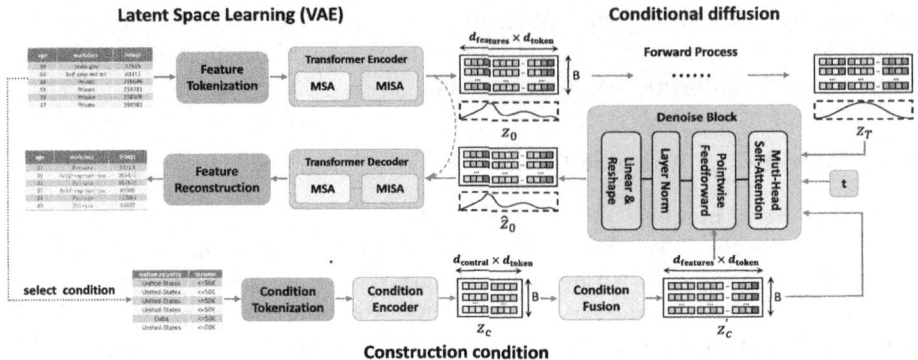

Fig. 1. ConDTab Framework. Tabular data and conditional columns are tokenized and encoded by VAE encoder with MSA and MISA into latent representations. A forward diffusion process adds noise to $z_0 \to z_T$, and the reverse denoising process is conditionally guided by z_c through a condition fusion module. The final denoised latent z_0 is decoded and detokenized into synthetic tabular data.

transformation matrix $W_{num} \in \mathbb{R}^{(d_{num}+1) \times d_{token}}$, while the categorical features $X_{cat} \in \mathbb{R}^{B \times M_{cat}}$ are encoded via a trainable embedding layer. This process yields a unified token representation for both feature types, and concatenates the numerical and categorical tokens into a single feature token matrix:

$$E = [E_{num}, E_{cat}] \in \mathbb{R}^{B \times (M_{num}+1+M_{cat}) \times d_{token}}. \tag{2}$$

Here, B denotes the batch size and M_{num} denotes the number of numerical features, 1 is prepended as the [CLS] token. M_{cat} denotes the number of categorical features. The token embedding dimension is given by d_{token}.

Transformer-VAE for Column and Sample Representation. We construct a unified latent representation for tabular data by leveraging the structured latent variable learning capability of Variational Autoencoder (VAE). The mean and variance encoders output the mean matrix and the log standard deviation matrix, respectively. The latent variable Z is then obtained via the reparameterization trick:

$$Z = \mu + \sigma \cdot \varepsilon, \quad \varepsilon \sim \mathcal{N}(0, I). \tag{3}$$

To capture both inter-feature and inter-sample relationships, we employ a dual-attention Transformer shared across the VAE's mean and variance encoders. The self-attention branch captures column-wise dependencies within each data point using standard multi-head self-attention (MSA) and feedforward layers. In contrast, our added inter-sample attention module (MISA) concatenates feature embeddings within each sample and computes attention across samples in a batch, enabling the model to capture global sample-wise dependencies. This combination facilitates comprehensive representation learning by integrating both intra-sample feature interactions and inter-sample relationships (Fig. 2).

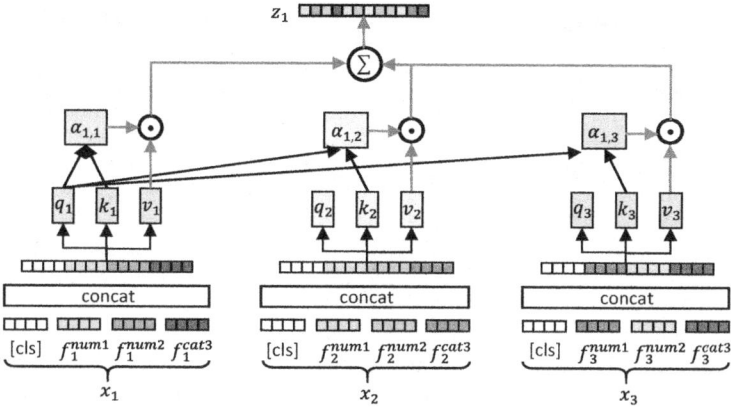

Fig. 2. Inter-sample attention mechanism. Each row is represented by concatenating its feature embeddings into a single vector. Attention is applied across the batch, enabling each sample (e.g., x_1) to aggregate information from others (e.g., x_2, x_3).

$$Z^{(1)} = \mathrm{LN}(\mathrm{MSA}(E)) + E, \quad Z^{(2)} = \mathrm{LN}(\mathrm{FF}_{\mathrm{col}}(Z^{(1)})) + Z^{(1)}. \tag{4}$$

$$Z^{(3)} = \mathrm{LN}\left(\mathrm{MISA}\left(\{Z^{(2)}\}_{i=1}^{B}\right)\right) + Z^{(2)}, \quad Z^{(4)} = \mathrm{LN}(\mathrm{FF}_{\mathrm{row}}(Z^{(3)})) + Z^{(3)}. \tag{5}$$

Reconstruction of Representation. The VAE decoder shares the same architecture as the encoder and takes the latent variable Z as input during training. It employs a multi-layer self-attention mechanism to generate intermediate hidden representations $\hat{E}$. We adopt the same mechanism as feature tokenization to map $\hat{E}$ back to $\hat{X}_{\mathrm{num}}$ and $\hat{X}_{\mathrm{cat}}$.

3.3 Conditional Diffusion

The tabular data and its condition are encoded by the VAE into latent variables Z_x and Z_c. To generate samples conditioned on Z_c, we model the posterior $p(Z_x|Z_c)$ using a score-based diffusion model in latent space. During training, noise is injected via a forward process; during generation, a reverse stochastic differential equation recovers clean samples from noise.

The conditional reverse process is formulated as:

$$dz_t = -2\sigma(t)\dot{\sigma}(t)\nabla_{z_t} \log p(z_t \mid z_c)\, dt + \sqrt{2\sigma(t)\dot{\sigma}(t)}\, d\omega_t, \tag{6}$$

where the score function $\nabla_{z_t} \log p(z_t \mid z_c)$ models the gradient of the log-density under the condition z_c, and the reverse-time SDE guides the sample trajectory from the noise space toward the data manifold conditioned on z_c.

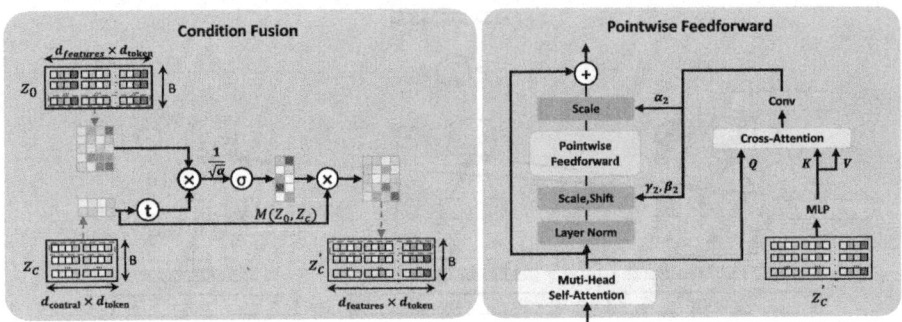

Fig. 3. Fine-grained conditional Model. Generation of fine-grained condition fusion (Left) and fine-grained conditional control in the denoising network (Right).

To estimate this conditional score function, we train a neural network G to recover the original noise ϵ from the perturbed data $z_t = z_0 + \sigma(t)\epsilon$. The training objective is formulated as a denoising score matching loss:

$$\mathcal{L}_{\text{denoise}} = \mathbb{E}_{z_0 \sim p(z_0),\, t \sim \mathcal{U}(0,T),\, \epsilon \sim \mathcal{N}(0,I)} \left\| G(z_0 + \sigma(t)\epsilon, t, z_c) - \epsilon \right\|_2^2, \qquad (7)$$

where the G acts as a denoiser, estimating and recovering the clean sample z_0 from the noisy input z_t, conditioned on the categorical latent representation z_c and the diffusion time step t.

Fine-Grained Conditional Model. To achieve precise conditional control, we first generate fine-grained guidance via a condition fusion module, which is then injected into both the input and intermediate layers of the model to dynamically align the generation process with the specified category constraints.

We first construct a weight matrix based on the correlation between the conditional information and the sample data. This weight matrix $M(Z_x, Z_c)$ can be formulated as Eq. 8. Upon obtaining the weight matrix, we use it to derive a fine-grained conditional matrix Z'_c based on the initial conditional information. This process can be formulated as Eq. 9:

$$(Z_x, Z_c) = S_m\left(\frac{1}{\sqrt{\alpha}}(\text{Linear}(Z_x) \times \text{Linear}(Z_c)^T)\right), \qquad (8)$$

$$Z'_c = M(Z_x, Z_c) \cdot Z_c, \qquad (9)$$

where S_m denotes the Softmax function, $Z_x \in \mathbb{R}^{(d_{\text{num}}+1+d_{\text{cat}}) \times d_{\text{token}}}$ represents the latent sample features, and $Z_c \in \mathbb{R}^{d_{\text{control}} \times d_{\text{token}}}$ represents the latent conditional features. The weight map is given by $M \in \mathbb{R}^{(d_{\text{num}}+1+d_{\text{cat}}) \times d_{\text{control}}}$, and α is a scaling factor.

Subsequently, the conditional information is injected into both the input and intermediate control layers to guide the generation of samples that align with the given conditions. The control layer structure is shown in Fig. 3(right), we use the conditional embedding as the query Q to match the key features K and value features V via the cross-attention mechanism. Furthermore, a convolutional layer is employed to refine and update the guiding embeddings. Here, we consider this conditional guidance as a modulation factor and utilize the Adaptive Instance Normalization (AdaIN) layer to generate the corresponding samples. Through this process, we obtain the latent features of the generated samples, as follows:

$$Z_X = \text{AdaIN}\left(Z_x, conv(CrossAttn(Z_x, Z'_c))\right). \tag{10}$$

4 Experiments

4.1 Experimental Setup

Datasets. We selected eight real-world tabular datasets containing both numerical and categorical features. These datasets span machine learning tasks, including binary classification(Bin): Adult[1], Default[2], Magic[3]; multi-class classification (Multi) : Obesity[4], Bean[5]; regression (Reg) : Beijing[6], News[7], King[8].

Baselines. To evaluate the effectiveness of ConDTab, we compare it with six advanced methods. CTGAN [20] and TVAE [20] are classical tabular generation models, while CTABGAN+ [23] is one of the most advanced conditional GAN-based approaches. TabDDPM [9] and CoDi [11] handle heterogeneous features through different diffusion processes, and Tabsyn [22] is the best-performing diffusion model for constructing a heterogeneous joint latent space.

Evaluation Methods. The evaluation of tabular data generation is generally conducted from three aspects: 1) Qualitative analysis (Sect. 4.2) includes distribution visualization, column-wise density estimation, and pair-wise column correlation to compare statistical similarity with real data. 2) machine learning efficiency (MLE) (Sect. 4.3) evaluates the model's effectiveness in downstream machine learning tasks. 3) privacy assessment (Sect. 4.4) is conducted using the DCR metric to measure data security.

---

[1] https://archive.ics.uci.edu/dataset/2/adult.
[2] https://archive.ics.uci.edu/dataset/350/default+of+credit+card+clients.
[3] https://archive.ics.uci.edu/dataset/159/magic+gamma+telescope.
[4] https://www.kaggle.com/datasets/fatemehmehrparvar/obesity-levels.
[5] https://archive.ics.uci.edu/dataset/602/dry+bean+dataset.
[6] https://archive.ics.uci.edu/dataset/381/beijing+pm2+5+data.
[7] https://archive.ics.uci.edu/dataset/332/online+news+popularity.
[8] https://www.kaggle.com/datasets/harlfoxem/housesalesprediction.

Table 1. Statistical Similarity Metrics. Average results across three task types datasets. (a) column-wise distribution distances (lower is better); (b) match rates (%) of pair-wise column correlation scores (higher is better). Results are reported on both balanced (Bal.) and class-imbalanced (Imbal.) versions of the datasets.

(a) Column-wise density estimation.

Data	Methods	Bin	Multi	Reg
Bal.	CTGAN	0.116±.002	0.124±.006	0.150±.002
	TVAE	0.106±.006	0.181±.006	0.178±.004
	CTABGAN+	0.083±.001	0.082±.003	0.228±.007
	TabDDPM	0.120±.005	0.073±.009	0.317±.003
	CoDi	0.119±.006	0.131±.014	0.145±.002
	Tabsyn	0.029±.005	0.036±.013	0.045±.004
	ConDTab	**0.022±.002**	**0.023±.003**	**0.042±.005**
Imbal.	CTGAN	1.064±.010	0.289±.004	–
	TVAE	1.173±.013	0.26±.003	–
	CTABGAN+	0.063±.006	0.225±.001	–
	TabDDPM	0.144±.009	0.238±.002	–
	CoDi	0.184±.016	0.318±.003	–
	Tabsyn	0.059±.003	0.220±.001	–
	ConDTab	**0.054±.002**	**0.135±.002**	–

(b) pair-wise column correlation score.

Data	Methods	Bin	Multi	Reg
Bal.	CTGAN	82.17±.046	85.35±.015	85.82±.008
	TVAE	83.93±.087	78.32±.040	85.99±.009
	CTABGAN+	89.13±.015	88.00±.026	71.30±.041
	TabDDPM	90.83±.018	92.44±.020	87.44±.010
	CoDi	67.19±.011	87.22±.017	83.26±.008
	Tabsyn	97.26±.019	96.24±.025	97.54±.018
	ConDTab	**97.33±.004**	**96.65±.002**	**97.62±.002**
Imbal.	CTGAN	80.36±.028	78.91±.021	–
	TVAE	76.63±.032	70.59±.041	–
	CTABGAN+	89.92±.024	78.25±.037	–
	TabDDPM	90.28±.013	81.34±.026	–
	CoDi	85.82±.016	69.28±.031	–
	Tabsyn	92.19±.017	80.69±.031	–
	ConDTab	**92.42±.016**	**90.25±.021**	–

4.2 Statistical Similarity

Column-Wise Density Estimation. To evaluate the statistical similarity between real and synthetic data at the feature level, we compute column-wise density estimation using Wasserstein distance for numerical features and Jensen-Shannon (JS) divergence for categorical features.

As shown in Table 1-a(Bal.), ConDTab consistently outperforms all baseline on column-wise density estimation across general-purpose balanced datasets. On average, ConDTab outperforms the most competitive baseline by 24.1%, 36.1%, and 6.67% on binary, multi-class, and regression datasets, respectively. Moreover, ConDTab demonstrates greater stability, while models like CTABGAN+ and TabDDPM perform well on classification but degrade on regression.

Pair-Wise Column Correlations. We evaluate structural consistency by computing the correlation match rate between real and synthetic data based on pairwise feature correlations, using Pearson correlation for numerical features, contingency similarity for categorical features.

Table 1-b(Bal.) demonstrates that ConDTab achieves the best pair-wise column correlation across all task types, demonstrating a strong ability to preserve inter-column dependencies. Both ConDTab and TabSyn adopt a joint latent space strategy, which leads to significant improvements over models that handle heterogeneous features separately. However, ConDTab still outperforms the strongest baseline(TabSyn), with improvements of 0.07%, 0.43%, and 0.08% across the three dataset types, respectively. We attribute this improvement to the effectiveness of the cross-sample attention mechanism.

Extended Experiment Under Class Imbalance. Additionally, we design an experiment on imbalanced datasets to assess the effectiveness of conditional generation. We simulate class imbalance by selecting one majority and one minority class, downsampling the latter with a random ratio between 1:5 and 1:10. The evaluation procedure follows the same protocol as in the standard setting.

As shown in Table 1-(Imbal.), ConDTab maintains strong performance on imbalanced datasets, outperforming the strongest baseline TabSyn in both binary and multi-class tasks. While most models suffer significant performance degradation when transitioning from balanced to imbalanced settings, ConDTab demonstrates superior robustness, with smaller average performance drops compared to all other methods. This highlights the importance of conditional modeling in mitigating distribution shifts caused by class imbalance.

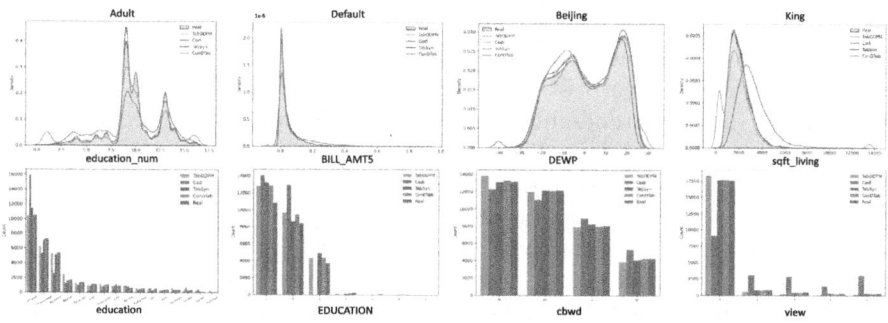

Fig. 4. Visualization of column-wise distribution densities for real and synthetic data (TabDDPM, CoDi, Tabsyn, ConDTab). Top: numerical; Bottom: categorical.

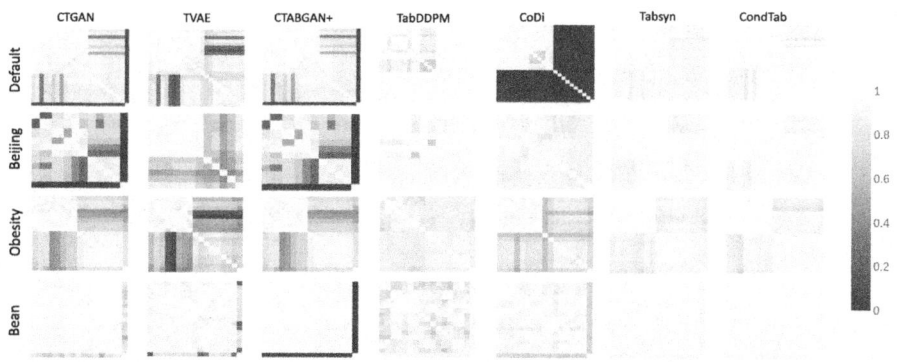

Fig. 5. The heatmaps of pair-wise column correlation matching between synthetic data v.s. the real data (the lighter, the better).

Visualization. Figure 4 presents the column-wise density distributions of eight features (one numerical and one categorical from each of datasets). Compared to TabSyn, which tends to produce exaggerated peaks, ConDTab more accurately preserves the shape of the real data distribution, generating smoother and more realistic outputs. Figure 5 shows the heatmaps of pair-wise column correlation matching between the generated data and the real data. It can be observed that ConDTab exhibits the fewest regions of low correlation match among all models, indicating its superior performance in capturing inter-feature dependencies.

4.3 Machine Learning Efficiency

Standard MLE Evaluation. To evaluate the practical utility of generated data, we adopt Machine Learning Efficiency (MLE) as the evaluation metric. Following the methodology of Tabsyn [22], the real dataset is split into training and test sets (1:9 ratio). A generative model is trained on the training set, and synthetic data of equal size is sampled to train an XGBoost classifier or regressor, evaluated on the real test set using F1 (classification) or R2 (regression). Furthermore, to reduce randomness, we conduct 20 runs with different seeds and report mean ± standard deviation.

Table 2(Bal.) presents that our method consistently outperforms baselines across eight real-world datasets, achieving an average 3.36% F1 improvement over the strongest competitor. Notably, on the Default and Magic datasets, it even matches or exceeds real-data performance, highlighting the high fidelity and utility of our synthetic data. In contrast, models like TabDDPM and CoDi fail notably on certain datasets (e.g., News), leading to large errors.

Table 2. F1 (classification task) and R2 (regression task) scores of Machine Learning Efficiency. ↑ (↓) indicates that the higher (lower) the score, the better the performance. Results are reported on both balanced and class-imbalanced versions of the datasets.

Data Type	Method	Adult F1↑	Default F1↑	Magic F1↑	Obesity F1↑	Bean F1↑	Beijing R2↑	News R2↑	King R2↑	Average Gap %
	Real	0.709±.004	0.467±.004	0.837±.005	0.968±.002	0.934±.001	0.822±.003	0.774±.001	0.871±.002	0.0%
Balanced Dataset	CTGAN	0.624±.011	0.406±.004	0.673±.006	0.172±.001	0.872±.008	0.196±.001	-0.145±.001	0.572±.002	46.0%
	TVAE	0.609±.003	0.345±.006	0.700±.014	0.377±.001	0.886±.009	0.321±.002	-0.356±.001	0.758±.002	43.6%
	CTABGAN+	0.642±.009	0.356±.004	0.644±.004	0.353±.001	0.912±.005	0.496±.001	-0.323±.001	0.817±.006	31.2%
	TabDDPM	0.657±.002	0.446±.003	0.807±.002	0.922±.014	0.923±.007	0.675±.002	–	0.690±.002	9.19%
	CoDi	0.560±.009	0.214±.002	0.801±.007	0.709±.012	0.921±.004	0.453±.001	–	0.808±.002	23.4%
	Tabsyn	0.664±.003	0.431±.002	0.819±.005	0.884±.003	0.922±.006	0.629±.006	0.121±.003	0.856±.001	17.5%
	ConDTab	**0.669±.002**	**0.473±.001**	**0.837±.003**	**0.949±.003**	**0.931±.001**	**0.769±.008**	**0.122±.001**	**0.862±.004**	**13.17%**
	Real	0.575±.001	0.402±.001	0.653±.002	0.756±.001	0.909±.001	–	–	–	0.0%
Imbalanced Dataset	CTGAN	0.501±.006	0.214±.002	0.549±.011	0.292±.004	0.755±.006	–	–	–	33.46%
	TVAE	0.463±.008	0.194±.003	0.515±.002	0.482±.004	0.814±.010	–	–	–	27.80%
	CTABGAN+	0.520±.002	0.220±.006	0.562±.004	0.517±.001	0.825±.004	–	–	–	21.92%
	TabDDPM	0.519±.008	0.318±.004	0.573±.004	0.522±.002	0.842±.009	–	–	–	16.24%
	CoDi	0.442±.007	0.264±.002	0.528±.001	0.472±.004	0.790±.009	–	–	–	25.45%
	Tabsyn	0.524±.002	0.237±.001	0.584±.001	0.539±.003	0.868±.003	–	–	–	18.73%
	ConDTab	**0.526±.002**	**0.401±.001**	**0.681±.003**	**0.667±.001**	**0.873±.002**	–	–	–	**4.46%**

Extended MLE Evaluation Under Class Imbalance. Similarly, We further extend the MLE evaluation under class imbalance by training the generative model on the minority-class dataset and generating data with the same class distribution. The synthetic data is then used to train a classifier or regressor, following the standard MLE evaluation procedure.

From Table 2(Imbal.), we observe that most baseline models suffer a significant performance drop across both classification (F1). For instance, the average performance gap from real data increases to 25.45% for CoDi and 18.73% for Tabsyn, indicating their limited ability to recover the minority class distribution. In contrast, ConDTab demonstrates the smallest average gap of only 4.46%, significantly outperforming all baselines under class imbalance.

4.4 Privacy

The Distance to Closest Record (DCR) is used to evaluate the privacy of synthetic data, defined as the 5th percentile of the L2 distances between synthetic samples and their nearest real data points. Higher DCR implies stronger privacy, but improved downstream performance often increases privacy risk. Therefore, based on the joint reporting of DCR and F1(R2) score, we use CTGAN as a reference baseline and propose the average F1 gain per 0.001 DCR reduction as a metric (F1/DCR) to assess the privacy-utility trade-off.

As shown in Table 3, ConDTab achieves lower DCR values on three types of datasets, indicating closer alignment with real data and thus higher privacy risk. Despite this, it delivers the best downstream performance, outperforming all baselines. ConDTab achieves consistently high F1-to-DCR ratios, while CTABGAN+ shows peaks but lacks stability, indicating that ConDTab yields greater utility gains per unit of privacy loss. In contrast, models like CTGAN offer stronger privacy but much lower utility. Overall, ConDTab achieves a better balance between privacy and utility, demonstrating strong practical value.

Table 3. Comparison of privacy risk (↑ for DCR) and ML efficiency (↑ for F1 or R2). Utility Gain per Privacy Loss (↑ for ML/DCR, $\times 10^{-2}$) represents the average F1 or R2 score improvement per 0.01 increase in DCR. CTGAN, with relatively high DCR and low F1 or R2, is included as a reference baseline.

Methods	Magic			Bean			King		
	DCR ↑	ML ↑	ML/DCR ↑	DCR ↑	ML ↑	ML/DCR ↑	DCR ↑	ML ↑	ML/DCR ↑
CTGAN	**0.078**	0.673	0.000	**0.196**	0.872	0.000	**0.128**	0.572	0.000
TVAE	0.044	0.700	0.0794	0.082	0.886	0.127	0.060	0.758	2.735
CTABGAN+	0.065	0.644	-2.231	0.034	0.912	0.247	0.102	0.817	**9.423**
TabDDPM	0.048	0.807	4.467	0.029	0.923	0.305	0.067	0.690	1.934
CoDi	0.046	0.801	4.000	0.030	0.921	0.295	0.062	0.808	3.576
Tabsyn	0.046	0.819	4.562	0.028	0.922	0.298	0.056	0.856	3.944
ConDTab	0.043	**0.837**	**4.686**	0.027	**0.931**	**0.349**	0.052	**0.862**	3.816

5 Conclusions

In this work, we proposed ConDTab, a conditional generative model for tabular data that addresses challenges in modeling heterogeneous features and generating minority-class samples. By combining a Transformer-based VAE with self- and cross-sample attention, ConDTab captures inter-feature and inter-sample dependencies within a unified latent space. A condition fusion diffusion mechanism further enhances class-conditional generation while preserving global distributional consistency. Extensive experiments show that ConDTab outperforms baselines in distribution fidelity, downstream performance, and privacy control, providing a robust solution for high-quality conditional tabular data synthesis.

References

1. Bahri, D., Jiang, H., Tay, Y., Metzler, D.: Scarf: self-supervised contrastive learning using random feature corruption. arXiv preprint arXiv:2106.15147 (2021)
2. Giuffrè, M., Shung, D.L.: Harnessing the power of synthetic data in healthcare: innovation, application, and privacy. NPJ Digit. Med. **6**(1), 186 (2023)
3. Gui, J., Sun, Z., Wen, Y., Tao, D., Ye, J.: A review on generative adversarial networks: algorithms, theory, and applications. IEEE Trans. Knowl. Data Eng. **35**(4), 3313–3332 (2021)
4. Ho, J., Jain, A., Abbeel, P.: Denoising diffusion probabilistic models. Adv. Neural. Inf. Process. Syst. **33**, 6840–6851 (2020)
5. Hoogeboom, E., Nielsen, D., Jaini, P., Forré, P., Welling, M.: Argmax flows and multinomial diffusion: learning categorical distributions. Adv. Neural. Inf. Process. Syst. **34**, 12454–12465 (2021)
6. Jolicoeur-Martineau, A., Fatras, K., Kachman, T.: Generating and imputing tabular data via diffusion and flow-based gradient-boosted trees. In: International Conference on Artificial Intelligence and Statistics, pp. 1288–1296. PMLR (2024)
7. Jordon, J., Yoon, J., Van Der Schaar, M.: Pate-GAN: generating synthetic data with differential privacy guarantees. In: International Conference on Learning Representations (2018)
8. Kim, J., Lee, C., Park, N.: STASY: score-based tabular data synthesis. arXiv preprint arXiv:2210.04018 (2022)
9. Kotelnikov, A., Baranchuk, D., Rubachev, I., Babenko, A.: TabdDPM: modelling tabular data with diffusion models. In: International Conference on Machine Learning, pp. 17564–17579. PMLR (2023)
10. Lederrey, G., Hillel, T., Bierlaire, M.: DatGAN: integrating expert knowledge into deep learning for synthetic tabular data. arXiv preprint arXiv:2203.03489 (2022)
11. Lee, C., Kim, J., Park, N.: Codi: Co-evolving contrastive diffusion models for mixed-type tabular synthesis. In: International Conference on Machine Learning. pp. 18940–18956. PMLR (2023)
12. Liu, T., Qian, Z., Berrevoets, J., van der Schaar, M.: Goggle: generative modelling for tabular data by learning relational structure. In: The Eleventh International Conference on Learning Representations (2023)
13. Peebles, W., Xie, S.: Scalable diffusion models with transformers. In: Proceedings of the IEEE/CVF International Conference on Computer Vision, pp. 4195–4205 (2023)

14. Schreyer, M., Sattarov, T., Sim, A., Wu, K.: IMB-DinDiff: conditional diffusion models for class imbalance synthesis of financial tabular data. In: Proceedings of the 5th ACM International Conference on AI in Finance, pp. 617–625 (2024)
15. Somepalli, G., Goldblum, M., Schwarzschild, A., Bruss, C.B., Goldstein, T.: Saint: improved neural networks for tabular data via row attention and contrastive pre-training. arXiv preprint arXiv:2106.01342 (2021)
16. Suh, N., Lin, X., Hsieh, D.Y., Honarkhah, M., Cheng, G.: AutoDiff: combining auto-encoder and diffusion model for tabular data synthesizing. arXiv preprint arXiv:2310.15479 (2023)
17. Suh, N., et al.: TimeAutoDiff: combining autoencoder and diffusion model for time series tabular data synthesizing. arXiv preprint arXiv:2406.16028 (2024)
18. Villaizán-Vallelado, M., Salvatori, M., Segura, C., Arapakis, I.: Diffusion models for tabular data imputation and synthetic data generation. arXiv preprint arXiv:2407.02549 (2024)
19. Wang, Z., Sun, J.: TransTab: learning transferable tabular transformers across tables. Adv. Neural. Inf. Process. Syst. **35**, 2902–2915 (2022)
20. Xu, L., Skoularidou, M., Cuesta-Infante, A., Veeramachaneni, K.: Modeling tabular data using conditional GAN. In: Advances in Neural Information Processing Systems, vol. 32 (2019)
21. Yoon, J., Zhang, Y., Jordon, J., Van der Schaar, M.: VIME: extending the success of self-and semi-supervised learning to tabular domain. Adv. Neural. Inf. Process. Syst. **33**, 11033–11043 (2020)
22. Zhang, H., et al.: Mixed-type tabular data synthesis with score-based diffusion in latent space. arXiv preprint arXiv:2310.09656 (2023)
23. Zhao, Z., Kunar, A., Birke, R., Van der Scheer, H., Chen, L.Y.: CTAB-GAN+: enhancing tabular data synthesis. Front. Big Data **6**, 1296508 (2024)

SentiAug: Adaptive Keywords Replacement and Confidence-Guided Self-training Selection for Robust Sentiment Classification

Luyuan Yang[1], Yan Chu[1(✉)], Qingchao Zhao[2(✉)], Hanlin Wang[3], Ximeng Zhao[1], and Zhong Chu[4]

[1] Harbin Engineering University, Harbin, China
chuyan@hrbeu.edu.cn
[2] Shenzhen Polytechnic University, Shenzhen, China
zhaoqc418@szpu.edu.cn
[3] MEDI GROUP STOCK LIMITED, Foshan, China
[4] Tencent Technology Company Limited, Shenzhen, China

Abstract. Current data augmentation methods for sentiment analysis predominantly employ random text transformations, which fail to preserve the semantic importance of emotion-bearing words and often generate low-quality training samples. To address these limitations, we present SentiAug, a unified framework that combines adaptive keyword replacement with confidence-guided self-training for robust sentiment classification. Our approach introduces two key innovations: (1) **Keyword Replacement Data Augmentation (KRDA)**, which employs a self-attention mechanism to identify emotionally salient keywords and performs semantically-aware replacements that preserve sentiment polarity; and (2) **Confidence-guided Self-Training Selection (CSTS)**, a threshold-based framework that dynamically filters and labels augmented samples based on model confidence scores. We further propose the **Augmentation Rate (AR)**, a novel metric to quantify the semantic diversity of augmented datasets, providing theoretical insights into model robustness. Extensive experiments across multiple benchmark datasets demonstrate that SentiAug achieves state-of-the-art performance, improving sentiment classification accuracy.

Keywords: sentiment analysis · data augmentation · augmented data selection · self-training selection

1 Introduction

The burgeoning field of sentiment analysis, pivotal in deciphering the emotional undertones of multimedia content, has witnessed a paradigm shift with the advent of sophisticated deep learning techniques [1,2]. These techniques have revolutionized our ability to parse and interpret the vast and ever-expanding corpus of digital textual content, from social media posts and customer reviews [3] to subcultures that artfully articulate the intricacies of human feelings [4]. Central to the efficacy of these deep learning models in sentiment analysis is the availability of extensive and varied datasets. Data augmentation, a technique used to expand the size and diversity of training datasets artificially, has emerged as a crucial tool in this context [5]. It addresses the perennial challenge of data scarcity and imbalance, a common hurdle in training robust and nuanced sentiment analysis models.

Data augmentation has been predominantly applied in the realm of computer vision, where it is typically achieved through geometric transformations and image mixing techniques [6,7]. However, the discrete and variable-length nature of textual data, coupled with its relatively low tolerance to noise, renders traditional augmentation methods less effective. Unlike visual data, introducing noise into text can result in unintended semantic alterations, complicating the augmentation process. The completion of the text data augmentation work can currently be divided into two streams: direct text manipulation [8,9] and feature-level fusion [10,11]. The former includes techniques such as synonym replacement, random insertion, deletion, and word swapping, which modify the surface form of text while attempting to preserve meaning. The latter approach involves combining features from different samples at word or sentence levels to generate new instances. However, both paradigms suffer from critical limitations in sentiment analysis contexts. First, random transformations often neglect the emotional significance of specific words, potentially altering sentiment polarity through inappropriate substitutions. Second, existing methods lack principled approaches for quality control, often generating augmented samples with inconsistent or mislabeled sentiment orientations. Third, current techniques provide limited mechanisms for evaluating the semantic diversity of augmented data, making it difficult to assess their contribution to model robustness.

To address these limitations, we present SentiAug, a unified framework that combines adaptive keyword replacement with confidence-guided self-training for robust sentiment classification. Our approach introduces two key innovations: (1) Keyword Replacement Data Augmentation (KRDA), which employs self-attention mechanisms to identify emotionally salient keywords and performs semantically-aware replacements that preserve sentiment polarity as shown in Fig. 1; and (2) Confidence-guided Self-Training Selection (CSTS), a threshold-based framework for dynamic filtering and labeling of augmented samples. Additionally, we propose Augmentation Rate (AR) as a novel metric to quantify the semantic diversity of augmented datasets, providing theoretical insights into the relationship between data diversity and model robustness. Extensive experiments demonstrate that SentiAug achieves state-of-the-art performance while generating semantically diverse training samples, establishing new benchmarks for data augmentation in sentiment analysis.

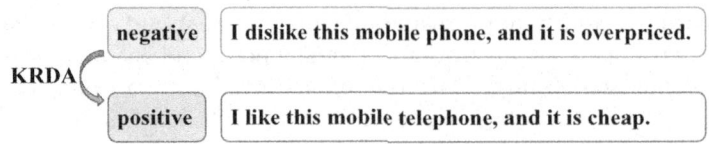

Fig. 1. An example of augmented samples generated by the KRDA method. Replace the top three words with WordAttention values, where red indicates antonym replacement and blue indicates synonym replacement.

2 Related Work

Text Data Augmentation. Text data augmentation has become a fundamental technique in natural language processing for addressing data scarcity and improving model generalization. Existing approaches can be systematically categorized into several paradigms: token-level transformations such as Easy Data Augmentation (EDA) [9], character-level noise injection [12,13], and adversarial perturbations [14]; sentence-level mixing techniques like MixText [15], SeqMix [16], SSMix [17], and DropMix [18] that combine information from multiple instances through interpolation or feature fusion [10,19,20]; and generation-based methods employing back-translation [21,22] or large language models for controlled text generation. However, these methods exhibit critical limitations in sentiment analysis contexts: token-level transformations often treat all words equally, ignoring the disproportionate importance of emotion-bearing terms and potentially altering sentiment polarity through inappropriate substitutions; sentence-level mixing can dilute emotional signals by blending samples with different orientations; and generation-based approaches lack explicit mechanisms for preserving emotional consistency. Furthermore, existing work provides limited theoretical analysis of augmentation quality and diversity, focusing primarily on downstream performance without examining semantic properties or developing principled metrics for emotion-specific evaluation. Self-training, while showing promise in semi-supervised text classification through iterative expansion of labeled data with high-confidence predictions, remains underexplored in combination with data augmentation for sentiment analysis, where label quality is paramount for maintaining emotional consistency. Our work addresses these gaps by proposing a unified framework that combines emotion-aware data augmentation with confidence-guided self-training, specifically designed for the unique challenges of sentiment classification.

Augmented Data Selection. Recent research has specifically addressed data augmentation challenges in sentiment analysis contexts. Hsu et al. [23] explore combinations of sentence-level transformations, paraphrasing, and generation methods for sentiment datasets. Kapusta et al. [24] have demonstrated effectiveness in leveraging unlabeled data for model improvement. Sah et al. [25] address the class imbalance problem in textual datasets by extracting keywords from minority class documents and learning the statistical and semantic features of important contextual words. Our approach integrates confidence-guided sample selection and dynamic label assignment to ensure augmented data quality, establishing a robust framework that maintains both semantic diversity and label accuracy in sentiment-augmented datasets.

3 Methodology

3.1 Keyword Sentiment Polarity Replacement Data Augmentation

Text data is fundamentally composed of individual **terms** (specifically referring to distinct word types), each carrying its semantic information and contributing to a network of intricate semantic relationships. These relationships are not only evident between the textual inputs and their corresponding labels but also manifest within the interactions of each word item within the text. In response to this complexity, we introduce the Keyword sentiment polarity Replacement Data Augmentation (**KRDA**) method. This method leverages the self-attention mechanism to more effectively discern the significance of each term in the text. By analyzing the distribution of self-attention values, it identifies and selects words with higher importance scores as candidates for augmentation.

Given that both individual words and sentence structures significantly influence the classification of text data, our approach aims to balance these elements. We have devised a word-attention calculation method to determine the self-attention distribution value for each word unit within a sentence. The formula is delineated as follows:

$$\text{WordAttention}(\boldsymbol{Q}, \boldsymbol{K}) = \text{Softmax}\left(\frac{\boldsymbol{Q}\boldsymbol{K}^T}{\sqrt{d_k}}\right) \quad (1)$$

where $\boldsymbol{Q}$ represents the vector representation of each word item in the sentence, $\boldsymbol{K}^T$ represents the transposition of the sentence vector $\boldsymbol{K}$. Since the sentence is composed of multiple word items, the sentence vector $\boldsymbol{K}$ is the sum of all word item vectors in the sentence, $\sqrt{d_k}$ represents the dimension of the word vector, and adjusts the inner product of word attention calculation. The greater the dot product between the term vector and the sentence vector, the stronger the correlation between them. We select the top k items in the sentence, arranged in descending order of WordAttention value, as the augmentation targets for subsequent data augmentation operations.

In the context of emotion classification tasks, KRDA is stratified based on the type of keyword emotional polarity replacement. This process is categorized into two types: antonym replacement and synonym replacement. The objective is to generate text data with the opposite sentiment label compared to the original sample, as illustrated in Fig. 1. Specifically, this paper selects words with high WordAttention values, computed via word self-attention, as keywords for replacement. Antonym replacement data augmentation is then performed by finding antonyms for these keywords using the WordNet, providing the model with augmented data of opposite polarity to the original samples for training. The keywords, identified based on WordAttention values, are grouped into antonym clusters. For augmentation, a word is randomly selected from these clusters and used for replacement, thereby enhancing the diversity of the augmented sample. This approach aligns with the fundamental goal of data augmentation, creating high-quality adversarial samples that challenge and improve model robustness.

When certain keywords lack antonyms, we turn to synonym replacement to maintain the efficacy of the augmentation. In such cases, synonyms are randomly selected from a predefined set to facilitate data augmentation, which ensures the augmentation process is not hindered by the absence of antonyms. Moreover, we introduce an antonym replacement counter to keep track of whether antonym substitution has occurred in a given text. If an antonym substitution is made, the label of the augmented sample is set to the opposite of the original. This systematic approach allows for a nuanced augmentation process that respects the semantic integrity of the text while expanding the emotional spectrum.

3.2 Confidence-Guided Self-training Selection

Considering the accuracy of the augmented sample, we propose Confidence-guided Self-Training Selection(**CSTS**), a threshold-based Self-Training augmented data Selection framework for augmented sample labeling and filtering. The model consists of three necessary modules: a data augmentation module, a self-training label setting module, and an augmented data selection module. Various standard methods can be used as data augmentation methods and training models for the framework.

For the given training set $\{(x, y)\}_i^N$, where x_i represents text input, and y_i is the golden label. The data augmentation module generates candidate samples. The augmented sample set $\{\hat{x}_i\}_i^{N'}$ to be labeled are generated by using this method.

Using the original dataset to train an initial classifier f, the self-training model relies on the pre-trained initial classifier to set labels for the generated augmented samples. The predicted label $\tilde{y}_i = f(\hat{x}_i)$ is obtained through this model.

Since the accuracy of the initial classifier cannot guarantee that all samples can be correctly classified, threshold selection is performed on the augmented samples to maximize the accuracy of training samples. Here, the threshold is set to g. For the augmented sample $\hat{x}_i$, the predicted label $\tilde{y}_i$ is obtained after passing the initial classifier. The augmented sample is selected with the confidence level of $\hat{p}(\tilde{y}_i \mid \hat{x}_i) \geq g$ to retain the prediction. Label $\tilde{y}_i$ serve as pseudo-label $\hat{y}_i$ and participate in subsequent model training, providing powerful data support for deep neural networks. After the augmented data are selected, the classifier f is retrained by mixing the qualified augmented samples with the original samples to obtain the final text classification model M.

3.3 Keyword Sentiment Polarity Replacement Augmentation in Multi-class Datasets

The KRDA method proposes to replace keywords with words with opposite emotional polarity in sentiment analysis tasks. This method considers the emotional polarity of keywords, which can effectively increase the semantic coverage and diversity of augmented samples. The KRDA method sets labels for the generated augmented samples based on the value of the antonym replacement counter. The basis of the label setting is relatively single, which may lead to the inability to assign accurate labels to multi-classification augmented samples, damage the quality of samples, and affect the subsequent training of the model.

Using KRDA as the CSTS framework data augmentation method, which is called SentiAug, can effectively achieve a more fine-grained label setting. This method enables keyword sentiment polarity replacement augmentation to be applied to multi-class sentiment analysis datasets. The overall structure of the SentiAug is shown in Fig. 2. The label of the augmented sample is set by a semi-supervised method and will no longer be limited by manual labeling.

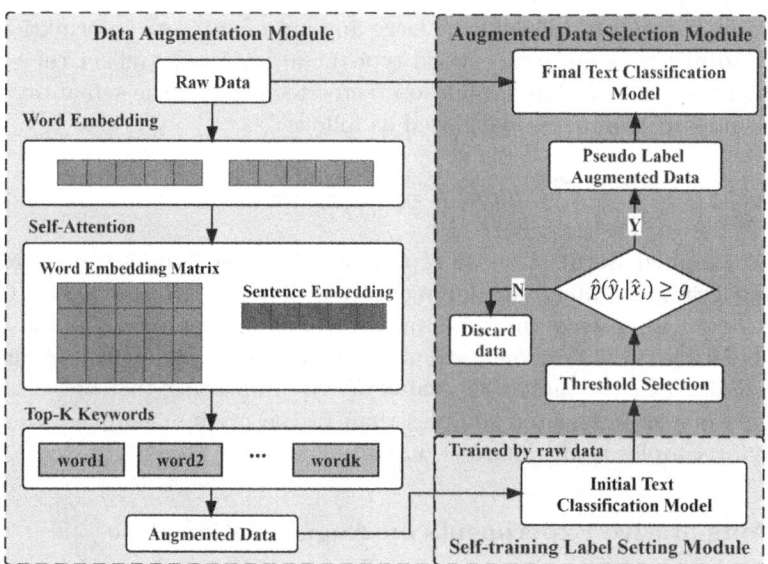

Fig. 2. SentiAug framework.

4 Experiments

4.1 Experiment Settings

The KRDA method is verified on three public binary sentiment analysis datasets. They are MR dataset [26], CR dataset [27] and SST-2 dataset [28], which all contain positive and negative sentiment polarities. A ten-fold cross-validation method is used to divide the datasets. Considering the short length and concentrated keywords in these datasets, which primarily consist of movie and product reviews, we selected the top three items in each sentence as keywords. We test the algorithm's performance under various data scarcity situations by using different sizes of datasets.

In our experiments, we compare the KRDA method with the current standard data augmentation methods, such as EDA [9] and AEDA [8]. We chose the KRDA method as the augmentation method and the CNN model as the classification model in the STS framework, called KRSTS-CNN. We compare KRSTS-CNN with text classification models with the Mixture models [29,30](including BGRU-CNN and CNN_BiLSTM_Attention). We also conduct comparative experiments with other models, and more details can be seen in the supplementary materials.

4.2 Augmented Data Diversity Evaluation Factor

We propose a new factor to evaluate the diversity of augmented samples - **Augmentation Rate(AR)**. Due to the large amount of semantic information in the text, the total number of items (word types) can intuitively reflect the semantic richness of the dataset. The evaluation factor to measure the semantic richness of the augmented sample is calculated as follows:

$$AR = \frac{ATC - OTC}{OTC} \qquad (2)$$

ATC (Augmented Terms Count) represents the total number of items in all augmented samples after data augmentation of the text, and OTC (Original Terms Count) represents the total number of items contained in the original sample before text data augmentation. Due to the fixed value of OTC, the larger the value of ATC, the higher the value of AR, indicating that there are more new terms in the augmented samples than in the original samples. Hence, the diversity of samples is also more abundant.

4.3 Comparative Experiments on Augmentation Rate

AEDA augments data by inserting punctuations, which cannot achieve the effect of enhancing the richness of the augmented samples. We mainly evaluate the augmentation rate of EDA and KRDA.

Table 1 shows that EDA and KRDA methods introduce new item information to the augmented samples. Observing the OTC and AR of the datasets, it can be found that the more initial items in the original dataset, the weaker the augmentation effectiveness of the EDA method. In contrast, the KRDA method has a better term augmentation effectiveness on the three datasets. On the CR, SST-2 and MR datasets, the KRDA method achieves an AR of 17.92%, 19.22% and 17.60%, respectively. In MR, the dataset with the most initial terms, the KRDA

Table 1. The augmentation rate of word in the augmented samples

Dataset	OTC	EDA$_{AR}$(%)	KRDA$_{AR}$(%)
CR	9654	14.97	**17.92**
MR	21425	7.57	**17.60**
SST-2	17574	12.97	**19.22**

method improves the AR over the EDA method by more than ten percentage points, proving the superior performance of the method on large datasets.

EDA introduces new terms through the synonym method, and the semantics of the augmented samples generated by this method remain unchanged. Especially when the initial number of items in the dataset is large, it is difficult to augment the rich corpus in a real sense. However, the KRDA method considers both synonym and antonym substitution to enrich the augmented samples. The introduction of antonyms, as a completely new corpus compared to the original semantics, truly enriches the semantics of the augmented sample items, rather than just reflecting it at the quantitative level.

4.4 Comparison with Augmented Dataset Size

The number of training samples influences the effectiveness of deep learning models. The essence of data augmentation is to expand the scale of dataset by performing augmentation operations in the case of insufficient data. To verify the effectiveness of the augmented data generated by the fusion of the KRDA method, we conduct comparative experiments with other data augmentation methods on multiple datasets of different scales. The percentage distribution of {1, 5, 10, 20, 30, 40, 50, 60, 70, 80, 90, 100} is the basis for dividing the dataset size. The number of augmented samples generated by EDA and AEDA methods is 4 times and 2 times that of KRDA method. Figure 3 shows each data augmentation method's classification performance at different sizes in the CR, MR, and SST-2 datasets. We also set up a no-augmented dataset as a control to ensure that the experiment is rigorous and reliable.

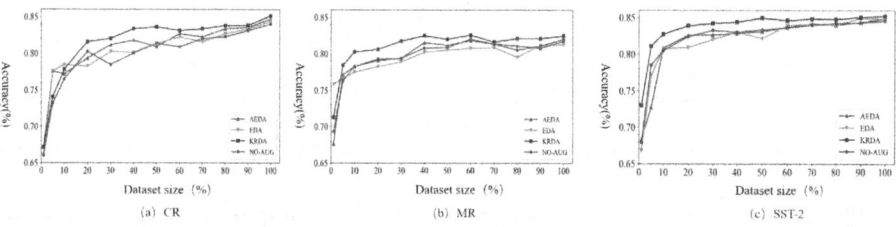

Fig. 3. The classification performance of data augmentation methods under different sizes of each dataset

We draw the following conclusions: the training effectiveness of the model using the data augmentation method is more evident when the amount of data is scarce than when it is sufficient. In the case of extremely scarce data, KRDA has a slightly lower effect because the generated sample size is less than the other two methods. In other cases, the KRDA method performs the best enhancement effect under each data size condition. This comparison experiment also fully demonstrates that the augmented data generated by the fusion of the KRDA method is effective for deep learning models and is superior to the EDA and AEDA methods in general.

4.5 Comparative Experiments on Classification Models

To verify the classification performance of the self-training text classification model KRSTS-CNN with an added augmented data selecting module, we compare it with the Mixture models on the CR and MR datasets. Meanwhile, we set up a model that removes the augmented data selection function to verify the effectiveness of augmented data selection. KRSTS-CNN uses a self-training model to set labels for augmented samples and does not perform threshold screening on augmented data. KRST-CNN-augonly means that the original data is not used during model training, but only the augmented data is used. In contrast, KRST-CNN-all means the model is trained using a mixture of original and augmented data.

Table 2. Accuracy (%) of different text classification models.

Model	CR	MR
CNN-static	84.1	81.0
CNN-non-static	84.3	81.5
RNN	82.3	77.2
BRNN	82.6	81.6
LSTM	78.4	75.9
BiLSTM	82.1	79.3
BGRU-CNN	86.0	82.3
CNN_BiLSTM_Attention	85.2	83.0
KRST-CNN-augonly	85.2	82.5
KRST-CNN-all	86.7	82.7
CSTS-CNN	**86.9**	**83.3**

Through the experimental results in Table 2, compared with the mixture models BGRU-CNN and CNN_BiLSTM_Attention based on CNN and RNN, our model is more accessible to implement and is used for better text feature extraction and learning capabilities. At the same time, the classification effect of KRST-CNN-all is better than KRST-CNN-augonly. Suppose only augmented samples are used to help model training. In that case, the role of original samples, which are opposite in polarity to the augmented samples, will be ignored, making the model unable to utilize the antonymous relationships between terms during the training process better, and the model cannot learn text more effectively—semantic information in the data. In addition, the volume of training data also has a corresponding impact on model accuracy. Adding raw data to participate in model training can effectively expand the size of training samples, provide sufficient corpus information for model training, and further improve text classification performance. CSTS-CNN includes an augmented data selection module, which provides original data support for the model during the training process and selects augmented data to ensure the quality of training samples. CSTS-CNN performs better than the hybrid text classification model without the augmented data selection module and the self-training text classification model KRST-CNN. It achieves good text classification performance on both CR and MR datasets, reaching the highest accuracy (86.9% and 83.3%).

4.6 Data Selection Threshold Settings

To obtain the optimal CSTS-CNN model, setting an appropriate threshold for the module is necessary to provide high-quality augmented data for future model training. We discuss the threshold setting in the augmented data selecting module on both the CR and MR datasets. In binary classification datasets, when the class prediction probability is 0.5, it indicates that the current sample has an equal probability of being assigned to either class, thus failing to achieve class distinction. Therefore, to effectively filter augmented data, this paper sets the initial value of threshold g in the augmented data selection module to 0.55. Subsequently, the threshold g is cumulatively increased by increments of 0.05. Since a class prediction probability of 1 is a relatively extreme case for label setting, its approximate value of 0.99 is chosen as the filtering threshold.

Table 3. The classification accuracy of CSTS-CNN model under different thresholds. Count represents the number of augmented samples after filtering by the current threshold, and Drop_rate represents the proportion of discarded samples to the total augmented samples.

		org	0.55	0.60	0.65	0.70	0.75	0.80	0.85	0.95	0.99
CR	Count	3666	3590	3531	3451	3388	3314	3241	3123	2780	2139
	Drop_rate	0	2.07%	3.68%	5.86%	7.58%	9.60%	11.59%	14.81%	24.17%	41.65%
	Accuracy	85.14%	86.25%	85.58%	85.58%	85.14%	85.58%	**86.91%**	85.58%	86.47%	85.58%
MR	Count	8527	8341	8157	7967	7780	7576	7305	7015	5919	4242
	Drop_rate	0	2.18%	4.34%	6.57%	8.76%	11.15%	14.33%	17.73%	30.59%	50.25%
	Accuracy	81.79%	**82.39%**	81.83%	81.83%	81.83%	81.64%	81.08%	81.46%	81.74%	82.20%

Table 3 shows that the number of qualified amplification samples decreases as the threshold increases, the number of discarded augmentation data at high thresholds is more significant than that at low threshold screening, and the number of amplification data discarded when the threshold is set at an intermediate value is more reasonable and the accuracy of the trained model is the highest. The setting of threshold g needs to weigh the impact of sample diversity and label confidence. When the threshold g is low, the criteria for screening the amplification samples are too low, and lower-quality data may also have a bad impact on training the classification model. When the threshold g is too high, a large proportion of amplified data is discarded, which is not conducive to ensuring sample diversity in the dataset. When the threshold g is a middle value, the augmented samples can maintain a high sample diversity and label confidence rate, and the model can achieve good classification performance when trained with such augmented data.

5 Conclusion

We presented SentiAug, a unified framework combining emotion-aware data augmentation with confidence-guided self-training for robust sentiment classification. Our approach contributes three key innovations: Keyword Replacement Data Augmentation (KRDA) leveraging self-attention for semantically-aware keyword replacement while preserving sentiment polarity; Confidence-guided Self-Training Selection (CSTS) using adaptive thresholding for dynamic sample filtering; and Augmentation Rate (AR) metric quantifying semantic diversity with theoretical insights into augmentation quality. Extensive experiments show SentiAug achieves state-of-the-art performance across sentiment analysis benchmarks, significantly outperforming existing methods. The framework provides both practical improvements and theoretical contributions through principled emotion-aware sample generation and adaptive threshold selection. Future work will extend this approach to broader emotion-driven NLP tasks and explore theoretical bounds of augmentation-based robustness.

References

1. Yang, J., Yu, Y., Niu, D., Guo, W., Xu, Y.: Confede: contrastive feature decomposition for multimodal sentiment analysis. In: ACL, pp. 7617–7630 (2023)
2. Tailored text augmentation for sentiment analysis. Expert Syst. Appl. **205**, 117605 (2022)
3. Lin, V., Morency, L.P., Ben-Michael, E.: Text-transport: toward learning causal effects of natural language. In: EMNLP, pp. 1288–1304 (2023)
4. Wang, Z., He, S., Xu, G., Ren, M.: Will sentiment analysis need subculture? A new data augmentation approach. J. Am. Soc. Inf. Sci. **75**(6), 655–670 (2024)
5. Yu, Y., Zhang, D.: Few-shot multi-modal sentiment analysis with prompt-based vision-aware language modeling. In: ICME, pp. 1–6 (2022)
6. Verma, V., et al.: Manifold mixup: better representations by interpolating hidden states. In: ICML, pp. 6438–6447 (2019)

7. Jiang, S., et al.: Explainable text classification via attentive and targeted mixing data augmentation. In: IJCAI, pp. 5085–5094 (2023)
8. Karimi, A., Rossi, L., Prati, A.: Aeda: an easier data augmentation technique for text classification. In: EMNLP, pp. 2748–2754 (2021)
9. Wei, J., Zou, K.: Eda: Easy data augmentation techniques for boosting performance on text classification tasks. In: EMNLP-IJCNLP, pp. 6382–6388 (2019)
10. Guo, H., Mao, Y., Zhang, R.: Augmenting data with mixup for sentence classification: an empirical study. arXiv preprint arXiv:1905.08941 (2019)
11. Dai, H., et al.: AugGPT: leveraging ChatGPT for text data augmentation. IEEE Trans. Big Data (2025)
12. Belinkov, Y., Bisk, Y.: Synthetic and natural noise both break neural machine translation. In: ICLR (2018)
13. Li, G., Wang, H., Ding, Y., Zhou, K., Yan, X.: Data augmentation for aspect-based sentiment analysis. Int. J. Mach. Learn. Cybern. **14**(1), 125–133 (2023)
14. Zhang, Y., Jiang, M., Meng, Y., Zhang, Y., Han, J.: Pieclass: weakly-supervised text classification with prompting and noise-robust iterative ensemble training. In: EMNLP, pp. 12655–12670 (2023)
15. Chen, J., Yang, Z., Yang, D.: Mixtext: linguistically-informed interpolation of hidden space for semi-supervised text classification. In: ACL, pp. 2147–2157 (2020)
16. Zhang, R., Yu, Y., Zhang, C.: Seqmix: augmenting active sequence labeling via sequence mixup. In: EMNLP, pp. 8566–8579 (2020)
17. Yoon, S., Kim, G., Park, K.: Ssmix: saliency-based span mixup for text classification. In: ACL-IJCNLP, pp. 3225–3234 (2021)
18. Kong, F., Zhang, R., Guo, X., Mensah, S., Mao, Y.: Dropmix: a textual data augmentation combining dropout with mixup. In: EMNLP, pp. 890–899 (2022)
19. Chen, J., Zhang, R., Luo, Z., Hu, C., Mao, Y.: Adversarialword dilution as text data augmentation in low-resource regime. In: AAAI, pp. 12626–12634 (2023)
20. Kim, H.H., Woo, D., Oh, S.J., Cha, J.W., Han, Y.S.: ALP: data augmentation using lexicalized PCFGS for few-shot text classification. In: AAAI, pp. 10894–10902 (2022)
21. Beddiar, D.R., Jahan, M.S., Oussalah, M.: Data expansion using back translation and paraphrasing for hate speech detection. Online Soc. Netw. Media **24**, 100153 (2021)
22. Taheri, A., Zamanifar, A., Farhadi, A.: Enhancing aspect-based sentiment analysis using data augmentation based on back-translation. Int. J. Data Sci. Anal. 1–26 (2024)
23. Hsu, T.W., Chen, C.C., Huang, H.H., Chen, H.H.: Semantics-preserved data augmentation for aspect-based sentiment analysis. In: EMNLP, pp. 4417–4422 (2021)
24. Kapusta, J., Držík, D., Šteflovič, K., Nagy, K.S.: Text data augmentation techniques for word embeddings in fake news classification. IEEE Access **12**, 31538–31550 (2024)
25. Sah, A., Abulaish, M.: Deepada: an attention-based deep learning framework for augmenting imbalanced textual datasets. In: Proceedings of the 19th International Conference on Natural Language Processing (ICON), pp. 318–327 (2022)
26. Hu, M., Liu, B.: Mining and summarizing customer reviews. In: ACM SIGKDD, pp. 168–177 (2004)
27. Pang, B., Lee, L.: Seeing stars: exploiting class relationships for sentiment categorization with respect to rating scales. In: ACL, pp. 115–124 (2005)
28. Socher, R., et al.: Recursive deep models for semantic compositionality over a sentiment treebank. In: EMNLP, pp. 1631–1642 (2013)

29. Feng, Z., Rongyu, L.: Convolutional neural network model for text classification based on BGRU pooling. Comput. Sci. **45**(06), 235–240 (2018)
30. Wu, H., Yan, J., Huang, S., Li, R., Jiang, M.: Cnn_bilstm_attention mixture model for text classification. Comput. Sci. **47**(23-27+34) (2020)

Real-Time and Personalized Product Recommendations for Large E-Commerce Platforms

Matteo Tolloso[1](✉), Davide Bacciu[1], Shahab Mokarizadeh[2], and Marco Varesi[2]

[1] Department of Computer Science, University of Pisa, Pisa, Italy
matteo.tolloso@phd.unipi.it
[2] H&M - AI, Analytics and Data, Stockholm, Sweden

Abstract. We present a methodology to provide real-time and personalized product recommendations for large e-commerce platforms, specifically focusing on fashion retail. Our approach aims to achieve accurate and scalable recommendations with minimal response times, ensuring user satisfaction, leveraging Graph Neural Networks and parsimonious learning methodologies. Extensive experimentation with datasets from one of the largest e-commerce platforms demonstrates the effectiveness of our approach in forecasting purchase sequences and handling multi-interaction scenarios, achieving efficient personalized recommendations under real-world constraints.

Keywords: Recommendation Systems · Graph Neural Networks · Parsimonious Learning

1 Introduction

Recommendation systems support users in their discovery of products, especially in online retail, through integration of preferences, behaviors, and trends. In digital marketplaces aspects such as personalization and responsiveness are paramount to maintain a competitive edge [2]. These requirements pose strong methodological and technological challenges on the learning and predictive substrate underlying the recommendation system. On the one hand, the learning model should be able to dynamically and swiftly update to respond both to changing behaviors and trends at a population level, as well as to personalize recommendations to the (possibly short-term) history of the specific user. At the same time, aspects of responsiveness and efficiency cannot be overlooked to avoid affecting the user experience on the digital platform.

With such motivations in mind, we propose a novel graph-based recommendation system [4] designed purposely for a fashion item recommendation scenario, characterized by the large scale of the item repository (and hence the graph) and tight needs of few-shot-like personalization of the recommendation to the personal taste and stock availability. Our framework is designed to target, specifically: (i) near real-time recommendations during e-commerce navigation with response times in the order of few milliseconds; (ii) scalability with respect to the number of users and reduction of cold-start effects; (iii) continual recommendation adaptation based on stock availability, with a maximum delay of a few minutes; (iv) personalized recommendations integrating historical and current session engagement; (v) efficient continual training limiting resource usage to few GPU hours per week.

Our approach builds upon the use of Graph Neural Networks (GNNs) [1] to process articulated user-item interaction patterns within real-world recommendation systems [3,4]. We specifically tackle the open-problem of working with multi-relational graphs [14] in a continuous update scenario in large-scale deployments. Such a challenging scenario requires integrating powerful GNN models, that can effectively extract information from complex multi-relational graphs, with knowledge distillation [5], which enables the transfer of knowledge from the large GNN teacher to smaller and efficient personalized student models. This is complemented with the use of few-shot [15] and continual learning [18] methodologies to allow efficient adaptation to new data, with minimal use of samples and without forgetting past knowledge.

The key contributions of this work are as follows:

- We introduce a novel distillation framework where the GNN is used to produce on-the-fly efficient personalized models capable of providing user-tailored recommendations in the order of 1 ms (on CPU) and with limited memory fingerprint (700 kb).
- We introduce an efficient approach to continually personalize user recommendation models, requiring on average less than 100 ms to complete adaptation (on CPU).
- We provide an empirical validation of the effectiveness of our approach in two large-scale benchmarks using real-world data (one publicly available, one proprietary).

2 Parsimonious Continual Adaptation of Personalized Recommendation Models

We build on a graph-based representation of historical product data, where items are assumed to be associated with visual information describing its nature (i.e. a picture of the product). In particular, we consider a heterogeneous graph $\mathcal{G}$ where nodes correspond to products, while edges mark the fact that users interacted with both products. Given an edge between two products (nodes), p and q, this edge will be associated with a weight, $a_{p,q}^{c_i}$, that quantifies the intensity of the interaction between these products, i.e. the number of users that interacted with both products. Edges are also associated with a type c_i that corresponds to one of the following four interaction events: *co-clicked*, *co-favorite*, *co-cart*, and *co-purchased*. Each node p has attached an initial label h_p^0 that is a vectorial embedding of the product image, obtained through the pre-trained Convolutional Neural Network (CNN) Resnet-18 [8].

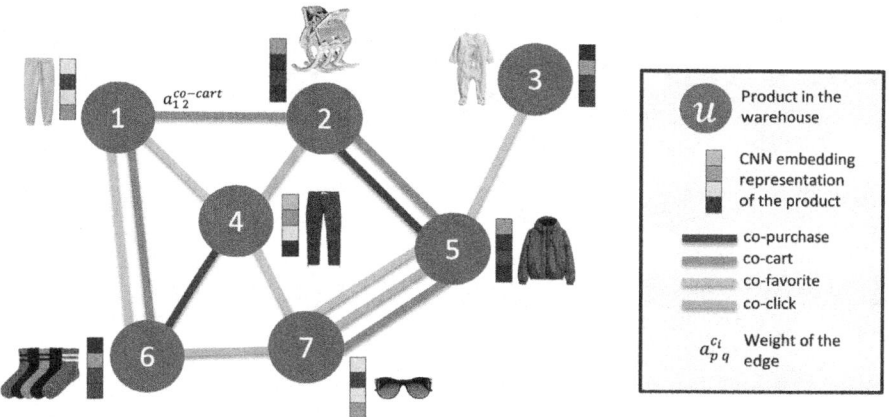

Fig. 1. Simplified example of a historical interaction graph used in our recommendation system. Nodes represent individual fashion products, each associated with visual embeddings derived from product images. Edges between nodes signify user interactions and are categorized into four interaction types: *co-clicked*, *co-favorite*, *co-cart*, and *co-purchased*. Each edge carries a weight proportional to the number of users who performed that specific interaction between the two products. The resulting heterogeneous graph encodes complex relationships among products, enabling the system to learn interaction patterns for personalized recommendations.

Figure 1 shows an illustrative example of the historical heterogeneous graph.

The overall architecture (Fig. 2) of our recommendation system comprises three components: (i) a *structural encoder*, (ii) an *attribute encoder*, and (iii) a personalized *meta model* for each user. The *structural encoder* processes the historical product graph using a Heterogeneous Graph Neural Network (HGNN) [20]. A Graph Neural Network (GNN) [1] is a machine learning architecture designed to handle graph-structured data. It employs a feedforward approach where each layer l generates node representation for a node p, named h_p^l, by aggregating information from neighboring nodes according to:

$$h_p^l = \Phi^l \left(h_p^{l-1}, \Psi \left(\{ \Omega^l(h_q^{l-1}) \mid q \in N_p \} \right) \right). \tag{1}$$

In this formula, N_p is the set of neighbors of node p, their representation in the layer $l-1$ is projected into a new space via the function Ω and aggregated into a single neighborhood representation using a permutation-invariant function Ψ (such as max, mean, or sum). Finally, the function Φ combines this aggregated neighborhood representation with the embedding of node p to produce the updated representation. Typically, Ω and Φ are Multi-Layer Perceptrons and the initial representation of a node p h_p^0 is the initial feature vector associated with the node. When dealing with heterogeneous graphs, a simple but effective approach to build an HGNN is to use multiple GNNs, one for each homogeneous subgraph within the heterogeneous graph, and combine the

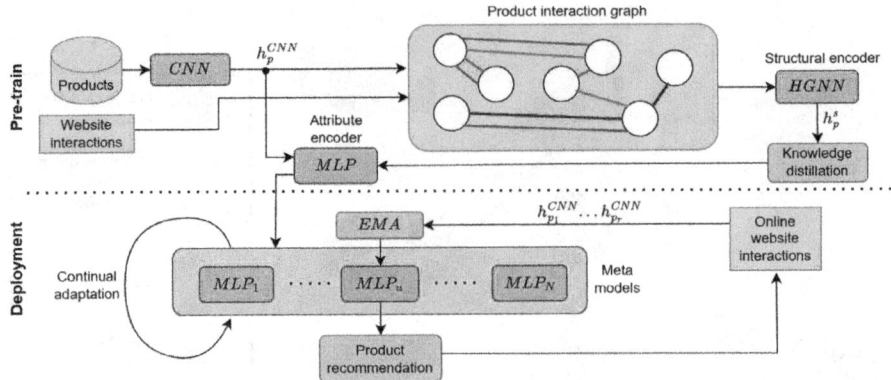

Fig. 2. Overall architecture of our proposed recommendation framework, consisting of three core components: (i) the *structural encoder (HGNN)*, which uses a Heterogeneous Graph Neural Network to process the historical interaction graph and capture intricate relational information between products; (ii) the *attribute encoder (Student MLP)*, a lightweight Multi-Layer Perceptron trained via knowledge distillation to approximate the HGNN embedding space using only product image embeddings; and (iii) the *personalized meta-model (Personal MLP)*, an individual user-specific version of the attribute encoder, continually fine-tuned on recent user interactions to personalize the embedding space. The system generates real-time product recommendations by efficiently finding the nearest neighbors to the dynamically updated user embedding.

multiple representations of a node p in each layer l [20]. The aggregation function is usually the mean, but more complex approaches exist [14].

The HGNN is trained via self-supervision similarly to [7]. The model learns to project the original product p representation h_p^{CNN} (obtained from the CNN) in an embedding space where similarly interacted articles are closer. For each node p the HGNN produces a structural embedding $h_p^s = HGNN(h_p^{CNN}, E_+)$, where E_+ are the edges of the graph, and its training is guided by the contrastive loss

$$\mathcal{L}_{cont}^{c_i} = \frac{1}{|E_+^{c_i}|} \sum_{(p,q) \in E_+^{c_i}} a_{p,q}^{c_i} ||h_p^s - h_q^s||_2^2 - \frac{1}{|E_-^{c_i}|} \sum_{(p,q) \in E_-^{c_i}} ||h_p^s - h_q^s||_2^2, \quad (2)$$

that is replicated for each different relation type c_i in the graph. Here, $E_-^{c_i}$ are negative edge samples (edges that are not in the graph) selected randomly with $|E_-^{c_i}| = |E_+^{c_i}|$, and $a_{p,q}^{c_i}$ is the weight of the edge between the nodes p and q. The final loss is:

$$L_{cont}^{tot} = \gamma_1 \times L_{cont}^{c_1} + \gamma_2 \times L_{cont}^{c_2} + \gamma_3 \times L_{cont}^{c_3} + \gamma_4 \times L_{cont}^{c_4}, \quad (3)$$

with γ_i hyper-parameters to assign importance to the different relation types c_i.

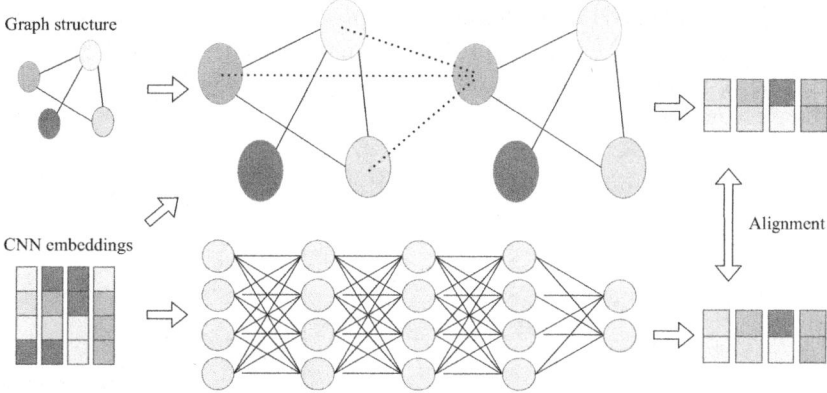

Fig. 3. Distillation process. On the upper part the GNN takes in input the CNN embeddings and the graph structure. On the bottom part the MLP takes in input only the CNN embeddings. The alignment loss pushes the two embeddings spaces to be similar. Note that the embeddings' dimensionality is also compressed by the two networks.

The HGNN serves as a teacher model to transfer knowledge to the lightweight student model, i.e. the *attribute encoder* (Fig. 3). The attribute encoder is a simple Multi-Layer Perceptron (MLP) that learns to map the original CNN embedding of the product into the embedding space generated by the HGNN (and that takes into consideration the relational inter-product knowledge) without having access to neighborhood information. From a recommendation systems perspective, such a student model is performing *hybrid filtering* [4] by integrating *content-based filtering* (the CNN embeddings) with *collaborative filtering* (the HGNN embeddings). Training of the student model minimizes the alignment loss

$$\mathcal{L}_{al} = \frac{1}{|V|} \sum_{p \in V} ||MLP(h_p^{CNN}) - HGNN(h_p^{CNN}, E_+)||_2^2, \qquad (4)$$

where $MLP(h_p^{CNN})$ is the embedding of the node p produced by the attribute encoder and V is the set of all the nodes in the graph.

The attribute encoder is then the model upon which we build the *meta-model* [17] for continuous personalization. Specifically, when a new user enters the shopping platform it is instantiated a personal copy of the attribute encoder (the meta-model). These personal MLPs project the products into a space that is continually adapted based on personal interactions with the website, and whose product embeddings are ultimately used to provide the personalized recommendations.

The recommendation process is very efficient: a user's representation is kept in memory as an Exponential Moving Average (EMA) of the user's interacted articles as

$$u_t = (1 - \alpha) \times u_{t-1} + \alpha \times MLP_u(h_{t,u}^{CNN}), u_0 = MLP_u(h_{0,u}^{CNN}), \qquad (5)$$

where $h_{t,u}^{CNN}$ is the CNN embedding of the product interacted by the user u at time t and $MLP_u(h_{t,u}^{CNN})$ is its projection made by the personal MLP of the user u. The K-nearest-neighbors to u_t, in the space projected by MLP_u, are the selected suggestions.

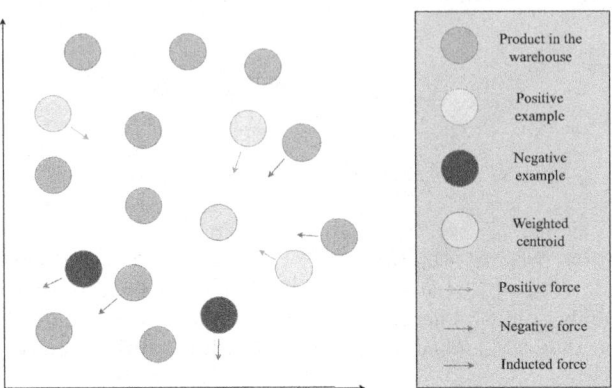

Fig. 4. Continual personalization process within the recommendation framework. When a user interacts with products (green points), the user's personal embedding space is adjusted so that these positively interacted items move closer to a calculated user preference centroid. Consequently, related yet unexplored products (nearby purple points) also shift within this personalized space, enhancing the likelihood that they become future recommendations. Products not interacted with (red points) serve as negative examples, guiding the model to maintain sufficient separation in the embedding space. This dynamic adjustment leverages recent user behavior to continuously refine personalized recommendations. (Color figure online)

To adapt the personal embeddings of user u, we collect a batch of interactions B_u and we calculate the weighted centroid h_u^{wc} of the CNN embeddings of interacted products h_{p+}^{CNN} as:

$$h_u^{wc} = \frac{1}{|B_u|} \sum_{(h_{p+}^{CNN}, w) \in B_u} h_{p+}^{CNN} \times w, \qquad (6)$$

where w weighs the importance of the interaction (for example purchase: 4, cart: 3, favorite: 2, click: 1). The centroid represents the current interest of the user. The next step brings positively interacted articles closer to the centroid and consequentially closer together. The hypothesis is that we are modifying the whole space in a way such that the related products, for the user's personal preference, are moved closer together. We also select negative examples h_{p-}^{CNN} among the products that the system proposes to the user but that are not interacted with. The process is depicted in Fig. 4. The adaptation of the user model MLP_u requires a few steps of SGD minimizing the triplet loss

$$\mathcal{L}_{tri} = \sum_{(h_{p+}^{CNN},\ h_{p-}^{CNN}) \in B_u} \max\left(0, \|MLP_u(h_{wc}) - MLP_u(h_{p+}^{CNN})\|_2^2\right.$$
$$\left. - \|MLP_u(h_{wc}) - MLP_u(h_{p-}^{CNN})\|_2^2 + \epsilon\right), \quad (7)$$

where the hyper-parameter ϵ, also named as "margin", has the effect of enforcing a minimum separation between positive and negative pairs in the embedding space preventing trivial solutions. The number of SGD update steps reflects the keenness to be pushing products closer. For instance, if all interactions in a batch are just click events, we may want to avoid the model changing too much; on the opposite, if all interactions are purchases we would like the model to project these articles very close together.

The underlying intuition of our method is that we are dynamically re-organizing the representation of products, particularly those unknown by the user, making it more likely to suggest those that will be appreciated, and doing so through a very efficient and scalable approach.

2.1 Technical Details

In Table 1 we report the computational and memory requirements to operate the system. The HGNN pre-training requires only a few hours of standard GPU computation; the response time for the recommendation part (1.5 ms) is compliant with our real-time objective, as well as the maximum memory occupancy of a few megabytes per user enables optimal scaling capability. It is fundamental to note that these phases are parallel and independent of each other; hence, the latency for the recommendations is unaffected by the time required for training and adapting the MLP. Additional details of how to maintain a constant memory occupation are discussed in Appendix A.1. For an example of an instantiation of the system, refer to Appendix A.2. We performed an exhaustive grid search to optimize hyperparameters for both the HGNN and the online personalization component, as described in the Appendix B.

Table 1. Range of frequency, time required, and memory required for each of the main parts of the system. The actual values depend on hyper-parameters such as the number of SGD steps and the batch size.[1]

	HGNN-MLP training (global)	MLP adaptation (per-user)	Recommendation (per-user)
Frequency	1–4 times/month	Every 1–9 interactions	At each interaction
Time	1.5 h (GPU)	3–150 ms (CPU)	1.5 ms (CPU)
Memory	16 GB (GPU)	2 MB	700 KB

Hardware configuration: Nvidia Tesla T4 16 GB GPU, AMD Epyc 16-core CPU, 32 GB RAM.

The framework is implemented in Python using Pytorch and Pytorch Geometric as main libraries.

3 Results

We assess our approach on a proprietary dataset, referred to as the "e-commerce dataset." For the sake of reproducibility, we also tested our model on a publicly available dataset released on Kaggle by H&M [10] for a global competition about personalization. The public dataset spans two years: from September 2018 to September 2020. It has 31 million transactions made by 1.3 million different users on 105,000 different articles; for each of those an image is available.

We simulate a realistic scenario by taking a temporal-based split, dividing the (simulated) past from the (simulated) future. The "simulated past" data are again split into train and validation in a user-based fashion. The training graph and the validation graph have in general different nodes and different edges since the users in the validation set may have interacted with a different set of articles compared with the ones in the training set. We used one week of data (simulated past) for training the HGNN and the following days (simulated future) for assessing recommendation and personalization in different scenarios: (i) day-by-day cold-start where at the end of each day the users' personalized spaces are deleted, (ii) multiple-weeks personalization, where the personalized embedding spaces are continuously adapted over time until the end of the tests. Three random weeks of data are sampled and used for pre-training (HGNN training) and for each of them, the following days are used for test (recommendations with continuous adaptation). The metrics used to assess the quality of the model are Precision, Recall, and F1 score. After each user's interaction, we predict K articles the user will buy, and the ground truth set is composed of the next T articles the user will actually buy. The values for K and T are set to 10 and 12 respectively, as it is common practice in these scenarios.

The results on the e-commerce dataset are shown in Table 2. The last-K baseline uses as a prediction for the next K purchases the last K interacted products. We also compared our approach with two of the most used recommendations systems in the literature: PinSage [19] and LightGCN [9]. Adapting these models to our use case is not straightforward, we discuss in details about the baselines in Appendix C. Table 2 shows that our model, after one week of adaptation, achieves the best results in F1 score. The high Precision and low Recall of LightGCN means that the model is accurate and conservative in its positive predictions but misses many true positive; its ability to find all relevant items (Recall) might be limited if those relevant items less connected in the interaction graph, or primarily discoverable through content features it doesn't use. In general a recommendation system with high Precision and low Recall is not optimal, as we discuss in more detail in Appendix C. It is worth noting that in our current experimental setting, adaptation is evaluated globally, with all user interactions constrained between fixed start and end dates. We hypothesize that adopting a more fine-grained approach, such as individually adapting for

Table 2. Performance comparison on the e-commerce dataset. All metrics (Precision, Recall, F1-score) are multiplied by 10^4 for readability. Standard deviations are reported. Best results are in **bold**. The last two columns show the F1-score improvement of each model relative to LightGCN and PinSage respectively.

Model/Baseline	Precision	Recall	F1-score	Improv. vs LightGCN	Improv. vs PinSage
Random Baseline	61	53	58	−74.7%	−80.2%
Last-K Baseline	174	145	158	−31.0%	−46.1%
LightGCN	**540**±39	147±6	229±4	-	−21.8%
PinSage	352±21	246±17	293±24	+28.0%	-
HGNN + Daily personalization	371±11	306±8	336±9	+46.7%	+14.7%
HGNN + 1 week personalization	448±61	**373**±51	**407**±56	+77.7%	+38.9%
HGNN + 2 weeks personalization	406±45	339±37	369±41	+61.1%	+25.9%
HGNN + 3 weeks personalization	389±45	324±38	354±41	+54.6%	+20.8%

one week starting from each user's first interaction, could further improve the resulting metrics.

Table 3. Performance comparison on the public dataset. All metrics (Precision, Recall, F1-score) are multiplied by 10^4 for readability. Standard deviations are reported. Best results are in **bold**. The 4th column is the F1 improvement with respect to the pretrained model (no personalization) and the 5th column is the F1 improvement with respect to the best public solution.

Model/Baseline	Precision	Recall	F1	Improv. no pers.	Improv. best
Random baseline	72	59	62	−77.5%	−76.3%
Best public solution [11]	289	241	262	−5.1%	-
HGNN No personalization	303±26	253±22	276±23	-	+5.3%
HGNN + Daily personalization	309±24	258±19	282±20	+2.2%	+7.6%
HGNN + 1 week personalization	**313**±20	260±18	284±18	+2.9%	+8.4%
HGNN + 2 weeks personalization	312±22	**285**±15	**298**±20	+8.0%	+13.7%
HGNN + 3 weeks personalization	**313**±22	260±18	284±20	+2.9%	+8.4%

In Table 3, we present the results obtained on the public dataset. All of our adapted models surpass the best publicly available solution [11]. The improvements over this baseline is more modest compared to the e-commerce dataset due to the limitations of this public dataset, which contains only purchase events, lacking richer user interaction signals such as add-to-cart, favorite, and click events. Additionally, it is important to highlight that the original Kaggle competition involved a different and simpler task: predicting a single set of K future purchases for each user based on their entire purchase history, without any time or memory constraints to compute the prediction, giving a strong advantage to non-real-time solutions.

3.1 Ablation Study

Table 4. Ablation study results for different configurations of our recommendation system on the e-commerce dataset. All metrics (Precision, Recall, F1-score) are multiplied by 10^4 for readability. Standard deviations are reported. Best results are in **bold**. The "Improv./Degrad." column shows the percentage change in F1-score relative to our "Complete" model HGNN + 1 week Personalization. The last two columns show the F1-score improvement relative to LightGCN and PinSage.

Model Configuration	Precision	Recall	F1-score	Improv./Degrad. vs Complete	Improv. vs LightGCN	Improv. vs PinSage
LightGCN	**540**±39	147±6	229±4	−43.7%	-	−21.8%
PinSage	352±21	246±17	293±24	−28.0%	+28.0%	-
HGNN + 1 week Personalization	448±61	**373**±51	**407**±56	-	+77.7%	+38.9%
No Personalization	336±15	280±12	305±14	−25.1%	+33.2%	+4.1%
No Pre-training	396±17	330±21	360±13	−11.6%	+57.2%	+22.9%
No Pre-training and No Personalization	224±7	196±22	209±19	−48.7%	−8.7%	−28.7%

To assess the contribution of each primary component within our proposed recommendation framework, we conducted a series of ablation studies. These experiments systematically remove parts of our architecture to isolate their impact on recommendation performance. We evaluate these ablated models on the e-commerce dataset using Precision, Recall, and F1-score as described in Sect. 3. In Table 4 the following configurations are evaluated:

No personalization (Cold-Start Performance). This configuration removes the continual adaptation mechanism (i.e., the Personal MLP is not fine-tuned during the user's session). Recommendations are generated using the user's session history (via EMA) projected by the global, pre-trained Student MLP.

No Pre-training (Continual personalization Only). In this setup, the personalized MLPs are initialized without any knowledge distillation from a pre-trained HGNN. The Personal MLPs are then continually adapted based on user interactions as in the full model.

No Pre-training and No personalization (CNN-EMA Baseline). This represents a minimal pipeline, serving as a strong baseline. It directly uses the raw CNN image embeddings of items. The user's current interest is represented by EMA of the CNN embeddings of items they have interacted with in their session. This configuration ablates both the graph-based pre-training and the adaptive MLP personalization.

The results in Table 4 highlight the need of both the HGNN pre-train and the continuous adaptation to user's preferences to achieves the best F1 score. Note that the Cold-Start (No Personalization) performance of our model is comparable to PinSage; in fact, in both cases, we have a pre-train phase via GNN and an EMA-style recommendation setting. Our model outperforms PinSage even without personalization phase likely due to the fact that we explicitly take into account multiple interaction types. Finally, the fact that LightGCN (that does not consider visual information) is surpassed by the simple CNN-EMA Baseline in terms of Recall suggests that in this recommendations scenario visual appearances are in general more important than global interaction patterns.

4 Conclusions

We proposed a novel scalable recommendation system exploiting a graph-based representation of historical interactions and continual adaptation of lightweight distilled models personalized to each user. Our pre-personalization model reaches competitive performance also for cold-start users, by exploiting the richness of representation of historical interactions. Knowledge distillation effectively transfers information to smaller models making the system faster and more memory-efficient, enabling real-time personalization for each user. The recommendation module is distance-based, which means that the latency is in the order of a few milliseconds and it is independent from the update time of the personalized models, which, however, requires only a few steps of SGD on a shallow MLP. Results show that the continuous adaptation is effective and enables us to perform more accurate predictions on future purchases than the best available solutions. Future work includes experimenting with a replay memory for each user to transfer the knowledge after the model is discarded. In fact, results show that the best life span for the personalized models is 1 or 2 weeks, after which the performance begins to degrade. An increased stability, for example, a higher regularization could increase the service life of the models at the price of a lower plasticity (and possibly a worse performance in the short term). A replay memory would also allow seasonal replay, for example when the summer season arrives we could use the navigation data from the same period of the past years to recommend products from a new collection that match the user's personal style.

A Additional Technical Details

A.1 Sampling

The graph can have tens of thousands of nodes and millions of edges, is therefore impractical to compute all the nodes' embedding in a single pass due to GPU memory constraints. In this regard, inspired by Hamilton et al. [6], we follow a sampling approach to build graph batches, in addition we also experimented a weighted sampling procedure based on the edges' weights described in Sect. 2:

1. The set of nodes is partitioned in batches such that each batch has *batch_size* nodes.
2. Starting from each node in the batch, iteratively sample some edges giving more probability to edges with higher weighs.

3. Add the nodes to the other end of the selected edges (and the edges themselves) to the graph batch.

The number of iterations and the number of edges to add at each iteration is described by the *num_neighbor* list, for example the list [3, 2] indicates to sample three edges for each node in the batch, and for each induced node sample two additional edges, and so add the two new nodes to the batch.

Only the edges used for the sampling process are added to the final batch graph, if there are other edges joining nodes in the batch, these are not considered in order to avoid an uncontrolled exponential increase of the edges.

At the end of the sampling procedure, the maximum number of edges in the batch E_b will be the product of the elements in the *num_neighbor* list and the maximum number of nodes will be $|E_b| * batch\_size$. Consequently, the adopted batch sampling strategy ensures that we have a constant predefined memory occupation whatever is the size of the graph.

A.2 Instantiation

One possible instantiation of the system is the following:

- The HGNN-MLP training is done at the end of each week with data from the week just ended. It will require 1.5 h but in the meantime the system continues working with the old MLPs instantiated for each user.
- When the HGNN-MLP training is complete, the new MLP is copied to all the users and the old ones are discarded.
- The user continues to navigate the website, every 5 interactions the MLP adaptation starts and lasts about 100 ms, in the meantime the user continues receiving recommendations with the not yet updated MLP model[1]. For each user, there is always one available MLP model. Since the role of the MLP is to project the CNN embeddings in a different space, this can be done in batch just after the MLP adaptation is complete (the space is modified), hence the MLP is used once every adaptation, and the embedding produced are stored in memory.
- The computation of the recommendation is a K-nearest-neighborhood from the user's representation. Our implementation is a simple sorting-based one and it respects the specifics required. An advanced data structure could further reduce the latency but would require a pre-processing phase.

B Model Selection

We performed an exhaustive grid search to optimize hyperparameters for both the HGNN and the online personalization component (Table 5). The activation function was consistently set to ReLU across all experiments. Motivated by prior

---

[1] It is really rare that a new interaction arrives in less than 100 ms.

studies that indicate the superiority of Euclidean distance over cosine similarity in low-dimensional embedding spaces [12,13,16], we adopted Euclidean distance throughout.

For the HGNN, we instantiated Eq. 1 using SAGEConv [6], with a fixed batch size of 128 and neighbor sampling configuration of $[8,8,8]$ to ensure constant memory usage, as discussed in Appendix A.1. Additionally, we employed early stopping with a patience of 5 epochs and set loss weighting to $\gamma = [\gamma_1 = 1, \gamma_2 = 0.5, \gamma_3 = 0.5, \gamma_4 = 0.1]$.

All other hyperparameters listed in Tables 5 were optimized using grid search.

Table 5. Hyper-parameters for the heterogeneous graph model (left) and online personalization (right).

Heterogeneous Graph Model		Online Personalization	
Hyper-parameter	Values	Hyper-parameter	Values
structural layers	$[dim\_in, 256, 128, 64]$, $[dim\_in, 256, 256, 128, 64]$	SGD steps	$1, 2, 3, 4, 5, 10,$ $20, 35, 50, 65, 80$
attribute layers	$[dim\_in, 256, 128, 64]$, $[dim\_in, 256, 256, 128, 64]$	learning rate	$1e-2, 1e-3, 1e-4,$ $1e-5, 1e-6$
neighborhood agg.	$sum, mean$	weight decay	$1e-5, 1e-6, 1e-7, 0$
relation agg.	$sum, mean$	batch size	$1, 2, 3, 5, 7, 9$
weighted sampling	$True, False$	margin	$1, 100, \infty$
learning rate	$1e-2, 1e-3, 1e-4,$ $1e-5, 1e-6, 1e-7$	alpha	$0.1, 0.2, 0.3, 0.4, 0.5,$ $0.6, 0.7, 0.8, 0.9, 1$
weight decay	$1e-5, 1e-6, 1e-7, 0$		
margin	$1, 100$		

C Baselines

The last-K baseline is important because a poor recommendation system could simply suggest to buy all the previously clicked or added to cart articles. This achieves a moderately good performance in terms of Accuracy when simulating the streaming with website logs, in fact, a purchased product has certainly been clicked and added to the cart in the past, and the recommendation system could learn to predict as future purchase only the items added to the cart. However, in real-world usage, this behavior will not increase the users' satisfaction and the number of purchases in the platform.

Directly comparing our proposed method with real-time personalization against models like LightGCN [9] and PinSage [19] in their canonical forms presents inherent challenges due to fundamental differences in their architectural designs and primary objectives. LightGCN, as detailed by He et al. (2020), is explicitly designed for pure collaborative filtering, and thus does not inherently leverage item content features like image embeddings. This makes a direct comparison difficult when item content is a significant aspect of the recommendation task, as it is in our fashion e-commerce context.

PinSage, on the other hand (Ying et al., 2018), while capable of incorporating content features to learn powerful static item embeddings from large-scale item-item or item-board graphs, typically employs these embeddings in a downstream recommendation phase. Its core architecture focuses on generating these item representations, and user personalization is often achieved by querying these static embeddings based on recent user activity, rather than through real-time adaptation of a user-specific model component as in our approach. The original PinSage paper, for instance, details a method for learning these item embeddings primarily for item-to-item recommendation scenarios.

To address these disparities and facilitate a more equitable comparison for the purpose of evaluating the quality of learned item representations in a dynamic, session-based context, we standardizes the recommendation generation and evaluation protocol. Specifically, after training the models to learn item embeddings from an item-item graph constructed from user interaction sequences (and incorporating item image features as node attributes in PinSage), we evaluate these learned embeddings in a manner analogous to our main proposal's inference stage:

1. The user's evolving interest within a session is represented by an Exponential Moving Average (EMA) of the learned item embeddings corresponding to the items interacted with so far in that session.
2. Recommendations are generated by performing a K-Nearest Neighbor (K-NN) search against this session-specific EMA user profile vector within the global space of learned item embeddings.
3. The same session-based Precision, Recall, and F1-score metrics (comparing against the next T items, as detailed in Sect. 3) are then applied.

References

1. Bacciu, D., Errica, F., Micheli, A., Podda, M.: A gentle introduction to deep learning for graphs. Neural Netw. **129**, 203–221 (2020)
2. De Nadai, M., et al.: Personalized audiobook recommendations at spotify through graph neural networks. arXiv preprint arXiv:2403.05185 (2024)
3. Dukic, H., Mokarizadeh, S., Deligiorgis, G., Sepe, P., Bacciu, D., Trincavelli, M.: Inductive-transductive learning for very sparse fashion graphs. Neurocomputing **504**, 42–55 (2022)
4. Gao, C., et al.: A survey of graph neural networks for recommender systems: challenges, methods, and directions. ACM Trans. Recommender Syst. **1**(1), 1–51 (2023)
5. Gou, J., Yu, B., Maybank, S.J., Tao, D.: Knowledge distillation: a survey. Int. J. Comput. Vision **129**(6), 1789–1819 (2021)
6. Hamilton, W., Ying, Z., Leskovec, J.: Inductive representation learning on large graphs. In: Advances in Neural Information Processing Systems, vol. 30 (2017)
7. Hao, Y., Cao, X., Fang, Y., Xie, X., Wang, S.: Inductive link prediction for nodes having only attribute information. arXiv preprint arXiv:2007.08053 (2020)

8. He, K., Zhang, X., Ren, S., Sun, J.: Deep residual learning for image recognition. In: Proceedings of the IEEE Conference on Computer Vision and Pattern Recognition, pp. 770–778 (2016)
9. He, X., Deng, K., Wang, X., Li, Y., Zhang, Y., Wang, M.: Lightgcn: simplifying and powering graph convolution network for recommendation. In: Proceedings of the 43rd International ACM SIGIR Conference on Research and Development in Information Retrieval, pp. 639–648 (2020)
10. H&M: Competition on personalization, https://www.kaggle.com/competitions/h-and-m-personalized-fashion-recommendations/data
11. JacobCP: https://github.com/JacobCP/kaggle-handm-helpers
12. Ladd, J.R.: Understanding and using common similarity measures for text analysis. The Programming Historian (2020)
13. Mukherjee, S., Sonal, R.: A reconciliation between cosine similarity and euclidean distance in individual decision-making problems. Indian Econ. Rev. **58**(2), 427–431 (2023)
14. Sattar, A., Deligiorgis, G., Trincavelli, M., Bacciu, D.: Multi-relational graph neural network for out-of-domain link prediction. In: 2024 International Joint Conference on Neural Networks (IJCNN), pp. 1–8 (2024). https://doi.org/10.1109/IJCNN60899.2024.10650198
15. Song, Y., Wang, T., Cai, P., Mondal, S.K., Sahoo, J.P.: A comprehensive survey of few-shot learning: Evolution, applications, challenges, and opportunities. ACM Comput. Surv. **55**(13s), 1–40 (2023)
16. Tessari, F., Hogan, N.: Surpassing cosine similarity for multidimensional comparisons: dimension insensitive euclidean metric (diem). arXiv preprint arXiv:2407.08623 (2024)
17. Vettoruzzo, A., Bouguelia, M.R., Vanschoren, J., Rognvaldsson, T., Santosh, K.: Advances and challenges in meta-learning: a technical review. IEEE TPAMI (2024)
18. Wang, L., Zhang, X., Su, H., Zhu, J.: A comprehensive survey of continual learning: theory, method and application. IEEE TPAMI (2024)
19. Ying, R., He, R., Chen, K., Eksombatchai, P., Hamilton, W.L., Leskovec, J.: Graph convolutional neural networks for web-scale recommender systems. In: Proceedings of the 24th ACM SIGKDD International Conference on Knowledge Discovery & Data Mining, pp. 974–983 (2018)
20. Zhang, C., Song, D., Huang, C., Swami, A., Chawla, N.V.: Heterogeneous graph neural network. In: Proceedings of the 25th ACM SIGKDD International Conference on Knowledge Discovery & Data Mining, pp. 793–803 (2019)

A Two-Stage Framework Integrating Prompt Learning and Fine-Tuning for Code Summarization

Xiaoshu Sun, Siqi Lv, Wei Wan, Yiming Qin, and Gang Hu(✉)

School of Information Science & Engineering, Yunnan University, Kunming, China
hugang@ynu.edu.cn

Abstract. Source code summarization automates the generation of natural comments, enhancing efficiency in software development and maintenance. With the emergence of large language models (LLMs), significant progress has been made in this domain. However, current approaches either rely on manually crafted prompts or standard fine-tuning that fail to fully leverage the power of continuous embeddings. To address this gap, we propose StageCS, a novel framework integrating prompt learning and model fine-tuning for code summarization, featuring a strategic two-stage training process with a multi-branch transformer architecture. StageCS generates specialized continuous embeddings that synergistically guide LLMs to produce high-quality summaries while maximizing the benefits of targeted fine-tuning. Evaluations on the CodeSearchNet Java dataset show StageCS outperforms baselines in representative LLM architectures like PolyCoder and CodeGen. More importantly, our ablation studies demonstrate that both the multi-branch transformer and the strategic two-stage process contribute significantly. StageCS enables LLMs to excel in code summarization without extensive manual prompt engineering, delivering superior quality through specialized training.

Keywords: Code Summarization · LLM · Prompt Learning

1 Introduction

Source code summarization [18]—automatically generating natural language descriptions (comments) for source code—is crucial in software development, enhancing code understanding and reuse efficiency. However, existing research [6] highlights that the lack of high-quality code comments is a widespread issue in the software industry. Unfortunately, as software evolves, comments often become missing, mismatched, or outdated, leading to the software crisis.

Recently, large language models (LLMs) have impacted natural language processing (NLP). Alongside general LLMs like ChatGPT [4] and LLaMA [22], LLMs tailored for software engineering have emerged. Compared to traditional information retrieval and deep learning (DL) methods, LLMs like CodeT5 [23] and CodeGen [12] have shown progress, but effective prompt design remains challenging and requires programming expertise. Recent studies have explored instruction prompting, particularly zero-shot and few-shot learning. For example, [19] evaluate ChatGPT for code summarization, while [2] explore prompting annotation. Despite this, open-source LLMs lag behind fine-tuned models, which perform better, as shown by [11] with Codex fine-tuned on bug-fix data.

However, existing techniques often struggle to effectively integrate continuous embeddings or achieve optimal synergy between prompt-based guidance and model fine-tuning for code summarization. These limitations hinder the learning of task-specific patterns, leading to suboptimal performance. Consequently, a more sophisticated framework is needed to enable effective adaptation of LLMs for high-quality summary generation without prohibitive costs.

To address these challenges, we propose a novel two-stage framework for code summarization called StageCS. StageCS's core advantage is that summary-generating prompts are learned through training, eliminating the need for manual design and evaluation. Specifically, it uses a multi-branch transformer to generate continuous prompt embeddings, which are then adapted to the LLMs through targeted fine-tuning. This two-stage process effectively captures the semantics and structure of code. More importantly, during the prompt learning phase, only the parameters of the prompt agent are updated to reduce training costs, while the LLM parameters are updated during the fine-tuning phase to enhance task adaptability. By experimenting with the representative LLMS such as PolyCoder–160M and CodeGen-Multi-350M, StageCS achieves superior performance in generating accurate and comprehensive code summaries.

In summary, our main contributions are as follows:

1) **Efficient Multi-Branch Transformer**: A novel multi-branch transformer introduced for continuous prompt embedding generation. It uses parallel attention with residual connections and layer normalization to capture complex relationships between code elements at various abstraction levels, efficiently modeling both local details and global structure without the need for previous complex structural preprocessing.

2) **Synergistic Two-Stage Training**: A two-stage paradigm that enhances synergy between prompt learning and model fine-tuning. It first generates prompt embeddings with frozen LLM parameters, optimizing the prompt agent, then fine-tunes the LLM using these optimized embeddings, adapting the LLM. This separation of concerns – focused prompt optimization followed by targeted LLM adaptation – leads to more efficient training and superior performance.

3) **Using code representative LLMs**: We validates the framework using representative models, PolyCoder-160M and CodeGen-Multi-350M. However, it is, in fact, a general LLM-based code summarization framework that incorporates improvements in prompt learning embeddings and can be fine-tuned with various backbone code LLMs.

4) **Superior Performance on Dataset**: Our extensive experiments on the CodeSearchNet Java datasets demonstrate that StageCS consistently outperforms baseline models, including instruction prompting and model fine-

tuning. Ablation studies confirm that both innovations contribute significantly to the overall performance improvement.

2 Background

2.1 Source Code Summarization

Code summarization automatically generates natural descriptions to capture the functionality of code. These summaries describe the code's purpose, behavior, and usage, helping developers understand it without needing to examine the details. Effective summarization improves code comprehension, maintenance, and reuse, especially in large codebase with incomplete or outdated documentation. Traditional methods include template match [18,19], information retrievals, and statistical machine learning [1]. With the advancement of deep learning, neural methods have become predominant, utilizing architectures such as recurrent neural networks (RNNs), convolutional neural networks (CNNs), and more recently, transformer-based models. With the rise of LLMs in NLP, their application in code summarization [2] has also gained significant momentum.

2.2 Large Language Models for Code

LLMs [26] pretrained on large code corpora [26] have shown remarkable capabilities in understanding and generating code. Models like GraphCodeBERT and CodeT5 [23] utilize transformer architectures and self-supervised learning objectives to develop rich representations of code's semantics, syntax, and structure. LLMs can be fine-tuned for downstream tasks with task-specific data, but standard methods often lack the specialized mechanisms needed to effectively bridge the gap between source code and natural summary. Alternative approaches include few-shot learning [2], zero-shot learning, and continuous embedding methods, which aim to leverage the LLM's pretrained knowledge through different adaptation strategies.

2.3 Continuous Embedding Learning

Continuous embedding learning [20] adapts LLMs to specific tasks by learning representations directly in the model's embedding space, unlike discrete prompt learning that uses natural language instructions. These learned embeddings help guide the LLM by activating relevant knowledge stored within the model. For code summarization, continuous embeddings bridge source code representation and natural language generation. StageCS advances this field through a multi-branch transformer architecture and a strategic two-stage training process that leverages both prompt learning and fine-tuning, creating a synergistic relationship between embeddings and the LLM for superior summarization performance.

3 Motivation

StageCS addresses several fundamental challenges in code summarization:

1) One of the core challenges in code summarization is effectively capturing both local details and global structure, which requires specialized architectures. While [8] used RNN encoders and [1] adapted standard transformer architectures, both struggle with the hierarchical nature of code and face limitations in handling deeply nested structures. In contrast, our proposed multi-branch transformer architecture uses parallel attention mechanisms, with each branch focusing on different aspects of code semantics, enabling a comprehensive understanding across multiple abstraction levels.
2) Conventional fine-tuning treats the entire model as a single entity, failing to distinguish between embedding generation and text generation mechanisms. Our two-stage process first optimizes embeddings with a frozen LLM, then allows the LLM to adapt to these optimized embeddings in a targeted manner. This decoupling allows the prompt agent to first converge on optimal prompt characteristics without the confounding factor of a simultaneously shifting LLM, after which the LLM can be fine-tuned with greater precision using these stabilized, high-quality prompts. This focused learning approach is hypothesized to be more effective and computationally efficient for the prompt learning phase.
3) Source code has distinct structural and semantic characteristics compared to natural language. Recent approaches [21] incorporated Abstract Syntax Tree(AST) information but required complex preprocessing and had inconsistent results across languages. Similarly, specialized tokens were used, but they didn't fully capture semantic relationships. Our multi-branch architecture addresses this by using parallel attention mechanisms to capture different aspects of code semantics, leading to more accurate and comprehensive summaries.

4 Methodology

4.1 Overview

Figure 1 illustrates the overview of our proposed StageCS framework. StageCS involves a two-stage process: prompt learning and model fine-tuning.

4.1.1 (A) One Stage for Prompt Learning

In the first stage, we focus on training the prompt agent while keeping the LLM parameters frozen. It can be broken down into 5 steps: *In step 1*, the framework feeds code snippets to the LLM, utilizing its input embedding layer to generate the corresponding code embeddings denoted $\mathbf{e}^C$. *In step 2*, the framework feeds a pseudo prompt into our multi-branch transformer encoder to generate the prompt embedding denoted

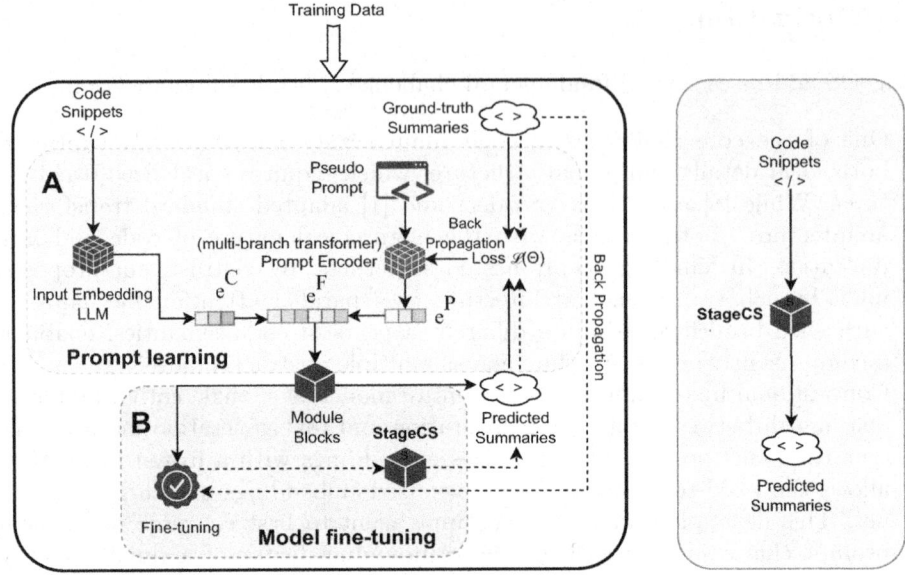

Fig. 1. Overview of the StageCS framework. It consists of two stages: (A) Prompt learning, where the best prompt is learned to obtain model blocks, and (B) Model fine-tuning, where the model blocks are fine-tuned with task-specific instructions.

e^P. The pseudo prompt is composed of learnable tokens with no actual meaning. *In step 3*, the framework concatenates e^C and e^P together to produce fusion embeddings denoted e^F. StageCS is non-invasive to input code snippets, meaning that the prompt embedding does not break the integrity of the code embedding. Hence, e^P will only be concatenated to the front or back of e^C. In the back-end mode, we concatenate the prompt embedding in front of the code embedding (i.e., $[e^P; e^C]$), while in the front-end mode we concatenate it at the back (i.e., $[e^C; e^P]$). Previous experiments have shown that the back-end mode generally offers optimal performance. *In step 4*, the fusion embeddings e^F are fed into the module blocks of the LLM to generate the predicted summaries. *In step 5*, based on the predicted summaries and the ground-truth summaries, StageCS computes the loss and updates the prompt agent's model parameters iteratively.

4.1.2 (B) Two Stage for Model Fine-Tuning After the first stage, we proceed to the second stage, freezing the well-trained multi-branch transformer prompt parameters and unfreezing the LLM parameters for fine-tuning. This sequential approach allows us to leverage the strengths of both prompt-based learning and model fine-tuning, resulting in superior performance across different model sizes and programming languages. In deployment, the fully trained system automatically generates a prompt embedding e^P for each new code snippet using the frozen prompt agent, guiding the LLM to produce high-quality summaries.

From the user's perspective, this process is seamless and imperceptible, requiring no manual prompt engineering or selection of few-shot examples.

4.2 Code Embedding Generation

As mentioned in Sect. 2.2, each LLM has three core components: a tokenizer, an input embedding layer, and module blocks. StageCS directly employs the first two components of the LLM to accomplish the task of code embedding generation. Specifically, given a code snippet, our prompt agent first utilizes the tokenizer provided by the corresponding LLM to convert various elements in the code snippet, such as identifiers and symbols, into index representations. Each index representation corresponds to a token in the LLM vocabulary. After tokenization, the prompt agent feeds the index representations to the input embedding layer of the LLM. The input embedding layer encodes these index representations to embeddings (i.e., $\mathbf{e}^C$) so that the module blocks can better understand their inner information. This process ensures that all syntactic and semantic information present in the code is preserved in the embedding space, allowing the LLM to effectively process the code snippet later in the pipeline. By leveraging the native tokenization and embedding processes of the LLM, we ensure compatibility and maximize the model's ability to interpret the code according to its pre-trained understanding.

4.3 Prompt Embedding Generation

Prompt embeddings guide the LLM. We use a multi-branch transformer encoder as shown in Fig. 1. The input is a pseudo prompt $p = \{t_0, t_1, \ldots, t_n\}$ of n learnable tokens. The prompt embedding generation process is formalized as:

$$\mathbf{T}_{pos} = \text{PositionalEncoding}(\mathbf{T}), \mathbf{T} = \text{Embedding}(p) \tag{1}$$

Here, p are learnable tokens; $\mathbf{T}$ is their d-dimensional embedding matrix; $\mathbf{T}_{pos}$ is $\mathbf{T}$ with added positional encodings.

Our core innovation is the multi-branch attention. For each branch b:

$$\text{Attention}_b(\mathbf{Q}, \mathbf{K}, \mathbf{V}) = \text{softmax}\left(\frac{\mathbf{Q}\mathbf{K}^T}{\sqrt{d_k}}\right)\mathbf{V}$$
$$\mathbf{H}_b = \text{TransformerEncoderLayer}_b(\mathbf{T}_{pos}) \tag{2}$$

where $TransformerEncoderLayer_b$ uses $Attention_b$ as the core computational component. Here, $\mathbf{Q}, \mathbf{K}, \mathbf{V}$ are the Query, Key, and Value matrices derived from the layer's input (e.g., $\mathbf{T}_{pos}$); d_k is the key vector dimension. $\mathbf{H}_b$ is the b-th branch output. Each parallel branch shares the same architecture, but independent random weight initializations enable them to learn distinct feature representations or transformations of the input pseudo prompt during training.

The outputs from all B branches are processed:

$$\begin{aligned}\mathbf{H}_{\text{concat}} &= \text{Concat}([\mathbf{H}_1, \mathbf{H}_2, \ldots, \mathbf{H}_B]) \\ \mathbf{H}_{\text{proj}} &= \mathbf{W}_{\text{proj}}\mathbf{H}_{\text{concat}} + \mathbf{b}_{\text{proj}}\end{aligned} \tag{3}$$

where $\mathbf{H}_{\text{concat}}$ is the concatenation of B branch outputs $[\mathbf{H}_1, \ldots, \mathbf{H}_B]$. $\mathbf{H}_{\text{proj}}$ is its projection using weights $\mathbf{W}_{\text{proj}}$ and bias $\mathbf{b}_{\text{proj}}$.

This process repeats for L layers, applying residual connections and layer normalization:

$$\mathbf{H}_{\text{layer\_output}} = \text{LayerNorm}(\mathbf{H}_{\text{input\_to\_layer}} + \mathbf{H}_{\text{proj}}) \qquad (4)$$

where $\mathbf{H}_{\text{input\_to\_layer}}$ is the current layer's input, and $\mathbf{H}_{\text{proj}}$ is its multi-branch projected output before the residual sum.

The final prompt embedding $\mathbf{e}^P$ is the L-th layer output, denoted $\mathbf{H}^{(L)}$:

$$\mathbf{e}^P = \mathbf{H}^{(L)} \qquad (5)$$

This multi-branch transformer architecture offers several key advantages:

1) Multiple parallel attention mechanisms, through independent random weight initializations, foster 'emergent specialization'. This allows each branch to learn distinct feature representations of the pseudo prompt, enhancing model capacity and providing a richer understanding of token relationships for the prompt agent. 2) Residual connections are crucial for training deeper networks by facilitating smoother gradient flow throughout the model. This helps mitigate issues such as vanishing gradients, allowing for more effective learning of complex hierarchies. 3) Layer normalization contributes to more stable and efficient training by normalizing the inputs to each layer. This process reduces internal covariate shift, leading to more consistent parameter updates and faster convergence.

Our experimental results confirm that this architectural improvement significantly enhances the quality of generated embeddings, leading to better code summarization performance across different LLMs and programming languages.

4.4 Prompt Agent Training

We introduce a novel two-stage training approach that further enhances the performance of our framework. In the first stage, we freeze the parameters of the LLM and only train the prompt agent. The loss function remains a categorical cross-entropy loss: The cross-entropy loss is formulated as:

$$\mathcal{L}(\Theta) = -\sum_{i=1}^{C} y_i \log \left(\frac{\exp(\hat{y}_i)}{\sum_{j=1}^{C} \exp(\hat{y}_j)} \right) \qquad (6)$$

where Θ represents the trainable parameters of the model, C is the number of tokens in the vocabulary, $\hat{y}_i$ denotes the predicted logit for the i-th token, y_i indicates the ground-truth label (1 for target token, 0 otherwise)

4.5 Model Fine-Tuning

In the second stage, we leverage the trained prompt agent as a foundation and perform model fine-tuning. This stage involves freezing the prompt agent parameters and unfreezing the LLM parameters. This two-stage approach allows the framework to first learn optimal continuous prompts while keeping the LLM intact, and then fine-tune the LLM itself guided by these learned prompts. Our experiments demonstrate that this sequential training approach yields superior results compared to either prompt learning or fine-tuning alone. Our experiments with prompt lengths of 10, 20, 50, 100, and 200 across different LLMs confirm that this two-stage approach consistently outperforms standalone methods while maintaining reasonable training efficiency.

5 Evaluation and Analysis

We conduct the experiments to answer the following research questions (RQs):

- **RQ1:** How effective is StageCS with the multi-branch transformer architecture and two-stage training process compared to baseline approaches?
- **RQ2:** How do the multi-branch transformer architecture and the two-stage training process each contribute to performance improvement?
- **RQ3:** How do different prompt lengths affect the performance of StageCS?

5.1 Experimental Setup

(1) Code Dataset. We evaluate StageCS on the widely used CodeSearchNet (CSN) [9] corpus, which contains code snippets and their comments in six programming languages (including Go, Java, JavaScript, PHP, Python, and Ruby). Due to noise in the original CSN corpus, we use the cleaned Java dataset from CodeXGLUE [15]. We select the training (164,923) and test (10,955) sets. **(2) Baseline Methods.** Instruct Prompting (zero-shot): Uses human-written instructions to prompt LLMs for code summarization without labeled data examples. Instruct Prompting (few-shot) [2]: Extends zero-shot by adding 10 randomly selected ⟨code snippet, summary⟩ examples from the training dataset. Fine-tuning [24]: Fine-tunes all LLM parameters using the entire training set of ⟨code snippets, summaries⟩ pairs. PromptCS [20]: Freezes LLM parameters and trains only a prompt agent (prompt encoder) on the full training set. **(3) Backbone LLMs.** We conduct experiments on two open-source LLMs: PolyCoder-160M, CodeGen-Multi-350M. PolyCoder, developed by Carnegie Mellon, is trained on 249GB of code from 12 languages using GPT NeoX. CodeGen-Multi, from Salesforce, is an autoregressive LLM for program synthesis. **(4) Evaluation Metrics.** We use 4 classic text summarization metrics (reported as percentages in [0, 1]) for evaluation, with higher values indicating better model performance. BLEU [16]: Measures n-gram precision with brevity penalty, aggregating 1–4 gram matches. METEOR [3]: Improves BLEU by combining precision and recall with the harmonic mean. ROUGE-L: Measures recall through longest common subsequence. SentenceBERT [17]: Computes semantic similarity using vector embeddings and cosine distance. **(5) Parameter Settings.** During training, we use a mini-batch size of 8 for computational efficiency on a single GPU, a learning rate of 2e-5 optimized with AdamW [14] (weight decay 0.01, epsilon 1e-8), linear warmup for the first 10% of steps followed by linear decay, and early stopping if the BLEU score does not improve for 4 consecutive epochs. Input sequences are truncated or padded to a maximum length of 512 tokens.

5.2 Experimental Results

5.2.1 RQ1: Effectiveness of StageCS

Table 1 presents a comparison of performance evaluation metrics (BLEU, METEOR, ROUGE-L, and SentenceBERT) for StageCS and several baseline methods on the CSN-Java dataset.

Table 1. Performance comparison of different baseline methods.

LLM	Method	BLEU	METEOR	ROUGE-L	SentenceBERT
PolyCoder	Zero-shot	7.98	11.55	16.12	47.58
	Few-shot	13.76	8.85	27.58	49.11
	PromptCS	16.01	11.68	34.04	56.44
	Fine-tuning	17.79	12.92	36.24	**59.21**
	StageCS	**18.24**	**13.12**	**36.61**	59.14
CodeGen	Zero-shot	6.13	7.46	13.76	40.26
	Few-shot	14.44	10.50	30.04	52.98
	PromptCS	17.38	12.97	36.37	58.84
	Fine-tuning	19.12	**13.69**	37.95	59.85
	StageCS	**19.63**	13.59	**38.55**	**60.26**

Results show StageCS significantly outperforms all baseline approaches across all metrics and LLMs. Compared to the PromptCS, our framework achieves an average improvement of 2.23 BLEU points, 1.14 METEOR points, 2.57 ROUGE-L points and 2.7 SentenceBERT points on PolyCoder-160M. Similar improvements are observed for CodeGen-Multi-350M. Most notably, StageCS outperforms fine-tuning. This demonstrates the effectiveness of combining the multi-branch transformer architecture with the two-stage training process.

> **Answer for RQ1:**
> StageCS consistently surpasses both baselines and state-of-the-art methods (e.g., instruction prompting, fine-tuning) on PolyCoder and CodeGen-Multi.

5.2.2 RQ2: Ablation of Two-Stage Contributions

We conduct ablation studies on the CSN-Java dataset using PolyCoder-160M and CodeGen-350M to assess the individual contributions of multi-branch attention and the two-stage training process, with the results shown in Table 2.

Table 2. Performance comparison of StageCS variants. TT: Traditional Transformer; MT: Multi-branch Transformer; PL: Prompt Learning; SBERT: Sentence-BERT. PromptCS*, Fine-tuning* is the improved first and second stage of StageCS.

LLM	TT	MT	PL	Method	BLEU	METEOR	ROUGE-L	SBERT
PolyCoder	✓	×	✓	PromptCS	16.01	11.68	34.04	56.44
	×	✓	✓	PromptCS*	**17.16**	**12.13**	**35.23**	**57.67**
	✓	×	×	Fine-tuning	17.79	12.92	36.24	59.21
	✓	×	✓	Fine-tuning*	**18.17**	**13.01**	**36.57**	59.18
	×	✓	✓	**StageCS**	**18.24**	**13.12**	**36.61**	59.14
CodeGen	✓	×	✓	PromptCS	17.38	12.97	36.37	58.84
	×	✓	✓	PromptCS*	**18.09**	**13.33**	**37.26**	**60.04**
	✓	×	×	Fine-tuning	19.12	13.69	37.95	59.85
	✓	×	✓	Fine-tuning*	**19.19**	13.52	**38.19**	**60.01**
	×	✓	✓	**StageCS**	**19.63**	13.59	**38.55**	**60.26**

The ablation study reveals that both innovations significantly improve performance. In PolyCoder, PromptCS* increases BLEU by 1.15, METEOR by 0.45, ROUGE-L by 1.19, and SentenceBERT by 1.23, confirming that the multi-branch attention mechanism with residual connections and layer normalization improves code semantics capture. The two-stage training process improves BLEU by 0.38, METEOR by 0.09, and ROUGE-L by 0.33, compared to fine-tuning. This suggests that using the well-trained prompt agent as a base for fine-tuning creates synergy, maximizing the LLM's code summarization ability. Combining both innovations in StageCS yields the highest performance across all metrics, demonstrating their complementarity. A similar pattern emerges with CodeGen-Multi, confirming the effectiveness of these improvements across different LLMs.

> **Answer for RQ2:**
> Ablation studies verify that both the multi-branch transformer architecture and two-stage training process are crucial for StageCS's performance gains.

5.2.3 RQ3: Effect of Prompt Learning Length

To investigate how prompt length affects performance, we conducted experiments with various prompt lengths (10, 20, 50, 100, and 200) using the back-end concatenation mode for our continuous embeddings. Table 3 illustrates the impact of prompt length on different metrics for both PolyCoder-160M and CodeGen-Multi-350M.

For PolyCoder-160M, optimal performance varies across different metrics. The highest BLEU score (18.63) is achieved with the shortest prompt length of 10, while METEOR and ROUGE-L peak at lengths of 100 and 50, respectively.

Table 3. Effects of Prompt Learning Length

LLM	Length	BLEU	METEOR	ROUGE-L	SentenceBERT	All. avg
PolyCoder	10	**18.63**	12.93	36.62	**59.6**	**31.95**
	20	18.35	13.03	36.93	59.16	31.87
	50	18.36	13.02	**37.00**	59.43	**31.95**
	100	18.24	**13.12**	36.61	59.14	31.78
	200	18.20	13.03	36.50	59.10	31.71
CodeGen	10	19.31	13.66	37.96	60.35	32.82
	20	19.52	13.41	38.06	60.07	32.77
	50	19.15	**13.82**	38.03	**60.63**	32.91
	100	**19.63**	13.59	**38.55**	60.26	**33.01**
	200	19.25	13.48	38.02	60.02	32.69

Overall, shorter to medium-length prompts (10–50) are most effective. In contrast, the larger CodeGen-Multi-350M benefits more from longer prompts, reaching its highest BLEU and ROUGE-L scores at a length of 100. This suggests that its larger capacity can better leverage the additional information in longer embeddings. In summary, optimal prompt length depends on the model. These findings provide practical guidance for configuring StageCS to maximize performance across different model sizes while balancing computational efficiency.

> **Answer for RQ3:**
> The experimental results show that there is an optimal range of prompt length, which depends on the specific model.

6 Related Work

(1) Code Summarization Research. Early methods relied on extractive summarization, identifying key statements and keywords from code. For instance, [5] introduced a technique for extracting essential elements. As large-scale code datasets and NLP breakthroughs advanced, deep learning, particularly Seq2Seq models (RNNs [5], LSTMs (Long Short-Term Memory) [10]), became prominent for capturing semantic relationships between code and text. Key works include [10], which used attention-enhanced LSTMs for C# and SQL, and [7], which combined LSTMs with Structure-Based Traversal(SBT) for Java method comments. However, RNNs struggled with long-range dependencies, leading to the adoption of Transformer architecture. For instance, [27] used a retrieval-enhanced Transformer, while [25] highlighted its effectiveness. **(2) LLMs in Software Engineering.** Traditional developer assistance through documentation and code adaptation has been augmented by LLMs. Initial explorations like

GPT-Neo (autoregressive architecture) and PolyCoder [26] (2.7B parameters/12-language support) established code generation capabilities. Subsequent innovations introduced multi-step program synthesis (CodeGen [12] via task decomposition) and zero-shot code infilling. Current advancements focus on scalability and efficiency, exemplified by StarCoder [13] (15.5B parameters, 80+ languages) with multi-query attention-accelerated inference. These LLMs collectively enhance code adaptation, generation, and contextual comprehension.

7 Conclusion

We propose StageCS, a novel framework for automatic code summarization using a two-stage training process. The first stage learns continuous prompt embeddings with a multi-branch transformer, while the second stage fine-tunes the LLM with these embeddings. StageCS reduces manual prompt engineering and enables LLMs to autonomously generate prompts for code summarization. Experiments on the CodeSearchNet Java dataset show that StageCS outperforms baseline methods using backbone LLMs like PolyCoder-160M and CodeGen-Multi-350M. Future work will involve applying StageCS to other software engineering tasks, conducting a more thorough theoretical analysis of its architecture, and evaluating its performance on larger models and diverse datasets.

Acknowledgments. The authors thank the General Program of Applied Basic Research of Yunnan Province (No. 202301AT070184), the Open Project Program of Yunnan Key Laboratory of Intelligent Systems and Computing (No. ISC22Y08), and the Open Research Project of the Yunnan University (YNU) Resilience and Excellence Children's Character Development Platform (No. K207003250006).

References

1. Ahmad, W.U., et al.: Unified pre-training for program understanding and generation. In: Proceedings of the 2021 Conference of the North American Chapter of the Association for Computational Linguistics, pp. 2655–2668 (2021)
2. Ahmed, T., Devanbu, P.: Few-shot training LLMs for project-specific code-summarization. In: Proceedings of the 37th IEEE/ACM International Conference on Automated Software Engineering, pp. 1–5 (2022)
3. Banerjee, S., et al.: Meteor: an automatic metric for MT evaluation with improved correlation with human judgments. In: Proceedings of the ACL Workshop on Intrinsic and Extrinsic Evaluation Measures for Machine Translation, pp. 65–72 (2005)
4. Brown, T., Mann, B., et al.: Language models are few-shot learners. Adv. Neural. Inf. Process. Syst. **33**, 1877–1901 (2020)
5. Cho, K., et al.: On the properties of neural machine translation: encoder-decoder approaches. arXiv preprint arXiv:1409.1259 (2014)
6. Gao, S., et al.: Code structure-guided transformer for source code summarization. ACM Trans. Softw. Eng. Methodol. **32**(1), 1–32 (2023)

7. Gros, D., Sezhiyan, H., et al.: Code to comment "translation" data, metrics, baselining & evaluation. In: Proceedings of the 35th IEEE/ACM International Conference on Automated Software Engineering, pp. 746–757 (2020)
8. Hu, X., Li, G., et al.: Deep code comment generation. In: Proceedings of the 26th Conference on Program Comprehension, pp. 200–210 (2018)
9. Husain, H., Wu, H.H., et al.: Codesearchnet challenge: evaluating the state of semantic code search. arXiv preprint arXiv:1909.09436 (2019)
10. Iyer, S., et al.: Summarizing source code using a neural attention model. In: 54th Annual Meeting of the Association for Computational Linguistics, pp. 2073–2083 (2016)
11. Jin, M., Shahriar, S., et al.: Inferfix: end-to-end program repair with LLMs. In: Proceedings of the 31st ACM Joint European Software Engineering Conference and Symposium on the Foundations of Software Engineering, pp. 1646–1656 (2023)
12. Li, H., Kuang, J., et al.: Codegen-search: a code generation model incorporating similar sample information. Int. J. Software Eng. Knowl. Eng. **33**, 1899–1921 (2023)
13. Li, R., et al.: Starcoder: may the source be with you! arXiv preprint arXiv:2305.06161 (2023)
14. Loshchilov, I., Hutter, F.: Decoupled weight decay regularization. arXiv preprint arXiv:1711.05101 (2017)
15. Lu, S., Guo, D., et al.: Codexglue: a machine learning benchmark dataset for code understanding and generation. arXiv preprint arXiv:2102.04664 (2021)
16. Papineni, K., Roukos, S., et al.: Bleu: a method for automatic evaluation of machine translation. In: Proceedings of the 40th Annual Meeting of the Association for Computational Linguistics, pp. 311–318 (2002)
17. Shi, E., et al.: On the evaluation of neural code summarization. In: Proceedings of the 44th International Conference on Software Engineering, pp. 1597–1608 (2022)
18. Stapleton, S., et al.: A human study of comprehension and code summarization. In: Proceedings of the 28th International Conference on Program Comprehension, pp. 2–13 (2020)
19. Sun, W., Fang, C., et al.: Automatic code summarization via chatgpt: how far are we? arXiv preprint arXiv:2305.12865 (2023)
20. Sun, W., Fang, C., et al.: A prompt learning framework for source code summarization. arXiv preprint arXiv:2312.16066 (2023)
21. Tang, Z., Shen, X., et al.: AST-trans: code summarization with efficient tree-structured attention. In: Proceedings of the 44th International Conference on Software Engineering, pp. 150–162 (2022)
22. Touvron, H., Lavril, T., et al.: Llama: open and efficient foundation language models. arXiv preprint arXiv:2302.13971 (2023)
23. Wang, Y., Le, H., et al.: Codet5+: open code large language models for code understanding and generation. In Proceedings of the 2023 Conference on Empirical Methods in Natural Language Processing (2023)
24. Wei, J., Bosma, M., et al.: Finetuned language models are zero-shot learners. arXiv preprint arXiv:2109.01652 (2021)
25. Wu, H., et al.: Code summarization with structure-induced transformer. In: Findings of the Association for Computational Linguistics, pp. 1078–1090 (2021)
26. Xu, F.F., Alon, U., et al.: A systematic evaluation of large language models of code. In: Proceedings of the 6th ACM SIGPLAN International Symposium on Machine Programming, pp. 1–10 (2022)
27. Zhang, J., et al.: Retrieval-based neural source code summarization. In: Proceedings of the ACM/IEEE 42nd International Conference on Software Engineering, pp. 1385–1397 (2020)

DialGACL: Nonlinear Graph Attention Reasoning with Contrastive Learning for Complex Dialogue Fact Verification

Wei Xia, Yu Zhong, Linfeng Gong, Yulong Yang, Sifan Zhao, and Shaoguo Cui[✉]

Chongqing Normal University, Chongqing, China
csg@cqnu.edu.cn

Abstract. Fact verification, as a critical technology for curbing the spread of misinformation, has garnered significant attention in recent years. However, existing methods in question-answering dialogues face two major challenges. Firstly, mainstream methods rely on sequential models or static attention and are often misled by redundant information. Secondly, inadequate utilization of label semantics results in difficulties in distinguishing fine-grained categories. To address these challenges, this paper integrates nonlinear **G**raph **A**ttention and **C**ontrastive **L**earning for fact verification in question-answering **Dial**ogues (Dial-GACL). The framework incorporates the K-GAT module, which leverages KAN-driven nonlinear attention to dynamically adjust edge weights while filtering noisy nodes, thereby constructing a deep semantic network. Additionally, to address deficiencies in label semantics, we propose a prototype contrastive loss that utilizes learnable label prototypes to enhance the discriminability of the feature space. Experimental results demonstrate that our DialGACL outperforms state-of-the-art methods on three benchmark datasets.

Keywords: Fact verification · Question-answering dialogue · Graph reasoning

1 Introduction

The explosive growth of misinformation and rumors has exerted serious negative consequences across society [1], affecting various areas such as politics, the economy, and public health [2]. In this context, fact verification, which automatically predicts claim veracity from evidence, has attracted significant research attention. Most existing studies focus on structured sources like news articles, structured tables [3], and Wikipedia [4], largely overlooking fact verification in the question-answer dialogue. Due to its high interactivity and diverse expressions, the question-answering dialogue often becomes a high-risk scenario for the spread of misinformation. Therefore, improving the robustness of fact verification systems requires ensuring that they can effectively verify claims in question-answering dialogue. Fact verification in question-answering dialogues faces multiple challenges. **Firstly**, the claim text is typically unstructured, with low fact

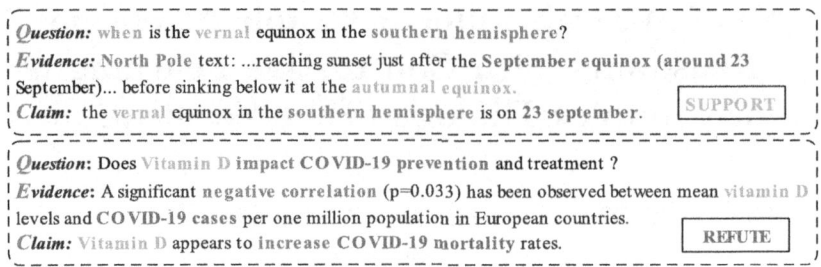

Fig. 1. Examples from the FAVIQ A dataset and the HEALTHVER dataset for fact verification. Different colors highlight different types of key information.

density and a mixture of opinions and colloquial language that obscures factual content (e.g., subjective phrases like *"I think"* or *"you know"*). **Secondly**, multi-level semantic interactions exist between the claim, evidence, and question. Previous PLM-based methods struggled to model these intricate, multi-granularity relationships. For instance, as Fig. 1 illustrates, in the vernal equinox example, it may be misled by the co-occurrence of *"vernal equinox"* and *"September"* without recognizing the critical contextual mismatch between the *"Southern Hemisphere"* claim and *"North Pole"* evidence. To better model these interactions, Graph Attention Networks (GATs) emerged to explicitly capture relational structures. Nevertheless, their linear mapping constrains deep logical reasoning, a limitation highlighted in the Vitamin D case (Fig. 1), where a model can identify shared entities like *"Vitamin D"* and *"COVID-19"* but fail to resolve the logical opposition between *"negative correlation"* and *"increase"*. **Finally**, approaches fail to mine inherent label semantic information, leading to blurry decision boundaries. To address the issues mentioned above, we propose a novel framework, nonlinear **G**raph **A**ttention and **C**ontrastive **L**earning for fact verification in question-answering **Dial**ogues (**DialGACL**). In summary, our contributions are as follows.

(1) We propose a non-linear graph attention network and an adaptive filtering mechanism to address the challenges of multi-level semantic modeling and noise interference in complex dialogue scenarios.
(2) We introduce a prototype contrastive loss with learnable label prototypes to enhance inter-class discrimination and sharpen decision boundaries.
(3) Extensive evaluations on three benchmark datasets demonstrate our model's superiority, achieving state-of-the-art performance across all tasks.

2 Related Work

Fact Verification. Early fact verification relied on natural language inference, matching claims with evidence from sources like Wikipedia [4,5] or structured tables [3]. The rise of pre-trained language models (PLMs) shifted this to fine-tuning encoders on concatenated claim-evidence pairs [6]. While effective, these approaches often capture only shallow keyword associations and struggle with complex reasoning. Graph Neural Networks (GNNs) were then introduced to address this, evolving from simple sentence-level graphs to more sophisticated structures. Despite these advancements, fact verification within dialogue contexts remains underexplored. Existing work in this area has primarily focused on dataset construction [7,8] and benchmarking [9], with few tailored solutions that can effectively model the tripartite interactions among claims, questions, and evidence [6,10]. Our study tackles these multiparty interactions by introducing heterogeneous node encoding and dynamic confidence adjustment to boost noise robustness and balance fine-grained semantics with complex reasoning.

Label Knowledge Embedding. In recent years, multi-task classification and contrastive learning have been widely employed to enhance fact verification performance. Label embedding, for example, enhances classification by integrating label semantics directly with the input text [6,11]. Concurrently, contrastive learning serves as an effective training paradigm that captures separable and distinguishable representations, thus significantly enhancing downstream tasks. Using losses like InfoNCE [12], it aligns positive samples and separates negatives, a principle refined by subsequent methods like SimCSE [13] and others designed for distant supervision. Building on this, our study employs a label prototype contrastive loss to heighten the model's sensitivity to subtle differences and enhance its generalization.

3 Task Statement

In this study, we investigate a question-answering dialogue-based fact verification task where we assess a claim's truthfulness using given evidence and related questions. Each sample is defined as $S = (c, (e, q), y)$, where c represents the claim to be verified, e denotes the evidence, q represents the corresponding question, and y indicates the label associated with the claim. Our objective is to verify c using the (e, q) pair. Possible labels y are SUPPORTED, REFUTED, or NEUTRAL (also known as NOT ENOUGH INFO, indicating insufficient evidence).

4 Methodology

4.1 Input Process

For each sample, we construct a claim-evidence-question triplet to form a unified input structure, facilitating subsequent tokenization and sequence processing. Specifically, we tokenize the triplet (c, e, q) into three token sequences C, E, and Q. The sequence input $S_{c,q,e} = [\langle s \rangle, C, \langle /s \rangle, E, \langle /s \rangle, Q, \langle /s \rangle]$, where $\langle s \rangle$ and $\langle /s \rangle$ serve as delimiters, indicating the start and end of each token sequence. For computational efficiency and a fixed input length, we truncate lengthy evidence and question sections and apply mask padding to all sequences.

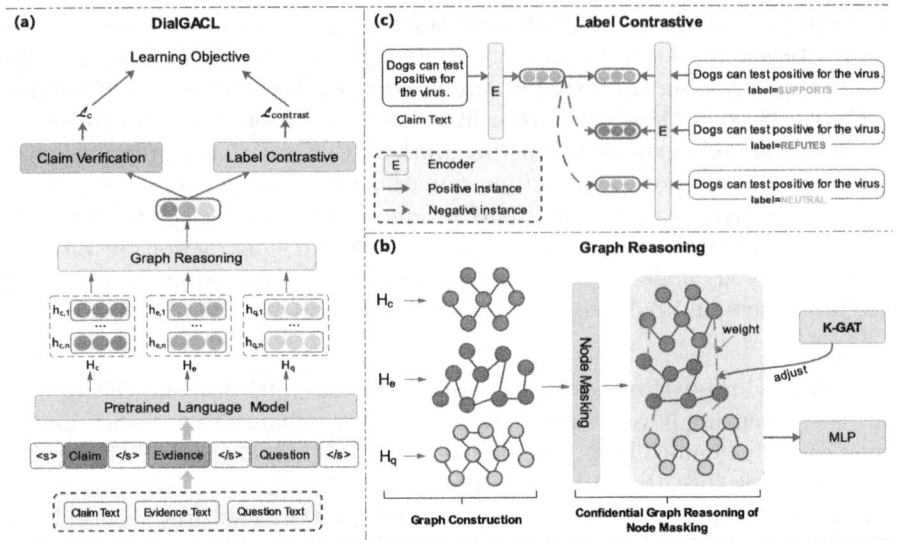

Fig. 2. (a) The overall architecture of DialGACL. (b) The Graph Reasoning Layer prunes nodes via Confidence Node Masking and captures their complex interactions using K-GAT. (c) The Label Contrastive pulls the distance of positive labels close while pushing the distance of negative labels apart.

4.2 Graph Construction

Node Encoding. We treat each word in the input sequence as a node and employ a pre-trained language model (PLM) to process the claim-question-evidence triplet, thereby generating the initial node representation, denoted as:

$$\mathbf{H} = f_{\text{PLM}}(\mathbf{S}_{c,q,e}) \tag{1}$$

where $\mathbf{H} \in \mathbf{R}^{n \times d}$ represents the learned joint semantic representation. Here, n denotes the maximum length of the input sequence, and d denotes the dimension of the representation vector. Specifically, we employ the RoBERTa model to encode the entire input sequence, generating the hidden state for each token and then extracting these hidden states from the output of the PLM as their initial node representation (as shown in Fig. 2).

Edge Construction. After creating word-level nodes, we define their connections. Instead of a noisy fully connected graph, we use positional and semantic edges to capture both structural and contextual information. Positional edges (C-E/C-Q/E-Q) are constructed using binary masks to preserve textual structure. Semantic edges based on cosine similarity (threshold 0.6) to capture meaningful context. Thus, the neighbor set $\mathcal{N}(i)$ of the node i is clearly defined.

4.3 Confidential Graph Reasoning of Node Masking

In fact-verification tasks, the initial node representations of evidence (e) and questions (q) often contain noise, such as redundant or irrelevant semantic details, which may mislead the model into focusing on secondary features. Inspired by Graph Structure Learning (GSL) [14], we design a node-masking mechanism that dynamically adjusts node representations by evaluating the nodes' confidence scores (CO-SCO).

Node Representation Adjustment. For each token i in the evidence (e) and question (q), we compute its confidence score CO-SCO$_i$ to quantify its relevance to the claim (c), indicating whether the token is meaningful for supporting or refuting the claim. The confidence score is calculated as:

$$\text{CO-SCO}_i = P(y_i = 1 \mid \mathbf{h}_i) = \text{Softmax}_{y_i=1}(\text{Linear}(\mathbf{h}_i)) \quad (2)$$

where CO-SCO $\in [0, 1]$. CO-SCO represents the relevance between the claim c and evidence-question $\mathbf{h}_i$. The $y_i = 1$ indicates that the token is recognized as relevant to the claim. We adjust its initial representation $\mathbf{h}_i$ by blending it with the blank node representation $\mathbf{n}_b$, weighted by its confidence score:

$$\mathbf{h}'_i = \text{CO-SCO}_i \times \mathbf{h}_i + (1 - \text{CO-SCO}_i) \times \mathbf{h}_b \quad (3)$$

where $\mathbf{h}_b$ is the node representation of the blank node $\mathbf{n}_b$. The blank node $\mathbf{n}_b$ only contains claim c without evidence and question. Finally, we obtain the denoised node representation $\mathbf{h}'_i$.

Confidence-Weighted Aggregation. Finally, we aggregate the adjusted representations to form the denoised representations of evidence ($\mathbf{h}_\text{evidence}$) and question ($\mathbf{h}_\text{question}$), weighting each token by its confidence score and respective mask:

$$\mathbf{h}_\text{evidence} = \frac{\sum_{i=1}^{L} \mathbf{h}'_i \cdot m_i^\text{evidence} \cdot \text{CO-SCO}_i}{\sum_{i=1}^{L} m_i^\text{evidence} \cdot \text{CO-SCO}_i + \epsilon} \quad (4)$$

where m_i^evidence is a binary mask for the i-th evidence token, and ϵ is a small constant. L denotes the total number of tokens in the input sequence. For the question representation, the same procedure is applied.

4.4 Kolmogorov-Arnold Nonlinear Graph Attention Reasoning

In graph neural networks, edge weights are crucial for effective information transfer and model performance. The traditional GATs are constrained by key limitations. Their attention mechanism, based on a shallow perceptron, struggles to capture complex non-linear dependencies and adapt to diverse graph structures, hindering generalization. Furthermore, this architecture is highly sensitive to noise in heterogeneous data, which can degrade its reasoning performance. To address these challenges, we propose **K-GAT** (Kolmogorov-Graph

Attention Networks), which integrates a dynamic edge-weighted attention mechanism, adaptive grid adjustment, and multi-head attention. Specifically, K-GAT employs a dynamic attention mechanism inspired by KAN [15], using B-spline basis functions:

$$\alpha_{ij} = \frac{\exp(\text{KAN}([\mathbf{h}_i\|\mathbf{h}_j]))}{\sum_{k\in\mathcal{N}(i)} \exp(\text{KAN}([\mathbf{h}_i\|\mathbf{h}_k]))} \tag{5}$$

where $[\mathbf{h}_i\|\mathbf{h}_j]$ denotes the concatenation of node features, and KAN is derived from the Kolmogorov-Arnold Representation theorem [16]:

$$f(x_1,\ldots,x_n) = \sum_{q=1}^{2n+1} \Phi_q \left(\sum_{p=1}^{n} \phi_{q,p}(x_p) \right) \tag{6}$$

where $\phi_{q,p} : [0,1] \to \mathbf{R}$, and $\Phi_q : \mathbf{R} \to \mathbf{R}$. This formulation illustrates that multivariate functions can essentially be decomposed into a well-defined composition of univariate functions, where the combination involves only simple addition. Building on this, K-GAT updates node representations through an attention-weighted aggregation of neighboring node features. This process is mathematically formulated as:

$$\mathbf{h}_i^{(l+1)} = \sum_{j\in\mathcal{N}(i)} \alpha_{ij}^{(l)} \cdot \mathbf{h}_j^{(l)} \tag{7}$$

where $\alpha_{ij}^{(l)}$ denotes the attention weight assigned to neighbor j for node i at layer l. This mechanism allows the model to dynamically assign weights to various nodes, thereby prioritizing the significance of neighboring nodes to ensure the central node receives more pertinent information.

After stacking L layers, we think each claim C fully understood the information through interaction with evidence E and question Q and has learned the potential reasoning paths between nodes. The model then aggregates these final node representations to predict the authenticity label y of C through a Multi-Layer Perceptron (MLP).

4.5 Multi-task Modeling Methods

Our final multi-task loss $\mathcal{L}$ combines the cross-entropy loss $\mathcal{L}_c$ for claim verification and the contrastive loss $\mathcal{L}_{\text{contrast}}$ for node prediction, with their contributions balanced by the hyperparameter λ:

$$\mathcal{L} = \mathcal{L}_c + \lambda \cdot \mathcal{L}_{\text{contrast}} \tag{8}$$

Claim Verification Loss. The cross-entropy objective is utilized to compute the claim verification loss:

$$\mathcal{L}_c = -\frac{1}{N}\sum_{i=1}^{N} y_i \log \hat{\mathbf{p}}_i \tag{9}$$

where y_i and $\hat{\mathbf{p}}_i$ denote the gold and predicted label of the ith claim, respectively. N denotes the number of samples.

Label Contrastive Loss. To enhance inter-class separability, we introduce a triplet contrastive loss, denoted as $\mathcal{L}_{\text{contrast}}$, leveraging learnable label prototypes. For each claim **c**, $\mathcal{L}_{\text{contrast}}$ maximize its cosine similarity (s_{pos}) with its correct label prototype $\mathbf{p}_{\text{label}}$ (positive sample) while minimizing similarity (s_{neg}) to a randomly selected incorrect prototype $\mathbf{p}_{\text{neg}}$ (negative sample):

$$\mathcal{L}_{\text{contrast}} = -\log\left(\frac{\exp(s_{\text{pos}}/\tau)}{\exp(s_{\text{pos}}/\tau) + \exp(s_{\text{neg}}/\tau)}\right) \quad (10)$$

where $s_{\text{pos}} = \cos(\mathbf{c}, \mathbf{p}_{\text{label}})$ and $s_{\text{neg}} = \cos(\mathbf{c}, \mathbf{p}_{\text{neg}})$. These prototypes are derived from a trainable prototype matrix $\mathbf{P} \in \mathbf{R}^{C \times d}$, where C is the number of classes and d is the prototype dimensionality. Unlike fixed class embeddings or batch-wise centroids, these prototypes are randomly initialized and updated directly via backpropagation, allowing them to dynamically adapt as optimal representations of each class. The temperature parameter τ controls distribution sharpness, with smaller values boosting contrast for difficult samples. This mechanism promotes feature clustering around true prototypes and away from irrelevant ones, thus sharpening decision boundaries.

5 Experimentation

5.1 Experimental Setup

Dataset and Evaluation Metrics. We utilize three datasets to verify our proposed model. Detailed statistics are summarized in Table 1. **HEALTHVER** [7] is a domain-specific dataset featuring medical claims paired with evidence from scientific journals, with instances labeled SUPPORT, REFUTE or NEUTRAL. In contrast, **COLLOQUIAL** [8] contains informal claims transformed from the FEVER dataset to include colloquialisms. To adapt it to our dialogue-based setting, we augment it with synthetic questions from QaDialMoE [10]. Finally, **FAVIQ** [17] is a large fact verification dataset from information-seeking questions, providing claims (from ambiguous questions for FAVIQ A or regular QA for FAVIQ R), Wikipedia evidence, and SUPPORT/REFUTE labels, with accuracy assessed on the FAVIQ A development set due to test set unavailability. Across all datasets, performance is evaluated using accuracy, supplemented by macro-averaged precision, recall, and F1-score for HEALTHVER.

Table 1. The statistics of three datasets

Dataset	Train	Dev	Test
HEALTHVER	10,590	1,917	1,823
FAVIQ A	17,008	4,260	4,688
FAVIQ R	140,977	15,566	5,877
COLLOQUIAL	41,000	28,900	8,400

Baselines. We compared DialGACL against various baselines on three benchmarks. (1) **HEALTHVER**: Baselines include BERT, its domain-specific variants SciBERT [18] and BioBERT [19], along with T5 [20] and RoBERTa. (2) **COLLOQUIAL**: The primary baseline is the graph-based KGAT model [21], using both BERT and CorefBERT as backbones. (3) **FAVIQ**: Baselines consist of several BART-based retrieval models [22], FiD, and its extension, FiD+EG [23]. Across all datasets, we also benchmark against recent state-of-the-art methods, including QaDialMoE [10] and LI^4 [6], for a comprehensive comparison.

Experiment Settings. Our models were implemented with RoBERTa-base as the primary encoder backbone. We apply the AdamW optimizer in training with a learning rate 2e5. The maximum input length is set to 512. All models were trained for 30 epochs on a single NVIDIA RTX 4090 GPU (24 GB) using a dataset-specific batching strategy. On the HEALTHVER dataset, the batch size was 32 (halved to 16 for RoBERTa-large). For other datasets, we enabled gradient accumulation with a batch size of 12. The number of gradient accumulation steps was 4 for the FAVIQ R dataset and 3 for the remaining datasets.

5.2 Overall Verification Results

Table 2, Table 3 and Table 4 summarize the experimental results of various models on HEALTHVER, COLLOQUIAL and FAVIQ, respectively.

Specifically, in the **HEALTHVER** dataset, as shown in Table 2, DialGACL (RoBERTa-base) achieves a 1.2%–1.8% accuracy improvement over the strongest baseline, LI^4 (RoBERTa-large), on the test set, marking the first instance of a smaller model outperforming larger models on this task. This result demonstrates that the model effectively captures complex logical chains in medical claims without relying on parameter scaling by incorporating a dynamic graph attention mechanism and a contrastive learning module. This approach mitigates the domain generalization limitations of traditional methods like LI^4, which depend heavily on pre-trained semantics.

This advantage extends to the **COLLOQUIAL** dataset (Table 3). Traditional methods (e.g., KGAT, LI^4+base) struggle with colloquial claims containing filler words (e.g., "you know," "yup") and unverifiable subjective expressions, limiting their accuracy to 67.7%–89.2%. By introducing a dynamic node-masking mechanism that adaptively filters non-critical nodes based on synthetic question generation, DialGACL surpasses QaDialMoE+large (89.5%) and LI^4+base (89.2%), achieving an accuracy of 89.7% under Evidence Oracle.

In the more challenging **FAVIQ** benchmark (Table 4), existing methods (e.g., DPR/BART, LI^4) are restricted to 66.9%–85.0% accuracy due to missing evidence (N/A fields) and static interaction mechanisms. Our model, leveraging a contrastive learning module, achieves a PE accuracy of 74.8%—a 7.9% improvement over DPR/BART—and establishes new state-of-the-art results on A/R test sets (R-Test: 85.5%; A-Dev: 74.8%). However, N/A fields continue to limit performance, underscoring the need for future exploration of multi-source evidence fusion strategies.

Table 2. Comparative performance on HEALTHVER dev and test set

Model	Dev-Acc	Test-Acc	Test-F1	Test-R	Test-P
BERT-base	-	74.82	73.54	73.70	73.45
SciBERT	-	78.11	77.12	78.15	76.62
BioBERT	-	76.52	74.59	75.73	74.07
T5-base	-	80.69	79.60	79.00	80.82
RoBERTa-base	81.89	78.24	78.60	78.81	78.46
QaDialMoE(Roberta-base)	82.36	78.60	77.18	76.79	77.78
LI^4(Roberta-base)	83.35	79.44	76.24	75.41	77.42
DialGACL(Roberta-base)	83.30	**82.33**	**81.55**	**81.02**	**82.49**
LI^4(Roberta-large)	85.44	81.51	80.54	79.99	**82.51**
DialGACL(Roberta-large)	**86.17**	**82.88**	**81.85**	**81.44**	82.50

Table 3. Fact verification label accuracy on COLLOQUIAL

Model	Retrieval +Selection	Acc
KGAT(BERT)	DPR+BERT	51.2
	Wiki+BERT	53.2
	Evidence Oracle	57.3
KGAT (CorefBERT)	DPR+BERT	61.0
	Wiki+BERT	60.9
	Evidence Oracle	67.7
QaDialMoE(large)	Evidence Oracle	89.5
LI^4(base)	Evidence Oracle	89.2
DialGACL(base)	Evidence Oracle	**89.7**

Table 4. Fact verification accuracy on FAVIQ

Model	A-dev	R-dev	R-test
Claim only BART	51.0	59.4	59.4
TF-IDF+BART	65.1	74.2	71.2
DPR+BART	66.9	76.8	74.6
FiD(base)	67.8	-	-
FiD+EG	69.6	-	-
QaDialMoE+DPR	70.8	78.0	75.3
QaDialMoE+PE	74.3	85.6	84.9
LI^4+PE	74.5	85.8	85.2
DialGACL+PE	**74.8**	**85.9**	**85.5**

5.3 Performance Analysis

Ablation Study. Our ablation study on the HEALTHVER test set (Table 5) validates the individual contributions of our core components. The K-GAT module proves its superiority over standard graph networks by outperforming GAT and GCN variants by up to 1.37% in accuracy; its removal causes a more drastic 3.45% drop, confirming its necessity for modeling complex semantics. Concurrently, removing the Label Contrastive Loss (LCL) decreases accuracy by 1.05%, underscoring its key role in refining class distinctions. These results confirm that both components are integral to our model's final performance.

Efficiency Comparison. To ensure a fair efficiency comparison, all model variants were built on the same RoBERTa-base backbone and trained for 30 epochs on a single NVIDIA RTX 4090 (24 GB) GPU. Table 6 presents our efficiency ablation study, demonstrating that the K-GAT module achieves significant performance gains with only a marginal impact on memory and training speed, confirming its high efficiency and feasibility on modern hardware.

Table 5. Ablation study on HEALTHVER test set

Model	Acc	F1	R	P
Complete model	**82.33**	**81.55**	**81.02**	**82.49**
w/o K-GAT & w GAT	81.45	80.60	80.33	81.07
w/o K-GAT & w GCN	80.96	80.02	79.77	80.36
w/o K-GAT	78.88	77.94	77.73	78.22
w/o LCL	81.28	79.91	79.49	80.64

Table 6. Training speed and memory usage on HEALTHVER

Model	Memory	Training Speed
DialGACL	15.35 GB	3.38 it/s
w/o K-GAT & w GAT	11.83 GB	5.55 it/s
w/o K-GAT & w GCN	11.74 GB	5.65 it/s

5.4 Error Analysis

To understand our model's limitations, we analyzed 200 randomly sampled errors from each dataset, with representative examples shown in Table 7. We found that on FAVIQ, almost 80% of errors were refuted claims misclassified as supported, mainly due to failures in common sense reasoning. For example, our model fails to refute the claim that Stacey's surname remains *"West"* after marrying (example 1), as it lacks real-world knowledge of surname changes and defaults to explicit textual evidence. A second critical challenge is distinguishing relevance from proof. Our model correctly captures the topical association between *"Dory"* and *"Pixar"* but then incorrectly extrapolates this general relevance to support a highly specific, ambiguous claim (example 2, COLLOQUIAL). This reveals its tendency to conflate strong thematic links with factual proof.

Table 7. Examples of claim verification errors

	Example
(1)	**Question:** what is stacey's surname in gavin and stacey after marrying?
	Claim: West was Stacey's surname in Gavin and Stacey after marrying.
	Evidence: ...The Bedmores representative he had to correspond with was a woman called Stacey West... within 9 weeks, they had gotten married.
	Gold label: REFUTES **Predicted label:** SUPPORTS
(2)	**Question:** Who was the lead by dory?
	Claim: dory was actually a lead by someone who works primarily at pixar.
	Evidence: Pixar content: Finding Dory, along with its predecessor Finding Nemo(2003), as well as Toy Story 3(2010) are among the 50 highest-grossing films of all time, with the lattermost film being the third all-time highest-grossing animated film with a gross of 1.063 billion.
	Gold label: NEUTRAL **Predicted label:** SUPPORTS

6 Conclusion and Future Work

We propose DialGACL, a novel model for dialogue-based fact verification that synergistically combines a KAN-driven non-linear graph attention with prototype contrastive learning. Our architecture effectively captures deep semantic dependencies while filtering informational noise, achieving state-of-the-art performance across three benchmarks with exceptional robustness in dynamic dialogue scenarios. While generative models offer a powerful alternative, our discriminative approach provides key advantages in efficiency, interpretability and reliability against hallucination. Future work will focus on integrating multi-source evidence and external knowledge, as well as a comprehensive benchmark against these generative paradigms.

Acknowledgments. Supported by the China National Social Science Foundation project (23XTQ009), the Chongqing Normal University Postgraduate Scientific Research Innovation Project (YKC24004), and the Sichuan Police College Key Laboratory for Management of National Security Risks 2024 Open Project (ZHKFYB2405).

References

1. Liao, H., et al.: Muser: a multi-step evidence retrieval enhancement framework for fake news detection. In: Proceedings of the 29th ACM SIGKDD Conference on Knowledge Discovery and Data Mining, pp. 4461–4472 (2023)
2. van Der Linden, S., Roozenbeek, J., Compton, J.: Inoculating against fake news about covid-19. Front. Psychol. **11**, 566790 (2020)
3. Gong, H., Xu, W., Wu, S., Liu, Q., Wang, L.: Heterogeneous graph reasoning for fact checking over texts and tables. In: Proceedings of the AAAI Conference on Artificial Intelligence, vol. 38, pp. 100–108 (2024)
4. Bekoulis, G., Papagiannopoulou, C., Deligiannis, N.: A review on fact extraction and verification. ACM Comput. Surv. (CSUR) **55**(1), 1–35 (2021)
5. Hu, X., Hong, Z., Guo, Z., Wen, L., Yu, P.: Read it twice: towards faithfully interpretable fact verification by revisiting evidence. In: Proceedings of the 46th International ACM SIGIR Conference on Research and Development in Information Retrieval, pp. 2319–2323 (2023)
6. Zhang, X., Wang, C., Zhao, G., Su, X.: Li4: label-infused iterative information interacting based fact verification in question-answering dialogue. In: Proceedings of the 2024 Joint International Conference on Computational Linguistics, Language Resources and Evaluation (LREC-COLING 2024), pp. 10488–10498 (2024)
7. Sarrouti, M., Abacha, A.B., M'rabet, Y., Demner-Fushman, D.: Evidence-based fact-checking of health-related claims. In: Findings of the Association for Computational Linguistics: EMNLP 2021, pp. 3499–3512 (2021)
8. Kim, B., Kim, H., Hong, S., Kim, G.: How robust are fact checking systems on colloquial claims? In: Proceedings of the 2021 Conference of the North American Chapter of the Association for Computational Linguistics: Human Language Technologies, pp. 1535–1548 (2021)
9. Gupta, P., Wu, C.S., Liu, W., Xiong, C.: Dialfact: a benchmark for fact-checking in dialogue. arXiv preprint arXiv:2110.08222 (2021)

10. Wang, L., Zhang, P., Lu, X., Zhang, L., Yan, C., Zhang, C.: Qadialmoe: question-answering dialogue based fact verification with mixture of experts. In: Findings of the Association for Computational Linguistics: EMNLP, pp. 3146–3159 (2022)
11. Du, C., Chen, Z., Feng, F., Zhu, L., Gan, T., Nie, L.: Explicit interaction model towards text classification. In: Proceedings of the AAAI Conference on Artificial Intelligence, vol. 33, pp. 6359–6366 (2019)
12. Oord, A.V.D., Li, Y., Vinyals, O.: Representation learning with contrastive predictive coding. arXiv preprint arXiv:1807.03748 (2018)
13. Gao, T., Yao, X., Chen, D.: Simcse: simple contrastive learning of sentence embeddings. arXiv preprint arXiv:2104.08821 (2021)
14. Chen, Y., Wu, L., Zaki, M.: Iterative deep graph learning for graph neural networks: better and robust node embeddings. Adv. Neural. Inf. Process. Syst. **33**, 19314–19326 (2020)
15. Liu, Z., et al.: KAN: Kolmogorov-Arnold networks. arXiv preprint arXiv:2404.19756 (2024)
16. Braun, J., Griebel, M.: On a constructive proof of Kolmogorov's superposition theorem. Constr. Approx. **30**, 653–675 (2009)
17. Park, J., Min, S., Kang, J., Zettlemoyer, L., Hajishirzi, H.: FaVIQ: fact verification from information-seeking questions. In: Proceedings of the 60th Annual Meeting of the Association for Computational Linguistics, pp. 5154–5166 (2022)
18. Beltagy, I., Lo, K., Cohan, A.: SciBERT: a pretrained language model for scientific text. In: Proceedings of the 2019 Conference on Empirical Methods in Natural Language (EMNLP-IJCNLP), pp. 3615–3620 (2019)
19. Schneider, E.T.R., et al.: BioBERTpt - a Portuguese neural language model for clinical named entity recognition. In: Proceedings of the 3rd Clinical Natural Language Processing Workshop, pp. 65–72 (2020)
20. Raffel, C., et al.: Exploring the limits of transfer learning with a unified text-to-text transformer. J. Mach. Learn. Res. **21**(1) (2020)
21. Liu, Z., Xiong, C., Sun, M., Liu, Z.: Fine-grained fact verification with kernel graph attention network. arXiv preprint arXiv:1910.09796 (2019)
22. Lewis, M., et al.: BART: denoising sequence-to-sequence pre-training for natural language generation, translation, and comprehension. In: Proceedings of the 58th Annual Meeting of the Association for Computational Linguistics, pp. 7871–7880 (2020)
23. Asai, A., Gardner, M., Hajishirzi, H.: Evidentiality-guided generation for knowledge-intensive NLP tasks. In: Proceedings of the 2022 Conference of the North American Chapter of the Association for Computational Linguistics: Human Language Technologies, pp. 2226–2243 (2022)

TimbreAdv: Timbre Adversarial Attacks on Speaker Verification Systems

Ye Xiao[1], Wenhan Yao[1], Zexin Li[1], Jinsu Yang[1], Yuhao Chen[1], Xiandang Luo[1], Fen Xiao[1], and Weiping Wen[2](✉)

[1] XiangTan University, Xiangtan, Hunan, China
xy@smail.xtu.edu.cn
[2] Peking University, Beijing, China
weipingwen@pku.edu.cn

Abstract. In recent years, speaker verification (SV) systems have become ubiquitous across security-critical applications. While these systems encode speaker identities into high-dimensional embeddings, they remain vulnerable to adversarial attacks that manipulate these embeddings, so it is essential for us to expose as many "blind spots" of speaker verification systems as possible. Existing attacks predominantly inject additive noise, which often compromises speech naturalness and lacks semantic control. In this paper, we propose the Timbre Adversarial attack (TimbreAdv), a novel paradigm that exploits vocal tract characteristics to deceive SV systems. Our framework introduces hierarchical feature disentanglement, feature-level timbre blending, and multi-object adversarial optimization to generate adversarial samples under the setting of black-box. We use comprehensive metrics to evaluate our method, and the results show great attack effectiveness and stealthiness.

Keywords: Adversarial Attacks · Speaker Verification Systems · Multi-object Adversarial Optimization

1 Introduction

Speaker verification systems [1], which authenticate individuals based on unique vocal characteristics, have become integral to modern security infrastructures. These systems are widely deployed in biometric authentication (e.g., smartphone unlocking, banking voiceprints), forensic analysis (e.g., courtroom evidence validation), and smart environments (e.g., personalized voice assistants). At their core, speaker verification pipelines involve two phases: enrollment and verification. During enrollment, a speaker's voice is converted into a high-dimensional embedding that captures vocal tract and prosodic traits. During verification, a similarity score is computed between the input voiceprint and stored references to accept or reject identity claims. The continuous and high-dimensional nature of voiceprint embeddings creates complex decision boundaries in feature space, which introduces fragility: minor perturbations(whether from environmental noise or adversarial manipulation) in the embedding space can shift samples across decision thresholds. This vulnerability renders speaker verification systems susceptible to *adversarial attacks* [5–10], where intentionally crafted perturbations induce misclassification. To avoid potential risks and further research the robustness of speaker verification systems, it is of great value to expose as many "blind spots" of speaker verification systems as possible at the current research stage.

Adversarial attacks aim at perturbing the system input in a purposefully designed way to make the system behave incorrectly. In general, adversarial attacks fall into two categories based on threat models: white-box attacks and black-box attacks. White-box attacks [5–7], such as the Fast Gradient Sign Method [2] (FGSM) and Projected Gradient Descent [3] (PGD), utilize gradient-based optimization to craft perturbations by leveraging full access to model parameters and training dynamics. In contrast, black-box attacks [8–10], exemplified by Zeroth-Order Optimization [4] (ZOO) and evolutionary strategies, rely on iterative queries to approximate gradients or heuristic optimization without direct model access.

The study of adversarial attacks originated in computer vision, where the differentiable nature of image pixels enabled systematic perturbation optimization. While adversarial attacks in computer vision have been widely studied, their application in the audio domain, particularly in speaker verification, remains underexplored for audio's temporal nature and human perceptual sensitivity. A critical constraint is stealthiness: perturbations must remain undetectable by humans, while preserving semantic content and temporal coherence. Also, while many existing adversarial attack methods operate under the white-box assumptions, their real-world applicability is limited for attackers typically cannot access model internals. Black-box attacks relying solely on query interactions or transferability are more practical but inherently challenging. To address these challenges, we propose TimbreAdv, a timbre-based adversarial attack framework that fills the gap in speaker verification robustness research. Our contributions can be summarized as follows:

1. We propose a novel adversarial attack framework leveraging timbre characteristics to implement adversarial attacks while operating under a black-box setting.
2. We propose the framework introducing hierarchical feature disentanglement, feature-level timbre blending and multi-object adversarial optimization to generate adversarial samples.
3. Our method generates adversarial samples that effectively deceive SV systems while preserving linguistic content, achieving great stealthiness.

2 Background

2.1 Adversarial Attacks

Adversarial attacks refer to techniques that manipulate machine learning models by introducing small but carefully crafted perturbations to input data, leading to

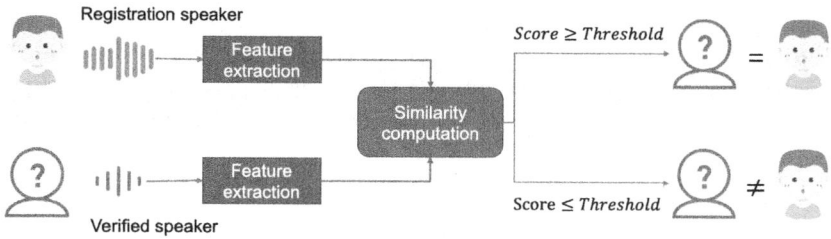

Fig. 1. Pipelines of speaker verification tasks.

incorrect predictions. These perturbations are often imperceptible to humans, yet significantly degrade model performance [2–4]. Formally, an adversarial attack aims to find a minimally modified input $x + \delta$ such that:

$$\mathcal{F}(x + \delta) \neq \mathcal{F}(x), \quad \text{s.t.} \quad |\delta|_p \leq \epsilon, \tag{1}$$

where $\mathcal{F}(\cdot)$ denotes the deep learning model, δ is the adversarial perturbation, and ϵ constrains perturbation magnitude under the ℓ_p-norm (typically $p = 2$ or ∞).

Adversarial example was first proposed in computer vision [2,14,15]. In recent years, researchers have proposed a variety of techniques in their attempts to challenge the robustness of SV systems [16–19]. These attacks can target a specific speaker or target multiple speakers, identify a speaker from a set of enrolled speakers, or identify a speaker if it is contained in this enrolled speakers set. Most attacks proposed in prior research are individual attacks [16,20], in which the attacker must generate perturbations specific to each genuine sample, reducing the attack's efficiency. Less common are universal perturbations [23], which although usually considerably more costly and difficult to generate, are more efficient during test time. In the study performed by Li et al. [22], a generative adversarial network (GAN) was trained to serve as a universal approach. In this paper, we focus on the challenging task of generating adversarial samples to implement universal adversarial attacks and work effectively on an unknown set of speakers.

2.2 Speaker Verification Systems

The goal of the speaker verification task is to judge whether a given utterance is from a registered speaker, as illustrated in Fig. 1. Let $F(\cdot)$ denotes the speaker embedding extraction function, which receives an input audio x and gives the speaker embedding $v = F(x)$. For two utterances x_1 and x_2, we use cosine similarity as a score to measure the distance between their speaker embeddings. The score $s(F(x_1), F(x_2))$ is calculated by

$$s(F(x_1), F(x_2)) = \frac{F(x_1)F(x_2)}{\|F(x_1)\|_2 \|F(x_2)\|_2}, \tag{2}$$

it will give a same speaker decision when the score satisfies $s(F(x_1), F(x_2)) \geq \theta$, where θ is a preset threshold, otherwise, it will give a different decision. This means that SV systems possess inherent defence capabilities and can resist weaker adversarial attacks, making it more difficult to craft suitable adversarial examples.

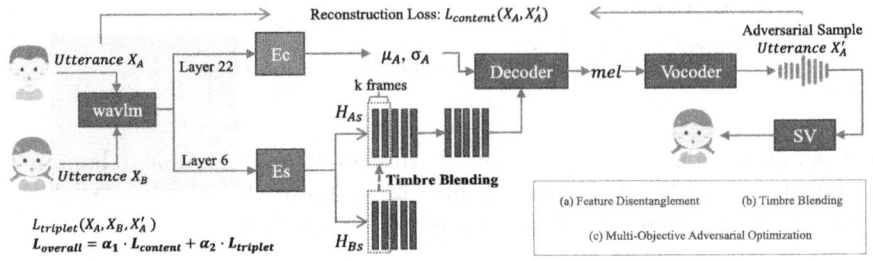

Fig. 2. Framework of TimbreAdv that adversarially misleads speaker verification models by confusing the timbre of speaker A and speaker B.

Table 1. Algorithm Symbol Definitions

Symbol	Description
X_A, X_B	Raw waveform inputs of source speaker A and target speaker B
f_{SSL}^n	Self-supervised learning encoder with n denoting layer index
E_s, E_c	Speaker encoder and content encoder
H_{As}, H_{Bs}	Speaker embeddings
μ_A, σ_A	Mean and standard deviation of source content features E_c
F	Speaker embedding extraction function
k	Critical frame length for timbre hybridization
$\mathcal{L}_{content}$	Waveform fidelity loss (L_1 distance)
$\mathcal{L}_{triplet}$	Triplet loss against SV model
α_i	Dynamic weights in MGDA optimization
η	Learning rate for gradient update

3 Methodology

3.1 Method Overview

Timbre serves as a fundamental attribute in speaker verification tasks, functioning as a unique auditory fingerprint determined by the physical characteristics of the vocal tract. The primary objective of SV systems is to distinguish between speakers based on timbre rather than the semantic content of speech. Consequently, altering timbre presents a direct and effective approach to disrupting SV systems, thereby increasing attack success rates. Furthermore, some speaker verification systems operate in a text-dependent manner, where authentication relies not only on the speaker's identity but also on the specific speech content.

This insight motivates a shift from traditional noise-based attacks to timbre-driven perturbations, which enable targeted speaker impersonation while preserving perceptual naturalness. We achieve this by altering the timbre of a source utterance X_A to resemble that of a target speaker X_B, generating adversarial examples that satisfy:

$$\text{SV}(\text{TimbreAdv}(X_A, X_B)) \neq \text{SV}(X_A), \tag{3}$$

where $\text{SV}(\cdot)$ denotes the output of a speaker verification model and $\text{TimbreAdv}(\cdot)$ denotes our attack framework. The generated adversarial sample retains the linguistic content of X_A but adopts the speaker identity of X_B, so that it can deceive SV systems while preserving the content and perceptual naturalness. The framework comprises three core modules: hierarchical feature disentanglement, frame-level timbre blending, and multi-objective adversarial optimization, as illustrated in Fig. 2. We define some description symbols in Table 1. Below, we detail each component.

3.2 Hierarchical Feature Disentanglement

Self-supervised learning (SSL) trained on a large-scale unannotated speech corpus shows considerable potential for Voice Conversion(VC) tasks that require feature disentanglement. Also, the WavLM model [11] effectively addresses comprehensive downstream speech tasks, encompassing speaker verification, speaker diarization, speech separation and speech recognition [12]. Also, the research demonstrates that the upper layers of the model have greater semantic information, while the lower layers of the model contain more speaker-related information. So we employ WavLM pretrained model to extract self-supervised feature information from speech and choose layer 6 and layer 22 of the model to capture speaker characteristics and encode content information, respectively.

3.3 Frame-Level Timbre Blending

After getting speaker embeddings H_{As}, H_{Bs} from E_s and getting content representation μ_B from E_c, we need to further deal with it to generate adversarial samples. As for speaker embedding, we employ frame-wise timbre blending to replace the k frames of H_{As} with those from H_{Bs} to inject target timbre features:

$$H_{As}[:, k :] = H_{Bs}[:, k :]. \tag{4}$$

Furthermore, for overall semantic consistency, we eliminate source timbre information from content features by whitening H_{Ac}^k with speaker A's statistics, then

Algorithm 1. Timbre Adversarial Samples Generation

Require: Utterance of speaker A X_A, utterance of speaker B X_B; SSL encoder f_{SSL}; speaker verification model SV; Frame number k; speaker encoder E_s; content encoder E_c; Decoder; Vocoder; learning rate η.
Ensure: Adversarial sample X'_A
1: Initialize model parameters θ
2: **while** Not Converged **do**
3: $\quad H_{As} \leftarrow E_s(f_{\text{SSL}}^6(X_A)), H_{Bs} \leftarrow E_s(f_{\text{SSL}}^6(X_B))$ ▷ Extract speaker features
4: $\quad \mu_A, \sigma_A \leftarrow E_c(f_{\text{SSL}}^{22}(X_A))$ ▷ Content encoder
5: $\quad H_{As}[:,k:] \leftarrow H_{Bs}[:,k:]$ ▷ Replace k frames of speaker A with B
6: $\quad$ mel $\leftarrow$ Decoder(H_{As}, μ_A) ▷ Generate Mel-spectrogram
7: $\quad X'_A \leftarrow$ Vocoder(mel) ▷ Convert to waveform
8: $\quad$ **if** $SV(X'_A) = SV(X_B)$ **then** ▷ Check attack success
9: $\quad\quad$ **break**
10: $\quad$ **else**
11: $\quad\quad \mathcal{L}_{content} \leftarrow \|X'_A - X_A\|_1$
12: $\quad\quad \mathcal{L}_{triplet} \leftarrow \max\left(\cos(F(X'_A), F(X_A)) - \cos(F(X'_A), F(X_B)) + m,\ 0\right)$
13: $\quad\quad$ Solve α_1, α_2 via: $\min \|\alpha_1 \nabla_\theta \mathcal{L}_{content} + \alpha_2 \nabla_\theta \mathcal{L}_{triplet}\|^2$
14: $\quad\quad$ Update $\theta \leftarrow \theta - \eta(\alpha_1 \nabla_\theta \mathcal{L}_{content} + \alpha_2 \nabla_\theta \mathcal{L}_{triplet})$ ▷ Optimization
15: $\quad$ **end if**
16: **end while**
17: **return** X'_A

---

rescaling with speaker B's distribution:

$$H_{Ac}^k = \sigma_B \left(\frac{H_{Ac}^k - \mu_A}{\sigma_A} \right) + \mu_B, \tag{5}$$

where μ_A, σ_A denote the mean and standard deviation of source speaker A's content features computed by E_c, and μ_B, σ_B of each layer denote the linear transformation of the output of speaker encoder E_s. This alignment ensures spectral compatibility between hybridized timbre and original content.

To be more specific, the content encoder employs instance normalization (IN) to standardize input speech features by eliminating speaker-dependent spectral characteristics while preserving abstract linguistic attributes. The speaker encoder extracts a low-dimensional timbre embedding from target speaker B's utterance. To blend timbre information into content features, the decoder transforms it into channel-wise affine parameters via fully connected layers and output mel-spectrogram further synthesized into a waveform via a neural vocoder, producing an adversarial example X'_A that exhibits deceptiveness and imperceptibility.

3.4 Multi-objective Adversarial Optimization

Generating effective adversarial samples for speaker verification requires simultaneously optimizing two competing objectives: (1) preserving the linguistic content and perceptual quality of the original utterance, and (2) altering the speaker identity by making the adversarial embedding resemble the target speaker rather than the source.

We formalize this as a multi-objective optimization problem with the following loss components: (1) $\mathcal{L}_{\text{content}}$: ensures the adversarial sample retains the original semantic content and waveform quality. We use the L1 distance between the original and adversarial waveform:

$$\mathcal{L}_{\text{content}} = \|X'_A - X_A\|_1. \tag{6}$$

(2) $\mathcal{L}_{\text{triplet}}$: encourages the embedding of the adversarial sample X'_A to be close to the target speaker X_B, and distant from the source speaker X_A. This is formulated as a triplet margin loss:

$$\mathcal{L}_{\text{triplet}} = \max\left(\cos(F(X'_A), F(X_A)) - \cos(F(X'_A), F(X_B)) + m,\ 0\right), \tag{7}$$

where $F(\cdot)$ denotes the speaker embedding extractor, and $m > 0$ is the margin hyperparameter.

These objectives inherently conflict as preserving content may hinder the ability to alter identity, and vice versa. To dynamically balance them, we adopt the Multiple Gradient Descent Algorithm (MGDA) to compute dynamic weights α_1, α_2 at each iteration to minimize the total loss:

$$\mathcal{L}_{\text{overall}} = \alpha_1 \cdot \mathcal{L}_{\text{content}} + \alpha_2 \cdot \mathcal{L}_{\text{triplet}}. \tag{8}$$

The weights are optimized via the Frank-Wolfe algorithm. MGDA allows the model to emphasize underperforming objectives early in training, and gradually converge to balanced weights as both objectives improve. This optimization is performed iteratively as shown in Algorithm 1.

4 Experiments

4.1 Experiments Setup

Dataset. We use LibriSpeech [24], VoxCeleb1 [25], and VoxCeleb2 [26] to evaluate the effectiveness of our adversarial perturbations. These three datasets collectively span both clean, studio-quality recordings and noisy, in-the-wild utterances, enabling a comprehensive assessment of attack performance under controlled and unconstrained acoustic conditions. LibriSpeech provides paired transcripts, allowing precise evaluation of content preservation via word error rate (WER). For VoxCeleb1 and VoxCeleb2, which lack ground-truth transcripts, we employ the Whisper [27] automatic speech recognition (ASR) model to transcribe adversarial and original audio, enabling WER computation in real-world scenarios.

Model. We adopt WavLM [11] to extract self-supervised learning (SSL) features, which have demonstrated strong generalization across a range of downstream speech tasks, including speaker recognition and content modeling. We employ HiFi-GAN [28] as the vocoder due to its ability to generate high-fidelity speech with low computational cost. To guide adversarial sample generation, we use the state-of-the-art speaker verification model ERes2NetV2 [29] as a proxy model. During optimization, the adversarial perturbations are iteratively updated to deceive this proxy system. For black-box evaluation, we attack ECAPA-TDNN model [30], which is not involved in adversarial generation.

Metrics. To evaluate both the effectiveness and perceptual quality of our adversarial perturbations, we compute the cosine similarity (Similarity) between the original clean input and the adversarial example, as well as the attack success rate (ASR) to assess attack effectiveness. We also calculate the word error rate (WER) using an automatic speech recognition system to verify linguistic integrity. For perceptual quality, we report the Perceptual Evaluation of Speech Quality (PESQ) score, which ranges from 1.0 (poor) to 4.5 (excellent). In addition, we conduct a Mean Opinion Score (MOS) test, in which human listeners subjectively rate the naturalness of adversarial sample on a 1–5 scale.

Baseline Methods. Our method was compared against with: (1) original clean utterances (Clean), (2) additive white Gaussian noise perturbations (Random), (3) white-box adversarial attacks based on projected gradient descent (PGD) [3], (4) GAN-generated perturbations (GAN) [22] and (5) universal adversarial perturbation (UAP) [23].

Training Details. Raw audio waveforms X_A and X_B are resampled to 16 kHz for consistent processing. Utterance lengths are standardized to 4s: shorter segments are zero-padded at the end, while longer segments are truncated at the end. The encoder and decoder are jointly optimized using the Adam optimizer with fixed hyperparameters: learning rate $\eta = 0.0005$, $\beta_1 = 0.5$, $\beta_2 = 0.9$, and batch size $= 8$. Training stops when any of these conditions is met: (1) The overall loss change $|\Delta \mathcal{L}_{\text{overall}}| < 10^{-4}$ for 10 consecutive iterations. (2) ASR $> 99.5\%$ against the proxy ERes2NetV2 model. (3) A maximum of 200 iterations is reached. The margin hyperparameter is set to $m = 0.4$ in our experiments.

Table 2. Cross-dataset evaluation of TimbreAdv

Dataset	ASR(%)↑	Similarity(%)↓	WER(%)↓
LibriSpeech [24]	96.91	46.86	13.3
VoxCeleb1 [25]	95.43	48.21	14.2
VoxCeleb2 [26]	93.87	51.05	15.8

4.2 Results

Results Analysis. Table 2 presents the cross-dataset generalization performance of TimbreAdv on three datasets. Across all datasets, TimbreAdv maintains consistently high ASR, demonstrating robustness in both clean and in-the-wild acoustic conditions. On the clean and studio-quality LibriSpeech corpus, TimbreAdv achieves a near-perfect ASR of 96.91%, with a low speaker embedding similarity of 46.92% and minimal degradation in speech intelligibility. When applied to the more challenging VoxCeleb1 and VoxCeleb2 datasets—characterized by background noise, varied recording channels, and cross-accent speech—TimbreAdv still achieves strong ASR values of 95.43% and 93.87%, respectively. As expected, the speaker similarity increases slightly, and WER rises moderately on VoxCeleb datasets due to greater acoustic variability.

As shown in Table 3, TimbreAdv achieves a high ASR of 96.91%, outperforming both GAN-based and UAP baselines, demonstrating its effectiveness in deceiving speaker verification systems under black-box conditions. The cosine similarity between adversarial and clean embeddings drops to 46.92%, confirming that timbre has been significantly altered. Meanwhile, the WER increases only marginally, indicating that linguistic content is largely preserved. For perceptual quality, TimbreAdv achieves a PESQ of 3.94, suggesting minimal audible artifacts. Furthermore, a small-scale listening study yields an average MOS of 4.2, confirming the naturalness and imperceptibility of the generated adversarial examples. Overall, TimbreAdv demonstrates a superior balance between attack effectiveness and perceptual stealth, outperforming both black-box and white-box attack baselines across all evaluation metrics.

Table 3. Evaluation of different attack methods on LibriSpeech.

Method	ASR(%)↑	Similarity(%)↓	WER(%)↓	PESQ↑	MOS↑
Clean	0.00	84.71	12.3	4.01	4.5
Random	13.26	80.05	18.7	3.58	3.7
GAN [22]	72.65	82.47	21.8	3.26	3.5
UAP [23]	82.10	76.98	19.2	3.42	3.6
PGD [3]	94.80	74.56	28.6	2.78	2.9
TimbreAdv (Ours)	96.91	46.92	13.0	3.94	4.2

Ablation Analysis. We perform ablation studies to examine the impact of two key factors: the frame selection ratio k/T and the loss weighting strategy.

As illustrated in Fig. 3, we investigate the impact of the frame selection ratio k/T on speaker similarity between clean and adversarial samples. The results show a clear decreasing trend: as k increases, the similarity score drops accordingly. This indicates that incorporating a larger proportion of frames from the

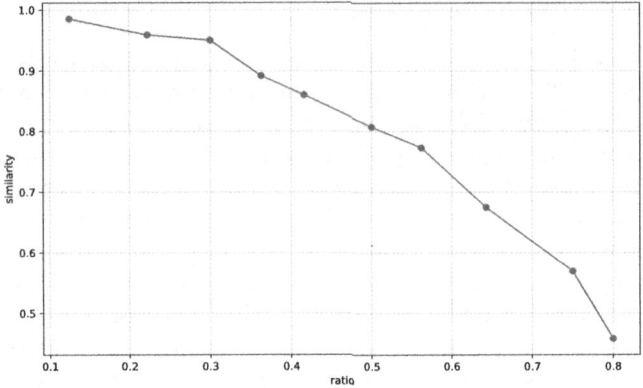

Fig. 3. Impact of frame selection ratio k/T on the same speaker similarity.

target speaker leads to more effective timbre transformation. In particular, higher k values inject more target-specific acoustic characteristics, thereby enhancing speaker identity manipulation. Conversely, smaller values of k result in more subtle, localized perturbations, which may better preserve perceptual naturalness while offering limited speaker obfuscation.

Table 4. Ablation Study on Loss Weighting Strategy (LibriSpeech)

Weighting Method	ASR(%)↑	Similarity(%)↓	WER(%)↓
Fixed ($\alpha_1 = 0.7$, $\alpha_2 = 0.3$)	91.82	53.48	13.7
Fixed ($\alpha_1 = 0.5$, $\alpha_2 = 0.5$)	94.17	50.13	14.2
MGDA (Ours)	96.45	45.63	13.1

We compare fixed loss weight configurations (α_1, α_2) with our adaptive strategy based on Multiple Gradient Descent Algorithm (MGDA), as shown in Table 4. Fixed ratios, such as (0.7, 0.3) or (0.5, 0.5), are static throughout training and cannot adjust to shifting optimization dynamics. In contrast, MGDA dynamically allocates higher weight to the underperforming objective during early training stages, allowing faster correction and more balanced convergence. Over time, MGDA weights tend to stabilize near (0.5, 0.5), reflecting equilibrium between adversarial strength and linguistic preservation.

5 Conclusion

In this paper, we present TimbreAdv, a novel adversarial attack framework targeting speaker verification systems by manipulating vocal timbre rather than introducing additive noise. Our method operates under black-box settings and comprises three key modules: hierarchical feature disentanglement, frame-level timbre blending, and multi-objective adversarial optimization. Extensive experiments across three datasets show that TimbreAdv achieves high attack success rates with low speaker similarity and minimal degradation in intelligibility and perceptual quality. Compared to both black-box and white-box baselines, our method consistently outperforms in terms of effectiveness and stealthiness.

Disclosure of Interests. The authors have no competing interests to declare that are relevant to the content of this article.

References

1. Bimbot, F., et al.: A tutorial on text-independent speaker verification. EURASIP J. Adv. Signal Process. **2004**, 1–22 (2004)
2. Goodfellow, I.J., et al.: Explaining and Harnessing Adversarial Examples. CoRR abs/1412.6572 (2014)
3. Madry, A., et al.: Towards deep learning models resistant to adversarial attacks. arXiv preprint arXiv:1706.06083 (2017)
4. Chen, P.-Y., et al.: Zoo: zeroth order optimization based black-box attacks to deep neural networks without training substitute models. In: Proceedings of the 10th ACM Workshop on Artificial Intelligence and Security (2017)
5. Li, X., et al.: Adversarial attacks on GMM i-vector based speaker verification systems. In: ICASSP 2020-2020 IEEE International Conference on Acoustics, Speech and Signal Processing (ICASSP). IEEE (2020)
6. Villalba, J., Zhang, Y., Dehak, N.: x-vectors meet adversarial attacks: benchmarking adversarial robustness in speaker verification. In: Interspeech (2020)
7. Luo, H., et al.: Spoofing speaker verification system by adversarial examples leveraging the generalized speaker difference. Secur. Commun. Netw. **2021**(1), 6664578 (2021)
8. Bi, X., et al.: Boosting question answering over knowledge graph with reward integration and policy evaluation under weak supervision. Inf. Process. Manag. **60**(2), 103242 (2023)
9. Liu, J., et al.: GNN-based long and short term preference modeling for next-location prediction. Inf. Sci. **629**, 1–14 (2023)
10. Jia, Y., et al.: Extrapolation over temporal knowledge graph via hyperbolic embedding. CAAI Trans. Intell. Technol. **8**(2), 418–429 (2023)
11. Chen, S., et al.: WavLM: large-scale self-supervised pre-training for full stack speech processing. IEEE J. Sel. Top. Signal Process. **16**(6), 1505–1518 (2022)
12. Lin, G.-T., et al.: On the utility of self-supervised models for prosody-related tasks. In: 2022 IEEE Spoken Language Technology Workshop (SLT). IEEE (2023)
13. Zhao, X., et al.: Adversarial speaker disentanglement using unannotated external data for self-supervised representation-based voice conversion. In: 2023 IEEE International Conference on Multimedia and Expo (ICME), pp. 1691–1696 (2023)
14. Feng, Y., et al.: Adversarial attack on deep product quantization network for image retrieval. In: Proceedings of the AAAI Conference on Artificial Intelligence, vol. 34, no. 07 (2020)
15. Wang, J., et al.: Dual attention suppression attack: Generate adversarial camouflage in physical world. In: Proceedings of the IEEE/CVF Conference on Computer Vision and Pattern Recognition (2021)

16. Shamsabadi, A.S., et al.: Foolhd: fooling speaker identification by highly imperceptible adversarial disturbances. In: ICASSP 2021-2021 IEEE International Conference on Acoustics, Speech and Signal Processing (ICASSP). IEEE (2021)
17. Kreuk, F., et al.: Fooling end-to-end speaker verification with adversarial examples. In: 2018 IEEE International Conference on Acoustics, Speech and Signal Processing (ICASSP). IEEE (2018)
18. Xie, Y., et al.: Real-time, universal, and robust adversarial attacks against speaker recognition systems. In: ICASSP 2020-2020 IEEE International Conference on Acoustics, Speech and Signal Processing (ICASSP). IEEE (2020)
19. Zhang, W., et al.: Attack on practical speaker verification system using universal adversarial perturbations. In: ICASSP 2021-2021 IEEE International Conference on Acoustics, Speech and Signal Processing (ICASSP). IEEE (2021)
20. Chen, G., et al.: AS2T: arbitrary source-to-target adversarial attack on speaker recognition systems. IEEE Trans. Dependable Secure Comput. (2022)
21. Xie, Y., et al.: Enabling fast and universal audio adversarial attack using generative model. In: Proceedings of the AAAI Conference on Artificial Intelligence, vol. 35, no. 16 (2021)
22. Li, J., et al.: Universal adversarial perturbations generative network for speaker recognition. In: 2020 IEEE International Conference on Multimedia and Expo (ICME). IEEE (2020)
23. Hanina, S., et al.: Universal adversarial attack against speaker recognition models. In: ICASSP 2024-2024 IEEE International Conference on Acoustics, Speech and Signal Processing (ICASSP). IEEE (2024)
24. Panayotov, V., et al.: Librispeech: an ASR corpus based on public domain audio books. In: 2015 IEEE International Conference on Acoustics, Speech and Signal Processing (ICASSP). IEEE (2015)
25. Nagrani, A., Chung, J.S., Zisserman, A.: Voxceleb: a large-scale speaker identification dataset. arXiv preprint arXiv:1706.08612 (2017)
26. Chung, J.S., Nagrani, A., Zisserman, A.: VoxCeleb2: Deep Speaker Recognition (2018)
27. Radford, A., et al.: Robust speech recognition via large-scale weak supervision. In: International Conference on Machine Learning. PMLR (2023)
28. Kong, J., Kim, J., Bae, J.: HiFi-GAN: generative adversarial networks for efficient and high fidelity speech synthesis. Adv. Neural. Inf. Process. Syst. **33**, 17022–17033 (2020)
29. Chen, Y., et al.: Eres2netv2: boosting short-duration speaker verification performance with computational efficiency. arXiv preprint arXiv:2406.02167 (2024)
30. Desplanques, B., Thienpondt, J., Demuynck, K.: ECAPA-TDNN: Emphasized Channel Attention, Propagation and Aggregation in TDNN Based Speaker Verification (2020)
31. Zolfi, A., et al.: Adversarial mask: real-world universal adversarial attack on face recognition models. In: Joint European Conference on Machine Learning and Knowledge Discovery in Databases. Springer, Cham (2022)

Time Series Generation for Augmenting Multi-channel Automotive Audio Data

Philipp Engler[1,3](✉), Ludger van Elst[1], Peter Schichtel[2], Andreas Dengel[1,3], and Sheraz Ahmed[1]

[1] German Research Center for Artificial Intelligence (DFKI), 67663 Kaiserslautern, Germany
philipp.engler@dfki.de
[2] Ingenieurgesellschaft Auto und Verkehr (IAV) GmbH, 10587 Berlin, Germany
[3] RPTU Kaiserslautern-Landau, 67663 Kaiserslautern, Germany

Abstract. One of the top limiting factors for machine learning applications in industry is the lack of data, as the training of powerful models often requires vast datasets. Acquiring data at large scales is generally expensive and sometimes not even possible, as it may depend on costly measurements with specialized equipment, trained personnel and possibly manual annotations by experts. Thus, augmenting or synthesizing data plays a key role in making machine learning solutions feasible and cost-effective for industrial applications. In this paper, we propose a diffusion model for synthesizing audio data in a real-world multi-label audio classification task from the automotive industry. Augmenting the training dataset with synthetic data, we obtain an improvement of 1.8 p.p. in mAP over training with real data alone. We discuss the difficulties in generating such domain-specific data and examine issues further by comparing our method to an alternative generative approach for environmental sound augmentation.

Keywords: Time Series Generation · Diffusion Models · Audio Analysis

1 Introduction

Time series data arises in various industries, such as automotive, medicine or information technology, as well as in our everyday life. This data can contain valuable information. Due to the amount or complexity of the data, it is often infeasible to analyze time series manually. Machine learning models can help to uncover the hidden information, but they often require large-scale datasets for training and in many applications manual annotations by human experts are required. The necessary amount of data is often hindering industrial applications of machine learning. Recent breakthroughs in machine learning with large language models and high-fidelity image generation models rely on enormous amounts of texts and images taken from the web, where they are essentially freely available [12]. Many industrial applications do not have comparable resources and are limited to internally gathered data. The amount of available data thus is typically magnitudes smaller, making it difficult to even train small-scale machine learning models. Acquisition of additional data is expensive and sometimes not even possible due to availability of resources. In order to enable machine learning solutions to such tasks, it is crucial to utilize data as effectively as possible.

One important technique to enable training with limited data is data augmentation, artificially expanding the data using transformations on the available data. The choice of transformations depends on the nature of the data and has implications on the behavior of the machine learning model. Handcrafted transformations, such as cropping, adding noise and mirroring data are popularly used for various problems. They are simple to apply and can lead to significant improvements already. However, such naive transformations often do not replicate the natural variations in the data well enough [11], lavishing potential for obtaining more diverse data. Improper transformations may imply wrong correlations and natural correlations fade as salient features are disturbed. An alternative to manually constructing transformations are generative approaches. A machine learning model learns to generate synthetic data, aiming to approximate the underlying distribution of the real data. Such models can replicate the natural variations in the data and respect class-labels to retain salient, class-specific features while generating diverse data [3,11].

In this paper, we develop such a generative approach for a real-world audio classification problem from the automotive industry. The amount of available data recordings is sparse to an extent that a trained machine learning model does not classify all labels in a satisfactory way. To tackle this issue, we generate synthetic data using a diffusion model. We extend the method CCATS [7] such that the model can deal with this specific use case effectively. The benefits of using such a generative model to augment the available data are assessed and we find advantages over using only real data or naive transformations. Our contributions can be summarized as follows:

- We propose a diffusion model to generate multi-channel audio data for a real-world industrial problem, overcoming limitations of off-the-shelf solutions
- Our model is able to learn from the strictly limited and highly-imbalanced dataset to augment the dataset
- We find significant advantages over real data alone and naive transformations, highlighting the potential for diffusion-based data augmentation on such complex, noisy and limited real-world datasets

2 Related Work

In this section, we discuss recent work on generative approaches comparable to our task. There are various types of audio data. Music exhibits specific features such as rhythms, chords and melodies. Speech on the other hand is composed of words following certain patterns to give them meaning. These modalities differ severely from our task, which deals with classification of sounds in vehicles. We deem environmental sound classification problems more comparable, as they exhibit various noise sources. Thus, the selection of related work is focused on such tasks.

GANs for Audio Augmentation. Generative Adversarial Networks [9] have been widely applied to generate data in various domains, such as computer vision [3] or natural language processing [18]. Data augmentation based on GANs has proven useful, specifically on imbalanced datasets [1] and domain-specific problems [16]. Thus, GANs have also been employed to generate audio data. Madhu et al. propose EnvGAN [11], a generative approach for environmental sound augmentation, which builds upon the more general audio generation approach WaveGAN [6]. Bahmei et al. [2] apply a DCGAN [14] structure to generate synthetic spectrogram images. The generated spectrograms are used to augment the environmental sound datasets, which are then classified by a combined CNN-RNN architecture.

DPM for Audio Augmentation. Guo et al. [13] propose DAG, which is a score-based diffusion approach for synthesizing general audio data. It is based on a full-band audio auto-encoder architecture and works directly in the waveform domain. MambaFoley [5] leverages a structured state-space model for Foley sound generation, which also includes several noises such as vehicle sounds. Chen et al. [4] propose a class-conditional diffusion model approach for augmenting single-channel environmental sound datasets with synthetic data. Using a diffusion model, they overcome the shortcomings of GAN-based methods. They further utilize guidance to improve the quality of generated samples. They additionally train a discriminator, which filters out poor quality samples. The generated data is incorporated in the training data in order to augment the dataset. They evaluate their model by comparing a classifier model trained on real data with traditional augmentation methods against the same model trained with the mixture of real and synthetic data. Similarly to our approach, their methods works with mel spectrograms. While they also use a U-Net architecture, their model is inherently different from ours. Their model is based on 2D-convolutions, treating the spectrogram like an image. Our model is based on 1D-convolutions, treating the spectrogram as a time-series. Additionally, our model includes multiple modifications to make it applicable to our automotive dataset. We need to deal with multiple channels and a multi-label problem. As code for their approach is publicly available, we use it as a comparison to our method. However, we still need to make necessary modifications to the approach in order to run with our data. The modifications are specified in Sect. 3.2. We refer to their method in the following as ESC-DPM.

Engler et al. [7] propose CCATS, a class-conditional diffusion probabilistic model (DDPM) for generating time series data. The denoising model is a U-Net model based on 1D-convolutions. It is conditioned on a joint representation, which is composed of embeddings for the class-label, the diffusion step as well as the different time-steps across the time dimension. Their code is also available publicly[1]. While their approach is evaluated only on univariate datasets from the UCR classification archive and it is not directly designed towards audio data, we use their method as a basis and extend it to work with our specific dataset.

---
[1] https://github.com/Engler93/CCATS.

Text-to-Audio Models. Recently, text-to-audio (TTA) generative models have been used for audio augmentation [8,15]. Auto-regressive models [15] or latent diffusion models [8,15] are leveraged to generate synthetic environmental sound data, either using template prompts or large language models (LLMs) for generating prompts. These may be difficult to apply in our scenario, considering that the noise sources are highly specific to the vehicles and the data contains multiple channels with unknown inter-channel characteristics due to the microphone setup. Still, such approaches are of high interest for future work.

3 Methodology

In this section, we give an overview of out method. First, the aforementioned audio classification problem is stated. Then, we detail our approach to generate data in order to augment the limited training dataset and finally, we explain our evaluation protocol.

3.1 Problem Statement

The task to be solved is the classification of some noises inside vehicles on a multi-channel audio dataset based on recordings by multiple microphones. It is a multi-label classification problem, meaning that the labels are not mutually exclusive. Thus, there can be multiple noises at the same time, which all need to be detected. There are five classes in total, which are unevenly distributed. In the training set, the most common class is present more than half of all recordings and the least common one is present in less than 10%. This motivates our task of generating synthetic data in order to augment the dataset and overcome the data sparsity, especially on the less common labels. In total, there are only 213 training samples, 70 validation samples and 58 test samples. A training data sample consists of an audio recording with a length of 20 s (longer recordings are cropped). Test samples are limited to 6 s and are ensured to be from different vehicles than the training set. For pre-processing, the raw audio data is converted to mel spectrograms with 128 frequency bins using 40 ms windows with a stride of 20 ms. The spectrograms are normalized per audio channel and frequency using Z-score normalization. The described pre-processing is also used in the downstream classification task and thus, the generation task can be simplified to generating the spectrograms rather than raw audio data. Vocoder techniques may be used to obtain an audio signal from the spectrograms again, which, however, lies not within the scope of this paper.

3.2 Our Approach

To tackle the sparsity of data, we generate synthetic samples in order to supplement the given dataset. Our entire pipeline, from training our diffusion model to the evaluation with the audio classifier is shown in Fig. 1. More details about the architecture, the training and evaluation procedure for the diffusion model as well as the audio classifier are given in this subsection.

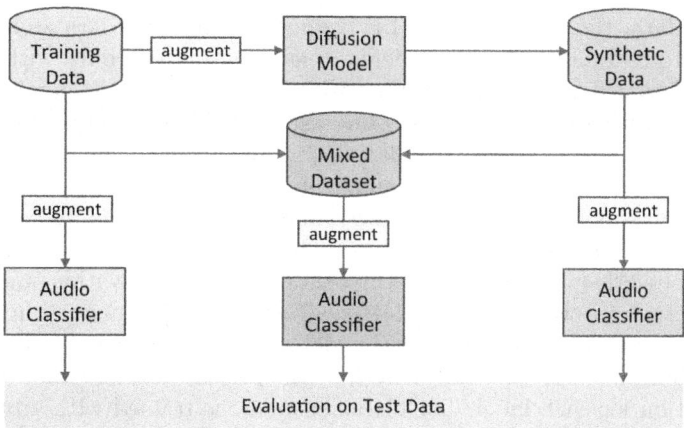

Fig. 1. Overview of our pipeline. A diffusion model is trained on the real training data with optional naive augmentations. The diffusion model then generates synthetic data. Audio classifiers are trained on the real training data, the synthetic data or a mixture of both datasets. Naive augmentations are considered again. The classifiers are evaluated on the real test set and results are compared.

Diffusion Model. Our approach for generating synthetic data builds upon CCATS [7] as described in Sect. 2. We include multiple modifications to suit the specific application. This includes some changes to the denoising model:

- the Mid-Block additionally receives the condition as input
- a linear layer is used instead of the embedding layer for the condition embedding, as it is a multi-label problem
- the number of channels is increased to 1024 across the entire model to account for the high dimensionality of the data

Real data samples, which are 1000 time windows long, are randomly cropped to 300 windows during training. For evaluation, we generate samples of 300 time steps, which correlates to 6 s of recording. Following CCATS [7], we train the diffusion model using an AdamW optimizer. We use a linearly decaying learning rate schedule with warm-up and a peak learning rate of 0.0002 and we choose a batch-size of 50. The diffusion model is trained for 16k epochs. As the training data is quite limited, we augment data samples with random noise and permutations for the training of the diffusion model to avoid overfitting issues. We also include classifier-free guidance with a guidance weight of $w = 0.5$ aiming to generate more label-specific samples. Other hyper-parameters remain unchanged. The hyper-parameters were optimized on the validation set.

Classifier Model. For evaluating the quality and benefit of the generated data, a classifier model is trained. As a baseline, the model is trained on real data only, either with or without naive augmentation strategies. To assess the quality of the generated data, the classifier model is trained on synthetic data and results are compared to real data. Finally, benefits of augmenting real data with generated synthetic data are assessed by training the audio classifier with a mixed dataset of real and synthetic data. The classifier architecture and the training protocol remain equal across the entire evaluation and all variants. The only difference is the data used for the training and augmentation strategies.

For the classifier model we tested several architectures. Finally, we decided on a CNN architecture with five stacks of 1-dimensional convolutions in the time dimension together with batch normalization, ReLU activation and dropout. The input mel spectrograms are flattened across the frequency bin and audio channel dimension beforehand. Lastly, global average pooling is applied across the time dimension. A final linear layer with spectral normalization then yields the prediction for each label. The classifier model is trained with a binary cross entropy loss with negative-tolerant regularization [17] to counteract a bias of the classifier towards negative predictions due to the strong imbalance between positive and negative samples in the dataset. In case of real data, the samples are cropped randomly to 300 time steps for each training epoch. The classifier is trained for 4000 epochs with a peak learning rate of 0.001, following a cosine annealing learning rate schedule [10].

Evaluation Metrics. As the method is developed for the real-world application of classifying noises, we also use the appropriate metrics for the use-case in our evaluation. We primarily measure precision and recall of the classifier model on the test data and subsequently compute F1-scores. We use the micro-average to aggregate results across all samples, meaning that every data sample contributes the same weight. As the classes are unevenly distributed, we are also interested in the per-class results. Thus, the metrics are also observed for the individual labels. In addition, we also use mean average precision (mAP), the Fréchet Inception Distance (FID) and Inception Score (InS) for comparisons.

3.3 ESC-DPM

We compare our method to ESC-DPM [4], a diffusion method for augmenting environmental sound datasets. To make this method compatible to our audio dataset, some modifications were necessary. Due to the multi-label nature of our problem, the embedding layer of the model has been replaced with a linear layer to support multiple true labels (or none) at the same time. Instead of rescaling the spectrograms to 128 × 128, we retain our spectrograms at 128 bins with 300 frames. The number of channels had to be increased from 3 to 8, which now take the numerical values from the spectrograms directly rather than the color channels of the visualization. As the data augmentation was not included in the published code to our knowledge and it is not being applicable to our dataset entirely, we default to the augmentation scheme that our model is training with, meaning random noise and permutations. Pitch shift and time stretching may be promising strategies to improve results, also with our method, but we leave such

Table 1. Test results for the classifier model trained on real data

Augmentation	Recall	Precision	F1-Score
No augmentation	0.680 ± 0.022	0.946 ± 0.028	0.791 ± 0.012
Random noise	0.704 ± 0.033	0.954 ± 0.022	**0.809 ± 0.023**
Permutation	0.724 ± 0.035	0.897 ± 0.034	0.800 ± 0.021
Mirroring	0.666 ± 0.040	0.812 ± 0.023	0.731 ± 0.025
Permutation & Noise	0.702 ± 0.016	0.941 ± 0.020	0.804 ± 0.009

open for future work. The discriminator model has also been reworked to comply with our dataset. For the multi-label training, we exchanged the cross-entropy loss with a binary cross-entropy loss.

4 Results and Discussion

The experimental results are structured in three parts. First, the baseline results are obtained using real data alone and different naive transformations. Then, synthetic data is generated and the evaluation is performed using synthetic data only. Lastly, we thoroughly assess mixed datasets of real and synthetic data. We consider our method for generating synthetic data samples and ESC-DPM [4].

4.1 Baseline

For the baseline, we train the classifier model on real training data only. To enable a competitive baseline for the evaluation with generated data, we also test multiple, naive augmentation strategies, including random noise, permutations and swapping of audio channels. We start by comparing the classifier performance when training with unaltered real data against the performance when applying simple transformations to augment the data. For *Random Noise* augmentation, we add Gaussian noise to the normalized spectrogram input data. The noise is added across all time-steps, channels and frequency bins different with a standard deviation of 0.1 and zero mean. For *Permutations*, we randomly split a spectrogram into 3 to 10 segments in the time dimension and shuffle them to build a new spectrogram. For *Mirroring*, audio channels of a data sample are swapped between left and right. The classifier is trained following the procedure outlined in Sect. 3.2. We train with each augmentation strategy for 10 individual runs and the average test results are reported in Table 1. The random noise augmentation and the permutations perform similarly. While the average F1-score is higher than without augmentation, the results lie within the standard deviation only. The combination of permutation and noise also shows similar results. However, in validation runs it more frequently resulted in less stable training. The mirroring augmentation alters the data too much and depletes the F1-score significantly. The results indicate that the naive augmentation strategies are not effective for the given dataset, motivating the use of a generative approach.

Table 2. Test results using synthetic data for training the classifier.

Dataset	Augmentation	Recall	Precision	F1-Score
Real data	Random noise	0.704 ± 0.033	0.954 ± 0.022	0.809 ± 0.023
Synthetic data (ours)	None	0.926 ± 0.026	0.725 ± 0.045	**0.823 ± 0.037**
	Random noise	0.903 ± 0.026	0.708 ± 0.038	0.794 ± 0.032
	Permutation	0.922 ± 0.041	0.700 ± 0.032	0.797 ± 0.039
Synthetic data (ESC-DPM [4])	None	0.549 ± 0.006	0.403 ± 0.002	0.465 ± 0.004
	Random noise	0.553 ± 0.000	0.406 ± 0.002	0.468 ± 0.001
	Permutation	0.525 ± 0.031	0.512 ± 0.115	0.509 ± 0.039

Table 3. Comparison of guidance weight w on validation set.

Guidance	F1-Score	FID
None	0.628 ± 0.016	47.1 ± 0.2
0.3	0.624 ± 0.010	41.7 ± 1.3
0.5	0.599 ± 0.007	39.8 ± 1.4
1.0	0.567 ± 0.009	39.2 ± 0.4

Table 4. Comparison of channel count in U-Net on validation set.

Channels per block				F1-Score
#1	#2	#3	#4	
1024	512	256	128	0.624
1024	1024	512	256	0.798
1024	**1024**	**1024**	**1024**	0.951

4.2 Synthetic Data

We train our diffusion model on the training set and generate synthetic data samples, as described in Sect. 3.2. We assess the quality of the generated data by training our classifier model with synthetic data only and then evaluate the performance on the real test set. We generate ten times the size of the training set, following the training label distribution. Different naive augmentation strategies are compared on top of the synthetic data. We generate three individual synthetic datasets, running the evaluation three times for each set and each augmentation strategy. The average test results are reported in Table 2. The results come close to the performance of real data. Interestingly, the recall is much higher than for real data, while the precision is much lower, resulting in a quite similar F1-score in total. The variant without augmentation on top of the generated data achieves on average the highest F1-score. However, the standard deviations are rather large. As the generative model was already trained with naive augmentations, a benefit from doing the augmentation again on top of the generated samples was not to be expected. Table 3 shows our ablation on the guidance weight, for which $w = 0.3$ seems to be a good compromise. Table 4 shows the F1-Score for different numbers of channel in the denoising model, which in this case is based on a classifier trained with real data and evaluated on the synthetic data. A high number of channels is required throughout the model. The original choice from CCATS [7] of (32,64,128,256) was just at chance level.

For additional comparison, data was generated using ESC-DPM [4]. Again, the number of generated samples is 10 times as large as the training set. However,

Table 5. Test metrics on the classifier model using 50% mixtures of real and synthetic data for training.

Dataset	Augmentation	Recall	Precision	F1-Score
Real data	Random noise	0.704 ± 0.033	0.954 ± 0.022	0.809 ± 0.023
Mixed dataset (ours)	None	0.842 ± 0.042	0.831 ± 0.057	0.836 ± 0.050
	Random noise	0.873 ± 0.034	0.840 ± 0.053	0.855 ± 0.032
	Permutation	0.864 ± 0.028	0.868 ± 0.050	**0.866 ± 0.031**
Mixed dataset (ESC-DPM [4])	None	0.492 ± 0.024	0.853 ± 0.012	0.699 ± 0.021
	Random noise	0.647 ± 0.000	0.884 ± 0.034	0.747 ± 0.012
	Permutation	0.643 ± 0.020	0.917 ± 0.022	0.756 ± 0.014

we only generate one synthetic dataset, which we evaluate three times with each augmentation strategy by training the classifier model. The results, shown in Table 2, essentially depict random chance. The quality of the generated data is not sufficient to train the classifier to properly classify real samples. This outcome is expected to some extent, as the distribution of our dataset has proven difficult to learn. The differences between labels are subtle and partly encoded in the relationship across channels. Our classifier architecture and training procedure required extensive tuning to recognize labels during training with real data at all. Similarly, careful optimizations were necessary for our diffusion model.

The Fréchet Inception Distance (FID) and Inception score (InS) are computed using a classifier model trained on the real training data. The FID between real training data and the test set is at 20.4 ± 0.7 just marginally lower than for our generated data with 22.2 ± 1.4. With ESC-DPM it is significantly higher at around 124.1. Real data exhibits an InS of 3.58 ± 0.01, our generated data 3.74 ± 0.10 and ESC-DPM around 1.56. The variations on the real data stem from randomly cropping the data.

4.3 Mixed Data

For the final assessment, we augment real data with synthetic data. In each epoch, we mix a random subset of real data with generated data from our model. Note that still all of the training data is used. The amount is only limited within each epoch. Test set results with 50% real data per epoch are shown in Table 5. While real data results in much higher precision than recall at the default decision threshold and synthetic data results in much higher recall than precision, our mixed dataset yields rather balanced results between both metrics. Training with additional naive augmentation shows a slightly higher F1-score on average than training without. This observation coincides with the findings on real data (cf. Table 1). Training the classifier on the mixed dataset with random permutations, the F1-score is 0.057 higher than when training with real data alone, which is a significant improvement. An independent samples t-test with nine samples for the mixed dataset and ten for real data results in $t(14.62) = 4.46$, $p = 0.0005$.

Table 6. Comparison of classifier model trained on mixed datasets or real data.

Dataset	Augmentation	mAP
Real data	Random noise	0.914 ± 0.016
Mixed dataset (ours)	Permutation	$\mathbf{0.932 \pm 0.014}$
Mixed dataset (ESC-DPM [4])	Permutation	0.838 ± 0.013

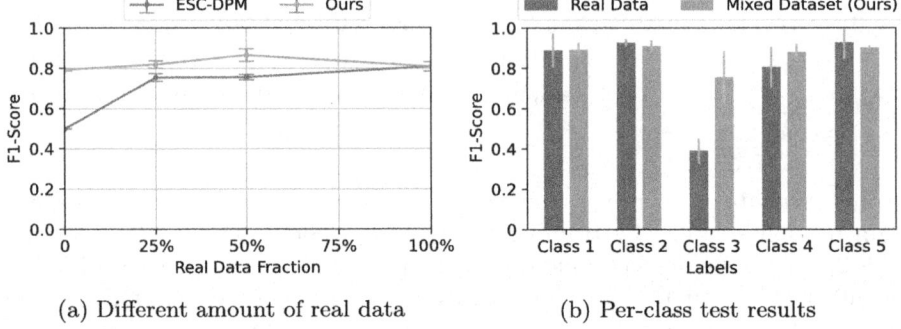

(a) Different amount of real data (b) Per-class test results

Fig. 2. F1-Score depending on mixing ratio (left) and per-class results (right).

Using ESC-DPM [4], the mixed dataset results are better than with training on synthetic data only. However, the results are still below the performance of real data, showing that the generated data also is not useful for augmenting the dataset. Again, the model does not seem to generate the fine-grained class differences well enough to benefit the training. However, we would expect to achieve better results, if the method would be further modified to deal with properties of the data. We have tested the performance also with our different variations of their discriminator model. Some slight improvements can be obtained with an F1-score of 0.775 using our classifier as discriminator and 0.786 with the original discriminator model. The F1-score only considers a single threshold for the classification. Therefore, we additionally evaluate the mean average precision (mAP) with our method. The results are summarized in Table 6. Augmenting real data with our synthetic datasets yields an improvement in mAP of about 0.018. This is a slight, but statistically significant improvement, $t(17.00) = 2.55, p = 0.021$.

We tested different mixtures between real and generated data for ESC-DPM and our model. Figure 2a shows results with different fractions of real data used per epoch. The results are based on the evaluation with permutation as additional augmentation strategy, as these were the best results with both generative approaches. With synthetic data generated by our model, the 50% mix seems optimal. With 25% or less real data, the average F1-Score is again similar to the results from real data alone. For ESC-DPM, the results were already below the performance of real data with the 50% mixture. The performance is similar still using just 25% real data, before the classifier performance depletes when using no more real data. Finally, we observe the per-class performance of the classifier (see Fig. 2b). We find that *class 3* is the most difficult for the classifier in either case. Interestingly, *class 3* is not the least frequent label in the training set, it is the second most frequent label. Augmenting the real data with our generated data significantly increases the F1-score for this class. It still exhibits quite a large standard deviation, indicating that it is still difficult to learn for the classifier and the improvement varies across training runs.

5 Conclusion

In this paper, we proposed a diffusion model for synthesizing audio data in a real-world application from the automotive industry. The model successfully learned to generate the highly domain-specific data. A classifier model based on synthetic data showed similar performance to training with real data alone. By mixing real with synthetic data, we have achieved statistically significant improvements over real data alone, also in comparison to handcrafted augmentation strategies. This benefit our use case and indicates potential for similar approaches in other industrial applications. While the improvement of 1.8 p.p. is not large, each vehicle that does not require manual examination due to wrong predictions means cost savings. Especially, the classifier shows increased robustness, as the most misclassified label had the biggest improvement. We compared our method to the approach by Chen et al. [4], which is designed for environmental sound classification. We fit their method to our data and discussed the difficulties of learning this dataset. The results imply that such a complex real-world dataset requires a well-fitted architecture and training scheme. Tailoring our method towards the given dataset with CCATS [7] as a basis, we have shown that it is possible to overcome these issues. However, some limitations apply. While still significant, the improvement is rather small considering the variance. Also, being specialized to our multi-label dataset, the model may not be directly suited for other applications, but in a similar way it may be adapted to other tasks. Our approach still has much potential left unexplored, e.g. using more sophisticated data transformations, such as pitch shifts and time warping. The classifier model is rather simple and a more developed model may yield better performance, more stable results and more possible gains through the augmentation. For example CNN-RNN architectures or transformers may be considered. Filtering strategies for generated data similar to the discriminator by Chen et al. [4] could also yield improvements and may be considered for future work.

Acknowledgments. This work was supported by a scholarship from RPTU Kaiserslautern-Landau. The research was conducted at the German Research Center for Artificial Intelligence (DFKI) within the transfer lab *Forschen und Lernen aus Prüfdaten* and was partially funded by IAV GmbH.

Disclosure of Interests. The authors have no competing interests to declare that are relevant to the content of this article.

References

1. Ali-Gombe, A., Elyan, E.: MFC-GAN: class-imbalanced dataset classification using multiple fake class generative adversarial network. Neurocomputing **361** (2019)
2. Bahmei, B., Birmingham, E., Arzanpour, S.: CNN-RNN and data augmentation using deep convolutional generative adversarial network for environmental sound classification. IEEE Signal Process. Lett. **29**, 682–686 (2022)
3. Brock, A., Donahue, J., Simonyan, K.: Large scale GAN training for high fidelity natural image synthesis. In: International Conference on Learning Representations (ICLR) (2019)
4. Chen, Y., Yan, Z., Zhu, Y., Ren, Z., Shen, J., Huang, Y.: Data augmentation for environmental sound classification using diffusion probabilistic model with top-k selection discriminator. In: Huang, D.S., Premaratne, P., Jin, B., Qu, B., Jo, K.H., Hussain, A. (eds.) Advanced Intelligent Computing Technology and Applications, pp. 283–295. Springer, Singapore (2023). https://doi.org/10.1007/978-981-99-4742-3_23
5. Colombo, M.F., Ronchini, F., Comanducci, L., Antonacci, F.: Mambafoley: foley sound generation using selective state-space models. In: ICASSP 2025 - 2025 IEEE International Conference on Acoustics, Speech and Signal Processing (ICASSP), pp. 1–5 (2025)
6. Donahue, C., McAuley, J., Puckette, M.: Adversarial audio synthesis. In: International Conference on Learning Representations (2018)
7. Engler, P., Koochali, A., van Elst, L., Dengel, A., Ahmed, S.: Ccats: moving forward with class-conditional time series generation. In: International Conference on Neural Information Processing (ICONIP) (2024)
8. Ghosh, S., Kumar, S., Kong, Z., Valle, R., Catanzaro, B., Manocha, D.: Synthio: augmenting small-scale audio classification datasets with synthetic data. In: The Thirteenth International Conference on Learning Representations (2025)
9. Goodfellow, I., et al.: Generative adversarial networks. Adv. Neural Inf. Process. Syst. **3** (2014)
10. Loshchilov, I., Hutter, F.: SGDR: stochastic gradient descent with warm restarts (2017)
11. Madhu, A., K., S.: Envgan: a gan-based augmentation to improve environmental sound classification. Artif. Intell. Rev. **55**(8), 6301–6320 (2022)
12. OpenAI: Introducing chatgpt (2022). https://openai.com/index/chatgpt/
13. Pascual, S., Bhattacharya, G., Yeh, C., Pons, J., Serrà, J.: Full-band general audio synthesis with score-based diffusion. ICASSP 2023 - 2023 IEEE International Conference on Acoustics, Speech and Signal Processing (ICASSP), pp. 1–5 (2022)
14. Radford, A., Metz, L., Chintala, S.: Unsupervised representation learning with deep convolutional generative adversarial networks. arXiv (2015)
15. Ronchini, F., Comanducci, L., Antonacci, F.: Synthetic training set generation using text-to-audio models for environmental sound classification. In: Detection and Classification of Acoustic Scenes and Events 2024 (DCASE2024) (2024)
16. Sandfort, V., Yan, K., Pickhardt, P., Summers, R.: Data augmentation using generative adversarial networks (cyclegan) to improve generalizability in ct segmentation tasks. Sci. Rep. **9** (2019)
17. Wu, T., Huang, Q., Liu, Z., Wang, Y., Lin, D.: Distribution-balanced loss for multi-label classification in long-tailed datasets. In: European Conference on Computer Vision (ECCV) (2020)
18. Yu, L., Zhang, W., Wang, J., Yu, Y.: Seqgan: sequence generative adversarial nets with policy gradient. In: AAAI Conference on Artificial Intelligence (2017)

PGD: Probe Guided Decoding for Alignment

Changxin Chen[✉]

Shanghai University of Finance and Economics, Shanghai, China
xccanxin@gmail.com

Abstract. Aligning LLMs with human preferences is widely recognized as a foundational factor in their recent advancements. This alignment process often necessitates substantial quantities of annotated data, the collection of which is both time-intensive and laborious when relying solely on human annotators. To mitigate this, previous work has introduced the concept of LLM-as-judge. However, this approach has limitations, including the considerable financial costs, privacy leakage, challenges in reproducibility caused by frequent model updates, and potential biases inherent in proprietary systems. An alternative line of research has explored fine-tuning open-source models using feedback data generated by proprietary models like GPT-4 to improve alignment capabilities. While these methods have demonstrated effectiveness, they typically depend on large-scale synthetic training datasets.

To address these challenges, we propose Probe Guided Decoding (PGD), a novel approach that enhances alignment capabilities while requiring only a minimal number of training samples and simple linear classifiers. PGD consistently surpasses the LLM-as-judge paradigm across diverse settings and significantly mitigates potential biases on two publicly available datasets with different LLMs. Notably, on the JudgeBench benchmark, PGD achieved a remarkable 11.8% improvement with as few as 10 training samples, compared to LLM-as-judge.

Keywords: LLM · LLM-as-judge · probe · guided decoding

1 Introduction

In recent years, large language models (LLMs) have exhibited exceptional proficiency in addressing a wide range of NLP tasks [1–3]. The alignment of LLMs with human preferences is widely regarded as a pivotal factor contributing to their success. Nevertheless, a major challenge in achieving such alignment lies in the substantial requirement for human-annotated preference data, as the quality of this data plays a crucial role in the effective alignment of LLMs [3]. The process of acquiring large quantities of high-quality preference data is not only resource-intensive but also time-consuming [4].

To address this challenge, prior research has proposed utilizing LLMs to generate annotated preference data, which can then be leveraged to improve alignment capabilities. AlpacaFarm [4] and LLM-as-judge [5] introduced the use of GPT-4 [1] to simulate human feedback, significantly reducing the time and cost of human annotation and demonstrating that data annotated this way is comparably effective to human-annotated data.

These approaches suggest that trained language models possess latent and interpretable structures that are intrinsically related to their ability to align with human preferences. While proprietary LLMs such as ChatGPT and GPT-4 demonstrate robust performance in emulating human preferences, they face several practical limitations. These include considerable financial costs, risk of privacy leakage, challenges in reproducibility caused by frequent model updates, and potential biases inherent in proprietary models [6,7]. This highlights the growing importance of research into using open-source LLMs as judges.

Nevertheless, the alignment capabilities of open-source LLMs remain inferior to those of their proprietary counterparts. Some studies have employed a SFT approach, wherein evaluation feedback data is first generated by GPT-4 and subsequently used to fine-tune open-source models, thereby enhancing their alignment performance [8–12]. However, [7] argued that these methods continue to exhibit limitations that cannot benefit from prompt engineering.

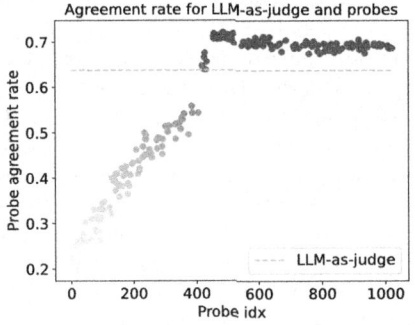

Fig. 1. The agreement rate of LLM-as-judge and probes. Some probes have larger agreement rate than LLM-as-judge.

To further explore the weaker alignment issue in open-source LLMs, we first define what it means for an LLM to "understand" human alignment, even if it does not directly produce accurate judgments. To this end, we employ probing techniques [13], specifically employing a linear layer to probe the intermediate representations of the LLM. By comparing the alignment performance of the LLM with that of the probe, we observe that certain intermediate model layers encapsulate richer alignment-related information. For instance, as shown in Fig. 1, we probe different layers and heads of the LLaMA model [14] on the MT-Bench dataset [5] and randomly sample 200 different probes to report their alignment agreement rate. A deeper model layer corresponds to an increasing probe idx. The highest probe agreement rate achieved was 71.23%, whereas directly prompting LLaMA model only achieved 63.8%.

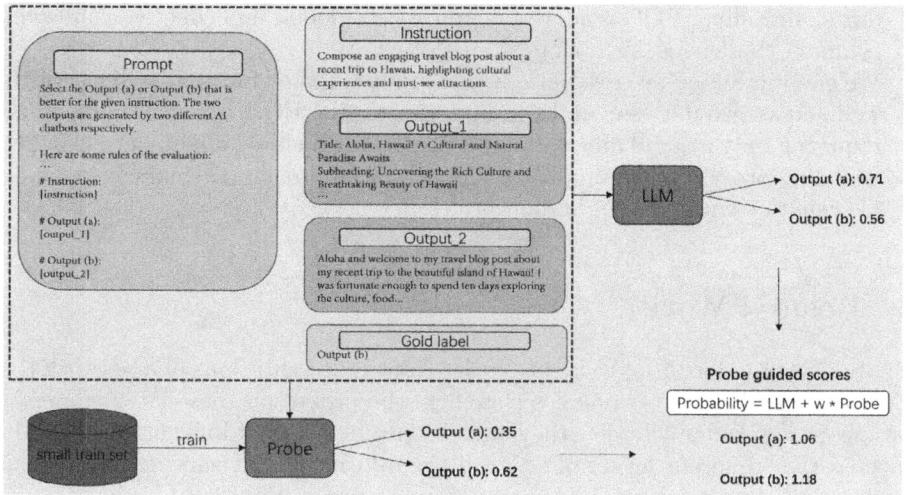

Fig. 2. Overview of probe guided decoding.

Based on this discovery, we propose Probe Guided Decoding (PGD), a novel framework designed to enhance the alignment of LLM-as-judge with human preferences. PGD uses probes that perform well on validation sets to guide the LLM during decoding, thereby eliminating the need for exhaustive retraining of the foundational model through SFT or RLHF.

The overview of PGD is in Fig 2. During the decoding phase, PGD utilizes probes containing richer alignment information to adjust the model's predicted probabilities. This approach enables the decoding process to (1) preserve and leverage the original semantic information of the LLM, and (2) achieve more precise alignment with human preferences while mitigating position bias. These two objectives can be balanced through a tunable weight parameter. The output probability distribution of LLM-as-judge implies the confidence of LLM on each sample. Samples with similar output probabilities can be calibrated by the probe and those samples with high confidence can affirm the original judgment. Compared to reinforcement learning algorithms such as DPO [15], which rely on large amounts of annotated data and retraining the entire model, PGD requires only a few dozen training examples to train simple linear probes. Despite this simplicity, it significantly enhances the alignment capabilities of LLMs.

The major contributions of this paper are as follows:

- We probe LLMs and discover that alignment capabilities are not uniformly distributed across all layers and attention heads. Certain layers and heads demonstrate significantly stronger alignment performance, while others exhibit comparatively poor performance.
- We propose Probe Guided Decoding (PGD), a novel approach that leverages probes with strong alignment capabilities to enhance LLM-as-judge alignment

during decoding. PGD is adaptable to various models and effectively mitigates common challenges, such as positional bias.
- We conduct extensive evaluations and analyses, showing that PGD performs well across two datasets and LLMs. Importantly, PGD is remarkably simple, requiring only a small amount of data to enhance model alignment during the decoding process. This simplicity renders our approach particularly beneficial in scenarios with limited human preference data.

2 Related Work

Probe is a standard tool to identify the latent representations of a network [13]. The core idea involves training a classifier (the probe) on these latent representations to determine whether they encode specific types of information. [13] discovered that different layers of LM capture information at varying levels. Some works use a linear probe [13,16] while others use a non-linear probe [17]. For simplicity and training efficiency, we employ a simple linear classifier to probe the alignment capabilities of the LLM following the previous work [13].

Guided Decoding. Our work is situated within the framework of token-level guided decoding. While some previous studies have explored token-level guided decoding [18,19], they have not established a direct connection between token decoding and the alignment problem. Other approaches have utilized Reward Models (RMs) for guided decoding [20,21]. However, RM typically requires a large amount of training data and is better suited for single-turn question-answering tasks. For multi-turn dialogue datasets, such as MT-Bench, there are numerous ways to define the input prompt due to the different choice of history messages. This variability makes training a suitable RM a time-consuming, trial-and-error process across different datasets. In contrast, PGD requires only a few dozen examples and can be applied to any dataset without extensive customization.

LLM-as-Judge. We focus on the pairwise judge. Given a prompt and two different responses, a LLM can generate a preference verdict between the two responses. Despite proprietary LLMs like GPT-4 [1] showing good performance in imitating human preference [4,5], there are limitations including high costs, risks of privacy leakage, irreproducibility, and inherent biases in the models [6]. Consequently, there is growing interest in open-source LLMs as alternatives. However, the alignment capability of open-source LLMs is limited [22]. To improve the ability, some studies have used GPT-4 to generate high-quality evaluation data, followed by SFT or RLHF to train open-source models [8,9,11,12]. However, achieving stronger generalization often requires collecting a large amount of data. For example, [9,11,12] used GPT-4 to collect around 100k examples, which is extremely costly. [7] argued that such methods have several drawbacks such as ineffectiveness of prompt engineering. In contrast, our method is much cheaper and simpler, requiring only a few dozen examples. By training multiple linear probes, we can enhance the alignment ability of LLMs. Moreover, our approach is plug-and-play for any open-source LLMs.

3 Preliminary

In this section, we briefly describe some key elements of the transformer architecture [23] and the probe [13].

Transformer Architecture. Simplifying for clarity, a transformer consists of a sequence of transformer layers, indexed by the variable l. We use x_l to denote the input of each layer, where $x_l \in \mathbb{R}^{DH}$. D is the dimension of vectors and H is the number of heads. Each transformer layer comprises two key components: a multi-head attention (MHA) mechanism and a standard multilayer perceptron (MLP). Specifically, MHA and MLP can be written as:

$$x'_{l+1} = x_l + \sum_{h=1}^{H} O_l^h Attn_l^h(P_l^h x_l) \tag{1}$$

$$x_{l+1} = x'_{l+1} + MLP(x'_{l+1}) \tag{2}$$

where $P_l^h \in \mathbb{R}^{D \times DH}$ maps representations into D-dimensional head space and $O_l^h \in \mathbb{R}^{DH \times D}$ maps it back. *Attn* is the standard attention operation [23].

Probe. Following the previous work [13], we simply use a linear probe:

$$p_\theta(x_l^h) = \frac{1}{1 + e^{-\theta \cdot x_l^h}} \tag{3}$$

where $\theta \in \mathbb{R}^D$ and $p_\theta(x_l^h)$ represents the probability that x_l^h be classified as certain label.

4 Probe Guided Decoding

4.1 Probe for Alignment Information

For an evaluation dataset $\{(question_i, response1_i, response2_i, y_i)\}_{i=1}^{N}$, we use prompts from [24] to concatenate the question and two responses as input x. Next, we feed x into the LLM and extract the representations of the final token across different layers l and heads h to construct probing datasets $\{(x_l^h, y)_i\}_{i=1}^{N}$. A linear classifier is then trained on the training set using Eq. 3, and the alignment capability of each head is assessed based on validation accuracy.

As illustrated in Fig. 1, we observed significant variability in probe accuracy across different attention heads. While many heads within each layer perform no better than random chance when evaluated with linear probes, a distinct subset of heads exhibits remarkably strong alignment capabilities, even surpassing the performance of LLM-as-judge.

4.2 Probe Guided Decoding

The probing experiment described above provides valuable insights into how LLMs process alignment information across and within their attention heads. Motivated by the phenomenon, we propose leveraging probes with strong alignment performance to guide and refine the decoded outputs of language models, improving their alignment with human preferences. This technique, which we term Probe Guided Decoding (PGD), adjusts the model's probabilistic predictions by incorporating probe-derived probabilities. By doing so, PGD steers the model toward producing judgments that more closely align with human preferences, while preserving the original semantic integrity of the LLM.

Given the probe probability $P_\theta(x_l^h)$ and the LLM judge logits of two responses $LLM(x)_t$, we formalize our probe guided scoring function as follows:

$$s(x) = LLM(x)_t + w \cdot P_\theta(x_l^h) \quad (4)$$

where $LLM(x)_t$ is the LLM output logits for the last token of x, which represents the score distribution of the model judging either *response*1 or *response*2.

This scoring function encourages the generated judgments to achieve two key objectives: (1) preserving the original semantics of the LLM and (2) aligning with human preferences. These dual objectives can be flexibly balanced through the weighting parameter w, which is thoroughly analyzed in Sect. 6.5.

5 Setup

5.1 Datasets and Evaluation Metrics

We evaluate our model over two commonly used public datasets, MT-Bench Human Judgments[1] and JudgeBench[2]. All dataset is divided into 80% test samples, with the remaining 20% split into training and validation sets in a 3:2 ratio. Following previous work [5,25], We use metrics such as Position Bias (PB) and LLM-Human Agreement Rate (Agr). PB measures the proportion of samples where the model's judgment changes after the two responses are swapped. Agr measures the proportion of samples where the model's judgment matches the human preference both before and after the swap.

5.2 Implementation Details

We develop PGD on top of multiple LLMs with varying scales and capabilities: LLaMA-3.1-8B-Instruct [14] and Qwen-2.5-14B-Instruct [26]. LLM-as-judge used vanilla prompt with rules from [24]. Self-consistency [27] is a technique for enhancing the reasoning ability of LLM. We set temperature=1.0, run LLM-as-judge five times and choose the most consistent judged answer. The combinations of w and linear probes that achieve the top 5 guided decoding accuracies on the

---

[1] https://huggingface.co/datasets/lmsys/mt_bench_human_judgments.
[2] https://huggingface.co/datasets/ScalerLab/JudgeBench.

validation set are then used for testing on the test set. Detailed tuning experiments are discussed in Sect. 6.5. The random seed for splitting the dataset into training, testing, and validation sets is set to 2024, 2025, 2026. We run three times and report the average agreement rate and position bias.

The accuracy of probes across different positions within the LLM exhibits variability. This phenomenon is explored in detail in Sect. 6.2. We ultimately select x'_{l+1} in Eq. 1 as our probing position, which is after the MHA and before the MLP, as it contains the most alignment-related information.

6 Experiment

6.1 Main Result

Table 1. PGD performance on Mt-Bench and JudgeBench.

Model	Method	Mt-Bench		JudgeBench	
		Agr	PB	Agr	PB
LLaMA-3.1	LLM-as-judge	0.6362	0.2427	0.2858	0.5931
	Self-Consistency	0.6191	0.2581	0.2597	0.5907
	Probe	0.7134	0.1359	0.3915	0.3903
	PGD	**0.7157**	**0.1313**	**0.4081**	**0.3832**
Qwen-2.5	LLM-as-judge	0.6916	0.1881	0.3926	0.4436
	Self-Consistency	0.6986	0.1872	0.4128	0.4234
	Probe	0.7187	0.1438	0.4353	0.3535
	PGD	**0.7265**	**0.1378**	**0.4674**	**0.3321**

Table 1 presents the performance on MT-Bench and JudgeBench with different LLMs. PGD consistently demonstrates superior performance compared to LLM-as-judge and self-consistency, making it a viable and promising solution for the lacking alignment problem. For example, PGD outperforms LLM-as-judge by 12.23% in agreement rate on the JudgeBench dataset with the LLaMa model. Besides, PGD can reduce position bias by 11.14% on the MT-Bench dataset with the LLaMa model. The significant improvement in performance and the reduction in position bias provide clear evidence of the effectiveness of our proposed Probe Guided Decoding approach.

6.2 Different Probing Position

Different positions within an LLM may contain varying amounts of alignment information. To further demonstrate the generalizability of PGD, we probe the representations at three distinct positions within the LLM: the representations after the *Attn* operation and before projected by O_l^h in Eq. 1, x'_{l+1} in Eq. 1

Table 2. Performance for different probing positions.

Model	Method	Mt-Bench		JudgeBench	
		Agr	PB	Agr	PB
LLaMA-3.1	LLM-as-judge	0.6362	0.2427	0.2858	0.5931
	Probe (mlp_input)	0.7134	0.1359	0.3915	0.3903
	PGD (mlp_input)	**0.7157**	**0.1313**	**0.4081**	**0.3832**
	Probe (o_proj_input)	0.6952	0.1615	0.3558	0.4412
	PGD (o_proj_input)	0.7021	0.1455	0.3737	0.4270
	Probe (layer_output)	0.6953	0.1514	0.3950	0.4021
	PGD (layer_output)	0.6938	0.1538	0.3986	0.3843
Qwen-2.5	LLM-as-judge	0.6916	0.1881	0.3926	0.4436
	Probe (mlp_input)	0.7187	0.1438	0.4353	0.3535
	PGD (mlp_input)	**0.7265**	**0.1378**	**0.4674**	**0.3321**
	Probe (o_proj_input)	0.7079	0.1596	0.4306	0.3487
	PGD (o_proj_input)	0.7239	0.1460	0.4520	0.3452
	Probe (layer_output)	0.6705	0.1965	0.3630	0.4911
	PGD (layer_output)	0.7108	0.1625	0.4520	0.3488

and x_{l+1} in Eq. 2. We denote these three probing positions as 'o_proj_input', 'mlp_input' and 'layer_output' respectively.

The results are shown in Table 2. We found that the optimal position is 'mlp_input', which contains the most alignment information. However, other positions also hold significant alignment information compared to the LLM-as-judge baseline. Furthermore, the PGD method consistently achieves improvements across these positions. These findings further demonstrate the effectiveness of PGD and suggest that alignment information is more likely to reside in positions preceding the mlp layer, offering valuable insights for future research.

6.3 Effect of PGD in Few Samples Scenarios

In this section, we further investigate the performance of PGD under varying numbers of training samples. Given our goal of enhancing the alignment capability of LLM-as-judge in scenarios with very few labeled samples, we aim to test whether PGD maintains its effectiveness even with as few as 1–2 training samples. Using the dataset splitting strategy described before, we first split the test set and then divide the remaining data into training and validation sets. The ratio of training to validation data is maintained at 3:2, while the proportion of the test set relative to the entire dataset is adjusted. For MT-Bench, we evaluate with test set proportions of [0.2, 0.4, 0.6, 0.8, 0.9, 0.95, 0.99, 0.995, 0.999]. For JudgeBench, the test set proportions are [0.2, 0.4, 0.6, 0.8, 0.9, 0.95, 0.99]. The test agreement rates with different test split ratios are presented in the Fig. 3.

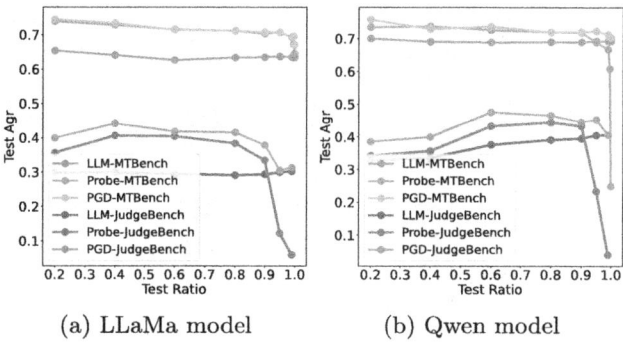

Fig. 3. Performace of difference testing ratio.

We observe the following phenomena: Firstly, PGD consistently outperforms LLM-as-judge across all dataset splits. Secondly, the performance of LLM-as-judge exhibits only minor fluctuations regardless of the number of training samples. Thirdly, the probe's performance surpasses that of LLM-as-judge when a large number of training samples are available, but it declines as the number of training samples decreases, which in turn impacts PGD's effectiveness. However, even when the training data is reduced to only 1–2 samples (test ratio > 0.95), where the probe's performance becomes less effective compared to LLM-as-judge, PGD continues to maintain a slight advantage over LLM-as-judge.

These findings demonstrate PGD's robustness in low-sample scenarios. For example, when the test ratio is 0.95 on JudgeBench using the Qwen model with approximately 10 training samples, the probe's agreement rate is 0.2342, which is significantly lower than the agreement rate of LLM-as-judge at 0.4054. Nevertheless, PGD achieves an agreement rate of 0.4535, surpassing LLM-as-judge by 11.8%. This performance can be attributed to PGD's ability to enhance alignment by leveraging the probe while simultaneously preserving the original semantics of the LLM, even when the probe's performance degrades.

6.4 Explaining the Effect of Reducing Position Bias

In previous experiments, we demonstrated that PGD effectively reduces position bias, a major obstacle for practical applications of LLM-as-judge. To build an intuitive understanding of how position bias occurs in LLMs, we analyzed the vocabulary vectors of two different response tokens, 'a' and 'b'. We calculated the similarity between these vectors and representations at various positions within the LLM. We used the same positions as in earlier experiments: 'o_proj_input', 'mlp_input', and 'layer_output', focusing on representations from the last layer in LLM. We conducted experiments on JudgeBench using the LLaMA model. As shown in Fig. 4, we found that position bias occurs in most positions. The proportion of sample representations more similar to the vector of 'a' reaches as high as 98% in the 'o_proj_input' position, 74% in the 'mlp_input' position, and 83% in the 'layer_output' position.

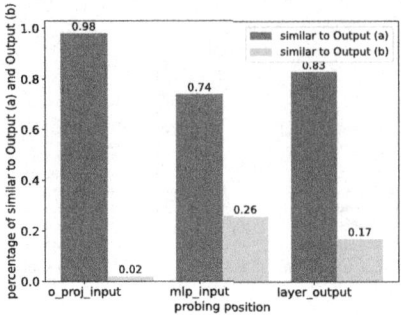

Fig. 4. The similarity between different representations and the two word vectors that correspond to the label.

These results indicate the following: Firstly, position bias is embedded in the intermediate representations of LLMs and persists throughout the model without diminishing. Secondly, this finding provides partial explanation for the observation that probing the 'mlp_input' position yields superior performance in Sect. 6.2, as this position inherently exhibits the least degree of prior position bias. Thirdly, the probe plays a key role in identifying a 'center' point within these biased representations, thereby effectively reducing the influence of position bias. Finally, it is important to acknowledge that numerous factors may affect the performance of LLM-as-judge. This study focuses exclusively on demonstrating that mitigating one specific factor—position bias—can significantly enhance the model's alignment performance. However, we do not establish a causal relationship between position bias and model performance.

6.5 Hyperparameter Sensitivity Analysis

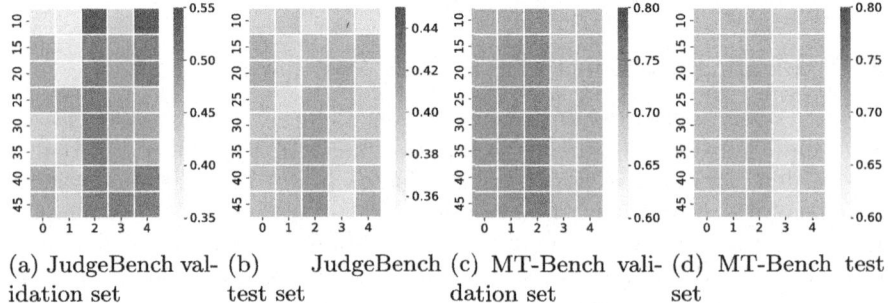

(a) JudgeBench validation set (b) JudgeBench test set (c) MT-Bench validation set (d) MT-Bench test set

Fig. 5. Performace of difference w and probe combinations.

To evaluate the model's sensitivity to hyperparameters, this section analyzes the agreement rates on both the validation and test sets across various combinations of w and probes. The analysis is conducted using the LLaMA model across two datasets. For w, we select values from range $[10, 15, 20, 25, 30, 35, 40, 45]$. For the probes, we select the top 5 based on their agreement rates on the validation set. A comprehensive grid search is performed on the validation set, evaluating the agreement rate for every combination of w and the selected probes. In practical applications, we select the top 5 parameter combinations from the validation set for evaluation on the test set. The results are shown in the Fig. 5. The X-axis is the indices of the probes, with smaller indices corresponding to higher agreement rates on the validation set. The Y-axis is the different values of w.

Figure 5a and Fig. 5b show that the optimal parameter combination identified on the validation set does not always correspond to the best performance on the test set. This discrepancy may stem from the limited size of the validation set, which can lead to less stable performance estimates. However, the best-performing parameter combination on the test set ($w = 45, probe\_id = 2$) ranks within the top 3 on the validation set, demonstrating the robustness and reliability of our parameter selection strategy. The results on MT-Bench exhibit greater consistency between the validation and test sets, likely due to the larger size of the validation set compared to JudgeBench. This experiment demonstrates that selecting the top 5 parameter combinations with the highest agreement rate on the validation set and applying them to the test set is a feasible approach. Notably, even the worst-performing parameter combination achieves results that are no worse than the LLM-as-judge baseline.

7 Conclusion

This paper presents a novel method, Probe Guided Decoding (PGD), to enhance the alignment capabilities of LLMs, addressing the challenge of requiring extensive training data. Through experiments on MT-Bench and JudgeBench, our proposed method demonstrated substantial improvements in human agreement rates, thereby validating the effectiveness of PGD. Notably, our findings indicate that alignment performance can be improved with as few as 10 training samples. Additionally, our analysis uncovered that position bias is widespread across various structural components of LLMs and represents a significant factor that compromises their reliability. Importantly, our method effectively mitigates the effects of position bias, thereby contributing to more robust and reliable model outputs.

Despite these promising findings, there remains potential for further improvement in our training methodology. Currently, we train linear classifiers using only binary (0/1) labels, which may constrain the richness of the supervision signal. In future work, we intend to integrate more detailed and nuanced supervision signals during the training process to further enhance alignment performance.

References

1. Achiam, J., et al.: Gpt-4 technical report. arXiv preprint arXiv:2303.08774 (2023)
2. Team, G., et al.: Gemini: a family of highly capable multimodal models. arXiv preprint arXiv:2312.11805 (2023)
3. Ouyang, L., et al.: Training language models to follow instructions with human feedback. Adv. Neural Inf. Process. Syst. **35**, 27730–27744 (2022)
4. Dubois, Y., et al.: Alpacafarm: a simulation framework for methods that learn from human feedback. Adv. Neural Inf. Process. Syst. **36** (2024)
5. Zheng, L., et al.: Judging llm-as-a-judge with mt-bench and chatbot arena. Adv. Neural Inf. Process. Syst. **36**, 46595–46623 (2023)
6. Gao, M., Hu, X., Ruan, J., Pu, X., Wan, X.: Llm-based nlg evaluation: current status and challenges. arXiv preprint arXiv:2402.01383 (2024)
7. Huang, H., et al.: On the limitations of fine-tuned judge models for llm evaluation. arXiv preprint arXiv:2403.02839 (2024)
8. Li, J., Sun, S., Yuan, W., Fan, R.-Z., Zhao, H., Liu, P.: Generative judge for evaluating alignment. arXiv preprint arXiv:2310.05470 (2023)
9. Zhu, L., Wang, X., Wang, X.: Judgelm: fine-tuned large language models are scalable judges. arXiv preprint arXiv:2310.17631 (2023)
10. Wang, Y., et al.: Pandalm: an automatic evaluation benchmark for llm instruction tuning optimization. arXiv preprint arXiv:2306.05087 (2023)
11. Kim, S., et al.: Prometheus: inducing fine-grained evaluation capability in language models. In: The Twelfth International Conference on Learning Representations (2023)
12. Kim, S., et al.: Prometheus 2: an open source language model specialized in evaluating other language models. arXiv preprint arXiv:2405.01535 (2024)
13. Tenney, I.: Bert rediscovers the classical nlp pipeline. arXiv preprint arXiv:1905.05950 (2019)
14. Dubey, A., et al.: The llama 3 herd of models. arXiv preprint arXiv:2407.21783 (2024)
15. Rafailov, R., Sharma, A., Mitchell, E., Manning, C.D., Ermon, S., Finn, C.: Direct preference optimization: your language model is secretly a reward model. Adv. Neural Inf. Process. Syst. **36** (2024)
16. Li, K., Patel, O., Viégas, F., Pfister, H., Wattenberg, M.: Inference-time intervention: eliciting truthful answers from a language model. Adv. Neural Inf. Process. Syst. **36** (2024)
17. White, J.C., Pimentel, T., Saphra, N., Cotterell, R.: A non-linear structural probe. arXiv preprint arXiv:2105.10185 (2021)
18. Li, X.L., et al.: Contrastive decoding: open-ended text generation as optimization. arXiv preprint arXiv:2210.15097 (2022)
19. Chaffin, A., Claveau, V., Kijak, E.: Ppl-mcts: constrained textual generation through discriminator-guided mcts decoding. arXiv preprint arXiv:2109.13582 (2021)
20. Deng, H., Raffel, C.: Reward-augmented decoding: efficient controlled text generation with a unidirectional reward model. arXiv preprint arXiv:2310.09520 (2023)
21. Khanov, M., Burapacheep, J., Li, Y.: Args: alignment as reward-guided search. arXiv preprint arXiv:2402.01694 (2024)
22. Yi, J., et al.: On the vulnerability of safety alignment in open-access llms. Find. Assoc. Comput. Linguist. ACL **2024**, 9236–9260 (2024)
23. Vaswani, A.: Attention is all you need. Adv. Neural Inf. Process. Syst. (2017)

24. Zeng, Z., Yu, J., Gao, T., Meng, Y., Goyal, T., Chen, D.: Evaluating large language models at evaluating instruction following. arXiv preprint arXiv:2310.07641 (2023)
25. Saha, S., Levy, O., Celikyilmaz, A., Bansal, M., Weston, J., Li, X.: Branch-solve-merge improves large language model evaluation and generation. arXiv preprint arXiv:2310.15123 (2023)
26. Team, Q.: Qwen2.5: a party of foundation models (2024). https://qwenlm.github.io/blog/qwen2.5/
27. Wang, X., et al.: Self-consistency improves chain of thought reasoning in language models. arXiv preprint arXiv:2203.11171 (2022)

Long Abstracts from the ICANN

Dimensionality Reduction of Protein Language Model Embeddings for Viral Clustering

Brendonas Stakauskas(✉) and Virginijus Marcinkevičius

Institute of Data Science and Digital Technology, Vilnius University, Vilnius, Lithuania
brendonas.stakauskas@mif.stud.vu.lt

Keywords: Protein language models · Neural networks · Dimension reduction · Clade assignment · Influenza

1 Introduction

Viruses continuously evolve, leading to the emergence of new strains. A critical component of monitoring viral evolution is the classification of viral strains. Monitoring viral evolution helps predict outbreaks and informs vaccine development.

Here, we investigate whether protein language model embeddings can be used for viral clade assignment, comparing their performance with existing methods and evaluating their potential for studying viral evolution.

2 Materials and Methods

For baseline scores, we used the findings of Nanduri et al. [3]. From the article, we picked PCA, t-SNE and UMAP as these dimensionality reduction methods performed best. Triplet neural networks were also evaluated. For clustering, we primarily used HDBSCAN, following the approach described in the aforementioned study. We used raw data (Hamming-distance matrices) and embeddings built by protein language models – the ProtT5-XL-UniRef50 [1] model and several variants (t33, t36, t48) of the ESM-2 [2].

The dataset consisted of 1,523 H3N2 hemagglutinin sequences. The original dataset and preprocessing steps are available in the referenced GitHub repository[1].

Results were evaluated using normalized variation of information (VI).

Supervised triplet mining was used to validate the method's usability. Triplets were built using original clade assignments. For self-supervised approach we used labels generated by t-SNE+HDBSCAN (as per Nanduri et al. [3]), to correct misclustered data points.

---

[1] https://github.com/blab/cartography/.

3 Results

Using embeddings from protein language models with standard dimensionality reduction methods did not outperform the baseline. The best score was 0.11 (using ESM2-t36 embeddings), while Hamming distance with t-SNE reached 0.08 (lower is better).

By visual inspection, we concluded that triplet networks are suitable for this task. This enabled continuation with the self-supervised approach. The self-supervised approach showed strong results, with normalized VI surpassing the base t-SNE+HDBSCAN score. For ESM2 models, VI was 0.06, 0.05, and 0.15 for the t33, t36, and t48 variants, respectively. ProtT5 embeddings scored 0.05. However, consistent with the previous method, the optimal results were obtained using only Hamming distances, yiealding a VI score of 0.03. As indicated by increased cluster consistency and a reduced Variation of Information (VI) score, the model effectively merged three clusters that were previously misclassified.

4 Conclusion

The use of protein language models for such tasks can be disadvantageous. Simple Hamming distance matrices proved more informative for grouping similar viral strains. Nevertheless, dataset size may be crucial, as matrix dimensions scale with each new element, while protein language model embeddings remain constant in size. There may still be advantages, as large dataset analysis using distance matrices becomes computationally expensive, while small datasets may lack sufficient information.

Our embedding strategy may also be flawed, as averaging can dilute subtle but important variations. More work is needed to develop representations of long protein sequences suited for fine-grained comparisons.

Self-supervised triplet mining could be improved: we sampled triplets from only one model's output. Sampling from multiple clusterings could enable an ensemble-like approach.

References

1. Elnaggar, A., et al.: ProtTrans: towards cracking the language of life's code through selfsupervised deep learning and high performance computing. bioRxiv (2020). https://doi.org/10.1101/2020.07.12.199554
2. Lin, Z., et al.: Evolutionary-scale prediction of atomic-level protein structure with a language model. Science **379**(6637), 1123–1130 (2023). https://doi.org/10.1126/science.ade2574
3. Nanduri, S., Black, A., Bedford, T., Huddleston, J.: Dimensionality reduction distills complex evolutionary relationships in seasonal influenza and SARS-CoV-2. Virus Evol. **10**(1) (2024). https://doi.org/10.1093/ve/veae087

Author Index

A
Abir, Nur-A-Alam 89
Ahmed, Sheraz 331
Ai, Xinbo 253
Alonso-Betanzos, Amparo 229
Attaoui, Zineb 192

B
Bacciu, Davide 279
Botev, Victor 151

C
Cai, Mingqi 53
Chen, Changxin 343
Chen, Su 41
Chen, Xiarun 180
Chen, Yuhao 319
Chen, Yuli 127
Cheng, Bo 127
Chu, Yan 266
Chu, Zhong 266
Correia, Adriana 151
Cui, Shaoguo 307

D
Dengel, Andreas 331
Dhaini, Mahdi 192
Dong, Yan 41
Du, Jun 53

E
Elst, Ludger van 331
Engler, Philipp 331
Erdogan, Ege 192
Esteban-Martínez, David 229

F
Fan, Liuyi 253
Fang, Jiaxin 16
Fang, Xin 53

Feng, Zunlei 65

G
Gao, Jing 164
Gong, Linfeng 307
Guijarro-Berdiñas, Bertha 229
Guo, Renzhong 139

H
Haq, Rafiul 89
Hu, Gang 294
Huang, Jin 77

I
Ivanov, Matyo 151

J
Jin, Ke 77

K
Kasneci, Gjergji 192

L
Lai, Nanhui 77
Lei, Jie 65
Li, Hao 16
Li, Minmin 139
Li, Shiying 253
Li, Wei 29, 241
Li, Xiaoyu 205
Li, Yuanming 164
Li, Zexi 253
Li, Zexin 180, 319
Liang, Ronghua 65
Liao, Mingke 1
Lin, Xixun 41
Liu, Xiaoliang 101
Liu, Xiaoqiang 65
Liu, Yumeng 164
Liu, Zhicheng 217

Long, Yingchao 77
Luo, Shutiao 164
Luo, Xiandang 319
Lv, Siqi 294
Lv, Xiongjian 205
Lyu, Xiang 217

M
Ma, Wei 253
Mei, Tong 16
Mokarizadeh, Shahab 279
Marcinkevičius, Virginijus 359

P
Pan, Li 101
Paz-Ruza, Jorge 229

Q
Qian, Yan 114
Qian, Yi 205
Qin, Yiming 294

S
Schichtel, Peter 331
Shang, Yanmin 41
Shen, Yiqing 114
Sheng, Xiaojun 139
Sun, Xiaoshu 294
Stakauskas, Brendonas 359

T
Tolloso, Matteo 279

V
Vankov, Ivan 151
Varesi, Marco 279
Vladika, Juraj 192

W
Wan, Wei 294
Wang, Hanlin 266
Wang, Lei 53

Wang, Qing 53
Wang, Ruoxuan 253
Wang, Weixi 139
Wang, Yafei 139
Wang, Yawei 217
Wei, Shilong 139
Wen, Weiping 180, 319
Wen, Yimin 205
Wu, Jiaqi 65
Wu, Peng 101

X
Xia, Wei 307
Xiao, Fen 180, 319
Xiao, Ye 180, 319
Xie, Yuxuan 101
Xu, Panpan 217
Xu, Xiaolin 41

Y
Yang, Jinsu 319
Yang, Luyuan 266
Yang, Qi 139
Yang, Yang 1
Yang, Yulong 307
Yao, Feng 1
Yao, Wenhan 180, 319
Yitagesu, Sofonias 89
Yu, Weihao 77

Z
Zeng, Hongji 164
Zhang, Xiaowang 89
Zhang, Yingying 127
Zhao, Qingchao 266
Zhao, Sifan 307
Zhao, Ximeng 266
Zhong, Guirui 53
Zhong, Yu 307
Zhou, Yun 217
Zinat, Kazi Tasnim 217

Made in the USA
Monee, IL
03 May 2026